THE ESSENTIAL ARTICLES SERIES

Pope: Recent Essays

by Several Hands

Edited by
Maynard Mack
and
James A. Winn

Archon Books   Hamden, Connecticut   1980

Library of Congress Cataloging in Publication Data
Main entry under title:

Pope, recent essays by several hands.

(The Essential articles series)
1.   Pope, Alexander, 1688-1744—Criticism and
       interpretation—Collected works.
I. Mack, Maynard, 1909- II. Winn, James Anderson, 1947-
PR3634.P66   821'.5   79-26345
ISBN 0-208-01769-0

© The Shoe String Press, Inc. 1980

First published in 1980 as an
Archon Book
an imprint of
The Shoe String Press, Inc.
Hamden, Connecticut 06514

Printed in the United States of America

FOREWORD

The resources available for the study of literature are so vast as to be almost overwhelming, particularly in the case of major authors. Few libraries have copies of all the important articles a serious student might wish to read, and fewer still can keep them easily accessible. The aim of the Essential Articles series is to bring together from learned journals and scholarly studies those essays on a standard writer or area of English literature which are genuinely essential—which will continue to appear on syllabus and reading list.

INTRODUCTION

The second edition of *Essential Articles for the Study of Alexander Pope* (1968) was an expansion of the first (1964), adding a number of important essays but retaining all those published in the first edition. This collection, by contrast, is entirely new, not because we believe the articles in the earlier editions are any less "essential" now, but because they have been widely circulated, while some of the more recent essays we reprint here have not been so readily accessible.

Selecting these essays was a difficult task. A typical year's work in Pope studies now includes some thirty-five articles, and we have attempted to survey the work of ten years. We limited ourselves at the outset by deciding not to reprint chapters of books, though we do include articles from *Festschriften* and other collections of essays; we also decided not to reprint more than one piece by any single author. Our selection was further influenced by our desire to include essays about as many of Pope's poems as possible. The generosity of authors and publishers in allowing us to reprint this material has helped us keep this volume inexpensive; however, we were unable to obtain permission from one publisher to reprint an essay we wanted. For all these reasons, many excellent essays are not included here, but we believe our selection will prove varied and stimulating, if it cannot claim to be exhaustive.

The many fresh discoveries, both historical and analytical, recorded in these articles should help lay to rest the curious notion that Pope's works have been "mined out." In fact, these essays show again the depth and richness of his poetry, which holds treasures enough for many subsequent collections; they also demonstrate the capacity of that poetry, after more than two hundred years, to stimulate active controversy and vigorous argument.

"Years following Years, steal something ev'ry day," and the years since the last volume appeared have stolen four of our authors: John Butt, Earl Wasserman, W. K. Wimsatt, and Rebecca Parkin. It is a pleasure to increase the indebtedness of all students of Pope to these scholars by reprinting an important late essay by each of them.

Our own debts to the living are no less great. Let us record our appreciation of the time devoted to this collection by the authors of the

essays, by Robert Balay of Yale University's Sterling Library Reference
Department, by James Thorpe III and Jeanne Ferris of The Shoe
String Press, and by typists Grace Michelle, Kimberly Kwaak, and
Barbara Shumway.

J. A. W.

M. M.

CONTENTS

ix

CONTENTS

POPE: THE MAN AND THE POET

John Butt

    Pope's career was exceptional in many respects.
His ability was recognized by the best judges of
poetry before he was twenty years old; and before he was thirty he was famous. Already at the
age of twenty-nine he was showing his concern for
his text and for the canon of his writings by
publishing *The Works of Mr Alexander Pope* in sumptuous quarto and folio editions, adorned with a
portrait of the author by Kneller and with head-
and tail-pieces to the poems by Gribelin, and
recommended by the verse addresses of Wycherley,
Parnell, the Countess of Winchilsea, the Duke of
Buckingham and others. This collection of poems,
containing the *Essay on Criticism, Windsor Forest,*
and *The Rape of the Lock,* besides many others, he
was inclined to look back upon in later life with
some measure of affectionate condescension; yet
it was a volume which both in poetical merit and
in physical appearance could rival what other
poets had achieved at the end of a life-time's
endeavour. Thus Prior's poems were to be published in an equally handsome format, but at the

This essay first appeared in *Of Books and Humankind*, ed. John Butt (London: Routledge
and Kegan Paul, 1964), pp. 69-79.

1

end of his career, and at the expense of friends;
and Congreve's early work had been almost equally
well received a few years before, but Congreve
did not live up to his youthful promise. It is
remarkable, however, that each of Pope's subsequent publications added both to his fame and to
his fortunes. At a time when a writer needed the
support or patronage of a political party to make
a living--and very good livings were to be had
that way, as the careers of Addison and Prior
bear witness--Pope was excluded from such patronage because he was a Roman Catholic. Yet in
spite of this disability he could claim that he
was the first poet to live at ease by his pen.
And if he was not the last poet who could make
such a claim, I suppose he has had few rivals
since in that respect. Though he was quite right
in admitting that it was

        Thanks to Homer that I live and thrive
        Indebted to no Prince or Peer alive,

we now know that he was also very skilful in mar-
keting the pretty little collected editions of
his works in octavo, which he published during
the last nine years of his life.
        His career was exceptional, too, in that his
success was not confined to this country. Mil--
ton had been known abroad during his lifetime,
but he was known as a prose controversialist;
Pope seems to have been the first English poet
to achieve contemporary fame by his poetry in
France, in Italy, and in Switzerland. And far
away in the American colonies he also had
admirers and correspondents.
        Such an exceptional reputation doubtless
derived some support from extraneous circumstances and from qualities in Pope's work that are
not essentially poetic. Thus he wrote at a time
when there seems to have been a considerable
growth in literacy and an unusually large market
for poetry, a market to be matched in size only
by the first twenty years of the nineteenth century, when Scott, Byron, and Crabbe made fortunes

for themselves and their publishers. Then, too,
it must be allowed that much of his later poetry
had a contemporary appeal to the inquisitiveness
of those who think they can detect a smell of
scandal. But when such allowances have been made,
it must be admitted that Pope's reputation rested, and still rests, upon sheer merit--the charm
of one who can handle common things with propriety (as in the *Moral Essays*), the skill (shown
both in the *Essay on Criticism* and the *Essay on Man*)
of one who can reconcile conflicting opinions
and achieve a new synthesis, the imaginative power (shown in *The Rape of the Lock* and *The Dunciad*) of
investing the social scene in a new light, of
presenting a new criticism of society; and, what
perhaps appealed most to the readers of his
generation, the conviction he gave them in the
Imitations of Horace, the translation of Homer, and
the *Essay on Criticism* that 'Still green with Bays
each ancient Altar stands'; in those and other
poems he was able to convince his generation
that the spirit of the ancients was still a living force in that latter age, that Homer and
Horace had still their relevance to eighteenth-
century life, that there was indeed such a concept as

   Unerring Nature, still divinely bright,
   One clear, unchang'd, and Universal Light.

And besides these qualities he was endowed with
peculiar charms of diction and versification; of
diction, in that he practised so skilfully the
doctrine of decorum, whether it be in judging
the exact degree of diminution required in *The
Rape of the Lock*, or the precise placing of a collo-
quialism in the elegant yet easy verse of the
Moral Essays and *Imitations of Horace*; of versification, in that he learned how to produce an in-
credible number of rhythmical variants in the
tiny space of the couplet. The charge of monotony is levelled against Pope's couplet only by
those who have not learned to hear it and to
read it.

Pope's achievement was substantial and widely
recognized. It brought him in his lifetime not
only literary fame but social fame. As a boy he
had been courted by the wits who survived from
Dryden's day, Wycherley, Congreve, Walsh and
Granville, and by the statesmen, too. William
III's Secretary of State, Sir William Trumbull,
took him out riding in Windsor Forest, and in a
charming passage of the *Epistle to Dr Arbuthnot* Pope
tells us how

> The Courtly Talbot, Somers, Sheffield read,
> Ev'n mitred Rochester would nod the head,
> And St. John's self (great Dryden's friends
>   before)
> With open arms received one Poet more.

It is not surprising that he should have taken
his natural place amongst his intellectual equals
like Swift and Berkeley, or with painters like
Kneller and Jervas, or with architects like Kent:
this is to be expected of a great writer in any
age. What is more remarkable is the ease with
which this Roman Catholic son of a wholesale
linen-draper entered the society of statesmen,
and counted amongst his closest friends lords
temporal and spiritual, generals, diplomats and
maids of honour. He could even conquer that formidable old dowager, Sarah Duchess of Marlborough:

> Had you sent away Sir Timothy, to re-call
> another [he writes to her in her still ac-
> tive 82nd year], it had been but a natural
> Change in a Lady who knows her Power over
> her Slaves; and that how long soever she has
> rejected or banish'd any one, she is sure
> always to recover him. But to use me thus--
> to have won me with some difficulty, to have
> bow'd down all my Pride, and reduced me to
> take That at your hands which I never took at
> any other; and as soon as you had done this,
> to slight your Conquest, and cast me away with
> the Common Lumber of Friends in this Town--
> what a Girl you are![1]

The range of his noble acquaintances and his
adaptability in meeting them is best conveyed in
two extracts from his poems, the first a few verses from a poem he never acknowledged, 'The
Court Ballad: to the tune of *To all you Ladies now at
Land*'. In it he shows his whimsical habit of
referring slightingly to his diminutive appearance (especially compared with the bulk of his
friend Gay), which he permitted also to the affection of his intimates, as when he reminds
Atterbury of Atterbury's likening him sitting in
a little chariot to Homer in a nutshell,[2] or when
in the January before his death he writes to
Bolingbroke: 'If your charity would take up a
small Bird that is half dead of the frost, and
set it a chirping for half an hour, I'll jump into my Cage, and put myself into your hands
tomorrow, at any hour you send':[3]

> To one fair Lady out of court
>   And two fair Ladies in
> Who think the Turk and Pope a sport
>   And Wit and Love no Sin,
> Come these soft lines, with nothing Stiff in
> To Bellenden, Lepell, and Griffin
>   With a fa.
>
> In truth by what I can discern,
>   Of Courtiers from you Three,
> Some Wit you have and more may learn,
>   From Court than Gay or me,
> Perhaps in time you'll leave High Diet,
> And Sup with us on Mirth or Quiet.
>
> In Leister fields, in house full nigh,
>   With door all painted green,
> Where Ribbans wave upon the tye,
>   (A Milliner's I ween)
> There may you meet us, three to three,
> For Gay can well make two of me.
>
> But shou'd you catch the Prudish itch,
>   And each become a coward,

> Bring sometimes with you Lady Rich
>   And sometimes Mistress Howard,
> For Virgins, to keep chaste, must go
> Abroad with such as are not so.

These verses are as well adjusted to three met-
tlesome young maids of honour as are the following lines to the noblemen for whose eyes they
were intended:

> But does the Court a worthy Man remove?
> That instant, I declare, he has my Love:
> I shun his Zenith, court his mild Decline;
> Thus Sommers once, and Halifax were mine.
> Oft in the clear, still Mirrour of Retreat,
> I study'd Shrewsbury, the wise and great:
> Carleton's calm Sense, and Stanhope's noble
>   Flame,
> Compar'd, and knew their gen'rous End the
>   same;
> How pleasing Atterbury's softer hour!
> How shin'd the Soul, unconquer'd in the Tow'r!
> How can I Pult'ney, Chesterfield forget,
> While *Roman* Spirit charms, and *Attic* Wit:
> Argyle, the State's whole Thunder born to
>   wield,
> And shake alike the Senate and the Field:
> Or Wyndham, just to Freedom and the Throne,
> The Master of our Passions, and his own.
> Names, which I long have lov'd, nor lov'd in
>   vain,
> Rank'd with their Friends, not number'd with
>   their Train;
> And if yet higher the proud List should end,
> Still let me say! No Follower, but a Friend.

If today we recognize that proud list ending in
no one more eminent than 'Poor Fred', who proved
so ineffectual a Prince of Wales, we should recall that when Pope wrote those lines Prince
Frederick was regarded as the nation's best hope
and in Bolingbroke's eyes was the very image of
a Patriot King. The Prince, who lived at Kew
Palace, was a neighbour of Pope's, and their

friendship was cemented by the gift from Pope of
one of the puppies of Bounce, his great Dane.
The puppy was accompanied by a collar on which
Pope had had engraved a motto that seemed to
epitomize the contemporary political situation
under Sir Robert Walpole:

> I am his Highness' Dog at Kew;
> Pray tell me Sir, whose Dog are you?

Intellectual and social success of such an
order might well be enough to turn a man's head,
and it is not surprising that Pope should exhibit
some measure of self-esteem. In him self-esteem
did not take its ugliest forms. He was never
addicted to ostentation; on the contrary, his
manner of life seems to have been studiously
modest: Lord Orrery, who frequently visited him,
reports that he 'treated his friends with a
politeness that charmed, and a generosity that
was much to his honour. Every guest was made
happy within his doors. Pleasure dwelt under his
roof and elegance presided at his table'. It
was never reported of him that he cut an old but
humble friend, or behaved with an air of offensive patronage towards modest worth, and he never forsook a friend in disgrace: his behaviour
to Oxford and Atterbury when imprisoned in the
Tower shows him as the sort of friend that any
man in distress would wish to have. No, his
self-esteem took more innocent forms. Thus he
was quite convinced that his poetry had achieved
a classical status, and he behaved towards it in
a way that I cannot recall any other poet behaving. Other poets, like Hopkins and Mr Eliot,
have written notes to their poetry, and others,
like Spenser, have engaged a friend to write a
commentary; but perhaps no other poet but Pope
has printed a selection of discarded readings
from manuscript and printed editions of poems no
more than two years old. Furthermore, a few
years before his death he had surrendered himself
to an editor, secure (it would seem) of his
matriculation amongst the Ancients: and he caused

the following announcement to be printed in the
revised version of *The Dunciad*:

> Speedily will be publish'd,
> In the same Paper, and Character, to be bound
>   up with this,
> The ESSAY ON MAN, the ESSAY ON CRITICISM,
> And the rest of the Author's Original Poems,
> With the commentaries and notes of
>   W. Warburton, A.M.

'You must be the vainest man alive', said Lord
Marchmont to Pope on this occasion; 'you must
want to show posterity what a quantity of dullness you can carry down on your back without
sinking under the load.'
  Yet in spite of this evidence, Pope affected
to slight his poetical achievements. He wrote
to Aaron Hill in 1731:

> I only wish you knew, as well as I do, how
> much I prefer Qualities of the Heart to those
> of the Head: I vow to God, I never thought
> any great Matters of my poetical Capacity; I
> only thought it a little better, comparative-
> ly, than that of some very mean Writers, who
> are too proud.

To this Hill replied:

> I am sorry to hear you say, you never
> thought any great Matters of your *Poetry*.--
> It is, in my Opinion, the Characteristic you
> are to hope your *Distinction* from: To be *Honest*
> is the Duty of every *plain Man!* Nor, since the
> *Soul* of Poetry is Sentiment, can a *Great Poet*
> want *Morality*. But your *Honesty* you possess
> with a *Million*, who will never be *remembered*;
> whereas your *Poetry* is a Peculiar, that will
> make it impossible, you should be forgotten.

Pope deserved the rebuke; but it was a rebuke that
was difficult to take amiss, and he was content
to reply that though his poetical talent was all

that might make him remembered, it was his morality only that would make him beloved and happy.
This was the idea of himself into which he had
grown over the years. His earlier notion of his
own character had baffled him. In 1713 he told
Caryll that every hour of his life his mind was
strangely diverted, one moment above the stars,
with a thousand systems round about him, looking
forward into the vast abyss of eternity, the next
below all trifles, 'even grovelling with Tidcombe
in the very center of nonsense':

> Good God! [he reflects] what an Incongruous
> Animal is Man? how unsettled in his best part,
> his soul; and how changing and variable in his
> frame of body? The constancy of the one,
> shook by every notion, the temperament of the
> other, affected by every blast of wind. What
> an April weather in the mind! In a word, what
> is Man altogether, but one mighty inconsisten-
> cy.

The kaleidoscopic nature of his personality in
these early years is delightfully illustrated
from a passage in a letter to his friend, Patty
Blount:

> Every one values Mr Pope, but every one for
> a different reason. One for his firm adher-
> ence to the Catholic Faith, another for his
> Neglect of Popish Superstition, one for his
> grave behavior, another for his Whymsicalness.
> Mr Tydcomb for his pretty Atheistical Jests,
> Mr Caryll for his moral and christian Sen-
> tences, Mrs Teresa for his Reflections on Mrs
> Patty, and Mrs Patty for his Reflections on
> Mrs Teresa.

But sobriety was to win the day. In so far as
anyone can resolve what character he will choose
to exhibit to the world, Pope had resolved upon
the character of the Good Man. He cannot be
shown in the act of trying on this character, as
we can see Boswell in his London Journal deciding

to adopt 'Mr Addison's character in sentiment, mixed with a little of the gaiety of Sir Richard Steele and the manners of Mr Digges'; but there can be little doubt that Pope designed the publication of his letters to exhibit this view of the dutiful son, the kind-thoughted friend, the well-bred host, the disinterested critic of society, yet warm in wishes for his country's good and patient under attack: in short, the man of plain living, high thinking and unimpeachable integrity. This is the view of himself that he discovered in his letters as he reread them, rather than the view that he designedly wrote into them. Not every critic of Pope in his own day or since has been able to see him in this light; and when allowance has been made for contemporary malice and subsequent prejudice, it must be admitted that his moral character was not perfect. He can be convicted of equivocation and of devious dealing; and though he was slow in replying to attacks, and not infrequently forgave the injuries done him, he hit harder than perhaps his profession as a Christian permitted; he hit hard, but deftly, in an age of hard hitting.

But though I think that his moral character has been unduly impugned, it is not my present purpose to defend it. Of greater interest is his employment of the character he had chosen. He had decided that goodness should be the profession of his mature years just as he had decided that wit was to be the profession of his youth. Doubtless he was aware from time to time that he did not always succeed in living up to his profession, just as a Christian is aware of committing sin; but either he had lived so long with his *persona* that he failed to recognize the mask he carried, or he was unable to abandon what had become the inspiration of his poetry.

He was as much accustomed as his friend Swift to the use of a *persona* in his writings. He had taught himself to write by imitating the styles of different masters, and most of his earliest surviving verses bear witness to this habit: 'Of

a Lady singing to her lute; in imitation of
Waller', for example, or 'To the author of a poem intitled Successio, in imitation of the Earl
of Dorset'; and though the famous 'Ode on Solitude' bears no similar subtitle, it is clearly
intended as an exercise in the manner of Cowley
on the popular theme of 'The Happy Man'. No one
is misled by these straightforward adoptions of
a poetic *persona*, and of others equally straightforward in such poems as 'Eloisa to Abelard' and
'The Dying Christian to his Soul'. But beginning with the 'Epistle to Miss Blount with the
Works of Voiture', which probably belongs to the
year 1710, and continuing in some later verse
epistles, that 'to Miss Blount, on her leaving
the Town, after the Coronation' (1714), 'to Mr.
Jervas, with Dryden's Translation of Fresnoy's
Art of Painting' (1715), 'to Mr Gay' (1720), the
noble epistle to the Earl of Oxford, with the
poems of Parnell (1722) and the affectionate
verses 'to Mrs M.B. on her Birthday' (1723)--in
all these poems there is evident a *persona* that is
clearly intended to resemble the features of the
historical Alexander Pope. Accustomed as he was
to model himself upon verse precedent, it is not
unlikely that Pope had his models here, too; and
they are not far to seek. There were the urbane
verse epistles of Dryden to Sir Godfrey Kneller
and to his 'dear friend Mr Congreve'; and behind
Dryden was the urbanity of Horace. In learning
to adjust his features to the mask of Horace,
Pope discovered a set of countenance and a manner
of behaviour that he felt suited him best of all;
the April weather of his mind was allowed to settle at last into an Horatian midsummer. Early
eighteenth-century society dictated its own modifications of the Horatian pattern. The predominant masculinity of Dryden's and Horace's
epistles were not altogether suited to a society
where women had begun to take a more prominent
place. But *The Tatler* and the letters of Voiture
served to teach Pope how to 'fairsex' it, to add
that touch of gallantry required. And how successfully the lesson was learned!

> But, Madam, if the Fates withstand, and you
> Are destined *Hymen*'s willing Victim too;
> Trust not too much your now resistless Charms,
> Those, Age or Sickness, soon or late, disarms;
> *Good Humour* only teaches Charms to last,
> Still makes new Conquests, and maintains the
>   past:
> Love, rais'd on Beauty, will like That decay,
> Our Hearts may bear its slender Chain a day,
> As flowry Bands in Wantonness are worn;
> A Morning's Pleasure, and at Evening torn:
> *This* binds in Ties more easie, yet more strong,
> The willing Heart, and only holds it long.
>   Thus *Voiture*'s early Care still shone the
>   same,
> And *Monthausier* was only chang'd in Name:
> By this, ev'n now they live, ev'n now they
>   charm,
> Their Wit still sparkling, and their Flames
>   still warm.
>   Now crown'd with Myrtle, on th' *Elysian*
>   Coast,
> Amid those Lovers, joys his gentle Ghost,
> Pleas'd while with Smiles his happy Lines you
>   view,
> And finds a fairer *Rambouillet* in you.
> The brightest Eyes of *France* inspir'd his Muse,
> The brightest Eyes of *Britain* now peruse,
> And dead as living, 'tis our Author's Pride,
> Still to charm those who charm the World
>   beside.

That is the tone he had already learned to use in
1710, at the age of twenty-three, learned it, before *The Spectator* could have taught it him, to
apply two years later in the greatest poem of his
juvenilia, *The Rape of the Lock*.
   We may watch the features settling both in
Pope's letters and in his poems. The reason why
the process can be watched in his poetry is that
as time went on he conducted an ever-deepening
exploration of his personality. His first massively personal intrusion into his own poetry is
in 'The Farewell to London' (1715), where 'the

gayest valetudinaire, most thinking rake alive'
sees himself against the background of a gay
society frequenting theatres and coffee-houses;
and from 1730 onwards there are few of his poems
in which the poet himself does not take up a prominent position. The *Moral Essays* are one and all
conceived as verse epistles, and the same is true
of the *Imitations of Horace*, while the presence of
an interlocutor in the epistles to Bathurst and
Arbuthnot and in the *Epilogue to the Satires*, with
their snatches of dialogue, emphasize even more
strongly the poet's presence. The *Essay on Man*,
too, is framed within the addresses to Bolingbroke that open and close the poem. These
addresses pay Bolingbroke the highest of compliments, but they are so arranged that we should
see his associate also. That attractive picture
of the two friends setting out on their shooting
expedition:

> Together let us beat this ample field,
> Try what the open, what the covert yield!
> The latent tracts, the giddy heights explore
> Of all who blindly creep, or sightless soar;
> Eye Nature's walks, shoot Folly as it flies,
> And catch the Manners living as they rise:
> Laugh where we must, be candid where we can;
> But vindicate the ways of God to Man--

What purpose does the picture serve but to define
the elegant yet easy spirit of debate in which
the discussion will be conducted? It will be
found on examination that every other personal
intrusion of the poet into these later poems,
whether he be conversing with friends in his
grotto in the first *Imitation of Horace* or offering
them hospitality at Twickenham in the second, or
the scene of domestic irritation with which the
Epistle of Arbuthnot opens or the deliberately contrasting scene of domestic calm at his mother's
death-bed with which it closes--each is designed
to control the mood of the poem, and to win the
reader to the poet's point of view.

A wide assortment of factors have combined to
produce this very personal poetry of Pope's maturity. Since 1711 he had been the victim of un-
remitting attacks that libelled both his moral
character and his personal appearance. 'If I am
not like that,' he seems to have asked himself,
'what am I like?' And he set himself to correct
the libels, encouraged by that sense of self-
esteem which fed upon his early success and
helped to determine what character he would
choose to exhibit to the world, not only in verse,
but on the canvasses of numerous portrait-paint-
ers and in the busts of Roubiliac and other
sculptors, whose work he seems to have directed
with attentive care. Then, too, he had the example of Horace before him, and a lifetime's
practice in poetical imitation which makes it
second nature to adopt a *persona*, as well as the
inheritance of a hundred years of experiment in
the Theophrastan character sketch; and finally,
perhaps, at some level of consciousness there
was the recognition that the personality that
charmed such a wide circle of friends could be
harnessed to his verse to charm an even wider
circle of readers.

And where in all this is the real man? Professor Maynard Mack, in an essay called 'The Muse
of Satire' has shown how closely modelled the
poet's *persona* is upon the traditional figure of
the satirist. Yet at the same time it is possible to annotate each incident from the satires
and show its derivation from the poet's own
biography. We are presented with a peculiar
blending of the artifact and the real, one of the
strangest confusions of life and letters. So
accustomed had he become to this blend that Pope
himself may not have known how precisely to distinguish the historical portrait from the literary one. That is the enigma that a study of his
life and writings offers.

INTEGRITY AND LIFE IN POPE'S POETRY

S. L. Goldberg

I

In the Preface to his edition of Shakespeare, Pope remarked that Shakespeare's work was 'inspiration indeed; he is not so much an imitator as an instrument of Nature; and 'tis not so just to say that he speaks from her, as that she speaks through him'.[1] It is easy to see what he meant. One mark of a very great writer is to present us with not so much a particular view of the world, as a 'world' itself--an imagined reality so large, so substantial, so free of any merely personal bias, that it seems continuous with our own. Things, places, actions, people assume an independent density and vigour; every particular seems alive; and the whole seems at once self-subsistent and yet everywhere animated by the same protean energy. As Pope said of Homer, ' 'What he writes is of the most animated nature imaginable; everything moves, everything lives and is put in action'.[2] It is what we call 'dramatic' power in its highest manifestation.

Pope himself is not often credited with this kind of power. He does seem to offer us a parti-

This essay first appeared in *Studies in the Eighteenth Century II*, ed. R.F. Brissenden (Canberra: Australian National University Press, 1973), pp. 185-207.

cular view of the world, and consequently it is
his Augustanism that draws most attention. But
to leave the emphasis there seems to me a critical mistake, for it is surely Pope's 'dramatic'
power that ought most to concern us. Whatever
Pope's conscious moral or philosophical intentions, he did not merely reflect his world, represent or 'imitate' it artistically, and comment
critically on it. As he matured, he also came
(as I think he saw) to 'represent' it in the
other sense of embodying its ideal possibilities
of self-awareness and self-criticism. His world
really 'speaks through him': to realise as he
did the significance of so many of its details
was also to make their reality visible--visible
and felt in all their stubborn but fascinating
actuality. Like all great 'dramatic' writers, he
makes his world conscious of itself and thereby
(as he suggests of Shakespeare) he partly re-
creates it. In fact, I think Pope re-creates his
world more substantially, ranges in it more
widely, and engages with it more profoundly, than
any English writer between Shakespeare and
Dickens. It is a remarkable achievement for one
who wrote so much formally in his own voice
(Chaucer's is perhaps the only comparable case
in English); and if Arnold had been able to appreciate what the great novelists of his own age
were doing, or had even understood the relationship between his own criticism of life and Pope's,
he might have discerned one or two important
truths in his otherwise silly remark that Pope is
a classic of our prose. If Pope's affinities
reach back to early seventeenth-century drama as
well as to seventeenth-century poetry and prose,
they also reach forward to the nineteenth-century
novel and to nineteenth- and twentieth-century
poetry and criticism.
   One such affinity is perhaps too obvious to
have been much noticed, though the nineteenth
century's myths about Augustanism did not help
anyone to appreciate it, nor do the twentieth
century's own myths about the 'dissociation of
sensibility' or the genealogy of 'modernism'.

For Pope is not only an intensely 'dramatic' poet, he is also an intensely self-conscious one.
By this I do not mean merely that he was a deliberate craftsman (though of course he was), nor
that he deployed his various self-images with
masterly skill (though he did), nor even that
references to himself form part of a quite remarkable number of his poems (though they do).
More than that, he was so serious about being a
poet that he obviously had something like a
sense of vocation about it--a consciousness from
first to last that his destiny, his very self,
was essentially that of a poet and Wit. He knew
the power of genius in himself; it was only half
a joke, for example, to assert that *The Dunciad*
'was not made for these Authors, but these
Authors for the Poem'.³ But as we might expect,
the degree to which he actually understood himself corresponded exactly to the degree of his
understanding of other people and of the ways in
which their lives were also fated. His view of
himself and his view of the objective world corresponded; and he clearly came to see this himself. But I think he also increasingly sensed
that to realise the objective world was simultaneously to realise, to fulfil, and thereby to
define himself--and vice versa.
     These may sound odd terms to apply to Pope,
as though he were some kind of prophet of
Romanticism or a secret crypto-modernist. But
it is worth remembering that Shaftesbury, for
example, even in 1710 could advocate 'soliloquy',
as he called it, or 'inward colloquy'--essenti-
ally, the creative *dramatisation* of inner conflicts
and possibilities--as a way of achieving moral
self-consciousness.⁴ As for poetic self-consciousness, the Romantics may have been the first to
philosophise about it systematically, but they
didn't after all invent it. Nor did self-definition become a problem only for writers in
the nineteenth and twentieth centuries, despite
the way some critics of modern literature talk.
To look no further back, it was problem enough
for some of Shakespeare's tragic heroes, or for

Donne, or Marvell, or even for Milton; and it was
no less so for Pope. Of course it is more usual
to regard his art, like so much else in his age,
as strictly--indeed, consciously--impersonal, and
to talk of his use of artistic *personae* rather than
different manifestations of his self. His age is
supposed to have rested upon a commonly accepted,
stable, comprehensive, and objective order of
moral values, natural laws, and social institutions, in which no man needed to be much per-
plexed abou who *he* really was or where *he* properly belonged; and Pope, it is assumed, simply
adopted a number of recognised traditional *personae*-- the social Wit, the easy Horatian Moralist, the philosophic Sage, the happy and virtuous
Recluse, the dignified Poet and Critic of life,
and so on--which are taken as devices, impersonal techniques, whereby Pope could get his personal self out of the way and bring traditional
and impersonal values to bear on the present.
    However much truth there may be in this view,
it is not really adequate to Pope. For one
thing, while it is obviously true that each of
his poems is a created object in its own right,
not a direct personal confession, it is also true
that it is created by, and embodies, a particular
mind, not some impersonal rhetorical process. In
the second place, it is hard not to agree with
Irvin Ehrenpreis in his suspicion of the term
persona as applied to Pope. No one at the time
thought the Alexander Pope inside the poems was
a quite different creature from the Alexander
Pope who published them; indeed, it is often the
very point of the poems that they are the same.
Clearly, it would be absurd to identify Pope
with any one of his self-images; nevertheless, as
Ehrenpreis argues, 'through his masterpieces a
man defines--not hides--himself', and this, I
think, was Pope's own view of it too.[5] Moreover,
a term like *persona* suggests that he was more assured of the certain certainties of his age, and
more self-possessed in confronting his material,
than he really was. His 'wit' constantly played
over those certainties; real self-possession--a

full, measured, and secure self-understanding as
a poet--was something he had continually to
strive towards and win. And for a mind like his,
as Johnson so well describes it, 'active, ambitious, and adventurous, always investigating, always aspiring', every success could be only partial and temporary.[6] In one sense, Maynard Mack
is obviously right to insist that the satiric
speaker in Pope's poems is a fiction. 'We may
call this speaker Pope, if we wish', he says--
though I cannot see what else we can call him,
even while agreeing with Mack's general point
that we can call him Pope 'only if we remember
that he always reveals himself as a character in
a drama, not as a man confiding in us'.[7] I
doubt if the matter is finally quite as clear-
cut as that, but in any case it is Pope the
"drmmatist' that matters, and the relevant kind
of impersonality to seek in his work is that
manifested in the greatest dramatic 'masterpieces'--an integrity and plenitude of dramatic
and personal realisation.[8]

II

     The impulse towards such self-possession ap-
pears long before the obvious cases of the 1730's
and 40s. In every one of his major poems up to
1717, Pope tries, more or less successfully, to
locate the self who writes the poem by defining
it in relation to his own personal experience on
the one hand, and to the particular subject of
the poem on the other. The reference to himself
at the end of the *Essay on Criticism*, for example,
hardly warrants even the term *persona*: it is little more than a conventional gesture imitated
from Boileau, a tactful claim to modesty and
moral integrity. But the actual spirit of the
poem is much less conventional; it corresponds
rather with the pervasive Longinian strain in its
argument. Words like *life, force, vigour, motion,
fire, ardent, teeming,* and so on, play against two
other sets of words. One comprises such terms as
glittering, chaos, gaudy, and the like. The other

is an even more significant group: *dull, malignant, slow, creep, sleep, lumber, dust, dullness.* Pope once remarked that 'of the two extremes one could sooner pardon frenzy than frigidity';[9] and the similarly contrasting terms of the *Essay on Criticism* point forward to his explicit understanding later on in *The Dunciad*: that it is essentially the 'Elasticity' and 'Fire' his own verse represents that is the measure of the fools and dunces.[10] Another interesting example is a passage he wrote as a young man to add to Wycherley's *Panegyrick on Dulness*, where he states, in a merely 'witty' and theoretical way, an insight that he fully realises only in the last Book of *The Dunciad*: that the poet's 'wit', the very principle of life in him, actually depends upon Dulness, not only as the substance it seeks to transform and enliven, but as that in which it 'last must end'. Being 'satisfy'd, secure, and innocent', Dulness is a reality both within and outside the self; being 'fit for all Stations', it is paradoxically the very element in which life manifests itself.

The consciousness of a power in himself less sedate, less controllable, less socially amenable, and far less modest, than a young man could fully understand, let alone express, is clearly part of the self that writes these early poems. It peeps out in *The Temple of Fame* (1715), for instance, where Pope measures the personal cost of seeking poetic fame. Once again, the opposition he sees there--between seeking a conscious moral integrity (which might well necessitate a psychic *retreat* from the world) and a conscious claim to public recognition (which is virtually the need to *master* the world)--is still rather crude, rather notional, in comparison with his later sense of the strains and difficulties involved. The finest of his early poems, *The Rape of the Lock* and the 'Epistle to Miss Blount, on her leaving the Town, after the Coronation', do realise their conflicting values with real vivacity and a delicate, even tender, sharpess; and Pope does hold them in a fine balance. All the

same, he achieves that balance only because his
sense of the opposing forces, and of what must be
sacrificed in balancing them, is limited--limited
in ways that Marvell's sense of them in 'The
Garden', for instance, is not. 'Annihilating' is
not a word Pope seems to need in either poem;
nor does Clarissa's 'good humour' quite answer
to the fate of those wretches who hang that jury-
men may dine.

Where Pope does reach out in these early poems towards such harsher, less tractable aspects
of life, his sense of them inevitably corresponds
to the extent and coherence of his self-understanding. *Windsor Forest*, for example, remains a
mess; his exercises in the 'pathetic' mode remain far more pathetic than passionate. As
Aubrey Williams has noted, in *The Rape of the Lock*
Pope was concerned with 'a "type" of human experience ... in which loss must be suffered if
... gain is to be at all achieved'.[11] In both
'Eloisa to Abelard' and the 'Elegy to the Memory
of an Unfortunate Lady' he is concerned with the
same thing within the individual; and as his
obvious self-identification with both unfortunate ladies suggests, he is trying not only to
express the centre of their fates, the centre of
each self as it confronted the world, but also to
explore how far it is also a centre to which his
own sense of himself could cohere. Certainly
he now realises the distinction between the self
and the world is more complex than it appeared
in *Windsor Forest*. There is no conventional cant
about 'home-felt Quiet', 'observing a Mean', '
'soft retreats', and the like. As he sees, human life asks more than 'the world forgetting,
by the world forgot'. But both poems remain so
merely rhetorical because what Pope realises, at
their centre and in his own self, is less the
need and the capacity to commit one's life to a
genuine passion than the *consciousness* of that
need and capacity. He sees his subject-matter
with a contricting kind of self-consciousness, as
though it were enough to indulge in emotional
rhetoric about it rather than to take emotion and

rhetoric as means to discover it. His sense of
himself has a correspondingly external pathos--a
not very engaging mixture, in fact, of self-pity
and self-congratulation on being a poet. And
once again it hardly encompasses the harsher,
more hostile feelings which give the poems such
life as they have, and which spring from a quite
different part of himself. One of the most revealing sentences in the Preface to his 1717
volume contains a metaphor that often recurs in
his work: 'the life of a Wit', he remarks, 'is a
warfare upon earth'. The word 'life', we may
notice, is as significant as 'warfare'.[12]
    This other side of him begins to take consci-
ous form in 'The Universal Prayer', which he
first wrote in 1715, or in the 'Hymn Written in
Windsor Forest' of 1717. One stanza of the
'Prayer', for example, deals with a temptation
that surely very few people can have felt strongly enough to think it warranted a place in a
'universal' prayer:

        Let not this weak, unknowing hand
            Presume Thy Bolts to throw,
        And deal Damnation round the land,
            On each I judge thy Foe.

Looking back from Pope's later work ('Yes, I am
proud; I must be proud to see / Men not afraid
of God afraid of me'), we can see why he might
have been troubled by some elements in himself.
Clearly, the simple integrity of innocence, retirement, identification with the conventional
ethical virtues, was impossible to one whose
genius had to take him into the world. Eventually, the losses he had to accept as the other
side of this destiny prompted a fuller, if more
difficult, understanding both of the world and of
himself, rather than driving him to moral retreat
or emotional indulgence.

III

Such integrity did not come just from Pope's
wanting it, however, nor was he always right in
thinking he had achieved it. He was only the
first to think (as some scholars still do) that
his mature work is really animated and shaped by
the values to which he consciously attached himself; reason, good sense, taste, nature, order,
and so on. But as a number of critics have
pointed out, his imagination draws most of its
vigour from the disorder, folly, irrationality,
dullness, grotesque and fantastic distortions
and extremes, that it realises as active forces
in the world around him. If Pope eventually
came to see this himself, he was not very clear
about it at first. His confusions in the *Essay on
Man*, for example, are most revealing. In so far
as the *Essay* has any poetic life, it does not lie
in Pope's repeated and rather strident assertions
of a cosmic plan, or his attacks on 'pride', or
even in his occasional perceptions of a scale of
being in nature.[13] His mind most fully realises
itself in realising the strange forms, the ambivalent energies, the self-entangled contradictions
of the world: the realities he tries to fix
within the bounds of a single cosmic idea. To
annihilate all that's made to a thought is to be
able to identify it as a whole, and therefore in
some sense to possess it all. Equally, it is to
possess all the possible forms of the self in a
single thought too--the self that can reach out
sympathetically to realise other forms of life
and in doing so fulfil itself, partly at least.
Nevertheless, it is an annihilation. Things are
drained of their actuality; the mind, in order to
rest in one ultimate idea, must (as Pope continually insists) 'cease' some of its activity. It
must 'desist' from curiosity and aspiration; indeed, it must voluntarily surrender part of its
life to fulfil a mysterious and impersonal order
outside itself. Pope's theme in the *Essay* has
been called 'constructive renunciation';[14] yet
what is 'constructed' becomes less real precise-

ly as the 'renunciation' becomes more insistent.
The vehemence with which he tries in the *Essay* to
assert an objective order--tries, that is, to
possess all possible experience and thereby secure both the world and himself within one self-
sufficient and demonstrable object of thought--
seems to be the reaction of a mind made inse-
cure, even anxious, by its very capacities. In
beating down 'pride', he seems to be beating down
an uneasy (and never quite acknowledged) sense of
the restlessly active, various, outflying, *cen-
trifugal* force of his own imagination. He seems
determined to rope the self down within the confines of a single, recognisable identity, and to
find in large, indisputable abstractions an imposing bastion, an impregnable centre, from which
to command all the confusions of life.

What I am suggesting is more than an attraction in Pope towards chaos, disorder, and eccen-
tricity, quite as powerful as that towards order,
form, and moral rationality.[15] It is more, too,
than a local conflict of the sort Reuben Brower
points to, between Pope's philosophy and his
sensibility.[16] It is an unavoidable problem
within himself--one that drew him forward to his
later work. For he cannot help responding to a
value in the disorder he sees. Its energy and
substance remain for him an irreducible part of
life; but if it prompts, it also seems to with-
stand, every formal paradox, every set of opposing terms, in which he tries to comprehend it in
a larger whole. Consequently he is driven to
seek a centre within himself where sympathetic
responsiveness, as well as true understanding,
authoritative judgment, and virtuous intent, all
coincide. The search for objectively 'real' values in the world is also the search for 'real'
identity--for a self that can and must and should
acknowledge the impersonal authority of those
values.

Thus the problem Pope stumbled into in the
Essay on Man is not simply to reconcile such opposing ideas as A. O. Lovejoy has traced all
through Western culture. For one thing, the op-

position Lovejoy saw between 'otherworldliness' and 'this-worldliness' ramifies much further than he noticed. Not only has the One been set against the Many, order against plenitude and diversity, peace and concord against abundance and fullness of being, the Idea against physical reality, universal Reason against idiosyncrasy, and so on. Because all of these have ethical implications, they have been accompanied by other opposites. Contemplation has been set against action, retirement against public life, country against city and court, the individual self against the fragmentations of society, rest against movement and aspiration, self-sufficiency against involvement with and dependence upon others, self-preservation and withholding against giving and self-consumption, character against sensibility, sincerity against being tactful and accommodating, fixed idenity against fluidity and the manifold potentialities of the self, the capacity (which Coleridge saw in Milton) to attract 'all forms and things to himself, into the unity of his own IDEAL', against the capacity (which he saw in Shakespeare) to dart forth, and pass 'into all the forms of human character and passion, the one Proteus of the fire and the flood'.[17] As Lovejoy suggests, such oppositions have generally been taken as dilemmas, terms that exhaust all the possibilities between them, and the Western mind has generally tried either to reduce one to the other or to reconcile both in some 'higher' third term. Moreover, the oppositions themselves have generally been taken as an inter-related set: any one opposition has tended to melt into others. This suggests, of course (as has been increasingly obvious since the early nineteenth century), that such oppositions are wholly or in part polarities of thought; the opposing terms are inter-dependent, so that to conceive the one is to conceive the other. But it also underlines another reason why Pope's difficulties were not merely local, philosophical ones. The opposing terms are more than 'ideas' in Lovejoy's sense. Their significance lies in their experiential content; and if for no other reason, this makes it necessary to distinguish (as many scholars, including Lovejoy, do not) between the different ways such oppositions may present themselves in literature. They may indeed appear as conceptual 'ideas', merely expounded or alluded to; but they may also appear as conflicts betrayed or exhibited by a work, or choices explored in it, or (as some Romantics wanted of all art) aspects of life that are absorbed in, and transcended by, the poetic imagination. We may recall Coleridge's famous description of the imagination as a power that, while activated and continuously controlled by the will and the understanding, 'reveals itself in the balance or reconciliation of opposite or discordant qualities'.18 With regard to these oppositions, it would be truer to say that the imagination seeks not so much a 'balance' or 'reconciliation'--which may all too easily take a form *dictated* by the will and the understanding: a conceptual paradox or an idea in which the poet invests his conscious belief (*discordia concors*, for example)--but rather a wholeness of life, a 'unity of being', an integrity, which the imagination itself achieves in responding fully to all the complexities of life, but which it may also see as impossible to sustain in ordinary life. Another of Coleridge's observations is perhaps even more to the point, for as he says, the poem apprehending the world truly, 'brings the whole soul of man into activity, with the subordination of its faculties to each other, according to their relative worth and dignity'.19

On one side, then, the temptation is to suppose order and value are merely data in the world, obscure but given facts of life to which the individual consciousness must submit, rather than possibilities of the world realised by the mind *in* its activity, forms in which the individual realises his identity as at once an individual, an inhabitant of a particular society, and a member of the human race. On the other side, the temptation is to equate an integral wholeness of of being with a visible, objective simplicity.

It is all too easy to think we have located our
'true' self when we have only lopped our experience back to some 'essential' or 'natural' pattern supposedly underlying all complexities:
locating it, for instance, in the consciousness
of our continuous and sincere attachment to a
number of basic virtues. Pope's struggle to get
free of both these temptations marks his artistic
development through the 1730s and 1740s.

IV

   It is interesting to see the change from the
Essay on Man in (say) the *Imitation* of Horace's
first Epistle of Book I, published in 1738. Here,
Pope speaks of the imprudence of galloping his
Pegasus to death, of the folly of writing at all,
and of the inconsistencies he shares with the
victims of his satire. But the poetry in which
he speaks of all this is anything but a Pegasus
'devoid of fire, or force', and anything but incoherent. He talks as if inside the public Poet
there was a simple, virtuous, wholly self-possessed Man struggling to get out--one who might
say what he says elsewhere, 'Let Us be fix'd, and
our own Masters still'.[20] But both the public
and the private selves here turn out to be only
manifestations of a yet deeper self: the one that
looks at the other two, laughs at the contrast,
and actually is its 'own master still', but *without* being 'fixed'. Bolingbroke may be most fully
himself in 'never' (as Pope puts it) 'changing
one muscle of his face' at the inconsistencies of
other men; the integrity Pope realises in the poem is of a different (and more valuable) kind.
For the self that writes these lines must laugh
at his other two manifestations, not only because
they are false, but also because they are not
wholly false. Each does simplify, and so reduce,
the whole of Pope's identity, but neither is insincere or a mere 'mask' or *persona*. As the
writer sees, the only way he can realise his
whole self is in the vivacious, critical, and coherent perception of those aspects of it--and of

the social and personal facts to which those aspects are the only honest, sincere answer he can
make in the real world.[21]
    All the *Imitations of Horace* and both the *Epistle
to Arbuthnot* and the *Epilogue to the Satires* are built,
more or less securely, on a similar interplay
between the public self (in his various forms--
the Wit, the Critic, the Sage, the Moralist, and
so on), the private 'real' self beneath that (in
his various forms--lisping in numbers, stooping
to truth, practising virtue, or piddling along
with broccoli and mutton), and the writer of the
actual poem in which the other two are portrayed
and defended. One common mistake with these poems is simply to equate all three figures, which
unfortunately tends to make Pope look something
of a hypocrite at times, or rather priggish, or
pompously self-important. Another is to separate
the three figures altogther, which unfortunately
tends to leave him with no specific identity at
all. But it is not always clear just how the
three figures are related to one another--largely
because Pope the writer was not always clear a-
bout it either. The *Epistle to Arbuthnot* is a case
in point, where the end of the poem seems quite
at odds with the rest. As a personal apologia,
the *Epistle* really depends on the brilliant 'fire'
of its poetry and the protean but steady 'force'
of its insight and judgment: on an imaginative
wholeness, that is, of which only a part consists
in the 'wit' and honesty of the public self, and
another part in the conscious moral intent of the
private self. This is clear enough even in lines
not directly about himself:

    You think this cruel? take it for a rule,
    No creature smarts so little as a Fool.
    Let Peals of Laughter, *Codrus!* round thee break,
    Thou unconcern'd canst hear the mighty Crack.
    Pit, Box and Gall'ry in convulsions hurl'd,
    Thou stand'st unshook amidst a bursting World.
                                    (lines 83ff)

The writer of these lines is obviously not one who
could stand unshook amidst a bursting world; indeed, he demonstrates his lack of folly in his
very responsiveness to Codrus's nature. His 'wit'
lies in seeing that the ability to stand in un-
shaken self-possession in all circumstances and
not to feel threatened or excited by the outside
world, is the mark of an ultimate lack of spirit
and intelligence. Obviously the writer here is
not the public figure, whose only wish is to
'maintain a Poet's Dignity and Ease'. Nor is he
the private man, who in the final section of the
poem claims that he only wishes to 'live my own!
and die so too!' (line 261) and to be like his
'innoxious' father, who 'held it for a rule / It
was a Sin to call our Neighbour Fool' (lines 382-
3). This latter self is quite sincere, of course,
in wanting only to 'rock the Cradle of reposing
Age / With lenient Arts extend a Mother's breath';
but in the final section of the poem, the writer
has come simply to identify himself with the
private man; and in doing so, he has stamped flat
all the vital antitheses in his own being--the
being who could respond with such insight and
such controlled, 'unlenient' art to Codrus, for
instance, or to Atticus, or to Sporus: 'And he
himself one vile Antithesis'. The last section
of the poem fails to sustain the bite and integrity of passages like those.
     Pope's impulse to 'fix' an identity that he
could *know* was continually at odds with his very
capacity to know anything--with his appetite for
life, his mobility, and his vivacious intelligence and wit. On the other hand, he could not
simply define himself as a bundle of contradictions either: he was conscious of a more significant kind of coherence than that. Thus, although
he was often led to identify himself in rather
conventional terms, this does not mean that the
impulse to do so represented something merely
conventional in him. It does mean, however, that
he is not reducible to any one of the self-images
he projects in his verse. In his satires of the
1730s, for instance, he is not, as Maynard Mack

and others tend to assume he is, 'really' the
virtuous Horatian Recluse, standing aside from a
corrupted society and opposing to it his ideal
vision of social life. Pope's poetry represents
that world too, quite as much as (if not more
than) those who corrupt it; and Mack's argument
in *The Garden and the City* seems to me based on an
insufficiently wide and critical grasp of the poetic facts.[22] As a matter of biographical fact,
Pope's retirement from the city in the 1730s was
obviously sincere; nor was there anything ignoble
in wanting to withdraw from a corrupt society and
to denounce its corruption. The long tradition
of 'retirement' to some simpler and loftier bastion of the spirit testifies to the perennial
need behind it. But it is also important to notice that Pope denounces that society *to itself*.
To identify him with any one aspect of him is to
mistake only one aspect of his poetry for the
whole. It is also to miss what his critical
imagination achieves at its greatest moments.
The poet that Mack depicts is hardly the one, for
example, who in the *Epilogue to the Satires* pene-
trates with such searching and creative disgust,
into the ambiguities of retirement:

>   There, where no Passion, Pride, or Shame trans-
>   port,
>   Lull'd with the sweet *Nepenthe* of a court...
>   (lines 7ff.)

   Mack does observe, in a footnote, that Pope
tends to take himself for a subject in the poems
of the 1730s, and that 'his favorite image of
himself' owes a 'transparent debt to Montaigne as
well as Horace'.[23] He dismisses the matter as a
'subject that has not so far been adequately explored', and indeed it has not. Yet this way of
putting it is no less misleading than Mack's own
emphasis. For if the best of Pope's poetry is
not written by a virtuous Recluse, neither is it
written by a man who (as Pope claims) loves 'to
pour out all myself, as plain / As downright
Shippen, or as old *Montagne*'. As he says, 'Fools

rush into my Head, and so I write',[24] but the
actual writing is certainly no pouring out of the
self nor the exercise of some favourite self-image.
Because the cast of Pope's imagination is so
thoroughly dialectical, the impulse to 'fix' his
true character is not merely a misguided attempt
to identify himself with some consciously chosen
persona or image, nor even a wish to play every
role in the text like Bottom the weaver. It is
the necessary reaction to the *out*going imagination, an attempt to find the centre in himself
from which the imagination darts forth and to
which it returns, the point where the personal
fuses with the impersonal, each giving life, definition, and authority to the other.

V

The full integrity of his own life was something Pope could realise only 'dramatically' (as
he does in most of *Arbuthnot*, for example, or in
the ending of the *Epilogue to the Satires*),[25] but I
think his greatest poetry is dramatic in a more
direct sense: where his imagination, his 'whole
soul', turns completely outwards to the lives of
other selves, and realises its own integrity only
in realising that of its object.
I have deliberately used the word 'integrity'
because it embraces various inter-related meanings, which we need to be clear about in order to
understand Pope's real achievement and importance.
In its most obvious sense, 'integrity' refers to
moral wholeness or consistency. An individual
has 'integrity' in possessing a single, unyield-
ing ethical core. That is, the word pertains to
the understanding and the will; to lack integrity
in this sense is to be insincere, or weak, or
just morally stupid. With an eye to Pope's rather confused ideas on the subject, we might also
notice that the word 'character' can have pretty
much the same meaning as 'integrity' here: 'a
man of integrity' is 'a man of character'.
In a second sense, 'integrity' refers to
psychological wholeness or consistency--the particu-

lar pattern of motives and causes that determine
the individual's feelings, attitudes and behaviour. Even a villain may have a human 'integrity'
in this sense; to lack it is to be mad, or un-
stable, or an incomprehensible mystery. And once
again 'character' can have much this same meaning
too: as in Pope's line, 'Most Women have no
Characters at all'.[26]
In yet a third sense, 'integrity' refers to
the realised *identity* of an individual--the completeness with which he is the particular human
being he is, his coherence, his Total disposition,
as a single being. Since this comprises all of
his particular ways of being alive in the world,
as distinct from those of any other person, the
word now includes what is meant by the existen-
tialists' term 'authenticity'. To lack this kind
of integrity is to fail in some vital respect to
be an individual at all, or to be oneself only
incompletely, to live (as the existentialist
would put it) in 'bad faith'. What makes the corresponding sense of 'character' hard to define
is that sometimes we regard a person's disposition as something he chooses, the effect of an
unconscious will in him to be what he is, while
at other times we regard his capacity to choose
as finally dependent on his disposition, so that
his 'character' seems less the visible effect of
his choice than the visible sign of his fate or
destiny. Nevertheless, there is a relevant sense
of 'character' here: if, for example, a man acts
gratuitously, he negates his 'character' in the
first sense I mentioned, and in another way the
second sense too, but he affirms it in this third
sense. Thus Macbeth's 'character' (or 'integrity')
lies in *everything* he chooses his fate to be--al-
though, as we see it, this is also everything he
is destined to choose.
But at this point the three senses of the word
obviously begin to coalesce. In the last analysis, we cannot separate destiny and choice, constancy and freedom; and we therefore give 'integrity' or 'character' a composite meaning to embrace all the ways that impersonal facts and

forces and values shape the individual person,
and are in turn given visible shape and significance by the whole, integral activity of the person. At the very roots of consciousness, and *a
fortiori* of self-consciousness, impersonal causes
seem both to determine, and yet to be transformed
into, personal motive and choice; impersonal
social traditions and pressures seem to condition, and yet to be subject to, the personal will
that accepts or rejects them; the possibilities
of an impersonal order in the objective world
seem to be realised only in the personal activity
of apprehending them.[27] In the end, the 'integrity' of any individual is nothing less than his
'whole soul' in active and passive engagement
with the whole of the not-self. It is the complex but elusive sense of 'character' corresponding to this that Shakespeare was concerned with
(as in *Macbeth* or *King Lear*); so in different ways,
have the great novelists of the nineteenth and
twentieth centuries been concerned with it too,
as in some of Dickens's so-called 'caricatures',
for instance, or (more consistently) in *The
Brothers Karamazov*, or *Daniel Deronda*, or *Nostromo*, or
in *Women in Love* and *Ulysses*. The tragic writer
is most aware of how *much* a man may choose to
experience in order to be what he is; the comic
writer (and theories of 'humours' or the like
are very much to the point) is most aware of how
little a man need choose to experience in order
to be what he is; but obviously these are not
mutually exclusive points of view: indeed, in
Pope it is almost impossible to distinguish them
at times. But it is finally in Pope's concern
with human 'character' in this sense that I see
the basis of his stature and importance.
   He tries to explain his ideas about it mainly
in the first of the *Moral Essays*, on the 'Ruling
Passion', and it is not hard to see why so few
readers have taken him seriously. All of Johnson's objections, for example, are thoroughly
justified; Pope's argument is confused, and does
look like 'a kind of moral predestination' doubly
confused with an absurdly simplified psychology.[28]

Nevertheless, it is worth asking if Pope was not
driving at something rather different from what he
seems to be saying, or even from what he thought
he was saying. He talks about both causes and
motives, but muddles them together; he talks
about inconsistencies both of behaviour and of
valuation, but muddles these together too; he
claims that social forces condition the individual's 'manners', but he also claims that social
phenomena are shaped and coloured by the 'manners'
of the individual perceiving them. But if I have
rather laboured the meaning of the term 'integrity' or 'character', it is because it may help us
see Pope's confusion here as the result less of
incompetence than of an insight he could not
quite express in the conceptual vocabulary available to him. As I see it, his real concern is
not to reduce human behaviour to a single psychological cause, nor (like Shaftesbury, and even
Montaigne perhaps)[29] to try to reduce all the individual's ethical activity to a single centre
where it assumes rational consistency. Nor is he
merely after a formula for depicting an individual's unique identity. His own principle, that
'all Manners take a tincture from his own',
applies to his analytic 'manner' here. The awareness of his personal inconsistencies and fluidity impelled him to try to 'fix' his full integrity in some concept of himself; just so, his very
responsiveness to others' inconsistencies impels
him to try to fix their full integrity: to fix
the point at which men's 'Manners with Fortunes,
Humours turn with Climes', which is also the
point where those fortunes and climes become des-
tinies men choose for themselves in choosing to
obey their pressure. The 'ruling passion' is the
name Pope gives the point at which the individual
is most intensely, most passionately, alive *as*
himself; and since it also *delimits* his being, it
is like the 'lurking principle of death' he receives at 'the moment of his breath'.[30] Thus the
term includes all its psychological, moral, and
even philosophical meanings, since it is what we
might call a 'dramatic' principle: for Pope, the

'ruling passion' is the shaping and animating
principle of an individual life as a dramatist
could conceive it simultaneously from within and
from outside.[31] Not surprisingly, Pope's meaning
emerges far more clearly in the way his imagination actually sees particular cases (in the examples at the end of the poem) than in the way his
intellect tries to expound the idea. With
Helluo, whose 'fate' was a salmon's belly, as
with the miserly old crone, or poor vain Narcissa,
or any of them indeed, the individual's integri-
ty--which is nothing less than the very principle
of life in him and therefore nothing less than
his whole destiny--can be seen as comic or heroic or tragic or (as Pope sees it here) something
of all three at once. But either way, Pope's
'Characters' here and elsewhere--Atticus, say, or
Sporus, or Villiers, or the main figures in the
fourth book of *The Dunciad*--are distinguished from
those of any writer of 'Characters' before him
precisely by this kind of integrity: the integrity of the imagination comprehending (and so also
judging) the integrity of the individual as at
once an ethical being, a social or psychological
type, and a unique consciousness, sensibility,
and will.[32]

Pope's judgments are therefore far more complex and searching than any reference to conscious Augustan norms would suggest. Some of the
finest examples come in the second *Moral Essay*, on
'the Characters of Women'--examples all the more
interesting for the hints here and there of a
conscious relationship between the subject and
Pope himself. Flavia, the 'Wit', whose whole
being desires 'while we live, to live', has so
much fire and force that she can only 'die of nothing but a Rage to live'. She has authenticity,
we might say, but no moral centre. The cases
that immediately follow have a moral centre, a
'fixed' character, but lack a necessary mobility
or 'fire'. With Atossa, Pope actually echoes the
phrase he had used of himself: 'with herself or
others', she 'finds all her life one warfare upon
earth'. She

Shines, in exposing Knaves, and painting Fools,
Yet is, whate'er she hates and ridicules.
                              (lines 117-18)

'Madame Atossa, c'est moi'. It is as if Pope is realising in himself the self-laceration he sees as
Atossa's 'character'. Again, at some points he
tends to think of women (rather simplistically)
as 'chameleons' that cannot be accurately painted
in 'white and black'--with the clear implication,
of course, that he has to be something of a chameleon himself to get them 'right'. At the end,
however, turning to Martha Blount, he sees not a
chameleon, but a 'blend' of the best (but opposing) qualities of each sex: 'Fix'd Principles,
with Fancy ever new', and so on. Heaven 'shakes
all together and produces--You'. Once again the
self-implication is clear. If Heaven gave her
sense and good humour, it also gave her a poet
whose own character--chameleon-like, but not
without 'fixed principles'--can realise the nature and value of hers. Pope makes the point a-
bout himself very delicately--and of course long
before Keats used the same word, chameleon, for
the 'dramatic' poet's lack of a fixed identity.
    Nevertheless, oppositions like that between
'chameleon' and 'fixed principles' are hardly
adequate to Pope's very greatest poetry, here or
elsewhere: for example, the passage here that begins, 'Yet mark the fate of a whole Sex of
Queens!', and ends with 'Alive ridiculous, and
dead, forgot' (lines 219-48). At first, the
lines do turn on the opposition between the 'foreign glory, foreign joy' that women seek--the
outgoing movement of life, against its integrat-
ing movement inwards towards a stable centre:
'Peace or Happiness at home', a 'well-tim'd Retreat' from the world, and so on. Yet (as always
with Pope) the word 'fate' introduces a more profound kind of insight and judgment, which transcends such polarities: 'As Hags hold Sabbaths'...
'their merry miserable Night'...'Ghosts of Beauty'
...'haunt the places where their Honour dy'd'...
'See how the World its Veterans rewards'. Com-

pared with the way Pope saw human 'fate' in *The Rape of the Lock*, this passage is not only more substantial, more deeply observed, felt, and considered; his object here, in all of its personal, social, and even metaphysical dimensions, wholly contains his response to it in all of *its* dimensions. Here, 'fixed principles' *are* 'fancy ever new', and 'sense' and 'good humour' the other side of horror and compassion. To know that the life of a Wit is a warfare upon earth can amuse him, but it can also lacerate him with the consciousness of his being not just an elusive chameleon but a scarred and vulnerable veteran of the world too. But it is the *life* of the Wit, wholly realised in seeing what it means for these women to be no more than veterans of the world, that finally prevents him from also being 'alive, ridiculous, and dead, forgot'.[33]

A comparable passage is the ending of the third *Moral Essay* (to Bathurst), 'Of the Use of Riches'. Whatever argumentative function the story of Sir Balaam has in the Essay as a whole, I think Pope's instinct was right to end with it, for it collects and fuses together all the various attitudes towards money and the power of money that go before. The Balaam passage is at once a 'life', a tale, a criticism of society, a brilliantly funny tragedy, a religious parable-- a whole drama, one might say, or rather a whole novel, concentrated under intensely creative power into a mere sixty-four lines. It is surely one of the greatest things in the language; certainly, it is characteristic of nobody but Pope. In theory, of course, his account earlier in the poem of the Man of Ross (lines 250-82) represents his ideals--the norm against which he claims to be judging the commercialisation of society. In fact, it represents only what he thought his central norm was. The difference in actual effect between that passage and the account of Sir Balaam could hardly be more striking: with the Man of Ross, rhetorical questions and vaguely general nouns, the verse deliberately flattening out its characteristic tensions and antitheses to

correspond with an ideal peace, an ideal single-
ness of purpose, and a human identity so ideally
simple that it is no more than the sum of its
virtuous deeds--and £500 per annum; with Balaam,
verve, spirit, a tone responsively alive to every
manifestation of life--'an added pudding', 'farth-
ings to the poor', 'his gains were sure', 'rouz'd
by the Prince of Air, the whirlwinds sweep / The
surge', 'lo! two puddings smoak'd upon the board',
'Behold Sir Balaam, now a man of spirit', 'Things
change their titles, as our manners turn'. All
through the passage, the rhythms evoke and comment simultaneously; the nouns are specific, and
they gather metaphoric generality like an elec-
trical charge. Pope's attitude is no less complex
than the complex relationship he sees between having one's soul 'secured', and 'being a man of
spirit' and 'wit'; between being acted upon and
choosing to acted on; between 'biting' and being
'bit'; between 'manners' and names and 'titles'.
The energy of the verse is that of the world it
evokes, even that of the Prince of Air who enters
this society through the soul Balaam opens to him.
Pope really *enjoys* Balaam. His detachment includes a certain complicity; his contempt is
mixed, though not diluted, with pity. The writing is more buoyant, less compassionate than the
passage on women; but the same edge of dismay
under the precision, the bitter taste of loss and
futility that gathers under the moralist's re-
lentless logic, make the last few lines on Balaam's end far more adequate a response to this
society than all the talk about moderation, general use, reconciled extremes, and the 'thrice
happy' Man of Ross. Here, the choices and deeds
and understanding of men (including Pope's own)
are seen as conditioned by inescapable forces--
psychological, social, moral and metaphysical--
and conversely those forces are seen as manifest-
ing themselves for good or evil only in the individual's life--in personal choices, deeds, and
understanding.

The greatness of the final *Dunciad* lies in this
kind of dramatic insight and power, much more

than in its forceful application of Augustan
norms to Augustan society and culture. Not that
the two features are wholly distinct, of course:
like Balaam's life, the life of Pope's poetry
obviously depends on the norms to which he gives
real (not merely notional) assent. It is significant, for instance, that *Dunciad* IV harks back
(sometimes in a seriously ironic way) to some of
his earlier works;[34] the poem itself announces
the personal implications right at the start.
The poet prays to the mysterious powers he celebrates and to which Time is also taking him:
'Suspend a while your Force inertly strong, /
Then take at once the Poet and the Song' (lines
7-8). As he sees it here, Dulness is not just
a possibility in the world he inhabits, a 'Seed
of Chaos, and of Night', but an actual reality:
it is the buzzing energy, the inert power, the
weird and crazy forms of the life Pope also
shares. It is the operatic singer, for example:

> Joy to great Chaos! let Division reign:
> Chromatic tortures soon shall drive them
>   hence...
> One Trill shall harmonize joy, grief, and rage,
> Wake the dull Church, and lull the ranting
>   Stage...
>
> > (lines 54ff.)

It is the bard and blockhead marching side by
side; the schoolmaster transforming boys into
pedants; pedants transforming verse into prose
again; the chef transforming 'Hares to Larks, and
Pigeons into Toads'; the florist transforming the
flowers of nature (including its human flowers:
'Each Maid cry'd, charming! and each Youth, divine!'); the fop transforming the education of
tastes into the mere eduction of tastes; and so
on. The verse is alive with their activity,
dense with their mental 'density', and integrated
by their creation of 'one mighty Dunciad of the
land'.
     Obviously, part of the joke is that Pope (and
we) realise perfectly well what he is doing here

in transforming the Dunces' life into something
else. The poet's creative 'character' is realising itself in realising theirs. His wit pounces
on their activities as the material of its own.
It too is buzzing with energy, vivacious, gaily
--indeed, hilariously--responsive to every crazy
object, exultant in its power to dart forth any-
where and everywhere so quickly and accurately.
But it realises 'madness' and 'chaos' for what
they are only because it sees them by the light
of its own sanity and order, its own integrity.
Pope, we should notice, does not now suppose that
sanity and order are objective realities outside
himself, divinely given facts merely obscured by
a 'maze' of appearances. The world he sees and
recreates here is not one of mere appearances,
any more than the values by which it is judged
are absolutes shining clearly behind the clouds.
The sun itself is 'sick'; it is precisely because
Dulness is real and alive that it is so much of
a threat to the fullest realisation of life.
Moreover, it is a double threat. On the one
side, the chaotic plenitude of 'madness', its
ever-multiplying forms, its 'bursting world',
draw the mind (Pope's mind, our minds, the Dunces'
minds) outwards, spinning the wits away from any
stable integrity, any morally coherent, psychologically whole, personally authentic being. On
the other side, its force is that of inertia; it
continually pulls the wits back, in towards the
single, fixed, impregnable centre of rest, of
inaction.
    In Pope's whole sense of it, the threat of
Dulness lies in the 'one trill' that 'harmonizes
joy, grief, and rage' as much as in its 'chro-
matic tortures', in the 'dull Church' as much as
'the ranting Stage'. The hour in which Dulness
triumphs is quite properly the 'all-composing'
hour. Peace, concord, and unity are achieved in
the 'one mighty Dunciad of the land'. If Dulness
is the necessary element of the poet's life as a
Wit, and all the figures in the poem like parodies of himself (and of the understanding reader),
it is also a 'resistless' power, one the Muse

must also 'obey'. It is the power that finally
composes everything in an all-inclusive unity,
in imperturbable self-possession, in absolute
integrity: in short, in the undivided, unviolated
chaos of boredom, sleep and death. The final
joke--and Pope clearly appreciates it to the full
--is that (like any man, but more objectively
than most) he realises his own life, his own
'character', in triumphing (with the fullest and
most passionately committed activity of his 'wit')
over the 'resistless' triumph he proclaims. Although the poem portrays the 'all-composing'
power of Dulness, the kind of 'all-composing'
power it actually embodies, the creative power of
human 'wit', remains to confront the triumph of
Dulness with a very different kind of composure,
energy, and integrity.[35]

VI

If there is any substance in the view of Pope
I have been advancing here, it has some more
general implications, of which I shall mention
only two. In the first place, it supports G.K.
Hunter's conclusion that in Pope's *Imitations of
Horace*, Pope is far more personal, more 'Romantic'
as Hunter puts it, than his original.[36] More
than that, we also find in Pope hints of the idea
of the poet-as-outcast (as William Empson has put
it),[37] and even a self-reflexive irony, both of
which are usually regarded as specifically Romantic characteristics. Again, Pope exhibits the
kind of interplay between a 'chameleon' self and
a 'central self' that Patricia Ball sees as a
crucial feature of Romantic and Victorian poetry.[38]
To say all this, however, is not to claim that
Pope was 'really' a Romantic, nor merely to repeat (what everyone knows) that 'Augustan' and
'Romantic' are very slippery terms. But it does
suggest that the English Romantics differed from
Pope less in *exhibiting* these characteristics,
than in being philosophically conscious of them
and of their fundamental importance, and so taking them as a conscious *program* for poetry. Indeed,

it may well be argued that it was just this philosophic and programmatic self-consciousness that limited nineteenth-century poetry. No matter how wide and subtle one's self-consciousness, to 'fix' it in *any* conceptual terms is to make it that much harder to sustain a full integrity of being; and this applies to the Romantics, who understood the point and worried about it, as much as to Pope, who never saw it in those terms. Perhaps the nineteenth-century novelists could achieve this kind of integrity more readily than the poets because they looked at the world more objectively, more dramatically; inasmuch as they were 'fixed' only upon seeking the full integrity of other people's lives, they could more fully realise their own.

As for the second implication, its relevance is illustrated in some recent works by two influential critics, F. R. Leavis and Lionel Trilling. Leavis, for example, has made some very large claims for Blake. He sees Blake's 'rebellion' against Augustanism as 'a vindication' of all that cannot be treated in abstract or quantifiable terms 'since it is "there" only in individual lives'; where, according to Leavis, the Augustans saw man only as a social being, Blake insists that 'a man is an individual, and his individuality is his reality'.[39] This dichotomy of 'abstract' and 'social' on the one side, and 'individuality' and 'particularity' on the other, surely rests on far too conventional a view of the Augustan age; indeed, if my view of Pope is at all tenable, it shows that the Augustan age could, and did, transcend the dichotomy altogether, and it also suggests that, if Blake could not transcend it, this can hardly be regarded as altogether a strength in him.

Much the same objection also applies to Lionel Trilling's recent book, *Sincerity and Authenticity*.[40] For Trilling, the two words in his title represent different stages of moral consciousness, and the shift from one to the other in the late eighteenth century represents one of the most important revolutions in the European mind between

the sixteenth century and the present. This is
not the place to discuss Trilling's argument as a
whole, but it does seem to be based on a view of
each literary period that, however valid for
French or German literature, is little more than
a conventional stereotype for English literature.
To put it bluntly, English literature from
Shakespeare onwards has been more profoundly and
more continuously concerned with what I have
tried to indicate with the word 'integrity' than
with, firstly, 'sincerity' alone, and then 'authenticity' alone. The polarity--or rather the
quasi-Hegelian dialectic--that Trilling sets up
with these terms seems to me not only false to
the history of English literature, but misleading
even about his main focus of interest: the nature
and genesis of 'modernism'. Anyone interested in
modern literature must inevitably look at earlier
literature in the light of that interest, but he
has to look more sharply, more perceptively, and
with fewer preconceptions than Trilling seems to;
and this applies especially to those writers
whose very stature lifts them beyond the commonplace attitudes of their day. It applies preeminently to Shakespeare, for example, and it
also applies to Pope. It may well be that literary history--which is a form of cultural his-
tory--can hardly proceed, as E.H. Gombrich has
suggested, without some quasi-Hegelian pre-sup-
positions about the field, or some quasi-Hegelian terms such as I have been using myself. But
as Gombrich goes on to say, these have to be
continuously *tested* in application, continuously
brought up against a critical attention to the
facts they are supposed to explain.[41] If any
conclusion is beginning to emerge from recent
critical studies of eighteenth-century literature,
it is that the old, essentially nineteenth-century stereotype of 'Augustanism' will no longer
do, nor will any history of English literature
based upon it. The relationship between integrity and life in Pope's poetry is a case in
point. If we look at it critically and without
preconceptions about Pope's art, it surely in-

vites a rather different view of English literature from Trilling's pretty conventional one, or
Leavis's, and of English literature not merely in
the eighteenth century, but in the nineteenth
and twentieth centuries as well.

SATIRE, AND POETRY, AND POPE

Ronald Paulson

Vision and Metamorphosis

My title means that, although my subject is
Pope's satire, I see no way of treating it apart
from his poetry, and in fact my intention is to
indicate some elements of a continuum between his
earliest and latest works, between the "poetry"
of his youth and the "satire" of his maturity.
The origins of his satire are not so much in the
models of Horace and Dryden as in his own early
non-satiric poetry written during those years
when he was making his Virgilian ascent from pastoral, georgic, and heroic epistle to epic, before settling in the 1730's in the foothills of
the Horatian sermo and epistola.
      Pastoral, of course, is an obverse of satire,
always implying the unpastoral world of the present, of the city and the court; the corrupt
world is present like the shadow of a wolf in the
shepherd's fold.[1] The young Pope followed Spenser in making his *Pastorals* (1709) seasonal, indeed simplifying twelve months into four seasons.
When the poet divides his pastorals into four
seasons, he is limiting the unfallen world, the

We reprint here only the first part of a longer essay which originally appeared in
English Satire (Los Angeles, 1972), by permission of The William Andrews Clark Memorial
Library, University of California, Los Angeles.

Golden Age, to spring, and each of the succeeding
eclogues must portray a further stage of decline.
"Spring," therefore, with its harmonious conjunction of contesting poets, their loves, alternat-
ing songs, and shared prizes, does not concern
us.[2] The other three pastorals, however, offer
indications of representative satiric modes.

The most obviously satiric is the "Autumn"
eclogue, dedicated to William Wycherley, the
dramatic satirist par excellence. Pope simply
steps back and overhears Hylas and AEgon, two
foolish shepherds, whose loves are absent and un-
faithful, maundering on about themselves and
projecting equally delusive visions of happiness
and suicide; the poet only returns at the end to
note that they sang this way "till th' Approach
of Night" and then went to bed without having
recovered the mistress or accomplished the suicide. This is a rehearsal for a satiric mode,
but not, as it happens, for Pope's. It acknowledges Wycherley's satiric drama[3] and may recall
Swift's straight-faced reporting of incriminating
documents. Pope, however, except in some of his
prose satires, never allows the reader to believe
he is merely overhearing the words of a Hylas or
AEgon. In his poetic satires we are always aware
of the "voice" and presence of a poet. It may be
a poet of many impersonations, or accompanied by
other voices or felt presences, but his voice remains normative, encompassing the dramatic scene.

"Summer," though a conventional pastoral complaint, is closer to this mode. The speaker
Alexis, associated by name with Pope, is the
young poet trying to write poetry to his beloved
in a world from which the muses have fled (to the
fashionable poets of Oxford and Cambridge); the
beloved is not to be found, and the only harmony
that remains is between the poet and his own rural setting. The dedication is to Sir Samuel
Garth, the satiric poet and translator of Ovid,
but Garth is invoked as a physician, a body-
doctor who cannot cure the "Disease" of love; and
mingled with the address to him are the references to the "You" of the ideal that is unattain-

able in this garden in which love is now a "Serpent." Only in the poet's complaint itself is
there an art, already prefigured in the bowl inscribed with the Four Seasons in "Spring," that
cures in a way that Garth's medicine cannot. The
present but inefficacious Garth, the absent but
longed-for ideal, and also perhaps the implied
busy poets of the universities are to reappear in
modified form in the satires of the 1730's.

"Winter," Pope's pastoral elegy, is a lament
for what was, the "You" of "Summer" no longer
missing but declared dead, with an Ovidian apotheosis in the afterlife but no hope of restitu-
tion in this world. It ends evoking a world in
which not Love but "Time conquers All, and We
must Time obey," and Thyrsis bids the shepherds
"arise" and withdraw. The tone of complaint--or
the sense of loss--with the only counter-efficacy
in the poem itself will also inform Pope's satiric writings, where the lost loved-one has become Astraea.

The crucial eclogue, however, is the fifth,
added later but intended as an integral part of
the *Pastorals*. "The Messiah" (1712), based on
Virgil's "Pollio," projects the future hope of
redemption and rebirth. The Messiah's presence
banishes the disjunctions of the fallen world
and reunites the contraries, including lions and
lambs as well as separated lovers, as they were
in the Golden Age. Pope had a genius for such
visionary passages, where the action is a slow
unfolding of apotheosis or apocalypse, and the
real action takes place in the smallest units of
meaning--the words, half-lines, lines, couplets,
and their interactions. The Messiah's miraculous
act of correction seems to have intrigued Pope
almost above all else in the poetic range. As
he recognized, one can either look patiently to
the future, here or in heaven, when lovers *will*
be reunited and the lion lie down again with the
lamb, or one can observe with dismay the pseudo-
poet, the self-appointed messiah, trying to invert or banish the distinctions inherent in the
fallen world. An inverted or pseudo "Pollio"

vision is the chief, the best-known mode of his
satire from *The Dunciad* to Vice's triumphal procession at the end of the first dialogue of *One
Thousand Seven Hundred and Thirty Eight* (the *Epilogue to
the Satires*). The other possibility is for the
poet to accept and understand the discontinuities
around him, recovering the real world through his
poetry in a way analogous to--but distinct from--
the Messiah's recreation.

If the "Pollio's" Messiah usually becomes an
inversion at the hands of dunces, the georgic's
farmer becomes the model for the poet or the
gardener who brings out the capabilities of restoration in fallen nature. He does this by
relying on the rhythm of the seasons that has
replaced the eternal spring of the pastoral Gold-
en Age, by ploughing, sowing, and reaping; most
dramatically (as in Virgil's fourth *Georgic*) by
regenerating his lost beehive out of the maggoty carcass
of oxen. In *Windsor Forest* (1713) Pope shows war
replaced by hunting, commerce, retirement, poetry, and contemplation. The poet does not create
afresh; he lets his art draw out the inherent
potential, develop the Genius of the Place,
whether in a landscape or in the texts of his
great predecessors Homer and Horace. The satirist, on the other hand, has to cope with the
false "Pollio" of those poets or gardeners or
farmers who are not content coming to terms with
nature.

The fiction Pope uses for these re-creations
and/or perversions in his early poetry is that
of metamorphosis.[4] His earliest translations and
imitations were of Ovid's *Metamorphoses*, and in
Windsor Forest the georgic readjustments are posed
in terms of metamorphosis. The central one is
of Lodona, fleeing from Pan, transformed into a
river, her flight into a smooth-flowing, contemplative mirror of nature, as war is transformed
into peace. The first two-canto version of *The
Rape of the Lock* (1712), written at about the same
time, emphasizes the form with a Belinda who is
essentially a Dryope or, better, a Lodona, who
goes too far, is pursued, her flight merely ex-

citing her pursuer the more, and when he has
seized her lock it is transformed. The Baron replaces Pan and, by implication, Belinda's coquett-
ishness replaces Lodona's vow to Diana. The
whole poem, it is clear from his preface, Pope
regarded as his own poetic metamorphosis of the
Petre-Fermor squabble into peace, of anger into
comedy and good feeling of chaotic reality into
art.

Metamorphosis is a fiction with which satirists are not usually concerned. Satire exposes
or reveals evil, or perhaps the knave transforming evil into false good and trying to convince
others that no transformation has taken place.
Swift wrote satire so completely and with such
ruthless efficiency that he carried exposure to
the brink of nihilism; even his norms are broken
and scattered. Ultimately almost everyone, including the reader, is caught in his subtle net
of incrimination. For Pope there is always a
final transformation into art: in the *Pastorals*
it was art that ordered fallen nature, as in his
own transformation of the quarrel in the 1712
Rape of the Lock; in the satires it is the gesture,
after the dunces have metamorphosed filth into
false art, of the poet himself metamorphosing
this into the true art of his poetry, so that
the ending of *Dunciad* IV, however hopeless a
sublunary world it evokes, by a kind of envelop-
ing action represents another apotheosis of the
fallible into something permanent and beautiful.
As satirist Pope never loses sight of himself as
poet; and in fact poet rather than satirist sums
up the man whose subject is primarily the perversion of God's good reality and includes its restoration.

I am proposing that the large action of Pope's
satires takes two general forms. One is the
emblematic, allegorical, allusive anti-Pollio
vision of chaos and disorder. The second action
concludes with the Horatian sermo in which "Pope"
converses with somebody; but it begins with the
pastoral Alexis, whose tone is never quite lost,
supporting the strong tendency toward apologia,

in which the satirist defends himself and at the
same time produces satire. One action is visionary, the other a dialogue interaction between two
or more people. And yet they usually join; the
latter is often a frame action for the vision,
an "occasion" created for projecting visions of
false-creation. Pope's career as a satirist begins and ends with fictions of a lone poet com-
plaining of the discontinuities of the world,
the victory of Time over love, and projecting a
vision of decline--his own and his society's--
expressed, however, in the form of something beautiful and lasting which contradicts (or qualifies)
the pessimistic conclusion of the vision itself.

The "Mighty Rage"

Pope's earliest known attempt at translation
is of Ovid's "Acis and Galatea," in which the
theme of unrequited love has been slightly complicated by the addition of a third party.[5] Acis
and Galatea love each other, and are not (like
pastoral lovers) separated; but Polyphemus the
cyclops also loves Galatea, and, seeing the lovers embracing, at last in frustration, "Frantick
with his pain, / Roar'd out for Rage" and
attacked Galatea's Acis, who is metamorphosed into a fountain.

If the "Acis and Galatea" introduces a metamorphosis which is separate from the protagonist,
it also introduces rage, which is another major
element of *The Rape of the Lock*. The rage of course
came as part of Pope's donné (and from the wrath
of Achilles), but both Belinda and the Baron are
invested with Polyphemus' fury--Belinda with his
"Rage, Resentment, and Despair," and the Baron
with his violent action. Pope's epic invocation
asks why "little men" engage in "tasks so bold"
and why "such mighty Rage" can dwell in "soft bosoms." Belinda's beauty and aloofness, plus a
drink of coffee which stimulates "New Stratagems,
the radiant Lock to gain," lead the Baron to commit the Polyphemus-like act of cutting the lock.
If his response is excessive, however, Belinda's

too is closer to Polyphemus' than to Galatea's.
At first she does not know what to do; Thalestris'
speech of poor advice is necessary to get her
started, and this is supplemented by Sir Plume's
expostulation, most unheroic by comparison, which
merely serves to provoke the Baron to a further
refusal to return the lock; and with this chain
of provocation Belinda initiates the battle of
the sexes, and "all the Prize is lost."

Although Pope does not always seek out causes,
the situation and, more, the effect (the "mighty
Rage") are subjects of concern for him: what are
the causes of passion and indignant outburst?
In this instance they are satirized as excessive
all around. But a basic pattern of Pope's satire
is established, a pattern not so much of cause
and effect as of action and response, provocation
and overresponse. Somewhere within the Baron
and Belinda and their overreactions is the later
obsessive question, What could make an innocent
well-brought-up poet, indeed one who has his own
soul to think about, attack such powerful men as
Hervey, Walpole, and even the king? This question is sometimes posed by enemies, sometimes by
friends, and sometimes by the poet himself. However different in evaluation, the outbursts of
Belinda and the Baron share with the poetic indignation of Pope's satires the apparently spontaneous emotion that has no place in the world
of Augustan society and art. While Pope's preparations for his satiric outbursts are carefully
constructed, the construction is based on that
of *The Rape of the Lock* and is both a way of getting himself into the position of uttering a
"Pollio" vision and perhaps the only convenient way
of creating a poetic effect of an intensity that
recalls the great poetry of preceding centuries.

The pattern is considerably clarified in the
five-canto version of the *Rape* published in 1714,
which adds explanations or motives for the
"mighty rages." It also attempts to distinguish
Belinda's rage from the Baron's, making it plain
that her rage reflects fear for reputation and
appearances ("Hairs less in sight, or any Hairs

but these!"), while his can be taken to represent
a touch of the real world which Belinda the
coquette needs--but which she rejects by simply
going over from the sylphs to the gnomes.

The addition of Ariel and the sylphs, in a way
developed out of Thalestris' speech of advice,
sets up a third agency which explains how "a gentle Belle" could "reject a Lord," and how "dire
offenses" can be related to "amorous causes,"
"mighty contests" to "trivial things." Within
this contrast of opposing worlds an action of a
different sort takes place, beginning with the
vision vouchsafed Belinda in which her guardian
sylph Ariel persuades her of (or supports her
belief in) her personal sanctity and ideality a-
bove "dire" reality. The *Rape* begins with these
contrasting worlds, or at least ways of interpret-
ing the real world, and a student and her mentor
who urges upon her the false interpretation. The
sylphs, whether we take them as a level of Belinda's consciousness or a social paradigm of
honor, make the essential mediating link between
Belinda and her imagined inviolability. Ariel's
speeches project a lovely, artificial play world
which is meant to replace the real world of marriage and deflowering--a world with its own laws
and games that Belinda must obey or be abandoned.
They also carry overtones of the temptation of a
deluded Eve into seeing herself as godlike when
she is a human in a humanly-limited situation of
courtship, and this temptation is followed by a
parody Mass with Belinda officiating before a
mirror altar at the "sacred Rites of Pride."

A result of making Belinda a tempted and fallen human being--fallen through pride--is to
produce the exulting hubris of her victory speech,
which is the direct stimulus to the Baron's overresponse (prompted only by coffee-dreams in the
earlier version) of breaking the rules of the
game and cutting the lock. The response of Belinda then is hysteria, followed by the Baron's
own exulting speech, which in the new context,
though excessive, illuminates his corrective
function. Because he has cut the lock, his

"Honour, Name, and Praise shall live." Echoing
Catullus' "Berenice" and its context of married
love, he apostrophizes his sword--his "steel"--
which "strike[s] to Dust th' Imperial Tow'rs of
Troy," confounds "the Works of mortal Pride," and
hews "Triumphal Arches to the Ground." In the
first version this was empty exulting; now with
the provocation of Belinda's pride and her own
exultant speech, it sounds more like a forerunner
of "O sacred Weapon! left for Truth's defense, /
Sole Dread of Folly, Vice, and Insolence!..." But
even in the first version Pope has indicated the
odds that are against the Baron, distinguishing
between "soon to obtain" and "long possess the
Prize"--which recalls the presence of the conqueror Time, with *his* "steel," as well as the
power of reputation.

A final addition, made in the 1717 version of
the *Rape*, is the speech of Clarissa, which balances Thalestris' angry outburst with counsels of
commonsense and moderation. She is the unheroic
and commonsense antithesis of Sarpedon, the hero
who goes off to death and fights on in a losing
cause. Given the same assumptions about a world
dominated by Time in which "frail Beauty must decay," he responds with "great Acts" and "Valour,"
she with "good Sense" and "Virtue."[7] Clarissa
speaks for the acceptance of truth, nature, and
reality; her handing the scissors to the Baron,
already present in the first version, represents
the same values, though with a militance that is
lacking in her 1717 speech. As Pope observed,
the latter was introduced to materialize the
moral of the poem; but in her realism there is
also the germ of a plea for the status quo. If
only, the echoes of the *Iliad* seem to say, there
were room for a Sarpedon in our world. Even poor
Belinda and the Baron are at least fighting for
their beliefs, however mistaken, in a losing battle with Time.[8]

At any rate, Clarissa's counsel of moderation,
even more than Thalestris' of rage, only serves
to provoke Belinda to attack, and the battle of
the sexes ensues. She rounds off a fiction of

a passionate person who brings down the paragon
of pride and affectation, even if it means dis-
rupting the structure around him, violating the
laws of politeness, and precipitating a battle.
In time, in the age of Walpole, it will become
necessary to rethink the alternatives of Clarissa and Sarpedon.

In so far as *The Rape of the Lock* is opposing a
world of reputation (Belinda's and Ariel's concern with her "honor," with appearances only) to
a real world of nature and flesh-and-blood passion, Pope's poetry is the truth that sets matters straight. He was much concerned with this
sense of poetry as truth, as his publication of
The Temple of Fame (1715) a year later shows. In
Pope's dream vision the young poet, who like the
Baron wishes that his "Honour, Name, and Praise
shall live," goes out to learn about the fame he
seeks as a poet, and discovers that instead of
his own fame it is the fame of others with which
he will be concerned. In the Temple the Homers
and Virgils of the past are not themselves celebrated but serve as pillars supporting the edifice of Fame. The poet's duty is to bring to
light those who do good by stealth, to repair the
reputation of the slandered, to bury in oblivion
those who do evil, but if they are falsely praised
or their wickedness made an object of emulation,
his duty is to show what they really are in the
strongest colors.

But the Temple of Fame is also complemented
by a Temple of Rumor, where there is no longer
any correlation between reality and fame or merits. From here emerge lies, or truths and false-
hoods mixed. Pope learns that his own essential
theme is the need to rectify the effect of the
Temple of Rumor with true fame. "Honest Fame"
will only come to him because he maintains its
truth in a world controlled by Time, liars, flatterers, and slanderers.

His career will be spent satirizing "the guilty Bays" that soothes Folly or exalts Vice, following Fortune and pandering to the great's
"Lust of Praise." As any reader of Pope's mature

satires must notice, vice itself is very vaguely
defined; it is often given particular names, but
Ward, Waters, and Chartres are names that are
virtually interchangeable. The vice they denote
is only a "mean Heart that lurks beneath a Star"
or a "Rich or noble Knave." The danger resides
in the phrases "beneath a Star" and "Rich or
noble," for the figure of Vice, vague in itself,
is defined in terms of its fame. Pope's satire
is less about Vice than about the reputation that
allows it to ride in Virtue's chariot or that
overpraises and awards honors to Colonel Chartres
and makes him an example to emulate. He is present in the satires not because he was a despica-
ble old rapist but because instead of punishment
for this simple crime he received royal favor.
Pope's real subject tends to be the people who
accept, flatter, and glamorize Chartres; people
who, beginning with party writers and hack poets,
shade off into attorneys, forgers of wills, and
swindlers, and rise to prime ministers and kings.
Pope's very earliest satiric imitation, of Donne's
second satire, is about the power of writing, focusing on a lawyer as a manipulator of legal contracts, deeds, wills, and other spiderwebs of
legalities which he employs to defraud heirs and
litigants and enrich himself rather than to order
the truth of human relationships.

The Temple of Fame was accompanied in the period
of 1711 to 1717 by a series of poems in which the
fame of someone admirable--an Eloisa, an "Unfortunate Lady," a Cleopatra--is in jeopardy, and
the poet rescues it by his poetical transformation. These require our attention because the
satires that began to appear a decade later merely shift the emphasis from the slandered to the
slanderers and libellers; and the slandered figure remains, sometimes peripheral and sometimes
central, in the figure of the poet himself or his
friends whose fame is put in jeopardy by the lies
of Sporuses, Dennises, and assorted dunces.[9]

The Rape and Eloisa to Abelard are both about
the questionable passion of a young girl in a
monastic community (whether of those now sexless

ladies, the sylphs, or of nuns), with "an earthly
Lover lurking in her Heart," and no outlet except
upward into self-worship or the true (Christian)
religion. Eloisa is a much more difficult, more
problematical case, however, because she is her
own speaker, and because value is patently on the
side of the absolute, the immortality of her soul,
vs. the mortal and sensuous life of love.[10] In
both protagonists the problem of loving to the
point of crime (breaking society's law) or sin
(breaking a religious law) is in the conflict
between a sensuous, "earthly" love and a love of
a higher sort, which is, however, associated to
a large extent with "the humanly unsatisfying,
empty promises of disembodied, airy, artful perfection" in the sylphs,[11] and with monastic re-
pression, a nun's cell, her vow of silence, her
confinement by the order's "rule," and emascula-
tion and sterility. On the side of the "Church"
and God's law are the all-too-human agents who
waylaid Abelard. It is hard to say how much emphasis Pope intends to put on "Church" as opposed
to God, but certainly in Eloisa's mind the monastic world, where only the statues can weep, is a
stifling equivalent of the world of bric-a-brac
and game rules as supervised by Ariel.
    Eloisa's dilemma is resolved in favor of with-
drawal to God, the settlement of her own salvation, but her rage is what has received the em-
phasis--what is down on paper, what is effect
remains.   Response is once again primary, from
the provocation of Abelard's letter, which
"awakening all her tenderness," makes her intensely aware of her divided allegiance, to her
vacillating outbursts and subsidences. The intensity of her yearning for Abelard outweights
her final resolution. Moreover, a reader cannot
help noticing that she really has no choice, for
Abelard's sexuality is only a memory now. Her
withdrawal, however difficult, is inevitable.
When she appears on the scene, writing her letter, she is speaking in the elegiac strain of the
"Winter" pastoral rather than the hopeful conflict of "Summer" (or *The Rape of the Lock*).   She

can regret her Abelard and curse his punishers,
or find a way to live within the possible, which
involves an emasculated and far-away lover. While
her choice, on one level, is between the absolute and the temporal, on another it is simply
between holding out for a lost love and accepting
her situation in the convent.

It is useful to recall another of Pope's translations, of Ovid's "Sappho to Phaon" (1712);
though in a sense a continuation of the complaint
of unrequited love in "Summer," it leads directly
into Pope's attempt at a heroic epistle. A possible reason for translating this particular
epistle from the *Heroides* is that in the story,
very much like Eloisa's, Sappho falls in love
with the beautiful youth Phaon, who however cannot return her love because in fact he is an
ancient boatman whom Aphrodite has transformed
only outwardly into a youth. But it is also the
only Ovidian epistle in which the speaker is a
poet, and her situation that of both lover *and*
poet.

For there is also the poet in *Eloisa to Abelard*.
He was, I have suggested, implicit in the *Rape*,
explaining and metamorphosing the rage, Belinda's
excessive response, and the brutal action of the
Baron; but in *Eloisa* he enters more directly in
the last lines as a parallel case--as the "future
Bard [who] shall join / In sad similitude of
griefs to mind," says Eloisa, for "He best can
paint 'em, who shall feel 'em most." The poet is
someone who has suffered as she has and therefore
will properly memorialize her, present her as she
was, order her writing-to-the-moment into heroic
couplets, so to speak. It does not matter whether Lady Mary was indicated or not in these last
lines; the point is that Pope himself comes in to
explain what he is doing, and he makes it clear
that his situation as a human is parallel to
Eloisa's, though as an artist it is quite distinct.

By the time he wrote the *Epilogue to the Satires*
Pope, by refusing to listen to his "friend," who
either urges him to write or not to write satire,

is behaving in a way analogous to Eloisa, expressing the urgency of his human duties while acknowledging the safety of his immortal soul in the
light of church doctrine. Pope has taken the aspect of church forms--of sylphish false pride--
and yet not forgotten the matter of the soul.   In
other words, the problem of the girl and the
length to which her love ought to be pursued in
relation to other commitments or forms, both
social and prudential, or in relation to her own
soul's salvation, may be reflected in the ostensibly different problem of the satirist vis-à-
vis a corrupt society, his duty as an active
citizen, and his duty to himself as a private man,
and tells something about Pope's habit of step-
ping back from his satire and framing it with an
explanation of how he was forced to respond with
this outburst.

In "The Elegy to the Memory of an Unfortunate
Lady," though the triangular relationship is the
same as in the *Rape* and *Eloisa* (there is a
young lady, her lover, and the force of social
and divine law),[12] now there is no conflict; her
"false guardian" is plainly repressive, separating her from her true love. Each of these poems
poses the question, explicitly or implicity, "Is
it a crime [or sin] to love too well?" Now the
"Unfortunate Lady" has "loved too well" in the
sense that she has rejected the world of repres-
sion and the way of those "sullen pris'ners in
the body's cage," and has, like Sappho (and, another hero admired by Pope, Cato), committed
suicide. Her response has taken her to the extreme of self-murder, and so (in terms of orthodoxy) to damnation.

Neither the Lady's conflict nor response is
the point here; it is the poet's response to her
example that has now become central. As was
hinted at the end of *Eloisa*, he has assumed the
role outlined for him in *The Temple of Fame* and is
setting the record straight. The emphasis in the
title is on "the *Memory* of an Unfortunate Lady"--
memory meaning that the poem will stand as a kind
of monument to her, because she is now slandered

or totally forgotten, "without a stone, a name."
The poet's function is to draw out her fame as it
should be and also stigmatize the "false guardian" and those who brought about her sad fate, and
this results in a passage of invective side-by-
side with the elegiac celebration. Immortality
therefore--which in *Eloisa* was in one sense on the
side of God and the Church *vs.* the "earthly lover"
in her heart--is here on the side of a suicide,
because her action raises her above the usual
limited responses of mortals, and because the poet is immortalizing her. The poet again takes
the closing lines of the poem to himself and
parallels one aspect of the Lady's fate with his
own: "Ev'n he, whose soul now melts in mournful
lays, / Shall shortly want the gen'rous tear he
pays."
     The poem ends with the Popean surmise that the
poet himself, as well as the memory of the Lady,
will be swept away by Time; but that the edifice
of fame he has constructed--by the very fact of
its existence, its being read--has granted both
passion in the face of an antithetical conclusion, so in the satires the fear of Time, which
is sweeping the poet away as well as the world
around him, is contradicted by the confidence
that the poem itself, which is being read, will
survive:

     Yet may this Verse (if such a Verse remain)
     Show there was one who held it [Vice]
        in disdain.

And of Chaos and Time, who "bears me on his rapid
wing," the poet requests:

     Suspend a while your Force inertly strong,
     Then take at once the Poet and the Song

--in a couplet that nevertheless remains a bul-
wark against Chaos and Time.
     "Cleopatra" (published 1717)[13] is another case
of a woman who plainly chose correctly. Her loving too well means preferring Antony to the val-

ues of Augustan Rome and, like the Unfortunate
Lady, committing suicide rather than walk in
Octavius' triumphal procession. She is, however,
speaking herself instead of being discussed as a
subject by the poet. And yet the poem is again
about the poet. Octavius, cheated of his prize,
has had a statue made of her as a surrogate to
ride in the triumphal procession and be set up in
the Forum in Rome. He has falsified her by omitting her tears: no one can now tell that she is
weeping, and that these tears are not for herself
but for Antony. She is thus both confined and
misunderstood in this statue as Eloisa was in her
cell and the dead and forgotten Lady in her un-
marked grave. Once again the poet is required:
here he appears in the form of Pope Leo X, the
great patron, the Man of Magnificence (whom Pope
will later parallel with the poet), who has her
statue transformed into a fountain, releasing her
tears which are her true fame, proving her not
cold marble but a warm, still-loving woman. It
is the poet's role to recreate the poetic truth
out of the statue, turning the triumphal simula-
crum into a nourishing fountain. Quite a different image from the bowl of the "Spring" pastoral,
this is a natural development from the idea of
metamorphosis in *The Rape of the Lock*. In both
cases, an artifact of ill fame, falsified, has
been remetamorphosed into something true and
meaningful.

Sylphish advice has developed in these poems
into Church Law, the repressiveness of the "false
guardian," and the tyranny of Octavius; its effect has fallen on hapless lovers from the Baron
to Abelard, the nameless lover of the Unfortunate
Lady, and Antony; and from Belinda to Eloisa, the
Lady, and Cleopatra. Clearly the constraining
force has become more repressive, has increasingly brought its weight down hard on both lovers,
as the subject has shifted from the protagonist's
dilemma to her correct choice of defiance. The
poet has developed from an implicit side issue to
a figure almost as important as the others: parallel with the protagonists but also able to

celebrate them. From these it is only a step to
the ethic epistles that begin with the *Epistle to
Burlington*.

To get a larger perspective on this series we
must go back to the "Ode for Musick" of 1713, in
which the poet is both the protagonist and the
lover, and which is specifically about the power
of music (poetry) and makes quite plain what the
alternatives are in terms of temporality and immortality. Here Pope ascends from the music that
arouses heroes to battle to the music of the poet
who is in love and, finally, to the sacred music
of the saint. He shows the alternatives as they
were in *Eloisa* --between defiant devotion to a
human lover and love of God--and admits that the
latter is the correct choice. But, since the
poem is about "fame," perhaps we should use
Pope's own words:

> Of *Orpheus* now no more let Poets tell,
> To bright *Cecilia* greater Pow'r is giv'n;
>   His Numbers rais'd a Shade from Hell,
>   Hers lift the Soul to Heav'n.

Orpheus' passion for Eurydice, which led him to
descend into Hades and continue to sing her name
even after his own dismemberment by the Bacchantes, is contrasted with Cecilia's renunciation of
her passion for Valerian, in order to convert him
to Christianity.[14] Pope knows that Cecilia is
right to love God more than her human lover-
husband; Orpheus is wrong to love his wife beyond reason. He also knows that Cecilia's is
therefore the higher poetry. But he cannot refrain from asking if it is a crime to love too
well, and giving Orpheus the most deeply-felt
lines of the poem--corresponding again to the
passion of Eloisa's feeling for Abelard, though
it goes against the grain of the poem's orthodox
conclusion:

> See, wild as the Winds, o'er the Desart
>   he flies;
> Hark! *Haemus* resounds with the *Bacchanals'* cries--
>   --Ah see, he dies!

> Yet ev'n in Death *Eurydice* he sung,
> *Eurydice* still trembled on his Tongue,
> *Eurydice* the Woods,
> *Eurydice* the Floods,
> *Eurydice* the Rocks, and hollow Mountains rung.

One part of Pope's feelings is more fully engaged by the human Orpheus, the archetypal poet, than by the saint, Cecilia.

As always, Pope is the poet of human possibilities—of Clarissa's world and the Baron's, and so of the poet who must do his best in the ordinary world; and though he is aware of the superior virtue of St. Cecilia and of her divine song, he writes his own poetry, from the *Pastorals* onward, about the ordinary world of hopelessly separated lovers. There is the poet whose "numbers raise a Shade from Hell" and the poet whose verses "lift the Soul to Heav'n." Pope knows the second is higher, but must himself choose the first. He has also set up in Orpheus the paradigm not only for his Cleopatras and Unfortunate Ladies but for his poet, who is willing to descend into hell in search of the one he loved too well, and, pursued and dismembered by Bacchantes, continues to sing about his lost love (which he will later call Virtue, Astraea, Bolingbroke, etc.) even as a bodiless head floating down the river; but who also asks himself if he should not rather be singing of God, lifting up his own or another's soul.

In a world where "Time conquers All," where Time, and not human love, is supreme, one can either accept the fact and choose divine love, turning his back on the world, or make a hopeless stand for human love against Time, the Church, the state, Walpolism, liars, and slanderers. Orpheus' severed head returns once again in the epigraph from Ovid attached to the final 1743 *Dunciad* . Preserved by the art of his patron Apollo in an everlasting agony with the gaping serpent's mouth that would devour it, the singing head figures the situation of the poet/satirist Pope himself in relation to the yawning abyss of Dulness as night descends.

*   *   *

POPE'S REASONABLE RHYMES

Hugh Kenner

The pun, which we used to be told was the lowest form of wit, is also the completest form of
rhyme. Not merely the vowels, not merely the
terminal consonants, but every phoneme in two
words will coincide. When Quintilian teaches us
the Greek word *homoioteleuton*--"like ending"--the
closest thing in his rhetorician's armory to what
we experience as rhyme, and then disconcerts us a
little by classifying it with the pun, which he
calls "a poor trick even when employed in jest,"[1]
he helps us frame a suspicion that the poet of
rhyme is playing with fire, flirting with triviality and unworthy coincidence, and justifying
John Milton's stern aversion from the mere exploitation of syllabic accident.[2] The problem
with such effects seems to inhere in their look of
randomness.

The centuries-old objection that one's point
should not depend on a pun seems related to the
principle that a plot should not depend on a coincidence. A coincidence, being uncaused, tells

This essay first appeared in *ELH* 41 (1974), 74-88. Copyright The Johns Hopkins
University Press.

us nothing, and we expect of the humblest story,
as of the humblest verse, some increment of enlightenment. From the very first pun we used to
learn as children--"When is a door not a door?
When it's ajar"--we may recall learning nothing
at all about doors, not even the answer to the
question, and if we do learn a fact about the
English language we may reject it as an annoying
fact. Why should a synonym for "open" make that
idiotic chime with the name of a kitchen receptacle? It seems a flaw in linguistic design, to
be tacitly overlooked.

So with rhyme, we may feel. If "ajar" and "a
jar" is unworthy, does not the pair "glade" and
"shade" verge on a like unworthiness? Or "descends" and "ends"? Or "twines" and "vines"? Yet
in the *Pastorals* written by the very young Pope,
which as a middle-aged man he still regarded as
"the most correct in the versification, and musical in the numbers, of all his works,"[3] there is
no difficulty in finding all these rhymes, and
many more just as obvious, and some of them more
than once.

> Where-e'er you walk, cool Gales shall fan the
>   Glade,
> Trees, where you sit, shall crowd into a
>   Shade....
>   (*Summer, 73-74*)

> But soon the Sun with milder Rays descends
> To the cool Ocean, where his Journey ends.
>   (*Summer, 89-90*)

> And I this Bowl, where wanton Ivy twines,
> And swelling Clusters bend the curling Vines....
>   (*Spring, 35-36*)

He used "glade" and "shade" again in *Windsor
Forest*:

> There, interspers'd in Lawns and opening
>   Glades,
> Thin Trees arise that shun each other's Shades.
>   (*21-22*)

In *Autumn* he rhymed "moan" with "groan" (15-16),
also "bright" with "light" (13-14) and "rise"
with "skies" (59-60), even "spring" with "sing"
(27-28). We may ask what it means, to say that
these rhymes are somehow obvious. The question
is worth a little pondering, because before we
have finished we shall be needing a category of
what we shall be calling "normal" rhymes, and the
principle of which rhymes seem normal is more
elusive than we might expect.

One's first thought is apt to be that their
senses concur, or at least grope toward one another. Unlike the puns to which the central objection turns on distaste for empty coincidence,
such words seem derived from a discovery about
the language. Shakespeare used such a discovery
when he terminated a famous stanza in *Cymbeline*:

> Golden lads and girls all must,
> As chimney-sweepers, come to dust.

Were the final word missing any native speaker
could supply it with near certainty. There is no
particular surprise to Shakespeare's rhyme. But
there is great authority. To find among the Germanic monosyllables that underlie our vocabulary
two utterances so similar denoting two notions so
solemnly allied is like confronting the wisdom
of our vanished ancestors, the more so when we
are assured that the two words have no etymological kinship whatever. Men once upon a time, we
are nearly persuaded, took great care over naming,
and like names go with kinship of perception.
Eliot drew from still deeper tarns *datta* and
dayadvham and *damyata*, give, sympathize, control,
unravelling from the one Sanskrit monosyllable DA
and hinting at a primeval imitation of the voice
of divine thunder.[4]

We might be tempted to class Pope's "spring"
and "sing" with Shakespeare's "dust" and "must."
Everybody understands their relationship, and we
may wish we could feel that ancestral wisdom pat-
terned the language to underwrite their effects.
What we are more likely to feel is that we have

heard these rhymes before. Far from incurring
Dr. Johnson's stricture against poets of another
school, that they yoked heterogeneous ideas together by violence, the Pope of the *Pastorals* --at
16 years of age--was taking care to join only
what joined easily because often joined. That is
part of what he meant by "correctness." If we
understand that "spring" goes with "sing" it is
because poets have taught us that it does, and
when William Carlos Williams--a non-rhymer--wrote
"Spring and All"[5] he was hoping to teach us that
such a coupling is mindlessly conventional, that
spring has deeper alliances with the stubborn
persistence of birth. And we may as well say of
"dust" and "must" that, far from echoing some
natural profundity, it rests on as literary a
base as "spring" and "sing." "Spring" goes with
"sing" because of a pastoral tradition; "dust"
goes with "must" because of a Biblical tradition.
Dust is not part of anyone's experience of death,
unless perhaps an archaelogist's. What Shakespeare's rhyme exploits is lettered experience,
derived from the third chapter of Genesis, the
19th verse: "Thou art dust, and unto dust shalt
thou return." The English text doesn't use the
word "must" but intends its force. Whatever poet was the first to use Shakespeare's rhyme simply found in the language a kind of pun that
corresponds to the Biblical meaning. It would be
a tiresome rhyme if it were much used. Probably
the strange word "golden" in Shakespeare's couplet is what takes our attention off this danger.
     When we find some inner congruity in a rhyme,
it is likely that we are being instructed by
literary tradition. This implies that we accept
rhymes we have heard before, but will stop accepting them when we have heard them too often.
Pope in his *Essay on Criticism* mocked poets who

     ...ring round the same *unvary'd Chimes*,
  With sure *Returns* of still *expected Rhymes*,

and immediately offered a sure-fire example:

> Where-e'er you find *the cooling Western Breeze,*
> In the next Line, it *whispers thro' the Trees.*
>   (II.348-51)

Pope dated this poem 1709, the same year in
which he published his Winter Pastoral, where we
are told of the dead Daphne how

> Her Fate is whisper'd by the gentle Breeze,
> And told in Sighs to all the trembling Trees.
>   (61-62)

Yet to notice this fact is not to catch the biter
bit. Readers of *The Dunciad* and of *Peri Bathous*
will know Pope's lifelong habit of mocking the
incapacity of others to do with judgment what he
has done himself,[6] and anyone whom the *Essay on
Criticism* prompts to look back at the lines in
Winter may admire Pope's skill in preventing fit
readers from supposing that he thought of "trees"
in consequence of having just written "breeze."
Pope's trees are sponsored by the fact that the
young lady whose fate they hear is named Daphne,
after Ovid's nymph who became a laurel, and they
tremble less at the breeze's agitation than at
its news of a relative's namesake's fate. The
poets Pope castigates in the *Essay* have not this
ingenious energy, nor this mastery of superintend-
ing coherence. They write "trees" because a moment ago they wrote "breeze," and their minds are
suggestible, not capacious.
Pope is at pains never to be thought suggestible. He means us, when we are reading lines of
his, to be visited by no suspicion that the first
rhyme of a pair has suggested the second, or even
vice versa: to judge rather that the rhyme vali-
dates a structure of meaning which other orders
of cogency have produced. When rhymes are as
copious as they were for Chaucer,[7] there is little harm in their seeming to suggest the next
turn a poet's meaning may take, one of very many
possible turns, but Pope seems to have thought it
fatal for us to suppose that this ever happens.
To let rhyme seem to be suggesting rhyme, hence

meaning, was to accede to empty banality, so scan-
ty was the stock of usable rhymes. But a rhyme
that seems to *validate* a meaning, that is something
else: whether by enforcing some plain congruity,
as between "high" and "sky," or by evoking the
literary tradition, as do "spring" and "sing."

These are what we shall be calling "normal"
rhymes, these rhymes that for one reason or another persuade us that they inhere in the workings of the normal mind. They are usually monosyllabic, and their meanings are in traditional
accord. To make them seem other than banal, Pope
then went to great labor: arranging that the
rhyme shall not seem to be producing the meaning
by making us see how other structures produce it;
rhyming different parts of speech, rhyming the
same part of speech in different syntactic functions, evading by many delicate devices any imputation that the line which closed the sense-
pattern was adding suspiciously little to the
line which opened it.[8] He paid nearly unprece-
dented attention to what each of two rhyme-words
meant, since to build a structure of some intricacy on their meaning was one way to forestall the
suspicion that nothing better than "the troublesom and modern bondage of Rimeing" had produced
them.

Yet his pains attest to the normality of these
normal rhymes, and the next thing to notice is
that Pope had a use for their feel of the normal.
A satirist works with chaos, and in his first extended venture into satire we can find Pope using the normal rhymes as tuning-forks.

A satirist works with chaos. No sooner does
Pope desert the decorums of Pastoral than we find
him rhyming "mankind" with "behind." One might
nearly base a theory of satire on a rhyme like
that. The satirist's occasion is unsatisfactori-
ness, and it is mankind in its unsatisfactory
condition that rhymes with "behind." We may
imagine how Swift would have used the opportunity.
But Pope on the occasion on which he uses it is
writing *The Rape of the Lock*, and writing it for
ladies. Accordingly he does not permit the rhyme

to grimace. He conceals it in a statement so
matter-of-fact that we barely notice the lurking
impropriety. He is telling us about the lock of
hair on which the action of his poem turns.

> This Nymph, to the Destruction of Mankind,
> Nourish'd two Locks, which graceful hung
>   behind....
>   (II.19-20)

The next verb is business-like, "deck": and it
rhymes with "neck," an exact rhyme though it does
not make a pretty sound:

>   ...which graceful hung behind
> In equal Curls, and well conspir'd to deck
> With shining Ringlets the smooth iv'ry Neck.

It seems a pity that "smooth iv'ry" can introduce
no more mellifluous a monosyllable than "neck,"
but the world, we are learning, is an imperfect
place. There exists, however, a more perfect
place, where amid a Platonic quiet the great moral *sententiae* utter themselves, and to this realm
Pope immediately transports us:

> Love in these Labyrinths his Slaves detains,
> And mighty Hearts are held in slender Chains.
> With hairy Sprindges we the Birds betray,
> Slight Lines of Hair surprise the Finny Prey,
> Fair Tresses Man's Imperial Race insnare,
> And Beauty draws us with a single Hair.

Here, as six maxims of ample scope unfold, the
lines seem almost to be writing themselves. Here,
where all fits, not as in Belinda's jumble of
"Puffs, Powders, Patches, Bibles, Billet-doux,"
here the great sage distillations of human sus-
ceptibility to enthrallment deploy themselves in
pairs linked by wholly congruous, wholly normal
rhymes, as though classic truths enjoyed the
validation of the language itself. That "detains"
belongs with "chains" we cannot doubt, nor "betray" with "prey," and as for "insnare"'s con-

gruity with "hair," it is validated by the very
meaning of "snare," an entrapment devised from a
single looped filament.   Here, in the domain of
principle, where one sees human folly with the
eye of eternity, here for once verything coheres,
down to the syllabification of the language, and
when we pass from principle to the special case
once more, when we turn to the Baron, still principle persists. It is the Baron's exemplification
of principle that the next rhyme insists on, another normal rhyme, "admir'd" with "aspir'd."

> Th'adventurous *Baron* the bright Locks admir'd;
> He saw, he wish'd, and to the Prize aspir'd.
>   (29-30)

But soon we are immersed in the Baron's particu-
late world, where "loves" can do no better than
rhyme with "gloves," and where, when the Baron
"to *Love* an Altar built," the rhyme denotes a
glittering speciousness, "gilt."
     This principle is wonderfully general, that
Belinda's world receives the incongruous rhymes,
while the world of maxim and principle, the world
that affords an overview of Belinda's world, receives what the reader of neo-classical verse has
learned to perceive as normal rhymes. Throughout
much of Pope's narrative the overview is entrust-
ed to the Sylphs, whose aerial council in the
second book yields a little thesaurus of normal
rhymes: sight / light; high / sky; even that
pastoral staple, flow'rs / show'rs. The principal Sylph is eloquent on the normal obligations
of Sylphs:

> Some guide the Course of wandring Orbs on high,
> Or roll the Planets through the boundless Sky.
> Some less refin'd, beneath the Moon's pale
>   Light
> Pursue the Stars that shoot athwart the
>   Night....
>   (II.79-82)

High / sky; light / night: perfectly normal. And
perfectly normal still, when the generic task of
safeguarding human beauties is anatomized, are
rhymes like "fair" and "care," "gale" and "ex-
hale."

> Our humbler Province is to tend the Fair,
> Not a less pleasing, tho' less glorious Care;
> To save the Powder from too rude a Gale,
> Nor let th'imprisoned Essences exhale;
> To draw fresh Colours from the vernal Flow'rs;
> To steal from Rainbows e'er they drop in
>   Show'rs
> A brighter Wash; to curl their waving Hairs,
> Assist their Blushes, or inspire their Airs....
>   (II.91-98)

Normal rhymes indeed, though we may expect that
some dissonance stirs beneath their surface.
"Gale" accords, by etymological wit, with "ex-
hale," yet a certain diminution is detectable under the wit. "Flow'rs" is so normal a rhyme for
"show'rs" that we may discover them paired in
Pope's Spring Pastoral--

> All Nature mourns, the Skies relent in Show'rs,
> Hush'd are the Birds, and clos'd the dropping
>   Flow'rs.
>   (69-70)

--but not quite as in the Sylph's speech. The
Sylph (for once) does not end his clause at the
line's end, on "show'rs." He goes on for three
runover words and comes to rest on a kind of low
synonym for "show'rs," the word "wash." As for
"hairs" and "airs," the hairs are "waving" and
the "airs," despite the etymological force of
"inspire," do not succeed in fixing our minds on
meteorology, only on demeanor. One more couplet,
and we see where this discourse is heading:

> Nay oft, in Dreams, Invention we bestow,
> To change a *Flounce*, or add a Furbelo.

When "bestow," augmented by Ciceronian "Invention," is able to prompt nothing better than "Fur-
belo," we are out of the world of normal rhymes,
the world where supernatural promptings in sleep
pertain to insights of some dignity; we are back
where Belinda lives. The catalogue of potential
disasters in the next paragraph pertains to her
shrunken world, and abounds in rhymed grotesquerie:

> Whether the Nymph shall break *Diana's* Law,
> Or some frail *China* Jar receive a Flaw;
> Or stain her Honour, or her new Brocade,
> Forget her Pray'rs, or miss a Masquerade;
> Or lose her Heart, or Necklace, at a Ball;
> Or whether Heav'n has doomed that *Shock* must
> fall....

(II.105-10)

"Shock" is her little dog, a tiny object for the
doom of Heaven to expend itself on. The even
verse is sustaining massive disequilibria. First
a whole line on the loss of chastity is paired
with a whole line on a damaged vase. Then the
disproportions commence running horizontally down
single lines--

> Or stain her Honour, or her new Brocade,
> Forget her Pray'rs, or miss a Masquerade;
> Or lose her Heart, or Necklace, at a Ball....

--while rather strange rhymes meanwhile run ver-
tically. "Brocade" and "masquerade" do not come
from the thesaurus of normal rhymes. And "law"
and "flaw," apparently standard monosyllables, do
not accord as "light" and "sight" accord; nor do
"ball" and "fall." And the rhymes get stranger.
We shall next find "note" rhyming with "Petticoat," and "fail" with "whale," and even "sins"
with "pins," rhymes of no use whatever for the
celebration of permanent truths.

At the very end of the poem we can watch Pope
returning to such truths as to a tonic key. Moving toward his peroration, he sweeps us upward to

the lunar sphere, where all things lost on earth
are said to be treasured. The inventory, true to
earth's incongruities, rhymes "ponderous vases"
with "tweezer cases," "sick man's prayers" with
"tears of heirs," even "flea" with "casuistry."
But Belinda's lock, it seems, has been carried
higher still, to the crystalline sphere where
the great laws obtain. As we follow its progress
thither we may note "air" rhyming once more with
"hair," and "bright" with "light," and "flies"
with "skies," and Pope's final compliment to the
pretty nymph closes on three resounding normal
rhymes, of the kind that offer to embody ineluctable maxims. Though his tone is mischievous, he
will have us postulate that the truths it plays
around are real:

> For, after all the Murders of your Eye,
> When after Millions slain, your self shall die;
> When those fair Suns shall sett, as sett they
>   must,
> And all those Tresses shall be laid in Dust,
> *This Lock*, the Muse shall consecrate to Fame,
> And midst the Stars inscribe *Belinda's* Name.

"Eye" and "die," the "quick eyes gone under
earth's lid" that attracted the talent of a later
poet; the Shakespearean "must" and "dust," trans-
posing a note of mortality to that of necessity;
and lastly the triumphant "fame" with "name,"
fame being but a breath and name but a shaped
breathing, made eternal when it is the utterance
of the Muse.
Incongruous rhymes for satiric observation,
normal rhymes for the realm of law: it is attrac-
tively neat, and one might think it the very
principle on which to erect a whole theory of
rhyme which should make it more than a "troublesom and modern bondage" directed toward the mere
"jingle of like endings." Alas, as a poetic system it seems not to be employed by anyone but
Pope, nor for that matter by Pope in later satires with anything like the schematic neatness
we find in *The Rape of the Lock*. It was a young po-

et's discovery, a good *provisional* system, something
not too tricky, we may surmise, which would zone
out the poem's orders and disorders according to
a sense of linguistic fitness his readers might
intuit but need not articulate.

What readers might be expected to intuit would
depend on what they were accustomed to read: not
only verse like Pope's own *Pastorals*, but all those
poems whose "sure *Returns* of still expected *Rhymes*"
impressed the normal rhymes on every literate
mind: "trees" and "breeze," "bright" and "light,"
"eyes" and "rise," those banal congruities which
Pope himself used and reused as though to imply
that they need not be banal though like the Bea-
titudes we have heard them rather often. Long
after he had written the *Essay on Criticism* the normal rhymes still seemed to him worth salvaging.
Though they were the overused rhymes, they were
also the rhymes through which one might glimpse
order: order as intuited by a general theory of
language which we no longer find it possible to
share. This is the theory, implicit in so much
seventeenth and eighteenth-century discussions of
usage and propriety, that languages are essentially taxonomic systems, and it underwrites the
persistent sense Pope apparently would have endorsed, that behind what we have been calling
normal rhymes there may be something more than
literary habit.

Any confident discussion of this theme would
be based on more knowledge than scholarship has
so far made accessible, especially knowledge of
that strangely scanted topic, the seventeenth-
century projects for synthetic languages. A
Bishop Wilkins, designing a language from scratch,
had the opportunity to order it thoroughly, and
if after hundreds of hours he had done no more
than construct a card-house of no conceivable use
to anyone else, still his work registers in mad
detail what might be expected of an ordered set
of signs.[9] It ought to reflect, we may gather,
the Creator's taxonomies.

Of Baconian science, which made a virtue of
examining particulars, one product was the need

to array what one had examined; one product of
this need was the construction of huge systems of
classification, often meant to delineate whatever
order the Divine Mind has imprinted upon Nature.
Parallel with such enterprises, reinforcing them,
was the growing conviction that languages were
essentially systems of names: that the normal
word was a noun. By the 1720's this linguistic
intuition was sufficiently accessible to common
readers for Swift to make jokes about it; everyone remembers the sages Gulliver met in Lagado,
who had decided that uttering words corroded their
lungs, but also that since words were merely substitutes for things they might converse without
any words at all by holding up things which they
fished out of huge sacks.[10] And as the fit between the system of language and the system of
the world became a more and more engrossing topic,
so did the habit of thinking of one's language
precisely as a system, a huge closed system which
might be examined from outside: which might be
ordered by an Academy, or inventoried in a dictionary: might have its excrescences trimmed,
its duplications cancelled, its synonyms discrim-
inated, its ambiguities purged. It was finally
Samuel Johnson who performed the heroic labor of
examining one by one every word in the language,
and he came reluctantly as he did so to the conclusion that there was only so much a dictionary
might accomplish. If words, he observed, were
the daughters of earth, things were the sons of
heaven.[11]

Still, the first man was closer to heaven than
we are. Adam once named all the things Heaven
had made according to their natures, which in his
unfallen state he perceived immediately. But at
Babel Adam's orderly language was shattered like
a looking-glass. The possibility remained that
man's new understanding, after Babel, of the order which Heaven had imparted to *things* might now
be mirrored in a new language constructed for the
purpose: a taxonomy of sounds and signs, to
match that of plants and rocks. Such, and not a
need to communicate with foreigners, would appear

to have been the deep structure beneath such projects; to communicate with foreigners learned men
already possessed a supplementary language, Latin, the language in which Bacon wrote his
Instauratio Magna and Newton his *Principia*.

So it is not surprising that the Royal Society, which had sponsored some famous directives
about the plain style of framing sentences, should
have involved itself in the project of John Wilkins for contriving a Universal Language exempt
from the disorders of uninspected usage. Wilkins'
scheme was but one of many; even Isaac Newton
made notes for such a project.[12] But Wilkins'
book, unlike many, was finished and printed, and
from his *Essay Towards a Real Character and a Philosophical Language* (1668) we may now learn in as much
detail as we please what intuitions guided such
endeavors. It can give us unexpected help with
the notion of "correctness," and with rhyme.

We start from the unstated premise that the
System of the World is closed, like its microcosm
the couplet. Hence the world's contents can be
submitted to inventory. "The first thing to be
provided for, in the establishing of a Philosophical Character or Language, is a just enumeration of all such things or notions, to which
names are to be assigned." This done, and the
items arranged in copious tables "by a Consideration of them *a Priori*," he accorded all them signs,
which indicated by their written form which
table an item belonged to, and its place in that
table. To join the signs he excogitated "such a
Natural Grammar as might be suited to the Philosophy of Speech,"[13] And now, having stablized
things on sheets of paper, he was ready to make
provision for his new language to be spoken.
This meant assigning to the characters a system
of sounds.

Such a system, we find him affirming some 400
pages into his vast project, will have five desirable characteristics, of which the fifth is
that the words "should be Methodical: those of
an agreeable or opposite sense, having somewhat
correspondent in the sounds of them."[14] The ac-

cords, the antitheses, will be encoded in sound.
And correspondence, for Wilkins, appeals not at
all to vague notions of onomatopoeia. No, letters and sounds are to be assigned analytically,
"beginning first with the *Integrals*, according to
their several varieties, and then proceeding to
the Particles." What we shall hear in the system
of sounds that make up a *word* is the place of its
thing in the Universal Taxonomy.

Wilkins was not thinking of poets, and his
next steps chanced to render the system useless
for rhymed poetry. No matter; what is interesting about the system is the fantasy of linguistic
order that guides it, a fantasy whose contours no
arbitrariness in the encoding system can hide.
To the forty Genera he assigned monosyllables;
thus *God*, the fifth Genus, is D*a*, the vowel *a* being equivalent to a short o as in "bottom." Pro-
ceding down the table of Genera, *World* is Da,
Element is De, *Stone* is Di, *Metal* is Do. The nine
Differences within each Genus are signified by
affixing consonants, taken in order from a list
of nine: B, D, G, P, T, C, Z, S, N. So to De,
Element, we affix the first of these letters to
signify the First Difference, which according to
the tables is *Fire*, and *Fire* will be Deb. Each
of the nine Species within a Difference we designate by vowel or diphthong affixes from a second
list of nine. The first vowel in this list is *a*,
the first Species of *Fire* is *Flame*, and Deba signifies *Flame*. We may now examine a word-cluster.
The fifth Difference under *Element* is *Appearing
Meteor*, Det, "meteor" denoting any brightness high
in the air. Its first Species, *Rainbow*, is Deta,
its second, *Halo*, is Deta. Hence Deba, Deta,
Deta: Flame, Rainbow, Halo: not rhymes, but an
audible phonetic kinship, whose details map a
kinship of phenomena, present no doubt in the
Divine Mind and certainly in the minds of all
candid men, which operate (Wilkins affirmed) in
the same way and have a similar "apprehension of
things."15

To generate normal rhymes of use to poets, we
should have to alter this coding system somewhat,

in the first place by starting from the latter
end of the word. One might expect normal rhymes
to affirm identity of Genus, for which Wilkins'
notation starts with the syllable's initial consonant, not relevant to rhyming. What "light"
and "sight" have in common is terminal, not initial.   Still, Wilkins helps us imagine how their
similarity might be felt, as the vestige of a
wrecked order of which "bright" is another sur-
vivor and "white" perhaps another, the termina-
tion affirming luminousness and the opening consonant a specific distinction. He also helps us
grasp how sounds need not "imitate" nor "echo"
senses, not when a language is working as it
should.   Rather, relationships between sounds
will map relationships of sense, within a frame
of reference fixed by the great Taxonomic Tables,
and according to encoding rules which would yield
useful rhymes if they were differently stated.
     Take the *Essay* as the paradigm of such a prin-
ciple, and look from that paradigm toward some
actual tongue. We see at once that "light" and
"sight" exemplify a shard of broken order, also
"sky" and "high," perhaps even "glade" and "shade."
But every pun is clearly a mistake, and in a
philosophical language it would be impossible to
amuse children by telling them that a door is not
a door when it is ajar. In such a language,
though adjusted on principles a little more accommodating to eloquence than were those of Wilkins, Pope would have been able to write the
sententious parts of *The Rape of the Lock* but not
the satiric parts, at any rate not in couplets,
since for the incongruities on which satire feeds
no rhymes would have been available. (But in
Adam's lost world, for that matter, where rhymes
are orderly, no satirist would have been needed.)
In such a language "pin" would not rhyme with
"sin," nor "fail" with "whale," pins and sins having no taxonomic intercourse. But "light" would
surely rhyme with "sight," and "fame" with "name,"
and perhaps some mortuary shading of "dust" with
"must," though not in Adam's lost time, exempt
from mortality.

In the light of such fantasies of linguistic order as Wilkins' project illustrates, every real language, every language accessible to poets, affirms hints of a shattered perfection. Order, congruence, universal truths, these a poet might hint at by careful exploitation of such few congruous rhymes as his tongue placed at his disposal. They are what we have been calling the normal rhymes, and the sense of propriety they denote can seem to come from beyond the world. How this sense of things, never clearly articulated, could validate the prevalence of the rhymed couplet itself we may easily guess, and why such tame criteria as "correctness" seemed of self-evident pertinence, conveying as they did hints of comprehensive wisdom, glinting from behind the aberrancies of speech.

That the world bespeaks order and congruence is an intuition as old as human record. That details of language should mirror this congruence was the intuition of an age that came and went, leaving a body of poetry in the most admired parts of which, the parts that seemed in their time to affirm order with especial vigor, it was natural for the next age to find something frigid and mechanical. Pope's great triumphs of normal and abnormal rhyming remain for us to admire, but no poet we can now foresee is likely to want to do more in that vein, so alien now is the intuition of language to which it appealed.

THE TRANSFORMING POWER
Nature and Art in Pope's Pastorals

Martin C. Battestin

Pope's poetic career began, as it ended, with
the idea of the Golden Age--not with the myth
only, but with its profoundest implications for
the poet and the man, inheritor of the classicism
that governed his conception of art and of the
great Christian humanist tradition that conditioned his view of life. The butt of one of
history's happier ironies, Pope found himself a
Romanist Virgil in no very Augustan time. Like
Virgil he began hopefully enough by celebrating
the Golden Age in pastoral, recreating a lost i-
deal through the magical efficacy of artifice and
the harmony of his numbers; but the promise of a
second *Aeneid* which this beginning implied--an
epic to immortalize the England of George Augus-
tus--could be fulfilled in parody only, in satire
proclaiming the grotesque apocalypse of "Saturnian days of Lead and Gold."[1] The distance between
the green world of the *Pastorals* (1709) and the
dark estate of *The Dunciad* (1728-1743) is, to be
sure, as immense as Pope's sad spiritual journey
from the relative optimism of his youth (he began his eclogues when he was sixteen) to the ut-

This essay first appeared in *Eighteenth-Century Studies* 2 (1969), 183-204.

ter disenchantment of his last years. But controlling and, in surprising ways, connecting both
poems is the idea of the Golden Age--an idea
comprehending both the Christian's conception of
Time and History and, within this context, the
poet's conception of the relationship of Art to
Nature.

Pope's Virgilian poems make clear a fundamental assumption of his art and theology: this is
the belief--as much moral and metaphysical as
aesthetic--that Order, Form, Harmony are the
sacred attributes of the highest reality, whether
in the universe at large, or in the micorcosm
man, or in the artifact. Hence his continuing
fascination with the creative act itself. Perhaps the simplest manifestation of this impulse
in his poetry is the frequency with which he
echoes and recalls the *fiat lux* of Genesis. When
Pope wishes to celebrate the institution of order in the body politic or in the physical sciences, or, conversely, when he wishes to deplore
the subversion of order in morality or in literature, his language returns us to that moment when
God's Word brought Light out of Darkness, Order
out of Chaos:

At length great *ANNA* said--Let Discord cease!
She said, the World obey'd, and all was *Peace* !

Nature, and Nature's Laws lay hid in Night.
God said, *Let Newton be!* and All was *Light*.

The skilful Nymph reviews her Force with
        Care;
Let Spades be Trumps! she said, and Trumps they
        were.

Lo! thy dread Empire, CHAOS! is restor'd;
Light dies before thy uncreating word:
Thy hand, great Anarch! lets the curtain fall;
And Universal Darkness buries All.

The awful close of *The Dunciad* thus signals the
triumph of Dulness, the death in a benighted

world of the sacred values the poet has cherished.
The forces of venality and barbarism, working
their own perverse alchemy, have transformed the
symbol of a golden age into the counterfeit of
itself, where lead is substance and gilt the only
value prized. But in *The Dunciad*, as in a negative
image, one may discern the true shape of Pope's
universe, the nature of his Christian vision of
time, and the significance of those symbols and
conceptual ideals that inform his work from first
to last. Though the action of that poem, in a
sardonic parody of Christian teleology, presents
the apocalyptic victory of Chaos and Old Night,
the *form* of the poem--Pope's nice control of
language and his system of allusion--is the
supreme assertion both of intellectual light, and
of an order in history and in art that not even
the prodigious incompetencies of a Cibber or the
grasping machinations of a Walpole can abolish.
The positive statement of these ideals had been
given earlier in those complementary works, the
Essay on Criticism (1711) and the *Essay on Man* (1733-
34), wherein the neoclassical conception of Nature and of the poetic imitation of her is set
forth discursively in couplets as finely wrought
and balanced as the poet's universe itself. In
the *Essay on Man* Pope had advised his reader that
"All Nature is but Art, unknown to thee; / All
Chance, Direction, which thou canst not see" (I,
ll. 289-290). Nature--according to Aristotle the
subject of the poet's imitation--is, in other
words, the perfect artifact; and history, even
more surely than any play of Sophocles, has its
own beginning, middle, and end. To Pope, as to
countless philosophers and divines of the Christian humanist tradition,[2] the poet of the creation,
of history, is the Deity himself, the Word who
brought Form and Order out of Chaos, beginning
propitiously enough what man has made a tragic
drama, and who at the final catastrophe will
speak again, dissolving time and the world into
eternity. Of this creative function of the Logos,
the imitator and surrogate in the fallen, sublunary realm of flux and decay is--or should be--the

poet himself, whose words and numbers have the
transforming power to restore to us a measure at
least of grace and harmony, the power, as it were,
to remind us of the identity of Art and Nature
that once obtained in Eden, in the Golden Age.[3]

As Frank Kermode and Edward Tayler have demonstrated,[4] the articulation of this theoretical
relationship between Nature and Art was long the
special province of serious pastoral poetry in
the Christian era. In Virgil, whom Pope made his
model, the essential paradox of the pastoral mode
is already clear; the most sophisticated literary
craftmanship has become the means of presenting,
and therefore of recommending, an image of perfect naturalness and simplicity. In Arcadia the
Golden Age is restored, Nature appears in her
original unfallen condition, and the artificial
manners and contrivances of civilization are
scorned. Yet it is only through the idealizing
powers of imagination and the refining powers of
a mannered artifice that this return to Nature
has been effected. Pastoral is the product of
the court, of an urbane, sophisticated society
very much aware that the loss of innocence and
simplicity is irremediable and that in this deca-
dent Iron Age, Art is the sole means of redeeming
Eden. As in the myth of the Golden Age recounted
in the *Georgics*, Art may thus be seen as man's
compensation for the Fall. In his "Discourse on
Pastoral Poetry" (1717), Pope insists on this redemptive function of artifice, asserting that the
Nature imitated by the pastoral poet is not that
discernible in the ordinary physical world of
actuality, but is rather that ideal realm available to us only through the imagination and ex-
pressible only in the images and harmonies of
poetry:[5] "If we would copy Nature," he declares,
"it may be useful to take this Idea along with
us, that pastoral is an image of what they call
the Golden age. So that we are not to describe
our shepherds as shepherds at this day really
are, but as they may be conceiv'd then to have
been...." The world of pastoral, he continues,
is realized only through "illusion" and by means

of the most exquisite verbal harmonies, by numbers "the smoothest, the most easy and flowing
imaginable."

The essence of pastoral, as Pope understood,
is the recognition of the Fall and of our desire
to repudiate the wretched legacy of Adam.   In
this life, in the final stages of Nature's decay
and of man's moral decadence, the Golden Age of
innocence and perfect harmony between man and
Nature is recoverable only through Art in the
formal world of the eclogue itself. At the end
of history, the true Golden Age will in fact be
restored to men through the redeeming efficacy of
Christ, the Logos and Messiah: this, as Christians from St. Augustine and Dante to Pope himself
believed, was the esoteric import of that greatest and most curious of all pastoral poems of
antiquity--Virgil's *Fourth Eclogue*. An awareness
of these profounder implications of the mode will
serve to clarify Pope's decision in 1717 to include his own sacred eclogue, "Messiah," as the
culminating poem in his series of Pastorals--a
decision most critics regard as ill considered,
but which was in fact necessary to the completion
of a coherent and quite remarkable design. Taken
together, Pope's poems on the seasons and his
"Messiah" comprise a unified, carefully developed
paradigm of the relationship between Art and Nature in the context of Christian time. Though
much useful scholarship has been published on the
subject of the pastoral in the eighteenth century,[6] in our understanding of the poems themselves we have not yet progressed very far beyond
Dr. Johnson's opinion that the form is "easy,
vulgar, and therefore disgusting"[7]--a mode suitable perhaps for juvenile versifiers to cut their
teeth on, but not, after all, very substantial
fare. To Johnson, the noblest prospect in Arcadia was the high road leading to something better; and to Pope himself, looking back as satirist
upon the decorous productions of his youth, the
Pastorals seemed little more than a holiday excursion in Fancy's maze.[8] Satire, after all, as the
French critics had decided, was a nobler and more

demanding genre than eclogue or georgic. However that may be, these five poems deserve a more
careful reading than they have been given, for
in them Pope realized, in some rather splendid
verse, the latent aesthetic and philosophical
implications of the pastoral mode.
If from Virgil Pope learned the function of
high artifice in pastoral, it was in Spenser that
he found a structure for the major theme of his
work--the theme of Time. In his "Discourse"
Pope explained his admiration for Spenser's device of the calendar:

> The addition he has made of a Calendar to his
> Eclogues is very beautiful: since by this,
> besides the general moral of innocence and
> simplicity, which is common to other authors
> of pastoral, he has one peculiar to himself;
> he compares human Life to the several Seasons,
> and at once exposes to his readers a view of
> the great and little worlds, in their various
> changes and aspects.

In adapting this structure to his own purposes,
Pope fully elaborated the comparison between
"the great and little worlds," between the universe at large and the microcosm man, viewing
both worlds from the perspective of Time implicit
in the idea of the calendar itself.[9] The dominant tension in these poems is that between permanence and mutability, between the Great Year
of Christian theology and the annual revolution
of the seasons taken as a metaphor of human life
and human history. In this way we are to understand Pope's assurance that he had improved upon
Spenser's design by relating the seasons to "the
several ages of man, and the different passions
proper to each age." In the movement of the
year from spring to winter is implicit not only
the idea of mortality, the troubled descent of
man from youth to the grave, but also the mythic
pattern of history, tracing mankind's sad decline
from the Golden to the Iron Age, from Eden to
the present moment. In this context of mortali-

ty and degeneration, Pope no less than Keats or
Yeats believed the artist to be the sole agent of
permanence and ideal beauty; for only in the Grecian urn or in the golden nightingales of Byzan-
tium or in the formal world of pastoral is Time
defeated, the fallen world perfected.

"Spring" depicts the Golden Age, the state of
innocence before the Fall when art and life mirrored the perfection of Nature. The situation is
a singing contest between the shepherds Daphnis
and Strephon, who, after staking a bowl and a
lamb as prizes and piously invoking Love and
the Muse, proceed in counterpoint to celebrate
the virtues of their sweethearts. Damon, the
arbiter, determines that the contest is a draw,
because, we may suppose, in this world judges are
wise, poets equally skilful, and lovers equally
fair and true: "Blest Swains, whose Nymphs in
ev'ry Grace excell; / Blest Nymphs, whose Swains
those Graces sing so well!" (11.95-96). Although
the poem develops according to a system of anti-
theses--Daphnis vs. Strephon, Sylvia vs. Delia,
Venus (goddess of Love and Beauty) vs. Phoebus
(god of poetry), the bowl vs. the lamb, Art vs.
Nature--these tensions imply not conflict, but
harmony. Like the genial debate of the shepherds
proceeding in counterpoint to a perfect resolu-
tion--indeed, like the balanced form and musical
repetitions of Pope's couplets--the opposing elements of the poem are happily reconciled; at the
conclusion they are poised in a state at once of
absolute autonomy and of mutual cooperation. In
this Arcadian world the agent of harmony, who
echoes the divine command of Genesis, is Damon,
the judge and mediator: "Cease to contend, for
(*Daphnis*) I decree / The Bowl to *Strephon*, and the
Lamb to thee" (11.93-94). *Concordia discors*--the
great principle of universal Order which Pope ex-
pounds in *Windsor Forest* (1713) and the *Essay on
Man*[10]--is in "Spring" the condition of life.

This, then, is the image of the world the poem
presents, the dramatic and formal expression of
the idea of the Golden Age. The explicit moral
of the poem is the one conventionally associated

with this idea: the recommendation of innocence,
of the naturalness and simplicity of the country
as opposed to the affectation and worldly ambition of the court. Addressing Sir William Trumbull in the second paragraph, Pope dutifully
declares his theme:

> *You*, that too Wise for Pride, too Good for
>   Pow'r,
> Enjoy the Glory to be Great no more,
> And carrying with you all the World can boast,
> To all the World Illustriously are lost!
>   (ll.7-10)

As Pope's footnote suggests, Trumbull--who "was
born in *Windsor*-Forest, to which he retreated
after he had resign'd the post of Secretary of
State to King *William* III"--is himself a living
parable of this softly didactic theme of pastoral, which addresses a courtly and urbane audience to recommend a return to original innocence
in the state of nature.

But all this is perfunctory. The intellectual
impetus behind these poems is not so much ethical
as aesthetic. What interests the poet is not so
much the folly of the English court (*that* would
come later!), nor, even at his tender age, any
sanguine expectation that he may effect the
wholesale translation of St. James to the Forest
of Arden. Appropriately enough on this, the occasion of his first essay as a poet, what interests Pope is the making of poetry and the meaning of his art. This is the theme announced in
the exordium and rendered in the emblem of Daphnis' bowl. The subject of the *Pastorals* is the
nature, the mystery, the efficacy of Art itself,
viewed in relation to those correlative concepts
with which the artist is most nearly concerned:
the meaning of Time and Nature in a fallen world.

> First in these Fields I try the Sylvan Strains,
> Nor blush to sport on *Windsor's* blissful
>   Plains:
> Fair *Thames* flow gently from thy sacred
>   Spring,

While on thy Banks *Sicilian* Muses sing;
Let Vernal Airs thro' trembling Osiers play,
And *Albion's* Cliffs resound the Rural Lay.

Ostentatiously mellifluous and thick with allusions to the poets whose example he meant to imi-
tate--to Theocritus and Virgil, Spenser and
Milton--the opening of the *Pastorals* declares
Pope's acceptance of the challenge of his art and,
further, it implicitly asserts the power of the
poet's song to transform "*Windsor's* blissful
Plains" into Arcadia, into Eden. In part, this
transformation is effected through allusion, to
Virgil and Milton in particular, with whom the
literary ideas of Arcadia and Eden are chiefly
associated: the "Vernal Airs" and "trembling
Osiers" that play along the Thames in Windsor are
echoes of Milton's description of Paradise and of
the sacred river Jordan.[11] But the ideal of harmony and perfect order that Eden signifies--and
which it will be the purpose of these eclogues to
keep constantly before the reader--can be *realized*
in the poem only through the music of Pope's numbers and his control of form. Hence the display
of sonic devices such as alliteration and assonance and of mannered rhetorical symmetries; and
hence, too, that elaborate fugal development of
the principle of *concordia discors* which, as we have
seen, is the formal expression of the idea of the
Golden Age.
　There is good reason, therefore, that Pope
should have labored to make these poems "the most
correct in the versification, and musical in the
numbers, of all his works." In this design he
succeeded so well that, in the opinion of his eighteenth-century critics, he effected a revolution
in English prosody: Joseph Warton, for instance,
found the *Pastorals* "musical, to a degree of which
rhyme could hardly be thought capable...the first
specimen of that harmony in English verse, which
is now become indispensably necessary";[12] and Dr.
Johnson, who saw little else to approve in them,
admired Pope's "series of versification, which
had in English poetry no precedent, nor has since

had an imitation."[13] What we have not appreciated is the *meaning* of the music. To a degree
unparalleled in any of Pope's later works, music
is the distinctive formal quality of the *Pastorals*
because music, defined traditionally as a *concordia discors*, is here the poet's symbol for the
Ideal, for order and perfection in Art and in the
world. Though, as Warton and Dr. Johnson remarked, the harmony Pope achieved in these poems
had no precedent in English verse, there was nothing novel about its symbolism. Thus, in his
illuminating analysis of Dryden's and Pope's
musical odes, Earl Wasserman observes that in the
Christian humanist tradition music was a conventional metaphor for ideal creation: like the
poet, God Himself is a "Musician, and the universe is the song He sang into existence."[14] In
the *Pastorals*, no less than in the *Ode for Musick*
(1713), formal harmony acquires an ontological
significance: it is the expression and embodiment of the poet's theme, the recreation of an
ideal order once, according to the myths of Eden
and the Golden Age, known to men on earth but
now attainable only through Art.
    Pope's belief in this redemptive potency of
poetry is clearly implicit in *Windsor Forest*: "The
Groves of *Eden* , vanish'd now so long,/ Live in
Description, and look green in Song" (ll. 7-8).
Because they possessed this deific power, Denham
and Cowley in the same poem are "God-like" (1.
270) and--though one could wish Pope's choice of
example were happier--Granville can effect a new
creation, through song achieving, as it were, a
second Nature[15] more perfect and durable than the
world of actuality:

> But hark! the Groves rejoice, the Forest rings!
> Are these reviv'd or is it *Granville* sings?
>   'Tis yours, my Lord, to bless our soft
>   Retreats,
> And call the Muses to their ancient Seats;
> To paint anew the flow'ry Sylvan Scenes,
> To crown the Forests with Immortal Greens,
> Make *Windsor* Hills in lofty Numbers rise,
> And lift her Turrets nearer to the Skies....
>   (ll.281-288)

Like Diana, who metamorphosed the ravished Lodona
into the chaste stream whose waters mirror an i-
dealized landscape, the poet has the power to
provide compensation for outrage, by a certain
nobler alchemy transforming the Iron into the
Golden Age.

In "Spring" the relationship between Art and
Nature is rendered by a different metaphor, not
by an allegory of transformation, but by an object of art. The Bowl of Daphnis is here Pope's
emblem for the *Pastorals* themselves. In the round
perfection of its form and in the symbolic devices wrought upon it, the bowl embodies the meaning of the poet's work, which, as I have suggested, is the attempt by exquisite artifice and harmony to imitate ideal Nature, to recreate Eden.
Though Pope has been more than once accused of
slavishly following his predecessors in the
pastoral tradition, the Bowl of Daphnis is no
mere transcription of similar devices in Theocritus, Virgil, and Spenser;[16] in the economy of
its representation and in its rich symbolic significance, it is quite unique--one of many
instances in these eclogues in which Pope dis-
closes new possibilities and new dimensions within the conventions of the genre. Here is the
passage as Daphnis stakes his prize against
Strephon's lamb:

> And I this Bowl, where wanton Ivy twines,
> And swelling Clusters bend the curling Vines:
> Four Figures rising from the Work appear,
> The various Seasons of the rowling Year;
> And what is That, which binds the Radiant Sky,
> Where twelve fair Signs in beauteous Order
>   lye?
>
>   (11.35-40)

The several emblems engraved on the bowl symbol-
ize the relationship between the poem and its
subject, between Art and ideal Nature. As is
clear from "Summer," for instance, where Pope
specifically identifies his work with "this
Wreath of Ivy" (1.10), the circlet of evergreen

ivy is one symbol of the poem, of the artifact itself; in contrast to this stand the "swelling
Clusters" of grapes that suggest both Nature's
rich fruitfulness and her powers of inspiration.
In the next line, the "Four Figures rising from
the Work" are immediately identified as an allegory of the seasons, and hence with the subject
and the form of the *Pastorals* themselves. Moreover, the thought of the poem's relationship to
the seasons and consequently to the theme of Time
("the rowling Year") leads to a final image--the
"beauteous Order" of the Zodiac, of the eternal
heavens, the realm not of seasonal change and
mutability, but of permanence and ideal reality.
The answer to Daphnis' question--"And what is
That, which binds the Radiant Sky...?"--is clearly, then, the power of the Deity, the supreme
Artificer of creation. As the bowl and its symbolism imply, the Art of God, binding the constellations in "beauteous Order," is in an essential sense analogous to the craft of the poet,
who fashions the "Wreath of Ivy" that binds the
materials of his art--Nature and the seasons--
within the ordered and lovely fabric of the poem.
In this context, the circle, traditional symbol
of perfection, becomes Pope's metaphor for the
power of art to unify, order, and contain: this
is the import not only of the bowl itself, but of
those images of roundness and encirclement it
depicts--entwining ivy, swelling clusters, curl-
ing vines, the rolling year, and God's binding of
the sky. The bowl of Daphnis is Pope's emblem
for those other artifacts, the *Pastorals* themselves and the sphere of the great creation. In
it is implied the relation of Art to Nature which
is the poet's chief concern in these poems.
    As we have seen, the theme of "Spring" is the
celebration of *concordia*--the condition of the
perfect harmony of life and art and nature in
Eden. In contrast, the following three eclogues
are elegiac in mood, depicting ever-worsening
stages in man's estrangement from Eden. In "Summer" the mourning song of Alexis for an unattainable mistress begins the theme of Time's victory,

of deprivation and mortality, which culminates in
"Winter." The poem is dedicated to the physician,
Dr. Samuel Garth, because the world it describes
is dis-eased. The sense of change and loss is
immediate: spring has passed into summer, dawn
into the heat of noon, youth into dissatisfied
maturity, the Golden into the Silver Age. Love
is here no longer a kindly god, but rather the
cause of torment and distress: it is "the sole
Disease" the skilful physician cannot cure (1.12),
the only "Serpent" in Eden (1.68).

That this eclogue may be read as something
more than a conventional love complaint is clear
from the identity of the singer and the nature of
his passion: Alexis is the figure of the Poet--
indeed, of Alexander Pope, author of these past-
orals--and the object of his unrequited desire is
nameless, that is, an abstraction. Through the
efficacy of the shepherds' songs and the symbol
of Daphnis' bowl, "Spring" presented the triumph
of Art, the mirror of ideal Nature; in the imperfect world of "Summer" this happy condition no
longer obtains. The opening lines echo Spenser's
"Januarye," Colin Clout's lament for the elusive
Rosalind, and remind us that here, as in *The
Shepheardes Calender*, the speaker is to be taken as
a projection of the author himself.[17] But the
despair of Alexis is caused by the discrepancy
between what he aspires to achieve as a poet and
what in fact is attainable. His ambition is not
to excel in the business of life, but to sing
true songs, songs what will gain him his mistress
and secure his reputation:

> Let other Swains attend the Rural Care,
> Feed fairer Flocks, or richer Fleeces share;
> But nigh yon' Mountain let me tune my Lays,
> Embrace my Love, and bind my Brows with Bays.
>   (11.35-38)

Yet, though he has inherited the flute of Colin
Clout, the master poet of English pastoral,
Alexis is sadly conscious of his own inferior
powers:

That Flute is mine which *Colin's* tuneful Breath
Inspir'd when living, and bequeath'd in Death;
He said; *Alexis*, take this Pipe, the same
That taught the Groves my *Rosalinda's* Name--
But now the Reeds shall hang on yonder Tree,
For ever silent, since despis'd by thee.
                              (11.39-44)

Seeking a cure for his disease, the burning after
a hopeless love that torments him, he has turned
to poetry and found himself inadequate. The
Muses have deserted him, gracing the groves of
Academe where Cam and Isis flow, while he sits
Narcissus-like, disconsolately scrutinizing his
face reflected in the crystal spring (11.23-28).
His art is good enough only to "please the rural
Throng" (1.49); for any higher purpose--to heal
his heart (1.34), to win the object of his pas-
sion--it is unavailing.

Such doubts concerning his powers are perhaps
understandable and seemly enough in a "Shepherd's
Boy" of sixteen, but properly to diagnose the poet's malaise, one must define the nameless mistress he longs for. In "Winter" we will find
that she is to be identified with Daphne--the
principle of ideal Beauty and therefore of true
poetic inspiration and power; according to the
Socratic view, she is the object of the higher
eros. In "Summer" she is defined only through
her attributes. Thus it is she alone who deserves
the poet's "Wreath," for in her "all Beauties are
compriz'd in One" (1.58). She is the source of
all that is benign and lovely in Nature:

Where-e'er you walk, cool Gales shall fan the
     Glade,
Trees, where you sit, shall crowd into a Shade,
Where-e'er you tread, the blushing Flow'rs
     shall rise,
And all things flourish where you turn your
     Eyes.   (11.73-76)

And, most essentially in this context, the ideal
harmony she expresses, like the song of Orpheus,
is the means of an absolute power over Nature:

But wou'd you sing, and rival *Orpheus'* Strain,
The wondring Forests soon shou'd dance again,
The moving Mountains hear the pow'rful Call,
And headlong Streams hang list'ning in their
    Fall!   (11.81-84)

Alexis longs in vain to live with this ideal,
to achieve the condition of perfect harmony enjoyed by the shepherd poets of "Spring." But in
"Summer" the Golden Age has passed; ideal Beauty
has "forsaken" (1.71) the green world, where now
"the Serpent Love abides"--Love unsatisfied and
insatiable. The poet cannot possess, though he
can woo, the Ideal--in his words and numbers e-
voking her imperfect image, always and painfully
aware of what he can never quite attain: "On me
Love's fiercer Flames for ever prey, / By Night
he scorches, as he burns by Day" (11.91-92). The
emblem for "Summer" may be found in the image of
Alexis viewing himself in the crystal spring,
while "Fresh rising Blushes paint the watry Glass"
(11.27-28). For this poem is the parable of
Alexander Pope's own self-scrutiny, the expression of the young poet's hopes and frustrations,
aware of both the ideals and the limits of Art.
    "Autumn," the next eclogue in the series, was
the last in order of composition, and we may add
that it is least successful in execution, least
interesting in content. One feels that in
"Spring," "Summer," and "Winter" Pope had completed his intellectual design for the *Pastorals*
and was now, for the sake of symmetry and wholeness, merely rounding out his Arcadian year. To
be sure, there is an occasional felicitous coup-
let--"Here where the *Mountains* less'ning as they
rise, / Lose the low Vales, and steal into the
Skies" (11.59-60)--but for the most part the
verse is, for Pope, undistinguished and the ideas
are of a sort to justify Dr. Johnson's opinion
that pastorals, "not professing to imitate real
life, require no experience, and, exhibiting only the simple operation of unmingled passions,
admit no subtle reasoning or deep inquiry."[18]

Still, the poem does carry forward Pope's parallelism between the gradual decline of the seasons toward the death of the year and the worsening condition of human life. In tracing the stages of man's estrangement from Saturnian felicity, we have in "Autumn" reached the Age of Brass, when folly first entered the world and men became their own tormentors. Since Pope's theme is for the first time moral, the usual topic of satire, the poem is appropriately dedicated to Wycherley, "Whose Sense instructs us, and whose Humour charms" (1.9)--a comic writer, indeed, "of infinite spirit, satire, and wit." Hylas and AEgon are the speakers, lovesick swains whose tribulations spring from different causes--"This mourn'd a faithless, that an absent Love" (1.3) --and whose folly manifests itself in the different ways of suicidal despair and euphoric self-delusion. For Hylas--as for Nature bereft of the warming sun--Delia's absence is death itself (ll.27-30). But his "melodious Moan" makes *"Mountains* groan" (ll.15-16), and the echoes of her name he has started at last induce the happy fantasy that she has returned to him:

> Go gentle Gales, and bear my Sighs away!
> Come, *Delia*, come; ah why this long Delay?
> Thro' Rocks and Caves the Name of *Delia* sounds,
> *Delia*, each Cave and ecchoing Rock rebounds.
> Ye Pow'rs, what pleasing Frensie sooths my
>   Mind!
> Do Lovers dream, or is my *Delia* kind?
> She comes, my *Delia* comes!--Now cease my Lay,
> And cease ye Gales to bear my Sighs away!
>   (ll.47-54)

AEgon, Hylas' fellow perpetrator of the "mournful Strain," laments a severer plight, the treachery of "perjur'd *Doris*," who has--one feels, understandably--abandoned him for another. In a tuneful paroxysm of grief and self-pity, AEgon questions heaven's justice (1.76) and leaves his flock a prey: "Ah! what avails it me, the Flocks to keep, / Who lost my Heart while I preserv'd

my Sheep" (11.79-80). Though the shepherds reprove him for his negligence and though Pan himself grows anxious at his ravings, believing him
bewitched, AEgon hugs his grief the closer,
threatening to "Forsake Mankind, and all the
World--but Love!" (1.88). Suicide, he promises,
will be his revenge on the world: "One Leap
from yonder Cliff shall end my Pains. / No more
ye Hills, no more resound my Strains!" (11.95-
96). Not Timon in affliction or Gloucester on
the brink at Dover presents a more moving spectacle, it would appear. But Pope's wry, hyperbolic language keeps us aware of the absurdity
of all this--of AEgon's ranting despair and of
Hylas' sanguine confidence in the efficacy of
his sighs. When the poet's voice is heard again
at the conclusion, it is to assure us that
Delia's return was, indeed, the soothing effect
of Hylas' frenzy, and that AEgon, despite his
threats of self-destruction, is still alive and
moaning in Arcady: "Thus sung the Shepherds till
th'Approach of Night...."
    Earlier I described the mood of "Autumn" as
elegiac, but it is so only with regard to the
complaints of the shepherds themselves and to
the sense, always a little distressing, of human
folly which the poet means to convey. Pope's
own attitude to the situation is rather one of
dispassionate amusement, a stance vaguely reminiscent of Wycherley's, let us say, or that of
the narrator of the *The Rape of the Lock*. In a
sense, "Autumn," though an eclogue, is Pope's
first essay in the satiric mode. Yet, though its
tone is lighter than the plaintive music of "Summer," "Autumn" continues to deepen the impression
of man's separation from Eden which is the dominant theme of the *Pastorals*. In these poems Love
is Pope's metaphor of life, of the way one fares
in the world; it is also the means of defining
the relation of the singers to ideal innocence.
In "Spring" Love was perfectly reciprocal and benign; in "Summer," though the source of spiritual dis-ease, it appeared as the higher *eros*--an
irresistible yearning after ideal Beauty, for-

ever elusive yet the source of all delight. In
"Autumn," where Pope first sounds his moral
theme, Love is a baser god whose nature is seen
in the faithlessness of Doris and in the passion,
either self-deluding or self-consuming, of the
shepherds. Though he is powerless to resist him,
AEgon knows his enemy:

> I know thee Love! on foreign Mountains bred,
> Wolves gave thee suck, and savage Tygers fed.
> Thou wert from *AEtna's* burning Entrails torn,
> Got by fierce Whirlwinds, and in Thunder born!
>   (11.89-92)

This is the destructive principle within man,
the source of all that is most inimical to his
true happiness and fulfillment. Pope's theme in
"Autumn" is the folly of men, is *human* Nature,
and the poetic imitation of this is the proper
subject of the satiric mode. "Oh, skill'd in
Nature!" the poet exclaims to Wycherley, "see
the Hearts of Swains, / Their artless Passions,
and their tender Pains" (11.11-12). Doubtless
Pope's design for the Pastorals, both formal and
thematic, demanded such a poem; but the delicate
frame of the eclogue strains under weighty matter it was never really meant to bear.
    "Winter"--before "Messiah" Pope's own favor-
ite and certainly the richest poem of the four--
completes the design. From the green, golden
world of "Spring" we have been plunged now into
darkest night and stormy weather, the situation
for mankind in the Iron Age. In this fallen
world, death is the condition of life, and death
is Pope's subject: the death of the day and of
the year, the death of Nature, and most especially the death of Daphne. Although the conceptual identity of Daphne is evident within the
eclogue itself--as Thyrsis reveals, she is the
one who inspired "sweet *Alexis'* Strain" (1.11)--
Pope's models for the poem make his meaning still
clearer. Among classical sources, she recalls
the Daphnis of Theocritus' *Idyll I* and of Virgil's
Eclogue V: in Theocritus, Daphnis is the legend-

ary inventor of pastoral song whose death all
Nature mourns; in Virgil, whose subject is Daphnis' death and apotheosis, he represents some
principle of cosmic Order which has disappeared
from the world but which still rules in Elysium.
Among the pastoral elegies of Pope's contemporaries, Walsh's *Eclogue V* in memory of Mrs. Tempest
provides a further analogue in the death of Delia, the figure of ideal Love and Beauty, whose
demise has disastrous consequences in the sublunary world: "Ev'n Nature's self in dire convul-
sions lies!" (1.26).   It was at Walsh's suggestion, we recall, that Pope dedicated his own poem
to Mrs. Tempest--an apt decision, certainly,
since in her name and in the circumstances of her
death (she died the night of the great storm of
November 1703), this unfortunate woman perfectly
exemplified Pope's theme of mortality and his
symbolism of winter weather, the climate of life
in this fallen world.
      In these poems Delia and Daphnis represent
some beneficent avatar of the Ideal whose death
leaves the world diminished and forlorn. Daphne
is Pope's own expression of this concept. Ideal
Beauty, that unattainable abstraction which demanded Alexis' love and inspired his song in
"Summer," has here been given a name. And, be-
fitting the wretchedness of our condition in the
Iron Age, at this withered end of history, she is
no longer merely elusive, she is dead; our
estrangement from Eden is complete. As the
changes of Thyrsis' sad refrain declare, with
Daphne every positive value has vanished from the
world: Love, Beauty, Pleasure, Sweetness, Music
--once "our Glory" in Eden--are "now no more."
In "Spring," the recreation of the Golden Age,
all these values were enjoyed by men; perfect
justice and love and song were the conditions of
life, and Nature and Art were one. In "Winter"
this ideal relationship no longer obtains: "No
more the Birds shall imitate her Lays" (1.55).
Within the world of these pastorals, Daphne is
the equivalent of Astraea, goddess of Justice and
Order, who fled the earth at the deposition of

Saturn by Jove, when the Iron Age succeeded the
Age of Gold. Like Astraea, Daphne has been translated from this sublunary realm of disorder and
decay to the region of timeless beauty beyond the
stars. There--beyond "heaven's bourne," as Keats
would put it--the original perfection of the divine creation remains unaltered, and Nature and
Art are one, as they were in Eden:

> But see! where *Daphne* wondring mounts on high,
> Above the Clouds, above the Starry Sky.
> Eternal Beauties grace the shining Scene,
> Fields ever fresh, and Groves for ever green!
> There, while You rest in *Amaranthine* Bow'rs,
> Or from those Meads select unfading Flow'rs,
> Behold us kindly who your Name implore,
> *Daphne*, our Goddess, and our Grief no more!
> (11.69-76)

Daphne's death and the winter weather are Pope's
metaphors for Actuality, for the harsh conditions
of life in this fallen, mortal world. Thyrsis'
valediction presents this world as it is, desolate and decaying, inimical to man:

> But see, *Orion* sheds unwholesome Dews,
> Arise, the Pines a noxious Shade diffuse;
> Sharp *Boreas* blows, and Nature feels Decay,
> Time conquers All, and We must Time obey.
> (11.85-88)

This last line, a significant variation upon the
famous conclusion of Virgil's *Eclogues* ("*Omnia vincit
Amor: et nos cedamus Amori*"), points to the dominant
theme of Pope's *Pastorals* and to the spiritual
distance, at least, that separates him from the
Roman poet. Pope's eclogues record the triumph
not of Love, which has died with Daphne, but of
Time. In terms of the carefully elaborated parallelisms of the *Pastorals*, Time has carried us from
spring to winter, from dawn to midnight, from
youth to the grave, from Eden to the present moment. It is the inexorable process of degeneration and decay leading to death.

Playing against this theme--indeed, at once
containing and in a sense transcending it--are
the poems themselves, the music not of time but
of eternity, whose harmonies recall that ideal
relationship between Art and Nature that once obtained. Daphne's dying request implies this antagonism between mutability and permanence, between
the ugliness of life and the loveliness of art:
"'Ye Shepherds, sing around my Grave!'" (1.18).
In Thyrsis' elegy Daphne is honored and immortal-
ized, his song so moving that all Nature listens
in silence--"Such Silence" as "waits on *Philomela's*
Strains" (1.78). The analogy recalls that mythical power which changed the ravished girl into
the nightingale, giving music in compensation for
outrage. The poet's art, as Pope implies and
demonstrates in these poems, has this same transforming power to restore imperfect Nature and re-
deem the fallen world. "The Groves of *Eden,* vanish'd now so long, / Live in Description, and
look green in Song."
    Though recent criticism has brilliantly illu-
minated the assumptions and techniques of Pope's
other major poetry, the *Pastorals* continue to be
regarded generally as little more than trivial
exercises in versification and decorum with which
Pope amused himself while learning his craft as
a poet. Even those who admire his eclogues take
refuge in uneasy analogizing, preferring to deal
with them not as poems, but as expressions of
Pope's "choreographic sense" or as verbal paintings after the manner of Poussin or Zuccarelli.[19]
The *Pastorals* deserve a better fate. In them Pope
came to terms with the essential intellectual implications of the mode itself--the peculiarly
generic relationship it bears to the ideas of Art
and Nature, Permanence and Mutability--and, discerning the significance of Virgil's artificiality and Spenser's calendar, he devised a form and
a structure that enabled him to develop, indeed
to embody, these themes coherently in poetry. In
this respect--in their nice adjustment of meaning
and form--the *Pastorals* deserve not our condescension, but our warmest admiration. Far from con-

stituting a deviation from the more serious philosophical concerns of Renaissance pastoral, as
Edward Tayler has supposed,[20] they are rather the
consummation of that tradition.

Even though the four poems published in Ton-
son's now famous *Poetical Miscellanies* of 1709 have
a coherent shape and meaning of their own, they
did not complete Pope's larger design for his
Pastorals. As we have seen, these poems, in
tracing the seasons from spring to winter, developed an analogy between "the great and little
worlds," between the decay of Nature and the re-
grettable progress of human life and human history. The loss of Eden and the triumph of Time had
there been Pope's theme. But implicit in this
idea and in the calendar structure of the *Pastorals*
is the expectation of renewal--of a new dawn, a
new spring, restoring the Golden Age. In the
context of Christian teleology, the world's Great
Year leads to the apocalypse, not to Time's victory but to its ultimate defeat.

Published in *The Spectator* for 14 May 1712,
Pope's "Messiah" is thus the logical sequel to
the poems on the seasons, as he himself indicated
when, for the edition of his collected works five
years later, he made room for his "Sacred Eclogue"
under the heading of "Pastorals," giving it the
climactic position in the series. To come from
"Winter" immediately to the "Messiah," as readers
of this volume would have done, is to sense at
once the relationship of the two poems:

> Ye Nymphs of *Solyma!* begin the Song:
> To heav'nly Themes sublimer Strains belong.
> The Mossie Fountains and the Sylvan Shades,
> The Dreams of *Pindus* and th' *Aonian* Maids,
> Delight no more--O Thou my Voice inspire
> Who touch'd *Isaiah's* hallow'd Lips with Fire!
>   Rapt into future Times, the Bard begun;
> A *Virgin* shall conceive, a *Virgin* bear a son!

Whereas Pope's secular eclogues had focused on
the meaning of life and art in this world, his
"Messiah"--like its model, Virgil's "Pollio,"

which was construed by Christian interpreters as
a prophecy of the coming of Christ--turns to
"heav'nly Themes." Whereas the earlier pastorals
had carried us from the past to the present, from
the Golden to the Iron Age, "Messiah" will translate us "into future Times." Whereas "Winter"
left us with the image of death, this sacred eclogue heralds the birth of the Savior. Deliberately, the themes and symbols which had earlier
defined the temporal and spiritual condition of
fallen man are now recalled in order to be contradicted. The heat and disease of "Summer," the
tempests of "Winter," the moral disorders of
"Autumn"--all are remembered and their curse dis-
pelled:

> The Sick and Weak the healing Plant shall aid;
> From Storms a Shelter, and from Heat a Shade.
> All Crimes shall cease, and ancient Fraud
>   shall fail.   (11.15-17)

Astraea, whose benign influence was manifest in
"Spring" in Damon's wise decision, had with every
other virtue departed the earth when Daphne died
in "Winter"; now "Returning Justice lift[s] aloft
her Scale" (1.18). And Death himself is bound
"In adamantine Chains" (1.47).
     It is the desolate, fallen world of "Winter"
which the imagery of "Messiah" joyously transforms. With the coming of Christ, "the good
Shepherd" (1.49), a new and metaphysical spring
revives the barren landscape, and Daphne's
flower, the "od'rous Myrtle," replaces "the noisome Weed" (1.76):

> The Swain in barren Desarts with surprize
> See Lillies spring, and sudden Verdure rise;
> And Starts, amidst the thirsty Wilds, to hear
> New Falls of Water murm'ring in his Ear:
> On rifted Rocks, the Dragon's late Abodes,
> The green Reed trembles, and the Bulrush nods.
> Waste sandy Vallies, once perplex'd with Thorn,
> The spiry Firr and shapely Box adorn;
> To leaf-less Shrubs the flow'ring Palms succeed,
> And od'rous Myrtle to the noisome Weed.
>   (11.67-76)

After winter's midnight, a new dawn bathes the
world in "a Flood of Day" (1.98); but this day is
"eternal" (1.104), the spiritual glory of "The
LIGHT HIMSELF" (1.103). At the apocalypse we--
or rather "Imperial *Salem*" (1.85), the true Church
--shall be released from the tyranny of Time,
from the perpetual revolution of the seasons and
the succession of nights and days:

> No more the rising *Sun* shall gild the Morn,
> Nor evening *Cynthia* fill her silver Horn,
> But lost, dissolv'd in thy superior Rays;
> One Tyde of Glory, one unclouded Blaze,
> O'erflow thy Courts: The LIGHT HIMSELF shall
>   shine
> Reveal'd; and *God's* eternal Day be thine!
>   (11.99-104)

As "Winter" had closed with Thyrsis' complaint of
Nature's decay and the triumph of Time, the final
lines of "Messiah" envisage the dissolution of
the world into eternity:

> The Seas shall waste; the Skies in Smoke decay;
> Rocks fall to Dust, and Mountains melt away;
> But fix'd *His* Word, *His* saving Pow'r remains:
> Thy *Realm* for ever lasts! thy own *Messiah* reigns!

In the *Pastorals* the ability to transform Nature had rested, though imperfectly, with the poet himself--imitator of the divine creative power
and lover of ideal harmonies. It is the poet
whose music and mastery of artifice recreate the
Golden Age in "Spring" and in "Winter" recall the
higher reality of Elysium, where Daphne dwells
among "unfading Flow'rs." Yet, as Pope reminds
us in his "Discourse," we are finally aware that
the green world of Arcadia is only a pleasant illusion. Figured in the complaint of Alexis and
in the death of Daphne, the effect of the Fall
has been the irrevocable separation of Art from
ideal Beauty, and the passing of Order from the
earth. In "Messiah" the original Edenic harmony
between Art and Nature is restored in transcen-

dent perfection, the power of Art and the ideal of
Order being united eternally in Christ. Pope's
sacred eclogue is the celebration of the true
transforming power, the Logos, the divine Artificer who made the world and who will at last re-
deem it from imperfection. In terms of the conventions of pastoral and the metaphors of the
Christian tradition, Christ is the shepherd poet
whose Word will make the Golden Age a reality.

Viewed in this way, "Messiah" may be seen as
the completion of Pope's intellectual design for
the Pastorals--hence his decision in 1717 to include the poem under that heading. Despite his
tender years, Pope at the very start of his career had not only achieved that mastery of technique which, as Joseph Warton and Dr. Johnson
remarked, effected a revolution in English prosody; he had also formulated a coherent philosophy of art which in a sense demanded nothing less
than technical excellence. For the function of
art was to order the chaos of actuality--not to
deny the chaos, which was always real enough for
him, but to oppose it with music and form, which
alone can put us in touch with a higher reality.
Lytton Strachey had not many intelligent things
to say about Pope, but he sensed this at least
when he observed that Pope's "poetic criticism of
life...was simply and solely the heroic couplet."[21]
The eclogue provided him with a likely vehicle
for the expression of this aesthetic philosophy.
In the *Pastorals* Pope took as his subject the relation of Art to Nature (and to man!) within the
context of Christian time. And significantly,
the ideas he here first expressed continued to
inform his work. In the *Essay on Man* ideal Nature
is still the "Art" of God, and the harmony of
the Golden Age, from which man has fallen, is yet
remembered:

> Nor think, in NATURE'S STATE they blindly
>   trod;
> The state of Nature was the reign of God:
> Self-love and Social at her birth began,
> Union the bond of all things, and of Man.
>   (III.11.147-50)

Even in *The Dunciad*, which sardonically records
the triumph of Chaos, Pope's skilful couplets and
his control of form implicitly affirm the victory
of Art.

In *The Dunciad*, to be sure, Arcadia survives only as a bitter joke, as "the fresh vomit run[s]
for ever green" (A. II, 1.148). There, a different music from that of the pastorals is heard--
still regular, still precise, still opposing harmony to discord and disorder, but, as befits
Pope's theme, no longer merely lovely: an effect
rather like that of Stravinsky imitating Mozart.
Yet Pope's vision of life in "Autumn" and "Winter" is at least theoretically the same as the
vision that darkens the major satires--the difference being that in the later poems he has *felt*
the destructive consequences of folly and the
painful effects of mortality, and has found that
no retreat into Fancy's maze can make them toler-
able. The progress of history, of the world's
Great Year, has in *The Dunciad* led out of Arcadia
to the spiritual midnight and winter weather of
Georgian England, to a world of dunces for whom
the Messiah is the "uncreating word." The same
ideals of Art and Order, the same philosophy of
Christian time, connect the *Pastorals* and the poems of Pope's last years. What separates them
may be felt in the terrible metamorphosis that
has transformed the Golden Age of "Spring" and
"Messiah" into that of *The Dunciad*.

IMAGERY AND METHOD IN *AN ESSAY ON CRITICISM*

Patricia Meyer Spacks

"I will show more *imagery* in twenty lines of
Pope than in any equal length of quotation in
English poetry," Byron wrote.[1] Poetry, T.E.
Hulme pronounced, "always endeavours to arrest
you, and to make you continuously see a physical
thing, to prevent you gliding through an abstract process."[2] Both observations are relevant to an understanding of *An Essay on Criticism*,
that compendium of familiar quotations whose
meanings have been widely canvassed while its
poetic merits remain relatively unexplored.
Alexander Pope's assumptions about poetry are
far removed from Hulme's, but in this versified
investigation of abstractions he does seem concerned to prevent his readers from gliding
through a familiar body of doctrine. His method
depends on voluminous imagery, product of the
"wit" which is, with "Nature," a presiding power of the poem.
    One of the *Essay's* famous cruxes[3] suggests the
nature of Pope's poetic intent:

    Some to whom Heav'n in Wit has been profuse,
    Want as much more, to turn it to its use.
        (ll. 80-81)

This essay first appeared in *PMLA* 85 (1970), 97-106.

The poetic ambition of the *Essay on Criticism* centers in its attempt to demonstrate how wit can provide a controlling power for what wit creates. The attempt, if not entirely successful, is yet impressive.

That wit is--among other things[4]--the image-making faculty is apparent, both from tradition and from Pope's prose comments. In his notes to *The Iliad*, for example, he remarked, "There cannot be a truer kind of Wit, than what is shewn in apt Comparisons."[5] Wit is equivalent to invention,[6] the power of poetic discovery and creativity for which Pope admired Homer. Homer's invention, Pope feels, is marked in his imagery: "If we observe his *Descriptions, Images*, and *Similes*, we shall find the Invention still predominant. To what else can we ascribe that vast Comprehension of Images of every sort, where we see each Circumstance of art and Individual of Nature summon'd together by the Extent and Fecundity of his Imagination?"[7]

It is less obvious that this aspect of wit can supply control as well as energy, not only decoration but discipline; yet exactly this, I think, is what Pope tried to demonstrate in the *Essay on Criticism*. It is possible to see his use of metaphor as orthodox and ordinary. Thus Jacob Adler, writing of Pope's technique in the *Essay on Criticism* and *Essay on Man*: "The *Essays* depend upon comparisons to an extent which no other of Pope's poems can very well claim. In Pope's day there were of course two perfectly good reasons for this: first, didactic poems were cast in the 'middle' style, avoiding both the epic 'high' and the satirical 'low,' and were hence to be dignified but not elaborately adorned; second, the comparisons considered (and surely properly considered) essential to illustrating and illuminating precepts and theories could adorn or amuse as well as instruct, could appropriately provide the *dulce* as well as confirm the *utile*."[8] Pope's imagery in the *Essay on Criticism* fills these standard functions; but the poet strives to make it do more. If wit

can control wit, imagery can supply poetic or-
ganization. The structure of the *Essay* has long
been an issue in evaluating the poem. Aubrey
Williams has argued that Pope tried to supply
the "larger design" he found missing in Horace,
and has demonstrated how that design manifests
itself in the poem's broad divisions and in some
of its details.[9] On the other hand, Donald
Greene earlier pointed out--with equal truth--
that looking at the main heads of the contents
of the *Essay on Criticism*, one discovers that "there
is no real logical order in the poem at all, beyond that of simple enumeration."[10] It is my
contention that Pope wished to enlarge the function of imagery, to supply a logic of metaphor,
thus achieving an organic unity which would demonstrate wit's power to organize as well as to
decorate didacticism. The nature of the *Essay's*
imagery, the complexity of its interrelations,
its moral and emotional implications, all support
this thesis.

I

Early in Horace's *Ars Poetica* occurs a passage
which enlarges the physical, philosophical, and
emotional scope of the poem:

Ut silvae foliis pronos mutantur in annos,
Prima cadunt, ita verborum vetus interit
    aetas,
Et juvenum ritu florent modo nata vigentque.
Debemur morti nos nostraque, sive receptus
Terra Neptunus classes Aquilonibus arcet,
Regis opus, sterilisve diu palus aptaque
    remis
Vicinas urbes alit et grave sentit aratrum,
Seu cursum mutavit iniquum frugibus amnis,
Doctus iter melius, mortalia facta peribunt,
Nedum sermonum stet honos et gratia vivax.
    (ll. 60-69)

Man and his works and his language become a part
of natural process in the poet's presentation;
the elegiac note is as appropriate to a consid-

eration of the death of words as to contemplation of the transience of other noble accomplishments. The tone and reference of this passage establish a new context for Horace's consideration of poetic minutiae, insisting that
discussion of iambic meter or of the proper relation of beginning, middle, and end can be
understood as a concern of high seriousness.The
relevance of criticism, Horace suggests, is
finally human, not technical.

Although the *Essay on Criticism* rises to astonishing heights of poetic dignity and passion,
its expansion of reference--equivalent to that
achieved by Horace--depends less on individual
passages than on the cumulative effect of its
multitudinous imagery. Like Horace, Pope wished
to demonstrate that his concerns were human,
that criticism was in the fullest sense a moral
activity. The poem itself, considered as an
essay *in* as well as *on* criticism, is the demonstration of what criticism can be, and how it
can unite with poetry and morality. Its technique of employing images asserts the related-
ness of all modes of endeavor; the intricacies
of the poem bear some relation to the intricacies of human experience.

The special insistence of Pope's imagery derives partly from its repetitiousness. Maynard
Mack has called attention to patterns of reference to physiological and institutional health
and sickness. "Literary norms, these images
suggest, are not ultimately dissociable from
greater norms. A perverse criticism and a corrupt art are equivalent in their own way to
other symptoms and symbols of deterioration:
tyranny in the state; bigotry and schism in the
church; impotence, nausea, flatulence, jaundice,
in the individual organism."[11] Implicit reference from limited to greater norms occurs as
well through other image clusters. One may instance the frequent allusions to art and architecture, to sex, and to military activity.

The reasons for the association between art
and criticism are obvious: throughout the poem,

Pope maintains and demonstrates that "wit," the
power which produces criticism, is like the genius which makes art: equally mysterious, powerful, creative.   The analogies to sex associate
one of the most "natural" of human activities
with a more sophisticated form of behavior which
is in some sense equally natural, dedicated as
it is to the following of nature.   The sexual
metaphors refer to perversions or distortions
of natural sex: to eunuchs, mules, "equivocal"
generation, the wooing of maids when one cannot
win mistresses, the wife enjoyed by other men.
In a striking simile, Pope suggests that dullness
in combination with obscenity is "As Shameful
sure as *Impotence* in *Love*" (l. 533): failure in
the attempt at wit is equivalent to sexual failure, and should be felt as an equivalent disgrace.   The vulgar treat the muse like a mistress: "This hour she's *idoliz'd*, the next *abus'd*"
(l. 433).   Wit and judgment are "meant each
other's Aid, like *Man* and *Wife*" (l. 83), but the
rest of the poem stresses how seldom this simple sexual mutuality obtains.   If sex is natural
and universal, its misuses are correspondingly
abundant; the misuses of wit, as easy to fall
into as those of sex, are also as destructive--
and, like sexual misbehavior, they hinder generativity.
   If the sexual metaphors stress generativity
and its failure, the military references emphasize the precariousness of power.   Wits are
capable of turning poets' arms against them;
the productions of wit involve awareness of
military strategy: "Those oft are *Stratagems* which
Errors seem" (l. 179); the rewards of literature
resemble those of war; nonsense breaks out from
time to time "in full *Vollies*" (l.628); efforts to
consolidate one's literary gains, like their
military equivalents, may fail, and "Like Kings
we lose the Conquests gain'd before" (l. 64);
the weak heads of the vulgar resemble "Towns
unfortify'd" (l. 434); the rules and method prescribed by Quintilian are like properly arranged
arms, ordered "less to please the Eye, than arm

the Hand" (1.673). "Natural" though it is, criticism--like art and love--is also a struggle, in which victory is possible, but likely to prove fleeting.

Through metaphors of this sort the poet conveys an attitude toward the experiences from which his images derive as well as those to which they allude. We feel his sense of the high importance of art (partly because of further metaphors through which he dignifies his allusions to artistic creation), his Horatian awareness of the precariousness of human glory. We have been taken into his world, in which criticism is one among many possible human enterprises, to be attempted and judged always in the richest available context. But we have also been made aware, through imagery, of the complex bases of judgment, and of a hierarchy of value.

II

The interaction of imagery in the *Essay on Criticism* is as functional as the repeated emphasis on specific areas of reference. Images grow out of, comment on, modify one another; as a consequence, their felt significance may increase between one appearance and another. A case in point is the passage surrounding the perplexing definition of *"True Wit."*

Some to *Conceit* alone their Taste confine,
And glitt'ring Thoughts struck out at ev'ry
    Line;   290
Pleas'd with a Work where nothing's just or
    fit;
One *glaring Chaos* and *wild Heap of Wit*:
Poets like Painters, thus, unskill'd to trace
The *naked Nature* and the *living Grace*,
With *Gold* and *Jewels* cover ev'ry Part,   295
And hide with *Ornaments* their *Want of Art*.
True Wit is *Nature* to Advantage drest,
What oft was *Thought*, but ne'er so well
    Exprest,
Something, whose Truth convinc'd at Sight we
    find,

That gives us back the Image of our Mind: 300
As Shades more sweetly recommend the Light,
So modest Plainness sets off sprightly Wit:
For *Works* may have more *Wit* than does 'em good,
As *Bodies* perish through Excess of *Blood*. . .
But true *Expression*, like th' unchanging
     Sun,   315
Clears, and *improves* whate'er it shines upon,
It *gilds* all Objects, but it *alters* none.
Expression is the *Dress* of *Thought*, and still
Appears more *decent* as more *suitable* . . .
          (ll. 289-304, 315-319)

In this representative range of the poem's
pervasive light imagery,[12] "glitt'ring" and
"*glaring*" describe the false; true wit is simple
"Light," true expression, more specifically,
resembles "th' unchanging *Sun*." Almost as emphatic are the metaphors from painting (the
four-line comparison of poets and painters, the
suggested manipulation of shadow and light in
line 301, the idea of gilding in line 317) and
the two important metaphors of dress.   Then
there is an implicit metaphor of building in
line 292, the mirror image of lines 299-300
and the submerged analogy to people hinted by
modest and *sprightly*, and the blood simile in
lines 303-304.
     The multiplicity of reference in twenty-one
lines is bewildering and compelling.   John
Aden has demonstrated, with specific reference
to "Nature," how elaborate a battery of poetic
devices Pope brings to bear in this poem when
he wishes to make sure of engaging the reader's
attention.[13]   Such multiplicity of associated
imagery makes it difficult to paraphrase Pope's
meanings--indeed, the complex relation of images fills one with awareness of the inexpres-
sible richness of the poet's meanings, which
they help to create.
     In the passage quoted above, the first
painting metaphor is crucial to an understanding
of the "*True Wit*" couplet which develops from it.
The antithesis is not, as one may at first

suppose, between the skilled painter who can trace
"The *naked Nature*" and the unskilled one who loads
her with jewels; it is, rather between the painter
skilled enough to dress her properly--"to Advantage"--and the mere decorator. No painter, no
poet, is sufficiently skilled to duplicate nature without alteration; his choice concerns
only the nature of the alteration. Wit's mirror does not reflect the truth of the outside
world, only "the Image of our Mind."
   Meyer Abrams used the mirror and the lamp as
metaphors to suggest opposed views of the creative process, associating the mirror metaphor
with a more classic, the lamp with a more romantic attitude.[14] It is characteristic of Pope
to define wit as both a light-giving and a reflective power. Many metaphors in the *Essay on
Criticism* invite us to see Pope as a kind of Ur-
Coleridge, full of awe for a creative power
which he associates with the sun and with divinity, urging reverence for genius and its mysterious force. But other metaphors always qualify
such images, or in their elaboration they qualify
themselves.[15] Wit concerns itself with "The
naked Nature and the *living Grace*," it is equivalent
to the vast energy of Nature, it is analogous to
blood, the vital fluid. Substitute *imagination*
for *wit* in these instances, and we feel ourselves
with the Romantics. But wit can also produce
chaos, for which the poet has only contempt; it
creates proper dress, not nakedness, concerns itself more with expression than with thought; it
can (like blood) produce disease if its excessive energy is not controlled. The anti-romantic
images which stress the necessity of control
qualify the conception. Wit's function as ordering power is as important as its creative force;
different sets of images stress each aspect.
   Pope's awareness of the value of multiple
analogies emerges in many of his notes to the
Iliad. Although he admits the possibility that an
object may be "lost amidst too great a Variety
of different Images," he points out that in Homer
"the principal Image is more strongly impress'd

on the Mind by a Multiplication of Similes."[16]
His effort to impress the idea of wit on the
mind by multiplication of similes is different
in technique from the predecessors he may have
used as direct models. The Duke of Buckingham
and the Earl of Roscommon, with whose accomplishments Addison equated Pope's,[17] spell out
to the point of tedium the implications of a
single metaphor; rarely do they rely on diversity of reference. When they do, their purposes
are simpler than Pope's. Here is a sample passage from Buckingham's *Essay on Poetry*. It concerns
"genius":

> A Spirit which inspires the Work throughout,
> As that of Nature moves the World about;
> A Flame that glows amidst Conceptions fit;
> Ev'n something of Divine, and more than Wit;
> It self unseen, yet all things by it shown,
> Describing all Men, but describ'd by none.
> Where dost thou dwell? What Caverns of the
>   Brain
> Can such a vast and mighty thing contain?
> When I, at vacant Hours, in vain thy Absence
>   mourn,
> Oh where dost thou retire? and why dost thou
>   return,
> Sometimes with pow'rful Charms to hurry me
>   away,
> From Pleasures of the Night and Bus'ness of
>   the Day?
> Ev'n now too far transported, I am fain
> To check thy Course, and use the needful
>   Rein.[18]

The difference between this and the passage
quoted from the *Essay on Criticism* is the difference
between good poetry and bad; but the role of imagery in creating that difference is instructive.
Here, too, is variety of reference. Genius is a
spirit analogous to the divine spirit, a flame,
a light, a "vast and mighty thing," a possessor
of magic power, a horse. But the multiplicity
creates confusion rather than clarification, em-

phasized by the vagueness of "Ev'n something of
Divine, and more than Wit" and of "vast and
mighty thing." The inadvertent effect of the
poet's references to himself is to suggest that
his lines are intended to demonstrate what they
in part describe: the effect of the absence of
genius.

Pope's metaphors reinforce one another; Buckingham's cancel one another out. If a reader is
troubled, in the lines from *An Essay on Criticism*,
by a sense that the dress metaphor is unduly
"low," or that it does not relate coherently to
the exalted imagery of light, the poet deals
with such an objection by using one dress metaphor to explain the other. In the second use of
the image, the power of dress is directly associated with that of the sun, which "*gilds* all Objects, but it *alters* none." The typographical
stress on the verbs directs our attention to a
vital antithesis, and recalls the more elaborate
contrast between the painter who loads a human
figure with jewels and the true wit which presents reality dressed to advantage--not "The
naked Nature," but nature gilded rather than altered. The dress metaphors, light metaphors,
and art metaphors are closely related; Pope
demonstrates and insists upon the relationship.
In contrast, Buckingham's metaphors seem des-
perate graspings at a glimpsed idea, random
efforts at communication. Even if the horse of
genius is Pegasus, it is hard to feel any coherence between genius as flame and as steed.

II

"Images have efficacy to move a reader's
affections, to quite properly affect his judgments; they move him to feel intensely, to will,
to act, to understand, to believe, to change his
mind."[19] Miss Tuve's summary of the Renaissance
view sheds light also on Pope's poetic practice.
His purposes are emotional and moral as well as
more narrowly didactic. The conjunctions of imagery in the *Essay on Criticism* lend density to

the poetry and deepen its philosophic and emotional implications. Even an individual image
can participate in such a process. Such an
image is Pope's figure of the "good man," which
emerges gradually through the *Essay*. It demonstrates wit's controlling power by giving reality
and substance to abstract ideas. The poem's
central abstractions--wit, nature, sense, judg-
ment--achieve solidity through a variety of imagery, but much of its general moral doctrine depends on a single group of human images to generate the emotional energy that makes it real to
the reader.

The human image--a simplified human being who
embodies and summarizes a set of moral quali-
ties--is peculiarly important in Pope's work. In
his late satiric poetry--the moral epistles, the
Horatian imitations, *The Dunciad*--he makes people
into images by an artificial isolation and heightening of characteristics. "The *Poem was not made
for these Authors, but these Authors for the Poem*," Pope
would write of his victims, in the appendix to
the 1728 *Dunciad*. He suggests how living people
had become in his hands poetic devices; "And I
should judge they were clapp'd in as they rose,
fresh and fresh, and chang'd from day to day, in
like manner as when the old boughs wither, we
thrust new ones into a chimney."[20] In the *Essay
on Criticism*, his primary purpose is not satiric,
but his technique bears affinities to his latter
one. It is possible to study the way in which
he converts a general moral idea--the notion that
the good poet or critic must be a good man--into
a concrete embodiment of that idea: an idealized,
heightened figure, appearing in several guises,
who exemplifies the virtues Pope advocates.

This figure has no physical substance; its
function as image does not depend on direct sensuous appeal. Yet the way it works in the poems
is the way images work. Critics who have tack-
led the painful task of defining imagery usually
try to avoid limiting their definition to objects
of sensuous reality. Caroline Spurgeon's attempt
is representative. An image, she says, "is a

description or an idea, which by comparison or
analogy, stated or understood, with something
else, transmits to us through the emotions and
associations it arouses, something of the 'wholeness,' the depth and richness of the way the writer views, conceives or has felt what he is telling us."[21] The vagueness of this definition acknowledges the difficulty of pinning down the
term, and the fact that other forms of embodiment than physical ones ("idea" as well as "description") may solidify or enlarge the poet's
statement. The solidity which Pope's virtuous
figures (and, for that matter, his vicious ones)
possess is moral solidity. By summing up and
balancing moral qualities in an imagined individual, the poet gives them greater imaginative
reality than they can have when called to our
attention only by sententious adjuration.

As Pope found in Boileau the idea of a connection between the creation of literature and
personal uprightness, it took the form of general moral injunctions:

> Que les vers ne soient pas votre eternel
>   emploi;
> Cultivez vos amis, soyez homme de foi.
> C'est peu d'etre agreable et charmant dans
>   un livre,
> Il faut savoir encore et converser et vivre.
>   (IV, 121-124)

The lines imply a possible antithesis between
good man and good poet: one can be agreeable and
charming in a book without being so in life; to
devote oneself to the eternal occupation of verse
is to neglect the responsibilities of personal
morality. For Pope no such antithesis exists:
the identity between the good critic and the good
man is almost necessary, not just possible. Early
in the poem, he refers to "a Critick's noble
Name" (1. 47); the phrase's justification is moral, not literary. A succession of metaphors associates wit with good breeding. Then, as Pope
develops his injunctions for the conduct of

criticism, his language becomes increasingly moral. It still concentrates on the promulgation
rather than the embodiment of doctrine:

>   Avoid *Extreams;* and shun the Fault of such,
>   Who still are pleas'd *too little,* or *too much.*
>   At ev'ry Trifle scorn to take Offence,
>   That always shows *Great Pride,* or *Little Sense.*
>   (ll. 384-387)

The conduct of the good critic is that of the
good man. When Pope urges that one should not
"let the *Man* be lost" in the critic, he adds,
"*Good-Nature* and *Good-Sense* must ever join;/To Err
is *Humane;* to Forgive, *Divine*"(ll. 524-525). He
is urging his readers--in their roles as men and
as critics--to partake of divinity through high
morality. One is to "make each Day a *Critick* on
the last" (l.571): the line exemplifies the union
of literary and human concern. One need not
choose between human and literary activity; the
two are identical.
    None of the references I have mentioned gives
the notion of the good man concrete form. Even
the metaphors of good breeding are so general
that they lack the force of images: "As Men of
Breeding, sometimes Men of Wit,/T'avoid *great
Errors,* must the *less* commit" (ll. 259-260). Yet
an image lurks behind the moral injunctions, and
it finally achieves reality. It is strengthened
by the broad religious context that has been established. The last lines of the poem's first
section enunciate a mythology of art in the most
exalted terms:

>   Still green with Bays each *ancient* Altar stands,
>   Above the reach of *Sacrilegious* Hands,
>   Secure from *Flames,* from *Envy's* fiercer Rage,
>   Destructive *War,* and all-involving *Age.*
>
>   Hail *Bards Triumphant!* born in *happier Days;*
>   *Immortal Heirs of Universal* Praise!
>   Whose Honours with Increase of Ages *grow,*
>   As Streams roll down, *enlarging* as they flow!

Nations *unborn* your mighty Names shall sound,
And Worlds applaud that must not yet be *found!*
Oh may some Spark of *your* Coelestial Fire
The last, the meanest of your Sons inspire,
(That, on weak Wings, from far, pursues your
     Flights;
Glows while he *reads,* but *trembles* as he *writes*)
     (ll. 181-184, 189-198)

The tone resembles that of the visionary ending
of *Windsor Forest,* but the vision is artistic, not
political, and it concentrates on the past more
than the future. The energy of the account derives from the tension between Pope's sense of
the permanence of these deities and their monuments and his awareness of the unbridgeable gap
between past and present. The restoration of
order depends on looking to the past, to which
alone can be applied the emphatic language of
permanence. Always adorned, always young, always marked with the emblems of honor, the poetry of the past looms above the poets of the
present, impregnable and universal: "above the
reach," "secure," "triumphant," "immortal," "universal." As time passes, the bards become only
more secure, their fame enlarging like the flowing stream.

The result of contemplating the "monuments of
unaging intellect" is new moral awareness. The
speaker understands precariousness as well as
permanence; he knows the forces of destruction:
natural energies (flames); human passion, individual and collective (envy and war); the mortality of people and objects ("all-involving
Age"). Sacrilegious hands always reach to destroy; praise of *"happier Days"* implies the unhappy present. The possibility of enduring fame
is slender; the poet must therefore find a position which justifies his vocation independently
of the hope of fame.

It is in this context that Pope introduces a
version of himself--a preliminary and vague im-
age--into the poem. The exaggerated humility of
his pose ("The last, the meanest of your Sons")

is justified by the dilemma which produces it:
humility is the moral doctrine of this religion
of art. The resolution of the poet's problem
is moral, not artistic; the speaker declares his
aspiration "To teach vain Wits a Science *little
known*,/*T'admire* Superior Sense, and *doubt* their own!"
(ll. 199-200). He has learned humility from contemplating the past; he proposes to teach it. The
identification of poet-critic-good man derives
from the moral necessity created by the gap between present and past. Thomas Edwards, discussing the writer's role as hero in this poem,
remarks, "by his continuation of an 'epic' literary past, by his demonstration that the present
need not be wholly worthless when measured by
classical standards, the writer-hero in his own
person reconciles the actual and the ideal. His
craft perpetuates values, and it proves that time
can be challenged, if not conquered."[22] The
writer's perpetuation of values, I would argue,
comes less from his craft than from his character
--character which must, Pope suggests, both form
and be formed by his vocation. Commitment to the
realm of wit, like commitment to God, requires
discipline, self-knowledge, relinquishment of lesser ideals. Such a commitment, its full range
and weight recognized, is an important subject
of the *Essay*.

Toward the end of the poem, Pope gives his
moral doctrine a local habitation and a name--
several names. Now the standard of virtue takes
form in a hypothetical figure whose characteristics must be familiar to any reader of Pope's
later satiric poetry.

> But where's the Man, who Counsel *can* bestow,
> Still *pleas'd* to *teach*, and yet not *proud* to
>   *know?*
> Unbiass'd, or by *Favour* or by *Spite;*
> Not *dully prepossest*, nor *blindly right;*
> Tho' Learn'd, well-bred; and tho' well-bred,
>   sincere;
> Modestly bold, and Humanly severe?
> Blest with a *Taste* exact, yet unconfin'd;

A *Knowledge* both of *Books* and *Humankind;*
Gen'rous Converse; a *Soul* exempt from *Pride;*
And *Love to Praise,* with *Reason* on his Side?
     (ll. 631-636, 639-642)

Compare this later version:

The Sense to value Riches, with the Art
T'enjoy them, and the Virtue to impart,
Not meanly, nor ambitiously pursu'd,
Not sunk by sloth, nor rais'd by servitude;
To balance Fortune by a just expence,
Join with Oeconomy, Magnificence;
With Splendour, Charity; with Plenty, Health;
Oh teach us, BATHURST! yet unspoil'd by
     wealth! (*Epistle to Bathurst,* ll. 219-226)

In one case criticism is the subject; in the
other, wealth. More than twenty years lie between the composition of the two poems; yet the
form of the moral ideal--the balancing of extremes, the definition by finding the midpoint,
the idea of taking in and giving out as complementary activities--remains the same. And the
function of the figure who embodies the ideal is
the same in the satiric and the non-satiric poem,
although in one case he is a hypothesis from the
past ("Such once were *Criticks*"; l. 643), in the
other he has a specific modern identity. Both
figures function as images rather than realities
--like reverses of the images of Sporus and Bufo
in the *Epistle to Arbuthnot.* Pope's portrayals of
those he admires and those he detests alike are
heightened to emblematic proportions. They provide the most forceful indications of his standards and values.
     Beginning at line 724 of the *Essay on Criticism,*
Pope names two writers who embody the union of
intellectual and moral values suggested by the
earlier idealized portrait and by the moral
stress of the entire poem. They are Wentworth
Dillon, fourth Earl of Roscommon ("not more
learn'd than *good*"; 1.725) and William Walsh
("The *clearest Head,* and the *sincerest Heart*";l. 732).

Then he returns to self-description, personifying
himself as a muse. It is a daring way to end the
poem, and an appropriate one. He makes himself
an image, as he was to do again in the Horatian
imitations, and demonstrates, through his capacity to fictionalize in this way, his determination to embody the fusion of criticism, poetry,
and morality that has been the ideal throughout
the poem. Declaring his intention to confine
himself to "low Numbers," he elaborates,

> Content, if hence th' Unlearn'd their Wants
>   may view,
> The Learn'd reflect on what before they knew:
> Careless of *Censure*, nor too fond of *Fame*,
> Still pleas'd to *praise*, yet not afraid to
>   *blame*.
> Averse alike to *Flatter*, or *Offend*,
> Not *free* from Faults, nor yet too vain to
>   *mend*. (ll. 739-744)

The antithetical form of the verse heightens
awareness of the affinities between this description and the earlier account of the ideal man.
This mortal muse is subject to criticism himself,
in his role as poet ("Careless of *Censure*, nor
too fond of *Fame*"); he is a critic, who praises
and blames; his ultimate concerns are moral
("Not *free* from Faults, nor yet too vain to *mend*").
But the relevance of the final line expands: the
"faults" may be moral, poetic, or critical, it
hardly matters; all three, the poem's imagery
has demonstrated, are finally the same.
      The idea that the poet must be a good man[23]
is less important in the poem than the way in
which it is propounded: through embodiment in
images which engineer the reader's assent to the
proposition by making him feel the splendor, the
awe-inspiring power, of the fusion of qualities.
The poet-critic-hero emerges only gradually; by
the end of the poem he is a well-defined figure,
both the poet's persona and his central subject.

IV

The complex relations among Pope's images involve variations of form as well as content. For
example:

Others for *Language* all their Care express,
And value *Books*, as Women *Men*, for *Dress*:
Their Praise is still-- *The Stile is excellent*:
The *Sense*, they humbly take upon Content.
Words are like *Leaves*; and where they most
     abound,
Much *Fruit of Sense* beneath is rarely found.
False Eloquence, like the *Prismatic Glass*,
Its gawdy Colours spreads on *ev'ry place*.
     (ll. 305-312)

One notes the profusion of imagery, and the way
in which one image merges with or yields to another: a sexual implication combines with a reference to dress; both give way to an image from
external nature, then to a simile about the division of light (the poem's primal power) in which
science becomes art, as the glass spreads gaudy
color like a poor painter. Equally important is
the intricate relation of metaphor and simile.
Three of the four couplets contain both (the
second couplet, which elaborates the meaning of
the first, has neither). The effect is to make
the metaphors seem like literal statements, and
thus greatly to increase their force. That we
value books for dress;that sense is the proper
fruit of wit (a fresh approach to the generativity theme); that eloquence spreads gaudy
colors about--these are the truths to which
Pope's technique calls special attention. The
similes seem, by comparison, decorative. They
broaden the context and display a limited version
of the poet's wit; most of all, they heighten the
significance of the accompanying metaphors and
direct our awareness toward them.
     It may be argued that there is no essential
difference of effect between "Words are like
Leaves" and "Much *Fruit* of *Sense* beneath is rarely

found," that the *kind* of meaning is in both instances essentially the same. Certainly the
distinction between metaphor and simile is tenuous at best, and difficult to generalize about
even within an individual poem. In this case,
it seems to me, the context rather than the substance of metaphor and simile demands that a
distinction be made between them. The juxtaposition of contrasting syntactical modes forces
awareness of their difference. That difference
once noted, Pope's more detailed development of
his metaphors, in conjunction with the more manifest artificiality of the similes, suggests that
the metaphors carry more important messages.

It is notable that the pattern of equivalences
established by the crucial light imagery depends
largely upon metaphor rather than simile, a fact
which reinforces the sense of value created by
the religious implications of many of the equivalences. Two exceptions have been quoted above:

> As Shades more sweetly recommend the Light.
> So modest Plainness sets off sprightly Wit.
>   (ll. 301-302)

> But true *Expression*, like th' unchanging *Sun*,
> *Clears*, and *improves* whate'er it shines upon.
>   (ll. 315-316)

In both instances, the reference of the light
imagery is less weighty than in the dominant
structure of metaphors. The kind of "Wit" referred to in the first couplet is not the transcendent creative power, but a relatively trivial
deftness and economy of expression. The power
of *"Expression"* is important--bad expression can
nullify good thought--but less important than the
vast forces which light as metaphor defines. The
similes, in both cases, establish an analogy, not
only between the two terms compared but between
them and the other forces which have been defined in terms of light; but they also support a
hierarchy. In the metaphors, analogy moves toward identity. The similes, by their connecting

terms, insist that they describe *only* analogies,
and thus remind us that lesser powers, though
resembling greater ones, remain lesser.

It is through the light metaphors that Pope
makes the boldest suggestions in the poem. "And
indeed," he was to write, "they who would take
Boldness from Poetry, must leave Dulness in the
room of it."[24] By a series of equations he indicates that "Heav'n" (or alternately "Nature")
is the source of light, then that Nature itself,
"divinely bright," is "One *clear, unchang'd,* and
Universal Light" (l. 71), that Truth, another
source of light, is therefore equivalent to
Nature ("*Truth* breaks upon us with *resistless Day*";
1.212), that Wit is equivalent to both (see ll.
470-473, supported by ll. 648 and 659). Wit,
the imagery suggests, has a lower position in
the hierarchy than the cosmic forces: it is
identified with "fire" and "light" more often
than with the sun, and in one important metaphor
it is produced by, rather than identical with,
the "sun" of Nature or Heaven:

> Meanly they seek the Blessing to confine,
> And force *that Sun* but on a *Part* to Shine;
> Which not alone the *Southern Wit* sublimes,
> But ripens Spirits in cold *Northern Climes.*
>   (ll. 398-401)

The human creative force partakes of the divine
nature but does not duplicate it, although it
may be seen as itself a sun which "too powerful
Beams displays" (l. 470), producing by its energy
the clouds which obscure it.

The association of wit with divinity, substan-
tiated by the poem's many references to religion,
exemplifies the way in which Pope uses imagery
to make precise a set of complex implications
concerning value as well as meaning. William
Empson comments, "The performance inside the
word *wit*, I should maintain, was intended to be
quite obvious and in the sunlight, and was so
for the contemporary reader; that was why he
thought the poem so brilliant."[25] The perform-

ance is elucidated by the imagery, as Empson's
own discussion makes clear. Evaluative as well
as explanatory, that imagery becomes almost un-
imaginably complex. If one considers only the
term *wit* in connection with the images which describe it, he discovers a bewildering range. At
one extreme, wit is associated with divinity; at
another, it becomes

> The *Owner's Wife*, that *other Men* enjoy,
> Then most our *Trouble* still when most *admir'd*,
> And still the more we *give*, the more *requir'd;*
> Whose Fame with *Pains* we guard, but lose with
>   *Ease,*
> Sure *some* to vex, but never *all* to *please.*
>   (ll. 501-505)

The difference between the two versions of wit is
less in definition than in evaluation. Wit seen
from the point of view of its creator is an awe-
inspiring power, a duplication of the divine
"making" force. Considered from a broader,
"public" point of view, its value becomes more
ambiguous. Its audience may value it highly but
misapprehend its nature; it becomes a burden to
its possessor because it cannot remain private;
used, it must be displayed, and therefore misunderstood.

The sensitivity to varying possibility demonstrated by the poem's metaphoric implications
gives energy, complexity, and authority to *An Essay on Criticism*. It is tempting to speculate about whether Pope's mode of using imagery represents a new eighteenth-century direction. The
images, in their variety and inventiveness, may
recall the extravagances of metaphysical poetry;
the poem considered as a whole does not. Considering it in comparison with such a predecessor
as Abraham Cowley's *Ode of Wit*, one discovers that
Pope has employed many specific images from the
past, but changed the method of using them.

Pope's early letters reveal his preoccupation
with the relation between wit's method and its
extravagances. His comments on the metaphysical

poets suggest that he finds in them a troublesome lack of discipline; yet their creative
energy makes it difficult for him to arrive at a
negative final judgment of them. *"Donne,"* he
writes in 1706, "had infinitely more Wit than he
wanted Versification: for the great dealers in
Wit, like those in Trade, take least Pains to
set off their Goods; while the Haberdashers of
small Wit, spare for no Decorations or Ornaments."[26] To "set off one's goods" properly is
desirable; yet one would rather be a "great
dealer in Wit" than a mere "Haberdasher." Four
years later, Pope is more unambiguously negative
about Crashaw: "All that regards Design, Form,
Fable, (which is the Soul of Poetry) all that
concerns exactness, or consent of parts, (which
is the Body) will probably be wanting; only
pretty conceptions, fine metaphors, glitt'ring
expressions, and something of a neat cast of
Verse, (which are properly the dress, gems, or
loose ornaments of Poetry) may be found in these
verses."[27] Like Johnson after him, he notes
that Crashaw's thoughts, though pretty, are "of-
tentimes far fetch'd" (p. 110); he objects most
of all to the apparent carelessness of his writing. Care in poetry--as he was to insist in
the *Essay on Criticism*--is for him an important
desideratum. At the age of nineteen, he was re-
futing Wycherley's suggestion that "The spright-
liness of Wit despises method." "This is true
enough," Pope replies, "if by *Wit* you mean no
more than *Fancy* or *Conceit;* but in the better notion
of *Wit*, consider'd as propriety, surely *Method* is
not only necessary for Perspicuity and Harmony
of parts, but gives beauty even to the minute
and particular thoughts, which receive an additional advantage from those which precede or follow in their due places."[28]

The metaphor of expression as "the dress,
gems, or loose ornaments of Poetry," prominent
in the *Essay on Criticism,* appears also in Cowley's
poem. Superabundance of wit, the piling up of
decoration, is as distasteful to Cowley as to
Pope. Working toward a definition of true wit,
he writes,

> Yet 'tis not to adorn, and gild each part;
>   That shows more *Cost*, then Art.
> *Jewels* at *Nose* and *Lips* but ill appear;
> Rather then *all things Wit*, let *none* be there.
>   Several *Lights* will not be seen,
>   If there be nothing else between.
> Men doubt, because they stand so thick i' th'
>   skie,
> If those be *Stars* which paint the *Galaxie*.
>   (ll. 33-40)

Both the metaphors and the use made of them
seem strikingly to foretell Pope. The jewel
metaphor pays due deference to the surface effect of wit's displays while reinforcing a negative value judgment through its implication of
vulgarity and barbarism. It yields gracefully
to the light metaphor through the visual nature
of the images: jewels, as tiny lights, sparkle,
prepare for the idea of light in general and of
stars in particular. The movement, as often in
Pope, is from a trivial to a serious metaphor;
and, as in Pope, images explain and define abstract statements ("Rather then *all things Wit*,
let *none* be there"). In the poem as a whole, as
well as in this single stanza, one finds the insistence on varied but often related metaphor,
the movement back and forth between abstract and
concrete, even the suggestion of religious relevance apparent in the *Essay on Criticism*. Yet the
most superficial reading reveals that this is a
poem radically different in kind from Pope's,
and that the difference has something to do with
the use made of imagery.
   Design and form compose the soul of poetry;
consent of parts is the body. The soul and body
of Pope's poem differ so much from Cowley's that
the dress, gems, and loose ornaments come to
seem different as well. Cowley's poem exists for
its metaphors. The subject of wit is a pretext
for its display; the interest of the poem derives
from the ingenuity with which various metaphoric definitions are proposed and rejected. No
structure, no argument exists, other than the one

shaped by images. When the poet asks, "What is
it then, which like the *Power Divine/* We only can by
Negatives define?" (ll. 55-56), we admire the ingenuity which has led him to this crucial analogy,
we recognize its linguistic appropriateness, but
nothing in the texture or substance of the poem
makes us take the comparison more seriously than
the earlier one to jewels. The ode's penultimate
stanza develops comparisons between wit and the
results of divine power, but their force is self-
contained; "earned" only by the rejection of the
preceding series of extravagant images, they grow
out of no substantial development. The poem explicitly denies the possibility of meaning contained in language by its final lines. Moving
back toward the complimentary tone of his opening,
the speaker concludes that if anyone asks him
"What thing right *Wit,* and height of *Genius* is/I'll
onely shew your *Lines,* and say, *'Tis This.*" Wit can
only be displayed; it cannot be discussed. The
entire poem supports this idea.

Pope's poem, too, is a display piece, a young
man's work, an exuberant outburst of imaginative
energy; but it also has a prose table of contents
describing a scheme which bears little obvious
relation to its structure of imagery. The relation of substance to metaphor is more complicated
than in Cowley's ode. The "design" of the poem,
the consent of parts, involves a set of paraphrasable ideas which are more than definitions. Here,
as in Cowley, definition emerges through metaphor,
but the purpose of the poem is more complex than
definition. The poet wishes to tell us "that
most men are born with some Taste, but spoil'd by
Education," or "When Severity is chiefly to be used
by Critics," or to offer "Rules for the *Conduct of
Manners* in a Critic." He wishes also to make us
feel something about these ideas, suggestions,
rules, and to make us understand the assumptions
and convictions that lie behind them and the ramifications of implication buried within them.
The poem in a sense has two designs: to promul-
gate a body of doctrine, and to convey a system
of feeling and belief concerning issues wider
than doctrine.

Rosemond Tuve, writing of the traditional
metaphor of style as dress, reminds us that one
meaning derives from "the notion of style as a
garment in the sense that the flesh is the soul's
garment, its bodying-forth or manifestation."[29]
The ideal relation between metaphor and substance,
Pope suggests in the *Essay on Criticism*, is of this
kind.   The *Essay on Criticism* is an ambitious attempt
to unify the disparate, to demonstrate the operations of the unified sensibility. Pope starts
with an intellectual subject and with a traditional set of attitudes toward it. By the resources of figurative language, he attempts to
connect this subject with the widest reaches of
human experience. The images have a logic and
energy more compelling than the structure of
ideas about criticism which they are intended to
support; the relation between the pattern of intellectual discourse and the pattern of imagery
is not always perfectly lucid and expressive.
Wit is more apparent than judgement in the poem.
To a considerable extent it successfully replaces judgment, as Pope demonstrates through his
poetic practice that wit can be a principle of
control, that imagery can create as well as express ideas, that metaphor can provide organiza-
tion without comprising the sole substance of a
poem.

VIRGILIAN ATTITUDES IN POPE'S *WINDSOR-FOREST*

David B. Morris

A study of the poetical development of Alexander Pope yields one sure generalization:
although Homer and Horace were the masters
of his late and middle years, Virgil was the
poet of his youth. With the exception of *An
Essay on Criticism*, all of his major works written
before 1715--the *Pastorals*,"Messiah," *Windsor-
Forest*, and *The Rape of the Lock*--reveal a style
and vision dominated by Pope's familiarity with
Virgil. The highest praise he could bestow
upon his own youthful pastorals was the ironic
criticism that "Mr. *Pope* hath fallen into the
same Error with *Virgil*."[1] Significantly, the
passion for Homer which Pope felt from his
earliest days never expressed itself, as it
sometimes did among his contemporaries, in a
depreciation of Virgil's gifts. Virgil's
judgment and correctness, which Pope distinguished from Homer's characteristic fire and

This essay first appeared in *Texas Studies in Literature and Language* 15 (1973), 231-250.
By permission of The University of Texas Press.

invention, made the Roman in his view "undoubtedly the greatest Poet" after Homer (Note
to *Iliad* XX.270)--elevating him above Shakespeare,
Milton, and Dryden, all of whom Pope revered--
and the qualities of Virgil's work were in many
ways uniquely suited to Pope's own temperament and ambitions. In following Walsh's now
famous advice to become England's first "correct"
poet, he naturally looked to Virgil as the
classical paragon of correctness both in art
and in morality. A humane moderation consistent
with the ideals of Christianity saved Virgil's
works from a "Spirit of Cruelty which appears
too manifestly in the Iliad"(Note to *Iliad* XIII.
471), offering eighteenth-century readers an
opportunity to enjoy a stimulating exercise
of their moral faculties. In fact, Virgil's
correctness was thought to extend beyond
propriety to an almost devotional piety, which
helps to explain why throughout his life Pope
continued to use a handsome Elzevir *Virgil*, just
as many families used the Bible, to record the
names of his departed relations and friends.
Certainly this ritual suggests that his lines
addressed to Charles Jervas, who instructed him
in painting, express a kinship of spirit which
transforms his borrowings from Virgil into more
than exercises in literary allusion:

> Thou oer thy Raphaels monument should mourn
> I wait inspiring dreams at Maros urn.[2]

Pope composed the couplet about 1713--the year
in which *Windsor-Forest* appeared--when the conclusion of a tedious European war seemed to
promise a future worthy of a poet's dream. In
such an atmosphere of renewed hope, with
Augustan Rome providing a recognized model for
emulation and with some already comparing him
to Virgil, Pope published his georgic vision of
" *Albion's* Golden Days."
    Perhaps the very fidelity of Pope's imita-
tion of Virgil--including the dutiful allusion
to his own *Pastorals* in the final line--helped

to foster critical neglect of *Windsor-Forest*. Its
originality might seem vulnerable to the same
charge which Dr. Johnson leveled at the
Pastorals: "The imitations are so ambitiously
frequent that the writer evidently means rather
to shew his literature than his wit."[3] The view
that *Windsor-Forest* is a charming but vacuous
trifle prevailed until Earl Wasserman in *The
Subtler Language* (1959) demonstrated the intricacy
and coherence of Pope's design. Arguing that
Windsor-Forest, like Denham's *Cooper's Hill*, employs
natural description as a metaphorical language
of politics, Wasserman traced Pope's manipulation of the philosophical doctrine of *concordia
discors* --which held that harmony, in the state
as in the cosmos, requires the creative tension
of opposing forces. This is a reading which I
generally support. The effect of Wasserman's
lengthy analysis, however, is to stress the
political and philosophical aspects of *Windsor-
Forest*. My intention is to stress its equally
important moral and literary dimensions,
particularly by reopening the question of Pope's
imitation of Virgil.

The question deserves to be reopened,
especially in light of Wasserman's reading of
the poem, because most existing treatments of
Pope's debt to Virgil are brief and general.
The Twickenham editors, for example, rely mainly
upon E.K. Rand's *The Magical Art of Virgil* (1931) to
trace a sketchy parallel between *Windsor-Forest*
and the *Georgics*:

> The movement of Pope's poem from the shades
> and glades of Windsor Forest to the villas
> and public buildings of London and to the
> "Golden Days" inaugurated by Queen Anne is no-
> thing less than a direct imitation of the way
> Virgil in the *Georgics* moves "from crops to
> towns and from the works of men to the men
> themselves, the older heroes and the hero
> [Augustus] of the age, in which the golden
> days of Saturn have come again." Pope's sub-
> ject, too, is the same as Virgil's: his
> country's "need of peace, well typified by
> the simplicity of rural life."[4]

This broad pattern of similarity tells us nothing about the fluctuations of thought and of
feeling which give both poems an eddying as
well as a straightforward movement. Further,
it provides no hint that the "direct imitation"
was at all creative or original, whereas Pope's
imitations often embody a principle of metamorphosis: words, images, and even general
patterns borrowed from earlier poets--like
fragments of ancient stained glass set in a
modern window--assume a changed value through
their skillful integration with the contemporary.
While some of the defects of the Twickenham
account are corrected by Reuben Brower, who
adds a sensitive appreciation of Virgilian
qualities more elusive than theme and large
design, even he tends to emphasize Pope's use
of separable images, devices, and motifs--such
as the "Virgilian tradition of the Golden Age."⁵
I wish to offer a fundamentally different argument.

Windsor-Forest is Virgilian not primarily because Pope borrows certain structural, thematic,
and ornamental features from the *Georgics* but
because he expresses a general outlook upon
life--certain "attitudes"--characteristic of
the Roman poet. Although he may have begun his
apprenticeship to poetry, as he told Joseph
Spence, by "copying good strokes from others,"⁶
Pope soon advanced to a subtler and much more
fruitful idea of imitation. Both Longinus
among the Ancients and Roscommon among Pope's
immediate predecessors--two of the select
company of critic-heroes praised at the end of
An Essay on Criticism--recommended the ideal which
the young poet quickly adopted. As Roscommon
advised, an author, whether translator or poet,
must be careful to choose only those exemplars
which suit the *"Ruling Passion"* of his mind:

Then seek a *Poet* who *your* way do's bend,
And chuse an *Author* as you chuse a *Friend*:
United by this *Sympathetick Bond*,
You grow *Familiar*, *Intimate*, and *Fond*;
Your *thoughts*, your *Words*, your *Stiles*, your
    Souls agree,
No Longer his *Interpreter*, but *He*. ⁷

Like Longinus, Roscommon recommends imitating
the spirit of ancient poets rather than the
substance of their work, and the "*Sympathetick
Bond*" which he imagines linking two writers in
an agreement of soul might well describe the
relationship between Pope and Virgil in
Windsor-Forest. It is not sufficient to say that
Pope "uses" the *Georgics* in order to give his
poem a generic coherence or an allusive
resonance: his borrowings, in fact, extend over
the whole body of Virgil's work and are neither
necessary for generic identification nor
effective in creating a unity of tone. Instead,
as Pope's classically schooled readers would
have recognized, Pope embodies in his poem the
spirit of Virgil--not as an act of proud im-
personation or as a device of rhetorical
strategy but as an expression of the deep
affinity between their ways of viewing experience.
    Pope announces the main theme of *Windsor-Forest*
in a memorable couplet which imitates the
sublimity of Genesis:

    At length great ANNA said--Let Discord cease!
    She said, the World obey'd, and all was
        Peace!   (11.327-328)

The development of the poem, mirrored in these
pivotal lines, comprises a series of contrasts
between conditions of discord and of harmony,
leading ultimately to the vision of a new
Golden Age in post-Utrechtian Europe. Anna's
composing fiat, then, foreshadows the conclusion
of the poem, in which Discord, grown from an
intellectual abstraction to an allegorical
figure, suffers actual banishment at the hands
of Peace:

Exil'd by Thee from Earth to deepest Hell,
In Brazen Bonds shall barb'rous *Discord* dwell:
Gigantick *Pride*, pale *Terror*, gloomy *Care*,
And mad *Ambition* , shall attend her there.
There purple *Vengeance* bath'd in Gore retires,
Her Weapons blunted, and extinct her Fires:
There hateful *Envy* her own Snakes shall feel,
And *Persecution* mourn her broken Wheel:
There *Faction* roar, *Rebellion* bite her Chain,
And gasping Furies thirst for Blood in vain.
      (ll.413-422)

The accomplishment of Anna's merely verbal
command now assumes the concreteness of ritual.
Around the central figure of Discord, as in a
monumental statuary, Pope groups all the associate powers which have suffered similar exclusion. The notion of exile is significant.
Nowhere in *Windsor-Forest* does Pope imply that the
uncivilizing ("barb'rous") power of Discord
can be resolved into a creative harmony. He
nowhere states, as he does later in *An Essay
on Man*, that Discord is an essential component of
universal rightness: "Harmony, not understood"
(i.291). Rather, true harmony is possible only
when Discord and its associates have been
utterly overcome. Here Pope and Virgil are
completely agreed.
    Pope perhaps signals his accord with Virgil
by echoing, in his description of the exile of
Discord, two passages from the *Aeneid*. The cast
of personified terrors recalls the spectres,
from Book Six, which Aeneas meets just within
the jaws of the underworld. Even more explicit,
however, is Pope's evocation of another Virgilian scene. In Book One, Jupiter predicts the
triumph of Aeneas's Roman descendants, who will
transform an era of "impious War" into one of
peace:

Janus himself before his Fane shall wait,
And keep the dreadful issues of his Gate,
With Bolts and Iron Bars: within remains
Imprison'd Fury, bound in brazen Chains.[8]

The image of *Furor* chained within the Temple of
Janus, whose closed gates signified peace to
the Romans, clearly underlies Pope's bondage of
Discord. In fact, the poet who claimed to
have learned versification "wholly from Dryden's
works"[9] seems purposely to echo the language of
Dryden's famous translation: except for an
alliterative change, the "Brazen Bonds" of
Discord are surely the same "brazen Chains"
which manacle *Furor*. The similarity, an example
of Pope's characteristic allusive mode, serves
a purpose more serious than ornament or elevation. In this case, as so often in Virgil's
works, allusion superimposes one literary context upon another, creating a transparency or
a lucid fusion of the two. The effect here is
the creation of a composite figure: Pope's
Discord assumes the identity and function of
Virgil's *Furor*.

Why did Pope wish to associate the two
figures? Probably the best explanation is that
Pope thought of Discord as an effect or outward
manifestation: hence its central position in
the circle of exiles. The attendant and associate powers also merit inclusion, however, because they represent the main *causes* of discord.
In this sense, Patricia Meyer Spacks seems
correct in writing that the image of the Furies,
which concludes the list of personifications,
"finally sums up all of them."[10] From classical
drama to Restoration panegyric, the Furies have
regularly presided over scenes of chaos and
destruction, often accompanying the manifestation of Discord. But by Pope's time much of
the meaning behind the association had disappeared: too often the Furies are employed
merely as a grotesque decoration, the classical
equivalent of buzzards.[11] Pope renews the
significance of the Furies by using them to
suggest that the causes of Discord are located
fundamentally within the human heart. Faction
and rebellion, no less than pride, vengeance,
and envy, are to Pope and his age passions
deeply rooted in the dark interior worlds of

mankind. The traditional association between
Discord and the Furies, then, becomes in
Windsor-Forest a means of expressing the relationship between outer and inner, between disorder
in the state and its source within the individual. The evidence for this view consists partly in an unobtrusive pattern of reference
linking Pope's image of the Furies to the
Virgilian concept of *furor*.

Throughout his works Virgil depicts the
irrational power of *furor* as constantly threatening to destroy the precarious balance of
civilized values both within the individual and
within the state. Because of its direct
influence upon action, the role of *furor* is
particularly clear in the *Aeneid*, where it
represents the negation of the complex religious
and social virtues which Virgil symbolizes in
the *pietas* of his hero. When in a moment of
mindless rage Aeneas seizes arms amid the fires
of Troy, it is *furor* which blinds him to the
firm directive of the gods. When Turnus later
breaks faith with the Trojans, it is *furor*
(personified as Alecto, one of the Furies)
which thrusts the burning torch in his breast.
It is *furor* which dooms the heroic mission of
Nisus and Euryalus. These instances, reflecting
a general motif well known to scholars of Virgil,
give special significance to the image with
which Jupiter describes the peace of Augustus:
Furor impius (I.294) at last chained within the
sturdy temple of classical order. The epithet
impius epitomizes the basic antagonism in the
Aeneid between Aeneas, always described as *pius*,
and the power of *Furor*, whose bloody mouth
(*ore cruento*) denotes the same savage impulses
which Pope in *Windsor-Forest* embodies in the
figure of the blood-thirsty Furies.

The diction of *Windsor-Forest*, like the
contrasting episodes, helps to reveal Pope's
concern with the antagonism between civilized
peace and the irrationality of *furor*. The
adjective "furious"--which of course derives
from the Latin root *furor*--always occurs in

contexts which imply frenzy bordering upon
madness; nor does it seem coincidence that, of
nine appearances of the word in his poetry,
three are in *Windsor-Forest*, where the concept of
furor has thematic resonance.[12] When Pope describes the tyranny of William the Conqueror,
for example, his language suggests not only
the condition of the people but also the cause
of their oppression:

> To Savage Beasts and Savage Laws a Prey,
> And Kings more furious and severe than they.
>   (11.45-46)

It is the dehumanizing *furor* of its rulers which
initiates the transformation of England into a
"dreary Desart and a gloomy Waste" (1.44).
But the cottages and temples which crumble into
"Heaps of Ruin" (1.70), like the falling towers
of Eliot's *The Waste Land*, are more than images of
destruction. Just as Eliot's allusive mode
emphasizes the disintegration of the present
by recalling simultaneously the high civilization of the past, Pope's image of devastation
recalls the "heaps of Ruins" described in
Dryden's *Aeneid* (VIII.472), where the context
celebrates the continuity, rather than the
radical disruption, of civilized values.
  The loss of rational control is again Pope's
theme in the mythological Lodona episode.
Straying beyond her proper "Limits" (1.182),
Lodona discovers that excess does not lead to
the palace of wisdom but to the amoral world of
Hobbesian power. Transformed from huntress to
prey, she desperately flees the hot pursuit of
Pan:

> Not half so swift the trembling Doves can fly,
> When the fierce Eagle cleaves the liquid Sky;
> Not half so swiftly the fierce Eagle moves,
> When thro' the Clouds he drives the trembling
>   Doves;
> As from the God she flew with furious Pace,
> Or as the God, more furious, urg'd the Chace.
>   (11.185-190)

The description plays no favorites: the first
couplet reflects the eagle's view, the second
the doves', while the concluding lines--by
applying the same adjective to both Pan and
Lodona--suggest the blurring of distinctions
which inevitably follows the neoclassical sin
of excess. The repetition of "furious" is,
in fact, a significant addition to the 1712
manuscript, in which the simile concludes:

> As from the God with headlong Speed she flew,
> As did the God with equal Speed pursue.[13]

The revised couplet suggests causation as well
as speed. In disregarding her proper limits,
Lodona calls forth the violence of nature which
is always present in potential. But nature
can also serve man instead of opposing him--a
fact which Pope establishes early in *Windsor-Forest*
by introducing Pan in his peaceful role as
shepherd (1.37). Like the episode which
describes the hunting of William, Lodona's
frenzied chase and abrupt metamorphosis affirm
that discord in nature can often be traced
directly to the *furor* of man.

The relationship between discord and *furor*
is illustrated perhaps most interestingly in
the 1712 manuscript version of Anna's fiat:

> Till ANNA rose, and bade the Furies cease;
> *Let there be Peace* --She said; and all was
> Peace.[14]

The most important change occurring in the
published poem of 1713 would seem to be the
shift from direct to indirect means of creating
harmony: "*Let there be Peace*" becomes in 1713 the
oblique command "Let Discord cease!" As the
effect of both commands is identical, however,
the shift does not involve a basic change of
conception: the 1713 command is simply a more
effective (because less presumptuous) allusion
to the monarach's semidivine powers. The
fundamental shift is Pope's substitution of

Discord for the Furies: "bade the Furies cease" becomes in 1713 "Let Discord cease!" The change is consistent with the attitude Pope expresses throughout toward uncivilizing violence. Discord, as an effect or outward manifestation, can indeed be stilled by fiat. (Or, what is the same thing, by treaty.) But the causes of discord, represented by the Furies, cannot be corrected or contained merely by the promulgation of law. Like the extralegal offenses traditionally scourged by the satirist, the interior "sins" of pride, envy, ambition, and vengeance require a different language of correction. In *Windsor-Forest*, written before his recourse to the punitive and cautionary power of satire, Pope attacked the causes of discord through an indirect mode of correction particularly appropriate to a Virgilian idea of the poet's role. He employs the language of poetry beyond any single-minded purposes of praise or blame in order to mirror the complexity--and sometimes even the ambiguity--of human experience. He attempts to make men better by enlarging the vision and by refining the sensibilities of a fallen world.

For Pope, as for Virgil, the voice of the poet expresses a civilized *humanitas*: an awareness of man's potential dignity tempered by an understanding of his possible baseness. For both poets the range of human possibility inspires a special kind of poetic language in which complexity and occasional ambiguity are perfectly mimetic, reflecting the mixed condition of creatures who hang between two worlds. Because man exists in a state of constant potentiality--poised between the possibilities of civilization and barbarism, of virtue and vice, of wisdom and dullness--the poet's language frequently contains the possibility of multiple values and of variable signification. Words, like men, may pass from one state to another: often tone and context alone, as in Pope's use of "nature" and "wit" in *An Essay on Criticism*, can determine precise meaning.

"There is a vast deal of difference," he
insisted in the headnote to Book One of the *Iliad*,
"between the Learning of a Critick, and the
Puzzling of a Grammarian," and, while the mere
grammarian is "apt to fancy Two Meanings for
want of knowing One," the true critic in
Pope's view is always alert to the resources
of intelligent complexity. Presuppositions
about neoclassical diction, however, find many
readers still believing that Dryden lacked
"suggestiveness" (Eliot's view) and that Pope
is always clear. Such presuppositions, where
they mistake precision for simplicity, distort
the meaning and design of *Windsor-Forest*.

An equally distorting presupposition is the
view that *Windsor-Forest*, like the works of Virgil,
shamelessly flatters a contemporary regime and
whitewashes the sins of nascent imperialism.
Pope's epigraph from Virgil--*non injussa cano*--
recalls the Roman's unwillingness to celebrate
Varus's military exploits in epic verse; and,
although bidden to sing, both Pope and Virgil
carefully mix just praise with qualifying
intimations. Only the high opinion of his own
independence could inspire Pope, late in his
career, to misrepresent Virgil and Horace as
"party-writers" in the service of Augustan
propaganda. Further, any political optimism in
the works of Virgil and of Pope is usually
conveyed in a vision of futurity. Praise of
Augustus or of Anne never compromises their
absolute refusal to ignore the painful complexities of the past and present. The vision of
man's highest civilized potential coexists
with a compassionate awareness of the tears of
things which, in a world still far from
perfect or redeemed, accompany even the most
heroic victories over disorder. Virgil's praise
of Augustan Rome, itself rarely unambiguous,
hardly alters the dominant impression of loss
and perplexity conveyed by the *Aeneid*. If the
deaths of Dido and of Turnus are required by
fate, we are not allowed to dismiss their
human significance: in fact, Virgil forces us

to understand that empire exacts a painful toll
in human sorrow. Similarly, in the *Georgics*,
the advent of the mating season evokes sentiments which transcend any national pride in
the multiplication of livestock:

> In Youth alone, unhappy Mortals live;
> But, ah! the mighty Bliss is fugitive;
> Discolour'd Sickness, anxious Labours come,
> And Age, and Death's inexorable Doom.
>   (III.108-111)

Careful attention to *Windsor-Forest* shows that
Pope's attitude toward national grandeur is
very close to Virgil's. Both poets, of course,
associate a condition of general harmony with
enlightened government. Although both discover
in contemporary rulers grounds for hope in
future peace and order, however, they do not
encourage partisan or utopian claims, nor do
they forget that their subject is the unideal
state of fallen humanity. The reader moves
toward affirmation, but only through the
troubling experience of ambiguity.
    "We oftner think of the Author himself when
we read *Virgil*," Pope wrote, "than when we are
engag'd in *Homer*."[15] In place of Homeric
objectivity, the works of Virgil embody a
distinct yet restrained subjectiveness. The
narrative voice expresses a civilized sensibility which in effect enriches the action of the
poem by surrounding it with what one critic
has called an "empathetic style." "The most
obvious key to Virgil's 'psychological
identification' of himself with the characters,"
Brooks Otis asserts, "is the tell-tale phrase
or word which either describes the character's
feelings or Virgil's own feeling for him or--
what is nearest to the fact--a subtle blend
of both."[16] It seems likely that Pope understood
this aspect of Virgil's art, for he practices
it himself in *Windsor-Forest*. The language of
the poem, far from being impersonal and
chauvinistic, conveys the poet's individual

sense that the achievements of civilization
often require disheartening sacrifices of
natural beauty. Through the process of reading,
we share, if only momentarily, the poet's
heightened powers of sympathy and understanding.
   The best place to examine Pope's language of
ambiguity is in the seasons-of-sport passage
(ll.93-164) which employs hunting, in Wasserman's words, as "a metaphor for the recommended
norm of human activity, in contrast to the
excessive and uncontrolled activity of William."[17] Hunting also is regarded traditionally
as an art and, hence, can represent the general
process of artifice which redeems man from
the potential barbarity of his fallen state.
Pope's language, however, while praising the
hunt, manages at the same time to suggest the
ambiguity of most human norms. The "eager"
(l.148) youths who rush headlong to the "Sylvan
War" ominously recall, in retrospect, the
"eager" (l.181) huntress Lodona, especially
when Pope describes the "eager Speed" (l.157)
of their horses in a famous line from Statius's
epic about civil war. The energy compressed
in the word "eager" is reflected in Johnson's
definition: "Struck with desire; ardently
wishing; keenly desirous; vehement in desire;
hotly longing." Some readers, of course,
have argued that the excessive energies of
youth require the therapeutic exercise of
hunting. But Pope's language goes beyond the
insinuation of civic prudence. The scent of
the partridge carries on "tainted" breezes
which "betray" (l.101); the fields are "un-
faithful" (l.103); the beagles "learn of Man"
(l.124) the unnatural pastime of killing. Indeed, Rebecca Price Parkin rightly asserts that
the ambiguity of Pope's diction conveys one
of the principal insights of *Windsor-Forest*: "that
there is a case to be made for both the hunter
and the hunted. The reader is made to enter
imaginatively into the sentiments of both."[18]
By exercising our powers of sympathy, we also
enlarge our comprehension: we become civilized.

Pope's manipulation of perspectives in
Windsor-Forest is a deliberate attempt, reminiscent of Virgil, to represent the complexity
of life, and this intention also directs his
treatment of two related vignettes within the
seasons-of-sport passage. The first is the
famous description of the dying pheasant, a
scene simultaneously elegiac and objective. Its
objectivity derives mainly from Pope's brilliant
pictorial detail, similar to the often passion-
less virtuosity of a French or Flemish *nature
morte*:

> See! from the Brake the whirring Pheasant
>   springs,
> And mounts exulting on triumphant Wings;
> Short is his Joy! he feels the fiery Wound,
> Flutters in Blood, and panting beats the
>   Ground.
> Ah! what avail his glossie, varying Dyes,
> His Purple Crest, and Scarlet-circled Eyes,
> The vivid Green his shining Plumes unfold;
> His painted Wings, and Breast that flames
>   with Gold?   (11.111-118)

Pope, like the hunters, might seem to be treating the pheasant simply as an object on which
to exercise his art. But the description is
complex. The concurrent elegiac tone exerts
a humanizing counterbalance which prevents
us from viewing the pheasant solely as an
object for the sublimation of warlike energies.
In fact, as a closer analysis of the passage
will show, Pope's language successfully re-
creates the intricate blend of acceptance and
regret which characterizes Virgilian pathos.
A variety of techniques, providing an
emotional complement to the cold descriptive
skill, helps to awaken our sympathy: the jolting
inverted metrics of "Short is his Joy," the
emphasis upon pain, the pathos of "Flutters" and
"panting"--in contrast to the vigor of the
earlier verb forms--and the openly elegiac
"Ah!" But Pope's most subtle techniques are

implicit in the same painterly skills which
give the passage its objectivity. The opening
command "See!" might well have reminded an
eighteenth-century critic of the traditional
argument of rhetoricians, then being revived
with the discovery of Longinus, that feeling
is best evoked through the use of visual
imagery. By careful attention to pictorial
detail, the poet transforms the mere reader
into a spectator, making him respond with the
emotional immediacy of an eyewitness. For at
least one of Pope's admirers, who described
his reactions in a verse compliment, the
strategy worked to perfection:

> Ah! how I melt with pity, when I spy
> On the cold earth the flutt'ring Pheasant
>   lie;
> His gawdy robes in dazling lines appear,
> And ev'ry feather shines and varies there.[19]

Pity is induced not by maudlin diction but by
its opposite: by the precise, visual delineation
which transforms a reader of words into a see-er
of things.
    Pope's use of color, which assists in the
process of visualization, also implies a special
value throughout his work which helps to temper
with emotion the objectivity of the description.
As opposed to certain forms of immutable truth
which he consistently associates with the un-
refracted purity of light, color for Pope
frequently signifies the sad but inevitable link
between beauty and death.[20] The pattern is
flexible rather than fixed--elsewhere in
Windsor-Forest color suggests plenitude, order,
and stability--and, as with his use of language
in general, individual instances must be judged
in context: Pope's imagery never requires our
knowledge of a private system of consistency.
In this case, Pope's use of color to describe
the pheasant fits the larger pattern of his
works. The pheasant's "gawdy robes" are themselves an image of the mutability which its

death embodies. The brilliant lifelike colors
and the plain fact of death create a contrast
too striking not to affect us. Like the
"transient Colours" (ii.67) which pastel the
wings of Belinda's delicate guardians in
The Rape of the Lock, the purples, greens, and golds
of the dying pheasant reflect the fragility
of all sublunary beauty.

The very subtlety of these techniques, some
might argue, diminishes their usefulness. But
subtlety was justified--indeed required--on at
least two grounds. First, excessive or obvious
pathos evoked by a dead bird would have quickly
degenerated into sentimentality or ridiculous
solemnity. Second, Pope did not wish to over-
emphasize the elegiac nature of the passage but
to create a balanced counterpoint of feeling
and objectivity. His language, encompassing
the dual perspectives of hunter and hunted,
is intended to make us experience the death of
the pheasant as a complex rather than simple
phenomenon. We are made to sense the intricate
nexus of loss and gain which typifies the
progress of civilization. The tone of the
passage, then, depends upon Pope's intention
to confront us with a situation demanding an
ambiguous response. And, given his intention,
it is not surprising that two learned eighteenth-century commentators glossed Pope's description of the pheasant with different passages
in Virgil.[21] A direct source will probably
remain impossible to specify. The attitude
expressed in the passage, however, is unmistakably Virgilian.

A second vignette of equally disturbing
ambiguity immediately follows and complements
Pope's description of the pheasant: the capture
by English troops of an "amaz'd, defenceless"
(l.109) little town. Just as the sudden,
colorful flight of the pheasant parallels the
abrupt hoisting of the Union Jack, the situation of the town, ringed by attackers, resembles
that of the pheasant, trapped by dogs and hunters. The conjunction of raw power and harmless

insufficiency should be at least slightly
troubling to the most patriotic reader: England's
"eager Sons" (1.106) are hardly ennobled by such
an easy conquest. Further, in a poem ostensibly
celebrating peace, the almost gleeful tone
of the description seems to jar with other
passages which suggest the futility and madness
of war. The jarring, however, is intentional.
Pope employs ambiguity for a serious, civilizing purpose: to unsimplify our assumptions about
the clear-cut relationship between victor and
vanquished.
    Gilbert Wakefield, who edited Pope's works
in the last decade of the eighteenth century,
helps to explain the disquieting quality of
the "capture" passage by his comment on the
poem's later celebration of peace. "This fine
panegyric on *peace*, in opposition to the horrors
and devastations of war," he writes, "was
in part occasioned, I presume, by our author's
politics; by his hostility to the name of
Marlborough, and an uneasiness at the glory of his
victories."[22] *Windsor-Forest* says little about
the victories of war: what scant praise of
conquest there is Pope deliberately calculates
to evoke "uneasiness" in the reader. His
method is like Virgil's when he described
Aeneas, just on the point of killing Turnus,
as *furiis accensus et ira/terribilis*(XII.946-947): the
victory of force, even when force is justified,
is undercut by the language of the poet.
Indeed, Virgil's doubts about Rome's history of
blood and *furor* seem dramatized in the indecision
--the deep suspense between compassion and
vengeance--which seizes Aeneas as he hesitates
over his defeated enemy. "Turnus stands for
the world of Italy," writes Michael C.J. Putnam,
"that strange combination of wildness and
pastoral order. In spite of Juno's plea to
Jupiter, it is this world which Aeneas destroys,
and with a lack of mercy singularly pronounced
because it gives the lie both to Anchises'
utterances about the future nobility of Roman
conduct and to Jupiter's scarcely finished

declaration about the happy union to be attained.
The tragedy of the destruction of Turnus and
his world does much to negate any romantic
notion of the *Aeneid* as an ideal vision of the
greatness of Augustan Rome, and it negates,
too, the image of Virgil as its poet-laureate.'[23]
Similarly, Pope's analogy between warfare and
hunting is a means of expressing both ambiguity
and discontent. Not only Marlborough's
victories but the fact of conquest itself made
Pope uneasy. "True Courage," he wrote in
criticizing a passage in Homer, "is inseparable
from Humanity, and all generous Warriors regret
the very Victories they gain, when they reflect
what a Price of Blood they cost" (Note to *Iliad*
XIII.471). Of course, war, like hunting, is
one of the "various Arts" (I.217) which Virgil
in the *Georgics* views as a consequence of man's
fate. But, as the tone of *Windsor-Forest* attests,
both hunting and warfare are, for Pope, arts
unworthy of England's highest civilized
potential.

    Although Pope employs the capture of the lit-
tle town as an analogy to the pheasant-kill,
using both to emphasize the ambiguities of
experience, he also distinguishes between
them: an enlarged perspective, after all,
ought to create an improved sense of proportion.
The distinction between the two vignettes,
however, is not merely one of magnitude: "if
small Things we may with great compare" (1.105).
Beyond the formulaic comparison of great and
small, Pope also contrasts the realms of the
natural and unnatural, of the rational and
irrational. The fate of the little town, unlike
that of the pheasant, teaches a human imperative
which transcends the perception of complexity.
It warns us that peace has its dangers as well
as war.

    If aspects of Pope's description of the
capture are troubling, the main thrust of the
passage is affirmative, and close attention to
Pope's language reveals why. The town is described as "thoughtless" (1.107). While this

condition is natural in the pheasant, an irrational creature, it is both unnatural and
ominous in man, for whom civilization is the
outward expression of social reason. Further,
although the town seems happily blest with
"Ease and Plenty" (1.107), the phrase begs
comparison with Pope's earlier description
of the landscape of modern England:

> Rich Industry sits smiling on the Plains,
> And Peace and Plenty tell, a STUART reigns.
>   (11.41-42)

The phrase "Peace and Plenty" was a cliché of
contemporary political rhetoric, but Pope
might also have remembered it from Dryden's
description, in the *Aeneid*, of the Golden Age of
Saturn (VIII.436). Its similarity to the
phrase "Ease and Plenty" is a useful reminder
that times have changed: for fallen man, peace,
while inevitably creating a state of plenty, is
by no means synonymous with ease. As Virgil
himself expresses this fundamental creed in the
Georgics, the fate of Iron-Age man is labor and
art:

> The Sire of Gods and Men, with hard Decrees,
> Forbids our Plenty to be bought with Ease.
>   (I.183-184)

True peace requires effort, just as "True Ease"
--according to Pope's *Essay on Criticism*--is
always the result of "Art" (1.362). The specious ease and plenty of the little town is
merely the momentary product of chance--as
vulnerable as the pheasant, and as transient.
It offers an image of false peace which
complements the disquieting descriptions of
the hunt. Together both prepare a background
for Pope's reconciling vision of a truly civilized era of peace.
    "No writing is good that does not tend to
better mankind some way or other," Pope told
Joseph Spence, probably recalling a similar

assertion in Knightly Chetwood's "Life of
Virgil" which was prefixed to Dryden's translation.[24] Amelioration, of course, can take many
forms, and men are less likely to persecute
one another if they see that life is more
complex than they had thought. But Pope also
viewed experience as a theater of moral action
where the perception of complexity is debilitating if it induces, as it can, a paralysis of the
will. Thus, Pope is rarely content to leave
his readers in ambiguity, and *Windsor-Forest*,
like much of his work, moves toward a point
of reconciliation.[25] This movement is embodied
in the poem's deliberate plan of development:
from an idealized distant past, irrecoverably
lost, through a history vacillating between
eras of discord and peace, to a vision of an
idealized but attainable future, in which
ambiguity is transformed into affirmation.

The transformation of Lodona, as Wasserman
has shown, stands as the central, transitional
episode of *Windsor-Forest*, moving the poem from
the discord and ambiguity of hunting to the
peaceful activities of meditation, poetry,
and commerce. As huntress, Lodona represents
the energy appropriate to the active life; as
river, she mirrors and composes the beauty of
her surroundings, suggesting virtues appropriate to the contemplative life. Neither state
alone, however, is entirely satisfactory. Her
slow waters resume something of her former
energy only when they "rush into the *Thames*"
(1.218). Similarly, the Forest achieves its
greatest glory only when half its trees, as
Father Thames remarks, "rush into my Floods"
(1.386), forming the fleet of England's new
commercial navy. Wasserman, in fact, finds in
Lodona's progress an image of the poem's
thematic movement: from unsatisfactory conditions of discord represented by hunting to the
fulfillment of a true *concordia discors* through
"the strifeful peace of foreign commerce, instead of foreign war."[26] But, while the treatment of commerce resolves the poem's main

political and philosophical themes, Pope also
relies upon his consistent "imitation" of
Virgil to create an equally appropriate moral
and literary resolution.

   Although Virgil in the *Georgics* glorifies
agriculture rather than commerce, both he and
Pope are more interested in the symbolic uses
of industry than in particular occupations, and
they use commerce and agriculture as symbolic
occupations in a profoundly similar way. For
Virgil, the resurrection of the bees from
decaying carcasses, the concluding episode of
the *Georgics*, provides an image of natural
renewal which fittingly resolves the poem.   Its
full meaning, however, cannot be understood
apart from the contiguous myth of Orpheus and
Eurýdice. The art of Orpheus proves useless
without an accompanying discipline over his
passions: "What fury seiz'd on thee,/Unhappy
Man!" Eurydice cries out, "to lose thy self
and Me?"(IV.714-715). Both discipline and art,
nevertheless, themselves prove useless without
the regenerating cycles of natural change,
represented by the bees' rebirth from dead
matter. Like agriculture for Virgil, commerce
provides Pope with an image of man's artful
harmony with dynamic nature, and, again like
Virgil, he associates this condition with the
myth of the Golden Age. Father Thames's prophecy of an era of peace and commerce, in fact,
is modeled mainly on Anchises' prediction,
in Book Six of the *Aeneid*, of the peaceful
reign of Augustus:

   Sent to the Realm that *Saturn* ruled of old;
   Born to restore a better Age of Gold.
      (11.1081-1082)

The idea of a "better" Golden Age underlies
Pope's choice of commerce as a resolving image
and reflects an attitude wholly, if not exclusively, Virgilian. It affirms the lesson of
the *Georgics*: that the new Age of Gold will not
be achieved through nostalgia and pastoral ease
but through the noble discipline of art and

labor.

The symbolic values of commerce in *Windsor-Forest* can be best illuminated by tracing two related phenomena: Pope's references to blood and his creation of a "social myth." The former occurs with a consistency suggesting that Pope intentionally elaborated an imagistic and thematic motif. Until the intervention of Queen Anne introduces the prophetic vision of Father Thames, *Windsor-Forest* conveys the painful impression of a land virtually bleeding itself to death:

> Oh Fact accurst! What Tears has *Albion* shed,
> Heav'ns! what new Wounds, and how her old
>   have bled?   (11.321-322)

From early references to the "bloody Chace" (1.61) begun by Nimrod, Pope continually associates the actual and potential violence of *furor* with images of bloodshed. Not even the stilling power of Granville's art can alter the burden of the past:

> Still in thy Song shou'd vanquish'd *France*
>   appear,
> And bleed for ever under *Britain's* Spear.
>   (11.309-310)

Ironically, the poem suggests that Britain rather than France seems most likely to bleed forever. The pheasant which "Flutters in Blood" probably summarizes better than any other single image the revelation of the poem's historical survey: a pathetic spectacle of wasted potential. In order to understand how Pope resolves this particular motif through his use of commerce, it is necessary first to examine his related development of a "social myth."

An Essay on Man (1733-34), although a much later poem, offers the best view of Pope's ideas concerning the origin and progress of society which underlie his resolution of

Windsor-Forest. The movement of both poems is
curiously similar. "Beginning with a reminder
of a paradise man has lost," Maynard Mack has
written of *An Essay on Man,* "the poem ends with a
paradise he can regain."[27] *Windsor-Forest,*
likewise, begins with a reference to Eden--
"vanish'd now so long" (1.7)--and concludes
with the vision of a future Golden Age of
commerce. Both poems also establish a context
within which human discord is not merely an
aspect of universal harmony but a stage of
arrested moral growth. Far from offering only
a philosophical vindication of the status quo,
An Essay on Man charts a potential evolutionary
progress: from innocence, through corruption,
to possible regeneration. This progress,
applied to the development of man in society,
provides the basis for Pope's vision of future
amelioration in *Windsor-Forest.*

The initial premise of Pope's "social myth"
is that the original state of nature, which
Hobbes had described as warring, was in fact the
"reign of God" (iii.148), a Golden Age in which
self-love and social interest were in perfect
harmony: "Union the bond of all things, and
of Man" (iii.150). This unity extended even
to man's relationship with the animals--a fact
which bears upon Pope's use of hunting in
Windsor-Forest:

> Pride then was not; nor Arts, that Pride to
>   aid;
> Man walk'd with beast, joint tenant of
>   the shade;
> The same his table, and the same his bed;
> No murder cloath'd him, and no murder fed.
> In the same temple, the resounding wood,
> All vocal beings hymn'd their equal God:
> The shrine with gore unstain'd, with gold
>   undrest,
> Unbrib'd, unbloody, stood the blameless
>   priest:
> Heav'n's attribute was Universal Care,
> And Man's prerogative to rule, but spare.
>   (iii.151-160)

The passage foretells, through its use of
negative constructions, man's later fall from
harmony, and the linked images of gold and gore
achieve a kind of emblematic power in representing the baseness of human pride:

> Now Europe's laurels on their brows behold,
> But stain'd with blood, or ill exchang'd
>   for gold.   (iv.295-296)

Like the blood-stained pheasant of *Windsor-Forest*
whose breast "flames with Gold," the hero's
laurels suggest the essence of man's fallen
character: a "foe to Nature" (iii.163).
    The "murder" of animals in *An Essay on Man*
is not only a mark of man's fall from harmony
but also a prelude to grosser corruptions.
Hunting literally breeds war:

> The Fury-passions from that blood began,
> And turn'd on Man a fiercer savage, Man.
>   (iii.167-168)

Passion, of course, is a positive force in
An Essay on Man, the active principle which
inspires all human motion. But, although Pope
insists that passion is necessary to man,
without the guidance of reason man would be
"active to no end" (ii.62). The destructive
"Fury-passions," then, represent passion un-
guided or misguided by reason. They are another
name for the irrational power of *furor*,
which plunges man from a condition of innocence
and of charity into a nightmare of blood.
    An Essay on Man holds out two paradigms of
regeneration: one historical and social, the
other timeless and personal. The personal
regeneration comes through charity--not narrowly
conceived as alms but broadly interpreted to
signify a sympathetic union with all nature.
Self-love, directed outwards toward society,
works in the rational mind like a pebble drop-
ped into a peaceful lake, radiating ever-inclu-
sive circles of charity:

156

> Wide and more wide, th'o'erflowings of the
>   mind
> Take ev'ry creature in, of ev'ry kind;
> Earth smiles around, with boundless bounty
>   blest,
> And Heav'n beholds its image in his breast.
>   (iv.369-372)

The charitable man creates a paradise within
which is an image of the original harmony of
man's unfallen state. But personal charity is
not the only alternative to the "Fury-passions."
The Age of Patriarchs offers a historical
pattern of restoration achieved by heeding,
not opposing, the voice of nature:

> Great Nature spoke; observant Men obey'd;
> Cities were built, Societies were made:
> Here rose one little state; another near
> Grew by like means, and join'd, thro' love or
>   fear.
> Did here the trees with ruddier burdens bend,
> And there the streams in purer rills
>   descend?
> What War could ravish, Commerce could bestow,
> And he return'd a friend, who came a foe.
>   (iii.199-206)

The transformation of foes into friends, of
war into peace, of plunder into commerce
returns us to the modern world of *Windsor-Forest*,
where commerce again becomes both means and
symbol of harmony restored.

The reconciling power of commerce, which
creates the same union among nations that
charity creates among individuals, is pictured
in *Windsor-Forest* as initiating a new social era,
an image of man's primal unity. The new
Golden Age can justifiably be called "better"
than the first, however, because it boasts all
the fruits of art and industry which were
unknown before the fall. Best of all, it
implies a progressive social evolution, and
the wisdom earned by experience, which makes
the possibility of a second fall from grace

extremely unlikely. Thus, the negative construction of Father Thames's prophecy foretells
a future free from the bloodshed which followed
the first Age of Gold:

> No more my Sons shall dye with *British* Blood
> Red *Iber's* Sands, or *Ister's* foaming Flood.
>   (ll.367-368)

River gods, of course, may speak with a certain
extravagance which the poet does not share, but
neither has entirely abandoned his mind to
millennial predictions. Hunting--a pastime
which Pope did not admire but realistically
admitted had "Authority and Custom to support
it"28--still remains as a "Trace" (1.371) of
war, reminding man of his fallen past, just as
Pope's reference to the tyranny of Spain (1.409)
suggests the imperfection of the present. But
the commercial future, if not wholly utopian,
still promises an immense improvement over the
discord of the past, improvement epitomized
in Pope's image of the "gasping Furies" who
now "thirst for Blood in vain."
   The futile bleeding which characterizes discord is not merely stopped but is transformed
into a metaphorical image of man's new harmony
with nature. The elevated diction of Father
Thames's praise of commerce, then, appropriately reflects a sense of heightened civility:

> For me the Balm shall bleed, and Amber flow,
> The Coral redden, and the Ruby glow.
>   (ll.393-394)

Blenheim and Saragossa no longer stain their
waters with " *British* Blood" but coral and rubies
redden naturally for man's delight; now the
fruitful "bleeding" of balm and amber replaces
the useless bloodshed of war; and gold, formerly a mark of human corruption, becomes both an
image of natural process (1.396) and an emblem
of social regeneration, announcing the arrival
of "*Albion's* Golden Days." Individual nations

enjoy their freedom, while commerce unites
them in a circle of mutual self-interest. Even
natural forces of isolation are transformed,
through art and labor, into connecting links,
as "Seas but join the Regions they divide"
(1.400). The peace which Pope envisions in
Windsor-Forest is not merely the conclusion to a
specific war but the creation of a dynamic
harmony which spreads "from Shore to Shore"
(1.407). While the godlike power of Queen Anne,
in banishing Discord, accomplishes much of the
transformation, the promise of a "better"
Golden Age also depends upon the civilizing art
of the poet, whose *humanitas* helps to overcome
the internal sway of *furor* and whose invention
discovers a resolving image worthy of mankind's
highest potential for cultural growth.

"Pope's life-work," G. Wilson Knight has
observed, "is rooted in *Windsor Forest*."[29] A
corollary would also seem true: that Pope's
life-work is rooted in the Virgilian attitudes
which nourish his thought in *Windsor-Forest*. Although his methods later changed mainly to the
satirical, his goal is always the Virgilian
end of warring down the savage and taming the
proud. Thus, in his role of civilized and
civilizing poet, Pope, like Virgil, conceived
of "correctness" in its largest and noblest
sense. An early version of *Windsor-Forest*, for
example, described the flags of England's
commercial fleet in the phrase "bloody Cross."[30]
The later disappearance of the adjective
"bloody" (1.387) reveals more than Pope's
attention to a minor detail of imagery. The
correction suggests his general attitude toward
the craft of poetry: for Pope, as for Virgil,
the refinement of the poem prefigures and
advances the moral improvement of mankind. It
is in such general attitudes, rather than in
verbal echoes and structural similarities, that
Pope's most meaningful reliance upon Virgil is
to be sought. For the young Pope, Virgil was as
much a sage as a poet, and what Pope learned
from Virgil, above all else, involves a whole
outlook on the nature of civilized man.

'THE ENAMELLED GROUND': THE LANGUAGE OF
HERALDRY AND NATURAL DESCRIPTION IN *WINDSOR-FOREST*

Pat Rogers

It is now widely agreed that Pope's *Windsor-
Forest* is far more than a discursive topographical
poem--a sort of *Grongar Hill* with political reflections thrown in. Today we see the work as opera-
ting through a complex series of parallelisms,
symbolic relationships and thematic echoes.[1] I
believe, however, that one major thread in the
artistic design has been overlooked. The unity
of *Windsor-Forest*, I shall argue--the connection it
forges between the natural world and the moral
and political sphere--proceeds quite largely from
one particular verbal habit. This is the technique of heraldic description. Pope applies the
specialist vocabulary of armorial bearings to a
physical landscape. And in describing the actual
Windsor Forest as though it were a heraldic
'achievement' he makes the scene more finely expressive and more deeply symbolic.

I

Throughout *Windsor-Forest* there is a dazzling
array of primary colours. There is something al-

This essay first appeared in *Studia Neophilologica* 45 (1973), 356-71.

most Pre-Raphaelite about this display. Norman
Ault, who remarked that Pope carried the use of
colour 'to a pitch never before attained by any
poet', relates the extraordinary frequency of
colour-words (approximately one every seven lines,
as against a norm in poetry at large of one to
thirty or forty lines) to Pope's interest in
painting.[2] I agree with Ault that Pope is
attempting to extend 'the poet's vision', but it
is not self-evident that landscape painting was
his principal recourse in this undertaking. As
it happens, *Windsor-Forest* makes use of a restrict-
ed range of tones. An artist like John Wootton
employed a much subtler palette. Pope's spectrum
is divided up (like Newton's, in a way) into a
few bright, distinct hues. Apart from the 'rus-
set Plains' and 'blueish Hills' of lines 23-24,
there are virtually no half-tones within the
poem.[3] Its characteristic hues are silver, gold,
clear blue and bright scarlet.
     Now these, patently, are not 'natural' shades.
They are rather the colours of emblematic representation. They are tones artificial in their
gloss and purity: they suggest lapidary surfaces,
instead of the texture of living things. It happens that in the very first line of the poem, we
have been alerted to Pope's heightened colour-
sensitivity by the phrase, 'thy green Retreats',
strongly redolent of pastoral calm and meditative
retirement--green thoughts in green shades. But
as *Windsor-Forest* proceeds, we find the indigenous
verdure of the scene more and more concealed behind a coating of bright 'mineral' layers. Even
the groves of Eden, once so abundant in vegeta-
tion, now 'look green' only 'in Song' (8). The
implication is that the real site of Eden is now
parched and brown: only in the fictive techni-
color of poetry does its bloom survive. Consequently, the word *green*, usually connoting natural creativity, has here taken on the force of a
paradox: it alludes to the eternizing power of
art. This is an important juncture in what might
be called the lexical trajectory of the work. At
this early stage we are made aware that the green

of nature is a transient thing. When Pope writes
near the end,

> My humble Muse, in unambitious Strains,
> Paints the green Forests and the flow'ry
>   Plains...   (427-28)

we recall the opening section: *paint* has come to
suggest not just a distant mimetic act, but a
necessary bit of life-preservation. The forests
will remain green, the plains continue to blos-
som, only if the poetic imagination freezes them
in this state. In the context of the entire work,
paint means not only 'picture', but also something like 'wash over', as one paints a steel
structure to preserve it from corrosion.
   So we find in the text of *Windsor-Forest* a
strong emphasis on artificial coloration. This
is perhaps clearest in the description of angl-
ing:

> Our plenteous Streams a various Race supply;
> The bright-ey'd Perch with Fins of *Tyrian* Dye,
> The silver Eel, in shining Volumes roll'd,
> The yellow Carp, in Scales bedrop'd with Gold,
> Swift Trouts, diversify'd with Crimson Stains,
> And Pykes, the Tyrants of the watry Plains.
>   (141-46)

The point about words like *dye* and *stain* is that
they suggest a process of colouring on top of an
existing ground. Likewise with such terms as
'whiten'd' (126). What Ault and others do not
seem to have observed is that the riot of colour
in the text has one peculiar feature: generally
we see the colour being applied. It is as though
all things were of themselves opaque Lockian objects, with no secondary characteristics--it is
through poetic recreation that they come to possess tones and identities. Hence the importance
of the allegoric tableau depicting Peace and
Plenty 'smiling on the Plains' (37-42). This
scene, representing the prosperity of a Stuart
reign, is composed of successive layers, as indi-

cated by the line, 'Here blushing *Flora* paints
th'enamel'd Ground'. The Twickenham editors have
explained this reference in terms of the preparation given to a metal before it is suitable as a
painting surface.[4] But more directly we can see
how the usage draws attention to the *coating* effect of the bright pigments in flowers. Once
more colour is associated with (*a*) artifice;
(*b*) mineral substances; (*c*) an embossed effect;
(*d*) an emblematic meaning.

All these components are found in one particular mode of representation: heraldry. But the
suitability of armorial terms from Pope's point
of view does not end there. A number of motifs
and imaginative concerns within the text of *Windsor-Forest* receive a kind of implicit reinforcement from this specialist vocabulary. For example, heraldry was closely connected with royalty
and the genealogy of noble families, a fact of
some importance in a poem designed to celebrate
the Stuart line. Moreover, Windsor itself,
through its association with the orders of chivalry, provided another connection. Heraldry is
instinct with history and tradition, themselves
dominant strands in the poem. Yet again, many
heraldic emblems involve beasts of prey: this
suggests another recurring theme in *Windsor-Forest*,
namely the opposition of war and peace, aggression and submission, rapacious destruction and
fruitful cultivation.[5] Lastly, it is customary
to look on heraldry as a commemorative activity,
by which illustrious deeds and distinguished
pedigrees may be duly recorded for posterity.
All these attributes serve to enrich the imaginative design of the poem According to the Twickenham editors,

> Most important...was the position that Windsor
> and its Castle occupied as the centre of much
> in English history, and as the repository,
> second only to Westminster Abbey, for the
> bodies of those monarchs who made that history.
> With these associations Windsor Forest could
> serve to mirror England and its national life,
> recall its past, and perhaps suggest its future.

That is well said: but it might be added that
heraldry provided Pope with a symbolic repository
along these lines, and an idiom that could apply
equally to the forest and/or to Windsor itself.[7]

II

The key terms in *Windsor-Forest* relate to visual
phenomena, but they are not minutely descriptive.
Favourite words are *gold/golden* (nine occurrences);
silver (six) and *green* (eight). It should be noted
that Father Thames wears a 'Sea-Green Mantle'
(350), and therefore the hue evokes marine as
well as sylvan images. *Verdant* occurs three times,
and immediately suggests heraldic 'vert'. But
then Pope actually uses the technical terms on a
number of occasions: azure figures in the text
twice (as often as simple 'blue'), as does *sable*.[8]
Purple, suggesting 'purpure', is found four times,
usually in a transferred sense:

She saw her Sons with purple Deaths expire...
(322)
There purple *Vengeance* bath'd in Gore retires...
(417)

Evidently this is 'royal' purple, the traditional
garb of dignitaries. In this context it is interesting that *crimson* and *scarlet* appear once each,
that is as often as the basic term--which also
figures once as 'redden' (394). *Yellow* is used
twice. Otherwise, the sole colour words not already mentioned are metaphoric, e.g. *chalky*, *milky*,
sandy, *pearly*. From this it is apparent that Pope
is employing colours in a ceremonial, almost
ritualistic way.

There are other significant items in the poem's
vocabulary, suggesting the same non-descriptive
register. Especially prominent is the word *shade*,
most commonly in the plural. The noun has overtones of pastoral retreat (e.g. 135); of the
haunts of the muses (269, 279); and of decent obscurity (432). It is regularly opposed to concepts illustrated by *bright* (six occurrences) or

cognate terms, such as *shining* or *glittering*. Commonly these are metaphoric usages: as in 'the shining Page' (303) or 'Geraldine, bright Object of his Vow' (297). The opposition is most explicit at lines 235-40, where Pope embodies in the figure of the retired diplomat Trumbull a merging of the active and contemplative lives:

> Happy the Man whom this bright Court approves,
> His Sov'reign favours, and his Country loves;
> Happy next him who to these Shades retires,
> Whom Nature charms, and whom the Muse inspires,
> Whom humbler Joys of home-felt Quiet please,
> Successive Study, Exercise and Ease.[9]

The poetry has contrived to image two different orders of existence through terms that are basically visual, *bright* and *Shades*. This is the method of the poem in little. Pope makes optics serve moral and philosophic ends. And he is helped in this by the fact that much of his terminology had long-consecrated meanings of an emblematic nature.

It is not just the coloration which carries a heraldic tinge. In Pope's walk to the paradise garden at the outset, there is mention of 'a chequer'd Scene' (17). This recalls a strictly armorial term, 'checky', used to describe a chessboard pattern; and more generally it suggests the regular alternation of shades found in a heraldic device. The description which follows makes reference to 'Purple Dies', 'verdant Isles' and 'sable Waste': beyond this, the line, '... crown'd with tufted Trees and springing Corn' (27), has strong chivalric overtones.[10] 'Crown'd' appears later in the paragraph, which ends with 'rich Industry' as she 'sits smiling on the Plains' (41), like a beast 'sejant' on a heraldic ground. It may not be wholly irrelevant that the term 'Field' appears several times (e.g. 26, 56, 98). Apart from its literal applicability, this is the technical expression for the ground of a shield, upon which emblems are disposed. It is roughly equivalent to the 'canvas' in painting.

As we move through the poem, we encounter a
number of such instances. I do not say that Pope
was always conscious of the sense a given word
bears in heraldry; but in a large proportion of
these cases, the armorial meaning does supply an
additional thrust of thematic energy. Sometimes
the picture can scarcely be missed:

> Fair *Liberty*, *Britannia's* Goddess, rears
> Her cheerful Head, and leads the golden Years.
> (91-92)

One might possibly think here of a coin, itself a
species of emblematic art: but the verb *rears*
strongly suggests a quasiheraldic pose. Likewise
in the description of Father Thames:

> ...from his Oozy Bed
> Old Father *Thames* advanc'd his rev'rend Head.
> His Tresses dropt with Dews, and o'er the Stream
> His shining Horns diffus'd a golden Gleam:
> Grav'd on his Urn appear'd the Moon, that
>   guides
> His swelling Waters, and alternate Tydes;
> The figur'd Streams in Waves of Silver roll'd,
> And on their Banks *Augusta* rose in Gold.
> Around his Throne the Sea-born Brothers stood,
> Who swell with Tributary Urns his Flood. ...
> High in the midst, upon his Urn reclin'd,
> (His Sea-green Mantle waving with the Wind)
> The God appear'd; he turn'd his azure Eyes
> Where *Windsor*-Domes and pompous Turrets rise...
> (329-52)

I have omitted the description of the tributary
rivers, which includes words such as *silver*, *verdant*, *crown'd*, *stain'd* and so on. Basically, this
passage suggests a decorative frieze. The urn
may be 'graved', but 'figur'd' suggests the working on brocade, and 'rose in Gold' (336) in context means not just 'was erected' but 'stood out
as though embossed'. The lapidary quality of the
language adds to the sense that we are looking at
a piece of fine workmanship rather than a natural

landscape. ('Mantle', incidentally, might suggest 'mantling', the ornamental drapery or scroll-
work surrounding a coat of arms.) The colouring
scheme owes little to Jervas or 'Mr Alexander
Pope, Painter'. It is as conventional as the
blacks and reds of a pack of cards--another
branch of heraldic representation in which the
poet was showing unmistakable interest around
this time.[11]

Returning to an earlier point in the poem, we
come on the famous description of the pheasant's
death--something even the nineteenth century
(Elwin apart) could enjoy:[12]

> Ah! what avail his glossie, varying Dyes,
> His Purple Crest, and Scarlet-circled Eyes,
> The vivid Green his shining Plumes unfold;
> His painted Wings, and Breast that flames with
>   Gold?   (115-18)

It is unnecessary to draw attention here to the
'glossy' coat, the 'dyes', the 'painted' wings.
What may bear emphasis is the fact that other
terms are taken directly from the armorial lexicon. The crest is a device worn above a knight's
helmet, and by transference a motif appearing
over the shield in a bearing. Moreover, the word
Plumes is strongly redolent of chivalric lore. In
the passages immediately preceding, Pope has spoken of the spaniel 'couch'd close', an odd usage
unless one thinks of the common heraldic pose
'couchant'.[13] A metaphor drawn from war ends
with a reference to *'Britannia's* Standard' waving
high in the air (110)--such banners are of course
heraldic in origin, and in their true import.

There follows a section largely concerned with
the pursuit of the chase. Since hunting is an
activity overlaid with numerous historic (notably medieval) associations it is not surprising
that the idiom here is not so much classical--
for all the allusions to Diana and the *Metamorphoses*--as chivalric.[14] Pope employs a slightly
archaic diction, with *zone, charger, dart, quiver,
hart, buskin'd, steed* and similar poeticisms. As

sometimes in his Homer, the effect is to reduce
the direct physical impress of the scene, and to
replace it with a removed, almost Spenserian atmosphere. For our immediate purposes, the central point is that this post-classical world of
chivalry was specifically the birthplace of heraldry. At the end of the story of Lodona comes
a well-known passage:

> Oft in her glass the musing Shepherd spies
> The headlong Mountains and the downward Skies,
> The watry Landskip of the pendant Woods,
> And absent Trees that tremble in the Floods,
> In the clear azure Gleam the Flocks are seen,
> And floating Forests paint the Waves with
>   Green.   (211-16)

This beautiful evocation of landscape reflected
in water once more substitutes a transferred
image and a factitious green for the simple reality. Nature is mirrored at one remove.
    We may pass more quickly over incidental sug-
gestions in the lines that follow, e.g. the
'Wreaths' of Cooper's Hill (265)--this is another
specialised word used for part of a coat of arms.
Again, Pope calls on Granville to 'paint anew
the flow'ry Sylvan Scenes / To crown the Forests
with immortal Greens' (285-86); and finally

> To sing those Honours you deserve to wear,
> And add new Lustre to her Silver Star.
>   (289-90)

('Honour' is another technical term.) This leads
on to the celebration of the poet Surrey, and
once more the diction is that appropriate to
chivalric romance: *lance, lists, vow*. We then reach
the most explicit use of armorial matters found
in the text. It comes in the form of instructions to a heraldic artist:

> With *Edward's* Acts adorn the shining Page,
> Stretch his long Triumphs down thro' every
>   Age,

> Draw Monarchs chain'd, and *Cressi's* glorious
>   Field,
> The Lillies blazing on the Regal Shield.
> Then, from her Roofs when *Verrio's* Colours fall,
> And leave inanimate the naked Wall;
> Still in thy Song shou'd vanquish'd *France*
>   appear,
> And bleed for ever under *Britain's* Spear.
>   Let softer Strains Ill-fated *Henry* mourn,
> And Palms Eternal flourish round his Urn.
>   (303-12)

Here the language seems to be constantly strain-
ing away from the ostensible vehicle of the
metaphor (aural) to a visual image. This becomes unmistakable at lines 305-06, with the
verb *draw* and then a verse dense with heraldic
connotation--

> The Lillies blazing on the Regal Shield.

Now these of course are the fleurs de lis: it
may be noted that any regular patterning of such
a charge is called 'fleury' or 'flory' tincture
--compare Pope's *flow'ry* (343). The Twickenham
editors cite from *DNB* the comment that Edward III
'quartered the lilies of France with the leopards
of England'--surely a significant reminder.[15]
The 'glorious Field' is not only the site of the
battle of Crecy, but the illustrious heraldic
bearings made possible by the victories of
Edward. Nor should we forget that 'shield' is
also a technical term: or miss the overtones of
blazing, owing to its proximity to 'blazon', the
fundamental armorial act. Verrio's pictures
showed a figure in a mantle 'embroider'd with
Flower-de-luces', representing France. Pope has
put the emblems back on a shield, in their original functions as heraldic charges.
   Shortly after this juncture, the poem moves
into a rich mythopoeic section including the
catalogue of rivers already cited. The theme
then widens as Pope compares the Thames to other
great rivers of the world--as the stream widens

from its rural source to its ultimate passage into the ocean, so the poetry becomes more expansive and evocative. Phrases such as 'Tydes of
Gold' (358) bring with them a vivid, indeed exotic tinge; the vision of a new Augusta is ushered
in with burnished images, trumpets, horns, the
'Chrystal Tyde' (376). Bloodshed in warfare, a
reiterated theme, is associated as before with a
metallic surface and with artificial coloration:

> Let *Volga's* Banks with Iron Squadrons shine,
> And Groves of Lances glitter on the *Rhine,*
> Let barb'rous *Ganges* arm a servile Train;
> Be mine the Blessings of a Peaceful Reign.
> No more my Sons shall dye with *British* Blood
> Red *Iber's* Sands or *Ister's* foaming Flood...
> (363-68)

'Groves of Lances' is a beautifully sharp picture,
its paradoxical expression setting nature against
art with curt finality. We recall the groves
which, instead of 'glittering', 'look green in
Song' (8), and the stark contrast points up the
brittleness of military glory.[16] This was a
political innuendo, directed against Marlborough,
as Gilbert Wakefield almost redundantly insists.[17]
   Pope now apostrophises the trees in the forest, as 'hearts of oak' which will bear British
commerce to every corner of the earth. They will
carry Britain's thunder 'and her Cross display'--
the editors note that this refers to the cross of
St. George, and it might be added that 'cross' is
the technical as well as the popular term.[18]
Again the language is instinct with an opalescent,
almost lurid quality:

> For me the Balm shall bleed, and Amber flow,
> The Coral redden, and the Ruby glow,
> The pearly Shell its lucid Globe infold,
> And *Phoebus* warm the ripening Ore to Gold.
> (393-96)

Such tones are blatantly non-naturalistic; they
have the finish and gloss of sacramental objects.

In passing, an 'escallop' is one very common charge.

Immediately afterwards comes another splendid allegorical set-piece. Pope envisages a time when the peaceful world will see

> ...the freed *Indians* in their native Groves
> Reap their own Fruits, and woo their Sable
>   Loves,
> *Peru* once more a Race of Kings behold,
> And other *Mexico's* be roof'd with Gold.
> Exil'd by Thee from Earth to deepest Hell,
> In Brazen Bonds shall barb'rous *Discord* dwell...
> There purple *Vengeance* bath'd in Gore retires,
> Her Weapons blunted, and extinct her Fires...
>   (409-18)

Apart from *sable* and *purple*, it is worth observing the renewed association of blood with heraldic colouring. Pope then relates the theme of '*Albion's* Golden Days' (the metaphoric adjective having been filled out by much that has gone before) to his patron, Granville, now become Lord Lansdowne. Modestly, the poet allots to Granville the task of bringing 'the Scenes of opening Fate to Light', whilst his own 'humble Muse... / Paints the green Forests and the flow'ry Plains' --again 'fleury', suggesting a surface dotted with small flowers, is a not inappropriate mental connection. Then:

> Where Peace descending bids her Olives spring,
> And scatters Blessings from her Dove-like
>   Wing.   (429-30)

The scene is frozen, still, iconographic. The present participle, so characteristic of the grammar in *Windsor-Forest*, encourages us to look at the action as a ritual gesture rather than as a once-for-all event.

I do not claim that every possible armorial significance one could locate was in Pope's mind as he wrote. It is well-known that terms such as *painted* derive from an agreed attitude to po-

etic diction, with classical echoes prominent in
the whole connotative structure of the word. And
I have not mentioned a large number of expressions common in heraldry which chance to figure
in *Windsor-Forest*. That there is a heraldic meaning for *star* at line 231 can only be coincidental, although a star in some form constitutes a
part of every order of knighthood--notably in
'the Star and Garter', the order most closely associated with Windsor. And the word *Arms* itself
(374) clearly has no punning force, even if it
is juxtaposed with 'Birds and Beasts', those in-
variable features of the heraldic vocabulary.
And it would be fanciful to read a pun into line
396, though 'or' is of course the heraldic description of gold.[19] Nevertheless, when such
cases are dismissed from consideration, enough
remains. Whether or not Pope was aware of the
associations, they are consistently present. The
facts of language determine as much. Pope's concern with such matters as chivalry, warfare,
hunting, royalty, partly explain this presence.
But more important in the last analysis is his
emblematic method, and his attempt to portray the
landscape of Windsor and its environs in a non-
representational, hieratic fashion. The vision
partakes of a sort of historical stylisation.
And the texture of Pope's language is duly affected: it reflects a bright, tessellated, for-
malised world. Pope celebrates the Stuart line,
and its seat at Windsor, much as a coat of arms
dignifies a noble family. The only difference is
that the territorial claim, instead of being just
landed property, comes to include the English nation itself, as revived by the forthcoming peace.
Inevitably, Pope's idiom springs into quasiheraldic life.

III

Windsor-Forest is both a public act of celebration and a private compliment. On 10 January
1713 Pope wrote to his patron Granville in these
terms:

> I thank you for having given my poem of Wind-
> sor Forest its greatest ornament, that of
> bearing your name in the front of it. ... Yet
> my Lord, this honour has given me no more
> pride than your honours have given you. ... I
> am in the circumstance of an ordinary painter
> drawing Sir Godfrey Kneller, who by a few
> touches of his own could make the piece very
> valuable. I might then hope, that many years
> hence the world might read, in conjunction
> with your name, that of Your Lordship's, &c.[20]

Allowing for some dedicatory licence, this passage furnishes some valuable hints--one notices,
for instance, that the poem is to go down to
posterity 'bearing' Granville's name, as a kind
of badge of fame. However, I wish to concentrate
on the second sentence quoted. Sherburn's gloss
runs: 'Pope is honoured by his lordship's permission to dedicate *Windsor-Forest* to him. Lord
Lansdowne's honours (elevation to the peerage)
had come at the beginning of 1712, when the
twelve Tory peers were created.' Now of course
this is true, but it is not the whole story.
Pope's flattery goes a little deeper, as the o-
verall design of his poem required it to do.
   In the first place, Granville was Secretary
at War from 1710 to 1712, when the peace negotiations began. The successful culmination of the
war through the forthcoming treaty of Utrecht
therefore contributes to his greater glory. The
iteration of 'Eagle' and 'Dove', twice each in
four lines in the Lodona section (185-88), becomes significant in this light. Plainly such
birds have little place in the habitat of the
real forest. They are rather emblems of majesty
and peace--and described as such in the armorial
handbooks, because of their frequent appearance
as charges.[21] Pope is conveying by indirection
the paradoxical idea that 'the fierce Eagle' (or
hawk, we might say today) has conspired with the
'trembling Doves' to bring an honourable peace
into being. Now the episodes of the hunt, according to Earl R. Wasserman, 'constitute a com-

plete allegorical representation, the first in
historical and the last in mythic terms, of the
entire course of the War.'[22] Quite so: and the
fact that Granville could be given titular credit
for the coming of the peace integrates his role
within the main symbolic action of the poem.

Secondly, just before his accession to the
peerage, Granville had married Lady Mary Thynne,
who was by birth a member of the distinguished
Villiers family. This dynastic union could reasonably be described as an 'honour' accruing to
the bridegroom. That is the more so, in view of
the fact that the bride's own father, the Earl
of Jersey, had taken a very significant part in
the diplomatic negotiations leading up to the
peace. In the words of G. M. Trevelyan, 'The
responsibility for the basic principles of the
terms of Utrecht, and for the policy of an exclusive friendship with France, does not lie with
St. John in the first instance. It lies with
Jersey and with Harley who left him in charge of
the negotiations from August 1710 to April 1711.'
Trevelyan goes on to examine the oddity of per-
mitting 'a Jacobite nobleman not at the time a
Minister of the Crown' to handle so important a
matter.[23] But whatever Harley's motives, it is
easy to understand why Pope should see the additional connection as a further qualification for
Granville as peace-maker. It seems likely, then,
that Pope's reference to 'heav'nly *Myra* now'
(298) is more than a tactless recollection of
Granville's former mistresses. It is a delicate
compliment to the new Lady Lansdowne.

Thirdly, there is the major 'honour', the
barony conferred on Granville on 1 January 1712.
One significant factor here which previous commentators have missed is the revelation by Granville's biographer that he was *disappointed* with
the barony. His uncle, the Earl of Bath, had
died in May 1711 without a male heir. From early
1712 until March 1714 protracted litigation was
in progress to settle the succession. Granville
hoped to gain possession of the family estates,
if not the title itself. In the end, it was the

Earl's two surviving daughters who won their suit.
At the time of Pope's poem, however, the issue
was undecided. It was widely known that Granville
had aspirations to the earldom. In May 1711 he
had written to Harley in this spirit; and according to his biographer, he 'hoped to the last'
that his peerage when it came would be the Bath
title.[24] This gave a new richness of implication
to lines 289- 90:

>   To sing those Honours you deserve to wear,
>   And add new Lustre to her Silver *Star*.

The Twickenham editors rightly point out that
Granville never did achieve the Garter.[25] However, as an Earl he would have been much closer
to a stall at Windsor; and his disputed 'Honours'
would have been settled. It is worth adding that
Granville did not cease to chase titles. In 1729
he was granted a whole clutch of Jacobite peer-
ages: Vicount Bevel, Baron Lansdowne (his real
title), Marquis Monk and Fitzhemon, Earl of Bath.
There is a proleptic accuracy in Pope's line, even
though by a harsh irony it was only in the fantasy kingdom of James III that Granville was to
attain his 'Honours'.
  When he took his authentic peerage, Granville
seemingly adopted the arms of Granville, Earls of
Bath--with what degree of heraldic impropriety, I
do not know. The principal motif of their shield
was a device in gold of three 'rests', or clarions. Heraldic dictionaries define this charge as
'a shrill trumpet'.[26] In the text of *Windsor-
Forest*, 'the shrill Horn' is associated with the
peaceful hunt (96); and again, critically:

>   The shady Empire shall retain no Trace
>   Of War or Blood, but in the Sylvan Chace,
>   The Trumpets sleep, while cheerful Horns are
>   blown ...   (371-73)

Immediately preceding this, there is a reference
to 'the bearded Grain', recalling the earlier
mention of '*Ceres*' Gifts' (39). The family crest

was a garb vert: that is, a wheatsheaf depicted in green. Here we have two important threads in the texture of the poem. The brassy timbre of much of the language associated with active pursuits (war, hunting, etc.) is expressed by the three clarions, or. Against this are set the subdued tones of creative and contemplative living (agriculture, poetry, etc.), represented by a garb vert. It can be proved neither that Pope knew of such matters nor that he did not. It is certain that these heraldic notions were available to him and that they come to the aid of his symbolism.[27]

Apart from the rhetorical interest of this material, I believe that it does reinforce the interpretation of *Windsor-Forest* as a Jacobite poem, 'hardly short of treasonable' in much of its drift.[28] This is not just because its recipient, Granville, was to reveal himself in time as an open adherent of the Pretender. It is rather because Pope's metaphoric heraldry opens out to disclose a bold claim for the Stuart cause. We noted earlier the reference to '*Britannia's* Standard' (110). The great authority Edmundson supplies this definition of *standard*: 'a martial ensign, painted with the whole achievements of him who has the right to display them in the field'. An *achievement* is the full armorial design, including shield, crest, scroll, supporters and wreath. Pope, I am contending, made a sort of heraldic eirenicon; a peaceful ensign, painted with Stuart deeds and confirming their entitlement to their inheritance--Windsor, and by transference England. When he wrote to Caryll of 'endeavouring to raise up round about me a painted scene of woods and forests in verdure and beauty, trees springing, fields flowering, Nature laughing.' he emphasised the pictorial rather than the political.[29] Yet, as this article should indicate, the 'verdure and beauty' of the scene are far more than decorative. The sheen which Pope puts on nature sanctifies a divine dispensation and a moral order, closely identified with the existing royal family. Heraldry, like all subjects with a genealogical basis, makes for an innate conservatism.

I have left until last one striking item of
evidence. It concerns some famous lines already
quoted:

> Ah! what avail his glossie, varying Dyes,
> His Purple Crest, and Scarlet-circled Eyes,
> The vivid Green his shining Plumes unfold;
> His painted Wings, and Breast that flames with
>   Gold?   (115-18)

And now this entry for the pheasant in a heraldic compendium then current, Randle Home's *The
Academy of Armory, or, the Storehouse of Armory and Blazon*
(1688):

> A red or scarlet ... compasses the eye; the
> fore part of the head is black, showing with
> a kind of purple gloss; the crown of the head,
> and upper part of the neck round about, is
> dark green, shining like Silk and ... sheweth
> very changeable ... next to the purple is a
> most splendid gold colour ... the Wings are
> of an ash-colour ... spotted all over with
> white spots ...[30]

Doubtless, there is only a limited range of terms
one can use to describe a pheasant. Nevertheless,
it is surely interesting that Pope should echo th
the *Academy* in using the precise words *scarlet,
purple, gloss(ie)* and *shining*, besides a number of
synonyms (*varying/changeable: painted/spotted*). It may
be that Pope never set eyes on this account--
though it is quite possible he did. He may even
not have opened a single work on heraldry and
allied matters--though that seems unlikely. The
crucial thing is that he observably did fall back
on the long-consecrated vocabulary of armorial
description.[31] The 'symbolic eternities' in
Windsor-Forest are not those of landscape-paint-
ing:[32] they lie within the metaphor of heraldry
which Pope, knowingly or unknowingly, adopted.[33]

POPE'S BELINDA, THE GENERAL EMPORIE OF THE
WORLD, AND THE WONDROUS WORM

Louis A. Landa

   Pope's heroine in *The Rape of the Lock* has deservedly been the object of extensive attention
from the critics. From John Dennis in 1714 to
the present, no small part of the commentary on
the poem has been concerned with the character of
Belinda. To Dennis, unlike certain more recent
commentators, she was no goddess. As Edward
Hooker remarked, Dennis by temperament and
nature was incapable of understanding or enjoying "the exquisite trifling of the *Rape*."[1] He
was similarly incapable of appreciating Belinda's charm. Perhaps no one has been so
severe in judgment of this beguiling young
woman, who becomes for him a "Ramp and a Tom-
rigg," an *"artificial dawbing Jilt,"* an "errant
Suburbian," and, among other things, a "Lady of
the Lake," a fine flow of slangy denunciation
which we can understand without recourse to
precise definition.[2] In our day Belinda has her
detractors but in more benign terms, ranging
from Hugo Reichard, who maintains that she is a

This essay first appeared in *South Atlantic Quarterly* 70 (1971), 215-35. Copyright 1971
by Duke University Press.

coquette, to Aubrey Williams, who delicately
suggests that she is a hypocrite. For Williams,
too, Belinda undergoes "a kind of 'fall' in
the poem; her 'perfection' is shattered, and she
does lose her 'chastity,' in so far as chastity
can be understood, however teasingly, as a
condition of the spirit." And then there is
the well-known essay by Cleanth Brooks, who
is as sensible of the sexual aspects as Dennis
but with a considerable difference. Fully
aware of the subtleties and ambiguities of the
poem, Brooks finds that Belinda is engaged
in a "sexual war" with the Baron under recognizable social conventions, an encounter, however, that in no respect reduces her charm.
Finally, we may mention the apotheosis of Belinda by Rebecca Parkin, who maintains that
she is "a kind of sun goddess" with an Olympian
pedigree.[3]
     But there is another aspect of Belinda and
of the poem which, so far as I am aware, has
received little or no attention: Belinda as
(if I may be allowed recourse to Shakesperian
phraseology) the glass of fashion, Belinda
who takes some coloration from her economic
milieu. Although Pope has been very sparing
in depicting her attire, who can read what he
does say, both of her and the social ambiance,
without visualizing her as "the observed of all
observers," a fashionably attired young woman
whose dress matches her charm in taste and
costliness? We may begin most profitably
with the cosmetic rites, Belinda at the toilet
table, where "awful Beauty puts on all its
Arms."

> The busy *Sylphs* surround their darling Care;
> These set the Head, and those divide the
>   Hair,
> Some fold the Sleeve, while others plait the
>   Gown;
> And *Betty's* prais'd for Labours not her own.[4]
>   (i.145-48)

As the cosmetic rites proceed, we should not
miss one useful fact: as the sylphs enhance
Belinda's beauty by means of gems, combs,
perfume, patches, and belladonna, they also
play a role in her attire. In this brief and
shining vignette of luxury and indulgence, as
in earlier lines, Pope has set Belinda down
in a world of glitter and fine feathers; his
suggestiveness is such that we easily form an
impression not only of Belinda's physical
beauty but as well of her stylishness. A fine
lady (in the eighteenth-century sense of the
phrase) in fine clothes, she undoubtedly is.
If this is granted, I should like to examine
(at the risk of pretentiousness) one or two
aspects of the poem which have economic implications and which relate interestingly to
the economic milieu from which it emerged,
implications which a twentieth-century reader
may conceivably miss but which Pope's contemporaries, sensitive to mercantilist doctrines,
may have perceived. As I relate Belinda to
certain economic ideas of the times, I am, in
effect, presenting a gloss on some lines in
the poem.

The lines (i, 121-48) concerned with Belinda
at the toilette reflect an ideal which possessed the minds of many English economic writers and others in the seventeenth and eighteenth
centuries, an ideal which at the same time
generated apprehension in the minds of moralists.
Pope writes: "Unnumber'd Treasures ope at once,
and here / The various Off'rings of the World
appear." Belinda is decked "with the glitt'ring
Spoil," gems from India, perfumes from Arabia,
combs of tortoise and ivory from Africa—or,
as Pope says in Canto v, "all that Land and
Sea afford" (v.11). The mere mention of these
objects of the toilette would have provoked a
pleasing mercantile image in the minds of many
contemporary readers: they testify to the vast
expansion of England's trade in the seventeenth
century and to the search for exotic commodities
in remote lands. Belinda and her kind were the

wealthy consumers whose demands gave an impetus
to the merchants trading in all parts of the
known world. They are referred to briefly by
John Gay in his poem *Rural Sports* (1713): "So
the gay lady with expensive care / Borrows the
pride of land, of sea, and air" (11.135-36).
But for sheer pleasure in the spectacle of the
lady of fashion, the Belindas of the day, I have
found nothing to surpass Addison's remarks in
Spectator, No. 69 (19 May 1711). Here she becomes an illustration of England's greatness as
a trading nation and testimony to the universality of its commerce. Addison writes:

The single Dress of a Woman of Quality is often
the Product of an hundred Climates. The Muff
and the Fan come together from the different
Ends of the Earth. The Scarf is sent from the
Torrid Zone, and the Tippet from beneath the
Pole. The Brocade Petticoat rises out of the
Mines of *Peru*, and the Diamond Necklace out of
the Bowels of *Indostan*.

Earlier, in *Tatler*, No. 116 (5 Jan. 1709-10),
Addison touched on the same theme, again visualizing a world explored and exploited for the
purpose of adorning womankind. Mr. Bickerstaff
tells us that he considers

woman as a beautiful romantic animal, that may
be adorned with furs and feathers, pearls and
diamonds, ores and silks. The lynx shall cast
its skin at her feet to make her a tippet;
the peacock, parrot, and swan shall *pay
contributions* to her muff; the sea shall be
searched for shells, and the rocks for gems;
and every part of nature furnish out its share
towards the embellishment of a creature that is
the most consummate work of it.

   Addison's purpose in *Spectator*, No. 69, is
primarily to eulogize the merchant, particularly
Sir Andrew Freeport and others engaged in
foreign trade, whose activities have organized

the commercial world in such a fashion that an
Englishman may have everything at his doorstep,
no matter how remote its origin:

Traffick [i.e., trade] gives us a great Variety
of what is Useful, and at the same time supplies
us with every thing that is Convenient and
Ornamental. Nor is it the least part of this
our Happiness, that whilst we enjoy the remotest
Products of the North and South, we are free
from those Extremities of Weather which give
them Birth; That our Eyes are refreshed with
the green Fields of *Britain*, at the same time
that our Palates are feasted with Fruits that
rise between the Tropicks.

The theme is not a new one. It appears often
in the poetry and prose of the seventeenth
century and earlier, particularly in economic
tracts stressing foreign trade or calling
attention to the importance of the sea, provid-
entially granted to England for her special
exploitation, In *A Panegyrick to my Lord Protector*
(1655), Edmund Waller illustrates in a few
lines how the theme was assimilated into verse:

> So what our earth, and what our heav'n denies,
> Our ever-constant friend, the sea, supplies.
>
> The taste of hot Arabia's spice we know,
> Free from the scorching sun, that makes it
>   grow:
> Without the worm, in Persian silks we shine;
> And without planting, drink of ev'ry wine.[5]

Now this paean to the sea and its enrichment of
English life is not merely materialistic. It
reflects a romantic vision, a larger conception
widely prevalent in the century and later. We
may turn once again to Addison for its expression. Mr. Spectator writes:

Our Ships are laden with the Harvest of every
Climate: Our Tables are stored with Spices, and

Oils, and Wines: Our Rooms are filled with
Pyramids of *China*, and adorned with the Workman-
ship of *Japan*: Our Morning's-Draught comes to us
from the remotest Corners of the Earth: We
repair our Bodies by the Drugs of *America*, and
repose our selves under *Indian* Canopies. My
Friend Sir Andrew calls the Vineyards of
France our Gardens; the Spice-Islands our Hot-
Beds; the *Persians* our Silk-Weavers, and the
Chinese our Potters.[6]

Thus it is that Mr. Spectator confesses to a
secret satisfaction and vanity that the merchants of the Royal Exchange are making London
"a kind of *Emporium* for the whole Earth."

   In spirit and substance these words are very
much akin to those in *Windsor Forest* (1713), where
Pope presents a vision of "golden days" for
Albion once the Peace of Utrecht is approved.
It is a shining vision uttered by Father
Thames, who prophesies a new age of amity,
wealth, and greatness fostered by British
commerce, an enriching and unifying force:
"Unbounded Thames shall flow for all mankind"
(1.398):

   Thy Trees, fair *Windsor* now shall leave their
      Woods,
   And half thy Forests rush into my Floods,
   Bear *Britain's* Thunder, and her Cross display,
   To the bright Regions of the rising Day;
   Tempt Icy Seas, where scarce the Waters roll,
   Where clearer Flames glow round the frozen
      Pole;
   Or under Southern Skies exalt their Sails,
   Led by new Stars, and borne by spicy Gales!
   For me the Balm shall bleed, and Amber flow,
   The Coral redden, and the Ruby glow,
   The Pearly Shell its lucid Globe infold,
   And *Phoebus* warm the ripening Ore to Gold.
      (11.385-396)

In these lines and others, mingled with the

millennial and saturnian strains, Pope too shows
the influence of the prevalent vision of England
as a world emporium, the center of a universal
trade carried on by "universal merchants" (in
eighteenth-century phraseology), such as Sir
Andrew Freeport, of whom Mr. Spectator says,
"there is not a Point in the Compass but blows
home a Ship in which he is an Owner" (No. 2,
2 March 1711). Britain was "nature's annointed
empress of the deep." So Edward Young expresses
it, in his *Reflections on the Publick Situation of
this Kingdom*(1745),[7] echoing a view which had
firm roots in the preceding century, stated
typically by James Whiston, an obscure economic
writer, in 1696: "God and Nature [have] designed
this *Island* for the Grand *Market* of the Universe."
England, Whiston adds, has all the potentialities for becoming "the General Emporie of the
World."[8] At the risk of tedium I cite one
more poetical expression of this theme because
it has a special relevance to Pope. When he
was completing *Windsor Forest* in November 1712,
he was disturbed to find that some of his lines
were similar to those in Thomas Tickell's *On the
Prospect of Peace*, recently published. The lines
from Tickell's poem are relevant to my purpose,
reflecting, as they do, the conception of
England as "the General *Emporie* of the World" and
a land where its citizens could have "the
remotest Products of the North and South" while
free from "the Extremities of Weather which
give them Birth" (*Spectator*, No. 69). Tickell
writes:

> Fearless the merchant now pursues his gain,
> And roams securely o'er the boundless main.
> Now o'er his head the polar bear he spies,
> And freezing spangles of the Lapland skies;
> Now swells his canvass to the sultry line,
> With glitt'ring spoil where Indian grottoes
>   shine.
> Where fumes of incense glad the southern
>   seas,
> And wafted citron scents the balmy breeze.[9]

Now it may be true, as Cecil A. Moore has
maintained, that in these poems we have instances of Whig panegyric;[10] but it is simply
not accurate to hold that others, men of Tory
persuasion, did not praise commerce or engage
in it. In Tickell's poem, in *Spectator*, No. 69,
in other works praising the glories of maritime
commerce, something more than a partisan or
factional view emerged. As I have indicated,
what we do in fact have is a delectable vision
of England's greatness and glory, a vision of
splendor and magnificence shared by Englishmen
of all persuasions. It was nourished by
England's expanding trade and wealth; and it was
often expressed in rapturous language, with
examples and parallels drawn from antiquity and
the Bible. The symbols of mercantile greatness
in the past--the Phoenicians and the Carthagin-
ians, Ophir and Tarshish, Solomon and ivory and
apes and peacocks--biblical passages from
Ezekiel, Revelation, and Kings, in which
commerce and merchants are celebrated, these
are mentioned again and again in the economic
writings of the seventeenth and eighteenth
centuries. But not only there. In the homiletic literature as well England is praised with
extraordinary frequency as "the Mart of Nations"
and "the great Empory of the World." London's
resemblance to the ancient city of Tyre is a
constant refrain. Tyre, too, had achieved its
greatness and magnificence by a universal trade,
Tyre "whose merchants are princes, whose
traffickers are the honorable of the earth"
(Isaiah 23:8, a text often used to demonstrate
the antiquity and dignity of trade). Consider,
as typical, these words from a sermon by a
well-known divine, published in 1698:

That Antient flourishing City seated in the
Phoenician Sea was deservedly reckon'd the
Greatest Mart and Empory of that part of the
Universe: Thither was brought the Riches of
Asia, Europe, and *Africa*. In this also Britain
resembles her, and was justly stiled by

Charles the Great the Store-House and Granary of
the Western World. The Great City of this our
Isle may be call'd the Mart of Nations, as
Tyre is, Isai.xxiii.3....[11]

   London as Tyre--one more instance must
suffice, a sermon published in the year of Pope's
death, a characteristic one but of special
interest because it displays in homiletic
literature what may be called the mercantile
zest or hunger, the feeling for material
objects exemplified in Defoe when he writes
"the trading style." Alexander Catcott's
sermon, *The Antiquity and Honourableness of the
Practice of Merchandize* (1744), was preached before
the Worshipful Society of Merchants of the
City of Bristol, who doubtless liked what they
heard. It presents Tyre "as a queen among the
nations," raised to that eminence by its
commerce. Tyre

furnished all the western parts [of the world]
with the commodities of *Arabia, Africa, Persia,* and
India....Its fleets brought into *Tyre* all the
useful and rare commodities of the then known
world...silver, iron, tin, lead, brass, slaves,
horses, mules, ivory, ebony, emeralds, purple,
embroidery, fine linen, coral, wheat, pannag
[balsam], honey, oil, balm, wine, white wool,
bright iron [steel], cassia, calamus, precious
cloaths, lambs, rams, goats, spices, precious
stones, gold, blue cloaths and rich apparel....

Hence it became the mother of navigation, the
center of trade, and the "common mart of all the
nations of the universe."[12] It was not necessary for Catcott to draw the parallel between
Tyre and London: the theme had long been a
hackneyed one. And none of his auditors would
have missed the point: it was London which had
become, in biblical phrase, the "crowning city,"
and it was England which now sat "as a queen
among the nations."

I return now to the relevant lines depicting
Belinda and her maid at the toilette:

> Unnumber'd Treasures ope at once, and here
> The various Off'rings of the World appear;
> From each she nicely culls with curious Toil,
> And decks the Goddess with the glitt'ring
>   Spoil.
> This Casket *India's* glowing Gems unlocks,
> And all *Arabia* breathes from yonder Box.
> The Tortoise here and Elephant unite,
> Transform'd to *Combs*,   the speckled and the
>   white.
>   (i. 129-136)

In the background of these lines, this brief
vignette of luxury, is the conception of England
as "the great Empory of the World." If, as I
believe, this idea was deeply implanted in the
consciousness of Pope and his contempories, a
literate reader of the poem would have found a
dimension in the passage not immediately evident to a reader in the twentieth century. By
subtle insinuation Belinda's gems from India,
her perfume from Arabia, and her ivory from
Africa would generate in a contemporary reader
responses appealing to the geographical imagination and related to the romantic image of an
England made magnificent by maritime activity.
I would certainly hesitate to suggest that Pope
has deliberately made Belinda a kind of
economic symbol, but she and the objects of the
toilette may well have had symbolic overtones.
She, and others like her, were the beginning
and end, the stimulus to "the adventurous
merchant" whose ships roamed "securely o'er the
boundless main" from Lapland to "the sultry
line"; and they were the final recipients of
the exotic products, "the glitt'ring Spoil"
from Indian grottoes, from the frozen north and
the southern seas.

> For them the Gold is dug on Guinea's Coast,
> And sparkling Gems the farthest Indies boast,

For them Arabia breathes its spicy Gale,
And fearless Seamen kill the Greenland Whale.
For them the Murex yields its purple Dye,
And orient Pearls in sea-bred Oisters lye;
For them, in clouded Shell, the Tortoise
    shines,
And huge *Behemoth* his vast Trunk resigns;
For them, in various Plumes, the Birds are
    gay,
And *Sables* bleed, the savage Hunter's Prey!
For them the *Merchant*, wide to ev'ry Gale,
Trusts all his Hopes and stretches ev'ry Sail,
For them, O'er all the World, he dares to
    roam,
And safe conveys its gather'd Riches home.[13]

In this mercantile flight or progress we
witness the poetic imagination playing with the
theme I have been discussing; and as the theme
found expression in Pope's day and earlier, it
embodied an element of awe and wonder at the
spectacle of a world, infinitely complex,
organized to enhance the beauty of a Belinda,
of ships roaming the world:

Now visit Russia's Snows and Guinea's Soil.
Hence in Hesperia's Silks the Britons shine,
Wear India's Gems and drink Burgundia's
    Wine.[14]

In the passage depicting Belinda at the toilette
we see that Pope has assimilated this theme, so
vibrant and meaningful in his time. Both the
diction and the substance of the relevant lines
are traditional; they are part and parcel of a
well-developed convention in economic writings
and in literature.

At this point we must give our attention to
Belinda's petticoat, whose importance is
portentously announced by her guardian sylph:

To Fifty chosen *Slyphs*, of special Note,
We trust the'important Charge, the *Petticoat*:

> Oft have we known that sev'nfold Fence to
>   fail,
> Tho' stiff with Hoops, and arm'd with Ribs
>   of Whale. (ii,117-22)

If Ariel considers this garment so important,
we have some warrant for taking it seriously,
with a different intention, of course. I am
still concerned to gloss certain lines in the
poem in terms of prevalent economic thought
and to indicate reverberations or layers of
meaning likely in contemporary responses to the
poem, particularly in an atmosphere suffused by
mercantilist doctrine. The hoop petticoat is
too much to cope with fully in the compass of
this essay. Any student of eighteenth-century
literature will be aware of the attention it
received for half a century or more, in the
essay, in poetry, and in the drama. It was
celebrated facetiously by Mr. Bickerstaff,
by Mr. Spectator, by Henry Fielding, and by
such minor authors as John Durant Breval, in
The Art of Dress (1717) and Francis Chute, *The
Petticoat: An Heroi-Comical Poem* (1716). In the year
that Pope was writing *The Rape of the Lock* there
appeared anonymously a poem titled *The Farthingale
Reviv'd...A Panegyric on...the Invention of the Hoop
Petticoat* (1711).[15] Had Pope been more consider-
ate of a later generation, he would have been
more detailed in describing Belinda's petticoat.
As it is, I cannot establish beyond all doubt
the kind she wore. She had a choice of the
dome-shaped or the oval hoop (the "orbicular,"
as it was called in *Guardian*, No. 114,22 July
1713). The oblong hoop was probably too late
for Belinda; but we are on somewhat safer
ground with the inner petticoats, which served
as structural supports for the outer. These
might be made of silk or satin, paduasoy or
chintz, gingham or mohair, or any of various
Indian silks. It is well to keep in mind that
the gown consisted of a bodice and skirt joined
together, with the skirt open in front to reveal
the petticoat, which was not thought of as an

undergarment but as an essential part of the
dress.[16] Thus petticoats were often of the
richest material. We may reasonably assume, I
think, that Belinda's petticoat was of the most
fashionable and costly kind, of silk in some
form, as brocade (perhaps her "new Brocade"
mentioned in Canto II, l. 107), or damask, or
tabby, or lutestring, or satin. As an
indication of the expensiveness of such a garment, we have recourse to Richard Steele's list
of "absolute Necessaries for a fine Lady."
Among the objects are "A Mantua and Petticoat of
French Brocade, 26 Yards, at three pounds *per*
Yard" (Ь 78), and less expensive but still
costly, " A *French* or *Italian* Silk quilted
Petticoat, one Yard and a quarter deep, and six
Yards wide" (Ь 10).[17]

Now here we may view Belinda in a climate of
economic opinion markedly different from the
romantic one discussed earlier, from a more
austere mercantilist atmosphere less tolerant
of her indulgences. From this vantage the
lady of fashion was frequently the object of
criticism, a danger to the national economy.
In the mercantile philosophy perhaps the most
cogent doctrine was that a nation should have a
favorable balance of trade. As a corollary,
national frugality was deemed a virtue. Any
action that caused bullion to flow out of the
country was held to be harmful, particularly
the importation of luxuries. Though there were
arguments to the contrary from the apologists
of the great trading companies, many of the more
stringent economic writers complained often of
the fashionable lady who insisted on dressing
herself in calicoes, linens, velvets, laces,
damasks, brocades, and satins imported from
around the world, all at the expense of England's
great staple, wool:

Our own manufacks out of fashion,
No country of wool was ever so dull:
'Tis a test of the brains of the nation
To neglect their own works,

Employ pagans and Turks,
And let foreign trumpery o'er spread 'em.[18]

Perhaps the most objectionable of all the
"foreign trumpery" was silk, an economic evil
of the first order because of the large amount
imported, both raw and wrought, and because
imported silk hindered the endeavors to establish a flourishing domestic silk industry.
Furthermore, it was particularly galling to many
economic writers that England should depend so
heavily on its great trade rival, France, for
silk, though silk was also imported from Italy,
India, and Persia, even from Holland and
elsewhere. Belinda, I suggest, is an economic
sinner (in mercantilist terms), and in the
light of the French trade unusually so. When
Samuel Fortrey, addressing himself to Charles
II in 1663, examined England's trade with France
he found that England

transported out of *France* into *England*, great
quantities of velvets plain and wrought,
sattins plain and wrought, cloth of gold and
silver, Armoysins and other merchandise of
silk...made at *Lions*,and...valued to be yearly
worth one hundred and fifty thousand pounds.
    In silk, stuffs, taffeties, poudesoys,
armoysins, clothes of gold and silver, tabbies,
plain and wrought, silk-ribbands and other such
like stuffs as are made at *Tours*,valued to be
worth above three hundred thousand pounds a
year.[19]

We may pass over the cost to England of such
French products as buttons of silk, cabinets,
watches, perfumes, gloves, feathers, fans,
hoods, gilt looking-glasses, bracelets, and
"such like mercery," all listed by Fortrey and
some doubtless relevant to Belinda. But one
of his categories of imports must be mentioned:
"In pins, needles, box-combs, tortoise-shell
combs, and such like, [imported] for about
twenty thousand pounds a year."[20] These, we

recall, are among the objects on Belinda's
toilet-table. Little wonder that Fortrey
complains that "foreign commodities are grown
into so great esteem amongst us, as we wholly
undervalue and neglect the use of our own,
whereby that great expence of treasure, that
is yearly wasted...redounds chiefly to the
profit of strangers, and to the ruine of his
Majesties Subjects."[21]

Many economic tracts in the seventeenth and
eighteenth centuries echoed Fortrey's complaint,[22] and his tract itself was reprinted
in 1673, 1713, and 1714. One of the more
illuminating treatises, doubtfully assigned
to Sir William Petyt, was entitled
Britannia Languens, or A Discourse of Trade (1680).
It was much concerned with the way in which
the English merchant and shopkeeper might
"avoid Trading in Foreign Consumptive Goods."
The author, like Fortrey, reveals a special
bitterness over England's excessive importation
of silk and the women who are responsible:

The *English* formerly wore or used little Silk
in City or Countrey, only Persons of Quality
pretended to it; but as our National Gaudery
hath increased, it grew more and more into Mode;
and is now become the common Wear...and our
Women, who generally govern in this Case, must
have *Foreign Silks;* for these have got the Name
...Of the same humour are their Gallants, and
such as they can influence....Our ordinary
People, especially the Female, will be in Silk,
more or less, if they can....Whence hath followed a vastly *greater Importation, and home-Consumption
of the dear Silk-Manufactures* from *Venice, Florence,
Genoa, France,* and *Persia,* and of late from *Holland.*
This our Affectation and Use of foreign Silks
having apparently much increased...must produce a great Odds in the Ballance, and besides
hath much contracted the *home-vent* of our
Woollen Stuffs and *Cloths,* and *Beggered our own Silk-
Weavers.* [23]

It seems clear that we have, from the vantage of
certain economic writers of the period, not
merely Italianate and Frenchified men but
Italianate and Frenchified women as well.
Belinda's "new brocade" and her petticoat, and
of course the objects on the toilet table, must
be suspect. Thus Belinda and the ladies of
fashion would appear to have some relationship
to the contemporary controversy over the im-
porting of silk--and to the many discussions
concerning the development of a domestic silk
industry.

    To consider Belinda in relation to the silk-
worm has its risible aspects, I am the first to
agree. "'Twere to consider too curiously to
consider so," as Horatio said to Hamlet in a
quite different context. But then we must
recall Hamlet's reply: "No, faith, not a jot."
At least we may recognize that the neoclassical
bee has a companion in the neoclassical silkworm. The "apotheosis" of the silkworm in
economic and scientific writings of the seventeenth and eighteenth centuries occasionally
found its way into literature. One can take as
a point of departure a writer greatly admired
in England, Du Bartas, whose *Divine Weeks* (1578)
was much translated--and in which the silkworm
was referred to as "this wond'rous Worm":

    Which soon transforms the fresh and tender
        leaves
    Of Thisbe's pale tree, to those tender
        sleaves
    (On oral clues) of soft, smooth silken flax,
    Which more for us, than for her self she
        makes.
    O precious Fleece!

This was quoted by Pope's contemporary, Henry
Barham, a fellow of the Royal Society, in his
Essay upon the Silk-Worm (1719).[24] But Barham
thought that Du Bartas had underestimated this
"Miracle in nature": "Had *Du Bartas* fully known
all the virtues and rare use of this incompar-

able Creature, which is even a Miracle in
nature, he would have enlarged his poem in a
more ample manner in the praise of it, to the
great honour of the Creator, *Cui Gloria. Amen.*"[25]
It may be that Du Bartas prompted such effusions
in verse as *The Silkewormes and Their Flies: Lively
described in Verse by T.M., a Countrie Farmer and an
Apprentice in Physicke. For the Great Benefit and
Enriching of England* (1599). When Nicholas Geffe
published *The Perfect Use of Silk-Wormes and their
Benefit* in 1607, it was prefaced by laudatory
verses from three poets, including Michael
Drayton. Geffe, who had been attempting for
seven years to persuade his countrymen to develop a domestic silk industry, pleaded for the
planting of mulberry trees, the food supply
of the silkworm. This, he asserted, is "the
readiest and assuredest way...to reare up,
nourish, & feed Silk-worms, ye most admirable
and beautifullest cloathing creatures of this
world."[26] Drayton compared Geffe to Columbus,
who once offered to England the wealth now
possessed by Spain. In the silkworm Geffe
offers England comparable riches:

> So may thy Silk-wormes happily increase
>   From sea to sea to propagate their seed,
> That plant still, nourish'd by our glorious
>   peace,
>   Whose leafe alone, the labouring Worme
>   doth feed.
> And may thy fame perpetually advance
>   Rich when by thee, thy country shall be
>   made,
> Naples, Granada, Portugale, and France,
>   All to sit idle, wondring at our trade.[27]

The prefatory verses by George Carr are similarly eulogistic:

> The silken fleece to England thou hath
>   brought,
>   There to endure till Doomesday cut her
>   clue,

And when thy bones, the wormes have eate to
   naught,
   Yet shall the wormes thy fame still
      fresh renue,
And thy name, thy house, thy stocke, thy
   line,
Be highly honored by this great designe.[28]

From Geffe, early in the seventeenth century,
to Pope's day and beyond, the silkworm was
anatomized, eulogized, and "moralized." In his
Antidote Against Atheism (1653), Henry More included it among those animals useful "as an Argument of Divine Providence," and praised it also
as very useful to man: it seems to have "come
into the world for no other purpose, than to
furnish man with more costly cloathing, and to
spin away her very entrails to make him fine
without."[29] Robert Hooke, the distinguished
member of the Royal Society, examined this
"miracle in nature" in *Micrographia*, 1665 (Obs.
XLI, Sch. XXV); and his contemporary Edward
Digges contributed a paper in the same year to
the *Philosophical Transactions*, in which he set
down his "Observations" of the Silkworm
(*Abridgement*, i.12). Both of these works came a
decade after Waller had included the silkworm
in his poem, quoted above, to the Lord Protector.
Most of the literature on the subject is, as
one would expect, primarily practical, the
intention being to stimulate the development
of an English silk industry, in hopes of un-
burdening the country from the onerous expense
of imported silk. As it was sometimes stated,
England should domesticate or naturalize the
silkworm and free itself of dependence on
foreign worms. To those who thought that the
mulberry tree would not flourish in England,
Virginia and the American colonies offered
hope. Edward Williams, in *Virgo Triumphans: Or
Virginia Richly and Truly Valued* (1650), directed
his attention to this point, arguing that
England should develop Virginia as "a reservoir
of riches," since the mulberry tree flourishes

abundantly there. But even in those tracts
where the economic motive is primary, as in
Williams, the authors dwelt on the wonders of
the insect, "this Mystery of the Silkworme":

there is nothing in the world more proper than
this curious atome of Nature, the Silkworme: to
see this untaught Artist spin out his transparent bowels, labour such a monument out of his
owne intralls, as may be the shame, blush of
Artists, such that Robe that Solomon in all
his Glory might confess the meanness of his
Apparell.[30]

Williams is lost in admiration of nature, "who
hath abbreviated all the Volumes of her other
Miracles into this her little, but exact
Epitome, like that Artist who contracted the
whole body of Iliads and Odysses into a Nutshell" (p.34). He, too, considers the silkworm evidence of the hand of the deity in the
creation.
      For a hundred years at least this "curious
atome of nature" engaged the attention of
Englishmen; and we may bring it close to Pope
by glancing at Aaron Hill, poet, dramatist, and
essayist, who over a period of years was inter-
mittently Pope's friend and enemy. As the
latter he found a place in both *Peri Bathous* and
The Dunciad. Although Hill's "Essay on the
Silkworm" (1717) is later than *The Rape of the
Lock*, it is useful for establishing the climate
of economic opinion (I am not concerned with
sources) which may have influenced the responses
to the poem in Pope's day. Hill's essay reveals
the continuity of views from the preceding
century. Like those before him, he maintains
that the mulberry tree and the silkworm can
flourish in England, and like his predecessors
he gives information about the habits of the
insect--its manner of breeding, proper care of
the eggs, feeding habits, maladies it was
subject to, and methods of spinning the silk.
These were the usual subjects of the tracts of

the seventeenth century. But Hill has one novel
point: he pleads with the fair sex to plant
mulberry trees and spin their own silk. Women,
he writes, ought to "do Justice to the Industry
of this *busy* little Animal, to whose constant
Labours they are so highly *oblig'd*, that the
least they can do in *meer Gratitude*, is to form an
Alliance and take their neglected, poor Servant
into their Protection." By this means, he
continued,

the Benefit will spread with the *Practice*,
when some *one* has begun and makes visible *Profit*,
not to speak of the *Pleasure*, when some Lady
temptingly dress'd at a Visit, and shining in
the Ornaments of her own private Industry,
shall be able to answer to the Commenders of
her *Gown* or her *Petticoat*--*'Tis the Silk, which my
own pretty Spinners have presented me*: Then first will
Emulation, or *Envy* produce *Imitation*: *More* every Year
will fall into the Practice...till some happy
Charmer will be made Immortal by *Fame*, and be
admir'd in our Histories, as the *first Introducer
of the Silk Manufacturer in England.*[31]

In certain kinds of light verse devoted to
the social scene or to social customs, the
conjunction of the lady of quality or fashion
and the silkworm was inevitable, as in John
Durant Breval's *The Art of Dress* (1717):

For you, th'Italian Worm her Silk prepares,
And distant *India* sends her choicest Wares;
Some Toy from ev'ry Port the Sailor brings,
The Sempstress labours, and the Poet sings.[32]

Or as in Soame Jenyns in *The Art of Dancing* (1729):

For you the Silkworms fine-wrought webs
    display,
And lab'ring spin their little Lives away...
For you the Sea resigns its pearly Store,
And Earth unlocks her Mines of treasur'd
    Ore. [33]

Similarly we find it in James Ralph's *Clarinda, Or the Fair Libertine* (1729): "For them the Silk worm spins her silken store / For them Peru exports its silver ore."[34] In a more serious vein, R. Collins, whose poem *Nature Display'd* (1727) is, among other things, a justification of reptiles and insects in the deity's plan for the creation, includes the silkworm:

> All these their Uses have, when given ore,
> The Viper's Broth, the Patient will restore.
> Insects, tho' small, with larger Birds may vy;
> What raises Blisters, like the Spanish Fly?..
> How does the Silk-Worm, in her Bowels bear,
> And finely Spin, what finest Ladies wear.[35]

I will not resist the temptation to include a notable example of how the "incomparable worm" crept into the greatest prose satire of the times. In Part III of *Gulliver's Travels*, when Gulliver visits the Grand Academy of Lagado, he walks into a room where walls and ceiling are covered with cobwebs. Immediately a projector warns him not to disturb the webs. The projector, Gulliver informs us, "lamented the fatal Mistake the World had been so long in of using Silk-Worms, while we had such plenty of *domestick* [italics mine] Insects, who infinitely excelled the former, because they understood how to weave as well as spin. And he proposed farther, that by employing Spiders, the Charge of dying Silks would be wholly saved; whereof I was fully convinced when he shewed me a vast Number of Flies most beautifully coloured, wherewith he fed his Spiders; assuring us, that the Webs would take a Tincture from them; and as he had them of all Hues, he hoped to fit every Body's Fancy."[36] Thus it is that Swift, having fun at the expense of the Royal Society, set this satiric passage in the context of the many current discussions of the silkworms, turning the projector into one who sought to use "domestic worms" rather than foreign ones.

In view of the ubiquity of this insect, it
is not surprising that Richard Bradley, a
fellow of the Royal Society and a widely read
popularizer of science, should remark, in his
A *Philosophical Account of the Works of Nature* (1721),
that "*The Silk-Worm*, at present, carries the Day
before all others of the Papilionaceous Tribe";
and he commends the efforts of Henry Barham,
then engaged with others in planting mulberry
trees in Chelsea and, with missionary zeal,
endeavoring to domesticate this preeminent
member of the Papilionaceous Tribe.[37]   Barham
is referred to earlier in this essay. I have,
I trust, amply demonstrated that the silkworm
had a strong fascination for the seventeenth
and eighteenth centuries, not merely for
merchants and statesmen who realized its
potentialities for adding wealth to the nation,
but as well for philosophers, clergymen, and
scientists. It also caught the imagination
of literary men, poets and prose writers alike,
who assimilated it into their works, at times
lightheartedly, at times seriously. In Pope's
day the image of this "*busy* little Animal," this
"curious Atome of Nature," spinning luxury "out
of its owne intralls," was indeed a vivid one,
peculiarly related to the fine lady; and the
very idea of it--and of silk--was deeply
embedded in a whole cluster of ideas, economic
and ethical, touching foreign and domestic
trade, "a world emporie," economic rivalry with
France and Italy, the fabulous wealth of the
Indies, the universal merchant, and, along with
others, pride of dress and what the economic
writers called "the consumptive trades."

Belinda as a consumer, the embodiment of
luxury, whose ambiance is defined by the mere
mention of such objects as Indian gems, Arabian
perfume, ivory combs, a fluttering fan, diamond
pendants in her ears, a sparkling cross, a new
brocade, and the hoop petticoat, was, as I have
indicated, recognizably the final point in a
vast nexus of enterprises, a vast commercial
expansion which stirred the imagination of

Englishmen to dwell on thoughts of greatness
and magnificence. And I suggest again that for
many contemporary readers of the poem something
would accrue to the character of Belinda, an
additional dimension in their response to her
and to the poem, insinuated by the economic
milieu with its awesome dynamism and its vision
of a world emporium. This would be an affirmative response, which very likely would be
leavened by a negative one. Whenas in foreign
silks Belinda goes, she could not please the
austere mercantilist. Defoe would see her,
if I may adapt his phraseology for my purposes,
as one who has "dethroned your True-born
English Broadcloth and Kerseys." Even Addison
inadvertently gives us a clue in *Spectator*, No. 45
(21 April 1711), where he expresses his apprehension over the prospect of a peace treaty
with France: "What an Inundation of Ribbons and
Brocades will break in upon us?...For the
Prevention of these great Evils, I could heart-
ily wish that there was an Act of Parliament
for Prohibiting the Importation of *French*
Fopperies." And fripperies too, he might
have added, an addition which would have evoked
a sympathetic response in many of Mr. Spectator's readers. Although Addison's tone and
treatment in this essay are light and amusing,
the subject itself was a serious one, as we
may observe from its treatment by Defoe in the
Review two years later. Here this laureate of
trade is lamenting the change in London, "the
mighty alteration in the face of trade in this
city" in the past three or four decades. The
metropolis, as he sees it, is now given over
to the dealers in "baubles and trifles" and to
such products as coffee, tea, chocolate, to
"the valuable Utensils of the Tea-Table," to
gilded boxes, looking-glass shops, gilders of
leather, toyshops, pastry cooks, periwig
makers, china or earthenware men, and other
"Foreign Trifles." Ironically, Defoe remarks,
"how gloriously is [London] supplied."[38] In
this mood Defoe would look disapprovingly at

Belinda and her world.   But he had other moods
as well, moments in which he would have ac-
quiesced in the remark of an apologist for the
East India Company, who declared that in
return for bullion the Company brought in
commodities "both to adorn and entertain our
ladies. Are not these riches?"[39] Alexander
Pope, I'm sure, thought so.

BELINDA LUDENS: STRIFE AND PLAY IN
THE RAPE OF THE LOCK

W. K. Wimsatt

I

The two stones of the Roman Neoplatonist
Plotinus (*Enneads* V.viii and I.vi), one beautiful in virtue of a special form carved upon it
by an artist, the other endowed with being,
and hence in Plotinian terms with beauty, in
virtue simply of its being one thing, may be
considered archetypal for a sort of metaphysical
explanation which explains too much--that is to
say, which expands its focus upon a special
idea until that idea coincides with the whole
horizon of the knowable universe. The Plotinian system has had its modern inverted counterparts in forms of expressionist idealism,
notably the Crocean. I think it has another
sort of parallel in the view of art, or of the
whole of cultivated life, as a form of play,
which develops, from the aesthetic of Kant,
1790, to a kind of climax in the masterpiece of
Johann Huizinga, 1938. *Homo Ludens* asserts that
"play can be very serious indeed." "Ritual,"
for example, "is seriousness at its highest and

This essay first appeared in *New Literary History* 4 (1973), 357-74. Copyright The Johns
Hopkins University Press.

holiest. Can it nevertheless be play?"[1] The
trend of the argument is to say that play is
the generator and the formula of all culture.
It was not carrying things much further when
Jacques Ehrmann, the editor of a volume in
Yale French Studies entitled *Games, Play and
Literature*, 1968, protested that Huizinga and
some others were in fact taking reality too
seriously. "Play is not played against a background of a fixed, stable, reality....All reality is caught up in the play of the concepts
which designate it."[2] This Berkeleyan moment
in the philosophy of play idealism had been in
part prepared by the work of a cosmic visionary,
Kostas Axelos, whose preliminaries to "planetary thinking" (*Vers la Penseé planetaire*) of 1964
led to the simple announcement of his title
page in 1969 *Le Jeu du monde*. Man as player and
as toy; the universe as a game played and as
itself an agent playing.
     But the universe, of course, as Emerson once
pointed out, is anything we wish to make it:
"The world is a Dancer; it is a Rosary; it is
a Torrent; it is a Boat; a Mist, a Spider's
Snare; it is what you will..."[3] I myself must
confess to a double inclination: to take the
concept of play very broadly, yet to stop short
of making it a transcendental. It seems a more
useful and a more interesting concept if it has
some kind of bounds and makes some kind of
antithesis to something else. Surely we can
think of some things, some moments of action or
experience, that are not play--jumping out of
the path of an ondriving truck just in time to
save your life, for instance, or making out an
income tax return. The more spontaneous the
action, I suppose, the more certainly we can
distinguish play from what is not play. Thus
a sudden skip and gambol on the green is not
like the leap amid the traffic. But a person
filling out a tax form may conceivably, either
to relieve tension or to express resentment,
evolve some half-conscious overlay of irony or
ritual. Allow us a moment to feel safe and

BELINDA LUDENS   203

the same is true on the street. I have witnessed a very distinguished academic person--a
university president--confront the rush of
automobile fenders at a busy corner in New
Haven by turning sidewise, like a toreador,
and flaunting the skirt of his topcoat.
   We have the double sense that play is both
clearly different from certain other things,
and that it is a chameleon--or, as Wittgenstein
would put it, only a collection of family resemblances.[4] We know that in our everyday
usage *play* has not a single opposite, but a
medley--what is real, serious, or necessary,
what is work, war, or woe.
   Perhaps we can usefully conceive the area
approximately circumscribed by the term "play"
as a polyhedron, in which our divisions according to genus and species will be determined by
which side we think of the figure as resting
on. Immanuel Kant initiated the modern discussion with a slant toward fine art when he conceived the pleasure of art as a "feeling of
freedom in the play of our cognitive faculties."[5] Such a *play* of faculties may be analog-
ized very widely--to the play of water in a
fountain, the play of firelight on a shadowy
wall, the play of muscles in an athlete's
body, the play of Aristotle's taws "upon the
bottom of a king of Kings." The English term
"play" has that loose sort of connotation. And
so have the German *Spiel* and *spielen*. But the
Kantian tradition of art as free play of
faculties need not be frittered away in such
directions. As developed by Schiller and later
by Groos and Lange, it gives us a notion of
manifold and ordered freedom that makes an
appropriate fit for the established fine arts
and at the same time may extend to such plausible analogies as childish or savage forms of
mimesis, game, and ritual, and to numerous forms
of civilized gratification which Kant himself
snubbed as merely sensate and pleasurable or
amusing.[6]
   The aesthetic or artistic emphasis on the

concept of play invites us to conceive different
kinds of play as realizing, with different
degrees of prominence, three insistent aesthetic
features: that is, expression, mimesis, and
design (or pattern)--corresponding broadly to
the three Kantian divisions (and features) of
art: the speaking, the shaping, and the art
of the beautiful play of sensation.   The
Kantian general aesthetic requirements of dis-
interest and of purposiveness without purpose
reappear today in clauses concerning convention,
unreality, isolation, autotelism, and freedom
which make the definitions of play according
to Huizinga and his successors.

"Play," however, is only one of two terms
which commonly appear side by side, as if all
but synonymous in recent literature of play
theory.   The other term is "game."   The two
terms are used almost interchangeably--as the
French *jeu* is translated either *play* or *game*.   It
is my notion that the terms are not in fact
synonymous, and that "play" does not always
entail "game"--that "game" in fact is only
one very special kind of play.   Sometimes we
play games; at other times, as when we gambol,
or romp, or swim, or walk in the woods, or
yodel, or doodle, we are just playing.   At this
juncture another of the inheritors of Kant and
Huizinga, Roger Caillois, editor of the journal
Diogène, comes to our aid with his articles on
"play" and "games" published in 1955 and
1957.[7]   Whatever else we may say in general
about play and game, however many classes or
qualities of either we distinguish, two common
principles seem to Caillois certain: one a
childlike, spontaneous principle of improvisa-
tion and insouciant self-expression (*paidia*), the
other a sort of perverse complementary principle of self-imposed obstacle or deliberate
convention of hindrance (*ludus*).   It is never
enough, for very long, to skip and gambol.   We
play leapfrog or hopscotch.   "The unfettered
leap of joy," says Schiller, "becomes a dance;
the aimless gesture, a graceful and articulate
miming speech."[8]

With convention, and only with convention,
can the element of game enter into play. The
idea of convention might carry us also very
quickly in the direction of language, and into
language games (that is to say, into the logical
problem of shifting frames of reference). But
a different idea from that is more relevant to
my present purpose. And that is the idea of
game as competition. Convention in games is
the opportunity for and invitation to an orderly
and limited competition.

The game of pure competitive skill (or *agōn*),
and the game of chance (*alea*) are two forms of
play which Caillois is specially interested in,
which he would insistently distinguish, but
which nevertheless he sees as very closely
related. It is my own notion, though I think I
need not argue it here at length, that chance
has such a close affinity for competition
that it is just as often an element intrinsic
to some kind of competitive game (dice, poker,
bridge) as it is a pure form (lottery, Russian
roulette), where, as Caillois instructs us,
it may be conceived as inviting only the passive
surrender of the player to the decree of fate.

The relation of competitive game-play to
forms of conspicuously aesthetic play may be
very interesting and very difficult to state.
The concept of mimesis[9] may be the hinge on
which a comparison most instructively turns.
A tragic drama is a mimesis of a combat (involving often murder and war), but no combat
actually occurs in this drama, at least none
corresponding to that which is mimed. A game
of chess or a game of bridge may be conceived
as a mimic warfare (*Ludimus effigiem belli*). But
that is to say that such a game proceeds according to a set of conventions which are the conditions for a very strictly limited but nevertheless *actual* combat--one which bears a relation
of *analogy* to larger combats and is in that sense
a *mimesis* of them. (Let nobody be in any doubt
about the actuality of the combat in chess or
bridge or poker.)

At least two special sorts of connection can
obtain between these two sorts of play, the
aesthetic and the competitive. (1) The element
of combat in the sheer game can be stylized and
arrested in the shape of puzzle or problem,
and in this case it is altered in the direction
of aesthetic design. This happens notably in
the kind of compositions known as chess "problems." (2) A second kind of rapprochement is
of more direct literary significance: it
happens that the competitive game can appear
internally to the art play, as part of the
story. And here the game may be treated with
either more or less precise regard for its
technical details, and in either case it may
manifest either more or less formal and
aesthetic interest as it seems to function
either more or less as an interior duplication
or symbol of the gamesome or ludic nature
which, in some sense, we may discover as a
character of the work as a whole.[10]

II

Before I plunge more directly into the proposed topic of this paper--the game of cards
in Pope's *The Rape of the Lock*--let me attempt one
further classical perspective, this time invoking not Plotinus but Plato himself, in an
analytic mood which is pretty much the opposite
of anything Neoplatonic. I have in mind that
dialogue in which a rhapsode, that is, a professional declaimer of Homeric poetry and a
professor of poetry, is given a destructive
Socratic quizzing. The question insistently,
if engagingly, pursued is this: whether a
professor of poetry, or for that matter his
model and inspiration the poet, knows anything
at all, or has anything to teach, in his own
right. It appears that he does not. If he
knows anything about medicine, for instance,
or about steering a ship, or spinning wool, it
will be in virtue of exactly the same kind of
knowledge as the practitioner of those arts
would have. The mind of a poet--Homer, for

instance--who talks about nearly everything,
is just a grab bag of various kinds of knowledge which are the proper business of various
other kinds of experts. The application is made
even to the knowledge of epic games:

"...does not Homer speak a good deal about arts,
in a good many places? For instance, about
chariot-driving....Tell me what Nestor says to
his son Antilochus...."   "'Bend thyself in the
polished car slightly to the left of them;
and call to the right-hand horse and goad
him on, while your hand slackens his reins'"
[Iliad XXIII.355 ff.].... "Now, Ion, will a
doctor or a charioteer be the better judge
whether Homer speaks correctly or not in these
lines?" "A charioteer, of course." "Because
he has this art, or for some other reason?"
"No, because it is his art" (Ion,537-A).

Almost any modern reader, I suppose, is likely
to believe that this question raised by Socrates is unimportant for the study of poetry.
Forgetting perhaps that the Greeks of Plato's
time did actually look on Homer as a chief
authority about chariot racing, warfare,
generalship, and related topics, and that in a
sense he was such an authority, the modern
reader will think of poetry about games, either
outdoor or indoor games, most likely in the
light of some such passage as the following
near the end of the first book of Wordsworth's
Prelude, where he recalls some of his childhood
pastimes:

    Eager and never weary we pursued
    Our home amusements by the warm peat-fire
    At evening...
       round the naked table, snow-white deal,
    Cherry or maple, sate in close array,
    And to the combat, Lu or Whist, led on
    A think-ribbed Army; not as in the world
    Neglected and ungratefully thrown by
    Even for the very service they had wrought,

But husbanded through many a long campaign.
Uncouth assemblage was it, where no few
Had changed their functions, some, plebeian
    cards,
Which Fate beyond the promise of their birth
Had glorified, and call'd to represent
The persons of departed Potentates.
Oh! with what echoes on the Board they fell!
Ironic Diamonds, Clubs, Hearts, Diamonds,
    Spades,
A congregation piteously akin.
Cheap matter did they give to boyish wit,
Those sooty knaves, precipitated down
With scoffs and taunts, like Vulcan out
    of Heaven,
The paramount Ace, a moon in her eclipse,
Queens, gleaming through their splendor's
    last decay,
And Monarchs, surly at the wrongs sustain'd
By royal visages. (I.534-36,541-62)

The main thing we learn about that card game
is that the cards were dog-eared, very badly
beaten up--a medley of survivals from several
different packs, some of them having been
doctored or altered to raise their value. A
poet, we will of course say, looks on a given
technical routine, like playing cards, in just
the light needed for whatever he is trying to
say in his poem; and we will most likely imply
that the precise rules and play of the game--
certainly its niceties and finesses--are not
likely to be a part of the poet's concern.
Maybe a writer of stories about baseball--a
Ring Lardner, a Bernard Malamud--will have to
know what he is talking about in order to convey
the appearance and feel of the thing. A very
good story about Chess, Vladimir Nabokov's *The
Defence*, manages to create a vivid impression
of a boy's experience of learning to play and of
becoming a master. In Stefan Zweig's celebrated
Schachnovelle (*The Royal Game*), the psychology of
obsessive, schizoid game play seems to me less
finely informed with any authentic chess
experience.[11] A story involving a card game or

a chess game is likely enough to tell us something very indistinct about the game itself,
or else something utterly absurd. In one story
about chess that I remember, an old man is able
to cheat another old man, his inveterate rival,
by allowing his beard to curl about a rook
at one corner of the board, thus lulling his
opponent into a sense that the rook is not
there. Short stories have been written indeed
around the actual score of chess games--but
these are just that, chess stories, and they
appear for the most part in chess magazines.
In one of Samuel Beckett's zero-degree novels,
Murphy, there is the actual score of a chess
game, played in a kind of madhouse, but the
point of the game is its utter absurdity.
Niether player (neither male nurse nor mental
patient) is able to *find* the other--they play
simultaneous games of solitaire. Faulkner's
short story "Was" (*Go Down, Moses* [1942]) manages
two hands of poker, one "Draw" and one "Stud,"
with an artistic economy made possible in part
by the concealment and bluffing which are intrinsic to this game that gives a name to the
studiously inexpressive countenance.

Wordsworth, we are told by his friend
Coleridge, was a specialist in "spreading the
tone." Generalization, even vagueness, in
imagery, idea, and mood, was his forte. It is
difficult to imagine a poem by Wordsworth in
which a precise and technically correct narration of a hand at cards would have been
relevant to his purpose. Is the same true for
Alexander Pope? I have an idea that most of us,
if only from our general habit of reading poetry
would read into Pope for the first time with
no more expectation of finding an exactly
described card game than in Wordsworth. I
remember that when about twenty-five years ago
I first studied *The Rape of the Lock* closely
enough to realize fully the presence of the
card game, I was very much surprised. I had a
special sort of delight in the discovery--be-
cause I myself have always been moderately

addicted to table games, and so it gave me
pleasure to work the puzzle out--but also because the precision of the details seemed to
me in a special way an achievement appropriate
to Pope's art as a couplet poet and also a specially precise and exquisite miniature of this
whole poem. For the modern eye or ear, this
game may often pass in a somewhat sunken or
muted way beneath the very colorful and
rhythmic surface symbols in which the action is
carried. It seems difficult to say to what
degree it was hidden for Pope's readers, many
of whom presumably were better up on the game
of ombre than we are. For us, I think, part
of the pleasure can come from the fact that
the game is not awkwardly obtrusive or obviously
technical, but is woven so subtly into the
poetic fabric. It seems to me a merit of the
passage that one may well read it without full
awareness of what is going on.

III

   There is now no way for me to avoid a degree
of technicality in my exposition. The game of
ombre as Pope narrates it is an impressive
blend of visual technique and gamesmanship or
technique according to Hoyle--the Hoyle of
that day, a French book on ombre and piquet,
translated into English in a volume entitled
The Court Gamester, published at London only a
few years after Pope's poem, 1719.[12] Beginning
with a writer in *MacMillan's Magazine* in 1874 and
a certain Lord Aldenham, who somewhat frivolous-
ly devoted a large book to *The Game of Ombre* (3rd
ed.,1902), a succession of modern writers have
commented on Pope's game. Geoffrey Tillotson's
exposition in an appendix to his Twickenham
edition of *The Rape of the Lock* in 1940 triggered
a contentious correspondence in the columns of
the *TLS*.[13] A short essay of my own, published
in 1950, was an effort to tidy up the tradition
and improve on it. Take a deck of cards and
remove the 8s, 9s, and 10s of each suit (12
cards in all), leaving forty. Seat three

players at a table, Belinda and two male courtiers. The man to Belinda's left, probably her
chief antagonist, the Baron, deals nine cards
to each player (27 in all); he puts the remaining 13 cards down in a stock or kitty.
Belinda bids first, gets the bid, and declares
spades trumps. The players then discard weak
cards and draw an equal number of replacements
from the kitty. The order of strength in the
cards is not as in modern contract bridge. It
differs from hand to hand, depending on
which suit is trumps. For the present hand, the
top card is the Ace of spades, Spadillio;
next the 2 of spades, Manillio; next the Ace
of clubs, Basto; then the spades in order, King
down to three. The red Aces are lower than the
face cards in their suits. In order to win
the hand Belinda has to take more tricks than
her stronger opponent--5 against 4, or 4 against
3 and 2. Four tricks unroll smoothly for Belinda as she leads in succession Spadillio,
Manillio, Basto, and the King of spades--pull-
ing smaller spades from her opponents--except
that on the third and fourth tricks the third
player, the anonymous one, fails to come
through. So the Baron may well have the last
trump, the Queen. Belinda has two winning
cards left in her hand, the King of hearts and
the King of clubs. As the hand turns out, we
can see that it doesn't matter which King she
plays. She gets her fifth trick sooner or later.
But what of the possiblities at that apparently
crucial moment as she leads on the fifth trick?
Which King shall she play?--if she is to live up
to the epithet "skilful" bestowed on her by the
poet at the commencement of the scene. ("The
skilful Nymph reviews her Force with Care.")
We are not told every card in each player's
hand. The xs in my chart indicate the degree
of indeterminacy in Pope's specifications. But
the probabilities may be considered. In the
event, for instance, that the Baron has the
Queen of spades and four diamonds, then no
matter how the diamond tricks are divided
between the Baron and the third player, produc-

ing either a win with five tricks for the
Baron, or a 4-3-2 win for Belinda, or a
4-4-1 Remise or drawn game, the outcome will not
depend upon Belinda's lead. Certain more complicated suppositions about the Baron's holding
one or two low hearts or one or two low clubs
(but *not* both hearts and clubs) can be made,
and I have made them, I believe exhaustively.[14]
I will not recite them here. The upshot of my
analysis is that only if the third player captured a diamond lead on the sixth trick and then
went on to produce the 4-4-1 Remise by taking
three more diamond tricks himself (the Baron
throwing down low hearts or clubs--but *not* both),
could Belinda suffer an *unfavorable* outcome which
depended on her leading the wrong suit at the
fifth trick. But on this supposition, that the
third player held four diamonds, or perhaps
on any supposition at all, Belinda at the
fifth trick could suppose very little about
the number of either hearts or clubs in the
Baron's hand and hence would have little reason
to prefer either a club or a heart lead. A
test by the calculus of foreseeable possibilities would be the correct test of Belinda's
skill (of whether her play of the hand is, in
the terms of Roger Caillois, a true *agōn* or is
largely an instance of *alea*),but such a test will
not quite pan out. We fall back on a more
superficial, human, and plausible test by appearances. The discard of the Knave of clubs
(Pam, who "mow'd down Armies in the Fights of
Lu") by the third player on the fourth trick
does look like a discard from weakness. Possibly his only club? In that case, the Baron
may be thought somewhat more likely to have
clubs than hearts. Dramatically, if not
technically and mathematically, the Knave of
clubs, so conspicuously heralded as a discard,
advertises a certain plausibility in her next
lead of the King of clubs. Belinda is a society
belle and not a Charles H. Goren. It is by the
standards of the polite card table (not necessarily profound) that we shall measure her skill.

She is no doubt skillful in her own esteem.
She leads her King of clubs, loses it to the
Queen of spades. The Baron pours his diamonds
apace for three tricks, his Knave on the
eighth trick drawing even her Queen of hearts.
Then the Baron's Ace of hearts (lower than the
face cards) is forced out on the last trick,
to fall a victim to the King lurking in her
hand. "The Nymph exulting fills with Shouts
the Sky, / The Walls, the Woods, and long Canals
reply."
   The pictorial features of a deck of cards,
the royal faces, the plain plebeian spots, are
well calculated for the symbolism of an epic
battle (the "routed Army.../ Of *Asia's* Troops,
and *Africk's* Sable Sons"); for that of palace
revolutions ("The hoary Majesty of *Spades*...
The Rebel-*Knave*"); and for that of the most
important business of court life, the battle
of the sexes (the warlike Amazonian Queen of
spades, the wily Knave of diamonds, the"captive"
Queen of hearts). Belinda's hubristic first
sweep of four tricks, the sudden blow from
fate, or the peripeteia, of the fifth trick,
her narrow escape from the jaws of ruin and
codille, her last-trick triumph and exultation--
all these develop her portrait as the mock-hero-
ine of a melodramatized tragic-epic action.

IV

   An episode of epic games was one of the dozen
or so ingredients prescribed for the epic poem
by René le Bossu in his *Treatise* of 1675. But
what is the significance of such contests in
the epic structure? The answer, broadly, must
be that epic games are a miniature emblem of the
contest which is the heroic panorama of the
whole poem. Heroic fighters and leaders relax
and indulge themselves, not in games of tiddly-
winks, or even ombre, but in huge, manly,
spectacular, circus-like feats: chariot races,
footraces, boxing, discus-throwing, spear-throw-
ing, archery. The games have a kind of ready-

made or prefabricated relevance in the epic
context--as in post-Homeric Greece the epic
spirit is annually recapitulated in the
festival games.

 That general kind of significance, however,
is not all. The epic poets in the Western succession each seems to have treated the episode
of the heroic games in his poem in such a way
as to confer on it some much more special
slant. Happily for my purpose, I am not the
first to have thought of this. My colleague
Professor George Lord, for instance, has written an excellent essay[15] pointing out how the
funeral games in honor of Patroclus in *Iliad*
XXIII (which, we have seen, the rhapsode Ion
knew so well by heart) are not simply a résumé of
the anger, division, and discourtesy among the
Greek leaders with which the poem opens, but
a kind of image in reverse, where courtesy
and reconciliation--i.e., good sportmanship--
have their day as a countertheme to the "wrath"
of which the poet has been singing from the
opening word of the first book. Paris had long
ago *stolen* Helen from Menelaus, thus starting
the war. In the first book of the poem,
Agamemnon at first angrily refuses to give up
a captive girl ("Her I will not let go"),
then does so with bad grace and snatches another,
the property of Achilles. (Hence all that
gigantic sulking; hence the reverses of the
Greeks on the plains before Troy and the death
of Patroclus.) In the chariot race of the
funeral games, where the second prize is a fine
mare, Antilochus at first beats out Menelaus
for that prize by some dirty driving, but then
he turns around, concedes the point, and gives
the mare to Menelaus, who in turn gives her
back to Antilochus. Sports, after all, are the
appropriate arena for good sportsmanship--which
is a ludic image of such virtues as courtesy,
chivalry, and gallantry. *Iliad* XXIII, says
Professor Lord, is a comic recapitulation or
self-mockery of the tragic heroism of the whole.

 The games which are narrated, by perhaps an

elderly Homer or by perhaps a second Homer,
in Book VIII of the *Odyssey* at the court of
King Alcinous in the charmed kingdom of the
Phaeacians, have about them both something
of the healthy athletic mood of a college track
meet, and the reveries which today characterize
the secret life of Walter Mitty. In the *Iliad*,
battle-scarred warriors lay aside armament for
a moment of major league game-playing. In the
Odyssey, the shipwrecked stranger, handsome and
tall, but eldering, worn, and sorrowful, watches
as the younger men among the oar-loving Phaeacians compete in footracing, wrestling, jumping,
discus-throwing, and boxing. After a while
somebody throws a few taunts at the stranger:
"You old scrubby-looking sea captain, you
wouldn't be so good at games of skill and
strength like these, would you?" And then the
transformation--the sudden heartwarming assertion. "I don't know about that," says the
unrecognized hero of the Trojan-horse exploit.
And he picks up a big stone discus, bigger
than any the others have been handling; he
gives it a skillful whirl, and it flies out a
long way beyond what anybody else has done.
Then this old stranger utters a boast, telling
them what he can do if they wish to challenge
him in boxing, wrestling, or footracing. Or,
for that matter, in archery. He says he is
very good at handling the polished bow, sending
an arrow into a throng of foes. We all know,
of course, what that bodes for certain insolent
suitors who are at that very moment living high
in the halls of a house at Ithaca.
    It was a commonplace of Renaissance criticism
from the Italians of the sixteenth century, to
Samuel Johnson, that Homer was the more profoundly original epic poet, but that Virgil
achieved a greater degree of polished perfection. Virgil had no doubt a problem in how to
give some original twist to the funeral games
held in Book V of the *Aeneid*. The ideas of age
and youth, paternity, filial piety, reverence,
and a corresponding bright hope for the future

are the keys to what he did. The whole poem
is a prophecy and a preview of the history of
Rome; and the more poetically successful first
six books are prognostic of the more propagan-
distic second six. So in Book V, the boatrace,
footrace, boxing, riding exhibition, and shooting matches, are a genealogical celebration,
and both a rehearsal for war (like rugby at
Eton) and a prefiguration of events to occur
in the second half of the poem on the plains
of Latium. Virgil, it has been said, was
probably the first great writer to turn play
into work.[16]

This survey of epic games might go on for a
long time. But I compress it now by coming
down to Pope's immediate predecessor and a
major model and sounding board for allusions in
The Rape of the Lock--Milton, of course, in the
games resorted to by the devils in the second
book of *Paradise Lost*. *Paradise Lost* is remarkable
for the spiritualization and subtle internal-
ization which are pervasive throughout the
grand murky and spiraling baroque cosmological
structure. We read the war in Heaven or the
allegory of Satan, Sin, and Death at the gates
to chaos in our own hearts if we read them
vividly at all. "Which way I fly is Hell;
myself am Hell" (IV.75). So it is only just,
and the description is full of genius, when
Satan's legions, left to their own amusement,
express the consuming restlessness of their new
state by setting out on long exploring expedi-
tions through the dismal semichaotic realm of
fire and ice which they have recently colonized.
Even more acutely and poetically, Milton has
some of them, more philosophic souls, sit down
to animated disputes on the theological issues
of freedom and necessity which touch them so
closely. At these infernal games, there are
wing, foot, and chariot races too, there is
demonic harping and song. There is no card
game. Cards, gambling, and drinking are possible demonic associations in some anti-saloon-
league context, but such would be too low for

the heroic damned of Milton's scene. The parlor
game which *we* have in view would be obviously
too dainty.

V

   The contrasting wider context of the big epic
tradition does much of Pope's work for him.
The work is invited in a very special way by
the other main part of the context, the immediate social one. It is perhaps easiest to invest
literature with the colors of a game when the
life represented is courtly, artificial,
ritualistic, playful. Such a life, lived with
a high degree of intensity and burnish, *is* a
game--or a jest, as Pope and his closest friends
might have said. It can also be a special sort
of warfare. Pope's letter to Mrs. Arabella
Fermor, prefixed to his second edition, in
which the game of ombre first appears, may be
read as a language game of teasing and flattery.
It is not my idea that the poem itself can be
said, in any useful sense, to be a game played
by Pope either with himself or with his reader.
The poem, however, is in a very notable way a
poem about a gamesome way of life. The background life of the poem, the powders, patches,
furbelows, flounces, and brocades, the smiles
and curls, the china, the silver, the billet-
doux, the lapdogs, and the fopperies and flirt-
ations, are built-in elements of the higher
social gamesmanship. The poem absorbs and
represents this situation in a very immediate
and vivid image, and thus in a very thorough
sense it is a game poem.
   Here we may as well recall some relevant
insights of the late Dr. Eric Berne, whose
best-selling book entitled *Games People Play* (1964)
was developed from his less racy *Transactional
Analysis in Psychotherapy* (1961). "Games" in the
somewhat extrapolated but persuasive sense of
certain slantwise and fictive stratagems employed in a variety of neurotic types of aggression. Instead of facing each other on the

level, as adults, the role-players of Dr.
Berne's analyses suffered either from assumptions of parental hauteur and inquisition or
from childlike poses, sulks, and tantrums.
They played, among many others, certain "Party"
and "Sexual" games, to which he gave such names
as "Kiss Off," "Ain't It Awful," "Rapo,"
"Indignation," "Let's You and Him Fight," and
"Uproar."   "Favors to none, to all she smiles
extends."--"At every word a reputation dies."--
"The Peer now spread the glittering Forfex
wide."--"Then flash'd the living lightning
from her eyes."--"To arms, to arms! the fierce
Virago cries."--"And bass and treble voices
strike the skies." Let us think here also of
the stubbornly contested betrothal gambits
played between Congreve's Millamant and Mirabell.
Think of the somberly mythologized combat between mentor and pupil, the dark luster, of
Swift's *Cadenus and Vanessa*. In *The Rape of the Lock,*
we witness the gladiatorial aspect of sex and
courtship. Belinda "Burns to encounter two
adventrous Knights,/ At *Ombre* singly to decide
their Doom."

The other epic games we have noticed are all
highly episodic, off-center developments in the
vast poems where they occur. The game of
ombre occurs in a central or focal position
which could be appropriate only in a poem of
rococo dimensions. The game of ombre is the
least deadly and most conventionalized combat
in Pope's poem, and yet it is a real combat
(game combats I have said and will repeat are
real) and it is the most precisely delineated
and most complete combat of the whole poem,
appearing in the center as a kind of reducing
or concentrating mirror of the larger, more
important, but less decisive, kinds of strife
and hints of strife that both precede and follow
it.

Here perhaps we can invoke, with only a
slight and forgivable degree of exaggeration,
a pattern developed by Professor Cedric
Whitman for ordering the complicated and lavish-

ly repetitious procession of quarrels, councils,
speeches, feasts, libations, sacrifices, battles,
triumphs, defeats, and burials which make up
the *Iliad* of Homer.   There is a kind of center
for the *Iliad* in two anomalously conjunct night-
time episodes, the embassy to Achilles of Book
IX and the (perhaps genetically intrusive)
reconnaissance by the scout Dolon and his
violent end in Book X.   Coming up to these and
moving away from them are two sequences of
events and of days that unfold in mirror
(or butterfly) patterns of partly antithetic,
partly similar images, "ring patterns."   And
this is in the manner of those Grecian pottery
vases or urns that have friezes of figures on
them converging on some central figure in a
reflecting pattern (the hugh vases of Dipylon
ware, for instance, manufactured at about the
time when Homer most likely was writing,
750 to 700 B.C.).   (Or think of that "leaf-
fringed legend" or "brede of marble men and
maidens," priest and sacrificial heifer, that
move, no doubt symmetrically from two sides,
toward the "green altar" in Keats's "Ode on a
Grecian Urn.")
    The card game at the center of Pope's poem
is not only the most precise and least earnest
combat of the poem.   It is at the same time,
though animated, the least animate, the most
completely a work of art, in that the actors
described so lovingly, with such detail and
color, are neither supernatural nor human agents.
They are in fact only cardboard--though the
ambitious animus of Belinda and the Baron are
just behind them, and even the sylphs "Descend,
and sit on each important Card."   Move back
from this artful center toward the beginning
of the poem, into the second canto, and we find
the human epic element of a journey or expedition (as prescribed by Bossu), Belinda's boat
ride on the Thames, which is convoyed by swarms
of supernatural agents, the sylphs, in attitudes
of keen vigilance and readiness for combat.
Look then next in the opposite direction.   The

game of ombre *ends* in Belinda's moment of greatest
triumph.   And this is followed almost immediately by the Baron's counterattack and victory
as he snips off the lock.   This is *his* moment
of greatest triumph.   (If he loses the hand at
ombre, he wins the canto.)   Immediately thereafter, in the fourth canto, we return to the
motif of a journey, this time a descent into a
grotesque allegorical region of the underworld (much as at the end of the first canto of
The Faerie Queene of Spenser).   The element of
the supernatural, or preternatural, is
prominent again now, both in the destination
and in the traveler, who is an agent of earth,
a gnome, descending to the Cave of Spleen on
no benevolent mission.   Now move back to the
very beginning of the poem, the first canto.
After the opening epic invocation, we first get
our bearings in a scene of the human and comic
everyday, with Belinda and her dog, rousing at
noon to an afternoon of adventure.   In the first
canto, too, appear the epic elements of extended discourse and encyclopedic knowledge, and of
supernatural agency, as the doctrine concerning
the elemental spirits is expounded by the
guardian sylph, with premonitions of impending
disaster.   At the end of the canto, Belinda
with the assistance of Betty arms herself
like an epic hero for battle and at the same
time practices her ritual of self-worship at
the toilet table.   At the level of such motifs,
perhaps we must admit that a degree of sinuosity
complicates our pursuit of an overall symmetry.
The chief later moments of ritual, for instance,
occur in the second canto with the Baron's
piled up French romances, the gloves and garters
sacrificed to the power of Love, and in the
ombre canto with the ceremony of the coffee mill
and "altars of Japan."   We have what may perhaps
be called only a complementary pattern of different emphasis, when we observe that the
extended anaphoristic sequences of hyperbole
and bathos ("While Fish in Streams, or Birds
delight in Air, / Or in a Coach and Six the

British Fair,"), both in the author's own voice
and in the voices of Belinda, the Baron, Thalestris, and Clarissa, are a conspicuous feature
of the second half of the poem, beginning at
the end of the third canto and recurring through
the fourth and at the start of the fifth. But
with these sustained speeches, especially with
the inflammatory speech of Thalestris to Belinda near the end of the fourth canto and the
ensuing episode of the vacuous Sir Plume's
confrontation with the Baron, we are on lowly
human and comic ground again, in a position
roughly the counterpart of the opening of the
poem in our geometric scheme. (The speeches
as such may be set against the long initial
discourse of the sylph.) The comic vein is
conspicuously continued in the fifth and last
canto with the lecture on good humour delivered
by Clarissa and rejected by Belinda, and in the
closing furious pitched battle between the
belles and beaus.

     The fury of this combat has no counterpart
in the first half of the poem. We may say
that the airy hints of danger and the vigilance
in the first two cantos have been stepped up by
the gamesome duel of the third canto, to a
degree of violence where the Baron's rude
aggression and the ensuing turmoil are poetically plausible. And now Pope finds himself in
a special dilemma, and with also a special
opportunity for brilliance, in this noisy
combat. The more physically it is realized,
the less it can be satisfactorily resolved.
And so, as shouts "To Arms," clapping fans,
rustling silks, and cracking whalebones shade
into death at the eyes of fair ones, a show
of Homeric gods in epic simile, and an allusion
to Jove's "golden Scales in Air," weighing the
"Men's Wits against the Lady's Hair," the
strife shifts into the mode of metaphor and
symbol, or of myth--like so many irresolvable
combats we have known in story and on stage.
Belinda resorts to throwing a physical pinch
of snuff at the Baron and even threatens him

with a deadly bodkin. But the only injury
inflicted is a huge sneeze, which reechoes to
the high dome. Apparently on the waves of
sound or air generated by this sneeze, or by
Belinda's cry of *"Restore the Lock,"* which too
rebounds from the vaulted roofs, the Lock
itself mounts and disappears. "But trust the
Muse--she saw it upward rise,/ Tho' mark'd by
none but quick Poetic Eyes." Like a "sudden
Star," or a comet, it "shot thro' liquid Air,/
And drew behind a radiant *Trail of Hair."* Vanished,
it assumes the mythic proportions of the
founder of Rome, Romulus, who withdrew to the
heavens during a thunderstorm, or the constel-
lated locks of the Egyptian queen Berenice
(virtuously sacrificed for the safety of her
husband), or the planet Venus worshiped by
lovers at the Lake in St. James's Park.

    Variation in kinds of combat is one of the
main structural modes, or principles of progression, in this poem. The minutely delineated
cardboard combat of the central canto is the
concave mirror in which, as Samuel Johnson
might have put it, the ultimately sidereal
reaches of the rest of the poem (the sun of the
first three cantos, the stars of the last) are
focused--and clarified. Or, to shift my metaph-
or, and to bring in the concluding words of
the short essay which I wrote on the poem
twenty years ago: "The game of Ombre expands
and reverberates delicately in the whole poem.
The episode is a microcosm of the whole poem,
a brilliant epitome of the combat between the
sexes which is the theme of the whole."

	BELINDA		THE BARON		SIR ANONYM
I. BELINDA ⟶	Spadillio Ace ♠		♠		♠
II. BELINDA ⟶	Manillio Two ♠		♠		♠
III. BELINDA ⟶	Basto Ace ♣		♠		Plebeian Card ×
IV. BELINDA ⟶	King ♠		Knave ♠		Pam Knave ♣
V. BARON ⟶	King ♣		Queen ♠		×
VI. BARON ⟶	×		King ◇		×
VII. BARON ⟶	×		Queen ◇		×
VIII. BARON ⟶	Queen ♡		Knave ◇		×
IX. BELINDA ⟶	King ♡		Ace ♡		×

THE LIMITS OF ALLUSION IN *THE RAPE OF THE LOCK*

Earl R. Wasserman

The works of Pope are not likely any longer to
be read as "the poetry of statement": we have
become too sensible of their extraordinary
subtleties at the level of language and of
the wealth of their allusiveness, especially
to the classics, the Bible, and the commonplaces. But although we are no longer inclined
to reduce this poetry to versified statement,
the vestige of that critical conception has
possibly deterred admission of the full complexity of Pope's art. Disinherited as we
are from his referential systems it is reasonable to question whether we are adequately
aware of the scope of his allusions and their
part in constituting the fabric of his poems.
Hence, the ultimate question at issue here will
be whether only the text of Pope's allusion
acts upon his poem or whether it also imports
its own context. If the context is indeed
relevant, what are the permissible limits in
our bringing that context to bear? How allusive

This essay first appeared in the *Journal of English and Germanic Philology* 65 (1966), 425-44.
Copyright The University of Illinois Press.

are Pope's allusions? and how functional?
Take the case of *The Rape of the Lock.*

   Even superficial acquaintance with the
classical epic will inform us of its role in
shaping Pope's mock epic. The epic proposition
and invocation, the adaptation of the epic
battles and feasts, the Rosicrucian divine
machinery, the epic style and phrasal formulas
are all obvious enough; and even the function
of casting Clarissa's speech in the pattern
of Sarpedon's famous commentary on the hero's
raison d'être has been made familiar to us. But
perhaps Pope's reader is no longer sufficiently
conscious of how deeply embedded the Latinate
manner is even in his language. The Twickenham
edition may have taught us that the *Aeneid*
(II,390-91) is being echoed when the Baron plans

> By Force to ravish, or by Fraud betray;
> For when Success a Lover's Toil attends,
> Few ask, if Fraud or Force attain'd his
>   Ends;[1] (II,32-34)

that Belinda's visionary beau "said, or seem'd
to say" (I,26) because these are also Virgil's
words on an analogous occasion (*Aeneid*, VI,454);
and that

> Where Wigs with Wigs, with Sword-knots
>   Sword-knots strive,
> Beaus banish Beaus, and Coaches Coaches
>   drive. (I,101-102)

repeats a popular classical phrasal pattern.
But, with our loss of Latin, it is less apparent
that when Pope described the beaux and belles
passing the hours "In various Talk" (III, 11)
his mind instinctively reached out to the
phrase *vario sermone* with which Virgil described
how Aeneas and Evander lightened the tedium of
their stroll (*Aeneid*, VIII, 309); or that Ovid,
wittiest of the Roman poets, instructed Pope
in shaping one of his most famous instances

of zeugma,

> Here Thou, great *Anna!* whom three Realms obey,
> Dost sometimes Counsel take--and sometimes
>   *Tea.* [2]   (III,7-8)

Nor are we likely to sense that "fatal Engine"
(III,149) and "Voices strike the Skies" (V,42)
are Virgilian phrases;[3] or that "sacrilegious
Hands" (especially in the sense in which it is
used in the poem, IV,174, referring to theft of
a sacred object),[4] "Nourish'd ...Locks" (II,20),
"Thirst of Fame" (III,25), "painted Vessel"
(II,47),[5] "Fate urg'd" (III,151),[6] and "decks...
with the glitt'ring Spoil" (I,132)[7] are recurrent Latinisms. Of course the entire poem
is a tissue of such classical echoes, many
far more pointed and palpable than these; and
the phrases mentioned are not allusive in any
significant sense. But, by indicating how
radical Latin is even in Pope's language, they
serve to tell us that the mind that composed
The Rape of the Lock was less an English one
hearkening back to the classics for witty
references than one applying itself to an
English social situation from the viewpoint of
a deeply ingrained classicism. Classical
literature and its manners, together with
Scripture and its exegetical tradition, are
not merely Pope's acquired learning; they shaped
the character and processes of his though.
Correspondingly, his poems consistently ask
for a reader who is equally native to the whole
classical-Scriptural world, a Christian Greco-
Roman scrutinizing eighteenth-century English
culture. On that assumption I propose to
survey the poem in order to observe what may be
the consequences of setting various passages in
the contexts they evoke.
    Before doing so in any systematic way, how-
ever, I should like to examine a parenthetical
passage in the poem which illustrates the kind
of ready knowledge Pope demands of his reader
and which also can serve as a paradigm of the

significant interactions taking place between
his text and the allusion it calls up. The
time at which Belinda undertakes the contest
at Ombre is set by the poet as the hour when

> The hungry Judges soon the Sentence sign,
> And Wretches hang that Jury-men may Dine;
> The Merchant from th' *Exchange* returns in
>   Peace,
> And the long Labours of the *Toilette* cease.
>   (III,21-24)

Elsewhere the poet, striking a Beau Brummel
pose, equivocates between Belinda's world of
social elegance and the matter-of-fact world
that encompasses it--the Queen's taking counsel
and taking tea, the foredooming of "Foreign
Tyrants" and domestic tyrants ("Nymphs
at home")--until he has made a charming mockery
of the distinction between serious necessity
and frivolous artifice. But in the context of
the sheltered Petit Trianon world of conventionalized manners that the total poem constructs,
the lines on the judges and the merchant are,
as it were, the poet's one hard glance at
the Hobbesian state of nature raging outside,
so that he may expose the ugly alternative for
Belinda and her friends if they shatter the
fragile decorum that fences them in. In addition, Pope expects his ideal reader to recognize the Homeric character of the two couplets
if they are to have their full force. In a
note to a line in the *Dunciad* he wrote, "This
is to mark punctually the Time of the day: *Homer*
does it by the circumstances of the Judges
rising from court, or of the Labourer's dinner"
(A 11,258 n.); and this suggests that Homer's
two methods are expected to be known and that
Pope's reader is to recognize in the quoted
couplets the conjunction of both of these
Homeric time devices. The first couplet
reflects Homer's lines translated by Pope as

> What-time the judge forsakes the noisy bar
> To take repast, and stills the wordy war.[8]

But the dining of Homer's judges merely stilled
the windy arguments; Pope's transformation
makes something hideous and savage of their
eighteenth-century heirs, who sacrifice lives
under selfish compulsion of their own bodily
hunger. Homer's words, that is, provide a
standard of simple dignity against which Pope
ironically measures the degeneracy of his own
civilization. His second couplet is built on
the lines he translated as

> As the tir'd ploughman spent with stubborn
>   toil,
> Whose oxen long have torn the furrow'd soil,
> Sees with delight the sun's declining ray,
> When home with feeble knees, he bends his
>   way
> To late repast, (the day's hard labour done).
>   (Odyssey, XIII,39-43)

One need only recall Pope's opposition of
agrarian cultural values to those of modern
City capitalism in the *Epistle to Bathurst* to
recognize the significance of his displacing
Homer's ploughman by the merchant at the Royal
Exchange. In the effete London culture the
day's hard manual labor of Homer's ploughman is
not performed by the merchant but by the lady
at her dressing-table. Pope's lines of course
are explicit enough and carry their own satiric
force, but we lose the large historico-cultural
context in which Pope has placed them unless we
can see how they do violence to Homer's passages, adulterate them, because the weak and
sordid modern culture adulterates the simple
purity of the Homeric life. In fact, then, the
text cannot properly be separated from its
allusion, and the latter is present as a functional part of the sense.

The shearing of Belinda's lock, that trivial
thing giving rise to the poem's mighty contest,

is sufficiently colored by Pope, even in the
poem's title, to take on ambiguous sexual
nuances and to grant Belinda some seeming
justification for her tantrums. It would not
be irrelevant or unilluminating at this point
to invoke Krafft-Ebing on the role of hair in
primitive fertility and puberty rites, but we
might more pertinently ask what the loss of
maiden locks would more consciously have suggested to an audience whose natural and in-
stinctive reference was the Greco-Roman literature and culture. Readers of Apollonius'
Argonautica (IV,26 seq.) would have known that
when Medea planned to elope with Jason she
tore off a long tress of hair and left it in
her bedchamber for her mother, a memorial, the
poet says, of her maidenhood. The annotators
would have reminded the reader that Euripides,
Herodotus, Callimachus, Valerius, Flaccus,
Pausanias, and Lucian,[9] among others, also tell
of nations whose maidens cut their virgin locks
and sacrificed them to a deity of chastity as
a ritualistic preparation for marriage. In the
words of Statius, "by ancestral rite the
daughters of Iasus, so soon as their chaste
years grew ripe for wedlock, were wont to make
offering of virgin tresses and pray pardon for
their first marriage-bed."[10] Because the hair
had been dedicated in childhood to a deity, it
was regularly called *crinis sacer*--the "sacred
lock," as Belinda's is twice called (III,153;
IV,133). These were facts known to any serious reader: the major edition of Statius,
by Caspar Barth, contains an essay on the subject, and encyclopedias like Theodor Zwinger's
Theatrum humanae vitae and Johann Hofmann's
Lexicon universale treated it at some length.[11]
        In such a context of nuptial rites, what
the Baron has raped is not Belinda's virginity
but, like her fillet (IV,101), the ritualistic
sign of it. Since one normally subsumes the
other, Pope can equivocate by innuendo, and
John Dennis was on the right track without
knowing it when he complained that the poet

should have asked what strange motive could *induce* or *provoke* "A well-bred *Lord* t'assault a gentle *Belle*" (I,8). "The Word *compel*," Dennis astutely observed, "supposes the Baron to be a Beast, and not a free agent."[12] But from Belinda's point of view, although she has not lost her virginity in fact, she has lost what in her values transcends it, the totemic lock whereby society presumes her an unmarried maiden and grants her the corresponding rights and privileges. For her world is made up of the beau monde's conventional signs, decorative and playful, that substitute for flesh-and-blood reality--one in which a rouged cheek surpasses a real blush, sword-knots duel instead of swords, wigs contend instead of beaux, a card game takes the place of the contest of the sexes, China jars stand for virginity, and a mirror reflection transcends the viewer. Hence, because Belinda equates "honor" not with the facts but with society's presumptions formed on the basis of these signs, she would rather have sacrificed "Hairs less in sight" than those which totemically endow her with maidenhood's power to domineer heartlessly over men, a power she is determined to retain.

To preserve that dominance, Belinda is fortified with the means of sublimating any heterosexual impulse. The resolute coquette, according to the Rosicrucian theology, is rewarded for her virginity with the (purely imaginary) sexual embraces of ambivalent sylphs, the disembodied souls of deceased coquettes. In addition, Belinda is provided with a chaste surrogate for a husband in Shock, the lap-dog equated by the poem with lover and husband (I,15-16; III,158).[13] Notably a mass of hair, the breed derives its generic name from the Icelandic word whose sense we retain in "a shock of hair" and thus is related to the sexual symbolism of the lock. This theriomorphic husband-substitute, appropriately located in the lap, is Belinda's fetish, for, as the system of incubus-like sylphs makes clear, she is

wedded to and sexually gratified by her own
virginity; and the fact answers John Dennis'
objection that a lesser sylph is assigned to
guard the favorite lock while Ariel himself
attends this "vile *Iseland Cur*."[14]

The motive for the narcissistic coquette's
desire to remain seemingly inviolate and
therefore independent is obviously her pride,
and its quasi-theological quality is defined by
Ariel's whispering into her ear a dream of her
importance in the same way that Milton's Satan
tempts Eve in a dream:

<blockquote>

fair Angelic *Eve*,
...be henceforth among the Gods
Thyself a Goddess, not to Earth confin'd.
(*P.L.*, V,74-78)
</blockquote>

But Ariel--that is, the coquettish humor in
Belinda's feminity--also tempts her with words
that arouse other allusive reverberations
defining her pride more precisely. According
to the standard interpretation of the Gospel,
the "babes" to whom divine mysteries are
revealed through faith are the humble and modest
untainted by carnal wisdom, and the "wise and
prudent" from whom it is hid are those with
a swelling conceit of their worldly knowledge.[15]
This Scriptural metaphor for humble faith Ariel
perverts into its literal sense, childish
ignorance of human nature:

<blockquote>

Some secret Truths from Learned Pride
    conceal'd,
To Maids alone and Children are reveal'd.
(I,37-38)
</blockquote>

Then through this ignorant credulity, instead of
faith ("The Fair and Innocent shall still
believe"), he reveals to Belinda the mysteries
of a religion of unrealistic and antisocial
chastity. But the basic tenet of this religion
of the naive is not Christian humility but
pride: "thy own Importance know,/Nor bound thy
narrow Views to Things below" (I,35-36).

Now, "thy own Importance know" pointedly inverts the ubiquitous doctrine that it is essential to "Know Thyself," which was consistently interpreted as the true act of humility and regularly opposed to the pride of curiosity, especially about the stars--the things *above*. The common exemplar of pride in suprahuman learning as opposed to humble self-knowledge was the astronomer Thales, who, gazing on the stars above, nearly fell into a ditch. And of course the opposition accounts for Raphael's refusal to explain to Milton's Adam the motions of the stars:

                                        joy thou
In what he [God] gives to thee, this Paradise
And thy fair Eve: Heaven is for thee too high
To know what passes there; be lowly wise:
Think only what concerns thee and thy being
(*P.L.*,VIII,179-75)

--advice that leads Adam to tell of his own creation, loneliness for society, and union with Eve, whereas Ariel advocates antisocial self-sufficiency: know how important you are and disregard the human world below, together with its sexual and marital needs. The persistence of this moral antinomy and its relevance to Pope's social theme can be judged by Johnson's *Rambler* No. 24 (9 June 1750), which contrasts the "vanity or curiosity" of "calculating the weight of the terraqueous globe" and "adjusting successive systems of worlds beyond the reach of the telescope" with the self-knowledge leading to the performance of "those offices by which the concatenation of society is preserved, and mutual tenderness excited and maintained."

Moreover, if Ariel's advice to know one's own importance is a Satanic inversion of humble self-knowledge, so, conversely, is his instruction *not* to bind "thy narrow View to Things below." As Plutrach wrote in one of the major *loci* of the doctrine, to "know thyself" means

to "use one's self for that one thing for which
Nature has fitted one";[16] and exactly what
Belinda is most fitted for and what is radical
for Pope in the carnal world that Belinda ought
to accept is intimated by "Things below," a
term we may let Swift explicate for us.
Spiritual ascent (like that advocated by Ariel),
Swift wrote, "is not the Business of Flesh and
Blood; it must by the necessary Course of Things
in a little Time, let go its hold, and fall
into Matter. Lovers, for the sake of Celestial
Converse...pretend to see Stars and Heaven in
Ladies Eyes, and to look or think no lower."
Such lovers "seem a perfect Moral to the Story
of that Philosopher [that is, Thales], who,
while his Thoughts and Eyes were fixed upon the
Constellations, found himself seduced by his
lower Parts into a *Ditch.* " No one who had read
at least his Juvenal--to say nothing of the
Priapeia--would have failed to understand the
real meaning of *fossa,* or ditch,[17] any more than
he would have failed to understand Pope's
"Things below."[18]

Awakening from her dream vision of Ariel,
Belinda immediately proceeds to the "sacred
Rites of Pride" at the dressing-table. As
the fact that the toilet is "unveil'd" indicates,
we are here at the temple's inner shrine, where
the idol of the goddess is kept,[19] and the
silver vases of cosmetics correspond to the
sacred vases on the pagan altars. The mirror
in which Belinda sees herself as a goddess is,
of course, the traditional emblem of Pride, but,
given the whole context of the mystery rites,
it is probable that the scene Pope has painted
can be identified more precisely. Apuleius
described a procession of Isis in which some
women with mirrors on their backs walked ahead
of the priestesses and the idol of the goddess
so that the goddess could see the priestesses
as though they were advancing toward her.
Other priestesses, he adds, made gestures as
though combing and adorning the goddess' hair.[20]
Seneca ridiculed the women in the temple of Juno

who hold up a mirror to the goddess;[21] and
Augustine, quoting a lost work by Seneca on
superstition, similarly mocked the women who
hold up mirrors to Juno and Minerva and in
pantomime dress the hair of the goddesses.[22]
Not unexpectedly, the editors made cross references to these three *loci* of the theme, while
one encyclopedia quoted Apuleius' description
under the heading of "Speculum" as an example
of "Vanitatem Foventia,"[23] and another, referring to all three passages, defined "Speculum Junoni tenere" as "vanitas."[24] Supplied
with a topos for the rites of pride, Pope solved
the mystery of the immaterial goddess by identifying the attendant priestess who holds the
mirror with the goddess who appears in it, and
the ridiculed rite has become one of self-ador-
ation.

However exquisite the sylphan machinery, it
must also be recognized as demonic, and in
tempting Belinda to transcend the flesh-and-
blood world by lifelong chastity Ariel offers
her a Satanic substitute for Christianity,
complete with doctrine of immortality, angelo-
logy, psalmody, and cosmology. For example,
he promises that if she is faithful to his
doctrines of coquetry the sylphs will keep her

>   Safe from the treach'rous Friend, the
>   daring Spark,
>   The Glance by Day, the Whisper in the Dark;
>   (I,73-74)

and his words invoke Psalm 91, promising that
God "shall give his angels charge over thee"
so that "Thou shalt not be afraid for the terror
by night; nor for the arrow that flieth by day;
Nor for the pestilence that walketh in darkness;
nor for the destruction that wasteth at noonday"
--threats regularly interpreted as covert and
overt temptations.[25] And just as the same Psalm
promises the faithful that guardian angels will
"Keep thee in all thy ways,"[26] Ariel translates
the coquette's social whirl into the wandering

motions of the planets and the guardian sylphs
into those angelic Intelligences who are
supposed to guide the spheres:

> Oft when the World imagine Women [like the
>   planets] stray,
> The Sylphs thro' mystic Mazes guide their
>   Way,
> Thro' all the giddy Circle they pursue,
> And old Impertinence expel by new. (I,91-94)

What the metaphoric activity of the poem is
constituting is, of course, the prideful image
of Belinda as an independent world and female
society as a self-sufficient scheme. Belinda
is imaged as the ruling sun, a deity who creates
order by fiat ("Let Spades be Trumps! she said,
and Trumps they were," III,46), a mortal priestess who is her own divinity. As goddess of
Pride she receives offerings from the entire
world because she is its supreme deity. To
the world she governs, the cup and coffee are
"*China's* Earth" and its "smoking Tyde" (III,110);
for her "all *Arabia* breathes from yonder Box"
(I,134); and the Hindu emblem of the world,
the elephant mounted on the tortoise, becomes
her ivory and tortoise-shell comb. Female
society is an entire planetary system, or a
cosmos governed by the divine "*Cosmetic* Pow'rs";
and just as Belinda is her own goddess and is
urged by Ariel to be sexually self-sufficient,
the souls of coquettes are supposed to become
the guardian angels of coquettes in a self-
perpetuating scheme of female chastity and
immortality.

The religion of such an exclusively coquette
world obviously depends upon the rejection of
all men, for in this theology they, not woman,
are the cause of the Fall: "oh Pious Maid
beware!...Beware of all, but most beware of
Man" (I,112-14)--which also nicely misapplies
Christ's advice to the Apostles: "But beware
of men: for they will deliver you up to the
councils, and they will scourge you in their
synagogues" (Matt.10:16-17). The resolute

coquette both aspires to an exclusively female
society like that of the Amazons and inverts
hierarchy by usurping man's place. Consequently when Belinda seeks to overcome two adventurous knights she resorts to Ombre, a game
deriving its name from the fact that the
challenger, who also determines the governing
trumps, is called *ombre*--the man. The reason,
according to the standard handbook of that day,
is that the game requires "Thought and Reflection which are Qualities peculiar to Man."[27]
Endowed with a lock which is itself the
"Destruction of Mankind" (II,19), Belinda has
arrogated to herself man's role and in the sex-
game of Ombre plays her cards to vanquish him
at his own game. Not only is she aided in the
battle against the beaux by Thalestris, queen
of the Amazons--the "fierce Virago" (V,37), or
manlike woman--but in burning "At *Ombre* singly"
to defeat the knights (III,27) she identifies
herself with Virgil's Amazon, Camilla, who
volunteered "singly" to engage the opposing
cavalry.[28] Indeed, when Pope writes that the
Baron prayed "Soon to obtain, and long possess"
the lock and that

> The Pow'rs gave Ear, and granted half his
>   Pray'r,
> The rest, the Winds dispers'd in empty Air,
>   (II,44-46)

he exactly repeats Virgil's words when Arruns
prays to slay that same belligerent Camilla,
notable for her love of virginity and weapons
of war.[29] The Amazon is the perfect type of
the coquette, implying the fantasy of a self-
sufficient female society, ever victorious over
men in the sex-battle.
Marriage would of course shatter this proud
fantasy by subjugating the coquette to man and
destroying her power over fashionable society;
and the theme of marriage, explicit in Clarissa's
speech, hovers suggestively over the poem in the
allusive contexts. A notable instance is the

Cave of Spleen episode, which draws into its
ambience the section of Virgil's seventh book
in which Juno calls up the Fury Alecto to anger
Lavinia's mother, Amata.[30] Now, Belinda had
been equated with Juno at the very beginning
of the poem when the poet asked, "And in soft
Bosoms dwells such mighty Rage?"   (I,12), for
the line echoes Virgil's "tantaene animis
caelestibus irae?"   (*Aeneid*, I,11), which
questions how Juno, a divinity, can entertain
the human passion of hate. Consequently Pope's
adaptation not only expresses wonder that
anger can lodge in Belinda's feminine tenderness
but also carries an allusive oversense intimating Belinda's supreme divinity and attaching
to her Juno's unforgiving resentment of Aeneas
and his entire race. In *Aeneid*, VII, the source
of the Cave of Spleen episode, Umbriel-like
Alecto, on being called up by Juno, inspires
Lavinia's mother and her female friends to
Bacchic fury like that of Belinda and her
attendant belles and incites the war that
occupies the last half of the *Aeneid* as it does
the end of the *Rape*. What is centrally significant in the context of the allusion is that
Juno stirred up these angry battles because,
in her enmity to Aeneas, she wished to thwart
by that means his fated marriage with Lavinia.
    Given Belinda's Amazonian character, the
totemism of her "sacred" prenuptial lock, and the
fact that the Cave of Spleen episode alludes
to a context having to do with preventing a
marriage, it is implicit that Belinda is not
fighting off sexual union so much as the
humiliation of marriage and its degrading
social consequences. As a coquette, Belinda
"rejects Mankind" (I,68), seeking only "to
win hearts and throw 'em away, regarding nothing
but the triumph,"[31] and her antithesis is
Clarissa, who, adapting Sarpedon's rationale
for the heroic life, urges that she use "good
Sense" and "good Humour" to preserve the men's
admiration and desire that "Beauty gains,"
whatever maiden locks or maidenhood may be lost

in the process. The advice is open to jaundiced
interpretation, and the coquette's ally,
Amazonian Thalestris, chooses to take it as
that of a prude, who, by the poem's definition,
seeks suitors only to jilt them successively
in an insatiable hope for an ever more splendid
husband. But in fact Clarissa's speech does
"open more clearly the Moral of the Poem" by
calling on Belinda to recognize that the coquette's mastery over men cannot outlast her
transient beauty and that if she were to
accept with heroic good humor the rape of the
prenuptial lock as the inevitable risk of being
a seductive and most nubile belle she would
preserve, not lose, her glorious power over
men. Moreover, Clarissa openly acknowledges
the value of undertaking a "Huswife's Cares"
as the heroic sacrifice that makes female life
meaningful and glorious in a world where beauty
cannot last. Belinda's life of privileged
artifice cannot forever evade reality; indeed,
it tempts it, challenges it to break in.
Therefore only when Belinda rejects Clarissa's
advice out of hand does the conflict of belles
and beaux develop into a real and physical
sexual battle--the *nocturnum bellum*, as Virgil
styles it--in which a finger and a thumb can
provoke an orgasmic sneeze that subdues the
hero's "manly Strength"[32] and the hero, who had
sought only "on his Foe to die,"[33] admits to the
heroine,

> Nor think, to die dejects my lofty Mind;[34]
> All that I dread, is leaving you behind![35]
> Rather than so, ah let me still survive,
> And burn in Cupid's Flames,--but burn alive.
> (V,99-101)

Whether or not the coquette submits to marriage,
her pretty fantasy of self-sufficient virginity
will inevitably be invaded by fleshly appetites--
to give evidence of Clarissa's truism that "she
who scorns a Man, must die a Maid." On this
occasion, it is true, the heroine has foiled

the bodily assault with an epic trick, but the
true wretchedness of her state is made apparent
by her cry:

> *Restore the Lock!* she cries; and all around
> *Restore the Lock!* the vaulted Roofs rebound.
>   (V,103-104)

Despite her victory over the Baron, Belinda,
by scorning Clarissa's advice, has reduced
herself to the pitiable condition of Ovid's
young girls who fancy they are being earnestly
wooed, only to find that their elegant suitors
are inflamed only by desire to steal their
robes:

> *Redde meum!* clamant spoliatae saepe puellae,
> *Redde meum!* toto voce boante foro.[36]

Another allusion exercises a structural
control like that of the Alecto episode. When,
at Ombre, the virgin fends off the temptation
diamonds hold out to female hearts, halts at
the brink of losing her heart, and then defeats
the men, she exults with pride; and the poet,
playing on "Honours" as both trophies of war and
card honors, warns:

> Oh thoughtless Mortals! ever blind to Fate,
> Too soon dejected, and too soon elate!
> Sudden these Honours shall be snatch'd away,
> And curs'd for ever this Victorious Day.
>   (III,101-104)

As we know, this exactly echoes Virgil's prophecy when Turnus slays Aeneas' companion Pallas
and, exulting, seizes Pallas' belt as his
"honor," or trophy. Virgil's prophecy is
fulfilled, for at the end of the *Aeneid* when
Aeneas hesitates in pity over the fallen Turnus
it is the sight of the stolen belt that incites
him to slay his foe. Belinda similarly pays
for her proud honors, for the Baron later swears

never to return the severed hair:

> But by this Lock, this sacred Lock I swear,
> . . . .
> Which never more its Honours shall renew,
> . . . .
> He spoke, and speaking, in proud Triumph spread
> The long-contended Honours of her Head
> (IV,133-40)

--the *honores capitis*, as the Ancients described splendid hair.[37] The honor Belinda won at Ombre is the coquette's societal reputation defined by Thalestris as greater than virtue and by Ariel as the woman-created system of chastity. And it is lost as far as coquette society is concerned when the sign of virginal independence--the *honor capitis*--is removed. The multiple puns on "honor" link Belinda's card victory with the rape to reveal that the causal sequence in the *Aeneid* is implicit here: the coquette's tempting conduct whereby she "conquers" men and gains honors should, indeed, lead to her being conquered by a man and losing those honors, but in marriage, not in the *nocturnum bellum* of the last canto. Belinda's flaw, as Clarissa makes clear, is not her pretty and domineering coquetry, but her refusal to accept as its proper consequence the Baron's compulsion to rape the social insignia of her virginal independence.

But even if we recognize that Pope's applying Virgil's prophecy to Belinda does more than provide the reader the delight of recognition and is also a structural control relating her acquisition of honors to the price she must pay for them, the question remains how much of the allusive context may properly be brought to bear. If we can assume that it is the nature of Pope's poetry to incite the reader to search the allusive context for even those relevances not verbally engaged in his text, then it is strikingly apposite that Virgil's analogue to

the fateful honors Belinda won at Ombre--that
is, the belt that Turnus took from his slain
foe and that was eventually responsible for
his own death--had depicted on it the story of
Danaus' heroically coquettish daughters who
were forced into marriage by Aegyptus' sons
and slew their husbands on their bridal night
(*Aeneid*, X, 495-99).

A number of the allusive contexts, however,
prove curiously at odds with the poem's explicit
words. When, for example, the lock has been
stolen, the poet writes,

> But anxious Care the pensive Nymph opprest,
> And secret Passions labour'd in her Breast.

These words, opening the fourth Canto, exactly
repeat those opening the fourth *Aeneid*: "But
the queen [i.e., Dido], long since wounded
by anxious cares...is torn by secret passion."[38]
The parallel is exact, for Servius and the
commentators who followed him, troubled by
Virgil's beginning a book with "But," explained
that Dido's anxious cares are being contrasted
with Aeneas' easy indifference at the end of
Book III, just as Belinda's cares contrast with
the Baron's exultation over the rape at the end
of Canto III. Moreover, just as Belinda is
perturbed because the loss of her totemic
lock undermines her social authority as coquette
so, according to Servius' gloss, Virgil here
indicates Dido by her title (*regina*) rather than
by name because the source of her cares threatens her dignity as queen.[39] But Belinda
grieves because a rejected beau has ravished
her sign of maidenhood; Dido, who has vowed
to remain faithful to her dead husband and
never to remarry, grieves because she reluctantly finds she loves Aeneas. If the allusive
context is truly operative, it suggests that
beneath the outrage over the social offense
and a determination to avoid love and marriage,
Belinda, like Dido, feels a reluctant desire
for the man, a passion hidden from her conscious

mind. To what other feelings could Pope,
repeating Virgil's very words, be referring as
"secret Passions"? Surely not Belinda's
resentment over the rape, which her shrieks
have declared pubicly enough. The same relation
between Dido's failure to keep her lover and
Belinda's failure to keep her sign of coquettish
heartlessness is, of course, again developed
when Belinda's lament is made to echo Dido's
"Happy! ah too happy had I been if the Dardan
keels had never touched these shores!" (*Aeneid*,
IV,657-58):

> Happy! ah ten times happy, had I been,
> If Hampton-Court these Eyes had never seen!
>   (V,149-50)

It is likely therefore that when Belinda,
almost immediately after this cry, wishes,

> Oh had I rather un-admir'd remain'd
> In some lone Isle, or distant *Northern* Land,
>   (IV,153-54)

we are meant to hear Dido sigh, "Ah, that I
could not live a blameless life outside wedlock,
even as some wild beast, knowing not such
cares!" (*Aeneid*, IV,550-51). If so, the
oversense vividly comments on the unnatural and
antisocial character of Belinda's wishes to
avoid wedlock.[40]
    Later Belinda's grief over the rape is again
set in the context of Dido's love-griefs.
Pathetically she demands the return of the lock,
but although "the pitying Audience melt in
Tears, / ... *Fate* and *Jove* had stopp'd the *Baron's*
Ears" (V,1-2). This echoes the failure of
Anna's pleas on Dido's behalf--"but by no tear-
ful pleas is [Aeneas] moved...Fate opposes, and
Jove stops his ears" (*Aeneid*, IV,438-40)--and
Pope makes the allusion explicit:

> Not half so fixt the Trojan cou'd remain,
> When Anna begg'd and Dido rag'd in vain.

But Belinda, rejecting the Baron, wants her
maidenly honor returned; Dido's raging desire
is that her lover return. Pope's words and
their allusive context contradict each other,
and if we take the contradiction as the conflict
between Belinda's conscious and subconscious
mind, it only confirms Pope's psychoanalysis
of her elsewhere. When, for example, Ariel,
guardian of virginal coquettes, seeks to
prevent the rape,

> Sudden he view'd, in spite of all her Art,
> An Earthly Lover lurking at her Heart.
>   (III,143-44)

Surely it is irrelevant to ask whether the lover
is the Baron. Despite the conscious social
artfulness of her mind, Belinda is flesh and
blood, not a sylph, and in the Nature of her
heart lurks unconscious yearning for a mortal
lover, not the imaginary, disembodied one Ariel
offered. In Ariel's religion there is sin in
Belinda's Nature, and his powers over her
integrity fail. After all, Belinda never was
Ariel's star pupil: in spite of the dream in
which he taught her to beware of all men, when
her "Eyes first open'd on a *Billet-doux*...all
the Vision vanish'd from [her] Head"(I,118-20).
As Pope paints her, she is at that age when
she thinks she hates the boys and cannot understand what is really troubling her. "What
mov'd my Mind," she asks in all innocence,
"with youthful Lords to rome?" (IV,159).
Perhaps Thomas Parnell best saw how the allusive
contexts adumbrate Belinda's unconscious urges
when he wrote of the poem:

> But know, ye Fair! a point conceal'd with art,
> The Sylphs and Gnomes are but a woman's
>   heart:
> The Graces stand in sight; a Satyr train
> Peep o'er their heads, and laugh behind
>   the scene.[41]

Superficially, the elaborate comparison at
the end of the poem (V,129-40) of Belinda's
lock to that of Catullus' Berenice[42] seems only
a charming compliment: the severed lock, like
Berenice's, becomes a star; the astrologer
Partridge, like Catullus' astronomer, discovers
it; and lovers hail it in the heavens. But
in fact the comparison is highly paradoxical,
and the differences are even more functional
than the similarities. Belinda is outraged
by the beau's seizure of her lock, Berenice
volunteered to sacrifice hers to the goddess
of love for the safe return of her husband; and
Belinda is related to Berenice in the same way
that she is to Dido.[43] Even within Pope's text
it is incongruous that the "blest Lover" should
mistake for Venus, goddess of love, the stellar
lock of the coquette who had rejected a lord;
and the line must be read tongue-in-cheek.
     Moreover, Berenice's lock calls on wives
who reverence their chaste wedlock to make
offerings to it, adding, "But I want no offerings from those given to foul adultery"; Pope,
on the other hand, pretending flattery, calls
on the "blest Lover" to send up vows to
Belinda's lock from " Rosamonda's Lake"--a
curious choice in view of the Fair Rosamond's
adulterous affair with Henry. For under the
guise of flattering Belinda, Pope is subtly
giving body to Clarissa's axiom that "she who
scorns a Man, must die a Maid," and the conclusion of the poem is far less the glittering
tribute to Belinda than its bequiling surface
claims. But now, as a working hypothesis, let
us assume that by invoking Catullus' poem
Pope implicitly invokes all of it that may be
relevant. Just as Belinda's rejection of a
possible lover is cast in terms of Dido's yearning for her lover, so, in one of the most
striking passages of Catullus' poem, Berenice's
lock asks, "Do new brides really hate Venus? or
do they mock their parents' joys with hypocrit-
ical tears when they leave their virgin cham-
bers? By the gods, they do not really grieve.
This is what Berenice taught me by her real

tears when her husband left her bed for the
wars." Montaigne, incidentally, quoted these
lines to illustrate the paradox "That we weep
and laugh for the same thing." The bride's
lamentation is veiled jubilation.

Indeed, Pope's enigmatic epigraph has all
along been intimating the disparity between
Belinda's conscious rejection of mankind and
the unconscious stirrings of desire for a man.
Pope substituted Belinda for one Polytimus in
an epigram by Martial so that it translates:
"I was reluctant, Belinda, to cut off your
lock; but I am happy to have granted this to
your wishes." Perhaps Mistress Arabella
Fermor was to be beguiled into taking this as
a charming tribute: the poet regrets that,
poetically speaking, he has cut off her lock,
but he is happy to have written the poem as
she requested. But it is not what the lines
actually say: Polytimus begged Martial to cut
off his hair, and Martial did so, adding in the
two lines Pope omitted that now his real beauty
has been made visible, just as Pelops, by being
shorn, bared his beautiful shoulder to his new
bride.[44] Now, the standard commentary on
Martial in at least twenty editions up to and
including the handsome variorum of 1617 was
that of Calderinus, who explains that Polytimus
asked the poet to cut his lock because he
intended to get married.[45] In view of the
general tenor of the other allusive contexts,
the relevance of Calderinus' interpretation
to Belinda seems fairly obvious.

If this has been an admissible commentary
on *The Rape of the Lock*, it would imply that the
mode of existence of Pope's poetry--and probably of many other neoclassic poems--ought
to be defined broadly enough to include a
creative act by the reader. For it suggests
that the reader is not only to appreciate the
poet's invention in finding appropriate
allusions but is actively invited by them to
exercise, within poetic reason, his own invention by contemplating the relevances of the

entire allusive context and its received
interpretation. Instead of making the passive
assumption, for example, that Pope omitted the
last two lines of Martial's epigram because
they are not applicable, one is to entertain
the possibility that their omission is an
enticement to the reader to exercise as much
wit as the poet did in applying the first two
lines to his poem. Certainly when Pope, like
some others, printed the Latin originals along
with his imitations of Horace, he was prodding
the reader to discover for himself the ways
in which the Latin text implicitly acts upon
the English, synergistically qualifying, in-
crementing, and complicating its sense and tone.
Sterne was not the first to ask the reader to
"give me all the help you can" and to "halve
this matter amicably" so that both author and
reader have "something to imagine." One might
instance the function of the tunes in Gay's
Beggar's Opera in drawing their original lyrics
into significant interaction with Gay's words;
or, to select an especially complex example,
the consequences of placing Pope's line "And
one more Pensioner St. Stephen gains" (*Epistle
to Bathurst*, 1.394) in the *total* context both of
the Scriptural story of St. Stephen and of Juvenal's Third Satire, which it echoes. One
might also consider the fact that when Gulliver
wishes to testify to the truthfulness of his
book and to avow that he has followed the
virtuous example of the rational horses, he
quotes the lines from the *Aeneid* in which Sinon
protests that he is incapable of deceit. Surely the reader is expected to recall that Sinon
was, in fact, the most heroic of liars and that
through his deceitful protestation of truthfulness he persuaded the Trojans to admit another
kind of fictitious horse--to the destruction of
their city. Such literature as this is constituted not only by its own verbal texture but also
by the rich interplay between the author's text
and the full contexts it allusively arouses, for
these allusive resonances are not peripheral
but functional to the meaning of the artistic
product.

POPE'S *ELOISA to ABELARD* AND
"THOSE CELEBRATED LETTERS"

Robert P. Kalmey

In view of the customary austerity of Samuel
Johnson's critical judgment, his praise of Pope's
Eloisa to Abelard (1717) is memorable: "*The Epistle
to Eloisa to Abelard* is one of the most happy productions of human wit." Johnson then discusses
the history of Abelard and Heloise, and concludes
with an appraisal of Pope's poetical genius:

> the subject is so judiciously chosen, that it
> would be difficult, in turning over the annals
> of the world, to find another which so many
> circumstances concur to recommend. We regular-
> ly interest ourselves most in the fortune of
> those who most deserve our notice. Abelard
> and Eloisa were conspicuous in their days for
> eminence of merit. The heart naturally loves
> truth. The adventures and misfortunes of this
> illustrious pair are known from undisputed
> history. Their fate does not leave the mind in
> hopeless dejection, for they both found quiet
> and consolation in retirement and piety. So
> new and so affecting is their story, that it

This essay first appeared in *Philological Quarterly* 47 (1968), 164-78.

supercedes invention and imagination ranges
at full liberty without straggling into scenes
of fable.
  The story, thus skilfully adopted, has been
diligently improved. Pope has left nothing
behind him which seems more the effect of
studious perseverance and laborious revisal.
Here is particularly observable the *curiosa
felicitas*, a fruitful soil and careful cultivation. Here is no crudeness of sense, nor as-
perity of language.[1]

Johnson's image from gardening suggests an intimate relationship between nature and art, and
more particularly the integral unity of Pope's
subject matter and his art. If the story of
Abelard and Heloise offers "a fruitful soil," it
deserved the "careful cultivation" of Pope's art.
  Eloisa to Abelard remains to this day sufficiently esteemed to appear in anthologies of literature, yet some modern critics have not admitted a
central fact of Pope's poetical achievement--that
unity of subject matter and art implied by Johnson in his image from gardening.[2] Professor
Reuben Brower, for example, sees *Eloisa to Abelard*
as essentially a *tour de force*: "the essential poetic design of the poem is Ovidian," and Pope
has attempted, but only "very nearly succeeded in
doing the impossible, in naturalizing an alien
literary tradition and form."[3] To Professor
Brower, *Eloisa to Abelard* is thus merely an English
rendition of hybrid foreign materials, a French
story cast in the mold of the Latin heroic epistle of Ovid. The heroic epistle, however, had
been successfully written in English by Michael
Drayton in his *Englands Heroicall Epistles* (1597-99)
more than a century before Pope, and Drayton's
work had remained popular throughout his lifetime
and the seventeenth century.[4] If an "alien"
tradition had to be "naturalized" at all, it
would seem that Drayton's poems had already completed the process. In the present essay, we
will seek to elucidate the basic Christian fabric
of the poem in an effort to discover some of the

ways by which a "careful cultivation" helps to
create, out of a collection of old letters, a new
poem with its own significant meaning.

I

One of the most influential modern scholars of
medieval thought, Etienne Gilson, has praised
Pope's *Eloisa to Abelard* for capturing the essential
spirit of the twelfth century letters of Abelard
and Héloise: "I would not take an oath," Professor Gilson declares, "that Pope is always
faithful to the thought of Héloise. But I know
at least four of his lines which Héloise herself
would have been sorry not to have written, so well
do they express what the Abbess of the Paraclete
suggests on each page, without daring to give it
expression:

> Still on that breast enamour'd let me lie,
> Still drink delicious poison from thy eye,
> Pant on thy lip, and to thy heart be prest;
> Give all thou canst--and let me dream the rest.
> (121-24)

If this is not what Héloise was thinking as she
wrote Letters II and IV of the Correspondence,
then it is useless for other poets to try to express her experience. The last line, especially,
is priceless."[5] Professor Gilson thus notices
in Pope's poem the preservation of the passionate
intensity of Héloise's emotional struggle. The
correspondence of feeling that Professor Gilson
perceives between the original medieval letters
and Pope's poem suggests, in turn, the possible
existence of an important contextual and thematic
continuity between them.

In "The Argument" prefixed to *Eloisa to Abelard*,
Pope states that his poem is "partly extracted"
from "those celebrated letters" of Abelard and
Héloise,[6] and the profusion of parallels between
Eloisa to Abelard and John Hughes' 1713 translation
of the *Letters of Abelard and Heloise* (the first in
English) indicates Pope's immediate source.[7]

Many of these parallels, but by no means all, are cited in the introduction and notes to the Twickenham Edition of *Eloisa to Abelard*. In addition, Professor Geoffrey Tillotson and other scholars have reviewed at some length the complicated history of the late seventeenth and early eighteenth century translations of the Abelard and Heloise letters.[8] They seek to establish that the difference between the twelfth century letters and the later translations arises from the infusion of the popular seventeenth century rhetoric of romance into the twelfth century letters.[9] Certainly we can agree that obvious differences separate the seventeenth and eighteenth century translations from the medieval letters: Hughes himself knew that his translation had cast off the bulk of what he calls "School Divinity, and ... the Learning of those [medieval] Times."[10] Without exception, however, modern studies of Pope's poem have ignored the persistence of an enduring Christian context and theme in the medieval letters, in the seventeenth and eighteenth century French and English translations, and in Pope's *Eloisa to Abelard*. A summary of the history of the letters from the medieval originals to the form in which they reached Pope will not only suggest the alterations they suffered, but also may affirm the basic contextual and thematic continuity of the Abelard and Heloise story.

At Paris, in 1616, Francois D'Amboise published the first edition of the medieval Latin letters as part of a larger edition of Abelard's works.[11] The high regard of D'Amboise for the letters anticipates the esteem felt for them in later times especially for their warm and passionate confessions of ardent mutual love. But the confessions of love represent only a small portion of the letters, and even they usually appear within a larger Christian context of sin, suffering, and hope for redemption. Heloise and Abelard have committed a sin by loving each other without regard for the divine and eternal laws of the Church to which they previously had sworn their faith. Each has sinned by turning away

from God in favor of one of His creatures, and
they come to see the calamities separating them
irrevocably from each other as punishment for
their sin. The purpose of their punishment and
suffering is to re-direct their now fruitless
manifestation of human love to include God, its
source and end. Heloise's struggle in the *Letters*
reveals her attempt to see in her love for Abelard the seed of a renewed love for God. "Her
problem," as Professor Gilson explains, "is to
find in the passion this man inspires the strength
required for a life of sacrifice which is both
meaningless and impossible save on the level of
the love of God."12 Heloise, and Abelard too,
are sustained in this struggle by the faith that
what seems an impossible task for mere human will
can be effected with the assistance of God's
grace. Suffering attains meaning for Heloise and
Abelard from their conviction that God benignly
directs all human events toward human redemption
and salvation.13

Later in the seventeenth century, Roger de
Rabutin, Comte de Bussy (1618-93), translated into French three letters of the original eight--
two letters by Heloise (Letters II and IV) and
one by Abelard (Letter III).14 Bussy chose the
most passionate letters and added freely to the
Latin original, but his translation nevertheless
preserved the main Christian context and theme of
the Latin letters. And while Bussy, who wrote
The Amorous History of the Gauls (1666), certainly
emphasized the frankly sensuous and passionate
character of the letters, it surely is a distor-
tion to see in Bussy's Heloise, as Professor
Tillotson has done, "the dynamo of what amounts
to a 'romantick' novel."15 By heightening the
passion of Heloise for Abelard, Bussy actually
raises into sharper relief Heloise's struggle
between the love of creature and the love of Creator which we have seen to be a central conflict
in the Latin letters.

As an epistolary model for a passionate nun
deserted by her lover, Bussy had the letters of
Marianna Alcoforado, published at Paris in 1669

as *Lettres portugaises*.16 Although these letters
from a Portuguese nun do little to suggest a depth
of agony in the human soul, they provided Bussy
with an already popular and analogous subject
written in contemporary style.

Other French translations based on Bussy's appeared in the late seventeenth century,17 and
Pierre Bayle included many details of the Heloise
and Abelard story in his *Critical and Historical Dictionary* (1697; English trans., 1710).18 François
Du Bois used Bussy's MS translation, Bayle's
Dictionary, and an anonymous 1693 French translation (published at The Hague) to fashion a collection of the letters which included two entirely fabricated letters and a translation of Abelard's *Historia calamitatum*.19 It was the fifth edition of Du Bois' collection (1711) that John
Hughes translated into English.

The Latin letters of Heloise and Abelard had
suffered not only translation, but also trunca-
tion and accretion, before they came into the
hands of John Hughes. Yet in spite of this series
of alterations, the traditional Christian context
and theme of sin, suffering, and redemption survived. Hughes found this theme in Du Bois' edition, and he preserved it in his own translation
of the letters into English. The profusion of
parallels between Pope's *Eloisa to Abelard* and
Hughes' translation may therefore affirm more than
mere similarities of diction; they may affirm also
the continuity of the basic Christian contextual
and thematic fabric of the medieval Latin letters
in both Hughes and in Pope. Pope's *Eloisa to Abelard*, like the letters that serve as its source,
is distinguished, we shall see, by its emphatic
concern with human frailty and suffering and with
the problem of salvation. If in one sense Pope's
poem has lost the specific medieval tone of the
Latin letters, in another deeper sense it has retained what is essential to them: the Christian
view of man humbled by his own weakness before a
just but merciful God.

II

The Christian view of man in *Eloisa to Abelard*
appears in sharp outline when we consider some of
the more important ways in which Pope used Hughes'
translation of the *Letters*. In Hughes' translation
of the *Letters*, Heloise appears in her convent
fully aware of her guilt and sin in a love which
has no room for God: "I am here, I confess, a
Sinner, but one who far from weeping for her Sins,
weeps only for her Lover; far from abhorring her
Crimes, endeavors only to add to them" (p. 123).
Heloise confesses herself a sinner, but admits the
imperfection of her act of contrition. She admits
that she does not have "the sincere Desire of being
truly penitent. Thus I strive and labour in vain"
(p. 123). Without the perfection of the indispensable act of contrition, which depends upon the
firm intention of the will to return to God, Heloise
remains immersed, unrepentant and unforgiven, in
her crimes. She recognizes the weakness of her own
will: "I am conquered by my Inclination. My Love
troubles my Mind, and disorders my Will" (p. 124).
The specific disorder of her will that Heloise confesses is the exclusion of God from her devotion:
"Among those who are wedded to God I serve a Man;
Among the Heroick Supporters of the Cross I am a
poor Slave to a Human Passion; at the head of a
Religious Community I am devoted to *Abelard* only"
(p. 123). Pope's Eloisa, too, acknowledges the
impotence of a will that cannot return her to God
as long as she remains an absolute "slave" (178)
to Abelard, and the outlines of Eloisa's struggle
appear sharply drawn in the balanced antithesis
of his couplet:

Ah wretch! believ'd the spouse of God in vain,
Confess'd within the slave of love and man.
                    (177-78)

Like Hughes' Heloise, Pope's Eloisa recognizes
her "crime" (104, 185, 193), her "guilt" (230),
her "stain" (266), and her "sin" (191).[20]

Hughes' Heloise understands clearly that for their sin "of a Criminal Love" she and Abelard now suffer punishment at the hands of God: "the whole Wrath of Heaven fell on us in all its Weight" (p. 169). She perceives her own punishment to be particularly appropriate to the nature of her sin--the letters and conversation which before had given her happiness and pleasure now cause her misery and pain: "Those tender Letters I have wrote to you, and those passionate Conversations I have had with you, give me as much Pain now, as they formerly did Pleasure" (p. 185). Heloise admits the culpability of her wilful sin with Abelard, and she knows too that she could have avoided her punishment by abstaining from her sin: "I ought to have foreseen other more certain Evils; and to have consider'd that the Idea of lost Enjoyments would be the Trouble of my whole Life" (p. 173).

The "Idea of lost Enjoyments" recurs frequently in Pope's *Eloisa to Abelard*. For instance, the sudden loss of the enjoyment of love is woven into the very structure of line 37, where misery follows happiness by only the short breathless pause of a caesura: "Now warm in love, now with'ring in thy bloom." The first word of the following line seems to punctuate the loss of happiness with an abrupt finality: "*Lost* in a convent's solitary gloom!"[21] Eloisa then recalls the happiness she enjoyed in her passion for Abelard (55-96), but also immediately remembers the subsequent brutal revenge taken on Abelard:

> This sure is bliss (if bliss on earth there
>   be)
> And once the lot of *Abelard* and me.
>   Alas how chang'd! what sudden horrors rise!
> A naked Lover bound and bleeding lies!
>   (97-100)

Throughout much of the poem, in Eloisa's reminiscences and dreams, the "Idea of lost Enjoyments" haunts and tortures her. Her torture is all the more intense for she has lost, in addition to Abelard, her God.

The memory of all that has been lost through
her sin moves Eloisa to an intense awareness of
her misery. Her tears, which Professors Audra and
Tillotson somewhat jocularly see as a "deluge"
imitating lachrymose epics and romances,[22] are
moved by her recognition that her sin-damaged
world is indeed a vale of tears.

In the final sentence of Hughes' translation,
Abelard implores Heloise to shed tears which will
help prepare her for eventual salvation--tears of
contrition: "may you shed as many Tears for your
Salvation, as you have done during the Course of
our Misfortunes" (p. 218). But Hughes' Heloise,
like all Christians, remains uncertain whether
her tears will be effectual for her salvation.
In her final letter to Abelard she compares his
relatively peaceful seclusion with her torments:

> You *Abelard* will happily finish your Course,
> your Desires and Ambitions will be no Obstacle
> to your Salvation. Heloise only must lament,
> she only must weep without being certain
> whether all her Tears will be available or
> not to her Salvation. (P. 199)

Pope's Eloisa, haunted by memories of the image
of Abelard as her lover, fears the stubborn
strength of her love for the man will render her
tears useless for her salvation:

> Nor pray'rs nor fasts its [her heart's] stub-
>   born pulse restrain,
> Nor tears, for ages, taught to flow in vain.
>   (27-28)

Specifically, Eloisa questions whether her tears
of anguish at the loss of Abelard do not in some
way withhold her from full contrition at the loss
of God and, therefore, from final salvation. In
both Hughes and Pope, Eloisa recognizes that as
long as her continued desire for Abelard diminishes her love of God she remains in danger of
losing her own salvation.

As some of the notes to the Twickenham Edition
show, Pope readily borrowed hints and passages
from Hughes' translation of Abelard's letters,
and adapted them to Eloisa's expression of her
grief and suffering. Pope seems particularly to
borrow from Hughes' Abelard in order to emphasize
and sharpen the dramatic conflict in which Eloisa
finds herself engaged. For instance, when Hughes'
Abelard replies to Heloise's first letter, he recalls the solemn ceremony that marked her entrance
into the convent: "I saw your Eyes, when you
spoke your last farewel, fix'd upon the Cross"
(p. 154). Pope not only gives Abelard's observation to Eloisa, but also, in a radical contradiction of Hughes' translation, he alters the situation significantly. Eloisa fixes her gaze not upon
the Cross to which her sacred vows commit her,
but upon Abelard:

> Yet then, to those dread altars as I drew,
> Not on the Cross my eyes were fix'd, but you.
> 　　　　　　　(115-16)

Pope deepens the dramatic conflict within Eloisa's
soul by showing that her love for Abelard literally diverts her from her devotion to God.
　　Pope uses other passages in the same letter
from Abelard to dramatize within Eloisa the conflict between the love of Abelard and the love of
God. Lines 189-98 in *Eloisa to Abelard* are structured on a series of thoughts taken from Hughes'
Abelard. "To forget," according to Abelard, "in
the Case of Love, is the most necessary Penitence,
and the most difficult" (p. 147). To Pope's
Eloisa, the difficulty of forgetting becomes a
part of her suffering:

> Of all affliction taught a lover yet,
> 'Tis sure the hardest science to forget!
> 　　　　　　　(189-90)

Hughes' Abelard asks, "How can I separate from
the Person I love, the Passion I must detest?"
(p. 141). Pope, in a chiasmic couplet, adapts

Abelard's dilemma to Eloisa's own struggle in
order to distinguish her crime from the source of
her love and pleasure, or the "sin"--"offence"
from the "sense"--"offender":

> How shall I lose the sin, yet keep the sense,
> And love th' offender, yet detest th' offence?
> (191-92)

Hughes' Abelard continues to meditate upon the
difficulty of separating the person of Heloise
from the passion he continues to feel toward her:

> What Abhorrence can I be said to have of my
> Sins, if the Objects of them are always ami-
> able to me? ... 'Tis difficult in our Sorrow
> to distinguish Penitence from Love. The
> Memory of the Crime, and the Memory of the Ob-
> ject which has charmed us, are too nearly re-
> lated to be immediately separated. (P. 141)

Abelard's inability to separate the hateful crime,
or sin, from its beloved object, Heloise, reap-
pears in the antithetical balance of Pope's couplet:

> How the dear object from the crime remove,
> Or how distinguish penitence from love?
> (193-94)

When Hughes' Abelard laments the self-contradic-
tions that contribute to his sufferings, he veri-
fies what Heloise had written to him in her first
letter. Heloise had realized that "a Heart which
has been so sensibly affected as mine cannot soon
be indifferent. We fluctuate long between Love
and Hatred, before we can arrive at a happy Tranquility" (p. 129). Abelard admits to Heloise
that he suffers the same fluctuation of love and
hatred: "my Heart is at once pierced with your
Sorrows and its own ... in such different Dis-
quietudes I betray and contradict my self. I
hate you; I love you; Shame presses me on all
sides" (pp. 142, 135). From the preceding ex-

change in Hughes, Pope draws signal words and
phrases to frame Eloisa's conflict of passions:

> Unequal task! a passion to resign,
> For hearts so touch'd, so pierc'd, so lost as
>   mine.
> Ere such a soul regains its peaceful state,
> How often must it love, how often hate!
> (195-98)

Pope's Eloisa then contrasts the pain of suffering that springs from her love for Abelard to
the bliss offered to her by the love of God:

> But let heav'n seize it, all at once 'tis fir'd,
> Not touch'd, but rapt; not waken'd, but
>   inspir'd!
> Oh come! oh teach me nature to subdue,
> Renounce my love, my life, my self--and you.
> Fill my fond heart with God alone, for he
> Alone can rival, can succeed to thee.
> (201-06)

Pope draws most of his inspiration from Hughes'
Heloise to describe the effect of the love of God
on the tortured soul. However, he does respond,
it would seem, to the amplication of certain
phrases that appear in the letters of both Heloise
and Abelard. In her first letter, Hughes' Heloise
implores Abelard for help in overcoming her suffering: "Oh, for Pity's sake, help a Wretch to
renounce her Desires, her self, and if it be possible even to renounce You!" (p. 125). Later in
the same letter she declares to Abelard that God
exercises a singular power over him: "God has a
peculiar Right over the Hearts of Great Men,
which he has created. When he pleases to touch
them, he ravishes them, and lets them not speak
nor breathe but for his Glory" (p. 131). In her
second letter to Abelard, Heloise declares, in a
passage suggesting lines 205-06 of *Eloisa to Abelard*,
that Abelard's rival for her love is God: "When
I have told you what Rival hath ravished my
Heart from you, you will praise my Inconstancy.

... By this you may judge that 'tis God alone
that takes *Heloise* from you" (pp. 183-84). Pope
seems to recall what Abelard had revealed to
Heloise in his first answer to her: "My Jealousie
seemed to be extinguish'd: When God only is our
Rival, we have nothing to fear" (p. 152). Pope's
characteristic method, it would seem from the
examples above, is to use scenes and phrases from
Hughes' translation to sharpen by contrast and
antithesis the dramatic conflicts that make up
Eloisa's suffering. His borrowings from Hughes,
which here extend through the wide range of three
lengthy letters (pp. 125-84), are compressed into
an intensified and tightly-knit drama of suffering and potential redemption.

Hughes' translation does not permit the mere
recognition of human sin and weakness (with its
resultant suffering) to be a final pronouncement
on the human condition. In his first reply to
Heloise, Abelard points the way from weakness to
strength--the way of the Cross: "How weak are we
in our selves, if we do not support our selves on
the Cross of Christ?" (p. 135). Later in the
same letter, Abelard sees the work of God even in
human weakness: "Who does not know that 'tis for
the Glory of God, to find no other Foundation in
Man for his Mercy, than Man's very weakness?"
(p. 153). If man's very weakness becomes the occasion for God's revelation of His mercy to man,
Abelard implies that even man's weakness has a
purpose in the divinely created world. Heloise
had said as much in her first and most famous
letter to Abelard:

> I am ready to humble myself with you to the
> wonderful Providence of God, who does all
> Things for our Sanctification, who by his Grace
> purifies all that is vicious and corrupt in
> the Principle, and by the inconceivable Riches
> of his Mercy draws us to himself against our
> Wishes, and by degrees opens our Eyes to dis-
> cern the Greatness of his Bounty, which at
> first we would not understand.23   (P. 125)

Hughes' Heloise discovers here how God, by an act
of grace, empowers man's will and "draws us to
himself against our Wishes." When she cries out
for help, however, she is not certain whether her
prayer is inspired by God's grace or goaded by
despair: "What a Prodigy am I? Enlighten me, O
Lord! Does thy Grace or my own Despair draw
these words from Me?" (p. 123). Pope's Eloisa
echoes this doubt by questioning the source of
her own prayer:

> Assist me heav'n! but whence arose that pray'r?
> Sprung it from piety, or from despair?
> (179-80)

Eloisa's question about the source of her prayer
must be answered within the context of the traditional Christian understanding of prayer. The
ability to pray to God comes as a grace from God
to man. Prayer is an act of human will, and thus
the power of the will to seek God by prayer comes
to man as a grace from God.[24] In contrast to
prayer, the state of despair in Christian psychology marks the worst possible estrangement from
God--the utter loss of hope in the efficacy of
divine mercy. Despair itself becomes a state of
sin, for with the loss of hope man suffers the
loss of his power to repent and to be forgiven.[25]
The state of despair defines, in one way, the
locus, or mental place, of hell and its tortures.
In *The Faerie Queene*, the Redcross Knight feels the
tortures of hell as Despair, "that cursed man,"
seeks to convince him to commit suicide:

>   the Miscreaunt
> Perceived him to waver, weake and fraile,
> Whiles trembling horror did his conscience
>   daunt,
> And hellish anguish did his soule assaile;
> To drive him to despaire, and quite to quaile,
> Hee shewd him, painted in a table plaine,
> The damned ghosts that doe in torments waile,
> And thousand feends that doe them endlesse
>   paine
> With fire and brimstone, which for ever shall
>   remaine.   (*F.Q.* I.ix.49)

And in *Paradise Lost*, Satan, "rackt with deep despair" (I. 126), embodies hell:

>   Me miserable! which way shall I fly
>   Infinite wrath, and infinite despair?
>   Which way I fly is Hell; myself am Hell.
>   (IV. 73-5)

In contrast to Satan and his despair, Adam and
Eve receive "prevenient grace," the grace which
anticipates and empowers repentance:

>   Thus they in lowliest plight repentant
>   stood
>   Praying, for from the Mercy-seat above
>   Prevenient Grace descending had remov'd
>   The stony from thir hearts, and made new
>   flesh
>   Regenerate grow instead, that sighs now
>   breath'd
>   Unutterable, which the Spirit of prayer
>   Inspir'd, and wing'd for Heav'n with speedier
>   flight
>   Than loudest Oratory ...   (XI. 1-8)

Eloisa, like Adam and Eve, prays for God's assistance to help her combat her frailties. Her prayer comes from her recognition of her own weak-
ness--a state of self-knowledge which in Christian psychology marks the opening of the way to
God. Eloisa's prayer, then, most certainly does
not spring from despair, and if it does not
spring from her own "piety," it shows nevertheless her will to communicate with God.

In Hughes' translation of the *Letters*, Abelard
agrees with Heloise that, given the face of human weakness, men must seek assistance from God:
"We shall more certainly compass our End [of conquering temptations] by imploring God's Assistance, than by using any Means drawn from our
selves" (p. 208). Earlier, Abelard had declared
the necessity of divine assistance to free the
lovers from the bondage of their sin: "We must
have the Assistance of God, that we may break

our Chains; we have engaged too deeply in Love,
to free our selves" (p. 154). With the assurance
that the assistance of divine grace renders the
human will efficacious where it once was weak,
Abelard exhorts Heloise to resolve to correct the
mistakes of their past relationship: "Let us repair, as far as is possible, the Evils we have
done ..." (p. 155).

   We have seen earlier in this essay how Pope
adapted to his epistle passages on suffering from
the letters of Hughes' Abelard. Now we should
notice how Pope again borrows from Hughes' Abelard an intensely dramatic scene in which he
creates Eloisa's will to "repair, as far as is
possible, the Evils [she has] done."

   In Abelard's first letter to Heloise, he describes his own humility as a sinner before God,
and confesses his persistent weakness before the
temptation of his love for Heloise: "I am a
miserable Sinner, prostrate before my Judge, and
with my Face pressed to the Earth, I mix my Tears
and Sighs in the Dust, when the Beams of Grace
and Reason enlighten me. Come, see me in this
Posture, and solicite me to love you [.]26 Come,
if you think fit, and in your Holy Habit thrust
yourself between God and me, and be a Wall of
Separation. Come, and force from me those Sighs,
Thoughts, and Vows, which I owe to him only.
Assist the Evil Spirits, and be the Instrument
of their Malice" (p. 144). Shortly after summon-
ing Heloise, Abelard reverses himself and resists
the temptation that would separate him from his
God: "Let me remove far from you, and obey the
Apostle who hath said *fly*" (p. 146).

   Pope adapts Abelard's situation in Hughes'
translation of the *Letters* by responding to a hint
in the first letter of Heloise: "Even into holy
Places before the Altar I carry with me the Memory of our guilty Loves. They are my whole Business, and far from lamenting for having been seduced, I sigh for having lost them" (p. 175).
Pope expands the hint from Heloise with specific
details taken from Abelard. In the following
lines, Eloisa's visions of Abelard before the

altar interrupt her prayers at Matins and her devotions during the celebration of the Mass. Her
visions of Abelard disrupt the formal order of
the rituals of devotion to God, and in this way
become what Hughes' Abelard called "a Wall of
Separation":

> What scenes appear where-e'er I turn my view!
> The dear Ideas, where I fly, pursue,
> Rise in the grove, before the altar rise,
> Stain all my soul, and wanton in my eyes!
> I waste the Matin lamp in sighs for thee,
> Thy image steals between my God and me,
> Thy voice I seem in ev'ry hymn to hear,
> With ev'ry bead I drop too soft a tear.
>   (263-70)

Eloisa's vision of Abelard's "image" (268), in
effect, blots out the image of her suffering God
on the Crucifix. The image of Abelard becomes
"a Wall of Separation" between Eloisa and the
Image of God.
    Pope's Eloisa, like Hughes' Abelard, perceives
the light of divine grace within her soul when,
aware of her sinful submission to temptation during her devotions, she humbles herself in the
dust (279). Pope omits Abelard's conjunction of
"Grace and Reason" in favor of "dawning grace"--
an omission that avoids the blurring of distinctions caused by Hughes' conjunction, and focuses
sharply the Christian perspective in which *Eloisa
to Abelard* must be seen and understood. But at
the same time that Eloisa perceives the light of
grace in her humility, she also summons the
tempting vision of Abelard to "oppose thy self to
heav'n":

> While prostrate here in humble grief I lie,
> Kind, virtuous drops just gath'ring in my eye,
> While praying, trembling, in the dust I roll,
> And dawning grace is opening on my soul:
> Come, if thou dar'st, all charming as thou
>   art!
> Oppose thy self to heav'n; dispute my heart;

Come, with one glance of those deluding eyes,
Blot out each bright Idea of the skies.
Take back that grace, those sorrows, and those
    tears,
Take back my fruitless penitence and pray'rs,.
Snatch me, just mounting, from the blest abode,
Assist the Fiends and tear me from my God!
                          (277-88)

Pope follows Hughes' Abelard fairly closely in
this passage, with one important exception.
Hughes' Abelard calls Heloise to be near in her
"Holy Habit" (p. 144, quoted above), but this detail forms no part of Eloisa's analogous vision.
Only after Eloisa has rejected the temptation of
Abelard's opposition to God ("No, fly me, fly me!
far as Pole from Pole" [289]) will she summon him
to herself in his appropriate "Holy Habit." In a
vision of her own future death, Eloisa sees Abelard in the crucial role of a priest administering
the last rites and sacrament to her. As a priest,
Abelard is the agent of God, and a communicator
of God's grace to man. But even within her vision
of Abelard as a priest, Eloisa must suppress the
recurring temptation of Abelard as a lover who
sucks the last breath of her sexual "death":

Thou, *Abelard!* the last sad office pay,
And smooth my passage to the realms of day:
See my lips tremble, and my eye-balls roll,
Suck my last breath, and catch my flying soul!
Ah no--in sacred vestments may'st thou stand,
The hallow'd taper trembling in thy hand,
Present the Cross before my lifted eye,
Teach me at once, and learn of me to die.
                          (321-28)

When Eloisa sees Abelard in his "Holy Habit," his
"sacred vestments," he does not "blot out" the
Image of God from her, and he does not "steal
between" her God and herself. Instead, Abelard
now holds the Cross before Eloisa and functions
as the means by which she fixes her attention primarily upon the Cross and the love of God that
it signifies.

This dramatic scene, which Pope creates from a mere hint in Hughes' translation of the *Letters*, shows quite literally in its physical configuration that Eloisa no longer diverts her eye from the Cross to Abelard, but keeps the Cross foremost in her devotion. Behind and beneath the Cross, Abelard the man as priest, the agent of God, supports the new order of Eloisa's love—a love that now embraces first God, and then Abelard the sanctified man. In this new hierarchical order of love, Eloisa properly adapts her love for the creature to her devotion to the Creator. Eloisa's vision of Abelard the priest and agent of God marks the most vivid discovery in the poem of what in Hughes' translation of the *Letters* Heloise called "the wonderful Providence of God, who does all Things for our Sanctification" (p. 125).

THE ELEGY AS EXORCISM: POPE'S 'VERSES TO THE MEMORY OF AN UNFORTUNATE LADY'

Ian Jack

From the very beginning too much has been written about the lady, and too little about the poem. 'Pray in your next tell me who was the Unfortunate Lady ...', John Caryll wrote on 16 July 1717. 'I think you once gave me her history, butt tis now quite outt of my head.'[1] It is clear that Pope did not answer the question,[2] and Caryll's curiosity about the lady was soon shared by a great many other readers. 'What would I not give to know who she was', wrote a correspondent from Boston in 1728, 'and the remarkable circumstances of her History. But I presume too far, and must ask Your Pardon for my Impertinance.'[3] If Spence ever 'presumed' so far as to raise the question we must conclude that he received no answer, as his *Anecdotes* do not contain a single reference to the poem. It is hardly surprising that the problem of identification became something of an obsession with subsequent writers on

This essay first appeared in *Augustan Worlds: Essays in Honour of A. R. Humphreys*, ed. J.C. Hilson, M.M.B. Jones, and J.R. Watson (Leicester: Leicester University Press, 1978), pp. 69-83.

Pope, and it is necessary to glance at their conjectures before we consider the poem itself.

'This Lady seems to have been a particular
Favourite of our Poet,' wrote the unreliable
William Ayre, in the *Memoirs* which he rushed out
in 1745, 'whether he himself was the Person she
was remov'd from I am not able to say, but whoever reads his Verses to her Memory, will find
she had a very great Share in him.'[4] His account
of her appears to be no more than a fanciful
summary based on the Elegy itself: his embel-
lishments include the information that 'Spies
being set upon her it was not long before her
Correspondence with her Lover of lower Degree was
discover'd' and a description of how 'some Young
People of the Neighbourhood, who saw her put into
common Ground ... strew'd her Grave with Flowers',
a circumstance which 'gave some Offence to the
Priesthood, who would have buried her in the
Highway, but it seems their Power ... did not extend so far.'[5]

In 1751 a curious note was appended to the
poem in Warburton's edition:

> See the Duke of Buckingham's verses to a Lady
> designing to retire into a Monastery compared
> with Mr. Pope's Letters to several Ladies, p.
> 206. She seems to be the same person whose
> unfortunate death is the subject of this
> poem. P.[6]

While there is no justification for rejecting
Warburton's claim that this note is Pope's own,
or derives from information supplied by Pope, the
word 'seems' is disconcerting. We must assume
either that the first sentence is Pope's and the
addition Warburton's, or (as would appear more
probable) that the whole note is Pope's, and that
he is teasing his readers. In any event, neither
the poem nor the letter proves helpful. The poem,
as printed in the first volume of Pope's edition of *The Works of His Grace The Duke of Buckingham*
in 1723, begins with a rhetorical question which
forms a fitting introduction to a thoroughly conventional set of verses:

What Breast but yours can hold the double Fire
Of fierce Devotion, and of fond Desire?

There is no reason to believe that these lines
have any autobiographical or even historical
basis. As for the letter, it had been printed
in 1735, in the section of the 'Surreptitious'
edition of Pope's letters which contained 'Letters to Several Ladies'. It is undated, but described in the Contents as *To an unfortunate Lady*.
Pope assures her that she is 'the most valuable
thing I know', and congratulates her on the fact
that her brother 'will at last prove your relation, and has entertain'd such sentiments as become him in your concern'. He seems to be urging her not 'to rob the world of so much example
as you may afford it', but maintains that 'even
in a Monastery your devotions cannot carry you
so far toward the next world as to make This
lose the sight of you'.[7] There is nothing in
the letter to prove the reality of the addressee:
it could perfectly well be a purely literary
composition mischievously inserted to encourage
further speculation about the Unfortunate Lady.
A few months later, after all, the poem was to
be reprinted in the first volume of a new edition of Pope's *Works*, the edition in which (incidentally) the title was changed from 'Verses' to
the now familiar 'Elegy'.
    If the note was designed to provoke specula-
tion, it succeeded admirably. In *An Essay on the
Writings and Genius of Pope*, published in 1756,
Joseph Warton admits that 'We are unacquainted
with her history, and with that series of misfortunes, which seems to have drawn on the
melancholy catastrophe', but continues: 'She is
said to be the same person, to whom the Duke of
Buckingham has addressed some lines', referring
to the poem and letter mentioned in the 'P.'
footnote. A page or two later he commits himself to a statement of the dogma which lies behind a great deal of subsequent criticism of the
poem:

> If this ELEGY be so excellent, it may be as-
> cribed to this cause; that the occasion of it
> was real ... Events that have actually happened
> are, after all, the properest subjects for
> poetry.[8]

In the second edition of *An Essay*, six years later,
Warton elaborates on the biographical background.
He will now only admit that 'We are unacquainted
with *the whole of* her history', while he adds an
important passage at the end of the penultimate
paragraph of the book. Whereas in the first edition he had censured the last eight lines of
'Eloisa to Abelard' and commented that 'They
might stand for the conclusion of almost any
story', he now writes:

> They might stand *it should seem* for the conclu-
> sion of almost any story, were we not informed,
> that they were added by the Poet in allusion
> to his own case, and the state of his own
> mind. For what determined him in the choice
> of the subject of this epistle, was the re-
> treat of that lady into a nunnery, whose
> death he had lately so pathetically lamented,
> in a foregoing Elegy, and for whom he had con-
> ceived a violent passion. She was first be-
> loved by a nobleman, an intimate friend of
> POPE, and, on his deserting her, retired into
> France; when, before she had made her last
> vows in the convent, to which she had re-
> treated, she put an end to her unfortunate
> life. The recollection of this circumstance
> will add a beauty and a pathos to many pas-
> sages in the poem, and will confirm the doc-
> trine delivered above, concerning the choice
> of subject.

In 1769 Owen Ruffhead was content to rely on
Ayre, from whom he takes the picturesque detail
that the dead lady had been found 'yet warm upon
the ground': appropriately enough, as he considers that the poem 'came warm from the heart, and
does honour to [Pope's] sensibility'.[9] Johnson

clearly wished to be more specific, but failed.
'The lady's name and adventures I have sought
with fruitless enquiry,' he observes in his Life
of Pope, 'I can therefore tell no more than I
have learned from Mr. Ruffhead.' Failing to notice Ruffhead's indebtedness to Ayre, Johnson
describes him as a man 'who writes with the confidence of one who could trust his information'.
He complains that 'the tale is not skilfully
told: it is not easy to discover the character of
either the lady or her guardian ... On such an
occasion a poet may be allowed to be obscure, but
inconsistency never can be right.' While he allows the Elegy some merit, his irritation at the
absence of biographical information and his
strong disapproval of suicide--'Self-murder; the
horrid crime of destroying one's self'--leads him
to the unworthy observation that 'her desires
were too hot for delay, and she liked self-murder
better than suspence' and to the well-known conclusion that 'Poetry has not often been worse
employed than in dignifying the amorous fury of
a raving girl.'10
In the year of Johnson's death a pseudonymous
correspondent wrote to the *Gentleman's Magazine* to
record what he had heard 'long ago, from a very
worthy, but obscure, country parson':

> That the lady's name was *Scudamore*; that she
> and her family were Roman Catholics; that,
> having fixed her affections on a person not
> suitable to her, the match was steadily op-
> posed by her uncle and guardian. This cre-
> ated such uneasiness between them, that it
> was agreed they should separate, and the lady
> go abroad to a convent. It was to Antwerp, as
> well as I can recollect, that she was sent;
> not with a view of taking the veil, but to
> stay as a boarder, her friends hoping that,
> by the time she was of age, she might come to
> better judgement; that she was soon after
> seized with a fever, which ended in a state of
> melancholy; and that she some how or other
> procured a sword, and put an end to her life.11

Horace Walpole immediately commented on this 'pretended discovery' in a letter to Joseph Warton,
expressing his belief that the writer was 'quite
mistaken': 'at least, my Lady Hervey, who was
acquainted with Pope, and who lived at the time,
gave me a very different name, and told me the
exit was made in a less dignified manner--by the
rope. I have never spread this...'. He promised
to give Warton the lady's name when they next
met. By that time, as it would appear, Walpole
may well have given the name to at least one
other enquirer, as Sir John Hawkins wrote in
1787 that he had in his possession

> a letter to Dr. Johnson, containing the name
> of the lady, and a reference to a gentleman
> well known in the literary world for her
> history. Him I have seen, and, from a memo-
> randum of some particulars to the purpose
> communicated to him by a lady of quality, he
> informs me that the unfortunate lady's name
> was Withinbury, corruptly pronounced Winbury;
> that she was in love with Pope, and would
> have married him; that her guardian, though
> she was deformed in her person, looking upon
> such a match as beneath her, sent her to a
> convent, and that a noose, and not a sword,
> put an end to her life.

It seems clear that the gentleman in question
was Walpole (and the lady of quality Lady Hervey),
since in his MS. notes on Pope Walpole had written:

> The name of this Lady was Withinbury, pronounced
> Winbury: the seat of her family was Chiras
> Court, Vulgarly Cheyney's Court, situated un-
> der Fromehill, & forming nearly a triangle
> with Home-Lacy & Hampton-lacy. It is said
> that she did not stab, but hang herself.[12]

This information was duly passed on to Warton,
who wrote as follows in his edition of Pope:

The true cause of the excellence of this
elegy is, that the occasion of it was real;
so true is the maxim, that nature is more
powerful than fancy, and that we can always
feel more than we can imagine; and that the
most artful fiction must give way to truth,
for this Lady was beloved by Pope. After
many and wide enquiries I have been informed
that her name was Wainsbury, and that--which
is a singular circumstance--she was as ill-
shaped and deformed as our author. Her death
was not by a sword, but, what would less bear
to be told poetically, she hanged herself.

This is all remarkably circumstantial, and it
is certain that Lady Hervey had been in an excellent position to catch such rumours, while Walpole is a reliable retailer of gossip. 'Chira's
Court' appears on Isaac Taylor's *Map of the County
of Hereford* (1754), about a mile north of Castle
Frome, and at the time in question it was occupied by a Roman Catholic family (the Scudamores
being the principal aristocrats of the neighbourhood). Unfortunately, however, their name was
not any variant of Withinbury, Winbury or Wainsbury, but Slaughter, and an exhaustive search of
the County Council Records of Hereford and
Worcester has failed to reveal anyone with the
name required; while enquiries in the Public
Record Office have proved equally fruitless.[13]
We must assume that Lady Hervey gave Walpole a
more or less accurate account of an old rumour,
but the question of the truth of the rumour is
another matter. If a lady with some such name
as Withinbury had in fact lived at Chiras Court
it seems unlikely that she was more than just one
of various unfortunate ladies whose fates may
have been in Pope's mind as he wrote his poem.
   In 1806 a slightly farcical postscript was
provided by William Lisle Bowles who, after conceding that 'It is in vain ... perhaps, to attempt further elucidation', nonetheless continues:

> but I should think it unpardonable not to men-
> tion what I have myself heard, though I can-
> not vouch for its truth ... The story which
> was told to Condorcet by Voltaire, and by Con-
> dorcet to a gentleman of high birth and char-
> acter, from whom I received it, is this:--
> "That her attachment was not to Pope, or to
> any Englishman of inferior degree;" but to a
> young French Prince of the blood royal, Charles
> Emmanuel Duke of Berry, whom, in early youth,
> she had met at the court of France.

Bowles concludes, a little tartly, by observing
that 'it is most probable that incipient lunacy
was the cause of her perverted feelings, and
untimely end'.[14]

Incipient lunacy is certainly the danger
threatening any scholar who presses too far in
this particular enquiry, and one is tempted to
comment that criticism has not often been worse
employed than in pursuing the shadowy identity
of a largely imaginary girl. After more than a
century of fruitless conjecture that admirable
scholar, Charles Wentworth Dilke, pointed this
out. 'All we are told by the biographers', he
wrote in *The Athenaeum*, 'no matter how circum-
stantially, is merely conjectural, made up from
hints in the Elegy, fanciful interpretations of
passages in Pope's letters, assumption of dates,
changes of persons, and traditional or original
nonsense.'[15] Fortified by his example, Victorian critics proved harder-headed in this matter
than their predecessors. In 1871 the Rev. Whitwell Elwin, in his edition of Pope's *Works*,
gives copious extracts from earlier writers
(though not from Dilke) and comments: 'At variance in nearly every particular, the conflicting
histories of the unfortunate lady have the common
quality, that they are unsupported by a single
circumstance which could warrant the smallest
measure of belief ... The biographers and editors ... had no suspicion that she might be altogether a poetical invention.' It is his conclusion that 'there was no real victim in the

case'.[16] In *The Life of Alexander Pope*, published in
1889 as the last volume of the same edition,
W.J. Courthope adopts a similar point of view.
Although he claims that Pope's sympathy with Mrs
Weston provided a 'basis of sincere emotion' for
certain passages, he concedes that 'there is
scarcely a line in the poem founded on the actual circumstances of the case' and censures earlier critics for believing that 'such an animated
expression of feeling could only have been evoked
by a series of facts corresponding with the story
suggested in the poem'. It is revealing to
juxtapose his statement that 'What the "Elegy"
really establishes ... is Pope's right to be considered a creative poet of genuine pathetic
power'[17] and Warton's assumption that the powerful expression of pathos in the poem 'may be ascribed to this cause; that the occasion of it
was real'.[18]
     Although he is rather less than fair to Elwin
and Courthope, George Sherburn comes to a conclusion which is substantially theirs. While he
allows that 'the woes of various ladies with
brutal parents or husbands may have been subli-
mated into the tragedy of Pope's lady' (who could
allow less?), he concludes that 'no one alone
among all those suggested notably parallels her
woes'.[19] In his edition of the *Correspondence*, 22
years later than *The Early Career*, he comments
somewhat impatiently that the letter to which
'P.'s' note refers was addressed 'to Mrs. Weston,
Mrs. Cope, or some other worthy but hitherto
unappreciated lady'.[20] Tillotson dutifully repeats the names of Mrs Weston and Mrs Cope, and
suggests that the poem may constitute a highly
imaginative expression of Pope's love for Lady
Mary Wortley Montagu, but he clearly appreciates
that the literary context is more important than
the biographical or historical, although he re-
frains from pursuing the matter.[21] The most
stimulating discussion of the Elegy is that of
Reuben Arthur Brower, who is content to leave
the question of the lady's identity unresolved[22]
and stresses (perhaps following a hint of Sher-

burn's) that in the poem she 'is cast as a Roman lover' and that 'the accent of the poet in addressing her is Roman-elegiac'.[23]

As soon as we take the Elegy rather than the lady as the focus of our attention we are reminded that there was an element of fiction in the tradition of the funeral elegy as developed from the poets of antiquity through the neo-Latin and vernacular poets of the Renaissance, as there had been (more prominently) in the tradition of the love elegy from the earliest times. The experience of 'E.K.' with Spenser, almost a century and a half before the publication of Pope's Elegy, was similar to that of Caryll with Pope. 'In this xi. AEglogue', he wrote, 'he bewayleth the death of some mayden of greate bloud, whom he calleth Dido. The personage is secrete, and to me altogether unknowne, albe of him selfe I often required the same.'

The handsome folio edition of his Works which Pope published in 1717 contains the Pastorals and a brilliant collection of other poems in various genres more exacting than the pastoral but less ambitious than the epic to which he already aspired. Nothing could be more appropriate than the presence among such poems of a fine example of the classical elegy. It is true that the fourth Pastoral, 'Winter', is elegiac in form (and we notice ahat whereas in 1709 it is simply 'To the Memory of a Fair Young Lady', with nothing to prove the reality of the lady, in 1717 Pope yielded to the persuasion of Walsh and headed it 'To the Memory of Mrs. Tempest'[24]); but that was early work. He decided to write another elegy, an elegy (as I believe) which is no more about a particular lady than 'Winter' is about Mrs Tempest, an elegy which is the product of his imagination working upon his reading. A brief consideration of the art which he displays in it may help us to set it more firmly in the tradition to which it belongs.

In his introduction to the Elegy Tillotson did well to quote Pope's observation to Spence: 'Most little poems should be written by a plan. This method is evident in Tibullus and Ovid's elegies, and almost all the pieces of the ancients.'[25] An outline plan for a funeral elegy is provided in the *Poetics* of Julius Caesar Scaliger, which Pope described as 'an exceeding useful book in its kind, and extremely well collected'.[26] For Scaliger the constituent parts of an elegy are the Praise, the Narration, the Lamentation, the Consolation and the Exhortation. He stresses the importance of appropriateness--'The treatment is different according to whether the song is for an emperor ... for a private citizen, a man, a woman ... each one of whom must be treated in the appropriate way'--and points out that whereas an elegy sometimes 'begins with a calm proem' it may also commence 'with an exclamation or interroga- tion'. He insists on the need for 'A discourse of consolation ... which restores the mind of the mourner to tranquility'.[27]

Pope's Elegy was clearly 'written by a plan', and elements of Scaliger's scheme may be found it it--though less (one may conjecture) because of Scaliger's precepts than because of the exam- ples of the poets from whose work Scaliger de- duced his rules. The centre of Pope's plan is remarkably simple, but also remarkably audacious. His 'Elegy' is a rite of exorcism.

As Thomas Warton pointed out, the opening lines of the poem may well have been suggested by those of Ben Jonson's 'Elegy on the Lady Jane Pawlet',[28] but we notice that the ghost in Pope's poem requires more than the 'garland' which is sought in Jonson's. The Unfortunate Lady, like the ghost of Hamlet's father, cannot rest until a wrong has been righted. This is the principal business of the poem, and it is accomplished by line 68.

If we wish to understand how Pope came to make so uncanonical a use of a Christian rite we shall do well to turn to the discussion of 'Elegy' in Joseph Trapp's *Praelectiones Poeticae*. I quote from the English translation of a book which Pope knew in the Latin, and referred to in a characterist- ically precise instruction about the printing of

The Rape of the Lock. [29] 'The chief Subjects to
which Elegy owes its Rise', Trapp points out, 'are
Death and Love', and he concludes that 'That
Elegy, therefore, ought to be esteem'd the most
perfect in its Kind, which has somewhat of both
at once: Such, for Instance, where the Poet bewails the Death of his *Corinna*, his *Delia*, or
Lycoris, or of some Youth or Damsel falling a Mar-
tyr to Love'.[30] It seems likely that this passage contributed more to the inspiration of Pope's
poem than the misfortunes of any particular lady,
however 'beauteous', however 'friendly'.

The part of the poem which owes its structure
to the rite of exorcism consists of five verse-
paragraphs. In the first (ll. 1-10) the poet
describes the ghost which has appeared to him,
and wonders whether there is

> no bright reversion in the sky,
> For those who greatly think, or bravely die?[31]

The second (ll. 11-22) deals briefly yet powerfully with the traditional topos of Ambition,
with a glance at the sluggish souls that lack
this 'glorious fault'. In the third (ll. 23-8)
the poet speculates that Fate has snatched the
lady away because she was superior to 'her Race',
while the fourth (ll. 29-46) constitutes a curse
on her 'false guardian' and his family. The final paragraph consists of two parts: in the first
(ll. 47-62) the poet demands what can atone for
the lady's 'fate unpity'd, and [her] rites un-
paid', while in the second (ll. 63-8) he astonish-
ingly asserts that the ground in which she was
buried has been rendered 'sacred' by the very
fact of her interment there. The brief penultimate paragraph ('So peaceful rests ...') reminds
us that the exorcism has been completed, prepares
us for a noble rendering of one of the great
commonplaces--'pulvis et umbra sumus'--and allows
the poet to introduce himself in the double role
of mourner and future subject for elegy.

To analyse the poem in this way is to become
aware that part of Pope's 'plan' must have been

a variation of tone and tempo as one movement of
thought and emotion succeeds another. In a letter to Cromwell in 1710 he had written that 'there
is (if one may express it so) a Style of Sound'.[32]
While he seems to have had something relatively
simple in mind (as a reference to 'Alexander's
Feast' suggests), we may perhaps extend the meaning of the phrase as we consider the architec-
tonics of the Elegy. It opens, as Warton observed, 'with a striking abruptness':[33] the initial rhetorical question is followed, in rapid
succession, by four others, with two exclamation
marks thrown in for good measure--so exemplifying
one of the modes of beginning an elegy which had
been mentioned by Scaliger. The effect is dramatic, verging on the melodramatic. A further
exclamation, and a further rhetorical question,
introduce the paragraph in which the poet extols
ambition and satirizes the spiritually lethargic.
As we read lines 17-20--

> Most souls, 'tis true, but peep out once an
>   age,
> Dull sullen pris'ners in the body's cage:
> Dim lights of life, that burn a length of
>   years
> Useless, unseen, as lamps in sepulchres

--it is interesting to recall Pope's observation,
in the same letter, that 'Monosyllable-Lines, unless very artfully manag'd, are stiff languish-
ing, & hard'. Elsewhere he explains what he
means by 'artfully managed' by conceding that
they 'may be beautiful to express Melancholy,
Slowness, or Labour'.[34] Lines 17 and 19 'express
[a] Slowness' which is spiritual rather than
physical.
   The movement of the third paragraph might be
marked 'Andante', as the poet uses an image from
chemistry to express the notion that the lady may
have been 'snatch'd ... early to the pitying sky'
from a world which is unworthy of her. By way of
contrast, the paragraph in which her guardian and
his family are cursed opens with a mark of exclam-

ation and advances with cumulative ferocity as
couplet succeeds to couplet. Rhetorical questions and exclamations again characterize the
paragraph on the lady's burial, and lead up to
the climax in which the poet asserts that the
ground has now been rendered 'sacred' by her
'reliques'. In the two paragraphs which form the
coda the tone becomes much quieter (in spite of
the exclamation mark at the end of each). At
the same time the diction becomes strikingly simple, while 'Monosyllable-Lines' are skilfully
used 'to express Melancholy':

    'Tis all thou art, and all the proud shall be!

and:

    And the last pang shall tear thee from his
      heart.

The quietly controlled conclusion contrasts
strikingly with the rhetorical uncertainty of the
opening: the speaker remains deeply sorrowful,
but his passion has been brought under control,
just as the ghost of the lady has been exorcized
by his lines.
    Pope's poem incorporates one element of which
Trapp might have disapproved. 'With this Kind
of Poem', he had written, 'every Thing that is
epigrammatical, satirical, or sublime, is inconsistent. Elegy aims not to be witty or facetious, acrimonious or severe, majestic or sublime;
but is smooth, humble, and unaffected.'[35] While
the Elegy contains nothing 'epigrammatical ...
or sublime' and is certainly not 'witty or facetious', the fourth paragraph is undoubtedly
'acrimonious' and 'severe'. Yet this does not
indicate any departure from the tradition of the
classical funeral elegy as it had been interpreted by the poets and critics of the Renaissance:
if the poem had lacked a satirical passage it
would have departed from the elegiac tradition
as exemplified by poets as different from each
other as Donne and Milton, a tradition psycho-

logically justified because the death of a beloved
person predisposes the mourner to search for a
scapegoat, a world unworthy of a soul as pure as
that of a deceased girl, a Church the corruptions
of which do not deserve an upright minister. And
so Donne commemorated the first anniversary of
the death of a young woman by writing *An Anatomie
of the World* 'Wherein, By occasion of the untimely
death of Mistris Elizabeth Drury, the frailty and
the decay of this whole World is represented',
and the second anniversary by writing a poem *Of
the Progresse of the Soule* 'Wherein ... the incommod-
ities of the Soule in this life, and her exaltation in the next, are contemplated'; while in
'Lycidas' Milton not only 'bewails a learned
Friend' but also 'by occasion foretels the ruine
of our corrupted Clergy then in their height'.
Unlike the elegies by Donne and Milton, Pope's is
not a Christian poem: a fact which makes his use
of exorcism as a structural principle the more
striking. His satirical passage is less comprehensive than Donne's two sermons *de contemptu mundi*
and different in focus from Milton's attack on
the 'Blind mouthes' of the contemporary church.
The miscreants on whom he turns are sluggish souls
to whom passion and true ambition are alike unknown and in particular the lady's guardian and
family, whom he takes as examples of the proud
and pitiless among mankind:

> Thus, if eternal justice rules the ball,
> Thus shall your wives, and thus your children
>   fall:
> On all the line a sudden vengeance waits,
> And frequent herses shall besiege your gates.
> There passengers shall stand, and pointing say,
> (While the long fun'rals blacken all the way)
> Lo these were they, whose souls the Furies
>   steel'd,
> And curs'd with hearts unknowing how to yield.
> Thus unlamented pass the proud away,
> The gaze of fools, and pageant of a day!
> So perish all, whose breast n'er learn'd to
>   glow
> For others good, or melt at others woe.

The angry satire of this paragraph recurs for
a moment in its successor, in the lines describing the conventional 'mockery of woe' and the
meaningless way in which the 'hallow'd dirge' is
habitually 'mutter'd o'er [the] tomb'; but the
principal part of this, the triumphant climax of
the poem, is a brilliantly original version of
the *consolatio*. While he excludes the Christian
faith from this Roman elegy, Pope turns unhal-
lowed ground to hallowed by the very intensity
(as it were) of his admiration of a beautiful and
courageous woman. His use of anaphora in lines
51-3 compels our admiration:

> By foreign hands thy dying eyes were clos'd,
> By foreign hands thy decent limbs compos'd,
> By foreign hands thy humble grave adorn'd,
> By strangers honour'd, and by strangers
>   mourn'd![36]

The withdrawal from anaphora in the fourth line
is particularly striking. Whereas a lesser poet
would have continued the figure, Pope avoids
the obvious yet enhances our sense of the rhetorical unity of the four lines by the repetition of
the word 'strangers' and by the near-assonance of
'honoured' and 'mourned'.

A further reason for the variation in the
fourth line was no doubt a desire to avoid
rhythmical monotony. In his letter to Cromwell
Pope pointed out that 'in any smooth English
Verse of ten Syllables, there is naturally a
Pause either at the fourth, fifth, or sixth Syllable', and continued: 'Now I fancy, that to
preserve an exact Harmony & Variety, none of
these Pauses shou'd be continu'd above three
lines together ...; else it will be apt to weary
the Ear with one continu'd Tone'.[37] Since the
caesura or pause occurs after the fourth syllable
in the two lines immediately preceding the passage just quoted, the rejection of anaphora in
line 54 avoids an even more flagrant violation of
Pope's own principle. In lines 19-22 we find
another possible instance:

> Dim lights of life /that burn a length of
>   years
> Useless, unseen,/as lamps in sepulchres;
> Like Eastern Kings/a lazy state they keep,
> And close confin'd in their own palace sleep.

The pause in the last line must either occur after the fourth syllable or after the ninth: in
either case Pope is obviously intent on creating
a sense of mindless monotony. At lines 63-6 we
have an undoubted example of four successive lines
with the pause after the fourth syllable:

> What tho' no sacred earth allow thee room,
> Now hallow'd dirge/be mutter'd o'er thy tomb?
> Yet shall thy grave/with rising flow'rs be
>   drest,
> And the green turf/lie lightly on thy breast:
> There shall the morn/her earliest tears
>   bestow
>
> (ll. 61-5)

Here no defence can be offered, or required: one
has only to remember one of the most important
injunctions in *An Essay on Criticism*:

> If, where the rules not far enough extend,
> (Since rules were made but to promote their
>   end)
> Some lucky Licence answers to the full
> Th' intent propos'd, that Licence is a rule.
> (ll. 146-9)

The Elegy contains no example of the pause after
the sixth syllable 'continu'd above three lines
together'.
   Returning to the paragraph on the lady's burial, we notice that the movement towards the resolution of conflict is marked by a less concentrated use of the figure of anaphora, in lines
55-62:

> What tho' no friends in sable weeds appear,
> Grieve for an hour, perhaps, then mourn a year,

And bear about the mockery of woe
To midnight dances, and the public show?
What tho' no weeping Loves thy ashes grace,
Nor polish'd marble emulate thy face?
What tho' no sacred earth allow thee room,
Nor hallow'd dirge be mutter'd o'er thy tomb?

So we come to the hinge or turning-point of the
poem--

Yet shall thy grave with rising flow'rs be
    drest,
And the green turf lie lightly on thy breast

--with just the hint of an anaphora in the following couplet--

There shall the morn her earliest tears be-
    stow,
There the first roses of the year shall blow

--to prepare for the final statement that angels
will

                o'ershade
The ground, now sacred by thy reliques made.

In a widely-used American anthology we are assured that whereas 'Pope speaks in his own person' in the last eight lines of the Elegy, in the
preceding 74 lines he 'imagines the lover to be
addressing the ghost of the unfortunate lady',[38]
but surely few readers have sensed any change
of voice (as distinct from the beautifully
managed modulation of tone) in these concluding
lines. The poem as a whole may be regarded as
a dramatic monologue in which the speaker is a
poet, but not necessarily the historical Alexander Pope. Writing of the Latin love elegists,
Colin Macleod has recently reminded us that when
they 'suggest they are speaking of their own experience' we should not allow ourselves to be
misled: 'This does not mean the elegists are
describing real events or even real persons; but

their manner as love poets is autobiographical,
however fantastic their matter'.[39] Exactly the
same is true of Pope's Roman elegy, which is a
triumphant variation on a number of classical
themes. It is ironical that the poet who had
exorcized a ghost so unforgettably in a poem
should have raised it again in a mischievous
footnote.

THE MEDAL AGAINST TIME: A STUDY OF
POPE'S EPISTLE *TO MR ADDISON**

Howard Erskine-Hill

I

   Awareness of the achievement of Augustan
Rome, and of the great preceding periods of
Hellenistic and Greek culture, provided, in
post-classical times, a challenge and a model
for Renaissance endeavour. The goal of this
endeavour, and its fulfilment, was the achievement of a new Augustan Age. It follows that
the idea of a Renaissance and the idea of an
Augustan Age are integral parts of the same
concept. It is therefore logical to expect any
writer, who looks on himself as a new Augustan,
to attach special importance to the fallen
civilizations of classical antiquity, and to the
means by which they may be renewed. From the
time of Ben Jonson English poets, in different
ways and to different degrees, saw themselves
as emulating the poets of the Roman Augustan
Age.[1] Contemporaries of Pope clearly felt that
the English Augustan Age was either about to

This essay first appeared in the *Journal of the Warburg and Courtauld Institutes* 28 (1965),
274-98.

reach its zenith or was but a little way declined from it.[2] Alexander Pope himself, one
may conclude by strong inference, thought of
himself as an English Augustan.[3]

There are three places in Pope's writings
where he discusses the fall of Rome, the
Middle Ages and the Renaissance. These are:
the concluding passage of *An Essay on Criticism*
(1711), *To Mr Addison, Occasioned by his Dialogues
on Medals* (1720), and the greater part of Book
iii of the *Dunciad* (1728-43). The *Dunciad* passage,
appropriate to Pope's subject in that poem,
enlarges most upon the fall of Rome and its
usurpation by the Dark Ages; a Renaissance in
Britain is hinted at in one line only, while
the ultimate triumph of Dulness is hailed, with
powerful irony, as a kind of Renaissance in
reverse.[4] By contrast, the first of the passages mentioned, that in *An Essay on Criticism*,
dismisses the whole of the Middle Ages with
confident expedition. Since the ideas Pope
expresses here are germane to my present subject,
I shall quote the passage.

> Thus long succeeding Criticks justly
>   reign'd,
> *Licence* repress'd, and *useful Laws* ordain'd;
> *Learning* and *Rome* alike in Empire grew,
> And *Arts* still *follow'd* where her *Eagles flew*;
> From the same Foes, at last, both felt
>   their Doom,
> And the same Age saw *Learning* fall, and *Rome*.
> With *Tyranny*, then *Superstition* join'd,
> As that the *Body*, this enslav'd the *Mind*;
> Much was *Believ'd*, but little *understood*,
> And to be *dull* was constru'd to be *good*;
> A *second* Deluge Learning thus o'er-run,
> And the *Monks* finish'd what the *Goths* begun.
>   At length, *Erasmus*, that *great, injur'd Name*,
> (The *Glory* of the Priesthood, and the *Shame* !)
> *Stemm'd* the *wild Torrent* of a *barb'rous Age*,
> And drove those *Holy Vandals* off the Stage.
>   But see! each *Muse*, in *Leo's* Golden Days,
> *Starts* from her Trance, and trims her wither'd
>   Bays!

Rome's ancient *Genius,* o'er its *Ruins* spread,
Shakes off the *Dust,* and rears his rev'rend
    Head.
Then *Sculpture* and her *Sister-Arts* revive;
Stones leap'd to *Form,* and *Rocks* began to *live,*
With *sweeter Notes* each *rising Temple* rung;
A *Raphael* painted, and a *Vida* sung! [5]

It is in the context of this historical view
that Pope's concerns in *To Mr. Addison* must be
seen. This epistle is less well-known than the
two passages cited above. Apart from the establishing of its text and the details of its
composition, little scholarly or critical attention has been paid to it. [6] Yet the ideas it
expresses throw light on Pope's Augustanism,
and it is in itself a brilliantly accomplished
poem. It is my purpose here to discuss its
content and its form in relation to the relevant
background of ideas.

II

In his *Dialogues Upon the Usefulness of Ancient
Medals,* which Pope's epistle was designed to
introduce, Addison advances three chief arguments against those who think numismatics a
merely pedantic pastime. In the first place
the coins of an ancient civilization afford
sure evidence of its political history: the
names, dates, acts, and even appearance of its
rulers. Secondly, coins may convey information
on other aspects of antiquity; they may bear
images of buildings and statues long destroyed,
or of ancient weapons, or fashions of dress.
Finally, the allegorical personages depicted
on Greek or Roman coins may illustrate and
illuminate passages from the ancient poets, as
the poetry may help to explain the coins. [7] The
assumption underlying all these arguments, which
even Cynthio, the sceptic of the dialogues,
never seriously questions, is the familiar
humanist one: that it is a thing of value in
itself to study, and be familiar with, all as-

pects of our classical heritage. Addison's
subject in these dialogues might have led one
to expect, at some point, a sustained lament at
the fall of Rome, or at least a mood of regret
at the passing away of ancient grandeur. On the
contrary; the tone is equable to the point of
monotony throughout.

Pope, on the other hand, opens his prefatory
poem by evoking the broad vista of Rome in its
ruins, seen down the long perspectives of time;
his lofty rhetoric is designed to arouse in his
readers the emotion of pity.

> See the wild Waste of all-devouring years!
> How Rome her own sad Sepulchre appears,
> With nodding arches, broken temples spread!
> The very Tombs now vanish'd like their dead!
> Imperial wonders rais'd on Nations spoil'd[8]

Pope's lines have the authority of a traditional
view; the presentation of time in the first line
is a commonplace in literature, albeit an impressive one,[9] while the second line suggests
community of thought and feeling with Du Bellay,
in his *Antiquitez de Rome* (1559). Pope uses the
same figure that Du Bellay had employed in the
third sonnet:

> Nouveau venu, qui cherches Rome en Rome,
>   Et rien de Rome en Rome n'apperçois,
>   Ces vieux palais, ces vieux arcz que tu
>   vois,
>   Et ces vieux murs, c'est ce que Rome on
>   nomme.
> Voy quel orgueil, quelle ruine: et comme
>   Celle qui mist le monde sous les loix,
>   Pour donter tout, se donta quelquefois,
>   Et devint proye au temps, qui tout con-
>   somme.
> Rome de Rome est le seul monument...[10]

In Du Bellay, as in Pope, the traditional
meditation and lament at the passing away of
grandeur and at the omnipotence of time is lent

immediacy and force by the scene presented.
Both poets have been stirred by the ambition
and power of the Roman Empire, Du Bellay perhaps more than Pope, and Du Bellay is, I think,
the more eloquent on the subject. It is easy
to find an earlier example of the same attitude.
Petrarch, who devoted so much energy and
eloquence to the cause of restoring Rome's
past glory, could compose the following exchange between Joy and Reason:

> G. Sum Romanus Imperator, mundi dominus. R.
> Fuit quando id dici propè ueraciter poterat,
> quorsum uero redierint res uides...Non est
> amplius gaudii materia Romanum Imperium,
> sed humanæ fragilitatis & fortunæ uariantis
> indicium.[11]

The conceit of Rome as its own sepulchre, or
monument, goes back earlier still, as Pope
probably realized; it is used in two different
places by St. Jerome, writing contemporaneously
with the final break-up of the Roman Empire.
'Vera sententia est:' wrote Jerome, in the
preface to the third book of his commentary on
Ezekiel:

> Omnia orta occidunt, et aucta senescunt.
> Et alibi: Nihil est enim opere et manu
> factum, quod non conficiat et consumat
> vetustas. Quis crederet ut totuis orbis ex-
> structa victoriis Roma corrueret, ut ipsa
> suis populis et mater fieret et sepulcrum...[12]

Pope does in a sense span the centuries with
his description of the ruins of Rome; the reader who is attentive to the allusive mode of his
poetry here cannot but feel, behind its concise
summary, the accumulated testimony of 'what
oft was thought'. The echo of Jerome in
particular, a conscious inheritor of the
imperial civilization and a contemporary witness of Rome's fall, seems to confer a special
historical and human authenticity upon what

Pope has to say.

In the lines which follow, Pope may be seen
as expanding upon the concise, central words
of Du Bellay's sonnet: 'Voy quel orgueil,
quelle ruine:' yet more perhaps than in Du
Bellay moral appraisal from a Christian standpoint enters into Pope's description of the
'Imperial wonders' of Ancient Rome. The part
played by despoiled nations and by slavery,
including the labour of persecuted early
Christians, is not forgotten; upon this suffering Rome's glory was built.[13] The emotion of
pity, aroused by earlier lines, is modified
by Pope's suggestion that Rome suffèred a
chastisement of imperial hubris, and in the
following couplet compassion is blended with
ironic perception:

> Fanes, which admiring Gods with pride survey,
> Statues of Men, scarce less alive than
>   they;[14]

It is the unexpected introduction of the word
'less', in the second line of the couplet,
which at a stroke reduces the Roman pantheon
to the level of men long dead and disregarded.
At this point one is much aware of the Christian
poet writing of pagan Rome.[15] Christianity,
however, is far from being exempt from Pope's
critical appraisal; he had offended his fellow
Catholics by his references to monkish barbarism
in *An Essay on Criticism*,[16] but his condemnation
of Christian philistinism is even more explicit
here:

> Some felt the silent stroke of mould'ring
>   age,
> Some hostile fury, some religious rage;
> Barbarian blindness, Christian zeal conspire,
> And Papal piety, and Gothic fire.[17]

Pope's rhetoric serves him well in these lines;
the antithetic patterning of the verse becomes
progressively more marked, the juxtaposition
of apparent opposites, and the implication of

their actual affinity, progressively more bold;
the total effect is expressive of a fine critical detachment on the part of the poet. The
concluding lines of the epistle's first paragraph serve both to re-emphasize the theme of
mutability and to introduce the central problem
of the whole poem: how may the knowledge and
spirit of Rome be transmitted, through the
wastes of time, into posterity?

>   Perhaps, by its own ruins sav'd from flame,
>   Some bury'd marble half preserves a name;
>   That Name the learn'd with fierce disputes
>   pursue,
>   And give to Titus old Vespasian's due.[18]

III

An emblem in Ripa's *Iconologia* depicts History
as a winged female; she writes in a book borne
on the shoulders of Saturn who, carrying a
scythe, walks close at her side. Beneath her
right foot is a rectangular form, symbol of
constancy.[19] Saturn, with his scythe, is here
the personification of time,whose capacity to
destroy has been overcome and controlled by the
Art of History. Pope, when he speaks of 'the
wild Waste of all-devouring years', presents
time as a force of disorder, sterility and
destruction. This presentation is the more
appropriate, from Pope's viewpoint, because
the particular lapse of time he has in mind is
that between the fall of Rome and the revival
of learning. It is worth noticing that the
metaphors Pope employed for the Middle Ages
in An *Essay on Criticism*, a '*second* Deluge' and a
'*wild Torrent*', are also images of disorder and
destruction, though that of the deluge has
further implications.[20] History, then, is one
feature of those 'images of men's wits and knowledges', which, as Bacon wrote,

remain in books, exempted from the wrong
of time and capable of perpetual renovation.
Neither are they fitly to be called images,
because they generate still, and cast their
seeds in the minds of others...So that if
the invention of the ship was thought so
noble, which carrieth riches and commodities
from place to place...how much more are
letters to be magnified, which as ships
pass through the vast seas of time, and make
ages so distant to participate of the wisdom,
illuminations, and inventions, the one of
the other?[21]

As history is a branch of learning, so antiquities is a branch of history;[22] the paragraph
on it in *The Advancement of Learning* suggests the
closeness of Pope's thought to that of Bacon:

Antiquities, or Remnants of History, are,
as was said, *tanquam tabula naufragii*, when
industrious persons, by an exact and scrupulous diligence and observation, out of
monuments, names, words, proverbs, traditions,
private records and evidences...do save and
recover somewhat from the deluge of time.[23]

By the word 'monuments' Bacon understood:
buildings, statues, inscriptions, coins, and
the like. Du Bellay, having compared Rome to
a harvest mown and stacked, might well liken
the antiquary to 'le gleneur' gathering the
remains "De ce qui va tumbant apres le moisson-
neur'.[24] Addison said nothing new when he
pointed out the value of coins as historical
evidence. Enea Vico, in his *Discorsi sopra le
Medaglie de gli Antichi* (1555), and Antonio
Agustín, in his *Dialogos de medallas* (1587), were
among the first to put forward the same view;
it was to become a commonplace among historians and antiquaries.[25]

When, in the seventeenth and eighteenth
centuries, historians came to think that nonliterary evidence from the past was more reliable than literary, medals assumed an even
greater historical importance.[26] A representative expression of this view may be found in
Charles Patin's *Histoire des Medailles* (1665), a
treatise which Pope and Addison may have
known.[27] In the second chapter of this work,

> c'est l'Histoire, qui estoit appellée par un
> Ancien, la messagere de l'antiquité, &
> la maistresse de la vie, qui nous inspire
> tousjours de nobles sentimens, & qui nous
> fait connoistre l'experience des regles qui
> doivent former nostre Philosophie morale.
> Cette Histoire ne s'apprend pas seulement
> dans les Livres, car d'une part ils ne
> disent pas tout ce que nous devons sçavoir,
> & de l'autre il se faut bien donner de
> garde decroire tout ce qu'ils nous disent:
> Il faut recourir aux pieces qui la justifient,
> à qui la malice & l'ignorance des hommes
> n'a pû donner d'atteinte: Il en faut croire
> les monumens du temps, dont les Medailles
> sont les marques les plus asseurées, & les
> plus frequentes.[28]

In another place in his treatise Patin points
out that medals outlast statues and buildings,
and are able, alone, to bear the image of such
monuments into modern times. Addison makes
the same point.[29]
This is the context of thought in which Pope,
continuing his epistle, introduces the subject
of medals.

> Ambition sigh'd; She found it vain to
>   trust
> The faithless Column and the crumbling Bust;
> Huge moles, whose shadow stretch'd from
>   shore to shore,
> Their ruins ruin'd, and their place no more!

Convinc'd, she now contracts her vast design,
And all her Triumphs shrink into a Coin:
A narrow orb each crouded conquest keeps,
Beneath her Palm here sad Judaea weeps,
Here scantier limits the proud Arch confine,
And scarce are seen the prostrate Nile or
    Rhine,
A small Euphrates thro' the piece is roll'd,
And little Eagles wave their wings in gold.[30]

What is the precise character of Pope's personified Ambition? Emphasis is laid less upon a
desire for ever-greater conquests than upon a
desire to be remembered by posterity, a desire
that her conquests should achieve lasting fame.
In this respect she comes close to Ripa's
Historia, and it is interesting to note that
Ripa derived his personification from the Roman
figure of Writing Victory, to be found both on
columns and coins.[31] One such coin is illustrated and discussed by Addison in his *Dialogues*,
and would thus be known to Pope:[32] Pope's
'Ambition' is the desire to 'make history' in
both senses of the term. Yet Rome's very *ruins*
must undergo a second process of destruction
(Du Bellay has the same thought) and even their
sites will be forgotten.[33] Only medals will
remain.
    A successful ambiguity governs the meaning
of the next line. The dominant sense of the
word 'contract' is of course to restrict, to
draw in; the word 'shrink', in the line following, confirms this as Pope's primary meaning.
The 'vast design' is thus the Roman Empire itself which must be reduced to the dimensions of
a coin, that its fame may be transmitted to
posterity. There is at the same time a secondary meaning of the word 'contract' which also
contributes to the meaning of the poem. Here
the sense is to establish, with the implication
behind it of bargain and agreement.[34] The 'vast
design' is here the stratagem by which 'devour-
ing Time' is foiled, and by which the essential
knowledge of what humanity achieved in Rome is

conveyed to distant ages and lands. It is
however the startling diminution effect, taking
its origin from the primary sense of 'contract',
which occupies the remainder of the present
passage, and which is perhaps the one really
dazzling piece of poetic artifice in the epistle.
The abstract terms of line 23 are succeeded by
the spectacular visual effect of: 'And all her
Triumphs shrink into a Coin', which so boldly
juxtaposes the great and the minute: a live
procession, celebrating an imperial victory,
transformed into a graven emblem. The sense of
diminution is made more poignant by the phrase
'narrow orb' with which the next line begins.
Here too a successful ambiguity has been employed. Primarily, the phrase refers to the medal:
the narrow circle which is now the surviving
vestige and proof of Roman glory. The very
coupling of the words 'narrow' and 'orb',
however, has something of a surprise effect, and
prompts one to think of the great orb: the world
itself. The allusion, as Warburton rightly
noted, is to 'the pompous title of *Orbis Romanus*,
which the Romans gave to their Empire.'[35]
Jerome himself, writing of the sack of Rome in
410, used this 'title' with a mixture of irony
and sorrow: 'Romanus orbis ruit, et tamen
cervix nostra erecta non flectitur' and elsewhere without irony, he wrote that 'in una Urbe
totus orbis interiit...'[36] The secondary level
of meaning thus reinforces our sense of the
startling transformation which it is the
purpose of this whole passage to express. A
third level of meaning lies in the traditional
function of the circle as a symbol for eternity,
a point fully discussed and illustrated by
Addison in his *Dialogues*.[37] In particular
Addison speaks of 'the globe' as a proper 'emblem of Eternity'; it is therefore most unlikely
that Pope did not intend his 'orb' to have this
significance.[38] On this level, therefore, the
reference is firstly to the 'vast design' of
Rome itself, a city, empire and world sometimes
held to be eternal,[39] and secondly to the vast

yet chastising design whereby the pride and
glory of Rome *has* succeeded in defying 'the
wrong of time' and in perpetuating itself in
the minds of posterity.[40] The vaunted and the
actual 'eternity' of Rome are thus simultaneously alluded to by the single image. All
three levels of meaning here contribute to the
poet's purpose. Pope has, in one image, brilliantly contrived to compress a sense both of
what Rome once was, and has since become. The
transformation and diminution effect, from *orbis
Romanus* to medal, is completed in this image;
Pope has, as it were, succeeded in contracting the 'Waste of all-devouring years' which
separates his own age from Rome's original
glory, and has super-imposed Renaissance upon
Antiquity. The hand of the poet who could
parallel the arming of an epic hero with a
fashionable Queen Anne belle at her toilet is
here very much in evidence.[41]

It was important for Pope's purpose, as will
shortly be shown, that the 'narrow orb' of the
medal should not be allowed to seem a dead,
fragmentary thing, an inert remnant of past
grandeur which has fortuitously survived. Pope
has already given the medal a miniature completeness by calling it a 'narrow *orb*' [my
italics] and has thus precluded the idea that
it is a mere fragment. He has suggested,
rather, that it is the essence of Roman achievement in miniature. The remainder of this passage imparts a sense of life and movement to the
medal, miniature though it is. They are
'crouded' conquests that the scantier limits
of the coin confine; 'sad Judaea' is alive and
weeping; the natural movement of the Euphrates
has not been halted, and the eagles, most
common of all emblems of Roman rule, can still
wave their wings. All the precision, sensitivity and delight, with which Pope, in *The Rape of
the Lock,* described the beauty of small objects,
is lavished here upon the final couplet of the
passage, in many ways the central couplet of
the epistle.

A small Euphrates thro' the piece is roll'd,
And little Eagles wave their wings in gold.[42]

IV

Bacon spoke, as we have seen, of the writings
of men as able 'to generate still, and cast
their seeds in the minds of others', and to pass
thus, through 'the vast seas of time', to distant ages.[43] Du Bellay likened the student of
Roman antiquities to the gleaner of scattered
grain, after the harvest; and in another sonnet
he declares that 'Ces vieux fragmens encor
servent d'examples' and proceeds to describe
how Rome is reviving itself from its own
ruins.[44] If the spirit of Rome is to be reborn
in men's minds, it is clear that its antiquities must not only be authentic historical
evidence; they must also have the power to
inspire. Thus the necessity, in Pope's epistle,
for the medal to be made to seem alive.

In his insistence on the 'living' property of
medals, Pope is recognizing in old coins a power
attributed to them long before their importance as reliable historical evidence was argued
by Enea Vico and Antonio Augustin. Two centuries earlier, Petrarch, in his letter to Laelius, described how he had presented Roman coins,
with his *De Viris Illustribus*, to the Emperor
Charles IV. The letter is so important for an
understanding of Pope's epistle that the
relevant passage is worth quoting at length.
After describing his exhortation to the Emperor
to emulate, in his deeds, the lives of the
illustrious Romans, Petrarch tells how an
expression of favour and approbation animated
the face of the monarch:

Quod dictum serenis oculorum radiis et
augustæ frontis læto probavit assensu.
Itaque peropportunum aggredi visum est,
quod iamdudum facere meditabar. Sumpta
igitur ex verbis occasione, aliquot sibi
aureas argenteasque nostrorum principium

effigies, minutissimis ac veteribus litteris
inscriptas, quas in deliciis habebam, dono
dedi, in quibus et Augusti Caesaris vultus
erat pene spirans: et ecce, inquam, Caesar,
quibus successisti, ecce quos imitari studeas
et mirari, ad quorum formam atque imaginem
te componas, quos praeter to unum, nulli
hominum daturus eram: tua me movit auctoritas.
Licet enim horum ego mores et nomina et res
gestas norim, tuum est non modo nosse sed
sequi: tibi itaque debebantur. Sub hoc
singulorum vitae summam multa brevitate
perstringens, quos potui ad virtutem atque
ad imitandi studium aculeos verbis immiscui,
quibus ille vehementer exhileratus, nec
ullum gratius accepisse munusculum visus
est.[45]

Petrarch presented coins to the Emperor Charles
IV expressly to reinforce the gift of *De Viris
Illustribus*, to inspire him to meet the challenge
of their great deeds by emulation. The coins
are for the Emperor alone because, though others
might be instructed by them, only *he* is in a
position to vie with the famous figures they
depict. It is significant that one coin bears
the head of Augustus, and that the image is
noted to be lifelike almost to the breath. The
presentation of the coins has its due place in
Petrarch's rhetorical strategy, the purpose of
which is not primarily to instruct the Emperor,
but to inspire him to *act* (tuum est non modo
nosse sed sequi).

That this famous episode was remembered in
the earlier eighteenth century is shown by the
Preface de l'Editeur of J. Bimard de la Bastie to
the 1739 edition of Louis Jobert's *La Science
des Medailles*. 'Le gout pour les Medailles Antiques', wrote de la Bastie,

a commencé à la renaissance des bonnes
études. Petrarque, le Restaurateur des
Lettres, ne se contenta pas de remasser
autant d'Ouvrages des Auteurs anciens,

qu'il lui fut possible d'en trouber; il
rechercha avec le même empressement les
Médailles Antiques, & il crut ne pouvoir
offrir à l'Empereur Charles IV. un présent
plus agréable & plus digne d'un grand Prince,
que de lui donner quelques Médailles
Impériales en or, & en argent.[46]

The power of medals to inspire emulation is in
fact fully recognized by Charles Patin in his
Histoire des Médailles ; he discusses it in a
number of places, and clearly considers its
effect to be similar to that of History Paint-
ing--with the exception that the medal is also
the proof of what it depicts.[47] Louis Jobert,
in his *La Science des Médailles* suggests another
aspect of the living and inspiring quality of
medals when he notes how faithfully they
reflect the level of civilization--Augustan or
barbarous--in which they were coined.[48] It is
suggested even more strongly when Jobert allows
his exposition of the Figure and Legend of a
medal to lead him into using the human metaphor
of the body and the soul. 'It seems as if the
Ancients,' wrote Jobert,

> had designed to make Images and Emblems of
> their Medals; the One for the Common People,
> and those of duller Apprehensions; the Other
> for People of Quality, and the more refined
> Wits. Images to represent the Faces and
> Heads of Princes; Emblems, their Virtues
> and Great Atchievements. Thus the Legend
> is to be looked upon as the Soul of the Medal
> and the Figures as the Body; and just so it
> is in the Emblem, where the Device has the
> place of the Soul, without which we could
> never understand what the Figures were de-
> signed to teach us.[49]

The comparison between medals and emblems,
like that of Patin between medals and History
Painting, makes it finally clear that the
medal's living power to inspire is intimately

related to the idea of the persuasive and
transforming power of the visual image.[50] As
late as 1709 a work purporting to be an English
translation of Ripa's *Iconologia* could be introduced in the following terms:

> Here you will find abundance of Figures
> and Emblems of every thing imaginable;
> accompanied with curious and solid Morals,
> owing to very learned Authors. The under-
> standing Peruser of this Book will meet
> therein Things not only to divert the Mind,
> but to instruct it, and to *inspire him* [my
> italics] with the Love of Virtue, and Hatred
> of Vice; and to regulate his Manners, Be-
> haviour and Conduct.[51]

It is from this vital background of attitudes
towards the medal that the next lines of Pope's
epistle spring. In these lines the medal is
fully humanized:

> The Medal, faithful to its charge of fame,
> Thro' climes and ages bears each form and
>   name:
> In one short view subjected to your eye
> Gods, Emp'rors, Heroes, Sages, Beauties,
>   lie.[52]

The medal's human trait of fidelity is shown to
its 'charge': the burden of knowledge and inspiration that it carries inviolate through the
ages, as did the ships through 'the vast seas
of time' in Bacon's metaphor.[53] This 'charge
of fame' is not merely referred to but displayed; the final line, with its sense of an
opening out of abundant variety and richness,
has this effect. The line unfolds before us a
whole hierarchy, ranging down from the divine
to the spheres of human action, reflection and
beauty. Pope's amplification at this point is
in marked contrast to the diminution effect
carried out in the previous paragraph; with the
line 'And little Eagles wave their wings in

gold' the turning-point of the epistle has been
passed, the possibility of *translatio imperii* and
translatio studii has been asserted and accounted
for, and one would expect Pope to devote the
remainder of his poem to the unfolding of a
new Augustan Age to counter-balance the old.

This expectation is fulfilled--one of the
strengths of the epistle is its sense of deliberate procedure and controlled form--but not
before Pope has turned his attention to one
serious obstacle to such a rebirth: the un-
critical adulation of antiquity for its own
sake.

> With sharpen'd sight pale Antiquaries pore,
> The'inscription value, but the rust adore;
> This the blue varnish, that the green endears,
> The sacred rust of twice ten hundred years!
> To gain Pescennius one employs his schemes,
> One grasps a Cecrops in ecstatic dreams;
> Poor Vadius, long with learned spleen de-
> vour'd,
> Can taste no pleasure since his Shield was
> scour'd;
> And Curio, restless by the Fair-one's side,
> Sighs for an Otho, and neglects his bride.[54]

The rust upon medals was indeed, in some cases,
prized by antiquaries; Addison's Philander is
afraid of being laughed at for taking it
seriously,but Jobert, in *La Science des Medailles*,
is quite unashamed to do so.[55] Rare medals,
likewise, were coveted more than common ones.
An image of Augustus was more likely to inspire
emulation of antiquity than an image of Otho,
Pescennius Niger or the entirely mythical
Cecrops, yet these were most highly prized
collectors' pieces.[56] The last line of the
passage sharply juxtaposes such antiquarianism
with the real world; its utterly dead and un-
productive character is the more stressed by
the mention of the neglected bride. This
characteristic, comically presented, is the very
opposite to that for which medals should

rationally have been valued: an accession of
inspiration and knowledge. Medals, in short,
are to be prized for what they convey, not for
their actual antiquity or rarity. The
'sharpen'd sight' of the antiquaries is thus
ironical on the level of metaphor, though
literally true; they cannot discern wherein
lies the true value of antiquities, and where
there is no discrimination there can be no
new growth.

                              V

   In a letter to the Emperor Charles IV
Petrarch conjures up the Genius of Rome to
pleas for help in reviving her ancient importance and glory; in Canzone VI ('Spirto gentil
...'), addressed to Cola di Rienzo, his pleading was animated by genuine belief that the
moment for such a revical was at hand--that the
revival was indeed beginning.[57]   Du Bellay, as
we have seen, deviated from his dominant theme
of mutability to take note of the enduring
spirit of Rome and its capacity for self-renew-
al.[58] These references mark out the tradition
in which Pope is writing in the passage from
An Essay on Criticism already quoted--

   Rome's ancient *Genius*, o'er its *Ruins* spread,
      Shakes off the *Dust,* and rears his rev'rend
         Head![59]

and in the last part of the present epistle,
where he heralds the advent of a new Augustan
Age in England. It is therefore necessary to
the plan of Pope's poem that he should clearly
distinguish Addison's estimation of medals from
that of the blind antiquaries.

        Theirs is the Vanity, the Learning thine:
      Touch'd by thy hand, again Rome's glories
         shine,
      Her Gods, and god-like Heroes rise to view,
      And all her faded garlands bloom a-new.

> Nor blush, these studies thy regard engage;
> These pleas'd the Fathers of poetic rage;
> The verse and sculpture bore an equal part,
> And Art reflected images to Art.[60]

The distinction necessary to Pope's purpose is
made in the first line; the marked antithesis
brings learning and vanity into full contrast,
the one both outward-looking and critical, the
other inward-looking and without thought. The
allusion in the next line is specific; Philander in the *Dialogues* (who is for all intents
and purposes Addison himself) had described
how a medal might be redeemed from harmful
varieties of rust. The 'skilful Medallist...'

> will recover you a Temple or a triumphal
> Arch out of its rubbish, if I may so call
> it, and with a few reparations of the
> graving tool restore it to its first splen-
> dour and magnificence. I have known an
> Emperor quite hid under a crust of dross,
> who after two or three days cleansing has
> appeared with all his Titles about him as
> fresh and beautiful as at his first coming
> out of the Mint.[61]

Just as, in the first half of the epistle, Rome
was seen to shrink to a coin, so here the clean-
ing of the coin assists in Ambition's 'vast
design' and is a prelude to the swelling act of
new Augustanism. It is the peculiar character
of the writing on numismatics at this period
that so great a concept should be linked to so
mundane and precise an action as (for example)
the application of 'Vinegar, or the Juice of
Lemons' for the removal of rust from medals.[62]
The emphasis on the possibility of new life and
growth, expressed in the words 'rise' and
'bloom a-new' culminates in the final couplet
of the passage. Pope alludes here to Philander's contention, in the *Dialogues*, that the
medals, sculpture and poetry of the ancient
world had much in common, and that medals might

therefore assist in elucidating the obscurities
and heightening the appreciation of the ancient
poets.[63] To clean a medal, then, is not only
to reveal an object in itself a thing of beauty
and an emblem of antiquity; it is also to help
clear away the 'rust' from the literature of
antiquity, to reveal it as it would have been
understood at the time of its composition.
In this way medals demonstrate the fundamental
affinity, and possibility of cross-fertilization
between the visual and literary arts--a cross-
fertilization which can give birth to stirring
visions. It is significant that the last line
quoted anticipates a similar line in the *Epistle
to Mr. Jervas*--'While images reflect from art
to art'--expressive as the later line is of a
dialogue between poet and painter which leads
on to *'Rome'*'s pompous glories rising to our
thought','And builds imaginary *Rome* a-new'.[64]

The final paragraph of the epistle opens with
a stirring call to Britain to rise to the
challenge of ancient achievement. Here too,
as Warburton was right to note, there is a
specific allusion to Addison. In his *Guardian*
paper No. 96, which was reprinted in 1715 with
the revised English translation of Jobert's
La Science des Médailles, Addison had contended
that the modern world should adopt the Roman
practice of circulating medals as popular
currency.[65] 'This method', wrote Addison,

> published every noble action to advantage,
> and in a short space of time spread through
> the whole *Roman* Empire. The *Romans* were so
> careful to preserve the memory of great
> events upon their coins, that when any
> particular piece of money grew very scarce,
> it was often re-coined by a succeeding
> Emperor, many years after the death of the
> Emperor to whose honour it was first struck.[66]

Addison continues that 'This is one of those
Arts of Peace which may very well deserve to be
cultivated, and which may be of great use to
posterity'. He then appends a proposal, pur-

porting to be the work of a friend, and about
to be put into execution. It runs as follows:

    I   That the *English* farthings and half-pence
be recoined upon the union of the two nations.

    II That they bear devices and inscriptions
alluding to all the most remarkable parts
of her Majesty's reign.

    III That there be a society established for
the finding out of proper subjects, inscriptions and devices.

    IV That no subject, inscription, or device
be stamped without the approbation of this
society, nor, if it be thought proper, without the authority of Privy-council.
    By this means, Medals, that are, at
present only a dead treasure, or meer
curiousities, will be of use in the ordinary
commerce of life, and, at the same time,
perpetuate the Glories of her Majesty's
reign, reward the labours of her greatest
subjects, keep alive in the people a gratitude for publick services, and excite the
emulation of posterity. To these generous
purposes nothing can so much contribute
as Medals of this kind, which are of undoubted authority, of necessary use and
observation, not perishable by time, nor
confined to any certain place; properties
not to be found in books, statues, pictures,
buildings, or any other monuments of illustrious actions.[67]

This is more than the expression of regret that
'no nation among the moderns has imitated the
ancient Romans in this particular' which we
find in the *Dialogues*.[68] It is a specific and
practical proposal, the 'Society' mentioned in
clause three being a copy of the French
Academie des Inscriptions et Belles Lettres, of
which Racine and Boileau had been members.[69]

Addison is here quite seriously advocating that
Britain should adopt the Roman practice. He is
not, however, proposing an imitation of the
ancients merely for its own sake, but for good
reasons; by the means proposed Britain would
attain a heightened awareness of the quality
of her own civilization, and would at the same
time discharge an obligation to posterity. It
is an assumption which seems to underlie much
of the writing on medals at this time that it
is a mark of civilization to leave records,[70] a
characteristic of barbarism to leave none.
Hence Philander's observation in Dialogue iii:

> We ought to look on Medals as so many monu-
> ments consigned over to Eternity, that may
> possibly last when all other memorials of the
> same Age are worn out or lost. They are
> a kind of Present that those who are actually
> in Being make over to such as lie hid within
> the depths of Futurity.[71]

Little advancement of learning and civilization
could be hoped for in a world which had lost
its past. It is significant that Addison likens
the destruction of coins to 'the burning of the
Alexandrian Library' and that Pope was to include
this latter event in the *Dunciad*, Book iii, as a
sign of the triumph of Dulness.[72] These are the
issues to which Pope seeks to give poetic
expression in the final section of his epistle.

> Oh when shall Britain, conscious of her
>   claim,
> Stand emulous of Greek and Roman fame?
> In living medals see her wars enroll'd,
> And vanquish'd realms supply recording gold?
> Here, rising bold, the Patriot's honest face;
> There Warriors frowning in historic brass:
> Then future ages with delight shall see
> How Plato's, Bacon's, Newton's looks agree;
> Or in fair series laurell'd Bards be shown,
> A Virgil there, and here an Addison.[73]

These and the concluding lines counterbalance
the broad vista of Rome in its ruins, at the
beginning of the epistle, and complete the
symmetrical structure of the poem. The tone,
set by the phrase 'conscious of her claim' in
the first line, is one rather of confidence
than aspiration. The argument assumes that
Britain is already in a position to sustain
comparison with Rome. She has her patriots,
warriors and philosophers; she can afford to
measure herself by the standard of antiquity,
which is what adopting the Roman usage of
medals would mean. In keeping with this assumption, and the confident tone, the passage
moves to a recognition of Britain's duty to
the distant future, which can best be fulfilled
by the adoption of Addison's proposals. The
swift movement of 'Plato's, Bacon's, Newton's
...' grandly overleaps the mere hiatus of the
Middle Ages, and ranges Newton and Bacon with
Plato, as in a single series of medals laid
out before some antiquary of the far future.[74]
The very marked antithesis and balance of the
line: 'A Virgil there, and here an Addison'
(contrasting with the swift connected movement
of the line just discussed) is even more expressive of a new Augustan confidence; the
weighing of one age against the other, and the
resultant equipoise, is here specifically
enacted by the verse. In the same way Pope,
in his Horatian epistles, was to print Horace's
Latin and his own English opposite to one
another on facing pages, as though to invite
comparison and assert a balance; in the same
way, in the 1739 edition of Jobert's *La Science
des Médailles*, the profiles of 'Divus Augustus'
and 'Lodovicus Magnus Novus Augustus', side by
side, are to be found engraved.[75]

At this point, according to Pope's own
testimony, the epistle was once concluded.[76]
To have ended with 'A Virgil there, and here
an Addison' would certainly have been to impress the reader with a fine, bold note of
finality, almost a note of triumph. Yet it

would perhaps have been abrupt. By adding the
ten lines in tribute to his and Addison's
friend, the statesman James Craggs (1686-1721),
Pope has been able to improve the poem in
several ways. Firstly he is able to sustain
and expand his imaginary insight into the
future, thus imparting fuller and more satisfying symmetry to the range through time which has
been the theme of the epistle. Secondly, he
is able to expand upon the moral and human
qualities which seem to him to merit the term
Augustan. Thirdly, he is able, to the great
advantage of the poem, to take up and develop
the circle imagery which was so important a
part of the first half of the epistle.

> Then shall thy CRAGS (and let me call him
>   mine)
> On the cast ore, another Pollio, shine;
> With aspect open, shall erect his head,
> And round the orb in lasting notes be read,
> 'Statesman, yet friend to Truth! of soul
>   sincere,
> In action faithful, and in honour clear;
> Who broke no promise, serv'd no private end,
> Who gain'd no title, and who lost no friend,
> Ennobled by himself, by all approv'd,
> And prais'd, unenvy'd, by the Muse he
>   lov'd'.[77]

That the Whig statesman, whose profile is
thus imagined eternized upon a medal, should be
compared to the Consul Pollio of Virgil's
Fourth Eclogue is of the highest significance.
Not only is this a part of the conscious procedure by which Augustan figures are given
modern counterparts, but Pollio in Virgil's
eclogue, and, by analogy, Craggs in the present
epistle, is associated with the return of the
Golden Age.[78] The Fourth Eclogue, by virtue of
its very date and subject, unavoidably suggests
the identity of the Augustan Age with a returning Age of Gold, recurring on the completion of
a cycle of ages or the Platonic Year. It is

obvious that such an identification would be
attractive to Renaissance minds, eager as they
were to hail the dawn of a new Augustan Age.
Pope, by comparing James Craggs to Pollio at
this point in the epistle, makes it very clear
that Augustan and Golden Ages are associated
in his own mind.[79] Addison indeed had discussed
the Golden Age, in his *Dialogues*:

> The person in the midst of the circle is
> supposed to be *Jupiter*, by the Author that
> has published this Medal, but I should rather
> take it for the figure of Time. I remember
> I have seen at *Rome* an antique Statue of Time,
> with a wheel or hoop of marble in his hand
> ...and not with a serpent as he is generally
> represented...As the circle of marble in
> his hand represents the common year, so
> this that encompasses him is a proper
> representation of the great year, which is
> the whole round and comprehension of Time...
> To sum up therefore the thoughts of this
> Medal. The inscription teaches us that the
> whole design must refer to the Golden Age
> which it lively represents, if we suppose
> the circle that encompasses *Time*, or if you
> please *Jupiter*, signifies the finishing of
> the great year; and that the *Phoenix*
> figures out the beginning of a new series of
> time. So that the compliment on this Medal
> to the Emperor *Adrian*, is in all respects the
> same that *Virgil* makes to *Pollio's* son, at
> whose birth he supposes the *annus magnus* or
> platonical year run out, and renewed again
> with the opening of the Golden Age.[80]

This discussion, which Pope cannot but have had
in mind when he compared Craggs to Pollio, helps
to disclose the relevant meanings of the line in
which the symbol of the orb is once more introduced. In the first place it is clear that the
same levels of meaning discovered in the word
'orb' earlier in the poem are to be found here;
most obviously the orb is the medal which will

bear the features of James Craggs and whose
Legend will bear witness to his virtues; on
the next level it is the world itself, and here
the word 'round' does not refer to the Legend
which runs round the circumference of the medal
but rather suggests that medals will convey the
fame of James Craggs 'round the world'.[81] It is
when we come to the original third level of
meaning (the orb as a symbol of eternity) that
we realize a new complication has been introduced. The reference to Pollio now prompts us
to think of eternity as that cycle of ages
which periodically renews itself with the return
of the Age of Gold, and the 'orb' as that encompassing circle which, in Addison's words,
is 'the whole round and comprehension of Time'.
It is significant that Dryden used the word to
express this meaning, in his translation of the
Fourth Eclogue.

> The last great Age, foretold by sacred Rhymes,
> Renews its finish'd Course, *Saturnian* times
> Rowl round again, and mighty years, begun
> From their first Orb, in radiant Circles
>   run.[82]

It would thus appear that Pope is not thinking
of eternity as a simple concept of timelessness,
but rather as a recurrent series of new Augustan
Ages which as yet, in Addison's words, 'lie
hid within the depths of Futurity', but to which
his own age may communicate by medals just as
the spirit of Rome's original grandeur has been
communicated to him. In the future, as in the
past, a medal may conquer time. To all this
the phrase 'lasting notes' lends an appropriate
suggestion of harmony, and the qualities for
which Pope now proceeds to celebrate James
Craggs are not inappropriate to the rule of
justice, concord and peace with which the Golden
Age has traditionally been associated.

VI

The purpose of the foregoing analysis has
been twofold: firstly to investigate what seems
to have been Pope's concept of Augustanism,
secondly to display the structure and working
of one of his most accomplished yet commonly
neglected epistles.

Under the first head, I have shown that
To Mr Addison, though hardly a major poem, has
nevertheless a major subject; one which is
central to an understanding of Pope's conception of his own age and its relation to
classical antiquity. *To Mr Addison* is a poem
about Augustanism. It demonstrates that Pope's
concept of the Renaissance and his concept of
an Augustan Age were integrally related to one
another, and that both Renaissance and Augustan
Age, in his view, draw their vitality from the
proper understanding and the inspiration of
man's past achievement. This pattern of beliefs, as the poem clearly shows, depends for its
cogency upon the particular conception of time
that the poet holds. Man cannot afford to lose
touch with his past, yet the ravages of time
threaten his heritage. It is notable that, at
the beginning of *To Mr Addison*, time is presented
as a destructive power, and it is in this
connection that Pope so movingly evokes the
theme of mutability as it has descended to him
from Jerome through Du Bellay and Spenser. At
the end of the epistle, on the other hand, the
'all-devouring years' have been set in the
wider perspective of a cyclical theory of time:
the revolutions of the Platonic Year which
regularly bring round again the age of gold, a
new Augustan Era to emulate and counter-balance
the old. This evolution in the epistle expresses Pope's confidence in man's capacity to
transcend the destruction of time, and in his
civilized and civilizing duty to do so; it is
as much man's effort as it is providence that
brings round the new Augustan Age. At the very
centre of this complex of ideas lies the study

of antiquities and in particular of medals.
What Spence was later to speak of to Pope as
'so dry a study as Antiquities' stands out,
in this poem, as alive with the promise and
excitement of a revelation: a new access of
spirit and power.[83] This is the significance
of the medal; it is devised by providence for
man's active use in perpetuating his achievements, for preserving his heritage. In this
poem Pope is not, I believe, using the medal
primarily as a symbol; its wide import is
nevertheless abundantly clear and is comparable
to that of the bee in Swift's *Battle of the Books*;
both stand out against ignorance, against man's
capacity for self-satisfied isolation from the
past and the future: the forces of darkness
evoked by Pope in his *Dunciad*.

Under the second head, I have tried through
an exposition of the subject of *To Mr Addison*,
and the manner in which it is expressed, to set
out the evidence upon which the poem must be
judged as a work of art. On the basis of this
evidence it is clear that the raw materials of
this poem--the ideas and even many of its
phrases--are of an entirely traditional kind.
Pope is here very obviously an eclectic; the
artistic merit of the epistle lies, if any-
where, in the way traditional concepts, sentiments and phrases have been put together. It
is in this respect that the poem seems to me a
triumph of artistry. The perfect adjustment
of form to theme renders the epistle outstanding.
On the most obvious level the poem is lent form
by its logical procedure: a problem is stated,
a solution proposed, and then pressed through
to a successful conclusion. This elementary
pattern is reinforced by the expanding and
contracting of the focus of attention throughout the poem. At the beginning the focus is
at its widest; we behold Rome's ruins through
the wastes of time. Then gradually it narrows
as, with sight almost as sharpened as the
antiquary's, we concentrate more and more upon
the medal itself: the one means by which

Rome's past glory may be transmitted through
the dark ages into the future. Finally the
focus widens once more as Pope hails a new
Augustan Age to equal the old, and even looks
forward to successive Augustan Eras in the far
future. This narrowing down and broadening-out
effect is the peculiar form of the epistle. It
is admirably suited to a poem which seeks to
comprehend, in its subject, two widely separated
Augustan Ages and the expanse of time between
them. The structural pattern of the poem thus
enacts the historical pattern with which it
deals. And just as the medal was the centre
of the complex of *ideas* elucidated above, so
here it is at the centre of the total pattern
of the epistle: at that pivotal point where the
focus is at its narrowest:

And little Eagles wave their wings in gold.[84]

The poem is further shaped and unified, its
dominant form elegantly complicated, by the
circle symbolism which runs throughout. This
has an almost decorative effect; but it is very
far from being *merely* decorative since it arises
from the very heart of Pope's subject: his
concern with medals against time, and serves,
in a way a less widely employed symbol could
never have done, to sustain a number of
relevant meanings simultaneously in the mind
of the reader.
To Mr Addison,then, is a poem with a great
subject; further, Pope has seldom succeeded in
shaping the flexible poetic *kind* of the epistle
into so brilliantly appropriate an expressive
form. Why then *is* this not a major poem?
Largely, perhaps, because the actual poetry,
though never ineffective, has a certain thin-
ness about it. The poem triumphs in its design,
and for the rest one feels a little too readily
that 'Expression is the *Dress of Thought*'. [85] This
appears perhaps most obviously in one of the
culminating lines of the poem:

A Virgil there, and here an Addison.[86]

The line is in thought entirely consistent and
of a piece with the rest of the epistle, and
its clear balance well expresses the thought.
Yet there is a starkness about it which springs
not from restraint but from a lack of verbal
and poetic inventiveness. This lack is, I
believe, less obvious in the rest of the poem,
and I do not find it at all in the vivid lines
with which Pope carries out his spectacular
diminution-effect from *Orbis Romanus* to the
narrow round of the surviving medal.[87] Taking
the epistle *To Mr Addison* as a whole, however,
the reader coming to it from the later poetry
is likely to miss the richness, energy and
imperious strength with which Pope, at the end
of *To Burlington* (1731), affirms the Augustan
ideal--

> Bid Harbors open, public Ways extend,
> Bid Temples, worthier of the God, ascend;
> Bid the broad Arch the dang'rous Flood
>   contain,
> The Mole projected break the roaring Main;
> Back to his bounds their subject Sea
>   command,
> And roll obedient Rivers thro' the Land;
> These Honours, Peace to happy Britain brings,
> These are Imperial Works, and worthy Kings.[88]

TIMON'S VILLA: WALPOLE'S HOUGHTON

Kathleen Mahaffey

"We come now to the character (or rather description) of Timon: and it is in this I shall
principally labour, as it has chiefly employ'd
the pains of all the Criticks."[1] This sentence,
from Alexander Pope's own *Master Key* to his *Epistle
To Richard Boyle, Earl of Burlington*, is as timely now
as the day it was penned. For after almost two
and a half centuries the identification of Timon
still engrosses the attention of the critics.
   Pope's enemies were loud and positive--and as-
tonishingly unanimous--in their identification.
Timon, they said, was James Brydges, Duke of
Chandos, who lived in a princely fashion at Cannons, the baroque mansion built with part of the
fortune he had made as the Duke of Marlborough's
paymaster-general. This application was acutely
embarrassing to Pope because Chandos was a friend
of Burlington; and it had gained such wide currency within a week of the publication of the poem, 13 December 1731, that Pope felt constrained
to deny it.

This essay first appeared in *Texas Studies in Literature and Language* 9 (1967), 193-222. By
permission of The University of Texas Press.

On 21 December he wrote Burlington that, having been confined at home by the grave illness
of his mother, he had "never heard till two days
since of a most Extravagant Censure, which they
saw the whole Town passes upon the Epistle I
honourd myself in addressing to your Lordship, as
if it were intended to expose the D. of Chandos."
What, he asked, should he do "in this unaccount-
able affair"? The next day, probably upon Burlington's advice, he sent Chandos a letter, the
gist of which can be inferred from the Duke's
answer:

> Sir--I am much troubled to find by your favour
> of the 22d you are under any uneasiness, at
> the application the Town has made of Timon's
> Character, in your Epistle to the Earl of Bur-
> lington. For my own part I have received so
> many instances of the will they bear me, that
> I am as little surprized as I am affected with
> this further proof of it; It would indeed be
> a real concern to me did I beleive One of
> your Judgment had designedly given grounds for
> their imbibing an Opinion, so disadvantageous
> of me. But as your obliging Letter, is suf-
> ficient to free me from this apprehension, I
> can with great indifference bear the insults
> they bestow, and not find myself hurt by 'em.2

On the day Pope wrote to Chandos, there appeared in the *Post-Boy* another letter of his, this
one anonymous, but purporting to come from a
friend of the much reviled author of the *Epistle
to Burlington*.3 "I could not but hope better for
this small and modest Epistle," he writes, "which
attacks *no one Vice* whatsoever; which deals only
in *Folly* and not Folly in general, but a single
Species of it; that only Branch, for the opposite Excellency to which, the Noble Lord to whom
he writes must necessarily be celebrated." The
excellency commended in Burlington is taste in
building and gardening; and the opposite folly
satirized in Timon, false taste that manifests
itself in prodigality and ostentation. "I

thought," continues Pope's defender, "the Author
had the common Liberty to observe a Defect, and
to compliment a Friend for a Quality that distinguishes him? Which I know not how any Quality
should do, if we were not to remark that it was
wanting in others?"

In the next paragraph Pope defends the validity of personal satire: "Some fancy, that to
say a Thing is *Personal*, is the same as to say it
is *Injust*, not considering, that nothing can be
Just that is not *Personal*: I am afraid that all
such Writings and Discourses as touch no Man, will
mend no Man." After this tacit admission that
the satire of Timon is personal, and an emphatic
denial that the person aimed at is the Duke of
Chandos, Pope closes his letter with a thinly
veiled challenge to the real Timon:

> I know no good Man who would be more concerned,
> if he gave the least Pain or Offence to
> another; and none who would be less concerned,
> if the Satire were challenged by any one at
> whom he could really aim it. If ever that
> happens, I dare engage he will own it, with
> all the Freedom of a Man whose Censures are
> just, and who sets his Name to them.

No claimant to the title of Timon stepped forward to dispute the justice of Pope's censures,
and for two hundred years most of his editors and
biographers swept aside his protestations of innocence of maligning the Duke, setting this down
as one further instance of the spiteful little
hunchback's duplicity. The first thoroughgoing
attempt to get at the truth of the matter was
made by the late George Sherburn, who published
his findings, exonerating Pope, in the *Huntington
Library Bulletin* for October 1935.[4] Since that
time few, if any, Pope scholars have held Timon
to be a satire on the Duke of Chandos, but the
legend still persists in more general quarters,
as for example in Christopher Hussey's excellent
work *English Country Houses*, where Cannons is described as a house of "stately but mannered opul-
ence, satirised by Pope."[5]

Proving that Timon was not intended for Chandos, however, is not the same thing as proving
that the satire is impersonal. Nevertheless,
since Sherburn's study, which disqualified the
only serious contender as the original of Timon,
the tendency has been to consider the satire
general.6 And this in the face of Pope's repeated insistence that satire must be personal. One
of his most explicit statements on this head appears in a letter to Dr. Arbuthnot, who had urged
him to use more caution--at least to name no
names--in the *Epistle* about to be addressed publicly to the Doctor:

> To reform and not to chastise, I am afraid is
> impossible, and that the best Precepts, as
> well as the best Laws, would prove of small
> use, if there were no Examples to inforce them.
> To attack Vices in the abstract, without touch-
> ing Persons, may be safe fighting indeed, but
> it is fighting with Shadows. General proposi-
> tions are obscure, misty, and uncertain, com-
> par'd with plain, full, and home examples:
> Precepts only apply to our Reason, which in
> most men is but weak: Examples are pictures,
> and strike the Senses, nay raise the Passions,
> and call in those (the strongest and most
> general of all motives) to the aid of reforma-
> tion. Every vicious man makes the case his
> own; and that is the only way by which such
> men can be affected, much less deterr'd.7

The portrait of Timon, I shall argue, is no
exception. It is an imaginative satiric character made piquant by its resemblance in many
respects to a clearly recognizable individual.
But for the preoccupation of Pope's own generation with seeking out the similarities and dis-
similarities of Cannons and Timon's Villa, later
critics might have looked for the original more
diligently elsewhere. And the original was never
far to seek: it is pictured in detail in the
same volume of Hussey, ironically, that perpetuates the legend about Cannons.8 There, described

in fifteen pages of pictures and text, is Sir
Robert Walpole's Houghton Hall, the most conspicuous if not the most lavish country house in England when Pope sketched Timon's Villa as the
epitome of prodigality and false taste. If
Houghton is so obviously the model for Timon's
Villa, the skeptic will ask, why did none of
Pope's contemporaries remark the resemblance?
One of the oldest tricks in the politician's bag
--and Walpole was the consummate politician--is to
divert attention from something that cannot be
concealed by starting up a din and commotion in
another quarter. Almost immediately on publication of the *Epistle to Burlington*, and with one
voice, Walpole's Grub Street hacks and Pope's
dunces[9] raised the cry of "Chandos." Those who
perceived the deception were silenced by a willingness to have it succeed or by fear of incurring
Walpole's wrath or reprisal. Pope made his indignant protest--but more of that later.

The Timon of Pope's poem is not Timon the mis-
anthrope, but Timon the prodigal tyrant, before
his fall, hosting lavish entertainments attended
by crowds of sycophants. He lacks the humanity
and amiability of Shakespeare's prodigal, whose
extravagance springs from a native generosity.
Pride motivates the prodigality of Pope's Timon,
magnifying the folly into a vice.

In making pride the ruling passion of his
Timon, Pope adapts the dramatic character to his
living model. Walpole at the height of his
political power was pride incarnate.

He paraded his wealth with ever greater ostentation. He bought pictures at reckless
prices, wallowed in the extravagance of Houghton, deluged his myriad guests with rare food
and costly wine; his huge ungainly figure
sparkled with diamonds and flashed with satin.
And he gloried in his power, spoke roughly
if not ungenerously of others, and let the
whole world know that he was master.[10]

There is little in this portrait to remind one of
Robin the "gay companion" that Lady Mary Wortley
Montagu remembered from earlier years.[11] Only
the prodigality. That characteristic remained
constant.

It is that characteristic, primarily, that
recommends Timon as the appellation for him in
Pope's poem. But there are also telling similarities of circumstance. Walpole, like the Tyrant
of Athens, was the most powerful politician of
his day, and "tyrant" in its modern sense was a
title his enemies frequently bestowed upon him.
There is something of prophecy as well in Pope's
choice of a name for his prodigal: this Timon,
too, would face financial and political ruin.

The imminence of Walpole's fall from power was
a subject that had been on every man's tongue
since the summer of 1727, when George I had died
suddenly on his way to Hanover. Walpole himself,
when he heard the news, had considered his dismissal an accomplished fact.[12] For everyone knew
of the animosity that had existed between the
late King and his son, and it was a foregone conclusion that George II would rid himself of every
minister who had served in the old regime. But
by adroit maneuvering in the crisis, the First
Minister managed to avert his fall. Though the
event was to be delayed for fifteen years, his
enemies continued to predict his fall in broad-
sides and ballads.

The *Craftsman* for 12 August 1727 reports that
two nights previous "some persons were seized and
carried before the Lord Townshend for uttering
scandalous and seditious ballads, one of which is
said to be entitled, *The Honest Voters, or Robin's
Downfall*." In August of 1731, while hunting, as
was his custom on Saturdays, with the King and
his courtiers in Richmond Park, Walpole suffered
a fall from his horse, an incident which the bal-
lad-makers were quick to interpret as an omen of
political significance. The mishap was celebrated
in "The Statesman's Fall; or, Sir Bob in the Dust."
The same theme had been treated in a satiric drama
a little more than two months earlier. The *Daily*

Journal for 5 June 1731 carried under the heading
"This Day is Published" a notice of *The Fall of
Mortimer. An Historical Play. As it is now Acting at the
New Theatre in the Hay-Market*.13   In the broad satire
Walpole is easily recognizable as Mortimer, who
intrigues with the Queen and tries to seduce Maria
--not very subtle allusions to Walpole's liaison
with Maria, or Molly, Skerrit and his controlling
the King through his influence with the Queen.
    By 1731 the end of "Robin's Reign" was more
hoped for than expected, but the hope was kept
alive by the growing volume of criticism in the
press. Walpole, his detractors said, lived in a
more princely fashion than the King himself.
They noted the disparity between his private income and the obvious expense of such an extravagant manner of living. But Walpole had more resources than Shakespeare's honest Timon: "For
the true Sinking Fund," sang one balladeer, "Is
the bottomless Pocket of *Robin*."14   Even that
pocket was sorely taxed to maintain three resid-
ences--two in London, in Chelsea and Arlington
Street, and the fine new mansion in Norfolk. Besides these Walpole had the use of the Old Lodge
in Richmond Park, which he had renovated in 1724
at a cost of £14,000, and in which he installed
Molly Skerrit.15 All his houses were filled with
fine paintings and other works of art, some pur-
chased by himself, some given to him, and some
procured through government agents abroad.16
Wherever he went, he entertained extravagantly.

   Only the best claret was seen at his tables--
   Lafite, Latour, Haut Brion. He paid reckless
   prices for old burgundy, old hock and cham-
   pagne. His wine bill in 1733 with James Ben-
   nett--one only of the half-a-dozen merchants
   who supplied him, but perhaps the principal
   one--was £1,118 12*s*. 10*d*., and 540 dozen empty
   bottles were returned. The same profusion was
   to be found in food, clothes, jewels, carri-
   ages, chairs, presents, Christmas boxes, tips.
   Little Horace had his footmen, French-tailored
   silk clothes and writing master. His wife lived
   in the same high style and his mistress too.17

His levees were attended by great throngs of
friends, place-seekers, and hangers-on. And when
he migrated to Houghton twice a year, usually for
a fortnight in May and a month in November, he
took with him a sizable company of servants and
friends, and sometimes wavering supporters whose
loyalty he hoped to confirm in the atmosphere of
conviviality and lavish entertainment. John Lord
Hervey, a frequent guest, describes one of these
Norfolk Congresses in a letter to the Prince of
Wales:

> Our company at Houghton swelled at last in-
> to so numerous a body that we used to sit down
> to dinner a little snug party of about thirty
> odd, up to the chin in beef, venison, geese,
> turkeys, etc.; and generally over the chin in
> claret, strong beer and punch. We had Lords
> spiritual and temporal, besides commoners,
> parsons and freeholders innumerable. In public
> we drank loyal healths, talked of the times
> and cultivated popularity: in private we drew
> plans and cultivated the country.[18]

Walpole's critics shared none of Lord Hervey's
smug enjoyment of the sumptuousness of Houghton.
Another visitor, or pretended visitor, writing in
the *Craftsman* for 20 July 1728, feigns awe at the
ostentatious splendor:

> *To* CALEB D'ANVERS *Esq;*

> *SIR*,
> I am just returned from a Journey into N----k,
> where I have at length satisfied my Curiosity
> in viewing a *certain great Palace*, which hath oc-
> casioned so much Discourse in Town, and by
> far exceeded the most sanguine of my Expecta-
> tions. A particular Description of the Magni-
> ficence of the *House, Gardens*, and *Stables*; as
> well as the great Variety of *fine Pictures*, the
> vast Quantity of *massy Plate*, and other *costly*
> *Furniture* would require a Volume in Folio; which
> I hope some Person, who hath more Opportunity

and Leisure than myself, will undertake. But
I was so much delighted with the Sight of an
huge and most sumptuous LANTHORN, which immediately struck my Eyes, upon entering the
great Hall, that I could not forbear celebrating
it in a few Stanzas; which (as trifling as
they may seem) will serve to fill up a little
Vacancy in your Paper; and may, perhaps, do
well enough by way of Contraste to the Remarks
on a little *dark Lanthorn*, which we were lately
desired to take notice of in our *Common-Prayer
Books*.

I am, &c.

The Norfolk LANTHORN,
A New Ballad,
To the Tune of, *Which nobody can deny*.

I.
In the County of *Norfolk*, that Paradise Land,
Whose Riches and Power doth all *Europe* command,
There stands a great House (and long may it
  stand!)

Which nobody can, &c.

II.
And in this great House there is a great Hall;
So spacious it is, and so sumptuous withal,
It excels Master WOLSEY'S *Hampton*-Court and
  Whitehall.

Which nobody can, &c.

III.
To adorn this great Room, both by Day and by
  Night,
And convince all the World that the Deeds of
  Sir Knight
Stand in need of no *Darkness*, there hangs a
  great Light.

Which nobody can, &c.

IV.
A *Lanthorn* it is, for its Splendor renown'd,
'Tis eleven Feet high, and full twenty Feet
  round,

And cost, as they say, many a fair hundred
   Pound,
                    Which nobody can, &c.

                    V.
The King, Sir, (God bless Him!) who lives in
   the Verge,
Could hardly afford the exorbitant Charge
Of a *Palace* so fine, or a *Lanthorn* so large.
                    Which nobody can, &c.

                    VI.
Now let us all pray (though it's not much in
   Fashion)
That this *Lanthorn* may spread such an Illumina-
   tion,
As may glare in the Eyes of the whole *British*
   Nation.
                    Which nobody should deny.

The copper-gilt lantern for eighteen candles
that hung in the Stone Hall at Houghton occasioned
"much Noise," according to Horace Walpole, who
recognized "The Norfolk Lanthorn" as an allusion
to Ben Jonson's lines on Penshurst:

   Thou art not, *Penshurst*, built to envious show,
   Of Touch or Marble; nor can'st boast a Row
   Of polish'd Pillars, or a Roof of Gold,
   Thou hast no Lantern, whereof Tales are told.[19]

Just as Penshurst in Jonson's poem represents the
ideal of use, so Houghton's lantern in the *Craftsman's* verses symbolizes "envious show."
   That Houghton was a lively topic of conversation at court as well as in the town is evidenced
by the Prince of Wales' desire that Lord Hervey
give him "a very particular account" of the Norfolk mansion. Hervey gratified the Prince's
curiosity, in a letter of 14 July 1731, excusing
himself from interpolating any remarks of his own,
and concluding his description with a word of
caution: "I beg Your Royal Highness to remember
that whatever I wrote of, and from this place,

you gave me your word should go no farther than
of chaise-party in the morning: and must take
the liberty to insist on not being put into the
Burlington-inquisition for want of implicit faith."
Despite his intention to forbear comment, Hervey
could not resist adding an opinion on Sir Robert's
"deviating from orthodoxy in the proportion of
the windows" in the upper story.   By this innova-
tion, Hervey declared,

> he has not only dared to let in light enough
> for the poor inhabitant to be able to read at
> noon day (which the Palladian Votaries would
> fain have prevented), but he has made the
> building much handsomer on the outside than
> without this successful transgression it could
> possibly have been.   In short, I think his
> house has all the beauties of regularity with-
> out the inconveniences; and wherever he has
> deviated from the established religion of the
> architects, I believe Your Royal Highness
> would say he had found his account in being a
> libertine.[20]

From these remarks and the wry allusion to the
"Burlington-inquisition" it may be inferred that
Houghton had stirred up considerable controversy
between the adherents of the pure classic Palla-
dianism and the innovators who favored a synthesis
with other architectural styles.
    Sir Robert's new house came into even greater
prominence, in November 1731, as the setting for
the princely entertainments honoring the Duke of
Lorraine, afterwards Francis I, on the occasion
of his five-day visit to Houghton.   The state
dinner given by Walpole was a prime topic in the
press and in private correspondence, and in after
years was to become almost legendary.   A late
eighteenth-century journalist ventured the opinion
that it was "the most magnificent banquet that was
perhaps given in England, though there was not a
single foreign dish in the whole entertainment,
relays of horses being provided on the roads, to
bring rarities from the most remote parts of the
kingdom."[21]

This is only a sampling of the public and private comment excited by Sir Robert Walpole's dinners, his new mansion, and the imminence of his
fall from power.22 When, amidst all this commentary, Pope wrote his lines,

> At Timon's Villa let us pass a day,
> Where all cry out, "What sums are thrown away!"
>   (ll. 99-100)

it is hardly credible that no one thought of Walpole and Houghton. There were other great men
who built fine houses in the first part of the
eighteenth century, but none save Marlborough and
his Blenheim had called forth more than a frac-
tion of the verbiage expended upon Walpole and
his Houghton Hall. The Duke had been dead for
almost ten years when Pope published his lines,
and Walpole had no rival for the title of "Great
Man."

When the *Epistle to Burlington* appeared, on 13
December 1731, Houghton Hall was complete except
for some details of furnishing and decoration.
The corner stone had been laid on 24 May 1722, and
by 1726 a few rooms were habitable, though the
last ornament was not in place until 1735.23 Walpole's plan for his country seat was on a grand
scale, including not only a palatial new house to
replace the rambling red brick house of his ancestors but new stables, a new and enlarged park,
twelve miles in circumference, and a huge garden
of twenty-three acres. To accommodate the new
park, the whole village was removed and re-erected
outside the pale. No expense was spared in the
selection of materials for construction, ornamentation, and furnishing--from the fine Whitby
stone of the exterior to the exquisite Carrara
and Plymouth marble and imported mahogany of the
interior, and the costly wall hangings, some of
tapestry, one of silk and wool cut velvet. If
Pope could not admire the finished result, there
were many of his countrymen who did. Sir Thomas
Robinson's praise is unstinted:

It is the best house in the world for its size,
capable of the greatest reception for company,
and the most convenient state apartments, very
noble, especially the hall and saloon. The
finishing of the inside is, I think, a pattern
for all great houses that may hereafter be
built: the vast quantity of mahogani, all the
doors, window-shutters, best staircase, &c.,
being entirely of that wood; the finest chimnies
of statuary and other fine marbles; the ceil-
ings in the modern taste by Italians, painted
by Mr. Kent, and finely gilt; the furniture
of the richest tapestry, etc; the pictures
hung on Genoa velvet and damask; this one
article is the price of a good house, for in
one drawing-room there [these?] are to the
value of three thousand pounds; in short, the
whole expense of this place must be a prodigious sum, and, I think, all done in a fine
taste.[24]

There was and is wide disagreement about the
taste, but the expense is beyond question. The
single item of gold trimmings for the bed in the
State, or Green Velvet, Bedchamber cost ₤1,219
3ⅎ. 11d.[25] How much Walpole spent on this sumptuous house one can only surmise, for few records
remain. Walpole probably destroyed the accounts
on his fall from power in 1742 lest they be used
to substantiate the accusations of misappropria-
tion of funds.

To design his house Walpole chose Colen Campbell, to decorate it, William Kent, and to lay
out the grounds, Charles Bridgeman--all famous
designers, and all, incidentally, members of Lord
Burlington's artistic coterie. So that Pope,
though he never saw Houghton, had every opportunity for knowing the minutest details of construction. One might have expected from these able
men a work pleasing to Pope and wholly worthy of
applause. But the master of Houghton saw fit to
make important alterations in the designs, caus-
ing anguish, no doubt, to the designers, and illustrating for Pope one of the worst proclivities
of "Imitating Fools,"

    Who random drawings from your sheets shall
      take,
    And of one beauty many blunders make.
                    (ll. 27-28)

From the classical Palladian design submitted
by Campbell was constructed a house mainly
baroque. Hussey gives a succinct description of
the original plan:

    Campbell's plan provided a rectangular man-
    sion facing east, flanked by wings set back
    to the plane of its west front, each contain-
    ing an office court and connected by segmental
    corridors with colonnades. The design ...,
    largely derived from Inigo Jones' Wilton, has
    its corners, projecting to the fronts, carried
    up as pedimented pavilions. It is astylar,
    except on the west where an Ionic portico was
    intended. The plainness is relieved by mas-
    sive rustication of the basement, the inner
    faces of the wings, and the east main floor
    windows which also have heavy keystones be-
    neath entablatures. On both fronts extensive
    flights of steps led up to the State entrances
    to the *piano nobile*.

The most damaging alteration was the substitution
of stone domes for the corner towers, concerning
which Hussey says:

    As conceived, Campbell's design possessed
    architectural dignity and restrained cogency.
    The triangular silhouette of the pavilions
    echoed the angle of the eastern steps, and was
    not so emphatic as to set up an unresolved du-
    ality in a design in which the centre was not
    stressed. The substitution of the domes des-
    troyed this balance, and their proportions,
    lacking a drum, are clumsy.26

The graceful line of the segmental corridors was
also destroyed by the expansion of the corridors
in a square to the east front. A further alteration, on the west front, deprived the steps and

entrance of a shelter: the Ionic portico, with
free-standing columns, was replaced by engaged
columns. Thus what was to have been functional
was degraded to mere decoration--the kind of
thing that invited the mockery of Pope's couplet:

> Then clap four slices of Pilaster on't,
> That, lac'd with bits of rustic, makes a Front.
> (ll. 33-34)

To execute Campbell's design, Walpole chose
Thomas Ripley, a carpenter become architect whom
Pope satirizes in the lines:

> Heav'n visits with a Taste the wealthy fool,
> And needs no Rod but Ripley with a Rule.
> (ll. 17-18)

To the 1744 edition of the *Epistle to Burlington* he
added the note: "This man was a carpenter, employ'd by a first Minister, who rais'd him to an
Architect, without any genius in the arts; and
after some wretched proofs of his insufficiency
in public Buildings, made him Comptroller of the
Board of works." Whatever Ripley's competence as
a carpenter and superintendent of construction,
Pope clearly thought him out of his depth as an
architect. He deserves the appellation "fool,"
Pope implies, no less than his master--they deserve each other. A fool, as Pope uses the term,
is not a man utterly without abilities, but one
who misapplies those he has or pretends to those
he has not. It is this pretense that Pope again
satirizes in a couplet in the *First Epistle of the
Second Book of Horace:*

> Who builds a Bridge that never drove a pyle?
> (Should Ripley venture, all the World would
>   smile).27

Horace Walpole, though he concedes that Ripley
"wanted taste," attribtes Pope's censures in part
to "politics and partiality."28 Ripley has left
enough monuments to his architectural ability--

or want of it--to enable the twentieth-century
critic to form his own estimate.

Sir Robert's grounds, like his house, reflected
the taste of one man of talent and another of
mediocre ability. Bridgeman laid out the park,
but, according to Horace Walpole, the gardens
were laid out by "Mr. Eyre, an imitator."29 The
plan published by Isaac Ware shows in some detail
the plantations in the park, but only indicates
the garden area.30 It was probably this plan
that Sir Thomas Robinson saw when he spent a week
at Houghton in late November or early December
1731. Just four days before Pope published his
poem, Sir Thomas was writing his admiring account
of Houghton:

>   The enclosure for the Park contains seven
> hundred acres, very finely planted, and the
> ground laid out to the greatest advantage.
> The gardens are about 40 acres, which are only
> fenced from the Park by a ʄoʋʋé, and I think
> very prettily disposed. Sir Robert and Bridge-
> man showed me the large design for the planta-
> tions in the country, which is the present
> undertaking; they are to be plumps and avenues
> to go quite round the Park pale, and to make
> straight and oblique lines of a mile or two
> in length, as the situation of the country
> admits of.31

There was an earlier plan, published by Campbell in 1725, which bears some resemblance to
this, but which covers a much smaller area and
apparently was drawn before the decision was made
to remove the village. If Bridgeman was also
responsible for this early plan, his taste changed
greatly in the interim, for the design is formal,
and the lines of crisscrossing avenues make one
dizzy.32 The taste shown in this design might
well belong to "Sir Visto" (l. 15) and provoke
the ironic allusion to "proud Versailles" (l. 71).

With a few deft strokes Pope evokes a picture
of the Great Man and his villa that reduces both
to absurdity:

So proud, so grand, of that stupendous air,
Soft and Agreeable come never there.
Greatness, with Timon, dwells in such a
     draught
As brings all Brobdignag before your thought.
To compass this, his building is a Town,[33]
His pond an Ocean, his parterre a Down:
Who but must laugh, the Master when he sees,
A puny insect, shiv'ring at a breeze!
Lo, what huge heaps of littleness around!
The whole, a labour'd Quarry above ground.
                          (ll. 101-110)

Here the proud master, the huge, corpulent Walpole, is diminished to less than Lilliputian
stature and his pretentious grounds expanded to
include the whole of Norfolk--his pond the Wash,
his parterre the entirety of Houghton's barren,
windswept plateau. "Building" has both verbal
and substantive force, referring at once to the
house and to the re-erection of the town to
accommodate it. In the last couplet Pope improves
upon the Duke of Shrewsbury's phrase for Blenheim,
"a great *Quarry of Stones above ground*," and applies
it to Houghton. Though less than half the size
of Blenheim, Houghton, to Pope's mind, justified
the characterization by its violation of the
cardinal principle of design--that the parts must
contribute to the whole, which otherwise remains
formless: "huge heaps of littleness."
     The designation of Timon's pond as "an Ocean"
may be taken in a hyperbolic sense, as ridiculing
grandiosity, or in the sense that the ocean serves
in lieu of a pond--that Timon has no other. Houghton had its ponds, but no source of water to keep
them supplied, and they dried up in the summer.
There nature is harsh: water is almost nonexist-
ent, and the soil is thin and sandy. When Bridgeman began his plantations, reports Sir Thomas
Robinson, there was "very little full-grown timber, and not a drop of water for ornament."[34]
     Timon's droughty parterre illustrates the folly
of trying to turn a treeless, waterless desert
into a garden, thus violating the first principle
of gardening:

> Consult the Genius of the Place in all;
> That tells the Waters or to rise, or fall.
>   (ll. 57-58)

In Timon's gardens there are no waters to either
rise or fall, but

> ... here a Fountain, never to be play'd,
> And there a Summer-house, that knows no shade;
> Here Amphitrite sails thro' myrtle bow'rs;
> There Gladiators fight, or die, in flow'rs;
> Un-water'd see the drooping sea-horse mourn,
> And swallows roost in Nilus' dusty Urn.
>   (ll. 121-126)

This is no random list of tasteless garden ornaments: all do violence to nature, and all have
at least one common point of incongruity--the absence of water. The fountain stands idle for
want of water. For the same reason, it may be
inferred, there is no sheltering foliage to protect the summerhouse from the direct rays of the
sun. All the remaining ornaments are topiary
monstrosities, and their contribution to the
theme of aridity is more subtle. Water, not airy
branches or earthen beds, is the natural element
of Amphitrite and the sea horse, so that these
are particularly ludicrous examples of the sculp-
tured plants and floral pictures that Pope de-
tested. The sea horse is even more laughable
than the waterless nymph because the wilted
flowers give him an air of mourning for his proper habitat. Similarly, dying flowers enhance
the comic effect of the scene in which "Gladiators
fight, or die, in flow'rs." This is the most
complex of the images, in which ambiguity is compounded with ambiguity. The line calls up simultaneously two distinct mental images: an actual
combat in a field of flowers, and a floral picture of gladiators fighting. The interpolation
of "or die" adds a third dimension of meaning:
not merely gladiators dying in a field of flowers,
or a floral representation of the famous statue
of the *Gladiator moriens* (as Pope's note to the

line, taken at face value, implies), but the
flowers themselves dying, so that the death of
the flowers and the death of the gladiator become
one. The final piece of "verdant sculpture,"
the water pot symbolizing the life-giving waters
of the Nile, Pope turns ironically into a symbol
of aridity, "Nilus' dusty Urn."

The figure of the gladiators was most likely
suggested by the bronze statue of the "Gladiator"
by John of Boulogne, a gift of the Earl of Pembroke, which is the principal ornament of the
Great Stair at Houghton, occupying a plinth in the
well at the level of the *piano nobile*.[35] Pope
translated the statue from house to garden and
transformed its metallic substance to flowers.
Lest the particularity of his reference be missed,
he appended a note: "The two famous Statues of
the *Gladiator pugnans* & *Gladiator Moriens*."

How closely Pope followed the design of Mr.
Eyre the imitator in his description of Timon's
gardens, it is impossible to say precisely, for
the fate prophesied for Timon's gardens overtook
those at Houghton even more precipitously than
Pope had imagined:

> Another age shall see the golden Ear
> Imbrown the Slope, and nod on the Parterre,
> Deep Harvests bury all his pride has plann'd,
> And laughing Ceres re-assume the land.
>   (ll. 173-176)

The upkeep of Houghton proved too great an expense for Walpole's heirs, and in 1779 the parterres and terraces, overgrown from neglect, were
cleared away for the sake of economy.[36] It is
evident, however, from the plan published by
Campbell in his *Vitruvius Britannicus* that the principal parterre, divided into four approximately
equal triangles, resembled a "*flourished Carpet,*
where the greatness and nobleness of the piece
is lessened by being divided into too many parts,
with scroll'd works and beds."[37]

Though Timon's gardens resembled Walpole's in
important respects--in their size, the formality

of the parterres, and the absence of water--they
were not meant to be mere replicas, and many of
the details are invented, like the gladiators in
flowers, or copied from the follies exhibited in
other gardens of Pope's day. Whether Houghton's
gardens actually contained excessive walls, or
hedges having the same effect, "Trees cut to
Statues," or "Statues thick as trees" (l. 120), I
have not been able to discover. The house itself,
however, contains a great deal of sculpture, especially the Stone Hall, where Walpole's bust
occupies a proud place among the Roman emperors.38
The "Statues thick as trees" may therefore be one
more instance of transferal from house to garden,
for the sake of the interplay of words and images.
    Timon's house is an even better index to his
character than are his gardens. The three rooms
singled out for special attention--the library,
the chapel, and the dining hall--reflect his intellectual, spiritual, and social qualities.
There is no hospitality in his entertainments,
only overbearing pride. Pride makes a mockery
of the rites in his chapel, which has more the
atmosphere of a bagnio than of a place of worship.
His study is not furnished for reflection, but
for show.
    Among all the men in public life in Pope's
day it would have been difficult to find a less
bookish man than Sir Robert Walpole. Although
he spent two years at King's College, Cambridge,
he never developed a love for reading, and his
college books and the *Statutes of the Realm* were
almost his only additions to the library he inherited from his father. This was comprised of
the Latin classics, histories, and other factual
writings, there being few philosophers represented,
and almost no English poet save Spenser.39 There
is only a slight exaggeration of the literal
truth in Pope's lines

    For Locke or Milton 'tis in vain to look,
    These shelves admit not any modern book.
                        (ll. 139-140)

Timon is a man totally ignorant of books. His
only interest in them is pride of ownership. He
collects old editions but, being no antiquarian,
can identify them only by "their dated Backs"; and
he collects fine editions but, having no taste,
can recognize them only by the names of their
printers and binders. He has not looked inside
his books, and so has not discovered that many of
them are dummies with painted or covered backs.

> To all their dated Backs he turns you round,
> These Aldus printed, those Du Suëil has bound.
> Lo some are Vellom, and the rest as good
> For all his Lordship knows, but they are Wood.
> (ll. 135-138)

The satire on the man who appreciates neither the
intellectual nor the aesthetic appeal of fine
books is heightened by his being made a collector.
In this detail Pope abandons literal truth for
poetic truth; for Walpole was a collector, not of
books, but of paintings. This kind of deviation
from or addition to fact is not unusual in Pope's
"characters." The character of Atossa, for
example, gains imaginatively as a satire on the
Duchess of Buckinghamshire by the lines intended
originally for another imperious duchess.[40] Timon
is Walpole in much the same way that Atossa is
the Duchess of Buckinghamshire: not all the details are biographical fact, but they are all in
character.
    Timon's chapel reflects not only his pride and
lack of taste but his sensuality. On the painted
ceiling sprawl the fleshly "Saints of Verrio or
Laguerre."

> To rest, the Cushion and soft Dean invite,
> Who never mentions Hell to ears polite.
> (ll. 149-150)

This is the sort of chapel that Walpole might
have had, but the one at Houghton had not yet
been decorated and the artists named were no
longer living.[41] The "Saints of Verrio or

Laguerre" are therefore to be taken as types of
the paintings of French and Italian decorators
popular in the eighteenth century--types inappropriate for a chapel.

Walpole's sensuality and salacious wit, his
profanity and irreligion were notorious, even in
an age as unshockably secular as the early
eighteenth century. Pope makes gibes at his
keeping a mistress, and there is one in the opening lines of the *Epistle to Burlington*: "his fine
Wife ... or finer Whore" (l. 12).[42] Lady Mary
Wortley Montagu wrote to her sister an account
of "a bill cooking-up at a hunting-seat in Norfolk, to have *not* taken out of the commandments
and clapped into the creed, the ensuing session
of parliament."[43] Walpole's only concern with
the Church was the dispensing of patronage.[44]

Pope's "soft Dean" is identified in the "Twickenham" edition as Knightly Chetwood, Dean of
Gloucester, who during the reign of James II
preached a sermon at Whitehall in which he told
his congregation "that if they did not vouchsafe
to give their lives a new turn, they must certainly go to a place which he did not think fit
to name in that courtly audience."[45] No doubt
Pope meant to remind his readers of this anecdote
published by Steele in the *Guardian* for 31 March
1713. But this incident had happened forty-odd
years before, and Pope usually up-dated his
satire to give it a current reference. It seems
likely, therefore, that "soft Dean" in 1731 was
intended as a play on the name of Henry *Bland*,
Walpole's closest friend from his Eton days, whom
Conyers Middleton described enviously as "y[e] best
beneficed Clergyman in y[e] Kingdom."[46] Walpole
had given him numerous lucrative posts and in
1728 had had him made Dean of Durham. Bland, a
frequent visitor at Houghton, wrote the Latin
inscription for the corner stone and was present
at the laying.[47] His close ties with Walpole
would have made him the current "soft Dean" of
the Court. Pope satirized him by name in the
Dunciad Variorum (I, ll. 231-232) and again in the
Epilogue to the Satires (I, l. 75).

The music of Timon's chapel is jarringly
secular and makes "the soul dance upon a Jig
to Heaven" (ll.143-144). It befits the taste
of a rude country squire--a reminder that the
lordly First Minister has not left behind all
traces of his humbler Norfolk beginnings. Even
Horace Walpole found amusement in his father's
lack of musical appreciation. "You know how
low his ideas are of music and the virtuosi,"
he wrote to his cousin Horace Mann; "he calls
them all *fiddlers*." [48]
     Timon's state dinner, spread in the "marble
Hall" with its "rich Buffet," moves his
unsympathetic guest to exclaim:

     Is this a dinner? this a Genial room?
     No, 'tis a Temple, and a Hecatomb.
     A solemn Sacrifice, perform'd in state,
     You drink by measure, and to minutes eat.
        (ll.155-158)

This description seems to draw on Pope's knowledge of the State Diningroom soon to be completed at Houghton. Called the Marble Parlor,
it was to be furnished with marble sideboards
set in recesses flanking the huge chimneypiece--
the chimneypiece itself a hecatomb in marble,
Rysbrack's "Sacrifice to Bacchus." [49]
     Walpole's usual mode of dining was not so
stiffly formal, but his state dinner honoring
the Duke of Lorraine rivaled Timon's in pomp and
plenty. Although Pope was not at that banquet,
he had often attended Sir Robert's Sunday
dinners at Richmond. After 1728, however, he
went less frequently, and after the middle of
1730, not at all. [50] The reason for the estrangement seems to have been Walpole's harsh--or
what Pope considered harsh--treatment of John
Gay, whose *Polly*, sequel to the *Beggar's Opera*, was
banned in 1729. The needy Gay was subsequently
turned out of his lodgings and his small place
in the Exchequer. [51] It is significant that
Pope addressed his defense of the *Epistle to*

Burlington "To J.G. Esq.," thus publicly making
common cause with Gay.

Pope, whose relationship with Walpole at
its warmest could not be described by a term
stronger than "amicable," was revolted also
by the Great Man's increasing ostentation and
love of sycophancy. This revulsion finds
expression in the closing lines on Timon:

> In plenty starving, tantaliz'd in state,
> And complaisantly help'd to all I hate,
> Treated, caress'd, and tir'd, I take my leave,
> Sick of his civil Pride from Morn to Eve;
> I curse such lavish cost, and little skill,
> And swear no Day was ever past so ill.
>   (11.163-168)

The furore that broke on the publication of
the *Epistle to Burlington* may not have come as
a complete surprise to Pope, but he was genuinely amazed at the turn taken by the criticism.
After making the hasty defense in the *Post-Boy*,
he undertook to find out the particulars of
this campaign of misinterpretation, and to
counter it by exposing those responsible for
it.   This he did in *A Master Key to Popery, or
A True and Perfect Key to Pope's Epistle to the Earl
of Burlington*,   a satire in prose, written
probably during the latter part of January and
early February 1731/2.   Pope never published
this refutation, and its existence was unknown
outside a small circle of his friends, until
a fair copy made by Lady Burlington was discovered by the late John Butt among the family
papers at Chatsworth.[52]

The *Master Key* cannot be dismissed, as it
has been in the "Twickenham" edition, as an
"amusing 'irony'," "essentially a prolonged
parody of the far-fetched satirical allusions
that were being read into the poem."[53] For
it is a great deal more than a parody.   It is
a veritable master key, wherein Pope ironically
puts the identification of Timon into the mouth

of one of Walpole's closest allies in the
Commons, Sir William Yonge, "Sir William
Sweet-Lips," thus giving the lie to his
courtly critics by the implication that they
had understood him perfectly well and had
maliciously applied the character of Timon to
the Duke of Chandos. Pope had made substantially the same charge, but without naming Walpole,
in his first retort to his critics, the
anonymous letter printed in the *Daily Post-Boy*
for 22 December 1731: "No wonder those who
know Ridicule belongs to them, find an inward
Consolation in removing it from themselves as far
as they can; and it is never so far, as when
they can get it fixt on the *best Characters*." 54
This sentence was omitted--accidentally,
Sherburn suggests--when next day the *Daily
Journal* reprinted the letter, with some changes
obviously made by Pope himself. But the omission may well have been a concession to
prudence. For if Pope meant Timon as a
satire on Walpole, he is here charging Walpole
with the responsibility for getting the
ridicule fixed on Chandos in an attempt to
remove it from himself. The hoax may not
have originated with Walpole, but his hack
writers and his partisans at Court were,
according to Pope, its chief perpetrators.

The explicator in *A Master Key to Popery*
acknowledges his indebtedness for "many In-lets"
into the poet's meaning and thoughts to persons
who "either had been his Friends or call'd
themselves so, or had made some pretence to
his Acquaintance or Correspondence." Such, he
declares, are Lord Fanny, Mr. Dorimant, the
Lady De-la-Wit, and the Countess of Methusalem.
The first three have been identified as John
Lord Hervey, Bubb Dodington, and Lady Mary
Wortley Montagu, all allies of Walpole--or
former allies, for Dodington (Mr. Dorimant) had
deserted to the opposition party centering
around the Prince of Wales. "I confess
further," says the explicator, "that I am in

many instances, but the Collector of the
dispers'd Remarks of his Majesty's Poet Laureat,
his Illustrious Associate Sr William Sweet-Lips,
the Lady Knaves-acre & Mrs Haywood (those
ornaments of their Sex) and Capt. Breval, and
James Moore Esqr: and Mr Concanen, & M^r
Welsted, and Henry K--y Esqr of the two last of
whom I ought in Justice to say, we owe to the
one the most *considerable writings* & to the other
the *Longest Discourses* on this Subject."[55]
Concanen, Welsted, and "Kelsey" (Henry Kelsall)
owed their living, and Colley Cibber his bays,
to Walpole's government. Sir William Yonge
served, according to Lord Hervey, as "a ductile
courtier and a parliamentary tool" of Walpole.[56]
Lady Knaves-acre has not yet been identified.
The remaining three joined this motley crew
as Pope's dunces rather than Walpole's
friends.[57]

His acknowledgments made, the author of the
Master Key lays down his postulates for the
interpretation of the *Epistle to Burlington*:

> My First Position is, that this Poet is a
> man of so *Bad a Heart*, as to stand an Exception
> to the Rule of Macchiavel, who says 'No man,
> in any Nation, was ever Absolutely Wicked, *for
> nothing*'.[58] Now this Poet being so, it is fair
> to Suppose, that of *two* or *more* persons whom he
> may be thought to abuse, we are always to under
> understand it of the Man he is *most oblig'd to*:
> but in such cases where his obligations seem
> *equal*, we impartially suppose the Reflection on
> *both*. Secondly, when so malevolent a man draws
> any character consisting of *many Circumstances*,
> it must be apply'd, not to the person with whom
> *most* but with whom *fewest* of those Circumstances
> agree.

Proceeding upon these postulates to the
character of Timon,[59] the explicator declares:

> I shall enumerate the several opinions of all
> others, & shew the Malice & Personal Reflec-

tion to extend much farther than has hitherto
been imagin'd by any. It is shewing the Author
great & undeserv'd Indulgence to confine it
to any One, tho' that one were the Best Man in
the world: There are so many Bypeeps &
squinting Glances, besides the main View, that
instead of twenty things being aim'd at one,
every Circumstance is aim'd at twenty.

The latter part of this second sentence has
been quoted repeatedly in support of the opinion
that Timon was not intended as a satire upon
any particular person. But this interpretation
ignores an important qualification--"besides
the main View." What is the "main View" if
not the profile or prominent features of the
subject? Pope is here reiterating in paradoxical language his contention that satire, though
it is universal in application, must, if it
is to be effective, be aimed at follies and
vices as exhibited in particular persons.
That this is his meaning is to be inferred
from what follows.
    The delineator first takes "a View of Timon's
character in *all its Circumstances* "(italics mine):

    A Proud, haughty Man, with no other Idea of
Greatness but Bulk and Size, but himself a
little contemptible Creature. His House consists of Unequal Parts, heap'd one upon another like a Quarry of Stones. His Gardens are
choak'd up with Walls, every where in sight,
which destroy all Appearance of Natural
Beauty. The Form of his Plantation is stiffly
regular, & and same repeated. A vast Lake-
fall to the North: an immense Parterre with
two Small Cupids in it: Tress cut into human
figures, & statues as close as Trees: his
Fountains without Water: a Terras of Steep
Slopes with a Study opening upon it, where he
receives his guests with the utmost Affectation: his Books chosen for their Printers or

Binders, no good Modern Books, & (to make them
perfectly a Show) the upper Shelves only Wood-
en and painted ones. He has a Chappel, with
Musick & Painting in it, but the Musick consists of Jigs and loose Airs, and the painting
of indecent or naked figures. He gives Entertainments attended by an hundred Servants,
in a Hall paved with Marble; his Bufet is orna-
mented with Serpents & Tritons; his Dinner
is a solemn, formal, troublesome thing, with
so much Pride & affected State, as to make
every man Sick both of his Dinner & of Him.

The author of the *Master Key* then makes a
detailed comparison of all these "Circumstances"
with those obtaining at Cannons, which he has
been at pains to visit out of his "great Love
to Truth," and where he has discovered "no
one Particular resembling." This is all the
more reason--invoking the second postulate--
for imputing the character of Timon to Chandos.
Mr. Dorimant, Mr. K--y, and Lord Fanny are
the chief exponents of this interpretation,
which "has been affirmed with Oaths by M^r
C--^{r} and very publickly by Mr Theobalds, M^r
Goode, Mr James Moore, the whole Herd of
Criticks, & all the honourable Gentlemen of the
Dunciad."
But there is one dissenting voice. Sir
William Sweet-Lips is struck with the salient
features in the portrait of Timon:

Why (says he) for God's sake may not this be
Sir Robert? are not his works as great as
any man's? Who has more Groves nodding at
Groves of his own plantation? I cannot say
much as to his Chappel; but who has rival'd his
Dinners? especially at the Time this Poem was
publish'd, when he was splendidly entertaining
the Duke of Lorain? Has he not a Large Bufet?
Has he not a hundred, nay near five hundred,
Servants? (In power, your Servants)[60] and who
oftener drinks the King's Health? How convinc-

ing are all these circumstances! I defy the
Partizans of the other opinion to match them.
And yet there is one which convinces me more
than all; the Author never Saw Houghton: and
how marvellously does it suit with his Impudence, to abuse the Things he never Saw?

This is not the character of Timon in "*all its
Circumstances*," but is it not the "main View"?
Sir William's conclusion is, of course,
illogical according to the crooked system in
the *Master Key*, for it ignores the second
postulate: that "when so malevolent a man
draws any character consisting of *many
Circumstances*, it must be apply'd, not to the
person with whom *most* but with whom *fewest*
of those Circumstances agree." All his arguments therefore but go to substantiate the
contention of the overwhelming majority--that
Chandos is the man. Such is the perversity
and malignity of his critics, Pope implies,
who persist in imputing to Chandos what they
can clearly recognize as belonging to Walpole.
    Pope also takes the occasion to call atten-
tion to other gibes at Walpole in the earlier
part of the *Epistle to Burlington*:   "But what
principally inclines Sir William to this opinion is, that unless Sir Robert be abus'd here,
he is not abus'd in the whole Poem."
    The diligent explicator now proceeds to
consider one of the "By-peeps & squinting
Glances":

To shew his wicked Impartiality, at the same
time he is squinting at Sir R. he has not
spared his old Friend the Lord Bolingbroke.

    A gaping Triton spews to wash y^r face,

is the exact Description of the bufet at
Dawley. Nothing sure can equal the Impudence
of such a Guest, except the Indifference of
that stupid Lord, who they say is not provok'd
at it.

This sounds like the literal truth; there may
well have been such a buffet at Dawley. In
admitting the borrowing of this detail of
inappropriate decoration to adorn Timon's
Villa, Pope indicates something of his satiric
method. While the "main View" looks very
much like Houghton, some of the details are
additions from other sources.

Throughout the *Master Key* the elucidator is
assiduous to "shew the Malice & Personal
Reflection to extend much farther than has
hitherto been imagin'd." At the same time
that Pope is squinting at his critics'
accusations that he attacks indiscriminately,
he is defending his own contention that
personal satire may have universal application.
He underlines this point in his expositor's
final comments on the portrait of Timon: "I
return to my first Position. The Extent of
this mans malice is beyond being confin'd to
any One. Every Thrust of his Satyr, like the
Sword of a Giant transfixes four or five,
and serves up spitted Lords and Gentlemen with
less ceremony than Skew'r'd Larks at their
own Tables."

The critic is "very sure," for example,
"that all he says of the Chappel, its Painting
& its Musick, is to be apply'd to his Grace
the Duke of R--tl--d's at Be--ir-Castle."
And why not, he asks, to others? He is "as
certain" that Timon's dining hall and dinner
are meant to ridicule a nobleman who "has
lay'd all his Vanities in the Grave"--"the
Companion in arms & Friend of the great Duke
of Marleborough." He "know[s] that the Building describ'd to be so huge, so like a Quarry,
such a Heap, &c. is the Immortal Castle of
Blenheim (to which the Spite of a Papist may
well be imagin'd)." This passage, and indeed
the whole of the *Master Key*, is replete with
innuendo. Pope gibes at the assurance with
which his enemies declare his meanings, their
charges that he makes mean, cowardly attacks
on dead men, and their abusive references to

his religion.

Why Pope did not publish his *Master Key to Popery* is open to conjecture. Perhaps, as Bateson suggests, he did not want to give his enemies the satisfaction of thinking "that his armour had been pierced."[61] And there may have been other, even stronger deterrents--fear of prosecution for libel and an unwillingness to further embarrass his friends Kent and Bridgeman, who were still in Walpole's employ.

Bridgeman seems to have been angry as well as embarrassed, for Pope made several attempts to placate him. Pope must have foreseen that it would be difficult to impugn Walpole's taste in gardening without reflecting on Bridgeman's, and he was careful to insert a compliment to Bridgeman in the earlier part of the *Epistle to Burlington*:

> The vast Parterres a thousand hands shall
>   make,
> Lo! Bridgeman comes, and floats them with
>   a Lake:
>   (ll.73-74)

an allusion to Bridgeman's ingenuity in converting into a beautiful lake the swampy portions of Lord Cobham's gardens at Stowe. Bridgeman, however, was not willing to have his name associated with the poem, and at his insistence Pope omitted it from the 1735 and later editions, substituting that of Cobham.[62] That Pope meditated further amends is evidenced by a fragment which he never published:

> Bridgeman, unskill'd in wit's mysterious ways,
> Knows not, good man, a satire from a praise;
> Yet he can make a mount, or turn a maze.[63]

It was undoubtedly from Kent, who was responsible for much of the decoration and furnishing, that Pope learned most of the details concerning Houghton Hall. Though Kent's taste ran to the baroque, Pope seems to have

respected him as an artist. At least he valued
him as a friend, and so refrained from
satirizing him. Nevertheless, the *Epistle* placed
Kent, and indeed the whole Burlington coterie,
in an anomalous position--their poet, in an
attempt to vindicate their aesthetic principles, inveighing against the very works to
which they had contributed.

Could it have been this situation that
inspired William Hogarth's famous sketch of
Pope whitewashing Burlington Gate?[64] Certainly
the attempt, as Sherburn remarks, is carica-
tured as awkward rather than malicious.[65] And
the artist understood, if none of his contemporaries did, that the bespattering of Chandos
was unintentional so far as Pope was concerned.
The print, which was immensely popular, was
suppressed almost immediately. Pope has
generally been held responsible for the
suppression, but his influence at Court, never
very great, by 1731 was nil.[66] There is little
likelihood that he even wanted the print
suppressed, for satiric though it is, it
places upon his *Epistle to Burlington* the kindest
interpretation then current, absolving him of
malice toward Chandos. The print could not
have been suppressed without Walpole's acquies-
cence; and if there was a conspiracy to divert
Pope's ridicule from Walpole by getting it
fixed on Chandos, the print might have been
suppressed at the instigation of the First
Minister.

Walpole was growing ever more resentful of
the criticism and abuse heaped upon him in
the newspapers, ballads, and pamphlets and was
taking harsh measures to suppress it and punish
the offenders. On 7 July 1731 an action was
brought in the Court of King's Bench against
"all the Authors, Actors, Printers, and Publishers" of seven of these "false, infamous,
scandalous, seditious, and treasonable Libels".[67]
Among them were some printed in the *Country
Journal* or *Craftsman*, Lord Bolingbroke's weekly.
This recent action, involving a close friend,

did not deter Pope from publishing his *Epistle to Burlington*, but may have been a consideration in his decision not to tempt Walpole's anger further by publishing the *Master Key*.

Lord Hervey implies in a letter to Stephen Fox that Pope's "last performance" has drawn resentment, and may draw punishment upon him:

Everybody concurs in their opinion of Pope's last performance, and condemns it as dull and impertinent. I cannot but imagine, by the 18 lines in the last page but one, that he designed ridiculing Lord Burlington as much as he does the Duke of Chandois. It is astonishing to me that he is not afraid this prophecy will be verified, which was told to him a year or two ago,

In black and white whilst satire you pursue,
Take heed the answer is not black and blue.[68]

This private communication to Hervey's closest friend might seem indisputable evidence that Hervey believed Timon to be a satire upon the Duke of Chandos. But the letter is a copy, the original having been lost or destroyed. It is doubtful that Hervey actually worte "the Duke of Chandois" and almost certain that he did not write "Sir Robert." What he wrote was, in all probability, "19," his code number for Walpole,[69] for which the copyist substituted the name that common gossip associated with Timon.

For once, Lord Hervey did not exaggerate when he wrote of the reception accorded Pope's poem. Still, though none came publicly to the poet's defense, there were at least a few outside the circle of his friends whose sympathies lay with Pope. The young Lord Orrery, who at this time had no personal acquaintance with Pope, was one of these. On 27 December he wrote from Bath to Lady Kaye, who apparently was of the opposite persuasion:

The Censures on Mr P..are universal & severe,
None to take his part, & All out of Envy, or
you may suppose Judgement, running him down.
He has wrote too many Things that have afforded me much Pleasure, for Me to join in this
clamorous Throng, nor dare I speak my Opinion
of so powerful a Man, but under y^r Lad^{ps} Roof
in Bond Street. I see he has vindicated him-
self(or endeavour'd at It) in the Daily Journal, I think of last Friday. I hope he'l not
be so intimidated as never to write again, for
tho' his Enemies are powerfull in their Tongues
they are not so in their Pens.

There is something here that looks like an
allusion, and may be evidence that both Orrery
and his correspondent understood Timon as a
satire on Walpole. Who is "so powerful a
Man"? Surely not Pope, whose credit, by
Orrery's own testimony, availed nothing against
the universal censure. And in this context the
phrase can hardly mean "powerful in his pen,"
for what Orrery would have said was obviously
in Pope's defense and could therefore have given
him nothing to dread from the satirist's pen.
There is the possibility, of course, that
the powerful man is Chandos, but Orrery seems
to have accepted Pope's denial that Chandos
was involved. Chandos, moreover, would have
had no way of knowing what was written in a
private letter. But there was one man who
had the means and who availed himself of it
unscrupulously--Sir Robert Walpole. His hirelings regularly opened private letters sent
through the post and reported to their chief
all that might be of interest to him. This
would have been reason enough for Orrery to
make his reference purposely vague and to
refrain from committing to paper his "Opinion
of so powerful a Man."
    Another letter from Lord Orrery to Lady Kaye
dated from Bath, 22 December 1731, just five
days earlier, also contains teasing references.
The Earl encloses "some Verses which I met with
at my Return hither last Monday," and adds:

"We have likewise a Houghton Tale by S^r
W..Y....g, & Satyrs and Lampoons without
Number, but that is a Ware I don't deal in, so
cannot tell your Ladyship who are the unhappy
Lott that are mark'd out for Destruction."[70]
Unfortunately the enclosed verses are not
preserved with the letter among the papers of
the Earl of Dartmouth, and I have been able
to find no copy of "A Houghton Tale." It is
fruitless to speculate about the verses, but
"A Houghton Tale" is worth a few conjectures.
All that can be said with certainty is that it
concerned Walpole's country seat, that it was
believed to be written by Sir William Yonge,
and that it was in existence nine days after
the publication of the *Epistle to Burlington*.
The company in which it is mentioned suggests
that it was a satire. All evidence points to
its having been an answer to a satire on
Houghton. Could it have been "A Houghton Tale"
that won for Yonge the role of Sir William
Sweet-Lips in the *Master Key*?

Pope cast the characters in his *Master Key*,
so far as can be ascertained, according to the
actual parts they had taken in the campaign
against his *Epistle to Burlington*. To Leonard
Welsted he ascribes "the most *considerable
writings*" on that subject, referring presumably
to *Of Dulness and Scandal* and *Of False Fame*.[71]
What is more to the point, he asserts that
Welsted has been converted to Sir William's
opinion--that Walpole, not Chandos, is lampooned
in the character of Timon--because "the Duke
does not take this to himself."[72] Chandos did,
in fact, on 1 January 1731/2, ask Anthony
Hammond to seek out Welsted and "acquaint him
I make it my request, that he will forbear
printing any thing, on my behalf, that may tend
to ye prejudice of a Person, who from what
he has wrote, I ought to beleive neither hath
nor had any ill will towards me."[73] Chandos
sent this urgent message on learning that
Welsted was about to publish an attack on Pope
for satirizing the Duke as Timon. The message,

Sherburn assumes, arrived too late, for *Of Dulness and Scandal* appeared on 3 January. But there is another possibility--that the message arrived in time, and Welsted, to avoid offending a lord whose patronage he had sought, was forced to make drastic last-minute changes in his intended publication, or to replace it altogether. Welsted's published attack on Pope is not made on behalf of Chandos, and thus observes the letter, if not the spirit, of the Duke's request.

Apart from the title, as Sherburn also observes, *Of Dulness and Scandal. Occasion'd by the Character of Lord Timon* makes no mention of Timon or his villa, though it parodies some of Pope's lines. Nor does it contain any reference to the Duke. It catalogues, under fictitious names, the alleged victims of Pope's various satires and protests at some length "Pollio's injur'd fame." The fulsome panegyric extols

> A mind sublime! where vice nor passion
>   reign;
> Nor proud in state, nor midst applauses
>   vain!
> The thousands weal, and the rich temple's
>   plan,
> His zeal to God proclaim, and love to man.[74]

The allusions, if any, are vague. But this passage suggests not so much a man retired from public life as a minister of state, responsible for "the thousands weal." Prevented from making his "defense" of Chandos, Welsted could only remain silent or couch his attack on the *Epistle to Burlington* in such terms as would augment the general clamor against Pope without pointing to a particular victim of his supposed injustice and ingratitude.

This was the dilemma faced by Walpole and his would-be defenders: so adroitly had Pope pointed to the Great Man in the character of Timon that the satire "could not be resented publicly without identifying Walpole as precisely that great man."[75]

The character of Timon illustrates Pope's
satiric method in greater detail than perhaps
any of his other full-length portraits. It is
compounded of fact and fancy, hyperbole and
understatement, and ambiguity that hits
unerringly. Though the satire may have been
motivated in part by private pique and resentment, it rises above the merely personal and
lashes universal faults in private follies.
Pope's method is epitomized by the anonymous
critic--perhaps Pope himself--who wrote in the
Gentleman's Magazine for January 1732: "It is a
known Trick amongst *Lampooners*, when a Man of
Distinction is to be *ridiculed*, to draw the remarkable Lines of his Picture beyond the Life,
yet with such a Resemblance, that all the
World may cry *'Tis He*."[76]

THREE PRINCIPLES OF RENAISSANCE ARCHITECTURAL
THEORY IN POPE'S *EPISTLE TO BURLINGTON*

William A. Gibson

Pope derived his aesthetic norms for the *Epistle to Burlington* largely from humanist architectural theory. The poem's form makes it possible for him to articulate major tenets of the theory, to illustrate the consequences of violating them, and to suggest the possibility of realizing them in architectural practice. His basic premise is that the rules governing architectural forms are the inevitable expression of the forms' uses and of the material and technical means available for satisfying them. Thus "Nature" dictates the essential interdependence of the useful and the beautiful. Vitruvius's rule of *decor*, as developed by his Renaissance commentators, provides most of the poem's specific key tenets. It demands uniformity of style and the observation of correspondences between the form and order of a building and its function, or its patron, or its inhabitants' station and moral traits. Decorum of "Situation" demands fitting a building to a healthy, productive, and convenient site capable of inspiring contemplation. A builder

---

This essay first appeared in *SEL* 11 (1971), 487-505.

who observes the rules, and thereby imitates cosmic design, can achieve "Magnificence," the effect
that evokes meditation of divine harmony, proportion, and order. Timon's Villa is the antithesis
of "Magnificence"; Burlington's principles and examples show how it may be achieved.

          PROFESSOR ALTENBERND'S remark that
"For Pope, poetry, gardening, painting, and architecture were all expressions of a whole mind"[1]
is as true for Pope's *Epistle to Burlington* as for
any poem he wrote. Although critics have examined the place of the *Epistle* in the tradition of
English poetry, the numerous biographical problems it presents, and various principles of
painting and landscape gardening, social and
ethical ideals alluded to or implicit in it,[2] yet
they have quite consistently ignored one important part of the "whole mind" that informs the
poem: the architectural principles whose abuse
occasions ridicule of Bubo and Sir Visto, Villario
and Timon, and whose perpetuation occasions Pope's
praise of Burlington.[3] Earl Wasserman points to
the need for specific attention to Pope's aesthetic principles in his discussion of the *Epistle
to Bathurst* where he shows that the "two poems,
taken together, constitute Pope's adaptation of
Aristotle's analysis of wealth." The virtue of
"magnificence," what Professor Wasserman sees
as the main subject of the *Epistle to Burlington*,
is possible only to a wealthy man; it has, he
says, "its proper decorum which requires that
the donor be an 'artist' in taste..."[4] The emphasis of this remark, with its implicit recognition of the virtual inseparability of ethics
and aesthetics, is certainly the right one. But
if Aristotle shows *what* the great man should be
and achieve, he does not show exactly *how*; he
does not specify the "rules of art" that will
enable a man of wealth to create a magnificent
architecture.
    Robert G. Shafer properly stresses the impor-
tance of knowing the aesthetic principles that
Pope defends with his satiric thrusts. He points
to the line "'Tis Use alone that sanctifies

Expence" (1.179) as the key to the poem, but in
trying to suggest that it shows Pope's anticipation of Benthamite utilitarianism he unfortunately
looks in the wrong direction, for Pope's appeal
to "Use" is but one indication of his great debt
to Renaissance architectural theory.[5] The *Epistle
to Burlington* is as firmly based upon a widely-ac-
cepted body of principles as the *Pastorals* or *An
Essay on Criticism*, and it is nearly as allusive as
these poems, although in it Pope alludes less to
Vergil, Horace, and the French neoclassical critics than to the architectural theory developed
by Vitruvius, his many commentators, and the
Renaissance architects, Andrea Palladio among them.
By the early eighteenth century many of the major
architectural treatises had become a part of
every learned gentleman's reading, and to these
works we must turn if we are to make clear Pope's
aesthetic norms.

That Pope planned the poem as an examination
and defense of one set of principles is apparent
from its very form, a form that must have been
familiar to Pope's readers from their acquaintance with Edward Young's recently-completed
"characteristical satires," *The Love of Fame* (1725-
1728). The first twelve lines provide examples
of eccentric "taste" in various arts and sciences--
from old books and manuscripts to butterflies and
antiquities; these serve as a general introduction
to the specific topic of the poem, the principles
of "taste" in building and planting. From line
13 through line 38 Pope gives examples of those
who reveal false taste and ignorance of the rules
of architecture, and of the arts directly related
to it; in these lines he introduces three subjects
which he develops later in the poem (and which I
shall stress in this paper)--"Magnificence,"
"Use," and decorum, including decorum of form,
ornament, and "situation." ("Use" and decorum are
architectural principles; "Magnificence" is an
effect in building that can be achieved by adhering
to "Use" and decorum, among other rules.) The
next thirty lines explain the necessity for
"Sense" and the basis for the certainty of the

rules, "Nature" (ll. 39-70). The examples of
Versailles, Villario, the young Sabinus, etc.,
in the following eighteen lines (ll. 71-98) illustrate violations of one rule or another,
preparing for the notorious depiction of Timon's
Villa (ll. 99-168), where all of the rules are
violated. (This sequence of brief satiric
sketches leading to a climatic fully-developed
one Young uses repeatedly in his satires, as
does Pope in other epistles.) The last lines
Pope devotes to suggesting the consequences
of violating and of observing the rules: first
an aside on the accidental benefits of Timon's
extravagance (ll. 169-172) and a reflection on
the transience of such vain displays as his
(ll. 173-176), and finally a catalogue of benefits resulting from both private and public
men's decorous projects, illustrating from those
of Bathurst, Burlington, and the King (ll. 177-
204). Here Pope is not simply paying an "architectural compliment"[6]; he is showing that the
aesthetic norms he adovcates--and the moral ones
they imply--are capable of being realized.

The key to Pope's moral interpretation of
architecture is neither, I believe, to be found
entirely in the couplet to which G.R. Hibbard
calls attention ("You [Burlington] show us,
Rome was glorious, not profuse,/And pompous
buildings once were things of Use" [ll. 23-24])[7]
nor in the line Professor Shafer cites. At least
as important is the passage quoted in a contemporary architectural treatise, probably by John
Gwynn[8]:

    To build, to plant, whatever you intend,
  To rear the Column, or the Arch to bend,
  To swell the Terras, or to sink the Grot;
  In all, let Nature never be forgot.
    (ll. 47-50)

"Nature" was as much the "aesthetic norm" in
architectural theory as in literary criticism,
and its meanings were very similar in both
disciplines. Nor was "Use" an entirely different

basis for aesthetic and moral judgment from
"Nature"; they were, in fact, believed to be inseparable. The proportions, dimensions, and
forms of plans, elevations, and various structural
members, as well as of the orders themselves, were
the necessary consequences of their uses and of
the limitations which building materials imposed
upon the designer. The architect was as much
bound by the laws of nature as the engineer and
the craftsman.

Behind this brief is a familiar Platonic commonplace, the identification of the good, the
useful, and the beautiful. Xenophon illustrates
it in his *Memorabilia* (III. viii. 6-8) when he re-
counts an argument Socrates advanced to prove
that a "dung-basket" is beautiful if it is shaped
to fulfill its function satisfactorily, whereas
a golden shield that fails to do so must be considered ugly. Socrates also applies the same
criterion to houses.

This principle appears frequently in architectural treatises of the Renaissance and the
eighteenth century, as well as in works of
philosophy and in poetry. Euphranor, for example,
in George Berkeley's *Alciphron* (1732) rejects the
idea that beauty is inherent in mathematical
proportions "pleasing to the eye." A door is not
beautiful, he says, simply because its height
is twice its width; it could be turned on its
side and still have the same proportions, but
it would no longer correspond with the human
form, and hence could not be considered beauti-
ful.9 Again, Shaftesbury in his *Characteristics*
(1711) insists that the appreciation of beauty
demands "the study and love of symmetry and order,
on which beauty depends...." This study will show,
he affirms, that "...the same shapes and proportions which make beauty afford advantage by
adapting to activity and use," and he concludes,
"Thus beauty and truth are plainly joined with
the notion of utility and convenience, even in
the apprehension of every ingenious artist, the
architect, the statuary, or the painter."10 To
explain and to provide authority for this interdependence of the beautiful and the useful he

quotes in a footnote a passage from *De Architectura*
in which Vitruvius shows that architectural ornaments imitate features of timber construction,
and thus that their forms and arrangements are
clearly dictated by the physical properties of
wood. For example, since small timbers cannot
be used to support large ones, the Greeks never
placed mutules over dentils because mutules imitate the ends of beams and dentils the ends of
rafters.[11] (It never seems to have occurred to
Vitruvius or his followers to explain why stone
buildings should obey rules deriving from the
properties of wood.) Shaftesbury refers readers
desiring further explanation of how propriety may
be deduced from the "true laws of Nature" to
Philander's commentary on the same passage in
his edition of Vitruvius.[12]
    The same "true laws of Nature" applied to all
the rules of architecture, from those dictating
the details of the orders to those dictating the
styles and forms of entire buildings, whether
prisons or garden temples, churches or palaces.
The architect Robert Morris, for example, in
his *Defence of Ancient Architecture* (1728) followed
Roland Fréart de Chambray in believing the
three Greek orders (the Doric, Ionic, and Cor-
inthian) adequate for all kinds of buildings, not
merely becuase of his veneration for their great
antiquity, but because they seemed to be the
product of the three possible "modes" of building,
the "strong," the "gay" (or "medium"), and the
"delicate." He insists that "The Necessity of
being conformable to those Proportions in our
Practices, is seen from their being prov'd to be
founded upon Nature and Reason," what he calls
"the Fountain of Order in general." To illustrate
the inevitable certainty of the proportions he
explains that "as Columns are more advanc'd in
height...they have...less power to sustain the
Bulk of the Weight with [sic] those whose Dia-
meters are equal, and of a less Height."[13] Thus
the properties of materials dictate the rules
that, as numerous architects and men of letters
insisted, "admit no medium." And this suggests
the basis for the confidence John Gilbert Cooper
later exhibits:

You very well know that every Rule, Canon, and
Proportion in building did not arise from the
capricious Invention of Man, but from the unerring Dictates of Nature, and that even what
are now the ornamental Parts of an Edifice,
originally were created by Necessity; and still
are displeasing to the Sight, when they are
disobedient, if I may use that Moral Expression,
to the Order, which Nature, whose Laws cannot
be repealed, first gave to supply that Necessity.[14]

Earlier in the century men of letters were less
reluctant than Cooper to see aesthetic principles
as morally binding, and just as ready to believe
them inviolable.

Most of the architectural principles that
Pope shows either being violated or observed in
his *Epistle* derive from Vitruvius's rule of
decor (although as considerably elaborated).
Vitruvius's definition is admittedly rather
vague: "Decor demands the faultless ensemble
of a work composed, in accordance with precedent,
of approved details. It obeys convention, which
in Greek is called *thematismos*, or custom or
nature."[15]

The rule implies more than "architectural good
manners or decorum."[16] The examples Vitruvius
uses to clarify the words *statione* ("convention"),
consuetudine ("fashion"), and *natura* suggest both the
means for deriving the rule's implications, and
many of its later applications--the decorum of
architectural plan and form, of the orders, and
of "situation" (from the sixteenth through the
eighteenth centuries this word was generally used
to denote all of the physical features of a building's whole site). Vitruvius expected to find
some analogy between a building's form and its
function, including correspondences between its
style or ornaments and the gods or persons to
whom it was dedicated. Hence a hypethral temple
(one open to the sky) erected on an open site is
appropriate to the sky gods, and so adheres to
"convention." This rule also required that the

architect pay heed to the "qualities" of the
orders and of the objects imitated in his ornaments; the "might" of Minerva, Mars, and Hercules
required that unadorned Doric temples be built
for them; the delicacy of Venus, Flora, Proser-
pine, Fountains, and Nymphs required the Corin-
thian order, adorned with "flowers, foliage,
spirals and volutes"; Diana, Juno, and Bacchus
required the "middle quality" of the Ionic order.
"Fashion" demanded that a building be uniform
in style inside and out, that neither "low" and
"high" styles be mixed, nor the ornaments of one
order with those of another. The last, "natural
decor," required that temples be erected on
healthy sites (to enhance the authority of the
gods venerated in them), and also that buildings
be placed and their rooms arranged to take advantage of available light.[17] Elsewhere in *De
Architectura* Vitruvius discusses sites in considerably more detail.

By the time Pope wrote the *Epistle to Burlington*,
the implications of these rules had been carefully examined, and the rules had been reinterpreted
to suit them to the needs of Renaissance--and
Christian--civilization. Using Vitruvius's pre-
scription of the proper orders for the various
pagan gods, Sebastiano Serlio, for example, in
his *Architettvra et Prospettiva in Sette Libri* (1537f.)
explains which orders are appropriate to Christ,
the saints, virgins, martyrs, etc.[18] Although
Daniele Barbaro in his influential commentary on
Vitruvius (1556f.) suggests that the rule of
decor may require new orders for Christian uses
("seruando il Decoro, & non seruendo a suio
[the architect's] capricci"), he remains consistent
with the sense of the rule.[19]

But Renaissance interpreters did not apply the
rule only to religious architecture; secular
structures were to observe *decor* as well. Pietro
Cataneo advised in 1554, "Debbesi per tanto fare,
che tutte le fabriche corrispondendo alla grand-
ezza & dignita del personaggio, & della città,
pendino sempre piu nel magnifico, che nel pou-
ero...."[20] In his much-read *Elements of Architecture*

(1624) Sir Henry Wotton says much the same thing:
Decor is the keeping of a due *Respect* between the
Inhabitant and the *Habitation*. Whence *Palladius* did
conclude, that the principall *Entrance* was never
to be regulated by any certaine *Dimensions*, but
by the dignity of the *Master;* yet to exceed rather in the *more* then in the *lesse*, is a mark of
Generosity...."

To clarify this Wotton relates a literary application of it in Sidney's *Arcadia:*

> And here likewise I must remember our
> ever memorable Sir *Philip Sidney,* (whose *Wit*
> was in truth the very rule of *Congruity*) who
> well knowing that *Basilius* (as he had painted
> the *State* of his *Minde*) did rather want some
> extraordinary *Formes* to entertaine his *Fancy,*
> then *roome* for *Courtiers;* was contented to
> place him in a *Star-like Lodge;* which other-
> wise in severe *Judgment* of Art, had been an in-
> commodious *Figure.*[21]

Wotton's emphasis here is not, like Cataneo's and
Palladio's, upon correspondences between the
social stature of the inhabitant and his dwelling,
but rather between the inhabitant's intellectual
(and, by implication, moral) traits and the form
of his dwelling. One might question whether
Sidney intended the configuration of Basilius's
"Lodge" to be a criticism of his fancy, but Wotton clearly believed he did, and long before the
end of the seventeenth century such a licentious
form would become a certain sign of a man's frivolity and lack of moral seriousness. John Evelyn
confidently declared in 1664, "It is from the
asymmetry of our *Buildings,* want of *decorum* and proportion in our Houses, that the irregularity of
our *humors* and affections may be shrewdly discern'd...."[22]

This same point was to be repeated many times
during the next century by writers as various as
John Dennis, Richard Blackmore, Shaftesbury,
James Thomson, Joseph Addison, Robert Morris,
John Gwynn, and, of course, Pope. And for all of

them novelty and violations of architectural decorum were not merely frivolous errors, but
destructive assaults on moral, religious, and
social order.

Pope displays the irregularity of his fools'
humors primarily through the violations of two
classes of rules, the decorum of form and
ornament, and the decorum of "situation," although
he freely intersperses his satire with many commonplaces of architectural criticism (for example in showing that Sir Visto's and Bubo's punishments are implicit in their follies [ll.15-
22]).

Pope realized that the mere existence of rules
does not make a Palladio of a common carpenter
any more than the existence of sound literary
criticism makes a Milton of a dunce. Burlington
may have shown in his *Fabriche antiche* (1730) the
uses of Rome's pompous buildings, but "just" and
"noble rules" will not necessarily improve architecture in England, not because the rules are
inadequate, but because "Imitating Fools" do not
understand them. They copy from models of sound
practice, including Burlington's, a number of
ornaments to apply to their structures without
any regard for the uses of them dictated by the
rule of *decor*. Burlington's publications, like
many of the great treatises, thus became mere
pattern books for ignorant workmen to pilfer. In
listing the deformities they created Pope echoes
the growing criticisms of the builders who con-
founded fasionable forms and ornaments with the
whole art of architecture:

> Reverse your Ornaments, and hang them all
> On some patch'd dog-hole ek'd with ends of
>   wall,
> Then clap four slices of Pilaster on't,
> That, lac'd with bits of rustic, makes a
>   Front.
>   (ll. 31-34)

This indecorum and incoherence results from
treating ornaments as if they were the building
blocks of architecture, from eccentically re-

versing and irresponsibly applying and combining
them. A decorated "dog-hole" surely does not adhere to "fashion"; Pope's sneering epithet "slices
of Pilaster" reminds one that pilasters combined
with rustic masonry are not to be found in Palladio's *Four Books of Architecture,* and that architects
who combine even engaged columns with roughened
stones, such as Serlio and Philibert de l'Orme,
carefully integrate them. But relying upon pattern books encouraged such medleys as Pope's verbs
suggest--"hand," "ek'd," "clap," "lac'd"--and
the subordination of design to ornamentation.
    Equally contemptible are those who, in attempt-
ing to follow the rules, subvert them, those who

> ...call the winds thro' long Arcades to
>   roar,
> Proud to catch cold at a Venetian door;
> Conscious they act a true Palladian part,
> And if they starve, they starve by rules of
>   art.
>   (ll. 35-38)

The pedantic imitation of Italian forms--the "long
Arcades" and Palladian door--is as worthy of
ridicule as the "patch'd dog-hold" because both
violate the rule English architects called "convenience," which Morris defines as "the just supplying of wants," and declares to be "the Handmaid to Nature."[23] In all of his remarks on
his arcades and loggias, Palladio, for example,
stresses their usefulness--their "convenience"--
for such purposes as protecting people and animals from the scorching sun, and crops and fire-
wood from the rain.[24] But he, like Vitruvius and
Alberti, also insists upon suiting design to climate and "situation." This "Imitating Fools"
cannot do, and so make the chilly English winds
"roar" all the more loudly, and their houses more
drafty; they violate a master rule to satisfy a
misunderstood fashion.
    In explaining what is needed to satisfy "con-
venience"--"Good Sense, which only is the gift
of Heav'n" (l. 42)--Pope again shows his debt to

contemporary architectural theory. The mere
possession of innate intelligence is not enough;
one who designs must apply it with steady attention to "Nature," inferring from the "Genius
of the Place" the proper orders, forms, and
arrangements for their gardens, grounds, and
buildings. Pope's insistence upon consulting
nature when raising a column or an arch, when
dressing "the Goddess," or when giving variety
to a landscape is reminiscent of a concern
running all through Palladio's Second Book;
Palladio carefully explains the appropriateness
of each design for its particular "situation,"
frequently calling attention to the proximity
of rivers, hills, and open prospects. English
architects elaborated upon "decorum of situation"
considerably, and Pope surely would have agreed
with Morris who insisted in 1736,

> SITUATION *has been my next Care, and in this I*
> *have been vigilant to appropriate my Design to the*
> *Imaginary Spot* [that he describes for each de-
> sign, often in blank verse imitative of
> Thomson's]. *If I have been poetick in Description,*
> *the Remarks are only from such Situations which I have*
> *frequently taken from* Nature *it self, and I esteem*
> *Situation so extensive a Branch of Architecture, that*
> *no Building should be design'd to be erected, without*
> *first considering the Extent of* Prospects, Hills,
> Vales, & c. *which expand or encircle it; its* Ave-
> nues, Pastures *and* Waters; *all which furnish*
> *the* ARCHITECT *with proper ideas, and the* Modus
> [crudely, the order] *must be shifted from one*
> *Scene to another, as Necessity requires.*[25]

This suggests, I believe, how narrow the modern
commentator is who stresses Pope's theory of
gardening in the *Epistle to Burlington* instead of
recognizing its place in the more comprehensive
humanist theory of architecture. When Pope assures his readers, "Still follow Sense, of ev'ry
Art the Soul,/Parts answ'ring parts shall slide
into a whole..." (ll. 65-66), he is not talking
only about gardens, but about the whole relation-

ship between a villa's buildings and its "situation," of which gardens are but a part.

Pope and Morris rely upon a fully-developed doctrine of a long tradition. Vitruvius most emphasizes the sites for cities, insisting that they be chosen for their convenience and healthfulness; the architect was to heed the availability of the materials for building, the prevailing winds, the cleanliness of the air, water, and soil, and the freedom from marshes, stagnant water, and "vapours."[26] Alberti elaborated upon Vitruvius in 1485, declared the country-house analogous to a small city, applied the same rules to the rural as to the urban "situation," and hinted at the benefits of a good site to the human spirit.[27] By the sixteenth century the requirements had become quite conventional. In 1542, for example, Andrew Boorde insisted upon the necessity of choosing a site with good air, water, soil, woods, and pastures, which would both provide "elbowe-rome" and content the mind.[28] Palladio repeats these and emphasizes even more the site's capability for inspiring contemplation.[29] While the physical requirements remained much the same in the seventeenth century, the effects on a viewer expected of a site became increasingly important, until John Evelyn smiled at a "humorous old knight" who displayed his insensitivity by erecting a barn-like house from which one could not possibly see "an incomparable prospect."[30] Pope's understanding of these demands and expectations is clear from a letter he wrote to Francis Atterbury in 1722: "The situation here is pleasant, and the view rural enough to humour the most retir'd, and agree with the most contemplative. Good air, solitary groves, and sparing diet, sufficient to make you fancy your self (what you are in temperance, tho's elevated into a greater figure by your station) one of the Fathers of the Desert."[31] Other of his letters make the same points.

The satire on Villario and the young Sabinus reflects these beliefs; it is not aimed just at the planting of a quincunx or of espaliers, the

creation of a forest or meadow. "Villario's
ten-years toil" is certainly a contrast to the
patient cooperation with Nature that in time
will produce "A Work to wonder at--perhaps a
STOW" (l. 70) just as Pope's catalogue of Villario's conventional devices in his formal garden suggests the same ignorant pedantry that
will "Turn Arcs of Triumph to a Garden-gate"
(l. 30). Yet Pope does not entirely scorn such
projects as Villario's, for he speaks with modest pride of his own quincunx in the *Imitation of
the First Satire of the Second Book of Horace* (l. 130),
and there is surely nothing abusive in having
"the parts unite" or "A waving Glow his bloomy
beds display" (ll. 81, 83). But it is not to
Villario's credit to lack so completely any fixed
principles as first to spend ten years constructing all the fashionable gimmicks of a formal garden, and then to discover "at last he better likes
a Field." He provies himself insensitive to the
"situation" in ignorantly imposing prescribed
forms upon it, and in readily destroying what he
has laboriously created. His acts are those of
builders and planters who love novelty, a passion
always seen in architectural treatises as destructive of the aesthetic and moral principles
essential to an ordered art and society.
    The young Sabinus is similarly whimsical. In
planting trees the elder Sabinus performed an
activity perfectly appropriate to a gentleman, one
that Alberti and Palladio assume to be a routine
part of the owner's management and development of
his estate, and one that had gained an especially
great prestige in England since the publication
of John Evelyn's *Sylva* (1664), in which he makes
the reforestation of the country a patriotic
duty.[32] Whereas the elder Sabinus is in tune with
Nature and his "situation," delighting in the
"thick'ning shade" and greeting "With annual joy
the red'ning shoots," his son is an insensitive
booby who follows his "fine Taste," unprincipled
as it is, and transforms the forest trees into
"ignoble broomsticks."[33] What is left provides
no occasion for that contemplation which the
decorous "situation" was supposed to inspire. The

young Sabinus has left only a "Monument to his
own Folly."[34]

But the greatest of such monuments is Timon's
Villa, where Pope brings together all of the violations of *decor* that he has introduced elsewhere
in the poem, and where he reemphasizes their moral as well as their aesthetic significance.
Timon's basic fault is ignoring the demands of
Nature and utility (or "convenience"); as a result
the Villa is improperly scaled either for its
"situation" or its inhabitant. Thus it must fail
to achieve "Magnificence."

Nothing in the Villa's "situation" is conducive
to the contemplation and comfort that architectural theory dictated, and that Pope expected.[35]
Instead, the house seems to be placed on an open
plain, unprotected from the winds. In fact, the
"Lake behind/Improves the keenness of the Northern wind" (ll. 111-112), an example of inat-
tention to a rule stressed by Vitruvius and most
Renaissance theorists, one explaining how to
locate a house and arrange its rooms so as to
avoid the dangers of chilling or noxious winds.[36]
And where Timon's landscape architect concerned
himself with the "situation," he violated it; he
has walled off the garden from the countryside
(l. 114), imposed a pedantic regularity and rigid
bilateral symmetry upon it (ll. 115-118), turned
trees into artifacts (ll. 119-120), and, because
inattentive to the "Genius of the Place;/That
tells the Waters or to rise, or fall" (ll. 57-58),
erected fountains and urns from which water cannot
flow (ll. 125-126).

Nor is there at the Villa any "keeping of a due
Respect between the *Inhabitant* and the *Habitation*."
The disproportionate size of the house and its
"situation" leave Timon "A puny insect, shiv'ring
at a breeze!" [(l. 108). The effect of the Villa's
pomp is ironically to diminish its builder's
stature instead of aggrandizing it; as for Bubo
and Sir Visto, the punishment is implicit in the
vice. And a similar lack of correspondence between architectural and human forms is apparent
in approaching the country house of Timon's Villa
from its gardens:

>   First thro' the length of yon hot Terrace
>   sweat,
>   And when up ten steep slopes you've dragg'd
>   your thighs,
>   Just at his Study-door he'll bless your eyes.
>   (ll. 130-132)

Pope's verbs "sweat" and "dragg'd" and the laborious slowness of the heavily-accented monosyllabic
verse (l. 131) make clear that the designer took
no account whatever of human needs, or the best
ways of satisfying them. Even walking--a simple
activity, believed conducive to a virtuous and
healthful life, that the villa is to encourage--
demands inordinate exertion.
   The dining room likewise violates the rule of
"convenience":

>   Is this a dinner? this a Genial room?
>   No, 'tis a Temple, and a Hecatomb.
>   A solemn Sacrifice, perform'd in state,
>   You drink by measure, and to minutes eat.
>   (ll. 155-158)

Here the ignorant application of an inappropriate
form contributes to the "formal regularity" that
destroys "all the pleasurable enjoyment of the
entertainment,"[37] and transforms hospitality into
an affront. The "Temple" may be a proper setting
for a sacrificial "Hecatomb," but it is surely
not one in which Timon can fulfill his responsibilities as a host and country gentleman, one
in which he can "amuse, & shelter a few friends...;
inspire a Political Acquaintance between a Sat-
urday Evening & Monday, with schemes for public
Good in Parliament; or receive with hospitality
a discarded Courtier."[38]
   Several of these violations of "convenience"
result from Timon's confusing mere size in architecture with "greatness" or "Magnificence." Hence,
instead of promoting its owner's virtue, encour-
aging social intercourse, and inspiring contemplation, the Villa's vulgarity "brings all Brob-
dingnag before your thought" (l. 104).

Addison in *The Spectator* No. 415 distinguishes
between greatness "as relating to the Bulk and
Body of the Structure" and, following Fréart,
"Greatness of Manner," which, he says, "has such
force upon the Imagination, that a small Building,
where *it* appears, shall give the Mind nobler Ideas
than one of twenty times the Bulk, where the Manner is ordinary or little."[39] He gives several
examples of the first one, and even attributes
to it a religious function; yet he is clearly
more interested in the second, which he believes
to result from the use of a few simple, bold
parts in a building, and especially the dome, for
"Among all the figures in Architecture, there are
none that have a *greater Air* [italics mine] than
the Concave and the Convex...."[40]

In his distinction between "greatness" and
"littleness" Pope surely relies upon similar beliefs. But Addison's conceptions of "greatness"
or "Magnificence" in architecture do not fully
explain Pope's meaning. It apparently never
occurred to Addison to specify analogies between
"natural" and "artificial" architecture, that is,
between the cosmos and the art. But by the time
Pope wrote his *Epistle* this commonplace of Italian
architectural theory found its way into English
theory, supported by the same scientific discoveries that Addison relied upon in his essays on
the imagination.

Morris silently borrows from and quotes Addison's essays on the imagination (especially
Nos. 415 and 420) in his *Defence of Ancient Architecture*, but he nearly ignores Addison's distinction between "greatness of bulk" and "manner,"
emphasizes the second one, and makes much clearer
than Addison the source for the "noble ideas"
architecture evokes. He sees architecture as an
imitation of the whole of created nature; "Magnificence" is therefore not achieved merely
through the use of a dome or a *"bold and ample
Relievo,"* but rather through the creation of an
ordered structure in which all parts are pro-
portionate to one another, and to the whole.
In emulating the Creator's attention to proportion and analogy the architect insures that his

design will be useful as well as beautiful, since
the Creator's wisdom is evident in his designing
each part of the cosmos--whether the orbit of a
planet or the limb of an animal--to satisfy its
function.[41] And besides this, the proportions of
a magnificent work of architecture should inspire a viewer to contemplate the proportions
and analogies which they imitate.[42] Given such a
conception, the distinction between sacred and
secular architecture can refer only to a building's
use, since the same systems of arithmetic and
harmonic proportions are to inform both; hence
any magnificent edifice should evoke religious
meditation.

Instead of this, Timon has, like Bubo, merely
provided "A standing sermon, at each year's expense,/That never Coxcomb reach'd Magnificence!"
(ll. 21-22)--in either the moral or aesthetic
sense of the word. The examples illustrating
features of Timon's "draught" reveal the dis-
proportion he has created: "To compass this,
his building is a Town,/His pond an Ocean, his
parterre a Down..." (ll. 104-105). These lines
make the false scale of the entire villa very
clear, and enforcing the point is the play upon
the Renaissance analogy between a country-house
and a city[43]; whereas a house should resemble
a city in being "healthy, furnished with all Manner of Necessaries, not defficient [sic] in any
of the Conveniencies that conduce to the Repose,
Tranquility or Delicacy of Life,"[44] Timon's
"building is a Town" only in its great size,
literally being as large as a city; its disorder,
inconvenience, and ill-government make it no
microcosm of a perfect city. Of it Pope exclaims,
"Lo, what huge heaps of littleness around!/The
whole, a labour'd Quarry above ground" (ll. 109-
110). Here is no magnificence, but its opposite;
the epithet "labour'd Quarry" suggests that
the littleness results from the materials not
being given a significant, ordered form, one capable of inspiring awe and reverence, the effects
of a truly "majestic" architecture. The only
benefit deriving from the Villa is entirely an

accidental one: "hence the Poor are cloath'd; the
Hungry fed ..." (1. 169).

Bathurst's planting and Burlington's building
contrast sharply with the tastelessness, vulgarity,
and violations of decorum illustrated by Bubo and
the young Sabinus, Villario and Timon, those who
are, to use Morris's words, "such Bigots to their
own unwarrantable selfish Opinions, that they
can't discern Light from Darkness, Truth from
Falsehood, nor the beauteous Paths which point
out the true and undoubted way to attain a com-
petent Knowledge in sound Building."[45] Bathurst
and Burlington point a way out of this architectural *Dunciad*, combining Nature and art so as
to create works both useful and magnificent. The
ideals Pope makes them represent are all a part
of the same intellectual heritage he has defended
throughout the poem. The "Lord" who plants useful forests and "Whose ample Lawns are not ash-
am'd to feed/The milky heifer and deserving steed"
(11. 184-185) is not merely being "practical"; he
is attending to the activities appropriate to the
"situation" and his station. Alberti suggests
that such concerns are more proper to "middling
People" than to the rich or nobly born, but Palladio assumes that every inhabitant of a villa
will actively manage his property.[46] By the
eighteenth century building and planting were
respectable and praiseworthy activities for the
gentleman living a life of decorum in the country,
and much encouraged.

Pope saves his highest praise for Burlington,
who mastered, Pope would have us believe, all of
the arts and learning essential to architecture.
It is he who can

> Erect new wonders, and the old repair,
> Jones and Palladio to themselves restore,
> And be whate'er Vitruvius was before....
>   (11. 192-194)

Besides undertaking such projects as rebuilding
Queen Anne's "new-built Churches" and designing
"new wonders,"[47] Pope expects Burlington to

teach the proper applications of the designs of
Inigo Jones and Palladio that earlier in the
poem (ll. 25-46) he has shown being perversely
rifled. These abilities qualify Burlington to
"be whate'er Vitruvius was before," that is,
the compiler of the rules of Greek architecture,
and the monarch's own architect (Vitruvius was
believed in the eighteenth century to have held
the post of architect to Augustus Caesar).
Burlington therefore, if called upon, can insure
that the King's projects--temples, bridges, high-
ways, and breakwaters--will attain appropriate
magnificence and utility, since he will apply
to them the same inviolable rules of art that
govern all the works of the humble as well as the
mighty, those in the country as well as in the
city.
    Thus at the end of the poem Pope holds out
great promise for the arts of both private and
public men in England, but only to those who
observe the traditional--and therefore tested--
rules governing their practice, what Morris calls
the "Ideas of a Community" that compensate for
the limitations of the individual mind, and for
man's "Pride, Avarice, Self Conceit," and "Un-
thoughtfulness."[48] But Pope has also provided
as a warning examples of the alternative, the
creation of a "false magnificence" destructive
of hospitality, ease, contemplation, productivity,
and social responsibility. Perhaps he would
not, like Morris, suggest that the destruction of
order in architecture can bring chaos to society
and to the structure of the cosmos itself,[49] but
he significantly includes architecture among the
arts extinguished by Dullness in *The Dunciad*. And,
as the *Epistle to Burlington* suggests, its inclusion
was inevitable, since it was an integral part of
the Renaissance whose achievements and demise
he darkly celebrates.

Alexander Pope by Jonathan Richardson. Courtesy The Beinecke Rare Book and Manuscript Library, Yale University.

Ut pictura poesis, AND POPE'S "SATIRE II, i"

Cedric D. Reverand II

In *The Sister Arts* (Chicago, 1958), Jean H.
Hagstrum has admirably and exhaustively demonstrated how it is that the Horatian tag, *ut
pictura poesis*, was a critical truism and working
principle for Pope's age. Yet of those critics
who, like Hagstrum, have concerned themselves
with pictorial elements in Pope, most have confined their attention to two points: first, that
Pope displays a penchant for talking like, and
often thinking like, a painter, which accounts
for the many passages wherein Pope talks of
prepared grounds, faded frescoes, hues subtly
mixed, lights and shades, lines justly traced
vs. ill-colors applied, and so forth; second,
that Pope creates detailed and extended pictorial
passages, such as the emblematic description of
Father Thames in *Windsor Forest*, the series of set
portraits in "To a Lady," or the elaborate historical or epic "paintings" scattered throughout
The Dunciad (Dulness ascending her throne, the
aspirants processing in state, etc.).[1] To discover this much is to recognize that Pope is
visual and that he is acutely aware of the analogy
between the sister arts. The next step, however,
is to explore what Pope's pictorialism, and the

This essay first appeared in *Eighteenth-Century Studies* 9 (1976), 553-568.

response it demands from us, can contribute to our
understanding of his individual works.

   This essay will focus on certain pictorial
elements of "Satire II, i," the first of Pope's
many Horatian Imitations, and his first real, full-
fledged *apologia*, a genre that was to occupy his
attention increasingly from the 1730s on.[2]   As
the poem opens, Pope portrays himself as the
"Tim'rous" (7) poet, misunderstood and disliked
by people his poetry has, in one way or another,
offended, and now led to seek legal advice from
his lawyer-friend, Fortescue. Usually, that
advice is for Pope to do the safe thing: if
writing has made life difficult for him, Fortescue advises, "I'd write no more" (11), and if,
as Pope claims, he *must* write, then Fortescue
suggests Pope "write CAESAR'S Praise" (21).
Such advice gives Pope the opportunity to proclaim his ideals, to explain the motivation behind his satire (and here he becomes anything
but timorous): he will not write flattering
verse, will not stoop to do the convenient and
safe thing, because he is dedicated to truth
and virtue, and his dedication is so strong that
"What-e'er my Fate.../I will Rhyme and Print"
(92, 100). Furthermore, he need not write
flattering verse because he is independent,
"Un-plac'd, un-pension'd, no Man's Heir, or
Slave" (116), and therein lies his strength.
Pope proceeds to describe the independent life
he wishes to live, apart from the "distant Din"
(123) of the real world, safe in his "Retreat,"
graced by the "best Companions" (125), devoted
to "The Feast of Reason and the Flow of Soul"
(128). In all, this idyllic grotto represents
a world distinctly apart from "the world of
stratagem and compromise and money-grubbing and
self-interest," as Maynard Mack describes it,[3]
that characterizes the real world of Cibber,
Walpole, Lady Mary, Lord Hervey, George II, the
world Fortescue had suggested Pope try to appease.

   Now comes the crux of the whole poem, and
here is where critics part company. Throughout,
Fortescue has suggested Pope behave so as to

please the prevailing social, cultural, and political orders; and throughout, Pope has argued
that he must remain independent of, and superior
to, all this. The question is, whose point of
view prevails in the end, Pope's or Fortescue's?
After talking about the ideal, independent life
he wishes to live in his grotto, Pope pushes home
his case: "This is my Plea, on this I rest my
Cause--/What saith my Council learned in the Laws?"
(141-42), and Fortescue is obliged to pronounce
his final legal opinion:

> F.   Your Plea is good. But still I say,
>   beware!
> Laws are explain'd by Men--so have a care.
> It stands on record, that in *Richard*'s Times
> A Man was hang'd for very honest Rhymes.
> Consult the Statute: *quart.* I think it is,
> *Edwardi Sext.* or *prim. & quint. Eliz*:
> See *Libels, Satires*--here you have it--read.
>   P. *Libels* and *Satires*! lawless Things indeed!
> But grave *Epistles*, bringing Vice to light,
> Such as a *King* might read, a *Bishop* write,
> Such as Sir *Robert* would approve--
>   F. Indeed?
> The Case is alter'd--you may then proceed.
> In such a Cause the Palintiff will be hiss'd,
> My Lords the Judges laugh, and your're dis-
>   miss'd.   (143-56)

By pronouncing the case against Pope "alter'd,"
Fortescue seems to be capitulating, but it is
scarcely an immediate and completely unambiguous
capitulation. Fortescue's immediate response
is consistent with the advice he gives throughout
the poem: Pope must beware the powers that be.
And Fortescue only pronounces the case altered
after Pope indicates he will write the kind of
satire a King, a Bishop, and Sir Robert would
approve--that is, after Pope suggests he will
appease the establishment. Read this way, the
poem's concluding lines suggest that it is Fortescue's attitude, rather than Pope's, that ultimately may prevail. The poem then becomes a

"virtual confession of defeat," as Thomas R. Edwards puts it; and Howard D. Weinbrot, whose
view is similar, sees Pope ending "in a dangerous
and unreliable alliance with forces that he will
soon bitterly attack."4
     It strikes me that such a reading is erroneous.
Pope's poem is not a confession of defeat, but
rather a satirist's forceful, resolute, and
convincing proclamation against a corrupt establishment; his vision of the ideal community,
epitomized by his grotto, is not a never-never
land, but rather a viable alternative. If we
read the poem with an eye toward Pope's use
of the pictorial, such a reading, it seems to me,
becomes inescapable. The key may lie in an
earlier section of the poem, where Fortescue tells
Pope that if he persists in rhyming and printing,
his "Days can ne'er be long" (101), and Pope
responds:

     P. What? arm'd for *Virtue* when I point the
         Pen,
     Brand the bold Front of shameless, guilty Men,
     Dash the proud Gamester in his gilded Car,
     Bare the mean Heart that lurks beneath a Star;
     Can there be wanting to defend Her Cause,
     Lights of the Church, or Guardians of the Laws?
     Could pension'd *Boileau* lash in honest Strain
     Flatt'rers and Bigots ev'n in *Louis'* Reign?
     Could Laureate *Dryden* Pimp and Fry'r engage,
     Yet neither *Charles* nor *James* be in a Rage?
     And I not strip the Gilding off a Knave,
     Un-plac'd, un-pension'd, no Man's Heir, or
         Slave?
     I will, or perish in the gen'rous Cause.
        (105-17)

This is the beginning of Pope's final plea and
has been justly called the poem's climactic
passage: Ronald Paulson says it is this passage "for which in effect the poem was written."5
It starts with a personification, something many
modern readers would regard as an artificial
device for making the abstract temporarily and

EMBLEMATA HORATIANA.

LA VERTU EST IMMORTELLE.

Tov qui pretend laiſſer à la poſterité
Un illuſtre renom durant l'eternité :
Eſcoute mon conſeil, il eſt ſeur & fidelle,
Embraſſe le fameux parti de la Vertu :
Pour arriver un jour à la Gloire immortelle ,
Il faut ſous ſes drapeaux avoir bien combatu.

V I R-

PLATE 1. Otto van Veen (Othonis Vaeni), *Quinti Horatii Flacci Emblemata*, 3rd
ed. (Brussels, 1683), p. 7. Courtesy of the Cornell University
Library.

EMBLEMATA HORATIANA. 17

.LA VERTU EST LE BUT DES TRAITS DE L'ENVIE.

Pourroit-on rencontrer un homme vertueux,
Qui n'eut jamais fenti les coups des Envieux,
Ils s'erigent d'abord en Cenfeurs de fa vie,
L'on en fait châque jour de differens portraicts,
Qui peut s'en eſtonner? le propre de l'Envie
Eſt d'avoir la Vertu pour l'objet de fes traicts.
                    C   AMOR

PLATE 2. Otto van Veen (Othonis Vaeni), *Quinti Horatii Flacci Emblemata*, 3rd
ed. (Brussels, 1683), p. 17. Courtesy of the Cornell University
Library.

conveniently concrete. However, in the eighteenth
century, as Henry Home, Lord Kames, explains,
personifications offer particular advantages to
the practicing poet:

Abstract and general terms, as well as particular
objects, are often necessary in poetry. Such
terms however are not well adapted to poetry, because they suggest not any image to the mind....
Upon that account, in works addressed to the
imagination, abstract terms are frequently personified.[6]

In short, personification was a means of rendering
abstracts visual, and Pope is not merely calling
upon his audience to recognize that he is a
virtuous satirist, but is asking his audience to
see this figure, Virtue, in whose "Cause" Pope
wields his pen.
    Virtue, in addition to being a minor classical
deity--Virtus to the Romans, Arete to the
Greeks--was also a figure widely depicted in
Renaissance art. She is perhaps best known as a
figure in the many paintings of "The Choice of
Hercules," or "Hercules at the Crossroads," a
popular theme for painters, in which Hercules
is depicted between the figures of Virtue and
Voluptas (or Vice), both of whom vie for his
fealty, and each of whom urges him to follow her
path.[7] Virtue is also a prominent figure in
emblem books, which is understandable, since
virtue itself is such a prevalent constituent
in the maxims and truisms that form the bases for
so many emblems. Consequently, when Pope
claims he is "arm'd for *Virtue*," he calls into
play an entire series of pictorial associations
which, though perhaps unfamiliar to us, would
have been commonplaces to his audience. As Hagstrum reminds us, since in the eighteenth century taste for graphically rendered abstractions
and mythological figures "was widely diffused,
and the appropriate and relevant iconography...
easily available," it remains the modern reader's
task to "learn the relevant iconographical

context" so that he can "respond to even slight
visual stimulus."[8]

As with any stock allegorical figure, no two
representations of Virtue are necessarily
identical feature for feature: Rubens, for instance, depicts Virtue wearing armor, whereas
Annibale Carracci omits the armor, and George
Wither makes Virtue a man who holds an Aescula-
pian staff.[9] Nonetheless, there is such a thing
as a traditional depiction, a more or less
standard set of details that an artist can rely
on to make the figure readily recognizable, a
set of what Chester Chapin calls "certain easily
comprehensible 'marks' distinguishing this or
that figure," marks which "the eighteenth-century
poet was usually careful to follow...in order to
take advantage of the emotional overtones and
image-making powers which such differentiae
possessed."[10] It would be tedious to enumerate
and discuss all the many drawings of Virtue, but
a close examination of one representative set
of drawings will help focus the issue, and for
this I turn to Otto van Veen's (Othonis Vaeni)
Quinti Horatii Flacci Emblemata, a widely disseminated
emblem book that maintained its popularity right
through the early years of the eighteenth century.[1]
Van Veen's drawings are particularly appropriate
for two reasons: first, his representations
of Virtue are traditional rather than eccentric
or atypical, and thus serve as a good index to
the "iconographical context" of the age; second,
there is evidence that Pope was familiar with
this book, if Spence's usually reliable anecdotes
are to be trusted. Spence records this Pope
observation, where Pope seems to be criticizing
van Veen's particular methods of allegorizing
Horatian mottos:

Otho Venius has published a picture-book which
he calls the *Emblems of Horace*. "Misce stultitiam
consiliis *brevem*" is represented by Minerva
leading a little *short* child with a fool's cap
on, by the hand. "Paulum sepultae distat inertiae
celata virtus" is Virtue in a dark corner, Lazi-
ness in a sepulchre, and only a thin partition
wall between them.[12]

Whatever Pope's opinion of van Veen's skill and
taste, Pope obviously recognizes the figure, and
would undoubtedly have been familiar with Virtue
from any of a wide number of representations,
not just from van Veen.

What, then, are the "easily comprehensible
'marks'" traditionally associated with this
figure, and what bearing might they have on
"Satire II,i"? Van Veen's Virtue is a helmeted
warrior, very much like an Amazon (and intentionally so); she carries in one hand a sheathed
sword (*parazonium*), while the other hand usually
holds a shaft or spear; at times there is a globe
beside her or under her foot, suggesting that it
is she who is responsible for protecting the
world. Often she is depicted in a forceful or
aggressive posture, suggesting her strength and
power, as in van Veen's emblem, "La Vertu est
Inébranlable" (p. 1). Here Virtue, who stands
in the center of the engraving, is the dominant
figure: she appears with helmet, staff, and
parazonium, with light seeming to radiate from
her, and she is surrounded by cherubs (representing Pity, Justice, etc.). She stands with one
foot triumphantly trampling a prostrate figure
representing Fortune. That Virtue should be depicted as strong, forceful, even potentially warlike, is in itself illuminating; indeed, in these
particulars--with helmet, sword, and staff--she
looks much like the traditional representation
of Minerva, so much so that on occasion the two
figures are virtually interchangeable, as in
Adriaan de Jonge's (Hadrianus Junii) *Les Emblemes*
(Antwerp, 1565).[13] When Pope in "Satire II, i"
claims he is aligned with Virtue, he does not
mean the rather pacific and often passive virtue
so inherent in our modern Christian ethic; he is
rather relying on a broader and more classically
oriented definition of virtue, one which would
have been readily perceived by anyone familiar
with this pictorial representation or the tradition behind it. As Cicero noted in his *Tus-
culan Disputations*, since *virtus* is derived from *vir*,
virtue, properly speaking, means "fortitude,"

that quality which is the prime requisite for
manliness.[14] The pictorial representations of
this figure preserve this definition, so that
Virtue in effect becomes a personification of
manliness, of courage--as certain latter-day
commentators have put it, "particularly courage
in battle."[15] The helmet suggests as much, as
does the sheathed sword, ready for battle but not
unnecessarily wielded. Similarly, Pope's weapon
of satire (69) is worn only in "a Land of Hectors,/Thieves, Supercargoes, Sharpers, and Directors" (71-72); that is, it is sheathed, but ready
if necessary:

> But touch me, and no Minister so sore.
> Who-e'er offends, at some unlucky Time
> Slides into Verse, and hitches in a Rhyme,
> Sacred to Ridicule! his whole Life long.
>   (76-79)

This parallel between the satirist's behavior
and that of Virtue is also explicit in the
Horatian original, which, one must remember,
Pope's audience would have read along with his
Imitation, since Pope's version was printed on
one page and the original on the facing page;
where Pope talks of his weapon of satire, Horace
explicitly likens the satirist's pen to a
sheathed sword (*"veluti custodiet ensis/Vagina tectus,"*
40-41). The point to be emphasized is that
Pope's being armed for Virtue is more than merely
a statement of the righteousness of his activities;
the pictorial and mythological context of Virtue
here employed suggests strength and power, for
to be armed for this Amazon, this personification
of manly valor, implies being both courageous and
strong in battle. Thus, many of Pope's claims,
which might seem at first glance arrogant over-
statements, grow quite naturally and logically
from that first claim; if he is armed for Virtue,
and if she is behind him, then of course he is
strong enough to

> Brand the bold Front of shameless, guilty Men,
> Dash the proud Gamester in his gilded Car,
> Bare the mean Heart that lurks beneath a Star.
>   (106-8)

There are other equally bold claims Pope makes which are similarly reinforced by this pictorial context. For example, in rejecting Fortescue's suggestion that he write harmless, Cibberesque panegyrics ("Then all your Muse's softer Art display," 29) rather than satire, Pope supports his case with a reference to Caesar:

And justly CAESAR scorns the Poet's Lays,
It is to *History* he trusts for Praise.
    (35-36)

The basic idea, clearly, is that Caesar and Pope care not for temporary glory, however conferred; no matter what happens in the here and now, "What-e'er my Fate, or well or ill at Court" (92), Pope "will Rhyme and Print" (100), for it is the absolute not the temporal scale against which Pope wishes to be measured. His interest in a lasting reputation rather than in temporary and consequently hollow success is apparent; what is not so immediately apparent to the modern reader is that Pope's alignment with Virtue gives him a substantial claim upon the permanent fame and lasting victory he seeks. One van Veen emblem (p. 7), entitled with a relatively ordinary apo-thegm, "La Vertu est Immortelle," rather vi-vidly emphasizes this: it depicts Virtue car-rying two men heavenward, and the text asserts that it is necessary to have fought under Virtue's banner to earn a name lasting to eternity.[16] And one might add that in the classical tradition, Virtue is inevitably victorious; as Petrarch claimed, "Viri enim egregii virtutis ope vincunt omnia," a truism that the pictorial tradition everywhere asserts.[17] Witness the van Veen em-blem previously discussed where Virtue is seen trampling on Fortune, or a Gabriel Rollenhagen emblem depicting Virtue turning a conquered For-tune who is bound to her own wheel,[18] or even the Hercules at the Crossroads representations mentioned earlier. Although the Hercules paint-ings and emblems depict the moment of choice rather than the outcome, every depiction contains the tacit assertion that it is Virtue who will

ultimately win over Vice, something Hercules'
subsequent accomplishments attest to. Thus, it
is the very nature of Virtue to achieve victory,
and to guarantee enduring fame, which is precisely what Pope hopes to achieve. When Pope
claims he will "Dash the proud Gamester" (107),
or "Bare the mean Heart that lurks beneath a
Star" (108); when he claims that, thanks to
satire, "no rich or noble knave/Shall walk the
World, in credit" (119-20); when he claims that
"Who-e'er offends" him shall end up "Sacred to
Ridicule!" (77,79), Pope scarcely sounds like a
man "in a dangerous and unreliable alliance with
forces that he will soon bitterly attack." Nor
does his poem sound like a "virtual confession of
defeat." On the contrary, by aligning himself
with Virtue, Pope gains a foothold on victory,
and more important, on a lasting kind of victory
that transcends the immediate successes that
knaves, fools, corrupt politicians, and the like
manage to achieve.

This mythological and pictorial context reinforces and clarifies themes and attitudes that
emerge later in the poem, where Pope, having left
the field of battle, the attacks on Blackmore,
Budgell, Cibber, Sappho, Judge Page, and so forth,
having completed his impassioned proclamation that
he is "arm'd for *Virtue*" and is "To VIRTUE ONLY and
HER FRIENDS, A FRIEND" (121), retreats to his
grotto and describes for us the peaceful endeavors
that are to ensue (122-32). In the midst of the
fray, Pope's energies had been directed toward the
battle itself, "My Head and Heart thus flowing
thro' my Quill" (63), but now that the quill has
done its work, his energies are directed in a
more urbane, peaceful flow; Pope and his friends
now enjoy "The Feast of Reason and the Flow of
Soul" (128). The elements of this peaceful
"Retreat" (125), the quincunx, vines, and stubborn
plain (130-31), all well apart from "the distant
Din that World can keep" (123), by virtue of
their quietness and inactivity serve as marked
contrasts to all the preceding suggestions of
noise and activity, Blackmore's rumbling and
his "tremendous Sound" (23,25), Delia's slander-
ing or poisoning (81), bulls readying to charge,

asses kicking (86), etc.; coming as it does just
after Pope's climactic speech of self-justification
(105-121), the description of his retreat re-
laxes the tension and creates for us a vision of
a life antithetical to those of Pope's adversaries.

Those who think of this poem as a confession
of defeat are likely to consider Pope's picture
of the retreat as defective. To them, the grotto
might seem to be a dreamed-for escape from a
world of conflicts, something fallen back upon
after the battle has become too tough; thus,
Pope's vision of this retreat, rather than representing a viable possibility, "seems tenuous,"
as Edwards puts it (p. 87). But the pictorial
tradition at Pope's disposal implies something
quite different. Another van Veen emblem (p.153),
this one with the motto, "La Vertu se respos apres
avoir bien travaillé," sheds some light; here, the
emblem depicts the reward to which Virtue is
entitled, a peaceful, pastoral setting of trees
and streams, where Apollo plays his lyre and the
nine Muses listen attentively. Such a world
represents not an escape from the fray, but a
reward for work well done. In a way, then,
Pope's assertion that he is Virtue's friend (121)
entitles him to the reward next described (122-
32), his grotto, something deserved after "avoir
bien travaillé." And the precedent implicit in
the pictorial context implies not that Pope is escaping from a battle that has become too rough,
but rather that he has completed his battle, has
come away with victory, and for his pains is entitled to this retreat, a state *achieved*, a state
that represents a positive accomplishment.

When Pope states that he is above "all the
distant Din that World can keep" (123), he is
depending on us to recognize that he has attained
just such an exalted state; in the next verse
paragraph, he pursues the point:

> *Envy* must own, I live among the Great,
> No Pimp of Pleasure, and no Spy of State,
> With Eyes that pry not, Tongue that ne'er re-
>   peats,
> Fond to spread Friendships, but to cover Heats,
> To help who want, to forward who excel;

> This, all who know me, know; who love me, tell;
> And who unknown defame me, let them be
> Scriblers or Peers, alike are *Mob* to me.
>   (133-40)

This might to some seem an exaggerated claim, for
Pope has dehumanized his adversaries and collec-
tively lumped them into a lowly mob; Pope is in
a higher sphere, "among the Great," condescend-
ingly looking down. But this is not merely
self-aggrandizement, or hyperbole, or undue condescension on Pope's part. The pictorial context of Virtue sets a precedent for his attitude
of superiority and immunity to the mob, thereby
reinforcing his stance and adding authority to
his claims. First of all, it is the very nature
of Virtue to be the object of envious attacks; to
quote the title of another van Veen emblem (p.
17), "La Vertu est le But des Traits de l'Envie."
The text accompanying the emblem puts the case
even more strongly: "le propre de l'envie/
Est d'avoir la Vertu pour l'objet de ses traicts."
Second, and even more important, it is also in
the very nature of Virtue to be immune to those
attacks and to be above the attackers. By "above,"
I mean literally as well as figuratively, for
the emblem just mentioned depicts Virtue seated
upon an elevated platform or pedestal, surrounded by six gesticulating members of the
mob, yet quite unconcerned, immune, and imperturbable, as Pope claims to be now that he is
apart from "all the distant Din that World can
keep."[19] The fact that Pope is subject to Envy's stings is, therefore, almost an inevitable
consequence of his alignment with Virtue; his
immunity to those attacks and his superiority
to the attackers are not unjustified claims, but
equally inevitable consequences of being "arm'd
for *Virtue*."

Many scholars have demonstrated what Pope
achieves by adding the weight of various authorities to his own arguments in "Satire II, i."[20]
Most obviously, the very act of imitating Horace
provides Pope with a respected precedent that
bolsters, and dignifies, his own claims, but

it doesn't stop at Horace; Pope also brings in
Dryden, Boileau, Juvenal, and Persius, each of
whom he cites, quotes, or echoes, and each of
whom is made to add his voice to Pope's own.
Thus, Pope cleverly manages to make his case seem
not an eccentric, peevish, individualistic outburst, but rather part of a historically recurring,
and hence sanctioned, pattern of behavior. My
point is that the pictorial tradition is no less
an authority, and that Pope's use of the pictorial
serves in much the same way as his use of classical
and contemporary precedents. An audience aware
of his pictorial context and willing to respond
to it will more readily accept Pope's claims of
strength, will more readily be able to see Pope as
strong, courageous, manly, victorious, as he
claims to be, and will be more readily inclined
to interpret his pictured retreat as a superior
state apart from the mundane and petty realities,
rather than a dreamed-for escape from a battle
Pope will ultimately lose.

Furthermore, an audience aware of this
pictorial context can perhaps see other Pope
poems in a new light as well, particularly certain poems of the 1730s where Pope is vigorously defending himself or where he is attacking
the world for its vicious and venal ways--where,
in short, he is concerned with the conflict between virtue and vice. He does not see these
merely as abstract principles, nor should we.
Notice how, for example, in Pope's "Epistle I, i"
(1738), it is not just the obvious opposition
of virtue to vice that intrigues Pope, but rather
the actual plight of choosing between the two, a
plight each man must face:

> Here, Wisdom calls: "Seek Virtue first!
>   be bold!
> "As Gold to Silver, Virtue is to Gold."
> There, London's voice: "Get Mony, Mony still!
> "And then let Virtue follow, if she will."
>   (77-80)

For Pope, the choice has been made: he is
"Still true to Virtue" (30), still fighting her
battles (27-29). But in the above passage
we are at the crossroads, watching mankind, like
Hercules, decide between Vice, which is now all
London and her venal song, and the other "song"
which "every child...will sing,"

> "Virtue, brave boys! 'tis Virtue makes a King."
> ....
>   And say, to which shall our applause belong,
> This new Court jargon, or the good old song?
>   (91-92, 97-98)

Even in a poem as different in genre and tone
from these satires as is the "Essay on Man,"
Pope can use this kind of pictorialism, and can
use it with a somewhat different emphasis. If,
in reading the second epistle, we put aside for
a moment our concern for this as a philosophical
document that is part of the theoretical treatises
of its age, can we not see behind this poem
another version of the Choice of Hercules motif?
Throughout, Pope describes man's predicament as
a choice between two things: he stands on the
"isthmus of a middle state" (3) and "hangs between"
(7) two alternative courses of action; he is
"Created half to rise, and half to fall" (15, and
we should bear in mind that in most of the Hercules
depictions, the path of Virtue is upward, often
to a temple at the top of a mountain, and that of
Vice is downward). Taking the preferred path,
the one that Pope in effect claims for himself in
the satires, is not all that easy:

>   Man's superior part
> Uncheck'd may rise, and climb from art to art:
> But when his own great work is but begun,
> What Reason weaves, by Passion is undone.
>   (39-42)

It is not easy because, given a "mixed Nature"
("Argument of the Second Epistle") ever tugging
him in both directions, man finds it difficult

to distinguish between Virtue and Vice; like
"light and shade" (208) in a painting, they

> oft so mix, the diff'rence is too nice
> Where ends the Virtue, or begins the Vice.
> (209-10)

Nonetheless, there is still a choice that has to
be made:

> Fools! who from hence into the notion fall,
> That Vice or Virtue there is none at all.
> If white and black blend, soften, and unite
> A thousand ways, is there no black or white?
> Ask your own heart, and nothing is so plain;
> 'Tis to mistake them, costs the time and pain.
> ....
> Virtuous and vicious ev'ry Man must be,
> Few in th' extreme, but all in the degree;
> The rogue and fool by fits is fair and wise,
> And ev'n the best, by fits, what they despise.
> 'Tis but by parts we follow good or ill,
> For, Vice or Virtue, Self directs it still.
> (211-16, 231-36)

Man's problem is that his built-in limitations
keep him from mounting (19) and soaring (23),
from taking the proper ascendant path of Virtue;
at times he cannot even see the path. Man is like
the Hercules in the Rubens painting who seems
about to give in to the charms of Vice. Pope
actually takes it a step further; given the
choice between these two, man is not as Herculean
as his superior part would have him be. Man is
inevitably "Virtuous and vicious," and, sad to say,
he is too often inclined to make the wrong choice:

> Vice is a monster of so frightful mien,
> As, to be hated, needs but to be seen;
> Yet seen too oft, familiar with her face,
> We first endure, then pity, then embrace.
> (217-20)

As these instances suggest, Pope can play with
the Choice of Hercules motif in two ways: he can
depict the consequences attendant upon the proper
choice, as he does in "Satire II, i"; or he can
turn things around and dwell on the other alternative, can show what happens when men embrace the
wrong goddess. As the "Epilogue to the Satires"
(1738) demonstrates, Pope can on occasion do both
these simultaneously. In Dialogue II, Pope dwells
on the consequences of aligning himself with
Virtue: as in "Satire II, i," Pope again wields
a "sacred Weapon" (212; see also 248); again he
claims, "I follow *Virtue*"; again Virtue radiates
light ("where she shines, I praise," 95); again
her force is irresistible--

> No Pow'r the Muse's Friendship can command;
> No Pow'r, when Virtue claims it, can with-
>   stand. (118-19)

--again she guarantees a fame lasting to eternity:

>   when diadem'd with Rays divine,
> Touch'd with the Flame that breaks from Vir-
>   tue's Shrine,
> Her Priestless Muse forbids the Good to dye,
> And ope's the Temple of Eternity. (232-25)

But if Virtue is victorious here, and if Pope
emerges with this kind of triumph, all is miti-
gated by the other dialogue where it is not
Virtue, but Vice who is seen to triumph:

> In golden Chains the willing World she [Vice]
>   draws,
> And hers the Gospel is, and hers the Laws:
> Mounts the Tribunal, lifts her scarlet head,
> And sees pale Virtue carted in her stead!
> Lo! at the Wheels of her Triumphal Car,
> Old *England*'s Genius, rough with many a Scar,
> Dragg'd in the Dust! his Arms hang idly round,
> His Flag inverted trails along the ground!
> Our Youth, all liv'ry'd o'er with foreign Gold,
> Before her dance; behind her crawl the Old!

> See thronging Millions to the Pagod run,
> And offer Country, Parent, Wife, or Son!
> Hear her black Trumpet thro' the Land proclaim,
> That "Not to be corrupted is the Shame."
>   (147-60)

This is a heavily emblematic passage, using the still familiar symbol of the triumphal chariot, a commonplace that many paintings and emblem books had made effective use of (Sambucus, for instance, in an emblem entitled "Voluptatis Triumphus," depicts Voluptas or Vice riding a horse-drawn victory chariot).[21] In effect, by portraying in one dialogue the triumph of Virtue, and in the other the triumph of Vice, Pope has it both ways; he asserts his optimistic hopes, and at the same time advances a pessimistic view of the world's accomplishments.

In all these poems the same pictorial tradition is at work; if we learn to "see" Pope as we have learned to "read" Hogarth (the literature-painting analogy, after all, works both ways),[22] we can better appreciate what Virtue represents, what being aligned with her implies, and we can more willingly accept some of Pope's claims. This is certainly the case in "Satire II, i," but we can go on from there. Pope elsewhere can invert the motif, can assign triumph to the wrong goddess, and to feel the impact of that most fully, we must be aware of the basic emblem Pope is inverting, as we are aware of the various epic authors, from Homer through Milton, whom Pope turns inside out in *The Dunciad*. To see things in such a light is to discover that poems of disparate genres and quite different tones can be considered variations of a single theme, a theme that Virtue-Vice depictions had made a visual commonplace, that of man's having to choose between two opposing ways of life. Pope, like the painters and emblematists of his time, plays with this theme repeatedly, consistently picturing himself on the side of Virtue, with all that that implies, and seeing the world at large as leaning in the wrong direction.

POPE AND DEISM: A NEW ANALYSIS

G. Douglas Atkins

Ever since Crousaz's excoriation of Pope's theodicy in the *Essay on Man* three years after its publication the question of whether Pope was a deist has troubled scholars and commentators, though in fact Pope's "orthodoxy" was questioned as early as the *Essay on Criticism* in 1711. Despite Warburton's heroic and often misleading efforts and Pope's own specific denunciation of deists and their views in the *Dunciad*, the matter has long been and is still being argued, and more often than not Pope is still called a deist. In one of the most recent detailed analyses of the *Essay on Man* Martin Kallich tends to assume, rather than argue, that Pope was a deist.[1] In this regard, indeed, Kallich's view is the rule rather than the exception. It appears again and again, as in Peter Gay's brilliant work on the Enlightenment.[2] Was Pope a deist?

A number of problems often overlooked in discussions of this question complicate the possibility of a solution. Religious currents in the late seventeenth and early eighteenth centuries were extremely muddied; the line distinguishing

This essay first appeared in *Huntington Library Quarterly* 35 (1972), 257-78.

orthodoxy from heterodoxy in the period is obscure, and, indeed, as has often been pointed
out, the opprobrious label of deist was applied
promiscuously.[3] But even at times when religious
positions are more clearly distinguished, it is
difficult--and dangerous to try--to establish what
is orthodox. As Warburton said, "Orthodoxy is *my*
doxy; heterodoxy is *another man's* doxy."[4] Further,
in dealing with the history of ideas, as one must,
to some extent, in this case, it is essential to
find sufficient differentiae for the application
of the *Geistesgeschichte* to be valid; that is, it
is not enough merely to show parallels between an
author and a putative source or analogue: some
grounds for inclusion or exclusion must be determined. With Pope such an attempt involves, in
its own right, certain problems. Purpose or intention has to be considered, as does the genre
in which Pope is at the time writing, for his
attitudes seem to vary depending on whether he
is writing a poem for publication or a letter,
and in the latter instance his opinions sometimes
vary according to the person addressed. Failure
to recognize and take into account many of these
problems considerably diminishes, especially for
our purposes, the value of such a work as A.O.
Lovejoy's "The Parallel of Deism and Classicism."[5]
     Though for these and other reasons it may be
impossible to decide conclusively whether Pope
was a deist, this should not prevent an attempt
to consider the available evidence and reach a
conclusion about the *probability* of Pope's being
a deist. Except for the diatribes pro and con
by Pope's contemporaries, which I shall consider
below, the work on the problem has been sketchy
and usually secondary to other concerns. Perhaps for this reason it has tended toward uncrit-
ical acceptance of established views of the matter. Heretofore, no inclusive study has been
attempted of what Professor Friedman has called
"the vexed question of [Pope's] relation to
deism."[6]
     The attempt I shall make will be more ex-
tensive than Friedman's valuable essay, "Pope
and Deism," which deals only with a short section

of the later *Dunciad* and is concerned solely with
pointing out Pope's adverse criticism of deists
and deism in that poem. Although Maynard Mack's
comprehensive introduction to the *Essay on Man* in
the Twickenham edition is generally viewed as
authoritative, it obviously has not been successful in persuading scholars to accept the view of
Pope that Mack himself holds. In that introduction Professor Mack never directly confronts the
question of deism in Pope. But though he does
maintain that at the time of the *Essay* "Pope had
leanings toward the fashionable 'natural' religion of the day,"[7] he plays down the possibility
that Pope actually was a deist.

What I propose to do is to examine the question from all angles possible, assembling the
relevant information (including some evidence
hitherto unrecognized), and then attempt an ad-
judication. There are three kinds of evidence
to be examined: first, opinions on the problem,
second, statements directly declaring Pope's
connection with deism, and third, Pope's own
statements in the poems and the letters. How
substantial is the various evidence for deism in
Pope?

Were it not for Jean Pierre de Crousaz, there
might not be a question of deism in Pope; for the
charge, despite the supposed heterodoxy earlier,
rests mainly on the *Essay on Man*. Crousaz's denunciation of Pope, if it did not initiate the cries
of deism, certainly gave such views their momentum.[8] Before Crousaz's publications, in French,
in 1737 and 1738, English reaction to the poem
had generally been favorable.[9] Indeed, the *Weekly
Miscellany*, an orthodox and officious Anglican
organ, praised its poetry and its theology.[10]
In France the Jesuit critic René-Joseph Tourne-
mine approved the work, as did an official
Jesuit publication, *Mémoires de Trévoux*.[11] Moreover, it is doubtful that Pope would have showed
the poem to Bishop Berkeley if it had been
deistic.[12] But Crousaz, anxious to find heterodoxy and to eradicate it, pounced on Pope first
in *Examen de l'essai de M. Pope sur l'homme* and then in

*Commentaire sur la traduction en vers de M. l'Abbé du
Resnel, de l'essai de M. Pope sur l'homme.* Crousaz was
far from objective. He was at the time particularly intent on discrediting Leibnitz, and his
first essay reflects this desire, even to the
point of reading Pope as Leibnitzian.[13] Further,
his access to Pope in the first essay was through
Etienne de Silhouette's prose translation, which
was not faithful to the poet's thought. His later essay was based on the inaccurate translation
by the Abbé du Resnel, which garbled the doctrines
ridiculously. Despite this, Crousaz's efforts
were widely influential in France and England, an
influence due in a large measure to his impressive
reputation.

Yet in the years following 1738, years of
hostile Popiana, the *Essay on Man* was generally
left alone by the "dunces"--this despite the
dedication of the poem to a "bad man" (Bolingbroke). It is curious that the first furore
over the *Essay* was so short-lived. Were it not
for Crousaz's personal inclinations, that furore
might well never have arisen. A possible reason
for the relative infrequency of charges of heterodoxy at the time is that religious distinctions were not clearly made and that many presumably orthodox Christians actually believed and
said much the same that Pope did in the *Essay on
Man*.

Though the question was considered by Pope's
early commentators, including Dr. Johnson, the
charge of deism (made prominently, as we shall
see, by Pope's contemporaries) was not vigorously
revived until the Elwin-Courthope edition of the
poet's works. Elwin of course sought to discredit Pope in every way possible. It is almost ineluctable, for some reason, that those
with an axe to grind find deism in Pope. It is
hoped that the rest of the present paper, together
with Pattison's analysis of the Elwin-Courthope
methods and intentions,[14] will be a sufficient
reply to these calumniators.[15] Here we shall
say only that the Elwin-Courthope comments are
merely opinions steeped in prejudice. They are

distinctly inferior in awareness of materials, in
discrimination, and in objectivity to the work
of the last three or four decades.

Among the commentators on Pope through at
least the first quarter of the present century,
those with the surest knowledge of Pope and his
ideas were, as Sherburn points out, Spence and
Warton.[16] Judgment by these men on the question
of Pope and deism is exactly what we would like;
but unfortunately they merely pass on comments
by others concerning the matter. It is these
statements and others that are used as evidence
for Pope's being a deist. From them comes apparent support, for instance, for the claim that
Pope had merely versified Bolingbroke's *Fragments
or Minutes of Essays*. That Bolingbroke was himself
a deist cannot be denied, nor that he significantly influenced Pope, who acknowledges his
debt both in the poem and outside it.[17] The
extent of the influence is the question. The
extravagant claim noted above is, as Warburton
and Dr. Johnson early recognized, patently
false. In fact, as Maynard Mack has shown,[18] it
is chronologically impossible, on Bolingbroke's
own statement in the introductory letter to his
philosophical writings, for him to have influenced, in the manner he himself described, more
than part of the Fourth Epistle. Moreover, we
must remember that the assertion that Pope had in
the *Essay* merely versified an earlier prose
version by Bolingbroke was made in 1763 by a then
aged Lord Bathurst.[19] Though such rejoinders
hardly remove the charge of deism in Pope, it is
true that Pope's *Essay* failed to satisfy Bolingbroke, just as it did Crousaz. Bolingbroke
wrote to Swift, August 2, 1731, "You will not
understand by what I have said, that Pope will go
so deep into the argument, or carry it so far
as I have hinted."[20] In his philosophical writings, Bolingbroke stated that Pope's caution
would somehow save him from direct heterodoxy.[21]
Bolingbroke felt, according to Warburton, that
Pope did not understand the implications of his
own principles.[22] Is there any validity to Bol-

ingbroke's expressed views of Pope and the *Essay
on Man*? At this point in our inquiry, all we can
say with assurance is that Pope in this work does
something quite different from Bolingbroke in
his; whether it is the result of ignorance, evasiveness, or difference in intention remains to
be seen. That there are obvious differences in
their thought, as Maynard Mack and John Laird have
pointed out, cannot be denied.[23]
     More telling than Bolingbroke's statements and
supposed influence, perhaps, are comments by
contemporaries directly affirming Pope to be a
deist. As Elwin reports, Mrs. Mallet told General
Grimouard that Pope, Bolingbroke, and their
friends were "a society of pure deists."[24] Of
course, Mrs. Mallet's husband was foremost in the
Bolingbroke group which tried to discredit Pope
after his death; further, we have already remarked
on the promiscuous use of the epithet at this
time. There are other, similar comments, however.
Lord Chesterfield says that Pope "was a Deist,
believing in a future state: this he has often
owned himself to me."[25] Though Chesterfield was
never, apparently, an intimate of Pope, Lord
Lyttleton was, and he too maintained that Pope
had often avowed his deism to him.[26] The younger
Richardson reported, in a similar vein, that Pope
acknowledged that he had never thought of inter-
preting the *Essay on Man* as Warburton did until the
furore over its supposed fatalism and deistic
tendencies began.[27] Few readers would view the
poem as Warburton did, and Pope's alleged statement to the Richardsons in no way necessitates a
deistic interpretation; but the assertions of
Chesterfield and Lyttleton cannot be lightly dismissed. Though we must remember how easy it is
to misinterpret a speaker's intention (and Pope
had the habit of accommodating comments to the
person addressed), these statements remain as
evidence for deism in Pope. Whether they are
enough, whether opposing evidence outweighs
them, are questions we cannot answer until we
have completed our examination.
     Actually, of course, the charge of deism in
Pope rests mainly on the *Essay on Man*; it is pro-

bably fortunate that the charge centers on a poem,
for Pope seems to reveal himself more fully in
the poems than elsewhere. Among the more suspicious passages, according to commentators,[28]
are expressions of optimism such as I. 294 ("Whatever is, is right");[29] III. 147ff ("Nor think, in
Nature's State they blindly trod;/The state of
Nature was the reign of God"); III. 317-318
("Thus God and Nature link'd the gen'ral frame,/
And bade Self-love and Social be the same");
III. 305-306 ("For Modes of Faith, let grace-
less zealots fight;/His can't be wrong whose life
is in the right"); and IV. 331ff ("Slave to no
sect, who takes no private road,/But looks thro'
Nature, up to Nature's God"). Similarly, in the
short companion piece to the poem, the *Universal
Prayer* (termed by Pope's enemies the "deist's
prayer"), isolated statements are labeled deistic.[30] It is often such comments, taken out
of context, which are used to support the deistic charge.

Even if we overlook, as we must not do, the
falsification and injustice involved in this kind
of procedure, we can easily see that such beliefs
as we have quoted cannot be used to convict Pope
of heterodoxy--unless we are willing to include
in the indictment such generally assumed orthodox
Christians as Sir Thomas More, Bishop Butler,
Edmund Law, and the Cambridge Platonists.[31]
The basic optimism which permeates the *Essay* is
by no means limited to Pope or to deism; similar
optimism appears in Shaftesbury but also in
Archbishop King, Law, and Bishop Butler.[32] Nor
is the idea of the innocence and goodness of the
state of nature confined to Pope.[33] Further, the
identity of self-love and benevolence is prominent in Bishop Butler, for instance.[34] On the
relative triviality of confessional or dogmatic
differences one can point to Erasmus, whom Pope
closely echoes:

> We associate Christ and devotion with certain
> places, with forms of worship, with a mode of
> living and with certain ceremonies. We think

> he is lost who has changed a white robe for a
> black one, or who has changed his cowl for a
> cap, and then changes his place. I would ven-
> ture to say that great harm to Christian de-
> votion has come from those orders which are
> called religions, although they were perhaps
> at first founded in pious zeal. Then little
> by little they grew and broke up into thou-
> sands of divisions. . . . How much more is it
> in accordance with the teaching of Christ to
> regard the whole Christian world as one house
> and, so to speak, as one monastery, and to
> consider all men as fellow-canons and fellow-
> friars.[35]

Virtually ubiquitous in Pope's time was impatience
with doctrinal niceties, at least among the laity.
Even the clergy was not, however, exempt from
this impatience; note Swift's sermon "On the Trinity," for example. People were tired of abstruse
theological disputes, having been through the period of the Commonwealth, the Trinitarian Controversy, and the disputations of the "free-thinkers."
Thus, in 1719 Defoe apologizes for inserting a
theological note into his paper.[36] But even the
allegedly heterodox view that what ultimately
matters is right living turns out, on examination,
to be precisely the position held by the Cambridge
Platonists. Note this statement by Benjamin
Whichcote: "The state of religion lies in a good
mind and a good life, all else is about religion;
and men must not put the instrumental part of
religion for the state of religion."[37] Note too
Ralph Cudworth's assertion that no man will be
kept out of Heaven "if he had but an honest and
good heart."[38]
     Worthy of notice is the extent to which the
"orthodox" had taken the idea of the similarity,
if not identity, of religions and of the universality of salvation. The Florentine Circle,
Nicholas of Cusa in *De Pace Fidei*, Ficino in *De
Christiana Religione*, and the Oxford humanists
steadfastly held that *una est religio in ritum varie-
tate*.[39] Indeed, belief in the universality of
salvation, indicated in Pope's lines, is a major
tenet of the Cambridge Platonists. As Cassirer

has said, "Undisturbed by all suspicions of the
sanctification of heathendom, they maintain that
he who bears within the true spirit of Christ,
even though he has never heard His name, deserves
far more to be called a Christian than those who
know and profess all the articles of faith in
Christendom, and yet do not exemplify and realize
them in their lives."[40] According to the Cambridge
Platonists, the angry zeal of a Christian is less
godlike than the goodwill of a heathen.

Further, as Friedman has demonstrated, the
deists in handling natural religion argued a
priori, reasoning "downward" from supposedly
self-evident first principles, deducing "the being and attributes of God *a priori* from 'the nature
and reason of things' and then from God's attributes [deducing] man's religious and moral duties."[41] The supposedly orthodox, on the other
hand, employed the a posteriori method, from observation of order and design in nature to "Nature's Cause," with the being and attributes of
God inferred from common experience. Apriority
cannot, it would seem, differentiate deism from
Christianity, for the Cambridge Platonists and
other "philosophizing divines" used this method.[42]
Moreover, in the *Dunciad* (IV. 465-472), Pope attacks those--apparently the deists--who "take the
high Priori Road,/And reason downward, till [they]
doubt of God."

As yet, then, we have found nothing peculiarly
deistic or even necessarily heterodox in Pope's
statements.[43] But more important, in the consideration of our problem, than particular
statements are fundamental views and assumptions
and the overall meaning and effect of the poem.
To decide whether Pope was a deist we need differentiae, some points that will serve for differentiation between deism and other forms of
thought, including Christianity. In the application of the history of ideas, such differentiation is all too frequently lacking, and one ends
with indiscriminate results like Lovejoy's "The
Parallel of Deism and Classicism" and Nancy K.
Lawlor's recent article on the *Essay on Man*. What

points and positions are peculiar to deism? Some
years ago R.S. Crane wrote that "the essence of
deism. . . lay in its radical assertion, against
Christianity, of the principle that any religion
necessary for salvation must be one that has always and everywhere been known to men."[44] According to E. Graham Waring, "Natural religion
contains all that is true in revealed religion;
where the latter differs, the differences are
either morally insignificant or superstitious.
This last position may most strictly be termed
'deism.'"[45] After quoting Crane's definition
of deism given above, Douglas H. White continues
as follows: "In order to show the relationship
of deism to natural religion, I define a deist
as one who espouses the *sufficiency* of natural
religion. An Anglican, therefore, who defended
the *excellence* of natural religion but did not
hold it to be sufficient for man's moral needs
would not be a deist."[46]

That the deists maintain the sufficiency of
natural religion, which "has always and everywhere been known to men," is apparent as soon
as we turn to the deistic writings themselves.
The necessity for universality is demonstrated
in this comment by "A.W." in "Of Natural Religion, as opposed to Divine Revelation," addressed
in the printed 1693 version to Charles Blount:
"It has been demanded of me, Whether I should be
convinc'd of my Opinion, and admit of supernatural
Religion in case the Gospel (*i.e.*) a supernatural
Religion had been promulgated to all the World?
I answer'd, I should."[47] Like so many Christian
thinkers, including the Cambridge Platonists,
the deists did not wish to believe that God would
condemn virtuous heathens or those who had been
denied access to the truths "revealed" in
Scripture. Too, they were suspicious that various
doctrines and ceremonies endorsed by revealed
religion were merely fabrications of a self-
seeking priesthood. The most reasonable approach,
then, was to fall back on natural religion,
specifically on the Five Catholic Articles, examples of the *"notitiae communes"* of Lord Herbert
of Cherbury, the first English deist.

This sufficiency for salvation of the natural
is at the expense of revealed or supernatural
religion. According to the deists, revealed religion, specifically Christianity, is simply a restatement of the Five Catholic Articles, along
with certain corruptions and various additions resulting from superstition and priestcraft. In
Christianity as Old as Creation, Matthew Tindal, whom
Pope attacked, says in response to the question
of why he favors deism:

> Because, if the eternal Reason of Things is
> the *supreme obligation*, must not that, if there's
> any difference between it and External Reve-
> lation, take place? And must not that Rule,
> which can annul any other, be not only the
> supreme, but the sole Rule? for as far as men
> take any other rule, so far they lose of their
> Perfection, by ceasing to be govern'd by this
> Rule, in Conformity to the Nature, and in Imi-
> tation of the perfect Will of God. And if
> this most perfect Will of God is to be thus
> known, can things that have another Original,
> and are of a later Date, be any Part of the
> most perfect Will of God? Or can the eternal
> Reason of things extend to things that do not
> belong to Reason; or, as Divines love to speak,
> are above Reason?[48]

Apparent in Tindal's statement is another
important element in deism. If natural religion
alone is sufficient for salvation, it is because
man has within him the capacity for discovering
those necessary truths, the tenets of natural
religion. Reason is that ability;[49] it is also
the test by which claims to truth are judged.
According to Tindal, expressing views representative of the deistic position generally, "Whatever
is true by Reason, can never be false by Revelation."[50] In a similar vein Charles Blount writes,
"What proceeds from common Reason we know to be
true, but what proceeds from Faith we only believe."[51] Elsewhere he says, "And Reason being
the first relation of God, is first to be believed, not depending on doubtful fact without
us, but full of its own light shining always in

us."[52]   It is, says Tindal, "our Reason which
makes us the Image of God."[53]
   Thus for the deists reason supersedes revelation. In *Christianity as Old as the Creation*, when
his interlocutor points out that "we Christians
have two supreme, independent Rules, *Reason* and
Revelation; and both require an absolute Obedience,"
Tindal replies:

I can't see how that is possible; for if you are
to be govern'd by the latter, That supposes you
must take every thing on Trust; or meerly because it's said by those, for whose Dictates You
are to have an implicit Faith: For to examine
into the Truth of what they say, is renouncing
their Authority; as one the contrary, if Men are
to be govern'd by their Reason, they are not to
admit any thing further than as they see it reasonable. To suppose both consistent, is to suppose it consistent to take, and not to take,
things on Trust.[54]

   Again divines, then, who urged a necessary
distinction between things above and contrary to
reason,[55] the deists argued that the Gospel contains nothing "above reason." The subtitle of
John Toland's famous book is indicative of the
deist view: *Christianity Not Mysterious: or, A Treatise
Shewing, that There Is Nothing in the Gospel Contrary to
Reason, nor above It: and that No Christian Doctrine Can
Be Properly Call'd a Mystery* (1696). On this point
Tindal echoes Toland.[56] One of the best sustained and most important discussions, other than
Toland's, of this ever-present concern in deistic
literature is in Anthony Collins' *An Essay concerning the Use of Reason* (1707). Collins' position is
apparent, I think, in this succinct and carefully
worded statement: "all Propositions consider'd as
Objects of Assent or Dissent, are adequately
divided into Propositions agreeable or contrary
to Reason; and there remains no third Idea under
which to rank them, as will appear more plainly
by examining the Senses assignable to the words
above Reason, which are applied to some Propositions,

as contradistinguish'd from Propositions agreeable to, and contrary to Reason."[57] A great many
things exist of which we have no idea, Collins
grants, but he argues that there is no ground for
applying a distinction between "above reason" and
"contrary to reason" when referring to objects of
man's understanding. What "we do not perceive by
the mediation of Ideas," Collins says somewhat
sarcastically, "may, if you please, be call'd
above Reason as a thing unknown to us, but not as
an Object of the Mind about which we may imploy
our Facultys: and 'tis to things as Objects of
the Mind, that the Distinction of above and contrary to Reason is [falsely] apply'd."[58] Thus,
Collins neither believes nor disbelieves in the
doctrine of the Trinity, frequently cited by
divines as one of those matters "above reason,"
for the terms of the proposition must be understood before we can assent or dissent. No
"particular doctrine can be assented to, where we
have no Ideas to the Terms that are suppos'd to
express it."[59]

Now, I believe, we have important criteria for
determining whether the *Essay on Man* is deistic. As
John Orr has said,[60] and as is implied in the
statements of Crane, Waring, and White quoted
above, one's position on revelation is the ultimate criterion for distinguishing deists from the
orthodox. Another trustworthy differentia, obviously, is what one believes about reason's
ability. In the words of E.C. Mossner, "the one
prime assumption of the validity and sufficiency
of reason to the discovery of ultimate truth" is
characteristic of the deists.[61] If, then, one
holds reason to be incapable of discovering
ultimate truth, he cannot be a deist. Let us
consider the *Essay on Man* in relation to these
questions of reason and revelation.

For at least one recent writer on the poem
(Lawlor), Pope's failure to claim the necessity
for supernatural revelation is a sign of deism.
Is this valid? Whereas it is true that in the
Essay on Man Pope's aim and scheme keep him from
mentioning revelation, he does leave the door
open for it. As Maynard Mack says, the *Essay*

"resembles in that respect those collections of
eighteenth-century sermons in which a first
series in defence of religion on natural grounds
is combined with a second series in defence of
revelation. Pope has telescoped the two and
submerged the second."[62] It was indeed common
for divines to treat of natural religion in the
body of a theological work and then to add a saving appendix--or perhaps second volume--on revealed religion. A Scottish clergyman, T. Haly-
burton, complained that in many sermons "heathen
morality has been substituted in the room of
Gospel holiness. And ethics by some have been
preached instead of the Gospel of Christ."[63]
Referring to Pope, Thornton is emphatic: "Pope's
method is much the same as that his Church employs. In the course of studies designed for
all clerics, natural theology is the proper introduction to dogmatic theology and revelation.
This procedure grounds theological studies in
their natural soil, in reason and reasonableness.
It is equally interesting that a tract *De Homine*
is one of the divisions of theology."[64]
     On the question of Pope's position on reason
we can be even more certain. Surprisingly, considering the large number of works opting for
deism in Pope, we find him clearly opposed to
the deistic belief in the sufficiency of reason.
Indeed, the *Essay on Man* is strewn with passages
dealing precisely with the insufficiency of reason. The mind is said to be unable to help us
mend our ways (II. 153-154), not a guide but a
guard (II. 162-163), by no means sufficient (III.
191-194). At various points throughout the poem
Pope indicates that, contrary to deistic belief,
man is incapable of discovering many truths: for
example, I. 147-164, and IV. 260-261: "Tell (for
You can) what is it to be wise?/'Tis but to know
how little can be known."
     In stressing the limitations of reason, Pope
argues that knowledge is limited to the senses:
"Say first, of God above, or Man below,/What can
we reason, but from what we know?" (I. 17-18).
Referring to the Platonists, who go beyond the
senses, Pope writes:

Go, soar with Plato to th'empyreal sphere,
To the first good, first perfect, and first
    fair;
Or tread the mazy round his follow'rs trod,
And quitting sense call imitating God.
    (II. 23-26)

Thus he differs from the deists, who hold
that reason is superior to sense. To quote
William Wollaston: *"In a word,* no man doth, or can
pretend to believe his senses, when he has a
reason against it: which is an irrefragable
proof, that reason is above sense and controlls
it."[65] Further, whereas the deists maintain, in
Toland's words, that "'tis from [reason] that
we are accounted Men,"[66] Pope argues that reason is not the principal characteristic of man:
"Two Principles in human nature reign;/Self-love,
to urge, and Reason, to restrain" (II. 53-54) and
"'Tis but by parts we follow good or ill,/For,
Vice or Virtue, Self directs it still" (II. 235-
236).
    In the passage with the fullest expression of
this skepticism concerning reason, Pope tells
what is the "unerring guide"--instinct:

Whether with Reason, or with Instinct blest,
Know, all enjoy that pow'r which suits them
    best;
To bliss alike by that direction tend,
And find the means proportion'd to their end.
Say, where full Instinct is th'unerring guide,
What Pope or Council can they need beside?
Reason, however able, cool at best,
Cares not for service, or but serves when prest,
Stays 'till we call, and then not often near;
But honest Instinct comes a volunteer;
Sure never to o'er-shoot, but just to hit,
While still too wide or short is human Wit;
Sure by quick Nature happiness to gain,
Which heavier Reason labours at in vain.
This too serves always, Reason never long;
One must go right, the other may go wrong.
See then the acting and comparing pow'rs
One in their nature, which are two in ours,

And Reason raise o'er Instinct as you can,
In this 'tis God directs, in that 'tis Man.
   (III. 79-98)

It is important to recognize, and emphasize,
that in diminishing reason and elevating instinct, Pope is not professing a kind of Shaftes-
buryanism that has also been called deism. Man,
Pope says, is characterized by self-love. The
virtue man is capable of does not come from within himself but depends rather on God and nature:

Thus Nature gives us (let it check our pride)
The virtue nearest to our vice ally'd;
Reason the byass turns to good from ill,
And Nero reigns a Titus, if he will.
   (II. 195-198)

Instinct reveals the workings of God: "And Reason raise o'er Instinct as you can,/In this 'tis
God directs, in that 'tis Man."
   As Robert W. Rogers has written, "To Pope
human character is a dual achievement of the Deity
and man. The Deity fixes the capacities of the
individual, prescribing the limits within which
he may act; and the Deity insures the good of
the whole, no matter what man makes of man."[67]
In Pope's own words: "God, in the nature of each
being, founds/Its proper bliss, and sets its
proper bounds" (III. 109-110). For Pope God
appears to be very much present and active in
the world He created. But as deism evolved, God
became increasingly more remote, transcendent,
and abstract.
   There are other, though less important, criteria
that distinguish Pope from deists. Among these is
the matter of faith, which, unlike the deists,
Pope takes quite seriously, as the *Essay on Man*,
IV. 341-352, indicates. Certainly, too, if Pope
had been a deist he would have wasted no opportunity to lambaste the priesthood for imposing
on the laity (out of desire for self-aggrandizement) various rites, ceremonies, and doctrines,
and in general for corrupting religion. Hatred

of the priesthood, as Peter Gay has said[68] and as
Leslie Stephen and John Orr have chronicled, is
prominent throughout deistic writings, from Lord
Herbert to Blount to Toland, Collins, Tindal,
Woolston, and others. The deists' position on
the priesthood is too well known to need detailing here; the titles of such prominent deistic
tracts as Collins' *Priestcraft in Perfection* (1710)
and Thomas Woolston's *A Free Gift to the Clergy; or,
The Hireling Priests* (1722) suggest the antipathy
the deists everywhere so vigorously expressed.
And whereas it is true that Pope took occasional
swipes at priests, it is equally apparent that
he was far from the hatred felt by the deists.
The seventeenth and eighteenth centuries were,
of course, highwater marks of abuse of the clergy,
if not of downright anticlericalism. Aversion to
the clergy is frequent, prominent, and vigorous
in Dryden,[69] who was not a deist. Even Swift,
himself a clergyman, was not above an occasional
jab at others among the clergy. Pope, though, is
mild in his "attacks." He notes, for instance,
the clergy's penchant for dullness (*Dunciad*, II.
387ff), drink (*Essay on Man*, IV. 202), and avarice
(*Epilogue to the Satires*, Dialogue I, 161) but hardly
goes further. Moreover, there are frequent but
unused opportunities for Pope to indulge in the
kind of spleen common to the deists, as in the
Essay on Man, III. 147ff. Further, in the *Dunciad*
he writes sneeringly of precisely this deistic
hatred of priests: "Toland and Tindal, prompt at
priests to jeer,/Yet silent bow'd to Christ's No
kingdom here" (II. 399-400; II. 367-368 in the
1728 version).
       Of course, no discussion of the question of
Pope and deism can be thorough or convincing
without close and careful attention to what it is
about Pope in general and the *Essay on Man* in
particular that has led to the charges of deism--
excluding those charges which were attempts to
discredit or simply to find fault. In reading the
Essay on Man, it seems to me, one feels that Pope
is concerned with man's place in the created order
and with the possibilities open to him--with,
as he himself says, vindicating the ways of God

to man, or showing that what God does is good.
The emphasis is clearly on man, on examination of
human nature; the poem confines itself to the moral, rather than the theological, realm.   Though
reference to revelation does not appear, there is
not the slightest criticism of revealed religion.
In the argument of the poem, revealed religion as
a topic simply has no place; it is irrelevant.
Moreover, as far as can be determined the poem
is free of all dogma, of all sectarian creeds.
Pope's comments in "The Design" to the poem are
completely consonant with the work itself. He
notes that there "are not many certain truths in
this world," but that study of the "large, open,
and perceptible parts" will be more beneficial
than disputes over minor points.   He concludes,
"If I could flatter myself that this Essay has
any merit, it is in steering betwixt the extremes
of doctrines seemingly opposite, in passing over
items utterly unintelligible, and in forming a
temperate yet not *inconsistent*, and a *short* yet not
imperfect system of Ethics."[70]   It seems clear,
and should be clearer below, that Pope's purpose
in the *Essay on Man* was to find a common ethical
ground for all religious sects--to steer between
Catholicism and Anglicanism, for example, and
find the principles of conduct on which *all*
could agree, an objective that Pope of course
shared with the deists.   In doing so, Pope was
obviously vulnerable to the charge of deism, so
frequently brought against him.   But Pope looks
for universals, I think, not because he was a
deist but because he simply wanted to avoid
sectarian particulars and the trouble they had
always caused and would very likely continue to
cause.   To talk of revelation, then, would have
immediately involved him in particular doctrines
and creeds.
    If we turn away from the poem itself, we can
begin to see that the antisectarianism in Pope
is very strong; and I suggest that it accounts,
at least to a considerable extent, for the misinterpretation which has produced the charge of
deism.   In considering this line of thought in
Pope we shall also find further grounds for

doubting that he was a deist. Throughout Pope
we find this opposition to sectarianism. As early
as 1711 he was accused of heterodoxy because of
statements in the *Essay on Criticism*, especially in
II. 396-397: "(Thus *Wit*, like *Faith*, by each Man
is apply'd/To *one small Sect*, and All are *damn'd
beside*)." In the famous letter to Atterbury (November 20, 1717), rejecting the bishop's invitation to join the Anglican Church, Pope writes, "And
after all, I verily believe your Lordship and I
are both of the same religion, if we were thoroughl
understood by one another; and that all honest
and reasonable Christians would be so, if they did
but talk enough together every day; and had nothing
to do together, but to serve God and live in peace
with their neighbour." He continues:

> In my politicks, I think no further than how
> to preserve the peace of my life, in any govern-
> ment under which I live; nor in my religion,
> than to preserve the peace of my conscience in
> any Church with which I communicate. I hope
> all churches and all governments are so far of
> God, as they are rightly understood, and
> rightly administered: and where they are, or
> may be wrong, I leave it to God alone to mend
> or reform them; which whenever he does, it must
> be by greater instruments than I am. I am not
> a Papist, for I renounce the temporal invasions
> of the Papal power, and detest their arrogated
> authority over Princes, and States. I am a Ca-
> tholick, in the strictest sense of the word. .
> . . In a word, the things I have always wished
> to see are not a Roman Catholick, or a French
> Catholick, or a Spanish Catholic, but a true
> Catholic.[71]

In a letter to Viscount Harcourt, May 6, 1723, he
tells "how different I am from what a reputed Papist is. . . *if to be a Papist be to profess & hold many
such Tenets of faith as are ascrib'd to Papists, I am not
a Papist.*"[72] In such letters there is no reason
to doubt Pope's sincerity concerning sects. Further, he explicitly condemns aspects of his own
church, as in the *Essay on Criticism*, II. 685-696,
and variously in the letters.[73]

But Pope never left the Catholic Church; he
refused to do so.[74] The spirit of the censures
of sects, and even of Catholicism, is like that
of the great antisectarian Erasmus, whom Pope
profoundly admired. In a letter to Caryll, June
18, 1711, defending his statements in the *Essay on
Criticism*, Pope said, "I will set before me that
excellent example of that great man and great
saint, Erasmus, who in the midst of calumny pro-
ceeded with all the calmness of innocence, the
unrevenging spirit of primitive Christianity."[75]
In the poem he had written of Erasmus as follows:

> At length, *Erasmus*, that *great, injur'd* Name,
> (The *Glory* of the Priesthood, and the *Shame!*)
> *Stemm'd* the *wild Torrent* of a *barb'rous Age,*
> And drove those *Holy Vandals* off the Stage.
>   (II. 693-696)

The basis for Pope's antisectarianism probably
lies in his Roman Catholicism and the situation
of Catholics at the time, which makes his fidelity
to that church, however nominal, all the more
significant. After the revolution of 1688--despite
William's personal aversion to persecution--not
only did the penal laws of Elizabeth and her
successors, designed to root out Catholicism, remain in force, but even more stringent laws were
enacted. The relative ease of James's reign
was abruptly ended. It should be enough to point
out, without documenting particulars of the legal
harassment, that Catholics paid heavy fines for
recusancy and were forced to conceal their assets,
vest property titles in alien hands, and live
outside London at inconvenient times. There was
also the denial of a university education. For
a man with Pope's personality and ambitions, always desirous of public favor, Catholicism was
in a particularly unfortunate state. Catholics
were always subject to ridicule and various in-
sinuations; Grub Street was a constant annoyance
for Pope, who told Atterbury, "It is certain, all
the beneficial circumstances of life, and all the
shining ones, lie on the part you would invite
me to."[76] Spence notes Pope's financial plight

and reports him as saying, early in his career,
that this condition was severe: "I had then [no
money]--not even to buy books."[77]   Yet Pope refused to leave the Catholic Church.

It is natural, I think, that a man reared in
persecution for his religion might later rebel
against the kind of sectarianism responsible for
it.   There is also philosophical justification--
in at least two senses--for this liberalism in
Pope.   He told Atterbury in 1717 that at fourteen
he began reading the controversies of the churches.
"I warm'd my head with them, and the consequence
was, that I found my self a Papist and a Protestant by turns, according to the last book I read.
I am afraid most Seekers are in the same case,
and when they stop, they are not so properly converted, as outwitted."[78]   Further, Pope knew the
antisectarian views of Erasmus and of the Cambridge Platonists, whom he read.   (The extent of
the considerable influence of Erasmus on Pope
has never been documented, nor has the not in-
considerable significance, for the poet, of the
Cambridge group.)   And whereas Pope had before
him the plight of his own tutor, Thomas Deane
(who was imprisoned, pilloried, and forced to
flee the mob of 1688 for his faith),[79] he had
also the geniality he had found at Binfield,
where there were many Catholics but also many
Separatists and a real spirit of toleration.[80]

Given Pope's great hunger for public acceptance and favor and the exclusion and persecution
in his background, it is hard to believe that he
would have wished to be a deist.   Deism too meant
regular denunciation--from the pulpit, in the press
in pamphlets, and elsewhere.   As Mossner says,
"The name of deist became a fashionable bogey
indicative of evil character.   Never in England
did the deist wear the badge of respectability."[81]
There was more than social obloquy.   Although
the Common Law decision of 1676 and the Blasphemy
Act of 1698 were not often resorted to, the
threat was nevertheless present.   That this
threat was not empty is indicated in the burnings
of the books of Toland and others and in the
pillorying and imprisonment of Woolston in 1730
and Annet in 1762, as well as in other actions
against deists.[82]

Of course, it is possible to turn this argument around and maintain that Pope declined to
become a convert to Anglicanism, not because of
fidelity to the Catholic Church, but because he
was at heart a deist.[83] Similarly, it could be--
and indeed has been--argued that the absence of
revelation in the *Essay on Man* is the deistic
trick of obliqueness or evasiveness. The only
way to answer is to point to the large amount of
evidence which makes acceptance of such arguments
all but impossible.

One final bit of evidence remains to be considered. This is the hitherto unnoticed fact
that Pope attacked deists and their beliefs
throughout his career. When Friedman wrote on
Pope and deism over twenty years ago, he dealt
only with a few lines of the later *Dunciad* (IV.
459-492) and failed to note the other, similar
attacks. Of the utmost importance here is the
time sequence. Were there only one such attack,
namely, the later *Dunciad,* Pope's repudiation of
deism would be less convincing than it in fact is.
One could argue either that by 1743 Pope's views
had changed or that, conscious of the ticklish
situation and desirous of the public's favor,
Pope was trying to extricate himself from implications of heterodoxy, whether or not he actually
held such views. But in fact Pope was denigrating
deists much closer to the time when the *Essay on
Man* was written. In 1737, in *The Sixth Epistle of
the First Book of Horace Imitated*, he wrote:

> But art thou one, whom new opinions sway,
> One, who believes as Tindal leads the way,
> Who Virtue and a Church alike disowns,
> Thinks that but words, and this but brick and
>   stones? (II. 63-66)

Here Pope's contempt is not aimed solely at
particular deists but also at their beliefs. The
objection brought against Pope's 1743 repudiation
could of course be made here, yet in neither the
Dunciad nor the Horatian imitation do the attacks
appear to be carefully calculated attempts to
ward off criticism. Instead, they are unobtrusive,

designed apparently for the immediate poetic purposes and nothing more. They are too matter-of-
fact and nonchalant to be more than the natural
expression of views long and firmly held.

That this is so is further attested by Pope's
comments long before the *Essay on Man* and the
charges of deism. Opposition to both Socinianism
and deism is apparent as early as 1711, from the
slurs in the *Essay on Criticism*: "The following
Licence of a Foreign Reign/Did all the Dregs of
bold *Socinus* drain" (ll. 544-545) and "Encourag'd
thus, Witt's *Titans* brav'd the Skies,/And the
Press groan'd with Licenc'd *Blasphemies*" (ll. 552-
553)--"Witt's Titans" signifying, as the Twickenham editors note,[84] deists. Further, the same
attack that appeared in the thirties and forties
occurs in the 1728 *Dunciad*. The digs are explicit:
"Toland and Tindal, prompt at Priests to jeer,/
Yet silent bow'd to Christ's No kingdom here"
(II. 367-368; repeated in the 1743 *Dunciad*, II.
399-400) and, in the voice of "the great Father
to the greater Son":

> But Fate with Butchers plac'd thy priestly
>   Stall,
> Meek modern faith to murder, hack, and mawl:
> And bade thee live, to crown Britannia's
>   praise,
> In Toland's, Tindal's, and in Woolston's days.
>   Thou too, great Woolston! here exalt thy
>   throne,
> And prove, no Miracles can match thy own.
>   (III. 205-210)

Thus the slurs on deists do not occur as a
result of the controversy over the *Essay on Man*.
On the contrary, Pope's views appear to be rather
consistent from 1711 through 1743. To argue still
that Pope was a deist commits us to one of two
possible positions, neither of which is defens-
ible: either Pope was willfully deceptive all
along or he became a deist, probably under Bolingbroke's influence in the early thirties, and
then by 1737 either abandoned those views or
falsified his true sentiments. At this point,

the wisest course is to employ Occam's Razor.

That Pope's thought involves elements common to the deists cannot be denied, for deism contains elements prominent in a great number of religious and philosophical positions. But clearly Pope condemned the principles, practices, and proponents of deism. Just as clearly, Pope fails to meet the criteria that would establish him as a deist. The point is that we must do what Pope himself did as early as the *Essay on Criticism*: we must carefully discriminate between his own liberalism, particularly his universalism and antisectarianism, and other forms of thought, including deism. This distinction can easily be blurred, especially when Grub Street hacks, and others with various axes to grind, deliberately set out to blur it. But as I have tried to show, the distinction is real. Careful attention to the various kinds of evidence must lead one to conclude, I think, that it is highly improbable that Pope was a deist.

ON THE LITERARY BACKGROUND OF THE *ESSAY ON MAN*:
A NOTE ON POPE AND LUCRETIUS

Bernhard Fabian

I

Pope's *Essay on Man* is usually placed among
his Horatian poems. This view is supported by
Pope's "prophetic" statement that after finishing the *Dunciad* he intended to write only Horatian epistles. The "system of ethics" of which
the *Essay on Man* was originally conceived to be a
part was to be carried out in the Horatian manner,[1] and unquestionably the work can be read
with Horace as backdrop; Reuben Arthur Brower
has demonstrated this possibility brilliantly.[2]
It is not my intention to challenge the fea-
sibility of this approach. Pope had a strong
affinity with Horace, and many characteristics
of the *Essay on Man* are given their specific profile by this Horatian background. The question
which I would like to ask is rather: Is Horace
sufficient? Does a "Horatian" reading adequately reveal the range of allusions and connotations of this text, which was written under the
premises of *imitatio* as an art form?

This essay first appeared in German, as "Zum literarischen Hintergrund des *Essay on Man*:
Eine Notiz zu Pope und Lukrez," in *Studien zur Englischen und amerikanischen Sprache und
Literatur*, ed. Paul G. Buchloh (Neümunster: Karl Wachholtz, 1973), pp. 176-187. It has
been translated by Kenneth Larson.

The answer can be found in Pope's correspondence. Lord Bathurst inquired about the *Essay on
Man* with an allusion to Lucretius: "When your
mind has shot through the flaming limits of the
universe, send me some account of the new discoveries."[3] Pope himself characterized the *Essay on Man* as a poem in the Lucretian manner:
"Whether I can proceed in the same grave march
like Lucretius, or must descend to the gayeties
of Horace, I know not."[4] And Bolingbroke,Pope's
philosophical mentor, made clear to him the difference between a philosophical treatise and a
philosophical poem based on Lucretius.[5]
It thus seems that it is not sufficient to
regard Horace as the sole background of the *Essay on Man*. The poem, at least according to the
author's own conception and that of his circle,
also implies *De Rerum Natura* as a text of reference. If a Horatian context can be inferred from
Pope's understanding of the work, this same understanding should lead one to apply a Lucretian context as well.[6] The following pages,
limited to the beginning of the first epistle,
represent such an attempt.

II

The beginning of the *Essay on Man* in its pre-
sently familiar form is the result of repeated
revisions. Pope originally wanted to begin the
work with an invocation. "In the Moral Poem,"
he told Spence in 1734, "I had written an address to our Saviour, imitated from Lucretius'
compliment to Epicurus, but omitted it by the
advice of Dean Berkeley."[7] These verses are not
preserved. One can thus at best speculate about their content. The *laudes Epicuri* are found
in several proems of *De Rerum Natura*, so it is
difficult to judge which motifs Pope presumably
adopted. The Lucretian invocation to Venus was
possibly also imitated in the original beginning of the *Essay on Man*. In many respects it was
well suited for the purposes of Pope's *imitatio*,
and in some places virtually offered itself for
a transposition of themes.

Warton thought he knew the reason for Bishop Berkeley's counsel: "because the Christian dispensation did not come within the compass of his plan."[8] Whether or not that was why Pope turned away from the invocation, an *imitatio Lucretii* was certainly precarious. The eulogium to the prince of atheists was hardly a suitable model for an invocation of God, even though Lactantius had supplied a tradition for using Lucretius in a Christian context.[9] The hymn could have entangled Pope in even more vehement controversies than those which the *Essay on Man* actually did cause among contemporaries.

Two things are notable about Pope's attempt to adapt Lucretius. First, the hymn would have changed the character of the poem. The *Essay* would have had a noticably closer relationship to the quasi-epic didactic poem (of which *De Rerum Natura* was considered a model, especially after Denis Lambin's reinterpretation of Lucretius)[10] than to the satiric-didactic epistle of Horatian origin. The fact that this relationship is present even without the obligatory epic invocation is almost univerally overlooked.

Secondly, the *Essay on Man* would have revealed its place in a tradition (until now largely unrecognized) which unites a considerable number of philosophical and literary works of the Restoration and the eighteenth century: the tradition of the "Anti-Lucretius." (The word is the title of a didactic poem by Cardinal Polignac.) The New Philosophy came to understand its ideas as a disengagement from the cosmological and anthropological teachings of atomism and atheism of the Epicurian and Lucretian variety which had been revived in the seventeenth century. Overcoming Lucretius in a didactic work of equal poetic achievement but of a different philosophical content was considered to be a symbolic task of literature. As late as 1815, Coleridge still expected the solution from Wordsworth.[11]

After deleting the hymn, Pope seems to have decided to use the pseudoinvocation which is familiar to us from the first two verses of the poem:

> Awake, my St. John! Leave all meaner things
> To low ambition, and the pride of Kings.[12]

This exhortation to his friend in place of the
invocation of a higher power sounds casual enough, but it is itself the product of several
steps of revision. Of the two manuscripts which
have been preserved, the Harvard manuscript
(closer to the printed version) has

> Awake my St. John! Quit all meaner things
> To puzling Statesmen, and to blust'ring
>   Kings[13]

for which Pope considered "puzzled" for "puz-
ling" and "flatt'ring" for "blust'ring." The
Pierpont Morgan manuscript, which is apparently
older, gives as the earliest version:

> Awake my Memmius, leave all meaner things
> To working Statesmen & ambitious Kings.

In other words, Pope took his starting point from
Lucretius here as well. Apparently the *Essay on
Man* was intended as an imitation of *De Rerum Natura*
in more than one respect.
      The parallel between Bolingbroke and Memmius
must soon have struck Pope as inaccurate. A
change is planned for "Awake my Memmius" even in
the Pierpont Morgan manuscript. And from the
earliest printed version onward the reminiscence
of Lucretius is deleted. Correctly sensing the
different nature of the relationship between
himself and Bolingbroke, Pope searched for another suggestive name before finally inserting
"St. John" in the third revision. The *Essay on
Man* clearly could not carry on the tradition of
De Rerum Natura on this point. Lucretius' poem is
characterized by a convention which can be found
first with Parmenides.[14] The poet and the recipient of the teaching are related by a dialogue in which the poet is an authoritative and
convincing teacher. This situation, which arises again and again, at least in the first books,

excludes the reader. The reader is hardly more
than a witness of a communication of doctrine,
which does not really include him.

The situation in the *Essay on Man* is quite
different. Here the poet receives rather than
gives. He does not communicate the teaching of
a third party. It is rather the friend whom he
addresses who takes the role of the teacher--in
life as well as in the poem. Bolingbroke was
"master of the poet, and the song" (IV, 374)
and is apostrophized as "guide, philosopher,
and friend" (390). Thus the relation of partner to poet turns around the relation between
Lucretius and Memmius. There is an anterior
agreement between them about the content and
importance of the teaching. The *Essay on Man* is
therefore "inclusive." Since the partner no
longer needs to be taught, the teaching loses
its private character. The dramatic speaker of
the poem turns outward and speaks to a general
audience.

In both separately printed editions of the
first epistle in 1733 "Memmius" was replaced by
"Laelius."[15] Here once again is a conscious
allusion which locates the *Essay on Man* in a literary context. Laelius Sapiens, as he was called because of his familiarity with Stoic doctrine, was well known to the contemporary reader from Horace. As a friend of the philosophers
and the poets, Laelius was a benefactor of Lucilius. The tacit allusion to Lucilius pushed
the *Essay on Man* into the vicinity of satire--or
rather, into an intermediate position between
epic, as incorporated by Milton and (in a philosophical and didactic variant) by Lucretius,
and satire, represented most notably by Horace.

If the planned invocation is reminiscent of
Lucretius, forgoing the invocation brings to
mind certain topical elements of the didactic
poem which had been developed since Virgil.[16]
The question of whether one may read into the
Essay on Man echoes of Horace's or Ovid's ironic
treatment of the ceremony of invocation or of
Tibullus' ironic invocation of a friend may be

left open. But it is obvious that the poem varies the didactic work's traditional renunciation
of epic themes in a characteristic way. Elevating the plan to view and comment on humankind
to a level above "low ambition, and the pride of
kings" is a new variant of the convention in didactic poetry of affirming the importance of its
subject while distancing it from that of epic
poetry.[17] Of course literary and personal motives are mixed here. Bolingbroke and Pope had
withdrawn from the events of the day with "a noble scorn of politicks,"[18] and now Pope emphasized their philosophical studies as a more-than-
royal occupation. The atmosphere of such a life
in contemplative leisure could be turned into
literature by the mere mention of Laelius:

> quin ubi se a volgo et scaena in secreta
>   remorant
> virtus Scipiadae et mitis sapientia Laeli
> nugari cum illo [Lucilio] et discincti ludere,
>   donec
> decoqueretur holus, soliti.[19]

The intimate tone of these lines from Horace contrasts effectively with the exhortation of Pope's
couplet.
     After the opening couplet Pope makes a new
start, and it seems as though he adopts the intimate, conversational tone of the epistle:

> Let us (since Life can little more supply
> Than just to look about us and to die)
> Expatiate free o'er all this scene of Man;
> A mighty maze! but not without a plan;
> A Wild, where weeds and flow'rs promiscuous
>   shoot,
> Or Garden, tempting with forbidden fruit.
> Together let us beat this ample field,
> Try what the open, what the covert yield;
> The latent tracts, the giddy heights explore
> Of all who blindly creep, or sightless soar;
> Eye Nature's walks, shoot Folly as it flies,
> And catch the Manners living as they rise;

>   Laugh where we must, be candid where we can;
>   But vindicate the ways of God to Man.
>   (I, 3-16)

Nugari et discincti ludere: such an impression can
easily arise on the surface. The sovereign resignation with which one is called to make an
expedition through the maze of life is expressed
in an atmosphere of detached play. The strict
claim of the didactic poem seems to dissolve in
the varied metaphors. The reflection of the moralist changes into the observation of the man
of the world. Everything seems to be directed
toward the pleasure of the hunt, culminating in
an expression of satiric delight. It is thus an
eminently Horatian passage: easy, relaxed, without the ceremony of the "grand" didactic poem.
    Nevertheless a more complex understanding of
these verses is possible with Lucretius in mind.
Pope's poem can be read as a confident imitation
of Lucretius. The point of departure seems to
have been the well-known beginning of the second book of *De Rerum Natura,* which had often been
translated and occasionally imitated: "Suave,
mari magno . . ."[20] To be sure, the sometimes
striking parallels of thought and formulation
are not easily seen if one confronts the *Essay
on Man* with the original itself. But Pope's Lu-
cretius--at least here and perhaps elsewhere--
was a mediated Lucretius. That might seem surprising, but it is a poetic technique which is
also characteristic of the *Dunciad.*[21] The parodies of the *Aeneid* which Pope inserted do not
correspond so much to the Latin text as to Dryden's translation. Pope's Virgil was the Virgil
of Dryden--a modern literary work shaped according to the poetic sensibilities of the age. In
the same way Pope's Lucretius was the Lucretius
of Dryden--the result of the particular art of
transposition which turned preclassical and post-
classical Roman literature into a component of
neoclassical English literature. Dryden expressed his intention clearly in reference to Persius and Juvenal: in his translation they were

to speak like contemporary Englishmen.[22] There
was no such statement of purpose concerning Lucretius, but the result is similar. The Latin
text is made smoother, and Lucretius' "masculine"
spirit which so fascinated Dryden[23] manifests itself in the expressions of the Restoration:

> 'Tis pleasant, safely to behold from shore
> The rowling Ship; and hear the Tempest roar:
> Not that anothers pain is our delight;
> But pains unfelt produce the pleasing sight.
> 'Tis pleasant also to behold from far
> The moving Legions mingled in the War:
> But much more sweet thy lab'ring steps to
>   guide,
> To Vertues heights, with wisdom well supply'd,
> And all the *Magazins* of Learning fortifi'd:
> From thence to look below on humane kind,
> Bewilder'd in the Maze of Life, and blind:
> To see vain fools ambitiously contend
> For Wit and Pow'r; their lost endeavours bend
> T'outshine each other, waste their time and
>   health,
> In search of honour, and pursuit of wealth.
> O wretched man! in what a mist of Life,
> Inclos'd with dangers and with noisie strife,
> He spends his little Span.[24]

The importance of the passage is less in the
individual literal parallels (although these,
such as "Maze of Life," are numerous) than in
the situation Lucretius describes. The observation is kept general, but above all it represents a self-portrait of the didactic poet. Such
self-portraiture is one of the means of construction in a genre in which the poet speaks in his
own person and creates his own role. The force
of the doctrine which is presented depends on
the authority which he can establish for himself. There could hardly be another text which
builds up such a superior position for expressing a dogmatic truth as this one. The poet
seems, to use Kant's phrase, "to speak down in a
decisive tone from the seat of wisdom"[25] because

he is privy to a higher knowledge. Every moment
he demonstrates his superiority and even bends
to a quasi-satirical contempt for the crowd,
which is trapped--blind and directionless--in the
maze of life. This is precisely the image of
the didactic poet presented in the exordium of
the *Essay on Man*. Here, too, one finds the playful
superiority of right knowledge; here, too, the
subdued smugness of the unassailable observer;
here, too, the potentially satiric stance toward
the person who does not know the real shape of
things. Bolingbroke's Lucilius, one might say,
adopted his stance from Lucretius.

Lucretius is also the source of the way the
dramatic speaker of the *Essay on Man* expresses his
doctrine: through metaphor. Along with his
friend he examines the human sphere and notes
down his observations. The hunting metaphors of
the exordium point toward the satiric nature of
some passages; but still more important, the metaphor of the common path provides a fundamental
convention of the poem. From start to finish one
is reminded that we are on the path to knowledge.
This image is strengthened by numerous exhortations such as "see," "look," "behold," which express the perception of new impressions which
have just come into view. The image is also
supported by the beginning of the third epistle,
"Here then we rest," and by a verse of the fourth
epistle, which anticipates the metaphor of the
stream of time to appear shortly thereafter:
"Come then, my Friend, my Genius, come along"
(IV, 373).

Not all these details can be found in Lucretius, but at the end of the first book, at a decisive point, the course of the poem is characterized as a path:

> nec tibi caeca
> nox iter eripiet quin ultima naturai
> pervideas: ita res accendent lumina rebus.[26]

These are the verses which immediately precede
"Suave, mari magno . . ." The poet leads his

disciple to the goal of knowledge of the "ultima
naturai":

Avia Pieridum peragro loca nullius ante
trita solo. iuvat integros accedere fontis
atque haurire. (IV, 1-3)

Pope altered the motif to fit his circumstances,
just as Lucretius had reshaped the "path of
songs" which Empedocles, "joining speech to
speech," had first conceived for his poem.[27]
Whereas Lucretius leads Memmius down the path, Pope
and Bolingbroke set out on a common expedition.

The echoes of Lucretius make up the nucleus
of the exordium with regard to technique. From
them derive such important characteristics as
the disposition of the dramatic speaker and the
convention of expressing the doctrine metaphorically. They form one unified stratum which is
connected to a second complex of motifs and allusions apparently more closely tied to the theme
of the work than to its technique. This complex
is dominated by a series of varied metaphors
for the concept of nature which is central to the
thought of the entire *Essay on Man* and which the
author apparently introduces here in intentional
anticipation of the rest of the poem. The range
of meanings which the eighteenth century connected with "nature" is explored subtly through
a series of suggestive metaphors: "maze," "wild,"
"garden," and "field." "Nature" seems to mean
the world of human beings, but also the cosmos--
created order as well as primeval wilderness.
The rhetoric of the couplet almost always joins
antithetical positions. The bafflement of the
ignorant and the vision of the knowledgeable poet
partaking of a higher insight are juxtaposed in
the image of the maze. Wilderness and garden (7
and 8) imply contradictory interpretations. And
the garden metaphor with its long tradition contains the contrast of spontaneous growth and
artificial design, of organic form and geometrical regularity, which was a living fact for contemporaries. Thus there are signs from the very

beginning of the disjunctive thought and the
attention to diametrical aspects which consistently characterize Pope's anthropology.[28]
     Two themes correspond to the ambiguity of the
metaphors. This differentiation begins at the
latest with the first appearance of the garden
metaphor. The image of the garden is associated
with that of the field and the terminology of
the hunt. The formulation refers almost wholly
to "negative" phenomena, to ideas and viewpoints
which seem to be folly from the chosen position
(I, 13). The reader is apparently being prepared
for the way the work as a whole will devote considerable space to representing false doctrines.
The essay does not fall into two parts, as Warburton supposed--one critical (which he saw in
the first epistle) and one constructive (which
he thought was constituted by the remaining three
epistles). But Pope does develop his own views
through conscious and literarily effective contrast with opposing thoughts. For Lucretius and
Pope, as De Quincey rightly observed, everything
is necessarily polemical. Their own arguments
are born of controversy and rejoinder.[29] In both
De Rerum Natura and the *Essay on Man* these polemics
often assume a satiric coloration. Pope in fact
seems to have aimed at the form of an inverted
verse satire. In making assurances of his uprightness and honesty (I, 15) he was at least
willing to make use of a conventional satiric
stance of the eighteenth century.[30]
     The second theme is announced with the allu-
sion to the Garden of Eden ("tempting with for-
bidden fruit") and reaches a commanding position
in the exordium with the adoption of the last
verse of *Paradise Lost*. It is Pope's "serious"
theme. It documents the intention of the poem to
carry on the traditional theodicy of the biblical
epic in a rationalistic age which demanded a new,
no longer mythological form of representation:
the discussion of the nature of the human being
and his relation to God. The two contrasting
themes are characteristically brought together
in the last couplet. Satire and epic appear as
the poles between which the didactic poem of the

age of ideas--oriented toward Lucretius--is realized. The often quoted "but" with which Pope
separates himself from Milton does not imply a
subordination of theodicy to satire, but rather
an emphatic stress on the mission of probing the
"ultima naturai."31   Milton's "justify" is also
changed to Pope's "vindicate," sounding the
fundamental tone which distinguishes *Paradise Lost*
from the *Essay on Man* and which assigns the poems
to two different spheres: one of religious justification, the other of rational proof.

III

I hope to have made clear that the relation
of the *Essay on Man* to *De Rerum Natura* is not of the
chimerical sort which Horatian interpreters of
the poem assume.   The impression that Lucretius'
poem was an implicit text of reference for Pope
is strengthened when one reads Pope consistently
against a Lucretian background.   The passage immediately following the exordium which culminates in the famous cosmic vision already shows
how close the relation is between the two works.
The importance of the Lucretian element in
the *Essay on Man* is not in the fact that allusions
can be found in isolated passages which an
eighteenth-century reader might have identified
to confirm his knowledge of classical literature.
What is important is that the poem as a whole is
a historically significant representation of
Lucretius in the way Pope's translations of the
Greek epics are a representation of Homer.   Ever
since the reinterpretation of Lucretius by the
sixteenth and seventeenth centuries *De Rerum Natura*
was considered more than an epic of ideas which
pointed beyond the traditional epic.   It was the
embodiment of the poetic expression of a philosophically founded world model.   One must thus
ask: is Pope's *Essay on Man* in the final analysis
an attempt to rewrite *De Rerum Natura* for the age
of Newton?

THE DILEMMA OF AN OBEDIENT SON: POPE'S
EPISTLE TO DR. ARBUTHNOT

Ripley Hotch

   The *Epistle to Dr. Arbuthnot* treats the dilemma
of a poet caught between the fear that he may
be (like the fools he satirizes in the poem)
cursed because he writes in a form that is useless or harmful, and the fear that his impulse
to write was itself a curse that his parents
may have caused by their own sin:

   Why did I write? what sin to me unknown
   Dipt me in ink, my Parents', or my own?
      (ll. 125-26)[1]

He therefore links the question of why he writes
to how he became the man that he is. By
choosing to connect the two questions, Pope also faces the recurrent charge that a satirist
cannot be a good man, a charge that was levelled at him from early in his career.[2] The
Epistle to Arbuthnot thus organizes itself around
an account of Pope's growth as a satiric poet.
He creates a rhetorically convincing portrait

This essay first appeared in *Essays in Literature* [Western Illinois] 1 (1974), 37-45.

of himself for the reader by the end of the
poem only because he has successfully faced the
apparent contradiction between his chosen form
and the character of a good man. What Richard
Onorato says of Wordsworth in the *Prelude* could
be said of Pope: "By finding poetic connections between the facts of growth and the causation and development of imaginative powers,
the poet invents himself as poet."[3]
     John Dennis delighted in connecting Pope's
physical deformity with a diabolical ancestry:
"'Tis the mark of God and Nature upon him, to
give us warning that we should hold no Society
with him, as a Creature not of our Original,
nor of our Species....his Original is not from
Adam, but from the *Divel*. By his constant and
malicious Lying, and by that Angel Face and
Form of his, 'tis plain that he wants nothing
but Horns and Tayl, to be the exact resemblance,
both in Shape and Mind, of his Infernal Father."[4] Pope notes in his Advertisement to
the poem that Lady Mary and Lord Hervey attacked not only his writings but his "Person,
Morals, and Family." Pope uses the attack on
his character to show that he is on the defensive, in order, as Elder Olson argues, "to
allay the fear of the reader that he may be the
next to be attacked, since such fear would make
it impossible for Pope to appear as one of good
will, and hence to persuade at all."[5] Part of
Pope's strategy is to show that what his attackers say about him is actually true of them.
In response to the accusation that he was a
toad, ape, wasp, and deformed, Pope shows us
the toads Bufo and Sporus, the ass Midas, and
the insect-like dunces who pester him; to the
accusation that he wanted to be a dictator, he
shows us real dictators in Atticus and Bufo; to
the accusation that he was avaricious and grew
rich, he shows us his own generosity in contrast to the avariciousness of the dunces.[6]
Pope creates his character for us through this
satiric combat, essentially through the negative images of the dunces to whom he bears a

close enough resemblance that even he is uncom-
fortable. The attacks of the dunces and his
counterattacks on them are important means of
self-definition for Pope.

Two contradictions in the poem point to his
ambivalence about his satiric mission. Although
he includes three devastating portraits (Atticus, Bufo, and Sporus), Pope insists that his
satire, which is supposed to make people change,
can in fact do nothing:

>   You think this cruel? take it for a rule,
> No creature smarts so little as a Fool
>   (ll. 83-84);
> Whom have I hurt? has Poet yet, or Peer,
> Lost the arch'd eye-brow, or *Parnassian* sneer?
>   (ll. 95-96)

He is sensitive to the charge that he has been
cruel and has hurt others. His defense is to
insist on their imperviousness. The contradiction between his own knowledge that the fools
are impervious and his insistence on writing
against them makes his compulsion to write look
at least superficially like theirs. We wonder
what the difference is between Pope's need to
write the *Dunciad* in order to obtain rest and
the madman "who lock'd from Ink and Paper,
scrawls/ With desp'rate Charcoal round his dar-
ken'd walls" (ll. 19-20):

>   Out with it, *Dunciad!* let the secret pass,
> That Secret to each Fool, that he's an Ass:
> The truth once told, (and wherefore shou'd
>   we lie?)
> The Queen of *Midas* slept, and so may I.
>   (ll. 79-82)

Pope can do nothing to stop the scribbler:

>   Who shames a Scribler? break one cobweb thro',
> He spins the slight, self-pleasing thread
>   anew;

Destroy his Fib, or Sophistry; in vain,
The Creature's at his dirty work again.
   (ll. 89-92)

On the one hand, Pope's character will not let
him rest without calling a fool a fool, yet his
calling them so does no good, and he is himself
made to look like them. Those who ask for favors or advice have no interest in it. And finally, by speaking Pope exposes himself to calumny, so that he is worse off than if he had kept
silent.

Pope distinguishes his compulsion from that
of the fools by showing that whereas they dis-
obeyed their fathers to become writers, he did
not. Unfortunately his obedience involves him
in another contradiction: he claims to be like
his father, yet he has chosen a career that
makes it impossible to have the life he longs
for. As he presents himself in the poem, he is
unlike his father in health, learning, and profession. In some ways, he seems even to be a
perversion of his father, as though his compulsion to write had cursed him. In order to distinguish his obedience from the fools' disobedience he must deal with the obvious curse his
life has been. It may in fact be possible that
he is sinning by his work, that he is not a proper son and is therefore cursed. Worse yet, his
parents may be the cause of the curse. His anxiety about obedience is therefore a part of his
anxiety about his own nature and consequently
about his mission as a satirist. He must find his
way from a naturally poetic childhood to the difficult adulthood of a moral satirist, from soft
numbers and inoffensive verses to the manly ways
of satire. At the beginning of the poem he wants
to retreat from his task:

Shut, shut the door, good *John*! fatigu'd I
   said,
Tye up the knocker, say I'm sick, I'm dead.
   (ll. 1-2)

By the end he is sure of his task and of his
obedience to his parents. The poem proceeds in
a way that builds his own assurance by facing
the real problems raised by the attacks on him,
so that his audience's confidence grows with his
own.

The behavior of the poetasters raises anxi-
eties about obedience at the beginning of the
Epistle to Arbuthnot. Without wanting it, Pope has
become a symbol of a widespread madness to write.
Fathers of would-be poets take him to be the
cause of this poetic anarchy, in which the mad
fools go beyond the bounds of decency, religion,
law, and obedience to families. "Is there," he
asks in despair,

> A Clerk, foredoom'd his Father's soul to
>   cross,
> Who pens a Stanza when he should *engross*?
>   (ll. 17-18)

Apparently a dissenter's son, the clerk exhibits the results of his own sect's belief in
predestination. His disobedience is not Pope's
fault, but Pope suffers the blame. A few lines
later occurs another case of filial disobedience:

> *Arthur*, whose giddy Son neglects the Laws,
> Imputes to me and my damn'd works the cause.
>   (ll. 23-24)

The son neglects both the study of and obedience to civil and poetic laws, an even wider
disobedience than to his father.

Faced with such actions, which bear some
resemblance to his own need to write, Pope
boldly treats the question of why he himself
writes. The lines that discuss his doubts draw
together personal growth, poetic mission, and
obedience to parental authority as different
parts of the same issue:

> Why did I write? what sin to me unknown
> Dipt me in Ink, my Parents', or my own?

As yet a Child, nor yet a Fool to Fame,
I lisp'd in Numbers, for the Numbers came.
I left no Calling for this idle trade,
No duty broke, no Father dis-obey'd.
The Muse but serv'd to ease some Friend, not
    Wife,
To help me thro' this long Disease, my Life,
To second, ARBUTHNOT! thy Art and Care,
And teach, the Being you preserv'd, to bear.
    (ll. 125-34)

The passage traces Pope's progression from baptism through childhood, his choice and discharge
of a profession, and his present old age. At
each of these stages Pope insists on the paradox
stated in the first two lines: he freely chose
what he had to accept. The parallel to baptism
suggests that, unlike Arthur's son, Pope was
anointed in his profession. The discussion
moves from the mere level of psychological com-
punction--the fools' madness to write--to the
level of moral and Christian duty by invoking
a parallel to John 9:2-3, in which Jesus cures
a blind man: "And his disciples asked him, saying, Master, who did sin, this man, or his parents: that he was born blind? Jesus answered,
Neither hath this man sinned, nor his parents:
but that the works of God should be made manifest in him." Behind the baptism also stands
the image of Achilles, whose mother dipped him
in the Styx to protect him in battle. These
three possibilities, baptism, the blind man,
and Achilles, strengthen our belief in Pope's
dedication to his craft.[7]
    But there is a movement in the lines that
runs counter to this one. Pope is not baptized
with water, but with ink; to be dipped in ink
like a pen is not to have sins washed away, but
to be stained. While his baptism may remove
the fault of being born to be a satirist, Pope
is as much dirtied as purified by his profession. This ambiguity of attitude catches the
complexity Pope is trying to convey about his
role: he knows fully the responsibilities and

the pain of the office he has no choice but to
accept. He is also different from the dunces
because they like the dirt. Insisting on the
parallel to the blind man in St. John and combining that parallel with the purpose of baptism
implies that it may be his parents' fault that
he suffers as he does. Their original sin is
devolved upon him instead of being removed by
baptism, and dominates his life. Such a slight
and comic expression of resentment helps us understand Pope's struggle to be obedient. His
childhood still finds him in an ambiguous relationship to a kind of parent: "As yet a child,
nor yet a Fool to Fame" means of course that he
was naive in his first utterances, and only later began to worry about reputation. But he is
also Fame's child, whom she makes her fool: she
gives him a gift, but she makes him suffer for
it. The line captures the ambiguity of Pope's
desire for fame but reluctance to accept it,
especially with its consequences in the form of
the demanding fools.

From the child whose speech was poetry, not
chosen but thrust upon him from no stated source,
he becomes a young man who must choose a profession. The previous four lines have made quite
clear, however, that there is no choice, or rather that it was made for him. Pope remakes that
choice, but negatively. He does not actively
seek a trade ("I left no Calling for this idle
trade"); he merely stays as he is. Unlike the
clerk, he is not "called" to a "trade" which he
forsakes. The line elegantly belittles his
choice of a profession by comparing it to a
trade rather than a high calling, but also suggests, as a country gentleman would, that he
does not worship the "idol, trade" as does, presumably, the clerk's father. The next line reflects on the earlier cases of disobedient sons,
as Pope, in contrast to them, "No Duty broke, no
Father disobey'd." His actions are therefore
qualitatively different from those of the fools,
but his choice still represents a passive yielding to his fate. He was not commanded by his

father to take up satire, he was simply not for-
bidden to do so. The lines protest too much, as
though Pope suspected that in fact his choice
was a form of disobedience, since it has clearly
led to a life of perpetual warfare totally unlike his father's, who "walk'd innoxious thro'
his Age" (l. 395). Pope cannot be sure, no matter how certain he sounds, that his choice has
been the right one.

The final four lines of the passage focus on
the ambiguities of creation. In line 131 ("The
Muse but serv'd to ease some Friend, not Wife"),
the gracefulness hides some ambiguity about the
muse's function. The placement of the phrase
"not Wife" suggests that the muse has served instead of a wife, not only that she eased a friend rather than a wife. The muse also serves
as a nurse for the physician, Arbuthnot, whose
care preserved the poet, and who is here being
eased by the man he preserved. The pleasures
of his poetry are essentially private, and he
has not really written for the public. The
muse, finally, serves to "teach, the Being you
preserv'd, to bear"--apparently to bear the sufferings of the long disease of his life. But
the verb "to bear" hints at a metaphor submerged in the passage: the muse in fact may be mid-
wife as well as wife. Without a wife, Pope has
no way to carry on his line, and his poetry becomes his only form of progeny. Deformed, he
can only give poetic birth, which is closely
connected to the long disease of his life. In
some way, he sees poetry as bound up with disease, so that it must relieve the very thing it
caused. Whether or not the reader agrees that
this metaphor is submerged in the passage, he
will probably agree that Pope displays here a
complex double view of poetry: his gift is
both a curse and a blessing.

I think that this analysis demonstrates how
much of the strength of the *Epistle to Arbuthnot*
depends on Pope's ambivalent attitude toward
poetry. Pope must relieve his fear that his
superficial resemblances to the accursed and

deformed attacking fools point to a fundamental
identity with them. Their very attacks are
therefore reassuring, for by them the fools admit Pope's difference and his superiority.   In
other words, even these persecutions are a blessing in disguise. When Pope asks the logical
question that follows "Why did I write?" which
is "why then publish?" the answer is already
inherent: it is to bear witness to the difference, even to reassure himself of the difference
between himself and the dunces by provoking the
attacks he claims to fear. In fact, we can take
him at his word when he insists that flattery is
worse than attack. Arbuthnot warns him:

> 'No Names--be calm--learn Prudence of a
>   Friend:
> I too could write, and I am twice as tall,
> But Foes like these!'--One Flatt'rer's worse
>   than all;
> Of all mad Creatures, if the Learn'd are
>   right,
> It is the Slaver kills, and not the Bite.
>   (ll. 102-06)

Flattery implies that he is like the fools.
Pope prefers the attacks, even needs them, and
his own satire helps to create them. They give
him the sense of righteousness that justifies
his painful mission. Their behavior as disobedient children is one of the sources of Pope's
righteousness. If he is different from them,
then he need not fear that he is disobedient
himself. They act out that possible fear, and
Pope has the pleasure of punishing them with
his satire as if he were their parent himself.
His attacks on them are a sign that he has
grown up and taken a place of responsibility.
  Sporus is Pope's major example of a dangerous fool. Arbuthnot considers Sporus disgusting and insignificant, but Pope insists on the
attack:

> Yet let me flap this Bug with gilded wings,
> This painted Child of Dirt that stinks and
> stings. (ll. 309-10)

Pope finds Sporus' childishness and apparent
harmlessness offensive. By discovering Satan
behind Sporus the toady, "at the Ear of *Eve*,
familiar Toad" (l. 319), Pope finds the venom of
the mad dogs at the beginning of *Arbuthnot* in
what at first seems to be one of the harmless
"well-bred Spaniels" who "civilly delight/ In
mumbling of the Game they dare not bite" (ll.
313-14). Thus by treating even the most apparently innocuous of cases, Pope defines a power
that is ultimately frightening. His behavior
towards Sporus seems unwarranted, and yet becomes warranted in the course of the portrait.
Sporus' attack on Pope calls the poet's attention to him, and that attention finds the devil
where he does not seem to be. As Pope insists,
it is the satirist's part to see evil where
others cannot.

If Pope's insistence on finding evil reminds
us of the self-fulfilling prophecy of a para-
noiac, we are making the same mistake Pope's
attackers do, assimilating him to the fools he
superficially resembles. The action of the
poem tempts us into making that mistake, as it
does Arbuthnot, to show us how difficult is
Pope's task. Still, we may be justified, with
Arbuthnot, in wondering about the violence of
Pope's response to Sporus. The reason seems to
lie in a resemblance between them that Pope himself recognizes. Pope at one time had the
choice of writing inoffensive, soft pieces, so
staying in the childhood of a poet, lisping in
numbers:

> Soft were my Numbers, who could take
> offence
> While pure Description held the place of
> Sense?
> Like gentle *Fanny's* was my flow'ry Theme,
> A painted Mistress, or a purling Stream.
> (ll. 147-50)

Yet the choice has already been made; the lines
mock themselves, and create a contrast to Lord
Fanny. Pope deliberately rejects this childishness in the lines following his portrait of
Sporus, that other version of Fanny, with whom
he contrasts himself:

> Not proud, nor servile, be one Poet's praise
> That, if he pleas'd, he pleas'd by manly
>   ways. (ll. 336-37)

Although adulthood seems the obvious goal of
the true poet, Pope still remains ambivalent
about it, insisting later that he is "soft by
Nature, more a Dupe than Wit" (l. 368).
Pope, then, cannot escape the fear that he
will be such a child as Sporus. When he insists on his manliness he is trying to contrast
himself with Sporus; yet he also insists on his
harmlessness. The poem suggests that in his
manliness there is as much danger to his attempt
to be obedient as in his childishness. He insists that his parents are themselves harmless:

> that Father held it for a rule
> It was a Sin to call our Neighbour Fool,
> That harmless Mother thought no Wife a
>   Whore...
> Stranger to Civil and Religious Rage,
> The good Man walk'd innoxious thro' his Age.
> No Courts he saw, no Suits would ever try,
> Nor dar'd an Oath, nor hazarded a Lye.
>   (ll. 382-97)

But Pope has been calling people fools throughout the poem, and the *Epistle to Arbuthnot*, as its
Advertisement says, is "a sort of Bill of Complaint" in the court of public opinion. Therefore, the reason for the contradictions would
seem to be this: Pope's duty to lash vice is
laid on him from birth by a higher authority,
and yet the representative of that authority,
his father, condemns the kind of attacks Pope
must make to carry out his mission. Obedience

seems to require disobedience. Carried to an
extreme, this dilemma would preclude any poem at
all; a weaker constitution might well lapse into
inaction. Pope, however, writes the *Epistle to
Arbuthnot*.

The most intense expressions of the dilemma
do not, however, occur in his treatment of his
parents, but rather with other authorities. For
example Pope constantly changes back and forth
from the naive to the lashing and manly satirist
before his audience, his public judges. But the
one figure who makes the ambiguities of Pope's
position most intensely felt is Atticus. Pope
stands in a special relation to Atticus, as he
does to Arbuthnot; if the fools are a distorted
version of himself, then Atticus is a distorted
version of the true friend Arbuthnot. Atticus
could have been another of those authoritative
older friends--Granville, Walsh, Congreve--who
"With open arms receiv'd one Poet more" (1. 142).
But unlike them Atticus plays the part of the
Asian monarch: "too fond to rule alone," he
bears "like the *Turk*, no brother near the throne"
(ll. 197-98). In this situation, the young poet
is like the son and heir, who is treated in such
a way that he does not know whether a given gesture is love or hate, approval or disapproval,
while he watches Atticus

    Damn with faint praise, assent with civil
        leer,
    And without sneering, teach the rest to
        sneer;
    Willing to wound, and yet afraid to strike,
    Just hint a fault, and hesitate dislike.
        (ll. 201-04)

Pope accuses Atticus of treachery, of an unten-
able combination of conflicting characteristics
that, by undermining the apparent relationship
he has with an admirer, destroys that admirer's
confidence in himself. Atticus is "A tim'rous
foe, and a suspicious friend" (1. 206). Atticus
has seemed to promise much, has raised hopes,

and like a bad parent dashed them out of jealousy: "so obliging that he ne'er oblig'd"
(1.208). Toward such a man, Pope's response
must be conflicting:

> Who but must laugh, if such a man there be?
> Who would not weep, if *Atticus* were he?
>   (ll. 213-214)

Someone unaffected might find his inconsistencies
laughable, but not the victim and would-be friend. The opposition between laughing and weeping
in the final couplet of the portrait focuses not
on Atticus or his conduct, but rather presents
the picture of the disappointed and bewildered
admirer.

There is no getting inside Atticus; for all
the explanation Pope seems to give, we are no
closer to understanding why there should be
such a man. But in working out the portrait,
Pope changes from the naive, besieged poet, forced by compulsion to write, into the monarch.
Pope tells us that he becomes, like Atticus, an
Asian monarch, but with emphasis on a different
quality:

> I sought no homage from the Race that write;
> I kept, like *Asian* Monarchs, from their sight.
>   (ll. 219-20)

The Atticus portrait would seem to be the turning point of the poem; it is precisely at its
center. It marks a direct treatment, though not
solution, of the ambiguities of Pope's position,
and allows him to make the image of retreat at
the beginning of the poem into a form of adulthood by the end. When he insists that the door
be shut at the poem's opening, Pope is, as he
knows, escaping his own poetic responsibility as
well as the nuisance of the poetasters. What
seems to be a joke actually turns out to have a
serious aspect: "Tye up the knocker, say I'm
sick, I'm dead." His retreat is a kind of death.

The poem becomes a way of finding his way back
to the world without leaving that important image of himself, Twickenham.

As Maynard Mack has demonstrated, Pope finds
useful the topos of the classical poets that
identifies a man with his house: "This analogy
has relevance to his works at Twickenham as a
whole, on which he impresses an image of himself as sharply as he impressed the head of Homer on the wax with which he sealed his letters."[8] Twickenham, as a sign of himself, is
a sign of his manliness, independence, adult-
hood--the place that fools may not enter. But
it is also, paradoxically, a retreat in which
his littleness is emphasized, as Mack points out:
"He drew amusement from considering himself a
miniscule inhabitant of a world tailored to fit
him. He is 'Homer in a nutshell,' to use the
phrase he appropriated from Bishop Atterbury,
who had thus described his appearance when driving in his little 'chariot.' ...He is prepared, if need be, to live yet more diminutively
than he does, shrinking back to his 'Paternal
cell.'"[9] Pope's parents, too, are still very
much a part of Twickenham, not only as Pope
built it, but at the end of the *Epistle to Arbuthnot*, so that his independence may be compromised
by his impulse to shrink back into childhood.
It is odd, too, considering Pope's health, the
state of the roads, and the comfort of Twickenham as an ideal place of retreat, that he spent
so much time away from it. The letters give the
impression of constant movement. Finally, his
most affectionate evocation of what Twickenham
meant to him as a poet, the *Epistle to Arbuthnot*,
was not even written there.[10]

Thus, even in the evocation of Twickenham
Pope faces the problem of the degree to which
his difference from his parents is still an obedience to them. His solution is their evocation
in the poem, where he recreates them within his
own symbol of adulthood, so merging the two that
he may now be said to be the creator of himself.
He has escaped them in one sense--he shows his

father dead and his mother dying--but he also
keeps them alive through his own verse:

> Unspotted Names! and memorable long,
> If there be Force in Virtue, or in Song.
>   (ll. 386-87)

They live because Pope chooses to write about
them, yet he also insists, perhaps heavily, on
their purity. That purity is a result of a rather extreme, even childish innocence about the
world which makes his parents look like infants.
This feeling about them is explicitly included
in the portrait of Pope's dying mother:

> O Friend! may each Domestick Bliss be
>   thine!
> Be no unpleasing Melancholy mine:
> Me, let the tender Office long engage
> To rock the Cradle of reposing Age,
> With lenient arts extend a Mother's breath.
> Make Languor smile, and smooth the Bed of
>   Death. (ll. 406-11)

The passage puts his mother in a special and
highly gratifying relationship to Pope: she has
become his child. Instead of his being her
helpless infant, she is his, and Pope has become
what his muse was earlier to him, a nurse. Whatever is fearsome about his parents and the rather terrible duty imposed on him through them is
entirely changed by this image.
    Joseph Warton noticed the change in the read-
ing experience which this transition created:
"The eye that has been wearied and opprest by
the harsh and austere colouring of some of the
preceding passages, turns away with pleasure
from these asperities, and reposes with complacency on the soft tints of domestic tenderness."[11] The tactic is rhetorically effective,
but also indicates the degree to which Pope has
redirected the ambivalence away from his parents. By the end of the poem Pope is no longer
in retreat from his mission, trying to escape

into the irresponsibility of childhood. In discovering the meaning of his mission he has discovered his own adulthood and independence even
in what seemed to limit him. The confidence he
has gained grants his voice authority; he no
longer needs to fear that his independence may
be disobedience. He becomes, not only the potential father of the dunces, with all the dis-
agreeable implications that contains, but the
parent of his parents. He gains his freedom by
accepting freely a task he could not avoid.

SATIRIC APOLOGY AS SATIRIC INSTANCE:
POPE'S *ARBUTHNOT*

J. Paul Hunter

    As personal apology and as defense of the sa-
tiric posture, Pope's *Epistle to Dr. Arbuthnot* is
justly praised. But the poem is more than a personal and professional manifesto; it is a *demonstration* of the attitudes and techniques proper to an
Augustan satirist. It defends righteousness and
sanity in a context of evil and absurdity, not
only by asserting, but by instancing the virtues
of justice, honesty, moral balance, restraint,
tenderness, and the gentle but firm stance one
must take against the malicious, the misguided,
and the dull. Pope exemplifies his propositions
in almost every line. His voice modulates from
puzzlement to anxiety, to disappointment, to
personal hurt, to moral indignation, to love for
the good and the just; the voice is ever balancing and testing, but Pope is always in control.
Even the lines sometimes thought to be too vehement, too unfair, too personal--the portraits
of Atticus and Sporus--demonstrate not Pope's
splenetic lapses from moral balance and human
compassion, but the judicious composure his po-

This essay first appeared in the *Journal of English and Germanic Philology* 68 (1969), 625-47.
Copyright The University of Illinois Press.

etic can maintain in the context of declared war,
even as the enemy fire breathes over him.

The composure of Pope's poem--its success as
an instance of proper satiric perspective--is the
more surprising when we recall circumstances behind the poem: the illness, soon to be terminal,
of Arbuthnot; the final months of life for Pope's
ninety-one-year-old mother; the vicious assaults
upon Pope by, among others, Lady Mary Wortley
Montagu and Lord Hervey. What Pope managed to do
was harness the multiple directions of each cir-
cumstance--balance their tensive energies--to
portray the universal plight of the satirist
trapped in love, hate, good, evil, violence,
tenderness--trapped, in other words, in life as
lived by postlapsarian man. In *Arbuthnot*, Pope's
art is as close as it ever comes to being life;
but here, ironically, is where he achieves his
finest statement (and instance) of the distinction between life and art.

In his advertisement for *Arbuthnot*, Pope
mentions two "facts" of the poetic occasion
which can lead us both to a better "siting" of the
poem and to a better evaluation of Pope's accomplishment. He says that he had composed the
poem "by snatches" over a long period of time,
and that he decided to publish it only after he
was attacked in two "extraordinary" lampoons,
Verses to the Imitator of Horace and *Epistle from a
Nobleman to a Doctor of Divinity*. [1] We can admit the
possible accuracy of Pope's first statement
without accepting the implications sometimes
drawn from it. We know that some parts of *Arbuthnot* (the Atticus portrait, for example) were
composed very early, and there is good reason to
believe that Pope had written, by 1733, more
than half the lines that ultimately appeared in
the finished *Arbuthnot* of January 1734/5. [2] But
Pope's description of his procedure has sometimes been translated into an admission of dis-
jointedness or into a rather naive description
of what *satura* is for an Augustan poet; readings
of Pope still suffer too frequently from an
admiration of parts--especially in *Arbuthnot*--

an admiration which implies that both the discrete poem and the poet's vision are ultimately
fragmented. Pope's second statement, when its
implications are carefully examined, can guide
us to a more accurate perspective for the first.
    Arbuthnot does answer *Verses to the Imitator* and
Epistle from a Nobleman; its answer to them is direct
and, unlike its implicit answer to other lampoons, almost point by point. But the answer is
different *in kind* from the attacks, providing an
instance of the difference between satire and
personal lampoon. Pope engages the particulars
of *Verses* and *Epistle* without engaging their method.
Where Pope answers their charges, he maintains
the patient attitude of a teacher toward a pupil
gone badly astray; underneath is disappointment,
exasperation, hatred of their acts, even a growing suspicion that perhaps, now, chiding is not
enough. But what he offers, anyway, is a lesson
showing how they have gone bad. He shows them the
difference between lampoon, a vehicle for the
vicious writer and an excuse for the vicious
reader to take pleasure in his lack of discrimination, and satire, which explores for the just
and the virtuous the reaches of righteousness and
of art.
    In this essay I wish to point to some of the
strategies Pope uses to make his distinctions
about the proprieties of satire. To do so, I
have combined three approaches to the poem: a
contextual examination of contemporary lampoons
and how Pope echoes them and turns them to his
own artistic uses; a critical examination of
Arbuthnot's major metaphors and how they are fused
into a satiric vision of poetic perversion; and
a genetic examination (through extant manuscripts)
of how *Arbuthnot* grew in Pope's mind.[3]

                          I

Verses to the Imitator appeared a month after Pope's
First Satire of the Second Book of Horace Imitated; the
first edition was signed "By a Lady," though
rumor quickly ascribed the poem to Lady Mary and
Lord Hervey jointly. In 112 lines, the poem

attacks Pope's understanding of Horace, knowledge
of Greek, family background, coarseness, motives,
injustice, friendlessness, and the impotence and
opacity of his poetry. It begins with an interesting and complex image of poetry as the cloth-
ing of fools, though the potential force of the
image is considerably blunted by Pope's distance
from the court:

> In two large Columns on thy motly Page,
> Where Roman Wit is striped with English rage;
> Where Ribaldry to Satire makes pretense,
> And modern Scandal rolls with ancient sense.
> (II. 1-4)

But the direct attack and simple assertion pall
quickly, and the images become less careful
and less effective as the attack becomes more
shrill. Beginning with shrewd perceptions about
Pope's difference from his model (Pope is more
"coarse" and "dark"--the reason, incidentally,
that the seventeenth century had preferred Juvenal and Persius to Horace),[4] the poem soon settles
for commonplaces stated with more anger than art.
The charges represent standard cliches about the
personality of the satirist (he is splenetic,
malicious, unjust, disloyal, etc.), but they are
larded with increasingly brutal remarks about
Pope's person. Pope, the poem asserts, is a
monster; his body is an emblem of his soul. But
the poem only shouts such correspondence and
becomes an instance of the libelous practice it
claims to be attacking. The violence of its
unrestrained and unchanneled personal abuse is
closer to the primitive curse than to a literature anxious to extirpate, a point that Pope
recognized and demonstrated in his answer.[5]

Two examples suggest the character of *Verses*.
The first passage emphasizes Pope's broken body
and seems to allude to a rather crude joke in *A
Popp upon Pope*, a 1728 pamphlet "describing" how
Pope was physically beaten:[6]

If none with Vengeance yet thy Crimes pursue,
Or give thy manifold Affronts their due;
If limbs unbroken, Skins without a Stain,
Unwhipt, unblanketed, unkick'd, unslain;
That wretched little Carcass you retain,
The reason is, not that the World wants Eyes;
But thou'rt so mean, they see, and they
    despise. (II. 66-72)

The couplets, flaccid and repetitious, develop
the plot tediously; the poetic texture is like
that of the poets Pope had entombed in *The Dunciad*.
But just as important is the tastelessness and
pointlessness. Even if *A Popp upon Pope* had been
intended as a kind of Bickerstaff-Partridge
prophetic joke, the allusion is dark and the joke
is five years old. Given the brawling humor of
the 1730's such a reference might be expected in
a London lampoon; but it is precisely this appeal
to expectation which defines the level of *Verses
to the Imitator*. Swift's satiric code, never to
attack natural limitations but only pretension
above them, asserts firmly the moral demands of
satire (demands which Pope consistently supported, and in *Arbuthnot* defended), and it is precisely
these demands which are lacking in *Verses to the
Imitator* and in similar contemporary lampoons on
Pope.[7]
    The second passage openly engages the curse
as strategy, and asserts analogies between Pope
and the origin of evil:

When God created Thee, one would believe,
He said the same as to the snake of Eve;
To human Race Antipathy declare,
Twixt them and thee be everlasting War.
    (II. 54-57)

But the logic is sloppy and the analogy distorted.
If Pope's deformity is a symbol and if the curse
precedes birth, Pope's guilt is denied, and Pope
is, at the most, parallel with evil, not responsible for it, nor a manifestation of it. But the
end of the poem disregards its original premise

and asserts a new curse; presumably God's original
curse had not worked, and *Verses* now has to reas-
sert it:

> Like the first bold Assassin's be thy Lot,
> Ne'er be thy Guilt forgiven, or forgot;
> But as thou hatest, be hated by Mankind,
> And with the Emblem of thy crooked Mind,
> Mark'd on thy Back, like Cain, by God's own
>   Hand,
> Wander like Him, accursed through the Land.
>   (II. 107-12)

The image of Pope's lonely wandering may be the
worst prediction of 1733, as Pope dramatically
shows in the opening lines of *Arbuthnot*. But more
significant is *Verses'* inept pursuit of a moral
dimension. *Verses to the Imitator* had gone to the
right fountain for its imagery, but the poetic
effort only muddied the water. In *Arbuthnot* Pope
returns to the Genesis context of evil, but he
does not indulge himself in simple vituperation
and easy but illogical parallels. Rather he
offers Lord Hervey and Lady Mary a lesson in how
to transform personal venom into a vision of
evil appropriate to the satiric posture.

Epistle from a Nobleman, scarcely disguised as
by Lord Hervey, appeared a few months after
Verses to the Imitator. The title page claimed that
it was "Written from H_____n-c_____t, Aug.
28, 1733"; the poem's greatest stroke of wit is
this self-effacing pretense of confirming Pope's
charge of "a thousand [lines] a day."[8] The tone
of the poem itself is less shrill than *Verses to
the Imitator*, but its attempt at a relaxed, detached urbanity results instead in a limp, flaccid
lack of intensity. It begins with the speaker,
as *ingenu*, describing his early life and his
entry among "the Great." Wits, he quickly notes,
are more concerned with showmanship than truth;
they lack humanity, and their exhibitionism advertises their weaknesses. Such generalities are
soon applied to Pope, who is directly charged
with inhumanity, vapidity, and lack of originality. And as in *Verses to the Imitator*, imprecations

are hurled at Pope's parentage and person:

> ...whene'er P___e writes, he's forc'd to go
> And beg a little Sense, as School-Boys do.
> For all cannot invent, who can translate;
> No more than those who cloath us can create.[9]
>   (II. 135-38)

Here is less vigor than in *Verses to the Imitator*;
yet the poem is not more subtle, but simply thinner. Sometimes the speaker seems pouty or piqued,
but never outraged; he declines to operate from
even the pretense of a moral stance and does not
claim the role of satiric hero. The total effect
is one of catty enervation; Pope remembered both
this effect and the amoral stance when he created
Sporus.[10]

II

The late John Butt has convincingly argued that
certain long sections of *Arbuthnot* were probably
written as early as 1731-32, a circumstance
that should neither surprise us nor lead us to
undervalue the structure of the much-expanded
finished poem.[11] In fact, the two lampoons just
described enable us to see how Pope gathers diverse circumstances and materials into a whole
which, though giving a surface impression of mazy
satura, is an exemplary instance of coherent
satiric form, of the cogency possible in Augustan
expansive poetry, and of the poetic analogue of
concordia discors. The "occasion" of *Arbuthnot* not
only provides Pope with important new subject matter and suggestions for devices, but guides him
toward a new organizing strategy which adds
major new sections to the poem (including its
climactic portrait) and which revises and re-
shapes parts already written.
    The explosive opening of *Arbuthnot*, Donnean in
its exaggerated sense of outrage at intrusion,
does exist in the 260-line Huntington-Morgan
Manuscript fragment, but there it is buried in
the midst of the poem. Its new prominence dramatically answers Lady Mary's and Lord Hervey's

charge of "loneliness," and that prominence becomes a crucial part both of the rhetorical
strategy of the poem and of the new motif which
Pope allows to control the poem. *Verses to the
Imitator* concluded that Pope was alone, barred
from the company of all: contemporaries

> Shall shun thy Writings like thy Company;
> And to thy books shall ope their Eyes no more
> Than to thy Person they wou'd do their Door.
> Nor thou the Justice of the World disown,
> That leaves thee thus an Outcast, and alone.
>   (II. 98-102)

Pope does not state the absurdity of the charge,
but rather dramatizes his problem as quite the
reverse:

> Shut, shut the door, good *John*! fatigu'd I
>   said,
> Tye up the knocker, say I'm sick, I'm dead,
> The Dog-star rages! nay 'tis past a doubt,
> All *Bedlam*, or *Parnassus*, is let out:
> Fire in each eye, and Papers in each hand,
> They rave, recite, and madden round the land.
>   (II. 1-6)

This much is in the early manuscript, but in the
completed *Arbuthnot* Pope considerably elaborates
the sense of oppression and clutter; the siege
now is on land and sea, the pursuers climb walls,
pierce thickets, board conveyances, and invade
groves, churches, and even Pope's grotto; and
they glut time (including sabbaths) as well as
space. The source of this oppression is the universal clamor for counsel; Pope builds the finished
poem on the motif of giving and taking counsel.
The satirist's exchange with his *adversarius*, the
scribblers' wish for critical "advice" and consent, the political relationships of court and
counsel--all illustrate the motif and work variations upon it. The shifts back and forth
between literary and political realms, and between proper and improper ways of seeking and
giving counsel, fuse the literary and political

implications into a cultural prophecy which develops a distinct and viable moral dimension.
The satirist here, as in *Epilogue, Dialogue I*, or in
The Impertinent, is isolated as the one positive force, the one honest man willing to take counsel-
seeking and counsel-giving seriously and treat
them as a vehicle of truth, not of self-seeking
delusion.

Three metaphors support Pope's motif, and he
interrelates them, in his finished poem, into
a rhetorical strategy culminating in the climatic
Sporus portrait--a portrait which gathers the
major strands of the poem's concern and offers a
horrendous prophecy of the eternal rhythms of
evil. Two of the metaphors--those of bestiality
and madness--are among the three most prominent
satiric metaphors isolated by Philip Pinkus,[12]
and they require extraordinary control to feed the
specific motif here. The third metaphor, that
of ears, ultimately controls and focuses the
other two, elaborating the bestiality of modern
counsel-seekers and the madness of modern counsel-
givers. Ears, imaged as receptacles, take on
passive, feminine connotations, and they accumulate a meaning of perverted sexuality, linking
bodies in a grotesque imitation of the distorted
modern means of communication. Miltonic allusion
imposes the moral dimension, and the whispering
madness of speaking is only matched by the asinine
satisfaction of listening in a world where words
are only substanceless froth and where flattery
reproduces evil. In this world truth can find,
among speakers or hearers, no takers at all.

Bestial metaphors take many shapes in *Arbuthnot*;
the dominant ones are those of dogs and of asses.
Dogs, because in the poem they are usually rabid,
connect the bestiality to the madness; asses,
because they shamelessly display their symbol of
stupidity, connect bestial imagery to ear imagery.
Thus the poem sets up its equivalences: bestiality
equals madness (both represent departures from
man's middle state in the chain of being), and
bestiality equals receptivity to false counsel.
In the Sporus portrait madness and ears are connected, and the equivalences are cross-referenced
in a cogent triangle of perverted horror: the

toad, frothing like the poem's mad dogs, spits
its counsel into the poised ear of Eve.
    The bestial metaphor here carries its usual
Augustan connotations of savagery, irrationality
and ignorance, and Pope implies that such animal
characteristics apply more or less indiscriminately
to the scribblers he portrays. But he keeps the
metaphor submerged most of the time, allowing it
to surface only at key places in the poem. The
opening passage, partially inverting the traditional hunt, establishes the metaphor and implies
its universality for the world of the poem; the
supernature in control here is the Dog Star. The
metaphor surfaces as a spider for one scribbler
(ll. 89 ff.), as a peacock for another (Bufo, ll.
231 ff.), and in a variety of shifting forms for
Sporus. But most of the time the metaphor only
lurks, subtly insinuating its implications without emerging onto the poem's surface. Once,
for example, the speaker alludes to "the Race
that write," sliding perilously close to semi-
scientific generic terms like "finny kind" and
"airy prey."[13] Such lurking omnipresence allows
the metaphor to suggest repeatedly the level of
imagination and taste which the scribblers possess. One couplet (ll. 275-76) illustrates Pope's
effect strikingly. In the early manuscript the
couplet began, "'I saw him walk with Swift'--
nay then no doubt," and the second line is incomplete. In the finished couplet, Pope's significant alteration is in one word: "'I found him
close with Swift,'" and the rest of the couplet
clarifies the image: "'Indeed? no doubt'/(Cries
Prating Balbus) 'something will come out.'"
The change in effect is enormous, for now the
couplet is phased with the pattern of submerged
bestial imagery, and the observer of Pope-Swift
is categorized in the full limits of his perception; he is unable to conceive normal human
relationships or the procedures of poetic creation, for he views everything through his perverted obsession with what a body, not a mind,
can make.[14]
    Pope controls the madness metaphor in a simi-
lar way. It bursts upon the poem at the beginning,

recedes, and then transmogrifies into several new
forms. The opening inversion of sanity establishes
the metaphor; the hot irrationality of the dog
days leaves no doubt that Bedlam has expanded to
fill the entire world of the poem. Poets rave,
recite and madden boundlessly; they seek Pope's
counsel "to keep them mad or vain." The metaphor
surfaces to describe the "slaver" of flatterers,
the "prose run mad" of bombastic poets, and the
general "madness" that urges scribblers into
print. More subtly it controls the madness implied in some of the rhymes, one of the relations
of rhyme to unreason which W.K. Wimsatt has
suggested.[15] Thus, Cornus blames his wife's
elopement on Pope because his name sounds like
her action; Lintot, similarly confused about the
relation of language to action, chooses his profession (print it) because of the sound of its
name; Phillips confuses the half-earned *renown*
of literary stealing with the monetary reward he
can make by half-invading a new kingdom; and a
confined poet writes because, in his necromantic
logic, the darkened walls suggest the charcoal
scrawls of black on black.

Pope's bestial and madness metaphors, while
subtly controlled and brilliantly extended, are
less significant in themselves than in conjunction
with the third metaphor. Pope's revision of the
early manuscript shows him beginning to find the
possibilities of the metaphor; its influence
later expands to the structure and meaning of the
whole poem. In the early manuscript the ear metaphor does not, in any significant sense, exist,
though one can see Pope toying with its possibilities. The story of Midas--an allusion which
comes to control the metaphor through two-thirds
of the finished poem--is added in the margin near
the end of the fragment; it is bracketed near
the lower right-hand corner of one manuscript
page, quite removed from the main body of the
poem on the left. Apparently, Pope inserted the
Midas story to illustrate the compulsive truthfulness of the satirist, and his first thought
was to place it late in the poem. Later, he
expanded the story and made it more pointed,

letting its particular historical reference suggest the counsel motif governing the shape of
the final poem. And he moves the story near the
beginning to let its allusive meanings reverber-
ate throughout the whole poem.

In the early manuscript there is no mention
of Queens, Ministers, or Kings, no allusion to
the contemporary government; instead the story
is told sketchily and in generalities, pointed
toward the analogy with the satirist's plight.
The section begins:

> His Asses ears if Midas would not hide
> What could his wife? She told it or had dy'd.

The finished poem shifts the focus and expands
the exposition:

> 'Tis sung, when *Midas*' Ears began to spring,
> (*Midas*, a sacred Person and a King)
> His very Minister who spy'd them first,
> (Some say his Queen) was forc'd to speak, or
>   burst.   (ll. 69-72)

Pope's new version describes an unholy trinity,[16]
and once he sets up the association of royalty,
bestiality, protruding growths, stupidity, self-
imperception, and calculated secrecy, he can let
the ear metaphor do several things. Ears, in the
Midas story, have outgrown normal proportions, but
their increased size results only in a decreased
usefulness; King Midas is the last to hear. The
protruding ears which scribblers extend toward
Pope bespeak bestial stupidity in the kingdom of
letters, but they also suggest the impossibility
of real communication.

This range of suggestion becomes an integral
part of the poem from the Midas story (ll.69 ff.)
to the Sporus portrait (ll.305 ff.), but Pope sets
up some preliminary association before Midas, and
draws out the implications more fully after Sporus. The beginning paragraphs of the poem present
an appalling sense of aural oppression. In this
noisy world, the airways are as glutted with intrusion as the personal time and physical space

456

surrounding Pope. This sense of aural oppression
is, in fact, characteristic of Augustan satire;
Augustan satirists--highly conscious of the oral
implications of poetry--found it hard to be detached about sound, for they were deeply sensitive
that poetry now had to compete in a kind of spiraling decibel race with entertainments that
used sound without sense: the threshings of Stephen Duck, the howls of the bear-pit, the mad
wails of the fanatic polemicists, the shrill cries
of the personal lampooner, the distorted unnatural
piercings of popular Italian opera. The year before *Arbuthnot* was published, Richard Savage had
described the "furious noisy Crew" of dunces in
this way:

> Their greater Right infer from louder Tongues,
> And Strength of Argument from Strength of
>   Lungs.
> Instead of Sense, who stun your Ears with
>   Sound,
> And think they conquer, when they but confound.
> *Taurus*, a bellowing Champion storms and swears,
> And drives his Argument thro'both your Ears;
> And whether Truth or Falsehood, right or
>   wrong,
> 'Tis still maintain'd and prov'd by dint of--
>   Tongue.
> In all Disputes he bravely wins the Day.
> No wonder--for he hears not what you say.[17]

One might argue that Pope picked up specific
suggestions here for his ear imagery in *Arbuthnot*;
but what seems to me more important is the Augustan typicality of the passage in citing aural
oppression. Pope early captures this sense of
oppression, but he quickly gives it an ironic
turn, even before the Midas passage. In Pope's
version the noisy scribblers feel oppressed by
calm voices of sense, even though they asked for
counsel, even when the voice has the authority
of Horace. Pope sets up the suggestion concisely,
mainly through the single phrase "unwilling
ears":

> I sit with sad Civility, I read
> With honest anguish, and an aking head;
> And drop at last, but in unwilling ears,
> This saving counsel, "Keep your Piece nine
>   years." (ll. 37-40)

Again Pope's procedures of composition are instructive. The early manuscript tries several
rhymes for "years"; Pope obviously was struggling
here for the right suggestion, and the two read-
able versions (both crossed out) are "these
words he hears" and "my author hears." But no
one hears good counsel in the world of metaphors
which the completed poem engages, and Pope's
final choice expresses the scribblers' ultimate
reluctance to confront themselves. The poem's
speaker--besieged, frustrated, anguished--finds
that honest counsel results only in anger and
misunderstanding like that which greets the published satirist; his attempt to use words mean-
ingfully is regarded not as poetic salvation, but
as physical rape.[18]

III

The Sporus portrait culminates the associations
I have described, fusing the metaphors and elaborating their moral implicaitons; it also provides the rhetorical climax for Pope's answer to
his attackers. The portrait is the poem's most
intense moment, channeling the poem's energy into
a lucid statement about the breakdown in verbal
communication at the same time as it provides
a model instance of what communication can do in
uniting the real with the ideal, the particular
with the universal.
  The portrait follows a paragraph on the moral
function of poetry, a paragraph which Pope had
thoroughly revised from a brief squib published
three years earlier.[19] Now he makes direct
comments about those who confuse art with life,
and--analogically--satire with lampoon. He concludes that

A Lash like mine no honest man shall dread,
But all such babling blockheads in his stead.
   (ll. 303-304)

Such concern brings him to Sporus, and the *adversarius* objects that Sporus is too trifling, too insignificant, too transitory an example to bother
with:

   ... "What? that Thing of silk,
   Sporus, that mere white Curd of Ass's milk?
   Satire or Sense alas! can *Sporus* feel?
   Who breaks a Butterfly upon a Wheel?"
      (ll. 305-308)

These lines set up much of the portrait itself,
for they enable the main speaker to contrast the
real insignificance of Sporus with his extraordinary influence in a modern world preoccupied
with the giving and taking of false counsel.[20]
In addition, the *adversarius*' imagery sets up the
interpretive machinery for the imagery that
follows.
   The "Thing of silk" places Sporus in the elegant court world and suggests the discrepancy
between the emperor and his clothes; the flossily
clad courtier had long been a symbol of elegant
corruption. The butterfly image suggests a gay,
fragile exterior recently imposed on grotesque,
crawling reality, and implies transience; according to the *adversarius*, this courtier need not be
satirically punished because his court life-
expectancy is not long anyway. Through such an
image Pope implies that the *adversarius* has not
fully understood the depth of the problem so
far described. The poem, as I read it, is not
only a high tribute to the goodness and high
personal standards of Arbuthnot, but a gentle
chiding for being willing to tolerate weakness
in others, for being confident that evil will go
away. The butterfly and silk images also introduce subtle hints of the effeminacy of Sporus.
The type of the effeminate courtier--foppish,
obsequious, narcissistic, affectedly graceful,

and amoral--is an old one (Shakespeare's Osric is
a typical example), and was frequently elaborated
by Pope's contemporaries; the butterfly image
standardly expressed the type.[21] And the "Thing
of silk" may well carry overtones of sexual impotence; later in the portrait, in a distinctly
sexual setting, Pope puns again on "thing" on
twice on "parts."[22]

The *adversarius'* third image is usually explained
by Lord Hervey's medicinal use of ass's milk, but
Pope's range of reference and tonal effect is far
more complex than that annotation suggests. Because Pope also used ass's milk, the reference is
self-mocking and adds a rather grim comic note
at a key rhetorical point. Such a reminder of
Pope's own infirmity functions thematically, demonstrating the common mortality of the satirist
and satiric object. The fact of physical infirmity is not, Pope implies, what separates the
just from the unjust; the difference lies in
what one does with one's mortality, and Pope
demonstrates quickly what has come of Sporus'.
The ass's milk here is curdled, almost the ultimate *reductio* of the bestial imagery the poem has
engaged; but even more important is the control
the curd asserts over the imagery that follows.
The curd is neither solid nor liquid, but in that
middle state of plasticity and shapelessness--a
quality that sets up the moral dimension of the
imagery soon to be used by the main speaker.
Ironically, the *adversarius* (trying to reduce
Sporus to an inanimate level, beneath the attention of the satirist) provides the perspective
from which to see the true insidiousness of this,
the most vicious foe of all.

The satirist begins his answer in the tonal
framework of the *adversarius'* objections, playfully feigning to meet the *adversarius* on his own
terms, but his voice shifts quickly to indignant
intensity:

Yet let me flap this Bug with gilded wings
This painted Child of Dirt that stinks and
    stings. (11. 309-310)

First accepting the *adversarius'* categorization, he
pretends only to swat, but by the second line the
wheel is moving. Bug, for Pope's contemporaries,
usually meant bedbug,[23] but Pope immediately begins to play with, and qualify, that expectancy
as he identifies just what kind of buggery is
here involved. Pope's lily-gilding swiftly introduces two major motifs in the portrait: the
perversion of Sporus (the oral pun on "gild" combines with the Roman allusion to clarify Sporus'
bedside manner), and his absurd willingness to
be more than one thing at once. But Pope quickly
reminds that Sporus' paint job does not hide his
origins. In the background here is Hervey's attack on Pope's birth, and Pope answers not by defense, but by instancing the way to handle such
a matter: the satirist, Pope implies, does not
impugn an innocent parent, but rather engages a
rhetorical device that both makes contextual sense
and focuses upon the character of the satiric object itself. Tonally, the first line of the
couplet seems to accept the *adversarius'* view of
the triviality of Sporus; the second line over-
corrects as the speaker becomes too intense and
loses himself for a moment in violent sound
associations (stinks-stings), as if he were showing the emotional hazards of confronting evil on
the one hand and of apathy on the other. But the
next line quickly straightens the bent, and re-
bent, stick; unable to sting, Sporus can merely
buzz and annoy, incapable of fully realizing
his intention. His inability to enjoy beauty or
to taste wit changes the focus of attack to the
mental and aesthetic; physical characteristics
had not been asserted as symbolic, but swiftly
and almost imperceptibly they had become *illustrative* of what lay beneath the gilded exterior.
The next three couplets elaborate the external-
internal relations by analogues which give Sporus
three new forms, each regressively lower than the
other. He is first a spaniel, tame and subdued,
his bestial desires masked by civility; then a
stream, seeming to live, but actually only reflecting narcissistic companions; finally a
puppet, lifeless and totally without personal

identity. The bathetic movement from ass to
butterfly to bug to stream to puppet is abruptly
terminated by Sporus' next form, higher in the
chain physically, but lowest of all morally; and
now the shapelessness of the curd and the shapeshifting of Sporus' roles are focused in a
crescendo of moral indignation.

The sights and sounds of the movement from
puppet to toad elicit the full response of the
poem's major metaphors. Pope now channels them
into a new violent statement about stupidity,
irrationality, malice, loss of identity, perversion and impotence in high places, establishing
an allusive context that enforces a moral judgment on Sporus:

> Whether in florid Impotence he speaks,
> And, as the Prompter breathes, the Puppet
>   squeaks;
> Or at the Ear of *Eve*, familiar Toad,
> Half Froth, half Venom, spits himself abroad,
> In Puns, or Politick, or Tales, or Lyes,
> Or Spite, or Smut, or Rymes, or Blasphemies.
> His Wit all see-saw, between *that* and *this*,
> Now high, now low, now Master up, now Miss,
> And he himself one vile Antithesis.
> Amphibious Thing! that acting either Part,
> The trifling Head, or the corrupted Heart!
> Fop at the Toilet, Flatt'rer at the Board,
> Now trips a Lady, and now struts a Lord.
> *Eve's* Tempter thus the Rabbins have exprest,
> A Cherub's face, a Reptile all the rest;
> Beauty that shocks you, Parts that none will
>   trust,
> Wit that can creep, and Pride that licks the
>   dust. (ll. 317-33)

The squeaky mummery of the puppet and the substanceless froth of the toad both demonstrate
what communication has come to--in conversation,
affairs of state, or the kingdom of letters.[24]
Venom replaces vertu; Milton's grotesque visual
vignette melts into the regular but meaningless
sexual rhythms of

Now high, now low, now Master up, now Miss.

The loss of identities (Sporus spits him*self*
abroad) and distinctions means that all the roles
are topsy-turvy, that clumsy attempts to communicate result only in a perverted demonstration
that man's first sin and fall predict his last.[25]
The toad and snake and the lisping sibilants
that hold them together take, of course, their
ultimate dimension from Eden via Milton, but Pope's
language makes clear one site of contemporary
relevance: the court. The allusive presence of
Lord Hervey starts the association, and it is
intensified by the description of the toad as
"familiar," by the account of the selfworshipping
fop, Lady, and Lord, and by the new analogue of
ears and whispering. The name Sporus also points
Pope's attack and underscores his moral, for Sporus was a handsome court favorite in Rome, so loved
that he was castrated and "married" to his emper-
or. The emperor was Nero; two years before his
Epistle to Augustus, Pope is already commenting on the
correct Roman parallel for George II's England.[26]
The other two major portraits of the poem comment similarly. Addison's christening as Atticus
is usually glossed as a mock-heroic device recalling the eminent judiciousness of Atticus,
friend to Cicero. But another Atticus (Vestinus)
was a consul under Nero; though opposed to the
corruption of Nero's Rome, he was left out of the
conspiracy because his friends did not trust him,
and at his death he found himself hopelessly between factions, suspected by all.[27] Even Bufo
draws on this unusual classical context. I have
said that Bufo is imaged as a peacock, but that
is not quite right, for it is only his apparent
form, "puff'd by ev'ry quill."[28] Again, Pope's
revision underscores his developed conception of
the poem's shape. Bufo was first Bubo, but sitting "full-blown" on "his forked hill," Bufo depicts his nominal identity, a Latin toad. By such
a device Pope both extends the sense of evil at
court and demonstrates that Sporus and Bufo are
not really important in themselves, for they have
no real identity; rather they are simply manifes-

tations, in temporary forms, of the continuing
oppressive presence of evil in high places. Pope's
uses of the past in *Arbuthnot* demonstrate the version of history that has imposed itself on modernity. Pope implies that modern scribblers imitate the tarnish of the Golden Age; their models
are degenerate rulers, untrustworthy judges, and
animal types of evil which, in whatever language
they are named, insinuate their shifting forms
finally to a kindred receptacle, corrupting by
false counsel all the bastions of Western cul-
ture--literature, law, the state, the social
structure, the dignity of human identity.
    Pope's final use of his structuring motif
comes as a clarifying anticlimax, just as the
main speaker sums up his detractors and just before he modulates to the touching *pianissimo* description of the satirist's private life. Here
the suggestive whisper still "vibrates on [the]
sovereign's ear," and the satiric hero tells why
he must continue to "insult the poor, affront
the great," calling an ass an ass.

>   A Knave's a Knave, to me, in ev'ry State,
>   Alike my scorn, if he succeed or fail,
>   *Sporus* at Court, or Japhet in a Jayl,
>   A hireling Scribler, or a hireling Peer,
>   Knight of the Post corrupt, or of the Shire,
>   If on a Pillory, or near a Throne,
>   He gain his Prince's Ear, or lose his own.
>   (ll. 361-67)

"Gain[ing] his Prince's Ear" by now bears a
resonance of meaning: "gaining" means not only
"getting access to" but also "acquiring." The
Midas story makes clear that one gains such a
mark of distinction through bad taste; Midas
had gotten his (and introduced the whispering asininity of the kingdom) by misjudging a singing
contest between Pan and Apollo.[29] The forces of
Lord Hervey and of Pope now offer a similar choice
in the kingdom of dullness, and the results are
predictable. And now, too, the relevance and
absurdity of the pillory are laid bare; cutting

off someone's ears is a kind of self-purgation,
but it is a treatment of symptoms, not of the
disease. And losing one's ear is not very important anyway in such a world of dizzying noise
and confusion, a world where, ironically, such
external projections can become merely receptacles
for the froth of substanceless selves.

IV

The perspective on modernity which Pope offers in
Arbuthnot is what is missing in the lampoonery of
the likes of Lord Hervey--where when history is
not ignored it is misunderstood or misapplied.
Pope's handling of the allusion to the Fall instances the distinction brilliantly; his footnote credits *Verses to the Imitator* with suggesting
the allusion, but what Pope is really doing is
calling attention to their comparative artistic
handling of the Fall--a handling that demonstrates
enormous disparities in their conception of both
life and art.
    Verses to the Imitator uses the allusion to try
to curse its enemy; to do so it violates chronology, fact, common sense, and good taste. Pope's
broken body and his lonely wanderings are asserted as accomplished results even before the causal
curse is delivered. But even more important, the
allusion bears no significant relation to the
rest of the poem, and instead of lifting the attack to a higher level it emphasizes a physical
characteristic which it fails to integrate with
any larger dimension. It may be witty to assert
that Pope hurts his head in bruising the heel of
his victims, but such imprecise inversion does
not add up to much. It asserts, again, Pope's
small stature, but fails to establish a connection
between the events of the poem and those of the
allusion. The method of *Verses* is to recall a
context, shout its relevance, offer a stroke or
two of wit, and hope. Satiric art is more complex and more precise, as *Arbuthnot* instances.
    If the emphasis in *Verses* is on physical ap-
pearance, the emphasis in *Arbuthnot* is on the

realities behind appearance. Pope's point is not
ultimately that Sporus is effeminate or homosexual,
but that Sporus is amphibiously willing to do
anything, to play any role, to assume any perverted
stance because he has no identity, because his
only essential characteristic is the formlessness
of evil itself. Pope uses various real characteristics of Lord Hervey to illustrate his point:
Hervey's contemporaries regarded him as effeminate
and shifty, his speech showed a tendency to the
reconciliation of opposites, he jealously guarded
his position near the ear of greatness. To
dramatize the shapeshifting, Pope accepts the
formulations of others (Pulteney had called
Hervey a Master-Miss),[30] and records Hervey's
conscious postures (Hervey "now trips a Lady and
now struts a Lord" in *Verses* ["by a Lady"] and
in *Epistle* ["from a Nobleman"]). Most important,
says Pope, the forms assumed by this shapeshifting
imitate in real life the mythic poses described
in traditonal accounts of man's fall.

Criticism of Pope for dwelling on historical
particulars ignores, I think, the nature of Augustan art and the precise distinctions that it
demands. What is important about Pope's por-
trayal of Sporus is where the emphasis lies--
not on physical appearance but upon underlying
significance. The contrast between Pope's emphasis and that of *Verses* is crucial: *Verses*
tediously asserts and reasserts a physical characteristic that is beyond the realm of choice,
while Pope presents a pattern of role-shifting
behavior which is a matter of choice--and a matter
of character. What Pope does *not* do is significant,
for some highly dramatic choices were open to him.
A bust of Lord Hervey shows a tiered chin and
puffy cheeks; his physical appearance offered
some amusing possibilities for elaborating the
toad comparison.[31] But Pope eschews such a method; a lampooner might wish to leave his emphasis
on a disgusting physical characteristic, but not
a satirist. And if a reader recognized the
physical relevance, the locus lay in the satiric
object, not in a poetic *assertion*.[32] One other

eschewed possibility must have been even more
tempting: Lord Hervey was an epileptic, but
Pope makes no reference to his seizures, even in
a poem that deals often with the seizures of
scribblers and madmen. Rather than trying to
assert such a physical characteristic as a symbol
Pope simply allows his dogs and toads to froth
their venom abroad. If a reader finds such imagery peculiarly relevant, it is *he* who invents
the insult. Like Dryden before him, and Sterne
after, Pope is a master at disclaimer; it is the
reader who draws the dirty pictures.

The allusion to Eden represents Pope's most
significant instance of how satire and lampoon
differ, but Pope also dramatizes, point by point,
an answer to the other charges of *Epistle* and
Verses. What I have already said suggests how
Arbuthnot offers proper satiric answers to charges
of friendlessness, poetic impotence, obscure
origins, and satiric motives. Two other charges
struck at the very basis of Pope's art, impugning
his knowledge of the past and his intengrity in
using the poetic tradition; *Epistle* and *Verses*
charged Pope with poetic theft, and *Verses*
questioned his knowledge of Greek.

Pope answers the charge of theft by noting
proper and improper ways to use the poetic tradition. His borrowing from Addison, "A painted
mistress, or a purling stream," illustrates echoic
characterization,[33] and his reworking of the
Addison portrait points to inept borrowing. Earlier
his summary couplet had read:

What Pity, Heav'n! if such a Man there be.
Who would not weep, if A---n were he?

In *Arbuthnot* Pope alters the first line to read
"Who but must laugh..." The change quotes Pope
himself (1. 107 of *Moral Essay IV* [1731]) but by
way of *Verses* , which had quoted and mangled the
original line. Pope's reinsertion of the line
into his own canon betters the couplet and extends
its evocative range. His proper use subtly implies *Verses'* improper use in quoting the line,
then trying to take over its images bodily.[34]

Pope's answer to the charges about Greek is, I
think, even more subtle, for he does not explicitly deal with the charge at all. But he appears
to give an implicit answer in the form of a challenge: Pope asks Hervey whether he knows enough
to recognize himself. Footnotes on Sporus in-
variably send Pope students to Suetonius, but I
think it more likely that Pope's "source" was
Dion Cassius, whose more detailed account of
Sporus was in Greek. Dion Cassius, unlike
Suetonius, offers the unsavory details about
Sporus' role, and includes the fact that Sabina,
the queen whom Sporus "replaces," bathed daily
in the milk of five hundred asses. If Pope had
this account in mind, it adds the dimension of
court luxury to his picture of Sporus' environment, and suggests an amusing reason why Sporus
is a curd. At any rate, there is good evidence
that Lord Hervey suspected Dion Cassius to be
Pope's source, for shortly after the Sporus portrait appeared, Lord Hervey (who admitted his own
ignorance of Greek) was frantically searching for
a Latin translation of Dion Cassius.[35]
We do Pope a disservice if we regard his
satiric art as too quickly "universal" and if we
view his portraits as portraits *only* of types.[36]
Pope's art is not merely topical, but is particular first, *then* comprehensive beyond its
time-space limits. The genius of Pope in satire
is precisely in his manipulation of timeliness
into a context of timelessness, offering his
contemporaries a vision that demanded perspective,
and offering posterity not only a way of seeing
how Pope and his rivals viewed themselves, but
also a vision of the shapes evil may assume when
it insinuates itself in human history.
The effect of such a vision on life may be
questionable, of course, especially if we confuse
art with life, or demand that the satirist, unlike other artists, be pragmatically effective
to be artistically successful. The idea of Lord
Hervey madly skimming Dion Cassius, searching
for self-recognition, may amuse us, and it would
have pleased the very real moralist in Pope. But

ultimately that kind of effect is irrelevant to
satiric art, as Pope well knew and as his aims
here demonstrate. Pope's artistic climax comes
in his destruction of Sporus. By the end of the
portrait, the angel in Sporus (the "Beauty" of
his "Cherub's face") has been completely cursed,
condemned to drag its pride along the ground.
Pride, wit, body (spiritual, mental, physical)
have been given the ultimate *reductio*, but through a
series of complex poetic maneuvers, not by simple
assertion. The portrait began in a shapeless
epitome of the poem's dominant physical image; it
ends by extending to that image a dimension both
mental and moral. The life that oozed from the
ground has been returned to dust--but only by
the satirist, only in the fantasy of his created
world. A lampooner may confuse life with art, but
not a satirist. Outside, Lord Hervey still
paints and flatters, trips and struts, stinks and
stings; and society still pretends to purge itself by trimming the ears of those it catches in
faux pas. But Pope does not choose here to give
that truth the final word. Here his last note is
to be peace and tenderness, and the evil is to be
treated as expunged, as if victory in art purges
not only the spirit of the satirist, but life
itself. Of course, Pope knew better, as the
Dunciad shows--as his entire dedication to the
satiric spirit shows. His satiric career demonstrates that artistic victory is not equivalent
to cosmic purification; but here he instances
what art *can* do. It may not win in the streets,
in the gross and brutal rivalries of London, even
at court; but the satirist can always use London
and George's court (or even Nero's) in his assault
on Parnassus--and on paradise.

THE ARGUMENT OF POPE'S *EPISTLE TO COBHAM**

John E. Sitter

The question from which this essay originates
may be posed simply: Why is there such disparity
between Pope's apparent regard for the *Epistle
to Cobham* ("Of the Knowledge and Characters of
Men") and two centuries of criticism in
which the poem has been regarded as a relative
failure? Pope's opinion is suggested by the
fact that he gave the poem a pivotal position
between the *Essay on Man* and the rest of the
"Second Book" of "Ethic Epistles," that he
viewed the arrangement of these poems as
significant, and that he told Swift (who had
already seen the epistles to Burlington and
Bathurst) that he was saving his "best silks"
for last.[1] On the other hand, the first of the
so-called Moral Essays has also been called
"the worst" of them in what is now something of
a venerable editorial tradition--Bowles to
Courthope to Bateson--and even the less invidi-
ous critical statements have, from Johnson on,
been largely negative.[2] The objections divide

This essay first appeared in *SEL* 17 (1977), 435-449.

basically into two kinds: critics examining
Pope's intellectual position tend to wonder why
he prized his theory of the "ruling passion"
so highly, while those who focus on Pope as
characterist frequently conclude that his best
character-sketches have little to do with the
reputedly "new hypothesis" of character which
he announced to Spence.[3] Put another way, the
objections are that Pope was influenced more in
formulating his theory than he recognized, or was
influenced less *by* it than he realized.

   All of this might be a curiosity rather than
a critical problem if we were not accustomed
to regarding Pope as a remarkably good judge
of his own work. Certainly poets before and
after Pope--perhaps Crashaw and Wordsworth may
stand as hoary examples--have written some very
good and some very bad poetry and have not
always known the difference. Despite his
usual tact and control, Pope may still be wrong,
of course; but it is worth reflecting that if
a poet who is also a good critic *is* wrong about
his work, such an error may well occur precisely when he is most intent upon combating
errors and when he is "about" his most important concerns as a poet. This is a difficult
line of inquiry, since it may quickly lead to
the temptation of claiming knowledge of the
poem's *real* meaning and the poet's *real*
intention. For the moment, at least, we need
only recall that the poem is largely about
books and men and how to read them, and that
to follow Pope's own simplest but difficult
advice on such judgments we need to try again
to read the work "in the same spirit its
author writ" and to be "candid where we can."
To do so it seems necessary to look more
closely at the poem itself, particularly its
first few paragraphs, and at Pope in the early
1730's--his own mid-forties--in an attempt to
understand better the grounds of his argument.

   That the poem is an argument appears to be
forgotten in much of the argument about it,
a phenomenon which may stem from two sets of

circumstances. The first is the 200-year-old
tradition of reading the poem in Warburton's
post-facto arrangement;[4] the second is the fact
that the epistle is addressed to Lord Cobham,
Pope's respected friend. This latter fact has
been influential because we tend to assume in
literature what we rarely assume in life,
namely that good friends do not have major
disagreements. Whether or not the historical
Pope and Cobham disagreed on matters philosophical, the epistolary "Pope" and "Cobham"
certainly do, and this need not surprise us.
The "Friend" of Pope's first Horatian imitation
both is and is not Fortescue and surely is in
disagreement with the poet. So even Arbuthnot
and Swift. All of these poems (*Satire II, i,
Satire II,ii,* the *Epistle to Arbuthnot*) date from
the same immediate period as the *Epistle to
Cobham* and stand as reminders of how frequently
Pope uses public debate as a medium for personal
philosophy.[5] In his last illness a decade later,
Pope sent copies of the "moral essays" to a
select circle of friends and, in doing so,
thought of Socrates dispensing morality as he
was dying. The analogy is drawn playfully,
even ruefully, but the image of Socrates lives,
for Pope as for us, because he liked to
argue with his friends.
    Warburton's pseudo-Aristotelian "ordering"
of the epistle has blurred its lively Socratic
process. That we no longer read the poem in
his text has not erased the poem's critical
heritage, nor has it erased for most readers
the assumption that the "essay" has (or should
have) a theoretical integrity apart from the
dynamics of debate. It has not been sufficiently stressed that the poem suffers as much
philosophically as artistically at his heavy
hands. But Pope's breezy opening also tends to
disguise argument in the act of revealing it--

    Yes you despise the man to Books confin'd
    Who from his study rails at human kind--

lulling us into armchair amiability and perhaps
"too easy a chair" at that. As in the *Epistle
to Bathurst*, the context of a friendly argument
is evoked, presumably one on a topic of long
standing; and here too Pope begins with a
witty concession as he quickly grants that the
cloistered railer knows little of the world.
Such a man is but "right by chance":

> The coxcomb bird, so talkative and grave,
> That from his cage cries Cuckold, Whore,
>   and Knave,
> Tho' many a passenger he rightly call,
> You hold him no Philosopher at all. (5-8)

The difference between the two epistles,
however, is that the position of Pope and "you"
do not amount, if only pushed far enough, to
essentially the same thing in practice. Their
disagreement is in fact more radical than the
easy gambit suggests, and it is doubtful
that we are meant to see the debates as involving merely the extremes of the urbane
observer and the scholar whose "study" is both
a physical and mental cloister. Whatever
significance those extremes possess is quickly
shown to be forensic and temporary. If for a
moment they take us back to the Wife of Bath's
opposition of "experience" to "auctoritee" (to
use an instance Pope had modernized 30 years
earlier), they also remind us that there is
something naive as well as perennial in the
tendency to create this black and white division:

> And yet the fate of all extremes is such,
> Men may be read, as well as Books too much.
> To Observations which ourselves we make,
> We grow more partial for th' observer's sake;
> To written Wisdom, as another's, less;
> Maxims are drawn from Notions, these from
>   Guess.   (9-14)

Men may be read--as well as books--*too much*.

The final surprise quickly sharpens an old saw
and hones the argument. For Pope, if not for
"Cobham," the debate has become more self-
conscious, and it soon grows more precise than
the general argument over written authority
and daily experience or over philosophy and
toothaches.

Aside from the poem's final paragraph in
which Cobham is addressed as Patriot hero and
model, "Cobham" is the generalized "you" of
the epistle. He stands for the most part in
the same relation to the poem as we do, and so
stands *for* the reader. He is a friend to be
sure, but he is addressed as a reader, not as
a fellow writer; nor is he invoked as a colleague in what is frequently Pope's imaginative
habit of alignment: Swift as fellow satirist,
Bolingbroke as peripatetic conversationalist,
Arbuthnot and Burlington as colleagues in
healing a diseased land. If the poem were more
political, Cobham's identity as Patriot would
make them fellow travelers in a context which
would color the whole; but the poem is clearly
concerned with individual rather than political
truths, and this emphasis enables Pope to
define the distance between himself and his
"you" with considerable aggression and starkness.
"Cobham" is the reader as reader, Pope is the
poet as poet, and between the two lies a gulf,
one which must be bridged by correcting the
casual skepticism of any reader unconvinced that
books have much to do with knowing men.

An awareness of this distance may help
explain Pope's reasons for assigning to "Cobham"
an argument essentially, and rather complacently
empirical and for quickly, and rather indecorou-
sly, proceeding to transcend that position. The
implications of the empirical argument would
discredit not only bookish railers but all who
are, in subtler fashion, "to Books confin'd."
This includes writers as well as readers,
those who speak through books as well as those
who speak from them. As one who lives in his
books--more fully than the scholar but, as

artist, no less "confin'd"--Pope carefully
broadens the challenge by shifting from "Books"
in the first paragraph to "written Wisdom" in
the second. This shift takes us from pictorial
caricature to perceptual scrutiny: in the first
instance the reader's prejudices are flattered;
in the second his pride is assaulted, politely
but firmly. We are no longer taking easy aim
at caged pedantry but confronting the more
difficult question of our resistance to
"another's" perspective in favor of the com-
placencies of egocentricity.

Perhaps a more challenging question from
Pope's point of view is whether poetry can
speak with real authority on matters of
individual psychology and concrete ethical
judgment, whether it can speak of men or merely
of Man. There is nothing necessarily so profound in the empiricists's distruct of "maxims"
(14)--even Rochefoucauld distrusted them--but
his position would, Pope argues, restrict the
speaker to "observations" based on "guess."[6]
It is a position which questions at once the
existence of order in the lives of individuals
and the reflection of such an order in literature. We can see this more clearly when we
assume with Pope that poetry depends upon
patterns by its very nature, that it tells
necessary truths about the nature outside of
itself by creating a nature "methodized." The
pure empiricist, however, assumes that human
natures cannot really be methodized, only
observed. If he is ultimately right, it is not
just the bookworms's rantings that are unreal;
the poet's efforts to catch and reflect
significant patterns in the lives of individuals
are likewise only so much illusion. These
efforts may be witty or forceful, but they do not
correspond to the real world; they too will only
be "right by chance." The poet's argument throughout is to admit variety but not meaningless chaos,
an aspect of Pope's temperament as well as his art
which Maynard Mack has described as "eschewing on
the whole the *thèse* and the *système*, cherishing the
ad hoc, recognizing the flux, variety, and disor-

derliness of experience," while "at the same time,
upholding the conviction that there *are* kinds, categories, precepts, maxims, schemes, and general
truths, and that experience in the long run adds
up to an order--or would, if one's perspective
were wide enough."[7]
    We do not need to look long to see that in
the poem's opening movement (1-50) Pope establishes a delicate but definite pattern of
inquiry and of widening perspective. After
the first two paragraphs he abandons the indirect discourse of debate (you vs. I), but
the process of debate is carried on by the
poet himself. The third and fourth paragraphs
in particular still carry the atmosphere of
dialogue, but it is dialogue internalized,
rigorous rather than competitive:

> There's some Peculiar in each leaf and grain,
> Some unmark'd fibre, or some varying vein:
> Shall only Man be taken in the gross?
> Grant but as many sorts of Mind as Moss.
>   That each from other differs, first con-
>   fess;
> Next, that he varies from himself no less:
> Add Nature's, Custom's, Reason's, Passion's
>   strife,
> And all Opinion's colours cast on life. (15-22)

The first of these highly compressed assertions
insists on recognition of human diversity,
resembling the epistle's opening lines in
hostility to cloistered theorists. But is is
significant that the ground has now shifted
just enough so that the appeal to experience
is made by and for the poet, the man who
deals as well in keenly visual discriminations
("some varying vein") as in imagistic analogies.
The appeal is based on essentially the same
foundations as Keats's complaint about Coleridge,
who pursued theories at the expense of missing,
according to Keats, many a "fine isolated
verisimilitude" from the world of fluid
experience.[8] And in Pope's particular climate,
"Grant but as many sorts of Mind as Moss," is

a more basic insistence that the urbane
auditor grant the poet what, certainly, any
reasonable man would grant the naturalist. The
next step, quickly taken, is to insist as well
on internal diversity, that each "varies from
himself" no less than from others. The phrase
is clearly a logical paradox, since it both
affirms and denies the existence of a single
self. But Pope feels little need to argue the
point, perhaps because he is now drawing upon
a skeptical and introspective tradition, at
least as old as Montaigne, which emphasized
man's own internal contraditctions, stressing
the paradox, more than the paradise, within.[9]
     The larger fact suggested by these two
brief paragraphs is that Pope has begun to
move swiftly from the issue of "observations"
and "maxims" about other people to questions
of introspection and self-knowledge. And
these beget the question of perspective:

> Yet more; the diff'rence is as great between
> The optics seeing, as the objects seen.
> All Manners take a tincture from our own,
> Or come discolour'd thro' our Passions
>   shown.
> Or Fancy's beam enlarges, multiplies,
> Contracts, inverts, and gives ten thousand
>   dyes.   (23-28)

     If one is alert to metaphor as well as logic
it is clear that Pope wishes to stress the
connection between self-knowledge and knowledge
of others. The categories are deliberately
conflated since the line immediately preceding
these--"And all Opinion's *colours* cast on life"--
relates internal inconsistency to optical
delusion. The "optics seeing," then, pertains
to the observer viewing others and viewing
himself. Warburton found such things untidy and
juggled this and the next section so much that
Pope's fine connections were severed. In effect,
Warburton "ordered" these paragraphs to say
that two discrete problems attend observation:

1) the complexity of the object, and 2)the limitations of the observer.[10] But the original structure suggests that these two problems are in fact one problem. The observer and the observed are both human, and the relationship is thus more intimate and chastening than the clinical relationship of the naturalist to his mosses. The complexity and mutability of those we observe should remind us of our own, and vice versa, so that proper inspection implies proper introspection.

A strenuous attack is well underway, then, on the complacency of the empirical stance which launched the poem's conversation. We begin to see that the worldly-wise position is founded on the assumption that the observer is steady and self-sufficient, on the illusion that the armchair will afford "sedate reflections." That foundation begins to shake when we confront "quick whirls, and shifting eddies" within our minds as well as without, and "When half our knowledge we must snatch, not take" (29-34).

"All our Passions are Inconsistencies, & our very Reason is no better," wrote Pope to Fortescue, six months before the poem appeared[11] and within the poem his insistence upon the fallibilities of reason outweighs his generally neutral and matter-of-fact description of the "Passions' wild rotation" (41). Again and again he emphasizes the blindness of the historian's "retrospective eye," the "dim" vision of "our internal view" in discovering motives (45-54), the difficulty of seeing even overt actions "in the dark" (74), and the weakness of "judgment" which, where man is concerned, "shoots at flying game" (155). This insistence moves the reader rapidly from the airy discussion of other people's inconsistencies to the mysteries of his own motivation and the feebleness of even his private vision of himself. Pope's intent, I believe, is to chasten the reader's skepticism--the pseudo-skepticism of the overly confident "you"--

and transform it into real and rigorous humility. The initial strategy is such that
the reader, if he grants Pope's exposition,
should enter the illustrative middle section
of the poem (51-173) with a strong sense of
his own inconsistency and self-delusion as
mirrored in the fickleness and folly of those
portrayed. We are shown a dazzling pageant of
"unthought of Frailities" (128, 135-153)
belonging as much to the character of observers
as to observed characters.[12] And so the brisk
parade demands a more profoundly introspective
skepticism than one thought.
    During most of the seventeenth century
moralists of many persuasions had frequently
stressed the insufficiency of common sense
empiricism, reaching the common conclusion
that man's senses are unreliable, his motives
elusive, and his empirical observation unable
to tell him much about his humanity. This
seems something of a truism, at least in
retrospect, but it is useful to recall the
instance of Malebranche (whom Pope elsewhere
placed in the heady company of Locke and
Bolingbroke) when he points out that the danger
lies precisely in regarding this truth as only
a truism. Pausing in his *Recherche de la Verite*
to reprove jesting Pilates, he attacks those
facile skeptics who believe "that it can only
be said in general, that our Nature is Infirm,
that our Mind is full of Blindness, and some
such things as these." The categorical
response is too easy: "They suppose that this
is enough to prevent being seduced by their
senses and not be deceived at all. But it is
not enough to complain that the mind is weak;
we must discover to her wherein her Errours
consist."[13] Although less scrupulously analytic
than Malebranche might wish, the section of
Pope's poem leading up to the Ruling Passion
(174) is nevertheless a full-color map locating
the mind's errors.
    I have treated the earlier sections of the
epistle at such length because that seems to be

where Pope's argumentative emphasis lies.
Given the critical tendency to think of the
epistle as "about the ruling passion," it is
necessary to recall that Pope does not mention
the ruling passion until the final third of
the poem; moreover, when he finally does mention
it the discussion is very brief, sliding almost
at once into portraiture:

> Search then the Ruling Passion: There
>   along,
> The Wild are constant, and the Cunning known;
> The Fool consistent, and the false sincere;
> Priests, Princes, Women, no dissemblers here.
> This clue once found, unravels all the rest,
> The prospect clears, and Wharton stands
>   confest.
> Wharton, the scorn and wonder.... (174-180)

And on quickly for 28 well-known lines dramatizing Wharton's "lust of praise." Only six
more lines of the poem, pointing out that the
ruling passion "sticks to our last sand" (225)
are devoted to psychological theory, and they
serve as preface to the series of short
"characters" which close the poem. If one
considers, then, the fact that the "theory"
is not presented in any detail and that it is
presented very late, it becomes clear that
much of Pope's energy has gone into what comes
before and, consequently, that the process of
education is at least as important to him as
the provisional answer.
   That process has consisted primarily of a
dizzying array of attacks on the complacency of
the self-styled Observer, as one by one the
apparently common-sense assumptions about
character and perception turn into blind alleys.
The pattern which remains is one of increasing
moral awareness. The reader is not offered
stability but the possibility of a momentary
"clue," a fleeting perspective: "The *prospect*
clears, and Wharton stands confest." And so to
himself and to the poet does the reader. Both

leave the full portrait and approach the
final sketches with the reflection that we
are "consistent in our follies and our sins"
(226), a reflection which does not permit the
luxury of Olympian detachment. In its light
even these brief caricatures can provide
occasion for self-scrutiny, particularly since
the shade of death falls on Cobham ("'Oh, save
my Country, Heav'n!' shall be your last") and
knaves alike. The reminder is necessary if
the "prospect" is to remain clear, since
self-knowledge begins and ends with the
recognition of mortality. This recognition
is what is missing in Wharton and the doomed
group at the end, all of whom live as it they
could defy death and whose fixations are an
attempt to ignore the motion in which mortals
have their being.

That man's condition is one of motion and
that, consequently, the self is best understood
as an energy rather than an entity is the basic
psychological truth which has made the poem's
energetic "search" (174) necessary in the first
place.[14] Both the process of the search and the
poetic use of the ruling passion are consistent
with this truth. Pope does not offer a
static explanation for a dynamic phenomenon;
instead his reader is conducted to a perspective from which he may comprehend the constancy
of motion. Although "Life's stream for
Observation will not stay," it is possible--
with the poet's guidance--to apprehend laws of
internal as well as external motion:

> Nature well know, no prodigies remain,
> Comets are regular, and Wharton plain.
>   (208-209)

The goal of such knowledge is not to be able
to gloat over Wharton, whose problem is not
that he *has* a ruling passion but his failure to
understand that "same spirit" with which he
adores and whores (188-189). His is a failure
of self-knowledge, since with both eyes on the

audience ("Enough if all around him but admire")
Wharton makes no attempt to view his own life.
"As the common punishment of the Condemned in
the other life will be to see themselves,"
remarked Pierre Nicole, "the general Character
of the Condemned in this here is not to see
themselves."[15]

The final group of miniature portraits are
all studies in symbolic gesture, lessons in
how to see, how to "read" personality. Each of
them, including Cobham's final gesture, is
presented so quickly and so much on the run as
to remind the reader, one final and dramatic
time, that "half our knowledge we must snatch,
not take." Moreover, it seems to be the better
half, for the poet's vision of character is
felt at once to be intuitive, disciplined,
artful. The powerful artist of the *Essay on
Criticism* is one who can "snatch a grace beyond
the reach of art." The genuinely moral
artist uses poetic form to penetrate social
forms and personal illusions.

All of this suggests, of course, that the
poem is highly self-conscious, and my reading
may seem to reduce it to self-congratulation
as well. But if the epistle is an effort to
demonstrate the poet's function, perhaps
self-justification is closer to Pope's intention within the poem, and perhaps such an
enterprise is motivated by a concern for
poetry as well as for himself. Certainly
such a preoccupation is evident in a letter
which may well have been written while Pope
was at work on the poem. He tells Swift:"There
is nothing of late which I think of more than
mortality, and what you mention of collecting
the best monuments we can of our friends, their
own images in their writings...I am preparing
also for my own; and have nothing so much at
heart, as to shew the silly world that men of
Wit, or even Poets, may be the most moral of
mankind."[16] What does it mean to be the "most
moral"? One meaning clearly is personal, and
anyone reading through Pope's letters of the

1730's is likely to be struck by the repeated
insistences that personal morality--charity,
hospitality, friendships--mean more to him
than literary acclaim. But there is a larger
insistence, too, on the morality of poetry.
This means not only that the poet is ethically
inoffensive but that his work is true, that it
pertains to life as it is actually lived, that
it comes home to "Men's Business and Bosoms."[17]
     The discussion of psychology in the poem is
essential in confronting the challenge Pope
creates for himself. Like most challenges, it
comes from within than without, and it is voiced
most explicitly elsewhere as something safely
conquered. The poet has "stoop'd to truth,"
has "moraliz'd his song," has left "fancy's
maze," left fancy itself in favor of the heart,
abandoned wit for nature, and turned "from
sounds to things." The phrases are from the
Epistle to Arbuthnot and the conclusion of the
Essay on Man, and they suggest the affinity of
both works to the *Epistle to Cobham*. Because of
the poem's discussion of the ruling passion it
is naturally linked in our minds with the
second epistle of the *Essay on Man;* but it is
connected as firmly and more interestingly
with the self-reflective ending of that poem
(IV, 383-392) and with the self-conscious
apologia of the *Epistle to Arbuthnot*. It may in
fact be seen as an even more fundamental and
self-conscious apology, not only for satire
and the satirist's morality, but for the
concrete truth of moral poetry: the experi-
mental truth to which Pope would soon claim to
have stooped when he moralized his song and
harmonized his mind. *The Epistle to Cobham* is a
significant part of what Pope is "about" in the
early 1730's and a crucial argument for his
"system of Ethics in the Horatian way."[18] That
"system" as a whole aims at a modern vindication
of the ways of God to man, but it is a vindication through poetry. Despite the example of
Milton, or more importantly *because* of it, one
might well wonder what room is left for a poet

in such matters.[19] I do not believe that Pope
formulated the problem in precisely these
terms; but both the procedure and placement
of the epistle imply an attempt to vindicate
the ways of poetry to men.

Regarding the poem as Pope's first serious
defense of a new and explicitly moral poetic
helps to account for its aggressive argument.
Within the epistle the territory of poetry is
deliberately redefined. When he remarks that
"Not always Actions show the man," Pope is
announcing the end of an era of poetic faith.
The remark itself is hardly radical, since
the assumption that actions reveal essential
character had long been disputed by moralists.
That same assumption, nevertheless, is the one
on which conventional narrative poetry
had depended. The epic is the most important
instance here because it represents the
traditional limit of poetic aspiration in
general and because, more particularly, it
is the form of the last attempt before Pope
to vindicate God's ways and to construct a
total world picture. The epic, however, is
largely external in perspective; its narrative
continuity and interest derive from the attitude
that actions *do* show the man, that what he does
is what he "meant to do" (54) and is what his
life means.[20] But from the late Renaissance
onward, ethical writers as diverse as Montaigne
and William Law centered more and more on
questions of motivation and intention rather
than visible action. They did so, in fact, with
such growing frequency and sophistication that
Pope's lines on the vanity of inferring "the
Motive from the Deed" (53) are thoroughly
commonplace.[21]

What is uncommon is the studied analysis and
self-announcement of this problem in poetry
itself. It is one thing for a philosophical
essayist to theorize about the gap between
external phenomena and "our internal view" (49);
it is another for a poet to define that space,
chart it, and then claim that territory as his

province. If Addison's desire was to bring
philosophy to the coffee house, Pope's is to
take poetry to philosophy, especially to that
branch of philosophy now regarded as psychology.
This desire is evident in the argument of the
Epistle to Cobham, as well as in numerous letters
of the same period, and it extends to the
Epistle to Several Persons as a group, where Pope
is frequently concerned with motivation and
perception. One purely intellectual superiority,
for example, of the *Epistle to a Lady* to Edward
Young's satires on women can be found in
Pope's scrutiny of his characters' dim "internal
view" of themselves. Similarly, in the *Epistle
to Bathurst* he proceeds to revivify the tired
topic of greed by coupling condemnation with
real, if ironic, sensitivity to how misers act
upon "some Revelation hid from me and you."[22]
The exploration of motives is essential if
the poet who has recently turned his energies
"wholly upon human actions"[23] is to gain the
confidence of modern and worldly readers. It
is no small enterprise, after all, to show the
world that *living* poets "may be the most moral
of mankind."

One assertion in Harold Bloom's recent
"Manifesto" with which Pope might have agreed
is the description of good criticism as the
"art of knowing the hidden roads that go from
poem to poem."[24] Bloom is primarily interested
in roads which are hidden indeed, those inroads
of influence which he sees Romantic poets
attempting to deny. But one of Pope's own
"romanticisms" is a Wordsworthian insistence
that there are "roads that go from poem to
poem" within his work and that his poems
should be viewed as parts of a larger structure.
In the same letter to Swift in which he speaks
of holding back his "best silks," Pope speaks
also of the "plain connexion" between his
epistles. "My works will in one respect be like
the works of Nature, much more to be liked and
understood when consider'd in the relation
they bear with each other, than when ignorantly

look'd upon one by one."

   Whether or not we wish to regard the *Epistle to Cobham* as one of Pope's best silks, a final "relation" may help us feel the texture of the fabric and understand the prominence with which it is displayed. The Second Book of epistles was originally conceived under the general idea "Of the Use of Things," [25] and this epistle stands as prologue to that book. By emphasizing the breadth of self-delusion and the narrow limits of self-sufficiency, the "man to Books confin'd" makes an ambitious and exemplary argument for the use of poetry.

THE ROLE OF TIME IN ALEXANDER POPE'S
EPISTLE TO A LADY

Rebecca P. Parkin

Pope's handling of time in the *Epistle to a Lady: Of the Characters of Women* merits careful scrutiny. In a poem where paradox is a primary reliance, it is not surprising to find time also presented paradoxically. On the one hand, the poem implies that the speaker and his companion have virtually unlimited time. This is in accordance with the Horatian convention of random, seemingly unhurried pace, as well as with the specific fiction that this poem is a leisurely tour of the portrait gallery. That the implied speaker and the lady he is addressing are not pressed for time may also be inferred from the minute and detailed dissection they make of a variety of feminine characters.

On the other hand, in portrait after portrait and in verse after verse, the poem insists upon the urgency occasioned by the passing of time. Linked with this paradox--and in fact a chief resource of the poem--is the polarization of time. This polarization, when presented with reference simultaneously to both absolute and

This essay first appeared in *ELH* 32 (1965), 490-501. Copyright The Johns Hopkins University Press.

ambivalent moral norms, at once complicates and
sharpens the moral crises. And these recurrent
crises, so presented, are responsible for much
of the tension and excitement of the poem.
     The speaker's attitude toward these crises
of conduct varies. Sometimes it is humorous,
sometimes elegiac, sometimes tragic. Taken with
the shift from absolute to ambivalent norms and
with the constantly shifting, ambivalent behavior of the ladies, the speaker's shifts in
attitude produce a substratum of turbulence
barely contained by the convention of the gallery tour. It becomes a kind of marvel that is
contained. The substantive paradox of all-the-
time-in-the-world and almost-no-time is contained in, as well as conditioned by, the procedural paradox.
     The opening lines of the poem present femin-
ine nature--and particularly corrupted feminine
nature--with reference to moral judgments made
within time:

     Nothing so true as what you once let fall.
     "Most Women have no Characters at all."
     Matter too soft a lasting mark to bear,
     And best distinguish'd by black, brown, or
          fair. (1-4)

In their relation to time, these verses are
partly elegiac and partly satiric. It is a
platitude that human beings find it difficult to
remain constant in the pursuit of virtue. Where
all efforts to lead a virtuous life are given
up, human beings may well sink to an animal-like
condition in which they can hardly be said to
have distinguishing criteria except for external
traits such as color of hair. To assert that
most women have indeed sunk to this level and
can be distinguished from each other only by
hair color is not complimentary. But because
all human beings experience lapses from ideal
virtue, neither is the observation purely satiric; it has an undercurrent expressive of
lachrymae rerum. Furthermore, there is a sense in

which the softness and adaptability associated
with the conventional feminine role reverse the
couplet's direction. Perhaps, after all, it
may be interpreted as in some measure a compli-
ment--at any rate, as polysemantic.

The celebrated lines portraying "Arcadia's
Countess" in a variety of poses have an oblique but effective time reference:

> Arcadia's Countess, here, in ermin'd pride,
> Is there, Pastora by a fountain side:
> Here Fannia, leering on her own good man,
> Is there, a naked Leda with a Swan.
> Let then the Fair one beautifully cry
> In Magdalen's loose hair and lifted eye,
> Or drest in smiles of sweet Cecilia shine,
> With simp'ring Angels, Palms, and Harps
>   divine;
> Whether the Charmer sinner it, or saint it,
> If Folly grows romantic, I must paint it.
>   (7-16)

That the poses range morally from saints to
sinners is a circumstance to which the lady
appears indifferent. There is historical range
as well. These poses stretch back through recorded history to embrace both Christian and
Greco-Roman frames of reference. And within
both of these historical traditions moral antithesis is used. But whether the Lady poses as
a pastoral innocent, a Roman adulteress, or the
Greek Leda, whether as the Magdalen or as St.
Cecilia--one effect of the allusions is to suggest woman's lack of character throughout recorded time. On the surface, the strategy in
this passage is primarily spatial-pictorial; but
at the same time, by carefully chosen examples,
the passage gives woman's indifference to morality a chronological dimension coinciding with
the history of Western Europe.

A double function with respect to time is exhibited by the delightful verses on the mock
preparations for painting Cynthia:

> Come then, the colours and the ground prepare!
> Dip in the Rainbow, trick her off in Air,
> Chuse a firm Cloud, before it fall, and in it
> Catch, ere she change, the Cynthia of this
>   minute. (17-20)

The stress on painting "the Cynthia of this minute" not only satirizes the lady's extreme
changeability but focuses attention on the pressure of time in a way that will later be utilized
to reinforce the pressure of moral crisis. And
linking the lady with the rainbow, air, a cloud,
and the moon emphasizes her feminine grace and
beauty in a context of transience. Her loveliness is all the more precious, in a way, because
of its fragility and short span. Ironically,
that loveliness is closely linked with woman's
besetting frailty.
    Stress on the short-lived beauty of the femi-
nine world continues in the couplet:

> Rufa, whose eye quick-glancing o'er the Park,
> Attracts each light gay meteor of a Spark....
>   (21-22)

Rufa's twinkling, irresistibly magnetic eye, together with the metaphors "spark" and "meteor"
for "beau," combine the strands of beauty and
transience with an accent on the diminutive. This
concern with the diminutive is carried on with in-
teresting--and ambivalent--moral implications in
the verses on Sappho. Rufa's coquetting, it is
said,

> Agrees as ill with Rufa studying Locke,
> As Sappho's diamonds with her dirty smock,
> Or Sappho at her toilet's greazy task,
> With Sappo fragrant at an ev'ning Mask:
> So morning Insects that in muck begun,
> Shine, buzz, and fly-blow in the setting-
>   sun. (23-28)

Both in the Rufa lines and these closely related lines on Sappho, extremes in action imply
the passing of time--a time gambit the poem makes

much of. Rufa cannot be flirting in the park
and studying Locke at the same moment. Neither
can Sappho be "at her toilet's greasy task" and
"fragrant at an ev'ning Mask" at the same hour
of the day. The time element is underlined when
Sappho is compared to an insect in its contrasted
morning and evening stages. But Sappho's own
moral depravity is accentuated by the same
stroke. The insect is born from muck in the
morning only to shine, buzz, and fly-blow in the
sunset. Sappho goes the insect one better--cos-
metic "muck" in the morning and the muck of lewd-
ness, to which her shining is only an enticement,
in the evening.

The pervasive comparison of Sappho to an insect not only scales down her nastiness and lust
but makes her appear shortlived, insignificant,
noisome, amoral, and a nuisance. The implication is that it is no less absurd to expect
to find character in Sappho than ethics in a
gnat. Scaling down the lady to insect size
works a kind of miracle of the boudoir in reverse. Along with the littleness and amorality
of the insect, Sappho has its evanescent beauty.
She too is fragile; she too shines. Besides,
the obvious implication runs, if we don't expect
anything of an insect except to shine, buzz, and
fly-blow, why should we expect more of woman?

In Silia we have another, though rather different, metamorphosis of the boudoir:

How soft is Silia! fearful to offend,
The Frail one's advocate, the Weak one's
     friend:
To her, Calista prov'd her conduct nice,
And good Simplicius asks of her advice.
Sudden she storms! she raves! You tip the wink,
But spare your censure; Silia does not drink.
All eyes may see from what the change arose,
All eyes may see--a Pimple on her nose.
     (29-36)

In this passage Silia's conduct, in relation to
time, turns on the word "Sudden." First of all,

Calista's fastidious--or perhaps hair-splitting--
justification of her conduct, as well as Simplicius's request for advice, imply leisure to
hear and consider serious matters--a reasonable
stretch of time. In contrast, it takes no time
at all for Silia to react with a storm of rage
at the rising of a pimple on her nose. The un-
expectedness, the violence, and the irrationality of Silia's change are reinforced by the
contrasted aspects of time. Superficially,
Silia seems almost Christ-like. She is the advocate of the frail and the friend of the weak.
Of course, Silia's advocacy and friendliness
stem not from compassionate concern but from
social and moral cowardice. And she is metamorphosed, in the wink of an eye, into a raging
shrew.

The verses on Papillia too present a charac-
terizing change within an ethically significant
lapse of time:

> Papillia, wedded to her doating spark,
> Sighs for the shades--"How charming is a Park!"
> A Park is purchas'd, but the Fair he sees
> All bath'd in tears--"Oh odious, odious Trees!"
>   (37-40)

Presumably it would take some time to look out
for and arrange for the purchase of a park.
The comparatively slow-moving and deliberate
world of business is contrasted with Papillia's
eponymous velleities. Actually these are as
charming--and just as morally serious, in this
context--as a butterfly's flitting from flower
to flower. Because of the connotations of her
name, Papillia's changeability takes on some
of the grace and fluttering of butterflies and
flowers--particularly the tulips mentioned in
the ensuing lines. Horticulturists prize certain streaks and spots on tulips. The Papillia
passage, then, presenting feminine inconsistency in a context of the lovely but absurd,
helps maintain the ambivalence with which
throughout the poem woman and her relationship
to time are regarded.

Narcissa's changeability with reference to
time is another matter altogether:

> Narcissa's nature, tolerably mild,
> To make a wash, would hardly stew a child,
> Has ev'n been prov'd to grant a Lover's pray'r,
> And paid a Tradesman once to make him stare,
> Gave alms at Easter, in a Christian trim,
> And made a Widow happy, for a whim. (53-58)

In line 56 the emphasis is on "once." In fact,
the semantic stress on "once" creates a cesura,
setting up an antithesis between all the times
Narcissa should have paid tradesmen and the
single occasion--to her shame--on which she did.
In the following lines, continuing her portrait,
the "now's" are pivotal:

> Now deep in Taylor and the Book of Martyrs,
> Now drinking citron with his Grace and Chartres.
> Now Conscience chills her, and now Passion
>   burns;
> And Atheism and Religion take their turns;
> A very Heathen in the carnal part,
> Yet still a sad, good Christian at her heart.
>   (63-68)

The "now's," conveying something like "one
hour this and the next hour that," reinforce
the moral comment on the polarized actions.
The colloquial, almost childish familiarity of
"take their turns" suggests the morally neutral
ground of a child's game. And this, of course,
belittles the importance of time, implying in
"Now this, now that" that "this" is equal to
"that."
    The ambivalence of "sad" in line 68 is es-
pecially relevant to the use of time in this
portrait. "Sad" has as one of its obsolete
meanings "steadfast." Taken this way, the line
implies that, in spite of natural frailty, Narcissa is at heart a good Christian. Actually,
this interpretation is undercut by two other
meanings of "sad"--one of the colloquial meanings of "bad, naughty, inferior in quality" and

the other "weary, sated." Narcissa, then is a
"sad" example of a good Christian; moreover, any
appearance of steadfastness she has at a given
time may, it is hinted, result from satiety and
depression rather than from sober virtue.

The irony turning on time in the portrait of
Philomedé is given a special twist. The lady
has first excused her promiscuity on the grounds
that, though her body betrayed her, her head was
not involved. But

>   Such this day's doctine--in another fit
>   She sins with Poets thro' pure Love of Wit.
>   (75-76)

Here it is not a question of this day's doctrine
being immoral whereas the next day's doctrine--
the lady having repented and amended--is moral.
The antithesis pointed up by time is that one
fashion of immorality has changed to another
fashion of immorality. The lady's lubricity
and hypocrisy alone remain constant. In the
following verses, continuing the portrait of
Philomedé, Helluo's gluttony is, of course, a
metaphor for Philomedé's gross and over-prompt
sexual appetite:

>   As Helluo, late Dictator of the Feast,
>   The Nose of Hautgout, and the Tip of Taste,
>   Critick'd your wine, and analyz'd your meat.
>   Yet on plain Pudding deign'd at home to eat;
>   So Philomedé, lect'ring all mankind
>   On the soft Passion, and the Taste refin'd,
>   Th' Address, the Delicacy--stoops at once,
>   And makes her hearty meal upon a Dunce.
>   (79-86)

"Late" in line 79 introduces the familiar element of contrast in time linked with contrast
in moral behavior. And in line 85 special
prominence is given "at once" by position and
rime, as well as by omitting to make the preceding couplet firmly closed and end-stopped.
Instead, the sense of line 84 runs over into

line 85, as no doubt the lady ran on in praise
of fastidiousness in love--until, without discrimination or time-consuming ceremony, she
stooped.

In the succeeding portrait of Flavia, time
functions, as it not infrequently does elsewhere, as metonymy for "life." In this passage
it does so with especial pertinency:

> Flavia's a Wit, has too much sense to Pray,
> To Toast our wants and wishes, is her way;
> Nor asks of God, but of her Stars to give
> The mighty blessing, "while we live, to live."
> Then all for Death, that Opiate of the soul!
> Lucretia's dagger, Rosamonda's bowl.
> Say, what can cause such impotence of mind?
> A Spark too fickle, or a Spouse too kind.
> Wise Wretch! with Pleasures too refin'd to
>   please,
> With too much Spirit to be e'er at ease,
> With too much Quickness ever to be taught,
> With too much Thinking to have common Thought:
> Who purchase Pain with all that Joy can give,
> And die of nothing but a Rage to live.
>   (87-100)

This lady's attitude toward time might be said
to vary from *carpe diem* to *tedium vitae*. She longs
both for the intensest possible use of time and
for death--which, for the individual, is the
cessation of time. In the "impotence of mind"
caused by these conflicting desires Flavia is
frustrated. She is trapped between the unwelcome attentions of her steady, enduring spouse
and the fickleness of her transient "Spark."
The Spouse becomes almost a metaphor for *tedium
vitae*, as the Spark does for desire born and lost
in an instant.

When with the poet we "turn...from Wits" and
observe the next five ladies--each briefly described and characterized in a couplet or so,
like lesser chiefs in the *Iliad*-- it is clear that
they are all linked in their relationship to
time by a certain ironic constancy. Words indicative of inflexibility within time pervade

the passage. "Simo's Mate" is said to be as
obstinate as an ass. The time-word "never" in
line 103 underlines the moral blindness of the
next lady, who "owns her Faults, but never
mends." "For ever" is used with equal emphasis
to stigmatize the ironic constancy of the third
lady

>   ......whose life the Church and Scandal share,
>   For ever in a Passion, or a Pray'r. (105-106)

The fourth lady

>   ...laughs at Hell, but (like her Grace)
>   Cries, "Ah! how charming if there's no such
>   place!" (107-108)

"Hell," of course, implies judgment within time
of ladies who alternately fear and laugh at the
concept. Incidentally, this couplet exemplifies
one of the rare explicit intrusions into the
poem of an absolute moral norm.
      Constancy, in the sense of being consistently
changeable, is also predicated of the fifth
lady:

>   ...who in sweet vicissitude appears
>   Of Mirth and Opium, Ratafie and Tears,
>   The daily Anodyne, and nightly Draught,
>   To kill those foes to Fair ones, Time and
>   Thought. (109-112)

The ambiguity of "Time" in line 112 is particularly meaningful. Time is a foe to these
fair ladies both in the sense of "something
boring which has to be lived through somehow"
and in the antithetic sense of something at
once very precious and very powerful which the
ladies ought to want to make the best possible
use of before it destroys their beauty and their
lives. This ambiguity in the aspect Time presents to the Fair is reinforced by the linked
antithesis of "daily" and "nightly" in line 111--
as well as by the linking of both these with the

ambiguous "sweet vicissitude" in line 110. The
metaphorical play of this passage among three
realms--time, drugs, and emotional stress--has
the effect of suggesting that such fair ladies
are meaningless, amoral whirligigs, turning frantically but to no purpose.
     The aphorisms following--

> Woman and Fool are two hard things to hit,
> For true No-meaning puzzles more than Wit.
>   (113-114)

--take the poem for a moment outside of time for
a reflection perennially true. A devastating
indictment of the brainless fair, this couplet
reinforces the opening convention of leisurely
speculation.
     In the portrait of Atossa, which comes next,
the paradox that a long life crowded with incident has only produced a wise fool is central.
These verses exhibit a particularly subtle concatenation of time and ethical relationships:

> Offend her, and she knows not to forgive;
> Oblige her, and she'll hate you while you
>   live;
> But die, and she'll adore you--Then the Bust
> And Temple rise--then fall again to dust.
>   (137-140)

"Then fall again to dust" is ambiguous in its
application. On the one hand, it is specific
to Atossa and illustrative of her character.
On the other hand, it is a general truth, elegiac in import. The implacable duration of
Atossa's memory while the offender or obliger
is alive is contrasted with her joyous triumph
over the person in his death, signalized by her
raising the bust or the temple and then promptly forgetting and neglecting them. The point
made is that it is impossible--by whatever action, even death--to secure a constant, ethically motivated response from Atossa. A further
indication of the passing of time used as the

means of displaying her illogicality and in-
stability occurs in the couplet

> Last night, her Lord was all that's good
>   and great,
> A Knave this morning, and his Will a Cheat.
>   (141-142)

This couplet is especially interesting in its
use of chiasmus to accentuate the presentation
of extremes in conduct within a very short
compass of time.

The aleatory painting techniques portrayed
in the following passage serve as a kind of
metaphor for the quickness with which women
change:

> Pictures like these, dear Madam, to design,
> Asks no firm hand, and no unerring line;
> Some wand'ring touch, or some reflected light,
> Some flying stroke alone can hit 'em right:
> For how should equal Colours do the knack?
> Chameleons who can paint in white and black?
>   (151-156)

"Touch," "reflected light," "flying stroke,"
"hit 'em right," "do the knack," and "Chameleons"--all these stress quick, unpremeditated
action and, of course, the pervading motif
Varium et mutabile semper femina. Against this is
played the convention which dominates the procedural strategy of the poem--namely, that the
speaker has all the time in the world for generalized reflective comment.

In direct contrast to the emphasis on quick,
unpremeditated, illogical feminine action is
the ironically climactic portrait of Chloe. By
the time Cloe's portrait is reached, the speaker and his companion have been touring the gallery for some time. They have seen many portraits which cannot be commended. The companion then proposes Cloe as an example of a woman
who does not exhibit the ceaseless irrational
and/or immoral changes inconsistent with character:

> "Yet Cloe sure was form'd without a spot--"
> Nature in her then err'd not, but forgot.
> "With ev'ry pleasing, ev'ry prudent part,
> "Say, what can Cloe want?"--she wants a Heart.
> (157-160)

The speaker's amplification, as he paints
the portrait is dominated by "never's" and
"forever's." These absolute time words emphasize Cloe's ruling passion--such a degree of
egocentric absorption that she is totally lacking in loving concern for others. She even has
to ask her footman to "put it in her head"
whether her so-called friends are alive or dead--
out of time altogether. And Cloe is a Pharisee:
she tithes the mint and cummin of minor social
niceties but is "Content to dwell in Decencies
for ever (164)"--her own peculiar timeless hell.
The most celebrated verses in this portrait involve a particularly intriguing use of time as
a vehicle of moral comment:

> She, while her Lover pants upon her breast
> Can mark the figures on an Indian chest;
> And when she sees her Friend in deep despair,
> Observes how much a Chintz exceeds Mohair.
> (167-170)

Simultaneity is used here primarily as a means
of focusing the enormity of these antithetic
actions. A further twist is given by the fact
that the situation in the first couplet is immoral anyway. But simultaneity also provides
the main source of the humor for which this
passage is noted.

In the ensuing portrait of the Queen, the
line of rising importance in presentation of
the portraits is still being followed--ostens-
ibly. In this royal portrait we have an attribution of feminine virtue that is absolutely
constant for all eternity: "The same for ever!"
But this attribution of constancy to the Queen
is mechanical; its mainspring is no more than
a tongue-in-the-cheek reluctance to commit
lèse majesté.

Constancy is indeed attributed to almost all
women in the lines:

In Men, we various Ruling Passions find,
In Women, two almost divide the kind;
Those, only fix'd, they first or last obey,
The Love of Pleasure, and the Love of Sway.
    (207-210)

But is constancy in these two ruling passions
praise? In the verse "But ev'ry Lady would be
Queen for life (218)" the ladies' constancy in
desiring sovereignty is shown as downright un-
reasonable compared with the reasonable recognition of differences in temperament by men in
the verse "Men, some to Quiet, some to public
Strife (217)." Moreover, since woman's purpose
in seeking life-long sovereign power is only to
make sure she doesn't lose pleasures, the constancy implied is undercut by the moral judgment in "But ev'ry Woman is at heart a Rake
(216)."
    Woman's pursuit of these two ruling passions
is bounded, of course, by time. And time itself executes judgment on feminine frivolity
and hedonism:

See how the World its Veterans rewards!
A Youth of frolicks, an old Age of Cards,
Fair to no purpose, artful to no end,
Young without Lovers, old without a Friend,
A Fop their Passion, but their Prize a Sot,
Alive, ridiculous, and dead, forgot! (243-248)

The moral judgment is voiced by polarizing time,
setting youth against age. Time is also involved in the ironic emphasis on frustrated
purpose, regardless of age, skill, or condition.
Time's final word on the worldly woman is indeed an absolute--death and oblivion.
    But time's judgment on the good woman, with
whose portrait the poem comes to a close, is
tempered. With this portrait the poem turns
from its negative to its positive pole, though
contrast is still the dominant mode. And a

combined astronomical and meteorological metaphor dominates the contrast.

The woman who wants to dazzle all day is a
sun who "Flaunts and goes down, an unregarded
thing (252)." The good woman is a moon: "Serene
in Virgin Modesty she shines (255)." Ordinarily, we expect the stronger or more valued of
two things to be compared with the sun, the
weaker or less valued to the moon. But the re-
versal of this expectation is especially appropriate in this context, where an essential
attribute of the good woman is her ability to
forego a meretricious immediate gratification
for the sake of a less showy but more apposite
and longer-lasting value. And what could be
more appropriate for the good woman than symbolic identification with Diana, the goddess
of chastity?

The good woman is, moreover,

> ...blest with Temper, whose unclouded ray
> Can make to morrow chearful as to day.
> (257-258)

Sun, moon, night, day, weather changes--all
these signals of the passing of time are used
to mark the distinctions between the good woman and the bad. But, good or bad, all women
live within a time continuum. When women are
unblest with good sense and good humor, time
takes on a retributive aspect: "Toasts live
a scorn, and Queens may die a jest (282)."

Even for the good woman the passing of time,
which means the passing of feminine grace and
beauty, can scarcely be contemplated without
some measure of regret. Yet in the closing
verses of this poem time is tamed, bent, and
gentled by the tone of chivalric compliment
the speaker adopts. Referring to a qualified
but basically auspicious future for the lady,
he says:

> This Phoebus promised (I forget the year)
> When those blue eyes first opened on the
>   sphere. (283-284)

Moreover, in the verse describing the good
woman as exhibiting "Fix'd Principles, with Fancy ever new (279)" one kind of feminine change-
ableness within time is depicted as captivating.
And time's "ripening" effect--so dreaded by frivolous beauties who lack fixed moral principles--
is shown as in many ways favorable to the woman
of character and good humor. The speaker assures
the virtuous lady he addresses that Phoebus
Apollo,

>The gen'rous God, who Wit and Gold refines,
>And ripens Spirits as he ripens Mines,
>Kept Dross for Duchesses, the world shall
>   know it,
>To you gave Sense, Good-humor, and a Poet.
>   (289-292)

In part, then, by the simultaneous mainten-
ance of two interpenetrating paradoxes--one
regarding time and the other regarding ethics--
Pope in this Epistle achieves, to a degree
scarcely surpassable, that adaptation of poetic
means to subject which was one of the ideals of
his age.

THE CISTERN AND THE FOUNTAIN: ART AND REALITY
IN POPE AND GRAY

Irvin Ehrenpreis

    Finding his satires "favourably received at
home, and abroad," Edward Young supposed he could
account for such good fortune by the remoteness
of his derogatory observations--where they oc-
curred--from specific human objects: "I am not
conscious," he said (introducing an edition which
was published the same year as *The Dunciad*), "of
the least malevolence to any particular person
thro' all the characters."[1] If Young sounds
commonplace in recommending Horatian or "laughing"
satire and condemning bitter, Juvenalian violence, he is equally representative of the critical truisms of his era in judging "general"
satire to be a higher form that "particular."
Like most satirists who flourished during the
lives of Dryden and Swift, Young did of course enrich his generalities with a strong infusion of
obvious particulars. Yet the structure and
meaning of the seven poems never depend upon these
changeable parts. In the final impression the
reader's mind is occupied with permanent moral
truths conveyed by vehicles or arguments that the
concrete instances only decorate. The external

This essay first appeared in *Studies in Criticism and Aesthetics*, ed. Howard P. Anderson
(Minneapolis: University of Minnesota Press, 1967), pp. 156-75.

realities surrounding the living poet are one
order; the internal elements that constitute the
poem are another.

In these prejudices Young curiously anticipates the widening practice of academic criticism
during recent decades, or since the pedantries
of philological and socio-historical research
were rejected by young American scholars a generation ago. That the true structure of accepted masterpieces never depends upon their reference to nonliterary reality seems a natural
law of learned criticism today. Ideally, it is
an internal pattern that the "trained" reader
hopes to find--a unifying design subtly harmoni-
zing the superficially disparate images in a
poem, or connecting the various rhetorical figures with the character of a person supposed to
speak the lines. To nourish the literary organism, one may indeed discover that profound intellectual traditions or ancient conventions of
symbolism serve as reservoirs of allusion. But
they in turn are self-contained imaginative or
mythological reservoirs, distinct from factual
history or from any science of observed human
nature. If a would-be critic should now ask, in
the style of Johnson, whether the argument of
the *Essay on Man* is intellectually respectable,[2]
whether it makes sense according to nonpoetic
logic or to principles of psychology, whether it
agrees with our knowledge of the external, historical events of the period to which it was
addressed, he would probably be censured for confusing literature with documentary evidence. The
praise that Johnson devotes to Shakespeare's understanding of human behavior[3] finds only a low-
keyed echo in the language of my colleagues.
From the study of art and poetry alone, they often
imply, we can learn what is most relevant to the
appreciation of literary structure, although the
accidents of a poem may receive helpful clarification from ancillary knowledge.

In the study of eighteenth-century literature
this view has gained coincidental strength from
the widely accepted belief that impersonal art
is the hallmark of Augustan craftsmanship. The

final pages of *Gulliver's Travels*, in which Swift
speaks out loud and clear, we are commonly asked
to regard as peripheral to the main design. Poems
like Johnson's elegy on Levet are passed under our
inspection to demonstrate that even the private
crises of an author are characteristically
generalized and purified before a truly Augustan
artist employs them in a work for publication.
As an attribute enhancing the ideal of a self-
contained literary structure, the value of impersonality is evident.

I am inclined to question the usefulness of
these postulates, not with any hope of destroying
them but rather in an effort to define the range
of their effectiveness. Nobody would like to
see us return to that mesozoic era when the biography of an author was indistinguishable from
the criticism of his work, or to that later
but glacial age when the history of the language
or the social development of the nation was
presumed to cast the ultimate illumination upon
both the import and the importance of a poem.
Yet if internal "literary" coherence has been
established, unconsciously, as the highest
principle that a scholarly critic can demonstrate
in a classic he admires, perhaps it would be
profitable to examine some consequences of that
assumption. My own hesitant, exploratory effort
can hardly generate a conclusive proof or dis-
proof, for my argument is not the sort that
knocks down one general proposition and sets up
a replacement. Rather I hope by using suggestive
examples to encourage others to test my case with
evidence of their own picking. In this effort I
shall take up a few masterpieces and failures
of eighteenth-century poetry, inquiring whether
the structural integrity of each does not depend
for its cogency, or deepest appeal, upon allusions
to reality--whether, in other words, the truly
successful imaginative structures do not reach
out like a fountain whose glitterling shape overflows into and thus vivifies the world around it.
Among the specimens to be examined here, two
Pope's *Epistle to a Lady* and Gray's *The Bard*, enjoy

a richness of self-contained form that has, I
think, seldom been adequately appreciated.

. . .

   Few of Pope's works pretend to exhibit throughout the sort of design which his couplets and
his verse paragraphs possess. I wish now to
argue that the second "Moral Essay," *An Epistle to
a Lady, Of the Characters of Women,* has just this
virtue in addition to its others. *To a Lady* is a
finished masterpiece such as Pope rarely created.
Parts of it have received famous praise from
Professor Empson, Dr. Leavis, and Lytton Strachey.[4] Yet little attention has fallen, I think,
on the elaborated form of the whole poem. So
I should like to consider this in terms of the
arrangement of parts and pattern of images, and
then to ask how it depends on allusions to reality. Through comparisons with similar poems
both by Pope and by Edward Young, I hope to show
that the achievement is remarkable.
   The *Epistle to a Lady* can be divided into three
parts: the first two hundred lines are a group
of portraits of women, mostly sinners; the next
fifty lines are a didactic analysis of their
sins; and the final forty lines are a eulogy addressed to a Lady listener, easily identifiable
as Martha Blount. Portraits, analysis, eulogy--
among these the connection seems obvious. The
concentrated praise in lines 249 to 292 balances
the distributed attacks in lines 1 to 198, and
the analysis in lines 199 to 248 forms a bridge
between the two. The virtues Mrs. Blount owns--
modesty, tenderness, fidelity--are conspicuously
those the sinners lack; and their vices--vanity,
avarice, ambition, lust--have no place in her
character.
   The structure of the first section will easily
be seen to have a formal order. Thus in the
series of portraits we find several kinds of
rising lines. For one thing, the poet surveys
his sinners roughly in order of size: a couplet
or two on each of the first few names; four

couplets on Silia; six on Calypso; eight on Narcissa; nine on Philomede, seven on Flavia; eighteen on Atossa; and twelve on Cloe, with some very
brief profiles interspersed. In the *Epistle to
Bathurst*, Pope had used the same rough order of
size: one couplet on Colepepper, eight on Blunt,
twenty-two on Sir Balaam, and so forth; the
principle seems ordinary enough. But in the
Epistle to a Lady Pope combines it with another,
which Professor Elder Olson has noticed in the
Epistle to Dr. Arbuthnot.[5] There, as the speech
progresses, the satire sharpens: the portrait
of Atticus is more severe than the ridicule of
fools at the beginning, and the portrait of
Sporus is more severe than that of Atticus. So
in the *Epistle to a Lady*, Atossa's portrait is the
climax of violence as well as the climax in length;
Philomede's is milder; Narcissa's, still milder.
But, as it happens, the sinners are also arranged
in degrees of reality. Out of the first six, five
seem fictitious: i.e., the poem does not invite
us to search for an original. But Sappho, the
next, can only refer to Lady Mary Wortley Montagu.
Four additional pseudonyms--Philomede, Flavia,
Atossa, and Cloe--have been associated with the
second Duchess of Marlborough, the Duchess of
Montagu, the Duchess of Buckinhamshire, and the
Countess of Suffolk. Finally, the Queen is
actually named, as is the Duchess of Queensberry
(who does not, however, count as a sinner).[6]
From the pseudonymous and fictitious, therefore,
through the pseudonymous but recognizable, Pope
moves to proper public names; and from a
countess and an earl's daughter, through duchesses,
he rises to the Queen. Admitting many irregular-
ities and interruptions, we may say that he moves
roughly through degrees of reality and degrees of
rank. In other words, as Pope gets further along
in the poem, and strengthens his grip on the
audience, he grows bolder.

There is a further meaning to Pope's order.
Those women who can be identified are peeresses
or royalty, in contrast to the humble station of
Mrs. Blount. Such targets of course give weight
to the poem, just as an imperial dramatis

personae gives weight to tragedy. They are
courtiers, natural focuses of national concern.
Lady Irwin had remarked of the *Epistle to Bathurst*,
"As the objects of [Pope's] satire are low,
people will be less offended, for who cares for
[Peter] Waters, Charters, or Ward."[7] One never
feels that the figures of *An Epistle to a Lady* are
too inconsequential to be worth reading about.
As we approach the peak of society, however,
we approach the peak of corruption: the poet
evokes an urgency suggesting a national crisis.
     Young has two satires on women which deeply
influenced Pope's work--numbers five and six of
The Universal Passion, which are commonly judged to
be the most satisfactory poems in that book.
Yet Young completely misses Pope's effect of
urgency because not only does he assign no particular ranks to his group of criminals but he
also singles out royalty as the example of virtue:

> 'Midst empire's charms, how *Carolina's* heart
> Glows with the love of *virtue, and of art?*[8]

But Pope, from the long sequence of portraits,
swings us up through the passage of didactic
analysis into the final eulogy of Mrs. Blount;
and there he shifts his point of view; for he
addresses the poem to the good woman and holds
up the vicious to her examination. Their corrupted natures are described in the third person; her virtuous self, in the second. They are
spoken about; she is present, to be saluted
directly. The effect gives to goodness, in its
limited space, an immediacy and a substance which
evil, though intensely realized and extended over
hundreds of lines, has lacked. On this drawn-out
moral contrast the poem is built. Like the
coils of a long spring, the vicious characters
are stretched at length and then let go to provide rebounding impetus for the final panegyric.
     The moral implications of this relationship
bear out the formal order. The Lady is both the
positive climax of the entire poem and the justification of the satire. Obviously, Pope wishes

to compliment Martha Blount. But in an age
when sincerity was the most imitative form of
flattery, and in a poem which singled out panegyric as the most suspect kind of literature,
he had to exert himself to give force to his
praise. By employing most of his lines in condemnation of dangerous women, he adds distinction
to the solitary approval bestowed upon Mrs. Blount.
Conversely, by loudly recognizing virtue as it
appears in a unique specimen, he gives energy to
his dispraise of vice. Years earlier, in the
Epistle to Burlington, Pope had followed the same
method; but there the attack on Timon is so much
longer than the neighboring eulogy of Burlington,
and so far more brilliant, that it submerges the
latter. In both cases, however, Pope is especially convincing because as a normal thing he
places an envoi or apostrophe, addressed to a
primary reader, at the end of a long poem. Since
this person is conventionally given his proper
name, as the subject of a public tribute, the
anonymous Lady inherits such authenticity. Here
Pope is in a sense merely expanding and heightening the envoi so that it becomes the positive
climax of his poem.

The apotheosis of Mrs. Blount also helps
Pope meet a demand normally attached to the
production of satire. By what right, a reader
naturally wonders, does any author take it upon
himself to expose so many faults in others?
Most satirists answer by making explicit their
moral principles and thereby establishing their
own integrity. Thus in *An Epistle to Dr. Arbuthnot,*
Pope displays the poet himself as *integer vitae
scelerisque purus,* to balance the ignobility of his
enemies. This makes sense rhetorically, but the
inevitable suggestion of vanity weakens his power as a satirist. In the *Epistle to a Lady* he
works less directly but places himself more
effectively under the banner of righteousness;
for here he embodies virtue in another person
and then aligns himself with her. To incarnate
his positive values, he invokes not a set of
propositions but the concrete description of
Martha Blount. Where he does have a long

generalizing, didactic passage--and that is to
bridge the great series of vicious women and the
final portrait of his heroine--he is not expound-
ing virtue but analyzing evil. By establishing
his friend as his standard, Pope not only makes
his ideal vivid; he also gives up implicit assurance of his own moral elevation. Since she appears as goodness itself, and he makes himself
out to be her wholesale and accepted admirer,
Mrs. Blount has the effect of a supreme character witness for him, and thereby encourages
us to accept his denunciation of the world.
Although Pope had employed a similar method at
the close of the *Epistle to Burlington*, the tie
between the earl and the poet is too thin, and
the effect correspondingly weak.

If the formal order of parts thus reveals
extraordinary internal coherence directed to a
significant rhetorical purpose, the pattern
of imagery in the *Epistle* supplies some fascinating reinforcement of that impression. We must
remember that *To a Lady* presents a dramatic situation in which the readers overhear the poet as
he talks to a woman friend about some paintings.
The pair are strolling through a gallery or
around a studio hung with portraits and sketches
of ladies. As they stop before the various pictures or studies, the poet delivers remarks on
the subjects. At the end of the tour and the
end of the poem, he turns to his friend and pronounces an encomium contrasting her with the
persons whose character he has just unmasked.

It was a traditional literary device, as
Professor Jean Hagstrum has shown, to use a gallery of painted portraits as the imagined scene
of a disquisition upon moral types.[9] Pierre
Lemoyne had employed it in his *Peintures Morales*
(1645). Farquhar staged the idea in the *Beaux'
Stratagem*, and Addison supplies an instance in a
Spectator paper (no. 83). Professor Hagstrum
also reminds us of the convention of satire
formulated as instructions given to a painter.
This was established by the Italian, Businello,
in his serious panegyric, *Il Trionfo Veneziano*, where
the poet does not describe scenes directly but

tells an artist how to represent them. Waller,
one of Pope's acknowledged masters, naturalized
the device to England when he composed a eulogy
upon the Duke of York's heroism during a naval
battle; here again the poet tells an artist how
to bring out the value of the scenes, and Waller
entitled his work *Instructions to a Painter*. The
formula was soon copied by satirists as a means
of pinpointing the corruptions of Charles II's
court. Although most of these bitter, libelous
pieces seem ephemeral, at least two are by Andrew Marvell.[10] Pope is only tangentially in-
structing a painter, and his scheme is far more
peripheral than either Waller's or Marvell's.
However, the tradition was familiar to him; and
for the reader who remembers the Restoration
poems, the overtone is there:

> Chuse a firm Cloud, before it fall, and in it
> Catch, ere she change, the Cynthia of this
>   minute.
> ....
> Some wand'ring touches, some reflected light,
> Some flying stroke alone can hit 'em right.
>   (ll. 19-20, 153-54)

All this is figurative, of course; for we
normally treat the Lady of the poem as a transparent screen between the poet and ourselves; we
treat the poem as a monologue; and we treat the
allusions to painting as metaphors. However, I
should like to indicate what the figurative setting contributes to the design and rhetoric of
the poem. Young, like Pope, states his theme
in terms of painting, and he makes casual use
of plastic similes:

> What picture's yonder loosen'd from its frame?
> Or is't *Asturia*? that affected dame?[11]

But he never hints at more, or connects the
separate similes to a general scheme. Pope, however, explores the symbolic value of treating
sinners this way; and he puts his meaning explicitly at the opening of the attack. In his

substitution of paintings for persons he implies
the vices of vanity, deceit, and--above all--
fickleness:

> How many Pictures of one Nymph we view,
> All how unlike each other, all how true!
>   (ll. 5-6)

Pope contrasts the corrupted women's dependence
upon visible charms with the Lady's reliance on
virtue within. The theme is a commonplace:
Juba's praise of Marcia in *Cato*, Swift's praise
of Biddy Floyd, Welsted's epilogue to Steele's
Conscious Lovers, all sing the same tune, exalting
not the visible but the moral, intellectual,
and domestic resources of the ideal woman; yet in
Pope's poem the implicit contrast, point for
point, with the tangibilities of the villainous
women who have just been observed, produces a
marvelous ironical transformation of the adjectives
associated with them--"art," :pride," etc.--when
these are applied to Mrs. Blount:

> Reserve with Frankness, Art with Truth ally'd,
> Courage with Softness, Modesty with Pride,
> Fix'd Principles, with Fancy ever new.
>   (ll. 277-79)

Young publishes similar aphorisms: "Your strongest charms are native innocence"; "Be kind and
virtuous, you'll be blest and wise." But he confuses his arguments by also praising good women
for appearances--for physical beauty and elegant
clothes; he never ties the moral contrast to a
pervasive metaphor; and his flattery of the
highest-born compels him to shun opportunities
for irony.

While Pope's objects of satire are present
only as paintings, his Lady appears as a living
being. The two-dimensional portraits therefore
enhance one's sense of positive climax, because
it is only after passing over these dozen surfaces that we meet the rounded heroine. To Pope's
remark that we distinguish such females by their
color--"black, brown, or fair"--Professor Hagstrum applies the principle, accepted by Pope's

generation of connoisseurs, that line is more
real and stable than color, that color is more
changeable and therefore like women.[12] The same
motif occurs in the *Essay on Criticism*, where the
"faithful pencil" is opposed to "treacherous
colours," and where the true lines of sound judgment are contrasted with he deceitful colors of
false learning:

> But as the slightest Sketch, if justly trac'd,
> Is by ill *Colouring* but the more disgrac'd,
> So by *false Learning* is *good Sense* defac'd.
> (ll. 23-25)

The motif appears again in the lines on Cynthia
in the *Epistle to a Lady*:

> Come then, the colours and the ground prepare!
> Dip in the Rainbow, trick her off in air.
> (ll. 17-18)

And later in the poem it is employed more generally:

> Pictures like these, dear Madam, to design,
> Asks no firm hand, and no unerring line.
> (ll. 151-52)

Pope even suggests that simple or unmixed (i.e.,
"equal") colors will not suit the problem; for
only blended paints, implicitly less pure than
the unmixed, can represent woman's evanescence
and superficiality:

> For how should equal Colours do the knack?
> Chameleons who can paint in white and black?
> (ll. 155-56)

Within the paintings Pope makes further
refinements. The pseudonymous women pose generally in costume or disguise, and not as themselves; and the costume is often of a mythological
rather than historical figure: false names,
false dress, false models. Or the sinners pose

ironically as saints--Mary Magdalen, Cecilia. To
such tokens of deception is linked the ancient
contrast between naked truth and overdressed vice.

> Artists! who can paint or write,
> To draw the Naked is your true delight.
> That Robe of Quality so struts and swells,
> None see what Parts of Nature it conceals.
>   (ll. 187-90)

Professor Hagstrum reminds us of Titian's *Sacred
and Profane Love*, in which sacred love is naked and
profane love cloted.[13] It is also obviously
symbolic that the same woman should adopt contradictory roles in different paintings. The
very syntax of such descriptions presses ambiguity
upon us:

> Arcadia's Countess, here, in ermin'd pride,
> Is there, Pastora by a fountain side.
>   (ll. 7-8)

The couplet seems deliberately paradoxical. Although she comes from Arcadia and should therefore
be a shepherdess, she poses for one picture in
the robes of a peeress; on the contrary, although
her husband is presumably Earl of Pembroke and a
great courtier, she disguises herself in the
pendant picture as a country lass.
    Finally, the metaphor of painting is borne
out in the use of color imagery to contrast the
Lady and the sinners. Gray and silver belong to
her; red and gold to them; her scene is shaded;
theirs is dazzling; she evokes the quiet moon,
they the beaming sun. Since the Lady happens
to be a spinster, the lunar tones appropriately
suggest Diana and chastity.

                    . . .

    If one were simply adhering to the principle
of self-contained art, this point might well be
the stopping place of criticism. The internal
structure of Pope's poem has been, however hastily

(I have not even mentioned the brilliant versification of the couplets leading up to the introduction of Mrs. Blount) set forth; his superiority
to a rival (and mentor) has been indicated. Yet
the power of the *Epistle* is obviously too great for
one to feel right about leaving it so soon: the
poem overflows, reaching beyond literature into
reality. It is in the very structure of the
Epistle that the overflowing occurs most beautifully, but the effect is evident as well in humbler
ways that may be noticed first. There is, for
example, a historical truth in the imagined situation. Pope had early experience of pictures
like those he describes; he took painting lessons
from Jervas; he was accustomed to thinking of
poetry in pictorial terms; and he was accustomed
to hearing an artist discuss painting in literary
terms.[14] Though for him pictorial art was divided, in the curious categories of his age, between portraits and history painting, it was of
portraits that he had the most experience; all
his own efforts were in that category. He had,
as it happens, seen pictures of some of the
women to whom he alludes in the poem; he had
himself copied one--the Duchess of Montagu--on
canvas; and he had commissioned and owned at
least two--Mrs. Blount herself and Lady Mary.[15]
Since Mrs. Blount spent much time in his house,
therefore, the setting of the poem is remarkably
close to reality. Of course, Pope shields himself by the use of misleading details. To
smother rumors and to protect the maiden Lady of
his poem, he gives her a husband and a daughter;
yet we all know she is drawn from the spinster
Martha Blount.

As it was originally printed, the poem suffered enormous excisions, the most sensational
characters being prudently omitted until Pope
felt secure enough to face the consequences of
releasing them--or else so near death that no
consequence could touch him.[16] He would hardly
have held back from publication the magnificent
lines on Philomede, Atossa, Cloe, and Caroline
if they were not allusions to the second Duchess of Marlborough, the Duchess of Buckinghamshire

the Countess of Suffolk, and the Queen. Sappho
has universally been taken as a lampoon on Lady
Mary Wortley Montagu. Arcadia's Countess is
probably Margaret, first wife of the eighth earl
of Pembroke. This employment of recognizable
people and events is one persuasive ground of
Pope's satirical appeal. Poetically, he keeps
hinting, "These things have really happened."
He does not mean that every name alludes to an
existing person, or that every rumored scandal
is true as represented. But since he claims that
his insights are worth our attention, he must
assume the wisdom of experience. By implying
that he has observed at first hand the profusion
of cases displayed in his argument, he encourages
the reader to take him seriously. As a corollary,
if the reader is to trust the obvious fables, he
must recognize some facts. Just as Pope's didactic propositions shade from overt convention-
alities to covert audacities, so his factual allusions shade from parables to direct reporting.
The truisms serve to win the reader's faith
so that he will respect the individual judgments; the facts season the legends so that the
reader may credit the author as both an experienced and a faithful historian.

A more special effect is also felt because
one never can be certain whether the poet has
created an example or witnessed it. Once the
reader thinks he can correctly name a pseudonymous character, he is bound to keep searching for
new clues; and this search adds to Pope's late
satires a vibrancy which deepens and strengthens
their rhetoric. Young, in his satires, both
sacrifices this special effect and weakens his
general argument by dropping clues to a subject's
name only when he is praising the person. His
topical allusions are, as a careful scholar remarks, "not malicious," and individuals, if
pointed out at all, are "generally mentioned in
flattering terms."[17] Our curiosity is therefore
dampened rather than aroused, and we infer that
evil has less power than good.

The most brilliant allusion to reality, and
the last effect I shall analyze in the poem, is

central to the structure. This occurs at the
negative climax and peripety, as Pope is completing and abandoning his collection of sinners;
and it shows how a rhetorical order can be determined by facts external to a literary work. With
the sequence of Atossa, Cloe, the Queen, and the
Duchess of Queensberry, Pope seems to plot his
path so as to reveal the sharpest contrast between the vicious and the good. He almost certainly intended the Duchess of Buckinghamshire to
be recognized in Atossa. Katherine Darnley,
Duchess of Buckinghamshire and Normandy, was the
illegitimate daughter of James II. All her life,
she exhibited a paranoid pride in her ancestry;
she had a long feud with her husband's bastards,
became famous for her megalomania, and ended up
insane by any definition. "Cloe" almost certainly points to Henrietta Howard, Countess of
Suffolk. She was at the same time both lady-in-
waiting to the Queen and *maitresse en titre* to the
King. But although, as Prince of Wales, he had
indeed made love to her, she was now superannuated,
overweight, and deaf. It was years since he
had shown her much tenderness. At court she en-
dured the contemptuous protection of the Queen,
who did not wish her to be replaced by a less
manageable instrument. The Countess of Suffolk
was Pope's neighbor and friend.

Of course, the lines on Caroline are cautious.
Pope discusses neither the Queen nor a painting
of her. Instead, he ridicules the stereotype
which always seems to be substituted for a description when a painter or author must represent
the majesty of Britain. There is a parallel
passage in Pope's version of Horace's *Satires*,
II.i, addressed to Fortescue (ll. 21-32). No
scholar seems to have observed that in both
places the poet was probably alluding to Young's
tinny tributes, in his satires, to the Queen and
her eldest daughter.[18] It is such cliché praises
and cliché poses that Pope pretends to be attacking, rather than the royal person. Because
of these screens of nonsense, he says, one cannot
look to the throne for a model of virtue.

As an alternative, however, he suggests, of
all people, an avowed enemy of the court, whose
title has a pun on "queen." Catherine Douglas,
Duchess of Queensberry, was celebrated not only
for her beauty and wit. She had bestowed the
most liberal patronage on Pope's friend, Gay; and
recently she had withdrawn from court because of
a furious quarrel with the royal household over
her grace's aggressive support of Gay's opera
Polly. Nevertheless, says Pope, this duchess is
too modest to act as a cynosure. He will therefore, pass on to the general fact that humble
persons are easier to see truly than the great;
and the humble, therefore, will better provide
us with examples. "If Queensberry to strip
there's no compelling,/'Tis from a handmaid we
must take a Helen" (ll. 193-94).

In giving us a king's bastard, followed by a
king's mistress, followed by the same king's
queen, to whom the same mistress was lady-in-
waiting, followed by a Duchess of Queensberry
who had thrown over the whole court, I think
Pope must be sounding a fanfare of innuendoes to
draw attention to his theme and to announce his
heroine.[19] Yet it is only by going outside the
poem, to external facts, that we can establish
the meaning of this sequence. We have touched
the point of the social pyramid and found it the
pinnacle of evil as well as of rank: the greatest vanity, the greatest lust, and the greatest
power appear together; and since it is here alone
that Pope uses proper names, we may also say this
marks his most direct appeal to reality.[20]

Applying to Young the test that Pope meets so
easily, one produces quite different results; for
at several points Young may be described as defeated by reality. As a comprehensive principle
the argument to which he tries to relate all the
instances of vice or frivolity in his satires
seems unpleasantly shallow: namely, that a desire for fame of one sort or another is the common source of foolish and vicious actions. Young
may perhaps have flattered himself that he had a
proposition to prove--and consequently more in-

tellectual coherence than Pope in the *Epistle* --
but the proposition is so weak and unconvincing
as to disgrace its asserter. Even if it should
be regarded not as a supposed truth but merely
as a structural device, it fails, because many
of the most effective passages in the poems
cannot be related to the central theme--the denunciation of patron-hunters:

> Who'd be a *crutch* to prop a rotten peer;
> Or living *pendant*, dangling at his ear.[21]

The failure of the poems to cohere as a general
argument would seem less offensive if Young allowed subordinate pleadings to move consistently
with themselves. But repeatedly when he claims
to fight for one doctrine, he wears the uniform
of another. In his own person, for example, he
reproaches venal authors and bemoans the willingness of poets to sacrifice truth to profit.
Yet in the dedications, compliments, and
apostrophes which intermit the satire, his
quivering eagerness for mercenary advancement
appears so openly that no reader can observe the
reproaches without sneering. Furthermore, the
portraits that seem to excite the poet's greatest energy do not exhibit threats to a real order of morality but reveal mere freaks or tri-
flers, such as Brabantio, who is proud of a reputation for absentmindedness.[22]   Normally, one
has little sense that the characters are drawn
from living people; they are too often governed
by meaningless whimsies, and Young too willingly
abandons the facts of human nature to satisfy
his love of paradox--as in the character of
Philander, who secretly loves his own charming
wife but publicly keeps a mistress to avoid an
unfashionable reputation.[23]   Young's supreme
blunder, in a work supposed to advance virtue
and ridicule vice, is to choose his objects of
admiration from the irregular circles of political power. Several of his eulogies would, with
no other change, become ironical insults if set
in the frame of some lines by Pope. The fawning

praise of Dodington, whom sober historians compare to a jackal, the exaltation of a pawn like
Compton--"the *crown's* asserter, and the *people's*
friend"! [24]--imply a contempt for the reality of
British public life that vitiates Young's attack
upon corrupt politicians.[25] As a final and wholly appropriate streamer to trail after his wob-
bling car, Young consecrates his closing "satire"
to the climactic and wildly indecorous flattery
of Walpole and the King.

· · ·

The two satires (V and VI) which Young allot-
ted to women rise to a far higher level of art
than the rest of the *Love of Fame* (or *Universal
Passion*), but no judge has yet accused Young in
these poems of an excess of craftsmanship. Probably the most brilliant piece of poetry between
the works of Pope and the works of Blake is
Gray's *The Bard*, against whose splendor the accusation might easily be brought. Once more, however, I think the astonishing internal, literary
coherence of the poem has been insufficiently
appreciated; and again I think the test of
reality can bring out aspects of the poem which
are fundamental to its value. The essential
design of *The Bard* has a deep similarity to that
of Pope's *Epistle*; for if we mark line 101 (two
thirds of the way through) as the turning point,
the ode comprises a long first part, aggressive
and denunciatory, which is balanced by a shorter
second part, affirmative and confident. Within
this general contrast Gray, like Pope, establishes a set of symmetrical parallels. Thus the
poem both opens and closes with a confrontation
between Edward I and the last of the Welsh
bards, on Mount Snowdon, with the Conway River
running below. After cursing the king, the bard
bemoans the deaths of his fellow poets, and
then foretells the miseries of Edward's descendants as far as Richard III. At the peripety,
the predictions of doom are symmetrically transformed into a paean of joy as the bard envisions

the triumph of Welsh blood in the Tudor dynasty.
This is symmetrically followed by a celebration
of the Elizabethan literary renaissance, to
match the lament over the singers murdered by
Edward.   Finally, in a gesture that reverses his
opening challenge when he looked down from a
beetling rock upon the descending army of invaders,
the bard leaps triumphantly to his suicide in the
"roaring tide" of the river.
     In its general movement the poem opposes im-
petuosity to formal restraint.   There is a boldness or extravagance in the action, imagery,
and language which is met by a fixed complexity
in the versification.   The mountain landscape
is deliberately sublime, anticipating the climactic
scene of *The Prelude*.[26]   Gushing under the peak, the
river bears connotations suggestive of the creative flow of the poetic imagination as detailed
in *The Progress of Poesy*.   The bard poses in a
style which recalls Raphael's representation of
God appearing to Ezekiel, as Gray himself notes.
It is therefore as an embodiment of the divinely
creative principle that the bard stands higher
than the king and the royal army.   To intensify
the terror that sublimity requires, Gray does
not entrust the prophetic verses merely to the
bard but rather gives them to a chorus of spir-
its--ghosts of the slaughtered poets--who are
seen and heard by their living confrere.   At
the turning point, they complete their prophecy
and vanish, to be replaced by the revelation to
the bard of a visionary pageant that displays
Tudor monarchs, courtiers, and poets, with Milton bringing up the rear.
     Gray's boldly inventive vocabulary, his sudden
shifts of point of view, the sensational choice
of historical detail (including royal murders,
civil wars, and infanticide), all strengthen the
rushing violence that marks the poem.   By ex-
aggerating his normally rich use of expressive
sound effects, Gray adds to the impetuosity of
the movement.   There is a quasi-onomatopoeia in
a line like, "He wound with toilsome march his
long array" (l. 12), or "Regardless of the
sweeping whirlwind's sway" (l. 75).   But the

elaborate use of alliteration, assonance, chiasmus, internal rhyme, and similar devices seems
dramatically appropriate as well, because Welsh
poetry is characterized by such intricacies:
notice, for example, the expressive contrast,
before and after the caesura in line 71, of the
same fricatives, sibilants, and liquids: "Fair
laughs the morn, and soft the zephyr blows."
On a modern ear the boldness of Gray's diction
is dulled by the freedom that recent generations
have exercised in altering old meanings and
creating neologisms. Yet expressions like "lyon-
port," "crested pride," and "hoary hair/Stream'd
like a meteor, to the troubled air" (ll. 117, 9,
19-20) still retain some of the shocking power
that disgusted Johnson in spite of Gray's care
to model his adjectival nouns and remote analogies
upon authoritative example.
    As a counter-vortex to the bursting richness
of action, scene, and style, Gray imposes upon
these elements the steady impulse of his formidable
metrics and rhyme scheme. By refining on the
form of the "true" Pindaric ode, he arrives at a
triple-ternary structure, the whole work comprising three main units each of which in turn contains three stanzas: a paired strophe and antistrophe, and an epode. To tighten the already
tight form, Gray requires not only that each
antistrophe match its own strophe (an elaborate
stanza form of his own invention), foot for foot
and rhyme for rhyme, but also that precisely the
same form be employed for all three pairs. Similarly, all three epodes possess a common, even
more complicated stanzaic pattern. In order to
clarify for the ear this articulated structure,
Gray ends each stanza with an alexandrine pre-
ceded by a rhyming pentameter. To give a sense
of burgeoning progression, he concentrates the
short verses at the beginning of the stanza and
makes the line-lengths expand near the end: thus
each strophe and antistrophe opens with five
tetrameter verses and closes with five pentameters
before the alexandrine. Combining brevity with
abruptness to give the effect of a sudden start

("Ruin seize thee, ruthless King!"), Gray omits
the first syllable of the first line of each
strophe and antistrophe, so that it sounds tro-
chaic and is shorter than any other line except
the fifth, which is heptasyllabic as well (I
suppose, to regularize the effect). In the epodes
each stanza begins with trimeters, has a heptasyllabic eighth line, and uses internal rhyme
in the fifteenth and seventeenth lines (enriching
the cadence of approaching conclusion). Although
the stanzas are long, Gray breaks them up into
distinct quatrains, sestets, and couplets. The
strophes and antistrophes work out curiously
like a Shakespearean sonnet; the epodes are
composed of a sestet at either end, joined by
two quatrains.

This whole, charted, subdivided apparatus of
verses and rhymes is worked in counterpoint with
the narrative of the poem. As in Pindar, the
meaning often ignores the breaks between stanzas,
and the pauses or transitions often occur at odd
points within a stanza. The reader cannot help
feeling the dancelike interplay of meaning and
form, boldness and restraint, motion and fixity.

In spite of its manifest brilliance *The Bard*
is widely acknowledged to be a failure. Why?
I think the essential reason will be found in
the weakness of the poem's appeal to reality.
Unlike Pope, Gray, so far from inviting such a
test, utterly evades it. This evasion appears
in the very structure of the story. Indubitably,
the poet asks us to treat the incident as fantasy.
For all the vividness of the representation, for
all the fullness of historical reference, the
episode has no claim to authenticity. The text
is largely devoted to the speech of the bard.
Yet this speaker kills himself as soon as his
monologue is over, and cannot, therefore, trans-
mit his account to any reporter. On the English
side no one is supposed to understand Welsh; and
if anyone did, the details of events that have
not yet occurred, and that are forecast with an
obscurity hiding their meaning even from the
bard, would be unintelligible. That Edward killed

the Welsh singers might be known; what one of
those singers prophesied alone, just before his
death, and to an uncomprehending audience, could
not possibly be preserved. The intellectual implications of the poem also remain as unreal today as they appear in Johnson's critique of *The
Progress of Poesy*.[27] Contrary to Gray's argument,
the true poet is not always patriotic; he does
not necessarily defend freedom; if he lives in a
"primitive" rural society, he will not write
more "sublime" songs than a cultivated, urban
poet (Milton and Caradoc make strange yoke-
mates to draw Gray's "presumptuous car"); and
finally, genius does not tend to flourish under
a good government or to wither under despotism.

On the other hand, Gray's most successful poem
has a positive bearing upon human life in general and the eighteenth century in particular.
The *Elegy* possesses the subtle appeal of flattering the reader into separating himself from the
redeemed, obscurely virtuous villagers and attaching himself to the toiling bearers of power.
The ultimate ironic implication of the *Elegy*,
that we gladly suffer the curse of greatness in
order to enjoy its fruits, is no misleading
account of human nature. In the vacuous lines
of the *Ode for Music*, Gray was to destroy the
power of this appeal by supplying only one, deadly conventional half of the dilemma:

What is grandeur, what is power?
Heavier toil, superior pain.
    (ll. 57-58)

Reality winces at the sound. But the theme of
wasted virtue, merit unrewarded, talents denied
expression (at the center of the *Elegy*) echoes
the cry of Swift, Fielding, and Johnson against
their common society: we hear it in *Gulliver's
Travels*, in *Tom Jones*, and in *London*.

There is nevertheless a sense in which *The
Bard* does make a profound appeal to reality.
In the final analysis Gray's contrast between
impetuosity and restraint becomes identified
with the meaning of the poem. The impetuous

bard, making propaganda for liberty and justice,
opposes the fixed, oppressive tyrant, who kills
the imagination; the gushing torrent of creation
streams beside the rocky, corpse-littered mountain; art confronts reality. Writing to Beattie
(years after this ode appeared), and discussing
the hero of *The Minstrel*, Gray recommended that
when Edwin was driven to become a bard, he
should perform some "great and singular service
to his country." Such an action, said Gray,
would constitute "the best panegyrick of our
favourite and celestial science" (i.e., of
poetry). There are several remarkable features
in Gray's statement. One is that he cannot himself specify what the sublime service might be;
another is that, according to Gray, simply
creating poetry was not itself enough. Yet the
deed must be one requiring the peculiar talents
of a poet--"some great and singular service to
his country? (what service I must leave to your
invention) such as no general, no statesman, no
moralist could do without the aid of music, inspiration, and poetry. This will not appear an
improbability in those early times, and in a
character then held sacred, and respected by all
nations."[28] Without telling us much about Gray
that Arnold does not intimate in his essay,
these remarks do point at both the source of
the energy the poet poured into the ode and the
cause of its failure. "In those early times"
the poet's character was truly sacred; in those
times he could perform services in the power of
no mere general, statesman, or moralist. But
now such a character would appear too improbable
to admit into the design of a serious literary
work. If the life of his own time represented
reality, Gray clearly felt that the poet's role
in it was nugatory. This is why *The Bard* never
reaches out beyond the limits of literature.
Just how remote Gray thought that a true poet
must be, in the middle of the eighteenth century,
from any deep influence upon his fellow countrymen,
just how far inferior he must remain to soldiers
(on the eve of the Seven Years' War and Pitt's
imperial victories), to politicians, and to priests

we may infer from the conclusion of this *chef
d'oeuvre:* the "celestial science" means prophesying to those who cannot understand you, and then
suffering martyrdom. Of course, during a regime
in which devotion to literature is itself a heroic act (as in Baudelaire's France), this would
be a significant relationship to one's time; but
Gray's gesture belongs in a different class. The
vision asserted by Collins in the *Ode on the
Poetical Character*, the vision reinterpreted by
Coleridge half a century later, was denied to
Gray. For all its splendor *The Bard* is an assertion
of its author's impotence.

· · ·

The slogan of the embattled critic-scholars
of the 1930's was that form is meaning. But this
cry becomes serviceable only when a degree of
tautology is implied: significant form, effective structure, has a direct bearing on meaning.
The corruption of the slogan by epigones produced
the assumption, which underlies the vast, unwieldy
bulk of academic critical analysis, that any discussion of formal structure is, by some mysterious
action at a distance, a discussion of meaning and
value. Johnson's Dick Minim the critic prides
himself on every instance of expressive form that
he can isolate. Yet the tendency disproves itself; for surely one cannot judge the expressive-
ness of a verse unless one grasps the meaning of
the poem, and surely the meaning depends upon a
relation to reality. To pretend that there are
such things as self-contained aesthetic objects,
or that poems are exquisite arrangements of the
sounds and the lexical implications of separate
words, is to deny the impulse that patently
drives every great artist. He is always trying
to say something of immense importance to him:
this is what *he* (not the poem) means; this is
his "intention"; this is what we must apprehend.
In every age the supreme geniuses have wished to
be measured against reality, against the truths
of human nature, the facts of the social order.

Wordsworth said he wished to trace, in the *Lyrical Ballads*, "the primary laws of our nature"; Coleridge said the merits of *The Three Graves* were "exclusively psychological."[29] When we narrow the grounds of their achievement and judge them by a simpler standard than they themselves proposed, when we reserve for Dostoevsky and Kafka the test of reality but limit the reference of the Augustans to terms of art, I suspect we may be not honoring the masters of our poetry but insulting them.

THAT IMPUDENT SATIRE: POPE'S *SOBER ADVICE*

John M. Aden

   Sober Advice from Horace has never fared well, and
the reason, one suspects, is as much related to
a failure to perceive its relevance as to any indecency, real or fancied, that is associated with
it. Why, in his fit of imitating Horace, did
Pope pitch upon this particular specimen, not especially reputable in the Horatian canon, and
subject to dogged misgivings on the part of the
Popeian constituency, including, apparently, even
Pope himself? I shall suggest that he did so
from motives neither perverse nor playful, as
generally supposed, but rather ethical and satirical, in keeping with his recently assumed role
of moral poet and imitator of Horace.[1] Such a
view will point, in turn, to the appropriateness
of a reappraisal of the poem *qua* poem, not only
the motives which led to it, but also the influences affecting its style and method, and the
quality of its wit.
   Sober Advice appeared anonymously in late 1734,
"from the house of a hitherto untried bookseller."[2] It was never quite acknowledged by Pope,

This essay first appeared in *Studies in Philology*, extra series 4 (1967), 88-106. Copyright The University of North Carolina Press.

though it did appear in the Octavo edition of his
Works in 1738, where it was retitled *The Second Satire of the First Book of Horace*, still "Imitated," as
Sherburn notes, "in the *Manner* of Mr. Pope."[3] It
was then reprinted, unchanged, in the reissues of
this edition in 1740 and 1743, but was, as remarked in the notes, omitted in both the old
standard editions.[4]

Pope is commonly supposed to have begun work
on the poem at least by mid-year of 1734, though
it is possible that its composition dates earlier
than that.[5] That he had completed a draft of it
by 27 June 1734 is evident from Bolingbroke's
letter to Swift so dated. Pope has, says Bolingbroke,

been imitating the Satire of Horace which begins
Ambubaiarum Collegia, Pharmacopolae, &c. and has
chose rather to weaken the images than to hurt
chaste ears overmuch. he has sent it to me, but
I shall keep his secret, as he desires....6

It was during August, at Lord Peterborow's, that,
according to Sherburn, Pope "polished" *Sober Advice* while also putting together the *Epistle to Dr.
Arbuthnot*.[7]

On 30 December, barely after its publication,
Pope began the series of equivocal disclaimers
of the poem which he had already anticipated by
its anonymous and ambiguous title-page announcement. He writes to the Earl of Oxford, "I am Lord
Duplin's humble Servant. I hope he will defend
me from the imputation which all the Town I hear
lay upon me, of having writ that impudent satire."
The next day (31 December) he is protesting to
Caryll:

Here is a piece of poetry from Horace come out,
which I warn you not to take for mine, tho' some
people are willing to fix it on me. In truth I
should think it a very indecent Sermon, after
the *Essay on Man*.

On 8 February 1734/5 he is still protesting to
Caryll:

The ludicrous (or if you please) the obscene
thing you desired me to send, I did not approve
of, and therefore did not care to propagate by
sending into the country at all. Whoever likes
it so well as to think it mine, compliments me
at my own expense.

Something under a fortnight later (18 February)
he explains to Caryll the Bentley development,
word of which had apparently gotten around:

The story of Bentley is this in three words. He
expressed a resentment as if I had injured his
father in a thing I disowned. I told him if he
was not satisfied in that, and if he required any
other satisfaction, I would give it. After a
three-weeks' hesitation, and messages, he gave it
under his hand he did not, and confessed himself
in the wrong.[8]

Why all this subterfuge and equivocation, and
how is it to be judged? Sherburn interprets
the matter bluntly: "Pope concealed his authorship because of the indecency of the poem and
the threats of Bentley's son to horsewhip the
poet, if he was the author."[9] Professor Rogers
is more inventive:

Various features of this work as published were
calculated to suggest that it was not Pope's
composition but a parody of his style. The
title page told readers that the poem had imitated Horace "in the Manner of Mr. Pope"; the
imprint, "Printed for T. Boreman...," implied
that the poem was the work of a Grub-street author. The general impression that such details
create is that *Sober Advice* is an attack upon the
satirist, an obscene parody of his manner in the
Imitations of Horace. Pope evidently hoped that if
readers could be made to think that *Sober Advice*
was an abusive lampoon, they would be prepared to
accept his apologia [the *Arbuthnot*] without
question.[10]

This theory, ingenious as it is (it is the Dunciad "ground bait" theory reapplied), is unsatisfactory on several counts. For one thing, it
ignores the likelihood that if such were indeed
Pope's motive, he missed a good opportunity to
give it currency by suggesting it to Caryll, or,
for that matter, to the Earl of Oxford. For
another, it overlooks, as nearly everyone does,
the testimony of Bolingbroke, who not only gives
no indication of being aware of any such stratagem
(only that Pope wished his authorship to remain
unknown), but who seems to feel, moreover, that,
far from being obscene, the poet has been rather
scrupulous in rendering Horace. But even without these objections, it would not follow that
because the poem is presented as parodic it was
to be understood as obscene and abusive, *i.e.*,
as damaging to Pope. That Pope himself feared
the imputation of obscenity is something quite
distinct from the supposition that the form of
the poem and its manner of publication were
calculated to provoke such a charge. The earlier *Imitations*, after all, were hardly innocent of
lampoon,[11] nor Pope himself of satiric obscenity,
from the *Rape of the Lock* through the *Dunciad*, to
the authorship of which last he would own up in
the very *apologia* that Rogers sees him preparing
for in the indecency of *Sober Advice*. Nor is it
easy to believe that Pope could (or would) have
seriously entertained the idea that his title-
page would really persuade anybody that the poem
which followed it was of Grubbaean origin:

> Poor guiltless I! and can I chuse but smile,
> When ev'ry Coxcomb knows me by my *Style*?[12]

Pope, we must recognize, is as much in earnest as
in jest here, and it is at some such point as
this that the ultimate objection to Rogers must
be made, for to accept his theory is to discredit
the poem out of hand, to regard it *prima facie* as
subpoetic, without sufficient wit or style to pro
tect it from false attribution--conclusions that
an unprejudiced reading of the poem will not, I

believe, support. It seems more reasonable--and
less costly--to assume that Pope's concern is not
to fob the poem off on another, but to get it
admitted to his own canon with as little embar-
rassment as possible.

As for the "indecency" of the poem, there both
is and is not a question. At no point in its
history has satire been distinguished for decency
of manner, and the age and page of Pope are no
exception. By the same token, at no point in its
history has satire been exempt from complaint on
that score, though the outcry has been perhaps
the keener since the advent of sensibility. But
indecency, as we know, is at least partly relative to time, place, and genre.[13] In Pope's case,
moreover, it is relative to a hostility bred as
much by his success (and politics) as by his
satire; and, in the particular case in hand, by
a new role he was striving at this point in his
career to create for himself. In the process
of building a reputation as a moral and philosophical poet, Pope had somehow to accommodate
his genius to that end. Such accommodation is,
of course, the problem of every satiric poet who
is, at the same time, a serious (ethical) poet,
but whose means (genius) is suspect. Hence the
apologia. Hence too perhaps the epistolary and
dialogic mechanisms. Hence even, as Rogers
suggests, Pope's imitation of Horace.[14] Hence,
finally, anonymity. However exalted his intent,
the satirist's genius is satiric (and to that
extent indecorous), and he must mediate these
factors--ethics and satire--in the face of a
stubborn reluctance on the part of the world
to view them as compatible. The task is difficult, and the satirist rarely succeeds except
in retrospect, and not always then.

This, at any rate, is something like the predicament of Pope at the time of turning to Horace's plain-spoken sermon on adultery. He is
intent upon dignifying his profession as satirist, and he must take pains to avoid any misunderstanding, intentional or otherwise, that would
compromise that aim. That Horace's poem is in

fact, as I believe Pope recognized, entirely consonant with his moral and philosophical program,
could have afforded little consolation, for Pope
was experienced enough to know that not many would
be so sophisticated as to realize it, or so candid
as to acknowledge it if they did. Just, therefore, as he had earlier published the *Essay on Man*
anonymously, while at the same time publishing
other pieces under his name, in order to outwit
his critics and gain an unprejudiced hearing for
his venture into dogmatic poetry, so in *Sober Advice* he may be thought of as resorting to a similar strategy in behalf of another radical venture. Pope's whole career, for that matter, was
a composition of just such defensive tactics
relative to the expression of his genius, and
there is no reason to suppose that (save for his
Catholic friends, whom he always tried to spare)
he donned the cloak of anonymity in this particular instance for any reason other than a lack
of confidence in the candor of his audience.
His adaptation is licentious, to be sure, but so
is its model. That is implicit in their nature,
as satires. It is, as Pope knew, no necessary
Friend of Virtue who protests,

> This filthy Simile, this beastly Line,
> Quite turns my Stomach--

and thus he rejoins,

> So does Flatt'ry mine;
> And all your Courtly Civet-Cats can vent,
> Perfume to you, to me is Excrement.[15]

Sober Advice is not gross, or nasty, but witty and,
in the best (satiric) sense of the word, shocking.
But Pope could not count upon the world knowing
or acknowledging the difference. Hence--and not
in some tacit confession of guilt or shame--the
anonymity of its publication.[16]

   A fair summation of the matter would, then,
seem to be this: that Pope indeed published *Sober
Advice* anonymously because he was accustomed to
proceeding in this fashion whenever he sensed dan-

ger, either to his reputation or to his person; but that he also resorted to anonymity because he wanted to venture his newly assumed profession of moral poetry in a genre, model, and tone he could not be certain would take, and so divested the experiment of such disadvantages as his name would almost certainly visit upon it. It is this last motive in fact which defines my basic proposition regarding the poem, that far from being an indecent excursion into the "pornographic," or even something so innocent as "a quickly written *jeu d'esprit*," *Sober Advice* is in reality an exercise in a different key in the very moral and philosophic scheme Pope had undertaken with the *Essay on Man* and *Ethic Epistles*.

It will not be necessary to rehearse the grand, complex, and shifting design of that ambitious undertaking. Pope expressed the essence of it in "The Design" prefixed to *An Essay on Man:*

Having proposed to write some pieces on Human Life and Manners, such as (to use my lord Bacon's expression) *come home to Men's Business and Bosoms*, I thought it more satisfactory to begin with considering *Man* in the abstract ...

. . . .

What is now published, is only to be considered as a *general Map* of MAN ... leaving the particular to be more fully delineated in the charts which are to follow. Consequently, these Epistles in their progress...will be less dry, and more susceptible of poetical ornament.[17]

Pope was anxious from the outset not to lose the poet in the philosopher, nor, as his performance makes clear, the satirist in the poet. Even the *Essay*, though it "stands apart from the satires ...[has] an obvious satiric flavor,"[18] and this flavor becomes more pronounced in the *Ethic Epistles*, which are generally acknowledged to be essentially Horatian satires.[19] Pope was, in short, in a Horatian mood of teaching and

speaking, and was expressing that mood in the
following sequence of publications:

Epistle to Burlington [Ethic Epistle IV], December
   1731
Epistle to Bathurst [Ethic Epistle III], January
   1733 N.S.
Imitation of Horace [Sat. II.i], February 1733
   N.S.
An Essay on Man [Epistles I-III], February-May
   1732/3
Epistle to Cobham [Ethic Epistle I], January 1734
   N.S.
An Essay on Man [Epistle IV], January 1734 N.S.
Imitation of Horace [Sat. II. ii], July 1734
Sober Advice from Horace [Sat. I. ii] December 1734
Epistle to Dr. Arbuthnot, January 1735 N.S.
To a Lady [Ethic Epistle II], February 1735 N.S.
   Etc.

Sober Advice, which gives back echo stronger or
fainter to every piece in the list, conforms
to Pope's general purpose in the series ("some
pieces on Human Life and Manners") and bears a
particular affinity to the Epistle to Cobham ("Of
the Knowledge and Characters of Men") and to the
Epistle to a Lady ("Of the Characters of Women").
To a Lady was composed by January 1733 N.S., but
not published until February 1735 N.S. Cobham
was composed, or was in composition, apparently
between April and October or November 1733 and
published the following January.[20] Depending
on how one looks at the question of the composition date of Sober Advice,[21] the order of composition of the three pieces would be either

To a Lady: by Jan. 1733 N.S.   To a Lady
Cobham:April to Oct.-Nov.   or   S.A.: 20 March
   1733   1733 N.S.
Sober Advice: by 27 June   Cobham
   1734

After To a Lady, or perhaps concurrently with its
composition, Pope turned to Horace: Satire II. i,

composed December-January 1732/3 and *Satire* II. ii, composed before the end of March 1733. He then turned either to the *Cobham*, as commonly supposed, or, as it may be--out of the momentum generated by *Satires* II. i and ii--to *Sober Advice* (I. ii). But in any case, *Sober Advice* comes either between or on the heels of *To a Lady* and *Cobham*. When, in other words, Pope turned to *Ambubaiarum collegia*, he was in the midst of his program of discourse on "Human Life and Manners" in "the Horatian way," and was more proximately engaged in studies of the "Characters" of men and women, both of which are at issue in Horace's satire and Pope's adaptation of it. What more consistent, given the Horatian reflex and the start on the *sermones*, than to turn at such a juncture to *Satire* I. ii? No other of the satires could have served Pope's purposes as well.[22]

Though not very like *Sober Advice* in style and technique, *Cobham* is thematically close to the Imitation.[23] It begins by acknowledging the baffling inconsistency in the characters of men, the inconsistency that leads one to this extreme, another to that, and the same man now to one extreme, now to another. This is the very point of Horace's complaint in *Sat.*I ii, which he expresses *Dum vitant stulti vitia, in contraria currunt*, and which Pope renders highlighting the sexual duality, "Women and Fools are always in extreme."[24] But the ultimate burden of *Cobham*, as more or less of the other parts of the *magnum opus*, is the idea of the Ruling Passion, which biases a man in some peculiar direction. *Sober Advice* addresses itself, on a more satirical level, to one of the commonest of such biases, the adulterous or venerean passion. To the folly of that passion, Horace, and with him Pope, brings a commonsense cure, of course, but beneath the urbanity of the one and the audacity of the other lies a common indictment of the expense of spirit in a waste of shame. Finally, though its scope extends beyond any single passion, *Cobham* amply alludes to the adulterous and venerean passions and persons with which and whom *Sober Advice* deals exclusively. Besides its mistresses (vv. 55-56), punks

(83-84, 190-91), and whores (212-13) *Cobham* affords
the following sobering spectacle:

> Behold a rev'rend sire, whom want of grace
> Has made the father of a nameless race,
> Shov'd from the wall perhaps, or rudely press'd
> By his own son, that passes by unbless'd:
> Still to his wench he crawls on knocking knees,
> And envies ev'ry sparrow that he sees.
>   (vv. 228-233)

To a Lady verges even closer on *Sober Advice*, partly
by virtue of its greater satiric particularity,
partly by virtue of its concern with women, but
chiefly by virtue of its basic device, the gallery
of satiric portraits, the latter of which almost
certainly influenced the opening of the Horatian
imitation, affecting the sex and manner of Pope's
adaptation, with its parade of Oldfields, Fufidias,
Rufas, and the like.[25] As Bentley is made to
complain in the footnotes, the corresponding
characters in Horace are male. Though Pope turns
to the male soon enough (v. 35 ff.), he com-
mences the Imitation in the spirit and manner
of *To a Lady*. The influence, as it turns out, is a
happy one, consistent with the different times,
habits, and vision of the English satirist. By
it Pope was able to update Horace to the eighteenth-century taste for satire on women, to
achieve a greater initial energy and impact than
his original, and, most significantly, to bring
to the forefront of the satire the object of the
folly that it decries and ridicules.

Among the ladies in this later, less glamor-
ous gallery, *Rufa* had appeared, by name at least,
in the earlier, where (vv. 21-23), though no
whore, she is perhaps but a coquette's remove
therefrom. Oldfield appears in the *Cobham* (242-
47), and *Fufidia* (under her more common sobriquet,
Sappho) in *To a Lady*, where she is no more wholesome
than here, though for different reasons. Peg and
bashful Jenny, though they have no counterpart
in the Epistle, qualify, in their fashion, for the
role assigned to Narcissa there:

A very Heathen in the carnal part,
Yet still a sad, good Christian at her heart.

Like the *Cobham*, *To a Lady* also takes ample notice
of the adulterous and venerean passions. We catch
a fleeting glimpse of them in Leda and Magdalen,
and we have already remarked Narcissa's weaknesses
that way. In addition there is *Philomede*, "Proud
as a Peeress, prouder as a Punk"; she "whose life
the Church and Scandal share"; and *Chloe*, with her
"Lover [panting] upon her breast." Every woman,
as Pope observes, "is at heart a Rake."

You purchase Pain with all that Joy can give,
And die of nothing but a Rage to live.
  (99-100)

For foreign glory, foreign joy, they roam;
No thought of Peace or Happiness at home.
  (223-24)

A Fop their Passion, but their Prize a Sot,
Alive, ridiculous, and dead forgot!
  (247-48)

To these observations on the folly of womankind
may be compared similar sentiments on that of
mankind in *Sober Advice*, especially verses 77-80,
96-101, and 143-46. It is as if after he had
done *To a Lady* Pope recalled in Horace the ideal
counterpart, "To a Man."[26] The parallels, at
any rate, are striking, and suggest a certain
continuity in design as well as theme. Pope
has not shifted ground in *Sober Advice*, but intensified what he was already about, thematically in
general and procedurally in aspects of *To a Lady*.
  It will be appropriate now to reopen the
question of the "art" of *Sober Advice*, as much misjudged, I believe, as its motives.[27] Since the
poem is an imitation, this question may best be
approached from that standpoint, *i.e.*, of what
Pope did with his original. As usual, he follows
his model fairly closely in substance and arrangement, but executes those local variations that
make the difference between translation and

imitation.[28] In this instance, apart from what
we have already remarked about the influence of
To a Lady, the variations will be found to be
chiefly, though not exclusively, a tissue of high
lampoon and *double entendre*. Pope, as always, in-
tensifies Horace: particularizes his reference
and sharpens his edge, scandalizes his nose for
satire, converts his Latin into racy English, and
draws him masterfully into those orbits of wit
so congenial to his own age and genius: the comedy and conscience of the Restoration, Swift and
the burlesque vein, and the happy malice and
audacity of Mr. Pope himself. But he saw his
imitative art precisely in proportion to these
innovations on his original, and he cannot be
judged except as they are taken into account.[29]

The imitation loses no time asserting its own
authority. Wit and lampoon converge at once
in the transformation of Horace's *Quippe Benignus
erat* (said of Tigellius) to the boldly ambiguous
declaration of what it is for Nan Oldfield to be
benigna:

> Engaging *Oldfield*! who, with Grace and Ease,
> Could joyn the Arts, to ruin, and to please.
>   (5-6)

Such heightening, variously enforced, lights up
the whole imitation. One sees it in the verses
on Con Philips:

> "Treat on, treat on," is her eternal Note,
> And Lands and Tenements go down her Throat
>   (13-14),

a vignette vastly more vivid than Horace's *in-
grata...ingluvie* or '*Sordidus, atque animi quod parvi
nolit haberi,*'/*Respondet*.[30] One sees it likewise in
the metaphorical re-creation of Horace's straightforward and literal *sunt qui nolint tetigisse*, etc.
(28-30):

> Some feel no Flames but at the *Court* or *Ball*,
> And others hunt white Aprons in the *Mall*.
>   (37-38)

It multiplies Horace's *mimae* (v. 56, the actress to whom Marsaeus gives his patrimony) into a veritable bed of actresses:

> To *Palmer's* Bed no Actress comes amiss,
> He courts the whole *Personae Dramatis*
>   (71-72)

Intensification is especially effective in the adaptation of Horace's *Adde huc ...turpia celet* (83-85):

> And *secondly*, how innocent a *Belle*
> Is she who shows what Ware she has to sell;
> Not Lady-like, displays a milk-white Breast,
> And hides in sacred Sluttishness the rest.
>   (108-111)

Pope adds to Horace's undenominated prostitute the playful irony of "Belle," against which he plays off (again to Horace's undenominated matron) the sarcastic paradox, "Lady-like," building up to the devastating oxymoron, "sacred Sluttishness."
   Where, as we see, Horace is generally content with the literal, Pope turns reflexively to metaphor, as in the handy pairing of figurative with literal in the following:

> ...*O crus, o brachia! verum*
> *Depugis, nasuta, brevi latere, ac pede longo est.*
>   (92-93)

> Goose-rump'd, Hawk-nos'd, Swan-footed, is my
>   Dear?
> They'l praise her *Elbow*, *Heel*, or *Tip o'th' Ear*.
>   (122-23)

Horace's *Matronae, praeter faciem, nil cernere possis* is made more pointed: "A Lady's Face is all you see undress'd" (124). *Interdicta* becomes "Charms more latent" (126) and *Custodes, Lectica*, etc., "Spies, Guardians, Guests, old Women, Aunts, and Cozens!"[31]

The uproar scene with which the poem ends finds
Pope intensifying his source with a burlesque of
the kind of thing one encounters in his own *Elegy*
and *Eloisa* and in Restoration She-Tragedy and
picaresque story:

> From gleaming Swords no shrieking Women run;
> No wretched Wife cries out, *Undone! Undone!*
> Seiz'd in the Fact, and in her Cuckold's Pow'r,
> She kneels, she weeps, and worse! resigns her
>   Dow'r.
> Me, naked me, to Posts, to Pumps they draw,
> To Shame eternal, or eternal Law.
>   (169-174)

There is even a touch of Restoration comedy in
the hubbub, an echo of the surprises, or near
surprises, in the cuckolding crises of that
drama.

We have seen a hint of Swift in the macaronic
rhyme quoted above (amiss-- *Dramatis*), and we have
remarked the Swiftian flavor of Pope's Moll and
Jack, Peg and Jenny. Something too of Swift may
account for the element of the boisterous in
Pope's adaptation, the frankness and occasional
impertinence of the style, and the impish delight
with which it pursues its serious purpose. One
of the episodes is particularly reminiscent of
Swift, the anecdote of Cato's encounter with the
rake emerging from the stews, soberly described
in Horace, but here given a Swiftian burlesque
turn--to which Pope adds what is almost certainly
an implied joke on himself and the Dean:

> My Lord of L--n, chancing to remark
> A *noted Dean* much busy'd in the Park,
> "Proceed (he cry'd) proceed, my Reverend
>   Brother,
> "'Tis *Fornicatio simplex*, and no other:
> "Better than lust for Boys, with *Pope* and *Turk*,
> "Or others Spouses, like my Lord of [York][32]

Swift too, of course, liked a joke on himself, and
that may also reflect his impingement on the adaptation.

Of the Restoration comic vein there is abundant evidence. We have caught a glimpse of it in the "Mall" (38) and in the cuckoldry that weaves in and out of the poem and that forms its climax. We see it too in the rendering of Horace's literal *moechos* (fornicators, adulterers) as "Cuckold-maker[s]" (48) and in the location of these offenders squarely in the "City." This impression is not lessened by the addition of venereal "Pangs" (51) to Horace's *dolore*, or by the substitution of a *Monsieur* and a "Sir *George*" (53,55) for Horace's noncommittal *hics, illes,* and *huncs.*[33] The vein persists in the witty adaptation of Horace's *merx...in classe secunda*: "*trades* in *Frigates* of the second Rate."[34] And this particular vignette concludes with the alteration of *Matronam* to "Dame[s] of Quality," another reminder of the comedy of wit. It is possible, finally, that Pope's adaptation of Horace's example of horse-trading harks to that Prince of Restoration rakes, Charles. Pope makes an interesting change in Horace's *Regibus* (86) which points in that direction. In Horace the word signifies *great men,* in the sense of *wealthy.* Pope takes it back to its root meaning, *king,* playing, we may suppose, with the idea of certain English kings, like Charles especially, who traded as shrewdly in the female as in the equine form:

> Our ancient Kings (and sure those Kings
>   were wise,
> Who judg'd themselves, and saw with their own
>   Eyes) (112-13)

That those kings are then described as trading in war-horses is no hindrance to the suggestion above, for the introductory couplet is nicely open-ended, and Pope has only recently (v. 82) alluded to Charles by name. Given that circumstance, and the subject of the poem, Charles could hardly ever be far out of mind.[35]

Of all the resources for adaptation in *Sober Advice,* the most notorious, however, if not the most conspicuous, is the *double entendre,* itself

reminiscent of the comedy of the last age. We
have encountered it already, if we may trust the
annotator, in the word *Cozens* of verse 129, where
it is innocent enough; and earlier, where it is
less innocent, in the "Flames" of verse 37 and
the phrase "comes amiss" of verse 71. What is,
unfortunately, too often overlooked about this
much criticized device is that its use, like
that of the metaphor, is as often a measure of
"decency" as it is of witticism, enabling the
poet, as Bolingbroke put it, to "weaken the images [rather] than to hurt chaste ears overmuch,"
though it is true enough that the device made it
possible for him to have it both ways, naughty
as well as nice, witty as well as sober. But
that, as we have said, is what the satiric genius
requires, if it is to function at its most effective. Pope, at any rate, accomplishes some
rather remarkable results with the device,
which it would be difficult to show he ever really uses irresponsibly.

One of the brightest of his *double entendres* is
his first, in vv. 35-36:

> But diff'rent Taste in diff'rent Men prevails,
> And one is fired by Heads, and one by Tails
> [.]

Though it has no counterpart in Horace, this would
I think, be counted wit by him, mounting, as it
does, the *jeu d'esprit* on a composition of gambling,
lust, and the price of whoring, all expressed in
a gay conceit.

Pope also triumphs in the alliance of metaphor and *double entendre* with which he meets the
challenge of Horace's *cunni albi* (36):

> ... *Nolim laudarier, inquit,*
> *Sic me, mirator,* CUNNI CUPIENNIUS ALBI [.]

"'I should not care to be praised, No Sir,' says
Cupiennius, admirer of *Cunni Albi.*" Thus literally.
Pope makes a conquest of it:

> May no such Praise (cries J---s) e'er be
>   mine!
> J [efferie]s, who bows at *Hi*[ll]*sb*[orọ]w's
> *hoary Shrine.* (45-46)

The *double entendre* arises from a pun, of course,
but the result is impressive under either rubric,
for it illustrates how, at his best, Pope can fuse
the scandalous and the serious without loss to
either, and with enormous advantage to satiric
penetration.

Toward the end of the poem Pope executes another skillful *double entendre.* LEPOREM, says Horace,

> ...*venator ut alta*
> *In nive sectetur, positum sic tangere nolit* (105-06)

Or, as Pope puts it,

> "The Hare once seiz'd the Hunter heeds no
>   more
> The little Scut he so pursu'd before (137-38)

Horace's *leporem,* left at *hare* in Pope's first
line, is wittily converted to the apt *double
entendre* of *scut* in the second. [36]

Verses 150-54 constitute a cluster of double
meanings. The Bentleyan footnote to Horace's
Pavonem (peacock) suggests that Pope was willing
to have his *Pea-Chicks* so understood ("*meaning a
young or* soft Piece, *Anglice* a Tid-bit"). [37] Horace would, I think, have been pleased with Pope's
"tight, neat Girl" for his own *Ancilla . . . verna*
(maidservant), and candor will surely credit
Pope for the distillation of *tument tibi cum in-
guina* through a tissue of ethical remonstrance,
Pauline proverbialism, and *double entendre:*

> Or, when a tight, neat Girl, will serve the
>   Turn,
> In errant Pride continue stiff, and burn? [38]

The passage concludes with *double entendre* contrived of good English homespun, rendering *parabilem*

amo venerem, facilemque (119), "The Thing at hand is of all Things the *best*." [39]

Part of the disaffection with Pope's *double entendre* belongs, properly, not to the poem, but to the *Notae Bentleianae*, which have contributed much to the poem's disrepute. But this objection is not only misplaced, but blown out of all proportion to the evidence. The notes number only seven, of which two are entirely innocent (the first two), two others essentially neutral (those on *consule Cunnum* and *testis caudamque salacem*), and a fifth--that on *Pavonem*-- not only inoffensive, but actually amusing. Only two of the notes are strictly indecent, that on *cunni albi* and that on *dum futuo*. But however the notes are scored, it is a mistake in the first place to regard them as convicting Pope, for they are clearly parodic and designed to convict Bentley. Even where they exceed the known evidence, as in the pruriency of the admittedly smutty ones, they should probably be thought of as falling under the license of satire to discredit by implied or express attribution of reprehensible motives or traits, whether such are actually in evidence or not. This is Swift's way, we know, with dissenters and zealots, and it has been the way with satirists from Aristophanes on. In resorting to it Pope was simply availing himself of an ancient and much exercised license.

But the poem is, after all, a thing essentially apart from the notes, and there, by means of witty and tactful *double entendre* and metaphor, apt allusion to Restoration comic symbolism, recourse to Swiftian facetiousness, and his own talent for happy descant and invention on Horace, Pope has appropriated *Satire* I.ii to his role of satiric moralist with a success that has too long gone unacknowledged.

In thus reevaluating *Sober Advice* it is not a matter of pretending that the performance is not "racy." That it is, and that is precisely much of its virtue as satire. But the view of the poem as nasty or pornographic, as a libel or a private diversion, or even as an indifferent piece, is neither warranted nor just, and deserves discrediting. *Sober Advice* is, as I hope I have shown, a serio-comic poem, relevant to both the moral and satirical vision of its creator, and no mean specimen of his genius. It deserves to be restored to the study of Pope.

POPE'S *EPISTLE TO AUGUSTUS*:
NOTES TOWARD A MYTHOLOGY

Manuel Schonhorn

"Into the *Dunciad* Pope artfully introduced a
frame of reference kept purposely elusive, even
secretive (as the above notes indicate). From
some of his notes it appears that the poet is
both anxious to reveal, and yet concerned to
hide, the theological metaphor that gives to his
subject its profoundest meaning."[1] In this manner, Professor Aubrey Williams somewhat cau-
tiously and hesitantly began his explication of
the *Dunciad*'s "extremely covert allusiveness" and
"theological hide-and-seek." Today, his cir-
cumspection and caution have been replaced by
our recognition of the almost infinite allusiveness of Pope's allusions. Biblical, classical, and continental exegetes, commentators,
and mythographers have been reread to open up
the larger context of his poems; and the poetic
resonance of Pope's lines has confirmed Professor Williams' earlier suspicion of the phe-
nomenal range of referential systems which make
his poems meaningful.[2] In the following pages I
would like to reconsider Pope's *Epistle to Augustus,*

This essay first appeared in *Tennessee Studies in Literature* 16 (1971), 15-33. Copyright
1971 by The University of Tennessee Press, Knoxville, Tennessee 37916. Reprinted by
permission of The University of Tennessee Press.

first by calling attention to an overlooked seg-
ment of the poem's structure, its notes;[3] and
second, by recovering the larger English and
contemporary context of two commonplace allusions which shows Pope reordering an exalted
theme, making the poem something more than an
obvious condemnation of the age of his own
George Augustus.

I

Following his salutation to Caesar Augustus,
Horace begins his castigation of the reactionary
literary attitudes of his contemporaries, who
accept as the best only that which is ancient.
His criticism of Rome's ridiculous admiration
for the mouldy relics of the past is particu-
larized and "Englished" by Pope in the following
lines:

> Chaucer's worst ribaldry is learn'd by rote,
> And beastly Skelton Heads of Houses quote:
> One likes no language but the Faery Queen;
> A Scot will fight for Christ's Kirk o' the
>   Green;
> And each true Briton is to Ben so civil,
> He swears the Muses met him at the Devil.[4]

There would, on the surface, appear to be nothing of special significance in Pope's citation
of wrong-headed antiquarian interest. His list
of earlier incorrect poets would get little more
than passing mention, were it not for the immediate introduction of the notes.

Skelton, Pope reminds us, was "Poet Laureat
to Hen. 8 a Volume of whose verses has been
lately reprinted, consisting almost wholly of
Ribaldry, Obscenity, and Scurrilous Language"
(l. 38n), and Christ's Kirk o' the Green is "A
Ballad made by a King of Scotland" (l. 40n),
variously attributed, the Twickenham editor tells
us, to James I and James V. Pope's own notes demolish the superficial surface of the poem, for

he has begun to tell us of laureates and of kings
and of the execrable taste which has consistently
linked them in the past. Pope's catalogue of
English poets--Chaucer, Skelton, Spenser, and
Jonson--is the pattern of laureates as tradition
fixed it into the eighteenth century.[5] His explicit references to poets, poetry, and kings,
now subsumed under the laureateship, indicate
moreover that significantly early in the poem--
these are his first notes--Pope is calling attention to the poet not as professional enter-
tainer but as the traditionally honored function-
ary of the Court and the Crown. If we have forgotten, we are reminded of the natural association of poetry with monarchy, and of the implicit obligations and spiritual significance of
the king's poet, as the laureate was once desig-
nated. More than a paid retainer of the king,
he is the surrogate for the Crown, the voice of
England.[6] What also has to be seen in the above passage is that Pope, following the literary
direction and theme of Horace's poem, refuses
to divert any emphasis from the political subject with which his poem began and which is, in
fact, its prevailing content.[7] Even the seemingly innocent reference to Ben Jonson's Devil Tavern is a particularly functional one, for it
concludes the series on a contemporary dynastic
note. Pope's London reader knew the Devil Tavern as the meeting place in Fleet Street where
Cibber the Poet Laureate's odes "are usually
rehearsed before they are performed at Court."[8]
Explicitly and implicitly, with past and present
memories and recognitions, Pope is passing
judgment on the office which is the symbolic extension of the Crown.
    Now it was inevitable that Pope's imitation,
given his concern for contemporaneity and particularity and given the literary theme of the
original, would have quite naturally included
the traditional appointees to the title. But I
find unusually sustained this deliberate reference throughout to the laureateship and laureates and their enervating connection with mon-

archy. Beginning with Chaucer, and with the
exception of Daniel and Tate, Pope follows the
tradition and mentions in one context or another every poet who had a strong claim to the
title. Indeed, when he calls attention to the
debauchery of the Muses at court, he specifically recalls for his reader the *Siege of Rhodes*
and William Davenant (l. 153n), who was publicly
and officially recognized at the time of Dryden's
installation as the poet laureate of two kings.[9]
Pope's poem, it must be seen, begins and continues with reference to the debasement of the
office of king's poet, and concludes with mention of the dirty leaves of Eusden, Philips,
and Settle, a triumvirate revealing the farcical
but essentially spiritual degeneration of a once
holy function, connected as all three are by
their public and private but always offensive
panegyrics to their Augustan king.[10] By extension I would argue that what Pope has seen degenerating is the office of kingship itself. The
poem's final lines on the complete loss of creativity in Eusden, Philips, and Settle, in the
poet-celebrant of the national consciousness,
may only tangentially seem to implicate the present king, but Pope's last glosses make clear
the import of the sterile poetic scene. Pope's
ultimate comment is an unexpected, almost gra-
tuitous, note on Horace's *munus Apolline dignum*:
"The Palatine Library then building by Augustus"
(l. 354n), a reminder of that storehouse of literary treasures near the temple of Apollo consecrated by the Emperor himself. What complements this is Pope's following gloss on his contemporary cultural equivalent, Merlin's Cave:
"A Building in the Royal Gardens of Richmond,
where is a small, but choice Collection of Books"
(l. 355n). Even without the knowledge that the
present monarchical repository of taste and tradition embraces such works as Cibber's and Stephen Duck's poems, the Persian Letters, an old
Bible, and Duncan Campbell's Predictions,[11] the
present-day reader can still delight in Joseph
Warton's controlled understatement of Pope's

editorial activity: "To mention Merlin's Cave,
for the Palatine Library, heightens the ridicule."[12]   But for us, Pope's notes juxtapose a
present of horrifying emptiness and a past of
imperial Roman majesty when the monarch was the
carrier of a special world-creating, world-sus-
taining power, whose word, wisdom, and vision
completely nourished a civilization. The allusionary world of Pope's *Epistle to Augustus* does
not present us with an evaluation of his Augustan
age alone. The persistent record in the poem's
lines, in the poem's notes, and in the poem's
fable of a crass art in a polluted Court, acknowledged by an uncreating king, presents the
mythic dissolution of that classical order and
harmony which once structured Pope's and his
sanctified ancient's vision of civilization.
Pope has shown us a dying world. The upholding
ideal of a moral and creative world community
has been lost forever, for the monarchy itself
has forsaken that vision which alone is the
mainstay of society.[13]

II

   Peter Dixon, in the most recent commentary on
Pope's Horatian epistles and imitations, remarks
about the uniqueness of the *Epistle to Augustus*, in
that it leaves implicit, as the other major poems do not, the honorific balance to the ethical
and cultural inadequacy of George Augustus and
his Court. That is, the Man of Ross, Lords
Bathurst and Burlington, and Martha Blount remind us of another reality of aesthetic, social,
and moral decency in which true standards and
values endure.[14]   Yet, in a masterstroke of
structural consistency, in his superlative ironic
statement, Pope has framed, in Henry James's
phrase, the rich and edifying other case in those lines to his dear friend who was born to introduce irony, "Refin'd it first, and shew'd its
Use":

> Let Ireland tell, how Wit upheld her cause,
> Her Trade supported, and supply'd her Laws;
> And leave on SWIFT this grateful verse
>   ingrav'd,
> The Rights a Court attack'd, a Poet sav'd.
> Behold the hand that wrought a Nation's cure,
> Stretch'd to relieve the Idiot and the Poor,
> Proud Vice to brand, or injur'd Worth adorn,
> And stretch the Ray to Ages yet unborn.
>   (ll. 221-228)[15]

Nothing could dramatize more the topsy-turvy
values of the immediate Augustan scene than
these few lines in praise of the Dean, the only
completely honorific comment of any length, it
might be noted, in the poem. The damning irony
of it all is that Swift and Wit, because of the
defection of the Crown, have found it necessary
to appropriate to themselves the inherent duties
of the monarch, that is, upholding the cause of
justice, providing for the economic welfare, and
dispensing mercy and grace to the sick. Justice
and Mercy, no longer the concern of the monarch
and forsaken by the Court, are served by an ex-
iled poet, ironically usurping the rights and
duties of the throne.[16] Pope's very pointed and
obvious allusion to the traditional functions of
the right ruler--in the midst of his imitation
insistently ironic at the expense of George II,
when supported by references to Merlin and Astraea, coordinate surrogates for monarchial ma-
jesty--finally provides us with Pope's considered
judgment of the Age of England's Augustus.
  A reexamination of Pope's neglected design
for an epic poem, which contains the Brutus fragment and the notes to his projected English epic
of 1743, has shown how it is related to the social, political, and philosophical concerns of
Pope's late years, and has shown in fact how the
themes exemplified his major preoccupations and
designs.[17] What I would like to suggest is that
years before this embrace of the Trojan legend
to project the restorative and redemptive possibilities of England, Pope had in the *Epistle to*

Augustus committed his theme, through an inversion
process, to that British myth which had once affected "the structure and ornamentation of some
of the greater works of Spenser, Milton, and
Shakespeare,"[18] as a means of illuminating the
manifold deficiencies of his mediocre present.

Brutus, the descendant of Aeneas, the reader
will recall, after years of exile, was destined
for English soil,

> There Fate decrees to raise a second *Troy*,
> And found an Empire in thy Royal Line,
> Which Time shall ne'er destroy, nor Bounds
>   confine.[19]

An integral part of this Trojan legend, ignored
by most commentators of Pope, as it was repeated
and reinterpreted again and again to suit the
various political factions, parties, and dynastic
crises of English history, was the figure of Merlin, magus, magician, and prophet of ancient
Britain.[20] It would be difficult to overestimate
the part played by Merlin in the *Historia Regum
Britanniae*, Geoffrey of Monmouth's unique twelfth-
century construct of England's past, which was
particularly essential for the Augustan period
because it was "the only coherent account of the
history of the Britons from the arrival of Brute
about 1100 B.C. to the death of Cadwallader in
689 A.D."[21] England's imperial destiny was given
validity and credence by the visions of her seer
and prophet, akin to the deific splendor of
Virgil and his projections of a golden Roman
civilization. During the Renaissance, Merlin
was soon cited by a political visionary who
sought to invigorate the fading Empire and make
Rome itself the capital city of a unified and
sacred Italian republic.[22] In England, Trojan
legend and British prophecy soon became the central preoccupation of Tudor and Stuart apologists
for monarchy. That legend, so much a commonplace
of Elizabethan thought, was altered and refas-
hioned into the seventeenth century, but one
thing remained constant: from the time of the

Faerie Queene and into Pope's day, Merlin and his
divinely inspired visions were employed to certify the monarch's claim to the crown.[23]
    Roberta Brinkley has shown how the Tudors'
claim to the throne was supported by their interpretation of Merlin's prophecy, and how "James
recognized the importance of establishing himself
with British prophecy."[24] While the growth of
parliamentary power and the seventeenth-century
researches of English antiquaries revealed the
hollowness of the British story, and the stren-
gthening evidence for England's Saxon heritage
reduced the prestige of the myth, the history
of that scholarship and debate reveals the extreme reluctance with which monarchists and
parliamentarians alike abandoned the Geoffrey
story and Merlin and his dreams of empire.[25]
"Even Milton began his *History of Britain Collected
Out of the Antientest and Best Authorities* (1670)
with the giant Albion, the Trojan War, Brut,
[and] the fables of the original colonization of
Britain,"[26] and in spite of his alignment with
Commonwealth reformation, never completely rejected a legend which supported Tudor and Stuart
absolutism. Despite the tainting of Merlin's
name during the Civil War, when quacks and prog-
nosticators used him to support diverse kinds of
visions, every dynastic crisis to the end of the
seventeenth century recalled the dignity of
Geoffrey's prophet and his imperial visions. "A
revival of the political usage of Merlin's prophecy took place just before the Restoration"
to emphasize the British lineage of Charles, and
Charles's ancestry enabled one to see "in the
Restoration, the culmination of England's glory."[27] Dryden's *King Arthur*, though produced in
1691 as a somewhat ethereal dramatic opera completely free of a partisan stance, was initially
a political adaptation of the Brutus legend,
celebrating Stuart peace and order after the fer-
ments of the succession crises of 1684 and
1685.[28] What perhaps can be surmised is that
Dryden, sensing the futility of his hopes for
encouragement and financial support of his plans

for an epic to honor his country, had utilized
his researches in British legend and Arthur and
Merlin for an opera whose purpose was still to
shadow, like the earlier epics of Virgil and
Spenser, "the events of future ages, in the succession of our imperial line...."[29] For in spite
of the alterations made necessary to avoid offending a foreign monarch on the throne, Dryden
has retained the British soothsayer of old, who
stabilizes the crown of England by rescuing
Arthur's bride, who provides the auspicious
prognostications of future fame and glory, and
the restoration of a British age of gold,

> And now, at once to treat thy sight and soul,
> Behold what rolling ages shall produce:
> The wealth, the loves, the glories of our isle,
> Which yet, like golden ore, unripe in the sun,
> Expect the warm indulgency of heaven
> To call them forth to light,[30]

and whose wand ushers in visions of a new Edenic
landscape of splendor, honor, and peace.

Further, one can see the plasticity of the
legend of Brut and Merlin in the ease with which
this essentially parochial story was resurrected
at the close of the century and infiltrated defenses of William's reign,[31] and how it was embodied immediately after in poems envisioning a
future of imperial splendor in the early years of
the reign of Queen Anne.[32] Sustained skepticism
by a growing number of respectable English historians and increasing scholarship in the Saxon
originals of English history during the following
century did not diminish the potency or belief
in the legend of Merlin, nor the political or
journalistic uses to which the prophecies could
be put. It will be recalled that Swift's
"discovery" and interpretation of them in 1709
was believed to be genuine as late as 1780, when
Samuel Johnson set about gathering material for
his biography of the Dean in his *Lives of the
Poets.*[33]

After Anne's reign Merlin virtually disappeared from the literary and political scene,
except for those ubiquitous notices in the London
almanacs of the day which helped to keep his name
alive.[34] His political restoration, or his restoration for avowedly political purposes, was
perhaps activated by and would appear to have
been a considered design of Court advisers who
suddenly attempted to vitalize an unpopular
Hanoverian royal house by aligning it, traditionally though belatedly, with the greatest
legend of England's past. Perhaps Lewis Theobald's new pantomine entertainment, *Merlin, or the
Devil of Stonehenge,* which was successfully presented during December 1734, provided the impetus
for Hanoverian propaganda machinery.[35] Perhaps
an additive was Hildebrand Jacob's epic, *Brutus
the Trojan, Founder of the British Empire,* published the
following year.[36] In any event, Queen Caroline,
fresh from her conquest over science and theology,[37] unexpectedly turned to poetry and prophecy, and in June of 1735 Londoners learned that
"A large subterranean building is by her Majesty's
Order carrying on in the Royal Garden at Richmond,
which is to be called Merlin's Cave, adorned with
Astronomical figures and Characters."[38] For the
remainder of 1735 and into 1736 London was bom-
barded with accounts of Caroline's cave, and excerpts in all the journals of the day detailed
Merlin's antiquity and prophecies. The Opposition press, led by Bolingbroke's *Craftsman,* which
was asserting the Saxon ancestry of English institutions and supporting the cause of a free and
independent Parliament, ridiculed this attempt to
dignify the existing dynasty by reference to
Britain's divine interpreter of the line of kingship. Nevertheless the Merlin of Spenser's *Faerie
Queene* and his ambiguous prophecies of empire dutifully appeared, initially to prove the historic
and literary antecedents for the Hanoverian grot
but later cited by Crown supporters as evidence
of the rightfulness of George's reign.[39] By 1736
Merlin, as counselor to King Arthur, was a household term; and by 1736, as one can see by the two

poems entitled *Merlin* which were heavily advertised and often reprinted, the Hanoverian discovery of Cambria's prophet served as a prelude
to a vision of restoration, to a coming age of
science, piety, and art equal to classical
Rome's.[40]

But the most significant consequence of and
response to the propaganda for the House of Hanover was the revival of Dryden's *King Arthur* by
William Giffard in the theatre at Goodman Fields.
First presented on December 17, 1735, Giffard's
spectacular and sumptuous production ran for
thirty-five nights, with all the attendant
publicity which one might expect from a work
which was clearly edited to proclaim what Dryden's
play had given only moderate voice to--the great
prophet's vision of the future in support of the
reigning royal family.[41] Its publication immediately followed the stage success, with the
title changed to emphasize the British wizard--
*Merlin: or, The British Inchanter. And King Arthur, The
British Worthy*-- and the new prologue and two
additional speeches reemphasize the theme, making
it pertinent to the raging contemporary debate:
In George II the nation was viewing again the
completion of British prophecy and the return of
a prince cut from the Arthurian cloth, sanctified
again by England's worthiest and most inspired
bard.[42]

The first alteration came in Act II, where
Merlin confronted the enemy spirits dangerous to
Arthur's safety:

> I must, I will be watchful for the State of
>   *Britain!*
> In Honour to a long Illustrious Race,
> Whose future Glory rises to my View.[43]

Later, when the victory over the forces of usurpation and evil is complete, Merlin projected
for Arthur his vision of the future:

And Lo, it opens to my wondrous View
A Glorious Scene of future Amity:
After the toils of long intestine War
Of Crowns Subjected, and Religion Chang'd
A Scaffold Blushing with the Blood of Kings
A Reign of many Tyrants--Restoration,
New Woes again--an Abdicated King
A glorious Stranger--born for Reformation
And Britain's peace--and Lo a little forward
Where from the German Shore a Stately Horse
Advances joining to our British Lyon
England date thence the whitest Hour of State,
Thence in a Gay Successive Order Shine
Peace and her Golden Train--nor can the Eye
Of long Futurity foresee a Change
But happiness must last till time Decay.[44]

But it is the prologue, spoken by Giffard himself, which fully and completely captures the excitement of ancient English grandeur resurrected:

Our Scenes no soft Italian Airs dispense;
Guiltless of Meaning; Innocent of Sense:
But lo! a Feast! for British Palates fit!
'Tis Purcell's Music, serv'd with Dryden's
    Wit!
Old Merlin's Ghost Rises with honest Rage
To mend your Taste, and vindicate the Stage:
Superior Magic here inchants your Souls,
And feeble Thrills with manly Charms contr-
    ouls!

    To Night the Sage my raptur'd Breast in-
        spires,
And the Muse labours with the Prophet's Fires!
Hear, Albion's Sons!--by me she shall unfold
What to fam'd Arthur he reveal'd of Old!

    Dire Wars shall waste our Realms, thro'
        various Reigns
Of conqu'ring Saxons and invasive Danes!
Lo! Civil Rage, and Discord light their Brand;
See! the fell Furies half consume the land!

--What Holy Fires, insatiate to devour!
Religious Butchery! and Mitred Pow'r!
--But, now--I see--wrapt into distant Times--
(He springs to Light) a Prince to purge our
    Crimes:
With Regal state to join the gen'rous Mind;
And rise the Benefactor of Mankind!

    See, Strife and Faction grin with hideous
        Yell!
See, the chain'd Monsters shrink within their
    Cell!
He comes, he comes!--Old Ocean hears the
    Word;
Smooths his rough Face, and hails his Sov'raign
    Lord!
To other Worlds the British Thunder rolls,
Beholds New Stars, and visits both the Poles!

    Now shall fair Commerce, Arts and Wealth
        explore,
And her Sails whiten Earth's remotest Shore!
While Heav'n-born justice breaks Oppression's
    Bands;
And lifts her Scales with un-inclining Hands!
Let Purple Tyrants the scourg'd Globe deface,
And riot in the Blood of Human Race!
War's Ravage; Thou, O warlike Prince, restrain!
Be thine the Glories of a Milder Reign!
Guardian, as Arbiter, of Peace restor'd,
Save bleeding Europe from the ruthless Sword!
Of Sacred Liberty great Patron Shine;
And prove by Godlike Worth the Right Divine![45]

To argue now for the integration of the total
allusive, albeit abstruse, world of Merlin into
Pope's poem to his monarch should present no insuperable problems, for, as Maynard Mack recently
stated, we are coming to appreciate "the complex
of attitudes, reminiscences, assumptions and
value symbols (everything that constitutes a
sensibility and habit of mind) on which his poems
draw from first to last,"[46] and we have ceased to
marvel at the manner by which Pope's poetry can

accommodate a multitude of meanings without
strain. As I have tried to indicate somewhat
cursorily in the preceding paragraphs and supporting notes, Merlin's prophecies and visions
of imperial grandeur constituted not only a convention that was still current in the eighteenth
century but one steadily popularized by poets,
playwrights, and historians, acknowledged by
Church and State, and, in the time of Hanoverian
rule, reasserting itself, sustaining its character of a national legend which, true or false,
was wholly sympathetic to the popular mind im-
bued with the spirit of British culture and in
perfect harmony with British poetic feeling. If
the figure of Merlin had lost the status of history, which cannot be conclusively argued, it had
sustained, even increased, its tremendous dignity
of myth.[47]
   If, as it must be pointed out, Pope had questioned the veracity of the Brutus myth in 1717,
Aaron Thompson's first English translation of
Geoffrey the following year did contain Pope's
versification of the prayer of Brutus to Diana.[48]
If, in 1740, Pope was to turn to the British myth
as the poetic structure in which to embody a vision of future English glory, it can be suggested
that the resurrection of Merlin by the Hanoverian
establishment triggered his own visionary thoughts.
Yet almost a decade before the *Epistle to Augustus*
we have a record of Pope's interest in English
antiquarianism, when he became an extra-regular
member of the Society of Antiquaries founded by
Maurice Johnson of Spaulding.[49] In addition,
Pope's Horatian poems were conceived during the
fervor of his developing relationship with Bolingbroke, who was directing the Opposition
attack on the King, and the *Epistle to Augustus* was
begun in the midst of an intense political struggle following the deployment of Merlin by the
Hanoverian Court.[50] Pope's mention of Merlin,
then, in the *Epistle*,

He, who to seem more deep than you or I,
Extols old Bards, or Merlin's Prophecy,
    (ll. 131-132)

and his gloss on Merlin's Cave following his
note that calls attention to the Palatine Library work in two ways: First, like his earlier
references to England's culture heroes, Alfred,
Edward, and Henry, Pope has recalled the glorious past, the unification of empire, the restoration of the British name, and the triumph of
British prowess, and the vision of universal
peace through that strength. The empty present,
a corrupt leadership, and a whoring King reveal
the total degeneration of British grandeur and
the failure of the dream. Again, by calling
attention to the debased use to which the Hanoverians had put this sacred and imperishable
legend, Pope enabled his reader to reflect that
this vision of empire which began in the classical past and which sustained the Tudor and
Stuart dynasties now served the infantile, out-
landish, and meretricious values of a Hanoverian
Queen, and was supervised by that fit measurer
of neo-Augustan taste, Stephen Duck.

Yet there is more to the story. For Trojan
history and Merlin's prophecies are linked via
Renaissance and British poetic practice to one
of the greatest and most enduring of classical
myths, a myth so familiar, as Marjorie Nicolson
has said, that Donne no more felt the need for
retelling it for his reader in *The Second Anniver-
sarie* than did Milton when he referred in passing
to the same legend in "On the Death of a Fair
Infant Dying of a Cough."[51] It is this conflu-
ence of English history, past and present, with
classical story which communicates the decay and
ultimate chaos of Pope's Augustan civilization.
For England's glory and Merlin's visions, the
restoration of piety and order, had long before
Pope's time joined with the legend of Astraea,
the goddess of Justice, whose return to earth,
from which she had fled after viewing the full
corruption of mankind, signalled the restoration

of the Golden Age. "In the course of history,
however, Astraea had acquired another meaning.
From Virgil, through Manilius and Dante, she had
been associated with imperial authority as well
as justice,"[52] and her reappearance on earth
implied the return of the just prince, and a
future of world harmony and peace. Her tenure
again connoted the return of law and kingly
power. In the Virgilian and Horatian tradition
the Golden Age was the Age of Augustan rule, of
the Augustan revival of piety, and of the far-
ranging peace of the Augustan empire. It is
this Virgilian manipulation of the myth of Astraea and empire which serves as an analogue for
Geoffrey's medieval materials, when he makes
Merlin the prophet of his country's golden future similar to Anchises' procession of Roman
heroes culminating in the form of Augustus
Caesar, and with him the vision of universal
sway and the return of Saturnian rule, at the
midpoint of the *Aeneid*.[53] By Renaissance times
in this golden world prophesied by Merlin, Astraea once more made her home.

To trace now the legend of Astraea through
British story and into the eighteenth century
is to retrace our steps over the Merlin landscape. Just as Merlin's prophecy, from Arthurian legend, was stressed to certify James's
rightful claim to the English throne, the presence of Astraea, "the idea of the return of
the golden age, which had been used effectively
by Elizabeth to emphasize the end of dissension
with her accession, was again stressed in the
reception of James, for the gift of peace was
one of the strong claims of James to popularity."[54] Not only did Dryden reinvigorate the
theme at the Restoration with *Astraea Redux*, ending the poem with a prophetic vision of England's
future glory under Charles II;[55] more significantly *Albion and Albanius*, his one-act opera introduction to the drama of *King Arthur*, the moral
of which "represents the double restoration of
his Sacred Majesty," continued the theme of
monarchical splendor and the return of Astraea

to English earth.[56]   As we have seen, it was
Merlin in the Arthur story who projected a Gold-
en Age again on England's shores; in *Albion and
Albanius* it is Juno, wife of Jove, who proclaims,
after hearing of the thunderous welcome accorded
the restored Albion (Charles II):

> Why stay we then on earth,
> When mortals laugh and love?
> 'Tis time to mount above,
> And send Astraea down,
> The ruler of his birth,
> And guardian of his crown.
> 'Tis time to mount above,
> And Send Astraea down.[57]

And with the apotheosis of Charles to the classical heavens and astrological divinity, and the
ascension of Albanius (James) to the English
throne, Venus, in phrases similar to those with
which Merlin addressed his monarch in the sequel
King Arthur, presents to the new king a similar
vision of future glory:

> Behold what triumphs are prepared to grace
> Thy glorious race,
> Where love and honour claim an equal place;
> Already they are fixed by fate,
> And only ripening ages wait.[58]

Consistently, in the following reigns of
William and Anne and into the Hanoverian period,
Astraea became the deity of imperial justice and
the proper companion of kings, intoned religiousl
albeit mechanically, and attesting always to the
renewal of Saturnian times and an Age of Gold.[59]
One example is a well-subscribed 1731 translation
of the second book of Horace's epistles by Charle
Carthy of Trinity College, Dublin, dedicated to
Thomas Lord Baron Wyndham, Lord High Chancellor
of Ireland. Carthy's praise of Wyndham concentrates on his administrative genius, but when
the classicist concludes with adulatory remarks
about his patron's more social hours, his lines

prove the easy and intimate association Pope's
age made of the deity and the monarch:

> So that from publick Cares when you unbend
> Your Thoughts, and to your private Self
>   descend,
> You're still admir'd, abstracted from the
>   State
> Of *George*'s and *Astraea*'s Delegate.[60]

Finally, *Merlin: A Poem Humbly Inscribed to her Majesty*,
which exults in the Hanoverian Queen's restoration of Merlin and British prophecy, concludes
by hailing his new guardian of Britannia in whom
"Astraea, and Minerva, joyn / To form one finish'd
CAROLINE."[61]

In spite of a single reference to the Goddess
of Justice, that mythic authenticator of the
reign of the just prince, in the whole of Pope's
poem, the ready knowledge of the least sophisticated of his contemporary readers would have provoked a recognition not unlike that detailed a-
bove. Pope, in spite of his eighteenth-century
milieu, still had the benefit of a mythology
through the use of which he was able to determine his reader's expectation and response. Imitating the finest of Horace's epistles to a
prince of celebrated taste and undisputed rule,
Pope would have been well aware of the range of
allusionary recognition which Astraea, as a
monarchical substitute or appositive, so to
speak, could sustain. In fact, the references
to monarchy and to Merlin earlier and Pope's
insistent commentary on kingly responsibility
would seem to determine his reader's inevitably
right disposition to the Astraea allusion.

So, then, Astraea and Augustus, the goddess
and the king, were inextricably linked by tradition both political and poetic. So, too, in
this unforgettably inverted poem to his king,
Pope's own Augustus and his Hanoverian civilization are linked to their own, well-deserved
Astraea. She enters the poem again from that
world in miniature, the stage, and Pope's own

gloss to her makes clear the diminution of monarchical rule and the complete perversion of a
once beatific vision: "*Astraea* A Name taken by
Afra Behn, Authoress of severall obscene Plays,
&c." (1. 290n). For Pope, the cycle is complete.
His Augustan Age has brought the return of a
demoralized and salacious goddess, signifying
through his allusive authority the full decay of
classical values for his time.[62]

HEROIC FOLLY: POPE'S SATIRIC IDENTITY

Thomas R. Edwards, Jr.

"Pope is the most fascinating of satirists,
because his poetry is so largely coloured by
his own personality; and his satires can only
be properly understood when they are exhibited with their conflicting elements of truth
and injustice; of vindictiveness and pathos;
of intellectual unscrupulousness and poetical art; of passion and irony; of bold invective and ambiguous evasion."

"In the character of Sporus the reader's
mind is kept so busy merely taking in the
baroque zigzag of beauty and nastiness that
Hervey is forgotten. Words like 'Beauty
that shocks you' provide too much to think
about, enlarge the mind too excitingly for
it to centre itself in narrow supercilious-
ness on a weak human character."

The first of these passages, written by W.J.
Courthope some eighty years ago, fairly represents a way of reading poetry that has gone
out of fashion. By "personality," we uneasily
note, Courthope means "the man himself," the

This essay first appeared in *In Defense of Reading*, ed. Reuben Brower and Richard
Poirier (New York: E.P. Dutton, 1962), pp. 191-205. Copyright 1962 by Brower and
Poirier. Reprinted by permission of the publishers, E.P. Dutton.

figure revealed by the kinds of evidence upon
which the biographer relies. Pope was a complicated person, and his poetry fascinatingly
reveals that personal complexity-the poems themselves become materials for biography. For us
this seems too simple. We doubt that the "self"
projected in a poem can confidently be equated
with the "self" that is the poet in his private
life; indeed, we may doubt that this latter self
is anything like a constant, objective fact, in
poets or anyone else. We are apt to feel more
at ease with the second passage, by Geoffrey
Tillotson. The emphasis still falls on the
"conflicting elements" Courthope noted, but for
Mr. Tillotson the conflict takes place in the
mind of the reader; it is not to be referred to
the real object of Pope's ridicule or to Pope's
personal feelings about him. The portrait of
Sporus is "baroque"-we contemplate it as esthetic event rather than biographical or historical document.

The shift in critical perspective Mr. Tillotson here reflects has unquestionably been for
the good; and yet I must confess that Courthope's
remarks tell me something true and important
about Pope as a poet, something I am not told by
critics who scrupulously avoid the issue of "personality." Courthope recognizes the complexities of tone in Pope's satires, and if he errs
in relating the complexities too easily to Pope
the man, he at least reminds us that in these
poems we listen to a speaking voice that is,
however indirectly, a *human* voice, one that reflects and gives edge to Pope's sense of the world
which was his subject.

This sense of the world, in Pope's late satires, is anything but the urbane, confident
one usually associated with his name. Consider
this astonishing passage from the second dialogue of the *Epilogue to the Satires* (1738):

[Fr.] The Priest whose Flattery be-dropt
      the Crown,
How hurt he you? he only stain'd the Gown.

And how did, pray, the Florid Youth offend,
Whose Speech you took, and gave it to a
   Friend?
 P. Faith it imports not much from whom it
   came,
Whoever borrow'd, could not be to blame,
Since the whole House did afterwards the
   same:
Let Courtly Wits to Wits afford supply,
As Hog to Hog in Huts of *Westphaly*;
If one, thro' Nature's Bounty or his Lord's,
Has what the frugal, dirty soil affords,
From him the next receives it, thick or thin,
As pure a Mess almost as it came in;
The blessed Benefit, not there confin'd,
Drops to the third who nuzzles close behind;
From tail to mouth, they feed, and they
   carouse,
The last, full fairly gives it to the *House.*
 Fr. This filthy Simile, this beastly Line,
Quite turns my stomach-P. So does Flatt'ry
   mine;
And all your Courtly Civet-Cats can vent,
Perfume to you, to me is Excrement.
   (164-184)

The Friend's reasonable, polite disapproval
("pray") is first countered by "Faith it imports not much"-the offhand indifference of a
speaker comfortably above his subject. But this
pose of superiority vanishes in the fierce obscenity that follows. The occasion scarcely
justifies such fury-politicians commit worse
offenses than borrowing one another's speeches.
The analogy between hogs and noble statesmen
would cut more insolently if it were merely
suggested; Pope's almost pedantic concern for
getting in every detail of the comparison, and
so magnifying the petty offense out of all reasonable proportion, seems oddly remote from the
gentlemanly insinuation with which the speech
began. By Augustan standards of social and
poetic decorum, the Friend's protest seems just.
It is indeed a filthy simile, and Pope's final

rejoinder sounds rather lame. He speaks with
the irrational, petulant defensiveness of a
child who knows he has gone too far.

Obscenity and other kinds of verbal indecorum
are important in Pope's satires. They convey
most immediately a general sense that cultivated
discourse cannot do full justice to a reality
which increasingly reveals itself as corrupt and
vile; there are after all no polite names for
evil. It stands as one of the great poetic
achievements that Pope was able to state his
revulsion with unsparing accuracy and yet contain and use it as a functioning element in
more complex poetic designs. The "Hogs of
Westphaly" passage is not a flaw in the *Epilogue
to the Satires* but a revealing moment of collision
between blunt moral speech and a more equivocal,
temporizing kind of utterance-opposing forces
whose conflict gives the poem its shape and direction. At the start of the first dialogue the
Friend complains about Pope's infamous lack of
political tact, and his own voice nicely demonstrates the "sly, polite, insinuating stile"
of the "artful Manager" Horace which he recommends to the poet:

> To Vice and Folly to confine the jest,
> Sets half the World, God knows, against the
>   rest;
> Did not the Sneer of more impartial men
> At Sense and Virtue, balance all agen.
>   (57-60)

Normal social equilibrium requires that sense
and virtue be kept in their place; the metaphor
of balance, which in the *Essay on Man* and the
Moral Essays expressed positive alternatives to
the apparent chaos of immediate experience, now
figures as an argument *against* the poet's position. *Fr.* is not imperceptive about behavior,
but it is enough for him to relish in private
the amusing discrepancies between "official"
and real virtue. He is virtually a caricature
of the Dryden of *Religio Laici*, preferring "common quiet" to unruly public disputes over unreal

issues. In him Pope gives his mature assessment
of the cool, disengaged urbanity of an Addison
or a Shaftesbury, which had been an ideal of his
own earlier days:

> Leave dang'rous *Truths* to unsuccessful *Satyrs*,
> And *Flattery* to fulsome *Dedicators* ....
> 'Tis best sometimes your Censure to restrain,
> And *charitably* let the Dull be *vain*:
> Your Silence there is better than your *Spite*,
> For who can *rail* so long as they can *write*?
> (*Essay on Criticism*, 592-599)

Fr. presents himself as a realist. His theme-
like the (at least professed) theme of Pope's
much maligned contemporary Bernard Mandeville-
is the inevitable and useful imperfection of
things as they are. His voice, at times indul-
gent and avuncular, at times maliciously feline,
at times shrill with shock at Pope's plain speaking, is the familiar voice of intelligence
debilitated by too much knowledge, sophistication that marks not moral subtlety but Geron-
tionlike moral paralysis.

This is more than the voice of a convenient
straw man. Both *Fr.* and *P.* are versions of
Pope himself, or of any man aware of the conflict between his social identity and his secret image of himself as autonomous moral hero.
The dialogue form articulates the inner debate
between the part of us which "knows better,"
which like Pope's *Fr.* stands by our indiscre-
tions murmuring "alas" with the sympathetic
disapproval that identifies our elders and
betters, and that other part of us which,
passionately committed to its own perception
of truth, will brook no compromises. Pope
controls both voices, to be sure, but the *Epilogue* moves not toward reconciliation of extremities, as do so many of Pope's earlier poems,
but toward acceptance of *P.*'s view, in all its
extravagant exaggeration.

The two dialogues develop various modes of
response to the politic voice of *P.* Until late

in the poem the mode of *Dialogue I* is ironic in
the textbook sense of the word: P. pretends to
defend "the dignity of Vice," and the terms of
the defense reveal the speciousness of any justification of things as they are. If, as *Fr.*
insists, the crimes of the well-born are not to
be dwelt upon by the satirist, the job still remains of keeping distinct the separation between classes. The vulgar are imitating the sins
of their betters with intolerable cheek: Cibber's son "swear[s] like a Lord," Ward "draw[s]
Contracts with a Statesman's skill," Bond and
Peter Walter "pay their Debts [and] keep their
Faith like Kings" (that is, not at all). The
joke is clear enough. It is indeed bad for the
lower classes to copy the behavior of the great,
but not because of any snobbish notion that
they may thus become *better* than they should be.
In this topsy-turvy society the highest are the
worst. Plebeians may have quite as much inclination to vice, to be sure, but in their proper condition they lack "know-how." For them
to learn the *style* of accomplished evil from
those who are naturally gifted is to make general an efficient viciousness that might otherwise be confined to the small world of aristocrats, where one expects it and is prepared to
cope with it.

But the indirections of irony fail to under-
mine *Fr.*'s complacence, and toward the end of
the dialogue P. is driven to a mere open kind
of speaking. Virtue is classless, he remarks,
and therefore it need not concern the satirist:
"She's still the same, belov'd, contented thing"
whether she "dwell in a Monk, or light upon a
King." (We note the barbed difference between
dwelling and lighting upon.) But Vice has more
delicacy. She is "undone, if she forgets her
Birth,/ And stoops from Angels to the Dregs of
Earth." The bitterness of "Angels" marks a
change of tone; conversational give-and-take
fades away in the concluding lines (145-172)
of the first dialogue, the chilling vision of
the Triumph of Vice. The everyday world is

revealed as an Inferno; every human activity
blurs into an ugly parody of itself as irony of
the cultivated sort is abandoned and the speaking voice trembles with shock and rage. *Fr.'s*
"political" view of a reality sustained and ordered by opposing evils has been a delusion.
Society collapses as nobles offer up their honor
and commoners their families, and established
religion abdicates its function as "grave Bishops" bless the Goddess of Vice: "hers the
Gospel is, and hers the Laws." The oxymorons
of Vice--innocence is shame and villainy sacred--
are only blunter versions of the moral evasions
and mystifications which *Fr.* has more elegantly
advocated.

     At the end of *Dialogue I* the debate between
Fr. and P., the political man and the moral hero, has been transcended:

     Yet may this Verse (if such a Verse remain)
     Show there was one who held it in disdain.
        (171-172)

The dialogue has been a fiction, and Pope admits
it--indeed, insists on it. Behind *Fr.* and P. is
another voice, one which closely resembles P.'s
and yet knows that P. is a character in a poem;
and this voice does not shrink from shattering
the dramatic illusion when gripped by such anger and disgust. Feeling takes precedence over
mere consistency of form, and we see Pope finally not as poetic maker but as passionate human
being. By asserting his independence of a corrupt social reality he defines his own isolation;
his lonely voice rejects the world in order to
maintain his moral integrity.

     Readers of Shakespeare's *Coriolanus* will find
some recognizable traits in Pope's satiric protagonist. Both Coriolanus and P. confront a
disparity between the moral ego and the demands
made upon it by political and social facts. Each
experiences these demands impatiently, in the
arrogant assurance that his personal nature affords a surer measure of truth and right than

does the politic compromising of Menenius or *Fr*.
And each, at the moment of crisis, turns upon
the political world and banishes *it*--a moment
of heroism and equally of supreme absurdity.
Coriolanus, I should say, is so terribly ambivalent a figure to us precisely because he himself shows no capacity for ambivalence. He can
feel only one way at a time. At his greatest
moment, the scene with his mother at the gates
of Rome, his language expresses not complexity
of feeling, which could save him, but alternation of feelings. He never finds the middle
ground where education takes place, where both
the reality and the incompatibility of conflicting motives are recognized and pondered; and
he dies, with a stubbornness which is at once
awsome and comically childish, insisting on the
very myth about himself which brought him disaster. Analogy is however not identity. Pope
in the *Epilogue* dramatizes himself as heroic
clown, but in a more knowing way than Coriolanus
does. Pope's satirist is both Coriolanus and
Shakespeare, in effect, understanding the comic
possibilities of moral heroism even as he insists on being a moral hero.

The conclusion of *Dialogue I* is Pope's equivalent to Coriolanus's insistence that "there
is a world elsewhere"; *Dialogue II* recalls his
awful discovery that there is no such thing.
Again Pope begins in the mode of ironic indirection, as if to make one last try at preserving his balance. The satirist would be a
hunter of vice, but in the face of *Fr*.'s knowledgeable explanation of the game laws the dignified possibilities of this role evaporate, and
P. is left as a kind of poacher, ruefully asking if there isn't *some* prey he may legally
take. As in *Dialogue I*, however, such irony is
inadequate to the gravity of the problem, and
P.'s voice again begins to take on the inflec-
tions of the serio-comic moral hero:

> I follow *Virtue*, where she shines, I praise,
> Point she to Priest or Elder, Whig or Tory,
> Or round a Quaker's Beaver cast a Glory.
>   (95-97)

The absurd possibilities of the last image are
not to be minimized. By urbane, "cultivated"
standards this involuntary morality is amusingly
close to madness, and Pope knows it. But to
express such intense conviction one can only
shrug off laughter and keep on talking:

> Enough for half the Greatest of these days
> To 'scape my Censure, not expect my Praise:
> Are they not rich? what more can they pre-
>   tend?
> Dare they to hope a Poet for their Friend?
>   (112-115)

Such insistent arrogance signifies much more
than personal egotism. The "I" of the poem is
not simply the man but the man as poet, with the
poet's traditional claim to dignity and virtue
that are qualities of his craft and not just of
his personality. But there is anxiety as well
as pride in his voice. Coriolanus at least inhabited a world of substance; his heroism is
founded on physical action, and his language
characteristically centers upon images of such
action--of himself or some natural surrogate for
himself breaking or overwhelming something. By
comparison, poetry is a pretty unsubstantial
weapon and vice a Protean object, and the exaggerated emphasis with which Pope defines the
satirist's role hints at uncertainty. His arrogance seems in some part a defensive mannerism,
an effort to exorcise the spirit of Vice by a
willful affirmation of faith in Virtue:

> Ask you what Provocation I have had?
> The strong Antipathy of Good to Bad.
> When Truth or Virtue an Affront endures,
> Th' Affront is mine, my Friend, and should be
>   yours.

Mine, as a Foe profess'd to false Pretence,
Who think a Coxcomb's Honour like his Sense;
Mine, as a Friend to ev'ry worthy mind;
And mine as Man, who feel for all mankind.
     (197-204)

P. here stubbornly rejects complication and moral subtlety. There is Good and there is Bad,
and their antipathy is as natural and inevitable
as magnetism. Moral categories demand large
letters--the Augustan habit of capitalizing abstract nouns to lend them solidity never did
more effective service. But "antipathy" is "feeling against," a negative, defensive emotion,
and P.'s image of himself as some almost Pro-
methean figure feeling for all mankind shows how
far he has been driven from the confident, ironic modesty that is the Horatian satirist's normal air:

     Fr. You're strangely proud.
        P. So proud, I am no Slave:
     So impudent, I own myself no Knave:
     So odd, my Country's Ruin makes me grave.
     Yes, I am proud; I must be proud to see
     Men not afraid of God, afraid of me:
     Safe from the Bar, the Pulpit, and the Throne,
     Yet touch'd and sham'd by *Ridicule* alone.
        (205-211)

This is impressively lofty--like Coriolanus he
seems "a thing/ Made by some other deity than
Nature,/ That shapes man better." Yet again the
assertion is significantly qualified. To have
even the slightest distaste for servility is to
be "strangely proud" by the standards of this
world, and the tone is rueful in its arrogance.
     Still, the positive aspects of the satirist's
pride are forcefully stated. If he has to some
extent been driven into this ultimate position,
this is only to say that the ground he now occupies is the center of his case, which no longer
need be qualified and compromised. Satire is a
"sacred Weapon," the "sole Dread of Folly, Vice,

and Insolence" in a world whose institutions are
too feeble or corrupt to enforce significant
order. The satirist, no longer able to speak
simply as a man among men, now assumes the role
of God's deputy, trying not by persuasion but
by sheer intensity of will to make an impious
society right the imbalance between its values
and divine ones. His instrument is "to all but
Heav'n-directed hands deny'd," and his target is
the falsity of official distinctions, "All that
makes Saints of Queens, and Gods of Kings." And
his heroic intensity affords him a vision of the
triumph of Virtue to counteract the vision of
Vice in *Dialogue I*:

>   ... diadem'd with Rays divine,
> Touch'd with the Flame that breaks from
>   Virtue's Shrine,
> Her Priestless Muse forbids the Good to dye,
> And ope's the Temple of Eternity.
>   (232-235)

The permanence of art is eloquently asserted.
Immortality rewards artistic virtue, and while
it is figurative immortality--fame--rather than
literal, still the petty achievements of the
worldly cannot earn it. The true moral scale
transcends time and death, to which even the
socially mightly are subject, and the poet speaks for a power that is ideal and eternal:

> Let Envy howl while Heav'n's whole Chorus
>   sings,
> And bark at Honour not confer'd by Kings;
> Let Flatt'ry sickening see the Incense rise,
> Sweet to the World, and grateful to the Skies:
> Truth guards the Poet, sanctifies the line,
> And makes Immortal, Verse as mean as mine.
>   (242-247)

But Pope recognizes, quite as clearly as
Shakespeare does, the ironies that adhere to the
heroic identification of self with natural virtue. The grand assurance of tone cannot dis-

guise the fact that this assertion of the artist's unique moral dignity represents a virtual
confession of defeat. Artists, Pope would be
the first to insist, have their significance in
a community, in relation to an audience. But
the heroic stature P. claims for himself is
clearly, like Coriolanus's, a function of ali-
enation. Coriolanus himself grows more awesome
and mysterious as his loyalties to other people
and their causes drop away, and he is most him-
self--most unlike *us*-- at the moment of his
death, when he has managed to detach himself
from every external limit to his freedom. (His
death is in effect a metaphor for the moral suicide his attempts to *preserve* his moral identity
have caused.) Pope's satirist would not need to
glorify his role so insistently if every other
kind of virtue had not disappeared from his
world. He simply has no one to talk to. The
select, understanding interlocutors to whom the
Moral Essays and the *Imitations of Horace* were largely addressed have been replaced by the anonymous and hopelessly cynical "Friend," who in
the ways that count is no friend at all. The
dialogue has become an oration, in fact a harangue, addressed to anyone who will listen, and
this provides a final twist of bitter comedy:

> Yes, the last Pen for Freedom let me draw,
> When Truth stands trembling on the edge of
>   Law:
> Here, last of *Britons*! let your Names be read;
> Are none, none living? let me praise the
>   Dead,
> And for that Cause which made your Fathers
>   shine,
> Fall, by the Votes of their degen'rate Line!
>   *Fr.* Alas! alas! pray end what you began,
> And write next winter more *Essays on Man*.
>   (248-255)

The grand tone has grown almost too grand.
("Pens" and "Votes" in this context are perilously close to the kind of anticlimax Pope

ridiculed in *Peri Bathous*, his ironic treatise "On
the Art of Sinking in Poetry.") And the discovery
that the good men are all dead--that the celebration of virtue must be an elegy--produces a
faltering of the voice that is close to the classic double-take of farce. Yet even this approach
to absurdity can't stop the last furious assertion of integrity.

The Friend's concluding rebuke fixes the problem for interpretation. Like him, we recognize
that P. has gone too far; such extravagance is
probably not only uncivilized but futile--to reject politics is to reject the possibility of
human adjustement on any but an authoritarian
basis, and poets scarcely command that kind of
authority. But unlike *Fr.* we feel, for all our
"liberal" reservations, that what has happened
in these dialogues is worth any number of cautious, generalized essays in moral definition.
It is true (and fortunate) that Pope's handling
of the *Epilogue* recognizes and explores the *comic*
aspects of the Coriolanus-like moral hero, the
man who will not compromise his vision of experience even though the world leaves him no positive
alternative to his bitter frustration. Yet finally, I think, we respond to P. with a warm approval that Shakespeare forbids us to feel in
any simple way about Coriolanus. While we recognize that heroism may be as absurd as it is
venerable, and as dangerous, the recognition
tellingly reveals the price of perfect virtue.
The price is painfully high; to pay it one may
have to abandon the defenses of urbane, ironic
civility and expose oneself to ridicule. But
while it is one thing to be a fool because you
are one, in all innocence, it is quite another
to decide that seeming a fool is preferable to
the moral evasions into which urbanity can lead.
(We may think of Lord Chesterfield.) Readers
of Blake and the "mad" poems of Yeats should
have no trouble recognizing Pope's satiric identity in the *Epilogue*, nor in understanding that,
for all its eccentric exaggeration, it expresses
a moral intelligence that is uncompromisingly
complex and mature.

I have been talking about the character called "P." in this discussion of "satiric identity." The question remains as to who P. is, what
relation he bears to Pope the author. My earlier
suggestion that both P. and Fr. are versions of
the poet may seem to be an endorsement of the
now rather common idea that Pope creates in his
verse a *persona*, a mask of rhetoric which is not
to be identified with the "real" personality
of the writer. In this view the comic aspects
of P.'s performance would indicate that Pope
projects not himself but an exaggerated figure
of "the satirist" for which he does not take
full responsibility, a fiction which exists to
convey certain general moral attitudes to the
reader but which may then be dismissed. Thus
the poet is to be seen as a kind of ventrilo-
quist, the Joycean artist who has refined himself out of existence--but not, apparently, for
the Joycean purpose of rendering life clearly,
without the interference of personal bias or
cultural accidents. Rather, Pope's use of
"masks" is treated as a rhetorical device for
efficiently manipulating his materials and his
readers.

But manipulation (by any name) suggests evasiveness or even dishonesty. Or, as so often
with Swift, it suggests a troubled uncertainty
about where one really is. As a critical metaphor, the "mask" emphasizes concealment and subterfuge quite as much as it suggests the creation
of imaginative roles for the artist himself, and
the metaphor seems ill-suited to the Pope of the
late satires, who so insistently presents his
subject in terms of moral conviction and urgency.
Rhetoric is, or ought to be, more than a way of
disguising the true grounds of an appeal so as
to implant in an audience attitudes that have
not been reasonably contemplated by all parties.
In a great speech or poem rhetoric is an agent
of responsibility, a means of clarifying and
qualifying the issues at stake. To the poet, as
to the orator, serious readers or listeners
might say: "If you want to move us, be moved
yourself, and let your rhetoric *reveal* your feelings as hesitant, tangled ordinary speech so
seldom can."

It thus becomes a matter not of whether the
voice in the poem is really Pope's, as Courthope
would say, or really a dramatic fiction, as we
so often hear nowadays, but of our tact in defining the relation of rhetoric to personal
feeling and thought. Perhaps we may imagine
that we read the poem in stages. (What we actually do when we read it is of course too mysterious to be perfectly expressed by this or any
other scheme.) First we listen to the voices of
P. and Fr., as we listen to real conversation,
innocently supposing that one of them is Pope's
and the other some unnamed real friend's; we
attend to tone, emphasis, idiom, syntax, just as
we do when we try to assess a human speaker.
Next we remind ourselves that the voices are not
"real," that we are overhearing not conversation
but a planned imitation of it in which, for our
benefit, a single intelligence controls and directs both voices. But having taken this critically all-important second step, we should go
further--which here, as it so often does, means
going back. The "mask" is not a false face, but
an identity quite as "real" as any of the poet's
other identities, including his private self
(or, more likely, selves); it is fashioned not
so that critics may admire its workmanship but
so that readers may come away with a heightened
sense of the motives which made the poem necessary to write. "P." is Pope--Pope provisionally
freed from the irksome restraints of social and
political moderation so that his deepest commitments may get something close to pure expression. Fr. is Pope too, but in him are combined
and punished just those elements of civilized
personality which necessarily yet tragically
thwart the full realization of one's best impulses. Pope the man could never quite live up
to the passionate moral conviction of P.--his
biography is full of the troubles he got into
by trying--but in the figure of P. he shows both
his understanding and his defiance of the truth
which R.P. Blackmur has tersely restated: "We
are never equal, so far as we have one, to our
view of life. Our lives are but a parody of our
best selves."

To limit interpretation of Pope's satires to
the configurations of his mask, without asking
what is revealed *through* it about the human
presence within, is to defeat the purpose of
poetry, if I am right in thinking that this purpose is to tell the truth about the world as the
poet sees it, with the fullest possible fidelity
to the peculiar angle from which he looks. This
angle will be peculiar, it should be insisted,
even for a poet as conscious as Pope was of the
conventions within which he works. We have
heard a lot--maybe too much--about the formality
of his style and the limitations of his subject
matter. The "conventional wisdom" (to appropriate a phrase of J.K. Galbraith's) about Pope's
neoclassicism should not prevent us from seeing
that in the *Epilogue to the Satires,* as in most of
the poems of his later career, he dramatizes a
fundamental clash between classical modes of
thought and expression and an increasing sense
that life cannot adequately be described within
the classical manner as his age understood it.
The clash is neatly epitomized by the beginning
of the "Sporus" passage in the *Epistle to Dr.
Arbuthnot:*

> A Lash like mine no honest man shall dread,
> But all such babling blockheads in his stead.
>   Let *Sporus* tremble--"What? that Thing of
>   silk,
> "*Sporus*, that mere white Curd of Ass's milk?
> "Satire or Sense alas! can *Sporus* feel?
> "Who breaks a Butterfly upon a Wheel?"
> Yet let me flap this Bug with gilded wings,
> This painted Child of Dirt that stinks and
>   stings...
>   (303-310)

The lofty assertion of the satirist's respect
for honesty begins to break up in the angry
alliteration of "babling blockheads" and the
ominous rise of the voice in the next line.
Arbuthnot's interruption tries to forestall the
explosion--his cool contempt for Sporus indi-

cates a classical confidence in standards of
judgment and an aristocratic sureness of superiority to those who do not measure up. But the
"Pope" of this poem, like the P. of the *Epilogue*,
will not be restrained. Sporus may be immune to
satire or sense, but Pope must flap him anyway.
No real good can come of it, but the inner pressure of moral outrage defies containment, and
the passage proceeds with its astonishing display of vituperative invention.
    What, then, does this struggle between clas-
sical restraint and personal intensity express?
I should say that it informs us of the difficulty
of believing in the positive power of satire, the
"operative irony" which, in a famous definition
of Henry James's, "implies and projects the possible other case, the case rich and edifying
where the actuality is pretentious and vain."
Positive satire, like pastoral, declares man's
"natural" innocence and virtue; behind our appalling misconduct stands an Eden which remains
at least ethically redeemable. It invokes an
agreed-upon scale of natural value. When we mis-
behave we are acting like animals, whereas we
are not animals but men, and more is expected of
us. The satirist exposes our errors by appealing
to or stylistically demonstrating the best human
possibilities, the mode of conduct appropriate
to our status in the whole scheme of things. But
the "Hogs of Westphaly" passage or the portrait
of Sporus, while they seem to criticize bad men
on just these natural grounds, can hardly be
said to encourage our belief that the satirist
speaks for an intelligible moral order he under-
tands and believes in. There is too much anger,
too little suggestion of what should be. Such
passages show Pope confronting a dreadful alternative to Eden, the possibility that "nature" is
not fundamentally good but meaningless--which to
a classically trained mind is virtually the same
as evil. If so, virtue must be seen (as Hobbes
saw it) to be a difficult and fragile construct
which *opposes* the natural tendencies of most men.
There is some complexity here. In dramatizing

himself as moral hero Pope invokes an ultimate
natural sanction for his integrity, just as Coriolanus does. But our sense of the comic aspects of his role marks the eccentric remoteness
of the satirist's "nature" from the regular,uni-
versal,publicly knowable nature which is the neoclassic norm. The satirist seems able to show
how shockingly Sporus and his beastly fellows
deviate from the norm only by himself departing
from it in the opposite direction. His violent
voice expresses anxiety, in short; he can't comfortably sustain the tone of the confident classicist who finds "civilization," at its potential best, an embodiment of natural and divine
law.

     And yet for all his comic possibilities, the
moral hero *is* heroic. While he cannot fully accept the classical view of the world, he resists
yielding wholly to its alternative. Some of the
classical breadth and impartiality of vision persists in Pope's recognition and acceptance of
the ludicrous aspects of his new role, his understanding that while moral clarity is worth
the sacrifices that must be made to it, the margin is at best a slim one. The satiric voice of
these late poems has rejected the perceptible
smugness of the *Essay on Man*. The satirist can
lose his temper, and while this marks his superiority both to impervious fools like Sporus and
bland "administrators" like *Fr.*, we know that he
can never see in himself the gratifying mastery
of reality that they see in themselves all the
time. The dramatic presence is ambivalent, neurotic, recognizably human.

     This is not the usual way of reading Pope,
but that scarcely matters. There is no serious
value in novelty per se. I have no wish to dismiss "conventional" formulations like this one
of George Sherburn's, from perhaps the best general history of eighteenth century literature:

     In the larger traditionalism of Pope's gener-
     ic patterns as well as in the preoccupation
     with public emotion eloquently expressed,

> Pope is the acme of "correct" neo-classical
> excellence. He is, perhaps permanently, our
> great example in English of "the poet of
> reason," of intellectuality in the poetic
> art.

Certainly the Pope I have been describing is far
from this. The emotion of the later satires is
preeminently private, not public; the expression
may be "eloquent" but hardly in the way Mr. Sherburn means; there is little reason and less in-
tellectuality in the passages I have cited. And
yet there most certainly is a Pope who conforms
to such a description; quantitatively there is
much more of that Pope than of mine. It depends
on the context in which you read. When you come
to Pope with Dryden in mind, as history invites
you to, and behind Dryden the Roman traditions
of epic, satire, eclogue, elegy, and amatory
verse which come into English poetry by way of
the continent in the sixteenth and seventeenth
centuries, you see that Pope is indeed a "neoclassical" poet. He thought of himself as such,
and we cannot understand him without knowing at
least generally how extensively his "sense of
the past" directed his procedure in particular
poems. But we resist our worlds even as we live
in them--living itself is a resistance, since
life never quite coincides with our ideas about
it. Pope's neoclassicism is important not only
because it tells us why he did things in certain
ways but also because it defines the limits
which as an artist he seems to have found increasingly intolerable.
    More important, as T.S. Eliot observed long
ago, "tradition" works both forward and backward
in time; in a significant sense it does not work
"in" time at all. The fact that,chronologically,
we do come to Pope through Dryden and European
neoclassicism should not unduly condition our
response to what is on the page, nor obscure our
understanding that for *readers* of literature history is a two-way street. When one has read
Blake and D.H. Lawrence, to name the two most

compelling moral poets since Pope himself, one
can never again read Pope's satires in quite
the same way. Without ceasing to be--in certain lights--"the poet of reason," Pope has an
eminent place in a "simultaneous order" of poet
moralists driven by an intractable reality into
a tragicomic intensity of private vision and
private conviction that has only remote connections with the public ideals and possibilities they began by asserting. In his uniting
of traditionally separate roles, the hero who
acts and the artist who observes and suffers the
complex consequences of action, he prefigures a
Romantic obsession with which our literature
has not yet come to terms. And he belongs among
the makers or users of systems, men who would
hold the world in a single imaginative whole but
who, grown old and shaken by experience, must
say with Yeats:

> Now that my ladder's gone,
> I must lie down where all the ladders start,
> In the foul rag-and-bone shop of the heart.

It is the acceptance of one's own vulnerability,
the unbreakable ties between noble principles
and the essential if often unlovely and ignoble
imperfections that unite us with other men, that
Pope finally comes to; and only this acceptance
can keep the moralist's voice a human voice as
well.

POPE'S "VIRTUE" AND THE EVENTS OF 1738

Paul Gabriner

"*Virtue* may chuse the high or low Degree,
'Tis just alike to Virtue, and to me;
Dwell in a Monk, or light upon a King,
She's still the same, belov'd, contented
    thing.
Vice is undone, if she forgets her Birth,
And stoops from Angels to the Dregs of Earth:
But 'tis the *Fall* degrades her to a Whore;
Let *Greatness* own her, and she's mean no more:
Her Birth, her Beauty, Crowds and Courts con-
    fess,
Chaste Matrons praise her, and grave Bishops
    bless:
In golden Chains the willing World she draws,
And hers the Gospel is, and hers the Laws:
Mounts the Tribunal, lifts her scarlet head,
And sees pale Virtue carted in her stead!
Lo! at the Wheels of her Triumphal Car,
Old *England's* Genius, rough with many a Scar,
Dragg'd in the Dust! his Arms hang idly round,
His Flag inverted trails along the ground!
Our Youth, all liv'ry'd o'er with foreign Gold,
Before her dance; behind her crawl the Old!

This essay first appeared in *Scripta Hierosolymitana: Further Studies in English Language and Literature* 25 (1973), 96-119.

See thronging Millions to the Pagod run,
And offer Country, Parent, Wife, or Son!
Hear her black Trumpet thro' the Land proclaim,
That 'Not to be corrupted is the Shame.'
In Soldier, Churchman, Patriot, Man in Pow'r,
'Tis Av'rice all, Ambition is no more!
See, all our Nobles begging to be Slaves!
See, all our Fools aspiring to be Knaves!
The Wit of Cheats, the Courage of a Whore,
Are what ten thousand envy and adore.
All, all look up, with reverential Awe,
On Crimes that scape, or triumph o'er the Law:
While Truth, Worth, Wisdom, daily they decry--
'Nothing is Sacred now but Villany.'

Yet may this Verse (if such a Verse remain)
Show there was one who held it in disdain."

The concluding passage of Pope's much admired
"Dialogue I," the first "Epilogue to the Satires,"
is generally regarded as one of the finest pieces
of poetry that Pope ever wrote.[1] Yet though
this short scene of only thirty-six lines (ll.
137-172) has been often remarked upon for its
"lofty indignation," no attempt has been made to
set the poem and its conclusion in the context
of dramatic events that attended its publication.
The first title of the poem, "One Thousand Seven
Hundred and Thirty Eight, A Dialogue Something
like Horace," could not be more clear in establishing a specific focus for its unabashed topic-
ality, and it is in this year that we find Pope
caught up as never before or after in the immediacy of a current political situation: in May,
1738, the month of the poem's publication, the
Tory Opposition, long favoured by Pope, suffered
what seemed to be a resounding and final defeat
in its decade-long fight to topple the King's
well-entrenched minister, Sir Robert Walpole.[2]
Of course none of this is explicit in the poem;
strict laws in regard to libel and sedition
necessitated allegory and innuendo as the principle modes of political comment, a state of affairs that gave the satirist no choice but to

trust his reader's quick sense for identifying allegorical figures with either persons or principles in the contemporary scene. Discerning that
a figure suspiciously shares characteristics in
common with Walpole or any one of a number of
other controversial public personalities could
make all the difference between seeing a work of
satiric comment with its intention fully revealed
or not seeing it at all; in an age of allusion
and innuendo, "decoding" was not only great fun,
but often enough, necessary fun.[3]
     As Pope was no stranger to this convention,
but rather a grand-master at exploiting its possibilities, we are well entitled to ask ourselves
if the unequal contest between "Vice" and "Virtue"
in the conclusion of "Dialogue I" may not be intended as an indirect reference to the then current political struggle between Walpole and the
Tories. The question may seem academically narrow, but an answer should also be able to provide
more than a simple gauge for the depth of Pope's
political involvement in May, 1738: our understanding of what Pope intends by the use of these
figures will colour the way we see the concluding
scene, and any interpretation of this scene must
of course have a bearing on the way we read the
"Dialogue" as a whole--more important, as the
"Dialogue" in question is not simply a poem in its
own right, but also an epilogue to a large body
of poems (the Horatian imitations), any new
reading we assign to it must inevitably affect
the way we see Pope's intentions as regards the
entire canon of which it and its successor,
"Dialogue II," are the conclusions.[4] To this we
may add that after the publication of "Dialogue
II," Pope, as he wrote to Swift, practically
ceased writing altogether.[5] Thus, the figures
of "Vice" and "Virtue" in "Dialogue I" stand at a
critical juncture in Pope's life: looking backward, they survey, in true epilogue fashion, the
Horatian imitations and a decade of increasing
political involvement; looking foward, they can
lay claim to explaining the silence of the poet's
last years. But whichever perspective may inter-

est us more, it is as a product of and commentary on the events of 1738 that "Dialogue I" first commended itself to the contemporary reader of Pope's own day. How this reader would have been most likely to perceive the figures of "Vice" and "Virtue" is the small question upon which the larger ones must depend.

We now know that the figure of "Vice" in this passage was meant to be seen as an allusion to Molly Skerrett, Sir Robert Walpole's mistress of long-standing whom he had finally married on March 3, 1738, three months before the publication of Pope's "Dialogue" in May.[6] Sir Robert's liaison with Miss Skerrett, who bore him two children while his wife was yet alive, was for many years a tolerated though notorious matter of public knowledge. So, too, was the political immorality of the Walpole ministry, and Pope, by dramatizing an element of private vice in the life of the minister, naturally casts expected aspersions on the public. Molly Skerrett, though she was liked personally, was nevertheless fair game for the Opposition: in the character of Vice Triumphant she equates misrule and dissolution with the administration of the man who finally made her "honest."

If the educated contemporary reader stood a fair chance of discerning the allegorical figure of "Vice" as a jibe at Skerrett and Walpole, it is fair to assume that this same reader paid equal interpretive attention to the figure of "Virtue."[7] In fact, he did not have far to look. In lines eight and ten of "Dialogue I," Pope's interlocutor establishes the compass of the poem's retrospective scope by quoting two lines (ll. 68 and 40, respectively) from the first Horatian imitation Pope published, "The First Satire of the Second Book of Horace Imitated" ("To Mr. Fortescue"), which had come out in 1733, some five years and thirteen publications earlier.[8] In this first Imitation Pope sets about to define and justify himself as a satirist, to draw the lines of battle, to hurl the challenge to Vice and to defend the precious interests of

Virtue. He is "arm'd for Virtue" (l. 105) and we
are given to understand that the "virtue" he
fights for refers, in its customary sense, to
good taste and clean morals. Thus, he proposes
"in a Land of Hectors, / Thieves, Supercargoes,
Sharpers, and Directors" (ll. 70-72) to "Brand
the bold Front of shameless, guilty Men, / Dash
the proud Gamester in his gilded Car, / Bare the
mean Heart that lurks beneath a Star" (ll. 106-
k08). This concept of virtue is an ethical one
only, and is based on a mixture of Christian
doctrine, the moderation of the classical "via
media" proposed by Horace, and Pope's own moral
sense. Whenever we see the word "virtue" in
Pope, at its heart is this kind of very general
ethical program.9
    But further on in this first Imitation, Pope's
reference to "Virtue" seems more exclusive. "TO
VIRTUE ONLY and HER FRIENDS, A FRIEND" (l. 121),
he proclaims in boldface, and he is not ashamed
to tell us who his friends are:

> Know, all the distant Din that World can keep
> Rolls o'er my *Grotto,* and but sooths my Sleep.
> There, my Retreat the best Companions grace,
> Chiefs, out of War, and Statesmen, out of
>   Place.
> There *St. John* mingles with my friendly Bowl,
> The Feast of Reason and the Flow of Soul:
> And He, whose Lightning pierc'd th' *Iberian*
>   Lines,
> Now, forms my Quincunx, and now ranks my Vines,
> Or tames the Genius of the stubborn Plain,
> Almost as quickly, as he conquer'd *Spain.*10
>   (ll. 123-132)

Here "Virtue" seems less strictly ethical in
meaning than political, and less political in a
broad sense than specifically partisan. Pope
wants us to believe that the word "virtue" can
act synonymously as a sign of moral worth *and* as
a descriptive label for his Tory friends.11 In
this ambiguous sense, he has behind him the
authority of a tradition that goes back to the

Romans and the understanding of contemporary
readers whose "Augustan" veneration of Roman
history "rest(ed) ... on the idealization of the
Roman Senate, and the semi-allegorical equation
of the 'Republic' with 'Liberty' or 'Virtue' or
'Patriotism.'"12 The eighteenth-century reader,
trained in this idealization, would understand
"virtue" as having a classical range of meanings
all of them centering around the main concept of
selfless political duty to the state:

> By "virtus" the Romans meant any character-
> istic that is appropriate and becoming in a
> man ("vir"). The word connoted not only a
> man's personal character and his ability, but
> also devotion to the state, and again effici-
> ency at his job, which was of special import-
> ance in the statesman and the general. But
> man, as the Romans conceived him, was first
> and foremost a citizen with duties to the
> commonwealth in which he lived, and unless he
> fulfilled these duties to the best of his
> ability he was not, from the standpoint of
> the Romans, or of Livy or Machiavelli, a
> virtuous man.13

The great interpreter of this ideal for the
1720's and '30's was neither Livy nor Machiavelli,
but rather Pope's idolized "guide, philosopher,
and friend" Henry St. John, Viscount Bolingbroke,
the "statesman out of place" complimented in the
passage beginning "TO VIRTUE ONLY and HER FRIENDS,
A FRIEND." It was he who appropriated the word
and its venerated heritage for the exclusive
political use of the Tory Opposition, and he who
trained the English reading public in the fine
art of understanding its proper application to
the contemporary scene. His Opposition newspaper,
the *Craftsman*, which commenced its attacks on
Walpole in 1727, had one of the largest circula-
tions of any newspaper of its day, and every
issue teaches the reader to distinguish between
"Virtue" as the attribute of all those who follow
the Tories in opposing Walpole, and "Vice" as the

only word that can fairly describe the minister,
his minions and his brazen system of government
by corruption.[14] It inveighs against those who
"debase moral Virtue into a meer Engine of State,
contrived and put into Motion by the Craft of
Law-givers and Politicians" and prides itself
that Tory Virtue "comes from a nobler Source ...
(the) Emanation of the divine Perfection, or the
original law of Nature, implanted in our Hearts
by the great Author of all Things."[15] "Bribery
and Corruption" are "Vices the most opposite to
all Virtue and good Government" and Englishmen
are warned that "as all Government began, so all
Government must end by the People; tyrannical
Governments by their Virtue and Courage, and even
free Governments by their Vice and Baseness."[16]
The *Craftsman* rails against those who "continually
harangue in publick Companies, in order to de-
preciate Virtue, to banish those glorious Principles from among us, which have hitherto preserved
us free, and to turn into Ridicule all those,
who rationally and nobly espouse the Cause of
Liberty."[17] In a clarion-call to political action, it urges that

> we ought every one of us, who have not bow'd
> our Knees to Baal, who have not been yet in-
> fected, to endeavor in our different Capa-
> cities to stem the Torrent, now breaking in
> upon us. Some may, by the Stations They are
> placed in, be able to be more eminently
> serviceable by a Virtuous Example. Others
> may have Opportunities and Talents to per-
> suade, or confirm their Fellow-Subjects in
> the noble Principles of publick Virtue.[18]

To his private friends (such as Pope) Bolingbroke
preached Machiavelli's notion that a corrupt
state can only be saved by "the virtue of some
one person who is then living, not by the virtue
of the public as a whole ..."[19] With George II's
mediocre son, Prince Frederick, as his candidate,
Bolingbroke formulated the concept of a Patriot
King who would "render public virtue and real

GABRINER

capacity the sole means of acquiring any degree of power or profit in the state ..."[20] "Virtue"" indeed, would triumph over "Vice," Walpole would be thrown out of office, for such a king "will want neither power nor inclination to cast out this devil, to make the temptation cease, and to deliver his subjects, if not from the guilt yet from the consequence, of their fall."[21] Bolingbroke concludes with a sweeping vision of a new Golden Age that uses Plato to justify "Virtue" as an "Idea" above the factions of party: "... let the imagination range through the whole glorious scene of a patriot reign; the beauty of the idea will inspire those transports, which Plato imagined the vision of Virtue would inspire, if Virtue could be seen."[22]

Significantly, the Tories, who made the word their own in the public arena, had a special affection for using it among themselves. To George Lyttleton, who was Secretary to the Prince of Wales (Frederick) and Parliamentary leader of the "Boy Patriots," or young Tories, Bolingbroke wrote: "I like you as an amiable companion and a fine writer, but I love you as a man of virtue, as one who is not only an ornament to his country, but who actually assists her cause and may in time be her savior."[23] In a letter of October 31, 1742, Pope encourages his anti-Walpole friend, Orrery, to come to the opening of Parliament, for "as there will be all other Orders of Angels"--a phrase that refers to the fallen or Walpolian variety--"methinks the 'Virtues' should not be absent."[24] On the subject of Bolingbroke himself, Pope is ecstatic: "There is so true a fund of all Virtue public & Social within You." he writes to the Tory leader.[25] The term was so much associated with the Opposition coalition as a whole that when certain of its factions betrayed the Tories' idealism by helping to form the "Broad-Bottom" administration in 1742, Horace Walpole could pointedly sneer at "two hundred men of the most consummate virtue setting themselves for sale for three weeks."[26] It was in vain that Walpole's paper, the *Daily Gazetteer*,

strove to convince the reading public that the
definitions of "Vice" and "Virtue" inculcated by
the Tory press were without foundation. Bitterly, it complains that the Opposition have "taught
even Jacobites to call themselves Patriots, and
to sanctify the Cause of Publick Destruction with
the Name of Publick Virtue," that "a ... favourite Maxim of these most wise and reasonable Men
is this, That Virtue, Probity, Wit, Learning, and
Common Sense, belong exclusively to themselves."[27]
Walpole's hacks were no match for the continual
barrage of repeated definitions that poured forth
not only from a broad spectrum of Opposition
journals and pamphlets, but also from the pens of
playwrights and poets, Pope among them, who were
sympathetic to the Tory cause. The public had
learned from Bolingbroke's primer, and were not
to be retaught.

Contemporary usage in the general period between 1727 and 1742 thus accorded to both "Vice"
and "Virtue" very specific political meanings
that were contained within the more generally-
understood ethical distinction between simple
"evil" and simple "good." But Pope's dramatization of these meanings in the concluding passage
of "Dialogue I" must be understood as the product
of a deepening personal involvement which had
preoccupied him for years and which only reached
its climax in the events of May, 1738. In the
Fall of 1732 Bolingbroke's press entered the
lists against Walpole's proposed Excise scheme
and succeeded in raising public opposition to such
a pitch, that when Parliament met in January
Walpole thought it prudent to put off his introduction of the scheme till March. It was at this
time (the latter part of January, 1733), as Pope
later recounted to Spence,

When I had a fever one winter in town that
confined me to my room for five or six days,
Lord Bolingbroke came to see me, happened to
take up a Horace that lay on the table, and
in turning it over dipped on the First Satire
of the Second Book. He observed how well that

would hit my case, if I were to imitate it in
English. After he was gone, I read it over,
translated it in a morning or two, and sent
it to the press in a week or fortnight after.
And this was the occasion of my imitating
some other of the Satires and Epistles after-
wards.28

But though the timing of this first Imitation may
have provided a convenient answer to Pope's "case,
it anticipates its successors by serving Bolingbroke's case as well.29 At the height of their
successful campaign against the Excise scheme,
the Tories were crowing with optimism; the Earl
of Stair had gone so far as to obtain a private
interview with the Queen on the hopeful premise
that she could be persuaded to lay Walpole
aside.30 At this juncture, Pope published his
Imitation, and its contents show that the poet
had caught some of the heady fever that was then
current among his Tory friends. While the
"Epistle to Bathurst," published just a few weeks
earlier, entertained a vision of "Britain sunk
in lucre's sordid charms" (l. 145) and forecast
that "... Corruption, like a gen'ral flood / (So
long by watchful Ministers withstood) / Shall
deluge all" (ll. 137-139), the "First Satire of
the Second Book," as we have seen, more boldly
states an optimism in the cause of "Virtue," and
lays out, in prologue-fashion, the groundwork
for a satiric assault on "Vice" that will be carried out in future imitations. The picture we
get is that of the satirist as hero, a man so
charged by the honest claims of his cause that he
is hurling challenges and baiting his opponent
before the battle is fairly joined. "Satire's my
Weapon" (l. 69), Pope declares, and he is "arm'd
for *Virtue* when I point the Pen" (l. 105). He will
write "grave *Epistles*, bringing Vice to light"
(l. 151) under any and all conditions:

Then learned Sir! (to cut the Matter short)
What-e'er my Fate, or well or ill at Court,
Whether old Age, with faint, but chearful Ray,

    Attends to gild the Evening of my Day,
    Or Death's black Wing already be display'd
    To wrap me in the Universal Shade;
    Whether the darken'd Room to muse invite,
    Or whiten'd Wall provoke the Skew'r to write,
    In Durance, Exile, Bedlam, or the Mint,
    Like *Lee* or *Budgell*, I will Rhyme and Print.
                                    (ll. 91-100)

This is indeed the Pope that "once with Rapture
writ," as he is tauntingly referred to by the
"Friend" in the opening lines of "Dialogue I."
In holiday mood, Pope reflects Bolingbroke's own
buoyancy. He is eager to imitate Horace's impersonal caveat, "clamo, melius non tangere" ("I
proclaim, it is better not to touch me"), in
order to give it a more specific, political twist:
"But touch me, and no Minister so sore" (l. 76).
He follows Horace, adopting the satirist's role
of impartial commentator--"Papist or Protestant,
or both between, / Like good *Erasmus* in an honest
Mean, / In Moderation placing all my Glory, /
While Tories call me Whig, and Whigs a Tory" (ll.
65-68)--and then, gaily oblivious to the contradiction, goes on to devote six lines of partisan
encomium to Bolingbroke, who, as "Virtue's" friend,
is just then busy pushing the Opposition advantage
in the Excise affair.
    If Bolingbroke and the Tories are to be under-
stood in the line "TO VIRTUE ONLY and HER FRIENDS,
A FRIEND," the fact that Pope is "arm'd for Virtue" when he "points the pen" is a statement of
political purpose as well as ethical program.
Pope's optimism, then, at the very start of the
Imitations, is closely associated with the political world; and although not primarily concerned
with politics, the "First Satire of the Second
Book" reflects in the timing of its publication,
in its spirit and its exclusive references to
"Virtue's" friends, a political point of view
that is unmistakably Tory in its sympathies. The
Excise affair failed to topple Walpole--he withdrew the proposal rather than risk its defeat in
a vote--but in its aftermath Pope's solidarity

with the Opposition cause was heightened and his
sense of exclusive fraternity with other members
of the group was increased; "the only praises
worth having," he writes to Swift later that
Spring, "are those bestowed *by* Virtue *for* Virtue."[3]
From 1733 to 1737 the intensity of Pope's publishing activity corresponds with the ups and
downs of the Opposition's sporadic attempts to
dethrone Walpole: the publication of the "Epistle
to Cobham," who had just been ousted from his
regiment for his part in the Excise affair, is
timed (January, 1734) to anticipate a bill the
Opposition was introducing in February to prevent
the dismissal without court-martial of army offi-
cers not above the rank of colonel; yet when a
disappointed Bolingbroke left England for France
in May, 1735, Pope published nothing for a period
of twenty-two months. That summer, however, he
was introduced at Lord Cobham's in Stowe to the
young Opposition leaders who would carry on in
their chief's absence--Lyttleton, Polwarth, Gren-
ville and Pitt, the so-called "Boy Patriots" or
"Cobham's Cubs," and to foster his interest,
Prince Frederick, who was soon to be the Patriot
King-figure at the center of the group, did "Mr.
Pope the honour of a visit at his home in Twickenham" in October.[32] Pope remained engaged, but
quiescent; with Bolingbroke gone and the "Boy
Patriots" still growing up, Walpole's star would
continue in the ascendant. The future looked
bleak. "What I gain on the side of philosophy,"
he wrote to Swift, "I lose on the side of poetry
... The climate (under our Heaven of a Court) is
but cold and uncertain: the winds rise, and winter
comes on."[33] When finally he broke his long
silence in March, 1737, it was at a time of renewed political activity on the part of the "new"
Opposition, who had resolved to embarrass the
government and strengthen their ties to Prince
Frederick by raising in the public forum the
delicate question of his allowance; this scheme
failed, but by April the political atmosphere
was pregnant with possibilities.[34] The government was already involved in the exhausting de-

bates relating to the imposition of penalties on
the city of Edinburgh for its alleged role in the
murder of Captain Porteus, and while Walpole was
in the midst of a struggle to prevent a dilution
of the government's penalties against that city,
Pope followed up his March effort with the publication on April 28th of the "Second Epistle of
the Second Book," addressed to an unknown friend
of Cobham; this was followed in turn by the famous "First Epistle of the Second Book" ("To
Augustus"), a masterpiece of anti-government i-
rony that had already been written and whose date
of publication, May 25, 1737, happened to coincide with the embarrassments then being suffered
by the royal prestige in Parliament.[35]

Thus, in the spring of 1737 Pope's concern for
Tory "Virtue" was once again fully awake, and we
may imagine, after four years in which to grow,
more mature, more expectant and more dedicated
than ever to the "gen'rous Cause." Events which
were to snowball in the summer and fall of 1737
must have increased in him a heady political optimism from which few members of the Opposition
proved immune. In July, when the town was empty,
Prince Frederick threw himself further into the
arms of the Opposition when he incurred his
father's wrath for having hurried his pregnant
wife from Hampton Court to St. James' in the dead
of night without informing either of his parents.
As the child was not born under his roof and its
mother's sudden removal was neither prepared for
nor announced, the King naturally took the incident as a personally-intended insult. Despite
the Prince's humble submissions, a complete rup-
ture was inevitable, and the affair at once became a public scandal. By September the Prince
had set up separate court at Norfolk House in
St. James' square, which became a meeting place
for the Opposition, and the King had issued an
edict forbidding those who paid court there admission to the royal presence. Here was an excellent opportunity for the Opposition to further
cultivate the interest of the Prince, upon whose
succession to the throne their hopes were pinned.

At the same time the *Craftsman* and other anti-
ministerial papers began to mount an attack on
Walpole's supine handling of the merchants' complaints in regard to the repeated seizure of
British ships by Spanish costa-guardas. Wishing
at all costs to avoid an unnecessary and expensive war with Spain, Walpole dallied in his
representations to the Spanish court while the
Opposition press, in the name of Virtue, Dignity
and Trade, busied itself raising the pitch of
public sentiment to coincide with the forthcoming
debate on the Spanish "depredations" in Parliament.

Such was the atmosphere that began to form in
the months directly preceding Pope's publication
of "Dialogue I" in May. The momentum of the Opposition's efforts gained a tremendous impetus
at the death of Queen Caroline on November 20th,
a loss which deprived Walpole of his most important confidante and rendered the political climate
more highly charged than it had been in years.
Sensing her end before it came, Chesterfield
exactly expressed the greatest hopes of the Opposition when he wrote to Lyttleton on November 12th
suggesting that

> in case the Queen dies I think Walpole should
> be looked upon as gone too ... and if the Op-
> position are wise, instead of treating with
> him, they should attack him most vigorously
> and personally as a person who has lost his
> chief support. Which is indeed true, for
> though he may have more power with the King
> than any other body, yet he will never have
> that kind of power which he had by her means.[36]

Bolingbroke, writing from abroad, concurred, and
only wished to remind his Opposition colleagues
that the Prince "if properly used" might become
a "center of union" enabling "men of different
characters and different views ... to draw together."[37]

The hopes thus expressed for a triumph of
"Virtue" were expected to find their destiny in

the forthcoming session of Parliament, which was
due to convene on January 24. The Earl of Stair
hopefully believed that if "Sir Robert's partisans should happen to be the minority, one single
vote of the House of Commons would make all that
enchantment, that deludes his Majesty, disappear."[38] The Opposition accordingly resolved
that "Walpole was to be thwarted in every measure
he introduced; his past policy was to be nightly
attacked; the King was to be poisoned against him
by those in the confidence of the Court; the
divisions in the Cabinet ... were to be widened
and encouraged by promises of support in the
future."[39] The convening of Parliament was consequently regarded with an unusually high degree
of anticipation, and political tension was high.
Bathurst, looking forward to the event in December, wrote to Swift "I mett our friend Pope in
town, he is as sure to be there in a bustle, as
a Porpus in a Storm ..."[40] Pope, indeed, was
following the turn of events closely.[41] He had
published nothing during the recess, his last
poem, the "First Epistle of the Second Book" ("To
Augustus"), having appeared in May, during the
last Session; to show where his sympathies lay,
on January 23, 1738, the day before the opening
of the Fourth Session of the Eighth Parliament,
he began his publishing year with the "Sixth
Epistle of the First Book" (*Griffith* no. 476), addressed to the young anti-Walpole lawyer, William
Murray, and pertinently concerned with the subjects of ambition, wealth and power. In it, Lord
Cornbury, who had spurned Walpole's efforts to
buy his support, is held up as a model of Virtue's
opposition to moneyed Vice (ll. 61-62). Pope's
beginning enthusiasm for an early Tory victory
must have been dampened, however, when, on February 3rd, the Opposition lost the first round of
the battle, their motion to reduce the size of
the standing army having been defeated after a
lengthy debate in which Lyttleton, Pitt and Polwarth all spoke.[42] On this same day Lady Murray
wrote her letter to the elder Marchmont, one of
the Tory leaders, prophesying "that all your con-

sultations will come to nothing, but Sir Robert
outwit you every one."[43]   The Opposition members
themselves had premonitions of doom, which they
confided to each other by letter.   The Duke of
Montrose wrote to Marchmont on February 17th:

> All I have to trouble your Lordship with now,
> is singly with concern to observe the deadness
> and want of spirit, which seems to prevail so
> universally in the present age.   I live, it
> is true, in ignorance of what passes, for I
> have no correspondence; but if there was vir-
> tue left amongst us; some instances of it be-
> hooved now and then to shine out; but indeed
> I am afraid it is all over with us ...[44]

On the 28th Marchmont replied "I know not what
posterity may think of us, but am of opinion they
can scarcely think worse of us generally, than
what we deserve."[45]

While Marchmont and others were gloomy, Pope
remained hopeful.   Two days before the Opposition
opened Parliamentary debates on the Spanish depredations, Pope on March 1st published the delightful "Sixth Satire of the Second Book" (Griffith, no. 479), a light satire originally written
in 1714 by Swift which he had reworked to include
the fable of the Town Mouse and the Country Mouse.
The moral of the poem had its present applicability, for "'Twas on the night of a Debate, /
When all their Lordships had sate late" (ll. 187-
188) that the Country Mouse learns how much better off he was before he came to London.   On
March 3rd the Opposition began its attack on the
government when Mr. Alderman Perry brought in
the petition of relief on behalf of the injured
merchants; an Opposition motion to see all the
papers relating to the ministry's negotiations
with Spain was defeated 164 to 99, and a less
comprehensive request proposed by Walpole accepted
without a division.[46]   On the plea that the ministry would have to search for the necessary documents, Walpole hoped to stall the momentum of the
Opposition attack.   A new date was set for March

15th, and both sides gathered their forces during
the interim; more merchants would present petitions and it was rumoured that Captain Jenkins,
who claimed to have suffered physical mutilation
at the hands of the Spaniards, would appear before
the bar of the House with his cropped ear.   It
was the general feeling that a decisive confrontation between Walpole and the Opposition was imminent.
     During this tense interim, Pope on the 7th
published his imitation of the "First Epistle of
the First Book, to Maecenas" (*Griffith* no. 480),
an intensely political poem which is openly
dedicated to Bolingbroke and scathing in its denunciation of city corruption, of the court, and
the ministry.   The poem is by turns aggressive
and humorous; above all, it is resilient and confident.   The opening lines imply that the poem
is a product of either Bolingbroke's request or
suggestion, as happened to be the case with the
"First Satire of the Second Book" in 1733:   "St.
John, whose love indulg'd my labours past /
Matures my present, and shall bound my last! /
Why will you break the Sabbath of my days?" (ll.
1-3).   Though the poem pronounces impartial
"philosophy" as its ideal, the government's arch-
enemy, Bolingbroke, is addressed in reverential
terms as

     That Man divine whom Wisdom calls her own,
     Great without Title, without Fortune bless'd,
     Rich ev'n when plunder'd, honour'd while op-
          press'd,
     Lov'd without youth, and follow'd without
          power,
     At home tho' exil'd, free, tho' in the Tower,
     In short, that reas'ning, high, immortal Thing,
     Just less than Jove, and much above a King,
     Nay half in Heav'n ...
                              (ll. 180-187)

Pope draws himself in the character of an Opposition patriot, such as those currently attacking
Walpole in Parliament:

> Sometimes a Patriot, active in debate,
> Mix with the World, and battle for the State,
> Free as young Lyttleton, her cause pursue,
> Still true to Virtue, and as warm as true.[47]
>   (ll. 27-30)

The entire poem constitutes an ethical and political definition of "Virtue" in tune with the current situation. "'Tis the first Virtue, Vices to abhor" (l. 65), but the ethical principle is founded on a political base: It is "here," at Pope's grotto, the meeting place for the Opposition in Twickenham, that Wisdom calls "Seek Virtue first! be bold! / As Gold to Silver, Virtue is to Gold" (ll. 77-78), while the city and court in London cry "Get Mony, Mony still! / And then let Virtue follow, if she will" (ll. 79-80). Only "Virtue makes a King" (l. 92), Pope ironically reflects, and compared to Virtue "a Minister's an Ass" (l. 96).[48]

A week later petitions and testimony, including that of Captain Jenkins, were heard before the bar in the House of Commons; the appointed day for a resolution of the whole affair was set for the 30th. Marchmont wrote to his ally, Tweeddale, on the 28th:

> ... Your Lordship will see from what has past and the present situation of affairs that they are come to a crisis, and nobody believes it possible for them to go on much longer under the present administration of our worthie ministers ...[49]

On the 30th the House resolved itself into a Committee of the whole House to listen to a report on the merchants' complaints submitted by Mr. Alderman Perry, and to an argument presented by their counsel, Pope's young friend, William Murray. Pulteney, one of the Opposition chiefs, then led off the final debate by moving for a resolution that was intended to force a war by forbidding Spain the right to search British ships; after an exhausting debate it was defeated 224-

163 and an amendment proposed by Walpole that
skirted the entire search issue was accepted without a division.[50]
   With this loss the Opposition could only hope
to raise the issue again toward the end of the
Session and in the meantime try to keep up the
tide of public clamour in their favour. Walpole's
Daily Gazetteer, in its issue for March 31, 1738,
correctly observed that "the Political Disputes
which have for many Years subsisted in this Nation, seem now to be drawing towards a Crisis ..."
But the crisis alluded to by the *Gazetteer*, high
as the level of national excitement was, took a
month in coming, and the whole of April proved a
relative lull before the storm. On the eve of
the Opposition's final effort, the *Gazetteer*
taunted that "Virtue is but a barren, unfruitful
Soil; but it is the Glory of great Patriots to
cultivate and improve it" (April 21), while on
the following day the Opposition newspaper *Common
Sense* triumphantly proclaimed that "the Nation
calls loud for War."
   By the 28th of April Pope was already writing
"Dialogue I," though probably not yet finished
with it, as seems indicated by a letter to Ralph
Allen on that date which requests the use of his
name for "a Poem of mine."[51] The line in which
Allen's name appears (l. 135) comes late in the
poem, just before the concluding passage, which
begins at l. 137--perhaps by April 28th the poem
was complete except for the concluding passage
and Pope was waiting to determine the outcome of
the final Opposition sally due in the last weeks
of the Session, before sending the completed poem
to the press in its final form three weeks later.
If the Opposition proved at last victorious, the
triumph of "Virtue" could be celebrated and the
satirist's cause justified in a conclusion of
some thirty lines; if, on the other hand, Sir
Robert should prevail, an optimistic conclusion
would be invalidated, and the last thirty lines
would then have to record the triumph of "Vice."
Once the outcome seemed faily certain, however,
either conclusion, if only thirty lines long,

could be written on short notice to make the poem's content and publication date in keeping with
whatever should prove the political event.

  In any case the latter was not long in making
itself apparent. On May 2nd the Opposition was
at first buoyed by a temporary note of success,
when the debate on the Spanish depredations in
the House of Lords culminated in resolutions
against Spain far stronger than Walpole's had been
in the House of Commons. The *Gazetteer* confidently
asserted on May 4th that "the Voice of Reason is
never heard till the Storm of Passion is over,"
while on the 5th the Opposition, attempting to
ride the crest of that storm, launched in the
Commons their last great attack on the minister,
an attack that was looked on as the culmination
of a year's policy and planning, and upon which
everything was banked. Pulteney led off for "the
Cause of Virtue" by moving leave be given to bring
in a bill "for Securing the Trade to America"
that would revive certain acts guaranteeing
British privateers prize money for the capture of
enemy ships; the bill was intended to oust Walpole by forcing against him a vote for going to
war with Spain, as its provisions were tantamount
to the declaration of war it had been Walpole's
policy to prevent. On the following Monday,
May 8th, the bill was read for the first time,
and on Tuesday for the second, when it was given
over to be considered on the 12th. On that day,
a Friday, took place the decisive confrontation
between the Opposition and Walpole that had been
expected by the nation for months. With so much
at stake, Pulteney was at his best. The design
of the bill, he declaimed, is to tell Spain that
unless

> those who have plundered us, grant us immediate
> satisfaction, we are resolved upon revenging
> ourselves by force of arms: That this is the
> resolution of Parliament, which no minister
> dare endeavour to disappoint ... By the passing
> of this bill they will see, that they have now
> to do with the Parliament of Great Britain,
> that the whole nation is roused, and that it

will be impossible even for our ministers to
stem the torrent of our resentment.[52]

Walpole, in his rebuttal, argued sensibly and
strongly against a bill that would "immediately
plunge us into an expensive, a dangerous, and a
destructive war."[53] Pulteney darkly suggested
that "ministers may sometimes have particular
reasons for being afraid of a war. By the breaking out of a war, secrets may be brought to light,
which would prove the certain overthrow of those
ministers that had been concerned in them."[54] The
measure would be brought up for a third reading
on Monday the 15th, but its fate already seemed
certain. In vain did the *Craftsman* on the 13th
quote from a contemporary play:

> What were Dominion, Pomp,
> The Wealth of Nations, nay of all the World,
> The World itself, or what a thousand Worlds,
> Compar'd with Faith unspotted, heavenly Truth,
> Thoughts free from Guilt, the Empire of the
>   Mind,
> And all the Transports of a godlike Breast,
> Firm and unmov'd in the great Cause of
>   Virtue?[55]

Marchmont knew better, and in a letter written
from Ealing on the 12th was already anticipating
Monday's outcome: "I look," he wrote to Montrose,
"as several others do, upon the Opposition as at
an end."[56] On the same day "Dialogue I" was
registered for copyright, having first been announced as forthcoming by the *Gazetteer* on the 11th.
The following Monday, May 15th, Marchmont's
pessimism was justified when, against all Opposition hopes, Pulteney's bill was thrown out on
the third reading by a vote of 106 to 75.[57] The
political outcome of the confrontation was no
longer a matter for conjecture, and the next day,
May 16, 1738, Pope's "One Thousand Seven Hundred
and Thirty Eight, A Dialogue Something like
Horace," with a concluding vision of "Vice's"
final triumph over "Virtue," was being offered by

the booksellers at the price of one shilling
(*Griffith*, no. 484).58
    Two months later, apparently realizing that
however impoverished a weapon satire might be in
the face of an omnipotent "Vice" it was still
something better than private disdain, Pope published "One Thousand Seven Hundred and Thirty
Eight, Dialogue II" (*Griffith* no. 494). At the
end of this Dialogue, however, he appended a
resolution that stated his intention to publish
no more poems of this "kind" in favour of entering a formal protest against "insuperable corruption and depravity of manners." "Bad men," he
wrote, "were grown so shameless and so powerful,
that Ridicule was become as unsafe as it was ineffectual." Instead, the Horation imitations as
a group would be recast as a memorial to the Opposition and his involvement in its fortunes: to
show that he wished the entire canon to be thought
of as one group unified by a common political
ideal, in the following year Pope added to his
advertisement prefacing all the Imitations the
Horatian motto "Uni aequus Virtuti atque ejus
Amicis," the Latin original for the partisan "TO
VIRTUE ONLY and HER FRIENDS, A FRIEND"; and in
1740 he re-titled both Dialogues to read in full
"Epilogue to the Satires: Dialogues I and II,"
thus fulfilling his prophecy to Swift that " ...
my works will in one respect be like the works
of Nature, much more to be liked and understood
when consider'd in the relation they bear with
each other, than when ignorantly look'd upon one
by one ..."59
    Yet despite such quiet reaffirmations of his
continued sympathy for "Virtue's" cause, in the
aftermath of May Pope's letters mirror an immediate and deepening sense of disillusionment.
The Opposition defeat and the publication of
"Dialogue I" mark a turning point in Pope's life;
he was never the same again. From this point in
time till his death six years later, his hopes for
a resurgence of "Virtue" are diminished to the
point of despair, and each of his correspondents,
as the months toll by, is informed of his exhaus-

tion and pessimism. In July, two months after
the debacle, he tells Ralph Allen

> I can but Skirmish, & maintain a flying Fight
> with Vice; its Forces augment, & will drive
> me off the Stage, before I shall see the Ef-
> fects complete, either of Divine Providence
> or Vengeance: for sure we can be quite Saved
> only by the One, or punishd by the other: The
> Condition of Morality is so desperate, as to
> be above all Human Hands.60--

This despite the imminent arrival of Bolingbroke,
who came two days after the letter was written
and would provide Pope with company for a year
while the sale of his estate was in progress.
Other correspondents received similar letters.
William Fortescue, Pope's lawyer-friend, was told
in September "I am as content to quit the clamorous Part of a Poet, Satire, as you could be to
quit that of a Pleading Lawyer ... *Quiet* is the
Life of Innocence & Good nature."61 When Lyttleton wrote, entreating him to help animate Prince
Frederick "to Virtue," Pope begged off with the
dispirited affirmation that "I love Virtue, for
I love You & such as you: Such are listed under
her Banners, they fight for her; Poets are but
like Heralds, they can only proclaim her, and the
best you can make of me, is, that I am her poor
Trumpeter."62 In February he writes to Allen that
"I want the Comfort of an honest Friend, in
these wretched Immoral times, when almost all the
Tyes that bind Man to Man, are Combinations of
Iniquity, or at best of mean Interest."63 His
"health is breaking more ways than one," he tells
Fortescue in March, adding that he "lamented not
any part of his fortune here, but that of living
to see an Age, when the Virtue of his Country
seem'd to be at a period."64 Swift, in May,
1739, is informed by Pope "I am sinking fast into
prose ... Since my *Protest*, (for so I call the
Dialogue of 1738) I have written but ten lines
..."65 Writing from Bath, where he wintered that
December, Pope tells Lyttleton "I think that ever

since I was a Poet, nay ever since I have ceas'd
to be one, I have not experienced so much Quiet
as at this place"; but before returning to London
he speaks of himself to Burlington as having left
the "Great World" because he has been, "like other
well meaning people ... much hurt by The Wickedness of the World he has past thro', & dealt
with."66   England's fate, he confides to Polwarth,
is now a matter of Divine Judgment, for "if God
had not given this Nation to Perdition, He would
not have removed from its Service the Men, whose
Capacity & Integrity alone could have saved it."67
The English, he writes to Polwarth again, on the
occasion of a Tory leader's death, are "the most
dirty, rascally Race on Earth":

> God Almighty certainly knows what he does,
> when he removes those from us whose lives we
> pray for; & leaves behind those Scourges,
> which a mercenary People deserve, tho' the
> Partiality of a few Virtuous or Brave men ...
> would save them.68

Each year, until his death in 1744, the sense
of depression grows greater.   In 1739 his publishing life is a blank.   "If any thing will a-
muse me at present," he writes to Robert Nugent
in 1740, "it must be playing the fool any way but
by Writing."69   In October of that year he explains to Warburton that "... all Satire is become so ineffectual, (when the Last Step that
Virtue can stand upon, Shame, is taken away)..."70
A year later the *Gentleman's Magazine* reprinted from
the *Craftsman* an anonymous poem that takes note
of Pope's unusually long silence, and refers to
the publication of the "Dialogues" as the point
in time from which it can be dated:

> Bless us! 'tis Strange, three tedious Years,
> They say, and not a Line appears;
> Not one Poetick Cobweb spun,
> From *Thirty-eight* to *Forty-one.*71

In this year his vision of the national scene is
as dark as ever. "My Mind," he confides in Allen,
"at present is as dejected as possible, for I
love my Country, & I love Mankind, and I see a
dismal Scene Opening for our own & other Nations
... God prosper your Particular, tho in General
Miseries no honest Man can be Easy."[72] Polwarth,
now 3rd Earl of Marchmont, is told "I am determined to publish no more in my life time, for
many reasons; but principally thro' the Zeal I
have to speak the *Whole Truth*, & neither to praise
or dispraise by halves, or with worldly manage-
ments."[73] Pope speaks in the same tone to Lyttleton: "I see no Uses to be drawn from the knowledge of any publick Events," he writes; "I see
most honest men melancholy, & that's enough to
make me enquire no more."[74] Four days later
Lyttleton answered with his usual patriotic injunction, urging Pope once more to write on behalf of the Opposition and not to "bury your
excellent Talents in a Philosophical Indolence,
but to Employ them, as you have so often done, in
the Service of Virtue ... some sparks of Publick
Virtue are yet Alive, which such a Spirit as
Your's might blow into a flame ..."[75] It is the
last surviving letter between them. Pope could
not be moved, though his political sympathies
remained the same: The day before George II created Walpole 3rd Earl of Orford, Pope shared with
Allen his opinion that "tho they call Kings the
Fountains of Honour, I think them only the Be-
stowers of Titles; which they are generally most
profuse of, to wh---s and kn---s."[76] Even Walpole's resignation failed to convince him to take
a more aggressive footing; there had been too
many compromises in the formation of the "Broad-
Bottom," from which his Tory friends had been excluded. Referring to the Minister's ouster that
February, Pope confines himself to the observation "*Accidents & Occasions* may do what *Virtue* would
not ... Whatever becomes of Publick Virtue, let
us preserve Our own poor Share of the private."[77]
The disclosures and disorderliness that followed
Walpole's overthrow tended, in fact, to confirm

Pope's growing feeling that "universal darkness"
was already descending.   "It is in vain I seques-
ter myself from the Action," he wrote to Orrery,
"when the Riot & the Ruin spread around me."[78]
He is "sick of This bad World," he writes to
Allen on December 1, 1742, "and I see it daily
growing worse."[79]   "Once more I tell you," he
writes again on the 8th, "I am sick of *this* World
& the Great ones of it, tho they have been my
intimate Acquaintance."[80]   To Orrery he confesses,
a year before his death, "as to any thing else I
shall write, it will be very little, and very
faint.   I have lost all Ardor and Appetite, even
to Satyr ..."[81]
    It was thus that the Opposition set-back in
May, 1738, marked a turning point in Pope's life
and work: it is in this immediate sense, as an
organic part of the history of its time, that
the conclusion of "Dialogue I" is to be understood not only in terms of an inversion of moral
values, but more urgently, as the dramatization
of a political debacle.   Actually, the two are
one, for Pope during the 1730's was increasingly
drawn to share the belief that morality was
capable of political expression; it was later a
happy convenience for him to seize on an established usage in political journalism according
to which "Vice" and "Virtue" were already understood in a double sense.   Both "Dialogues" (and
for that matter, the final "Dunciad" of 1743)
can only be understood properly when they are
set against the events and atmosphere of an entire decade of increasing political tension in
the struggle to overthrow Walpole.   Having sur-
veyed part of this history, we are in a better
position to understand why "Dialogue I" looks
back to the first Imitation of 1733: only a
history of the events which transpired during
the five-year period between them can explain why
the Horatian imitations begin on a note of aggressive and spirited optimism and end on one of defeat and disdain.   Pope took both Tory idealism
and the Opposition loss seriously, perhaps more
seriously than has been recognized; the "Epilogue

to the Satires" is not *only* an epilogue to the
satires. Finally, our discussion of Pope's
"Virtue" in "Dialogue I" sheds some needed light
on the disillusionment and resignation of the
poet's last years. It was for a war with Spain,
Burke correctly observed in his *First Letter on a
Regicide Peace,* that Pope "sang his dying notes";
his last years were spent in retirement, revising
his life's work and enjoying the solitude of his
Grotto. Above its entrance he affixed the Horatian motto *"Secretum iter et fallentis semita vitae,"*
from *Epistle* I xviii: "A secluded journey along
the path of an obscure life." Although he edited
and revised all previous editions of the *Dunciad*
so as to emphasize the political intent of the
1743 version, Pope's sense of "Virtue's" final
defeat never left him. A few months after the
publication of the *New Dunciad* (Book IV) in 1742,
he could still write to Allen, "my Sphere is
Resignation, not Action ... God preserve the
Few Good people that are left ..."[82]

POPE AND DULNESS

Emrys Jones

I

    The strangeness of Pope's *Dunciad* is a quality
that often gets lost from sight. During the last
few decades criticism has worked so devotedly to
assimilate the poem and make it more generally
accessible, that, inevitably perhaps, we may now
have reached the point of distorting it out of
its original oddity. The *Dunciad* is both a work
of art and something else: it is, or was, a
historical event, a part of literary and social
history, an episode in the life of Pope as well
as in those of his enemies. And its textual com-
plications--the different versions it went
through--present unwieldy problems to editor and
critic alike, which add to the difficulty of seeing clearly what it is. When the *Dunciad* is mentioned do we think of one, or more than one,
poem? And do we include the elaborate editorial
apparatus supplied by Pope, or do we suppress it,
as being inessential? Is it in fact necessary to

This essay first appeared in *Proceedings of the British Academy* 54 (1968), 231-63. Copyright The British Academy.

understand Pope's references to his now often
totally obscure contemporaries? The *Dunciad* is so
deeply immersed in history--the final version contains references or allusions to about two hundred
actual persons--that its status as poetry is
problematical, and has perhaps always seemed so.

In so far as the poem has been read at all,
and it has surely never been widely read, the real
critical effort has been to find in it some coherent meaning independent of its dead personalities. In the nineteenth century one tendency was
to see the poem so much in terms of Pope's private
character, to see it so confinedly within the
context of his war with Grub-street, that it was
impossible to take seriously any of its supra-
personal, cultural pretensions. In this period
the *Dunciad* was, so to speak, under-generalized.
In recent years, on the contrary, a prevalent
temptation--or so it seems to me--has been to
over-generalize it, or to generalize it in a
dubiously valuable way. I am thinking of the current tendency to praise the poem for taking a
stand against barbarism on behalf of civilization,
and to argue that, since such cultural issues are
always with us, Pope has given expression to a
permanent dilemma. The *Dunciad* may then be com-
pared--indeed has been--with Arnold's *Culture and
Anarchy*. The implication is that we read Pope as
we might read a cultural or educational treatise,
with a view to finding some guidance for practical
activity. There is of course something to be said
for this approach, for there is a genuine Arnold-
ian side to the *Dunciad* which comes out especially
in the fourth Book, and no doubt general issues
such as these may legitimately arise from a discussion of the poem. But it may be doubted
whether they are the reasons why we read the poem in the first place, or, more important, why
those of us who enjoy the poem return to it.

To say so much is certainly not to be ungrateful for such a scrupulous and thorough work of
scholarship as Aubrey Williams's *Pope's Dunciad: A
Study of its Meaning* (1955), despite some reservations one might feel about the limited sense in

which 'meaning' is being used here. In their
study of Pope's 'meaning' Aubrey Williams and
those who share his approach confine their attention to Pope's deliberate artistry, his conscious
intentions so far as these can be ascertained;
and for their purpose they are quite right to do
so. They emphasize the intellectual qualities
of the *Dunciad* and those parts of it which comprise statement or allegory or approximate to
either. And in such a treatment the great fourth
Book rightly gets pre-eminent attention. And yet
it is possible to read the *Dunciad* again and to
feel that there is something else to say, that
such accounts of the poem's 'meaning' do not
wholly tell us what it feels like to read, and
that the first three Books especially have a good
deal in them which seems to elude such treatment.
     The *Dunciad* on the page is a formidable *object*,
dense, opaque, intransigently and uncompromisingly itself. Its apparatus of prefatory material,
voluminous annotation, and after-pieces helps to
create something like a spatial sense of the area
occupied by the central object, the poetic text.
One can indeed contemplate it as something with
real physical dimensions. Just as the Lilliputians one day found the sleeping man-giant Gulliver within their kingdom, so Pope's contemporaries
can be imagined as discovering this strange
offensive object, lying in a public place like an
enemy weapon or a ponderous missile: essentially
not a set of abstract verbal statements but a
thing, to be walked around and examined, interpreted, and possibly dealt with. Certainly the
Dunciad when printed simply as a poetic text, without its surrounding paraphernalia, is not quite
itself; it has lost something of its solid three-
dimensional presence. This impression that the
Dunciad makes of being a thing, an object, is
important to our sense of a quality with which I
shall be particularly concerned here: its energy.
When we read the poem we can, I think, sometimes
feel that there is great energy and vitality in
it, that Pope transmits formidable waves of power
which affect us emotionally and psychologically,

and that this aspect of the poem's impact--its
emotional and psychological effect--is not really
accounted for in those descriptions of the *Dunciad*
which seem to have now become widely accepted.
Works of satire can often seem more emotionally
straightforward, the sources of their power less
mysterious than they really are. And when, as in
the *Dunciad*, the verse is crammed with the names
of actual persons and with references to real
events, the poetic end-product may all seem a
triumph of the controlled will--and of nothing
else.

If Pope were in complete control of his material, it would be easier than it is to speak of
the unity of the *Dunciad*. For critics still debate
whether it is one poem in four Books, or two in
three and one. Ian Jack concludes that Pope
shows 'a fundamental uncertainty about the subject of the poem, a fatal indefiniteness of purpose'.[1] He has been challenged by H. H. Erskine-
Hill,[2] who finds a satisfying unity of purpose in
the final four-Book version; but although his
argument is a highly interesting one he does not,
to my mind, altogether dispose of Ian Jack's
original objections. But whatever one thinks
about this question, there can be no doubt that
the poem did go through several stages after its
first appearance in print, that Pope did change
his intentions to some extent, and that this
happened with no other of his major poems with
the exception of that other mock-heroic *The Rape
of the Lock*. Uncertainty of purpose--if that is
what it is--is not the same thing as mysterious-
ness, but these external considerations might be
borne in mind when one tries to account for the
Dunciad's strange power. Pope himself may not
have been clear what it was he wanted to do.

Like some other great works of its age, like
A Tale of a Tub and *Clarissa*, the *Dunciad* seems to
engage us on more than one level. The first
level one might describe as a level of deliberate
artistry: the poet works in terms of play of
wit, purposeful allegory, triumphantly pointed
writing, in all of which we are made aware of the

pressure of a highly critical and aggressive mind.
But on another level the poetry works more mys-
teriously and obscurely: one seems to see *past*
the personal names and topical allusions to a
large fantasy-world, an imaginative realm which
is infused with a powerful sense of gratification
and indulgence. The first level is primarily
stimulating to the mind, while the second works
affectively in altogether more obscure ways. It
is indeed relevant here to recall Johnson's remark about the 'unnatural delight' which the poet of the *Dunciad* took in 'ideas physically im-
pure'--a notion to which I shall return.
     It seems altogether too simple to think of
Pope as a defender of cultural standards confronting an army of midget barbarians. It might be
nearer the truth to regard the *Dunciad* as having
something of the quality of a *psychomachia*, to see
Pope as dramatizing, or trying to reduce to order,
his own feelings, which were possibly more
divided and mixed than he was willing or able to
acknowledge. In what follows I shall be using
several approaches to justify the feeling that
the poem is often more deeply ambiguous than
Pope's overt purposes suggest; and I use several
routes because there are different ways of explaining this state of affairs.

                          II

     I shall begin by observing that the Scriblerus
Club has a markedly retrospective, even somewhat
archaic, character for the reign of Queen Anne.
In an age much given to club activity this one
stands out for certain qualities which recall
nothing so much as the circle of More and Erasmus: not only literary cultivation and critical
stringency but an almost conspiratorial intimacy
and high spirits. The admiration in which Swift
held More and the reverence which Pope more than
once expressed for Erasmus are too well known to
need insisting on: *Gulliver's Travels* is, of course,
an example of Utopian fiction, while in one or
two respects (which I shall return to) Pope's

Praise of Dulness, the *Dunciad*, recalls *The Praise
of Folly* (and was dedicated to Swift just as *The
Praise of Folly* was to More). But more generally
the later seventeenth and early eighteenth centuries seem to have been much engaged in taking
stock of the early and middle sixteenth century,
the age of the New Learning and the Reformation.
Bishop Burnet wrote a great *History of the Reformation* and translated the *Utopia*; during Pope's lifetime *The Praise of Folly* was available in two new
versions, Samuel Knight's *Life of Erasmus* appeared
in 1726, and Nathan Bailey's standard translation
of the *Colloquies* in 1733, while a few years
earlier (1703-6) the *editio princeps* of Erasmus's
collected works had been published at Leyden.
Montaigne was newly translated by Cotton in 1685,
and the great Urquhart-Motteux translation of
Rabelais--an important event for Augustan litera-
ture--was finally completed in 1708. The *Epistolae
Obscurorum Virorum* were not translated, but were re-
rpinted in 1710, dedicated to Steele. And Pope
himself edited a selection of Latin poetry of
the Italian Renaissance. Indeed when Pope wrote
the first *Dunciad* in the 1720s, he was not (as
readers fresh to the poem often suppose) simply
scoring off his enemies by adapting a few of
the incidents in Virgil, Milton, and others to
the degraded setting of contemporary Grub-street
--although he did of course do this. But he was
also fusing together certain other traditional
kinds of writing, some of which had previously
been associated with prose. Pope's concern to
preserve the names of men who would, most of them,
otherwise have been forgotten is comparable with
the intention of the authors of the prose *Epistolae
Obscurorum Virorum* (1515, 1517). And their satirical
interest in obscure men in turn gains definition
from such a work as Petrarch's *De Viris Illustribus*,
with its characteristic Renaissance concern with
true fame. Petrarch, who stands on the threshold
of the Renaissance, seems to have invented the
concept of the Dark Ages: at the end of his epic
poem *Africa*--the first Renaissance neo-classical
epic--he affirmed the hope that the dark age in

which he was fated to live would not last for
ever: posterity would emerge again into a radi-
ance like that of antiquity.[3] Pope, at the end
of the Renaissance, closes the cycle: his poem
ushers in an age of darkness more profound than
any envisaged by Petrarch:

   And Universal Darkness buries All.

The connections of the Augustan satirists, including Pope, with the early and high Renaissance
probably deserve more attention than they have
yet received.[4]
   More precisely, it is becoming increasingly
clear[5] that the *Dunciad* owes something to a literary tradition whose chief classical exponent was
Lucian. In the sixteenth century Lucian was
particularly associated with More and Erasmus;
who both translated some of his satires and whose
Utopia and *Praise of Folly* were in part Lucianic in
inspiration; and the same is true of the *Epistolae
Obscurorum Virorum* and Rabelais's *Gargantua* (except
that in them Erasmus's own influence is also
important). These Christian humanist works have
all caught something of the Lucianic flavour: an
elusive scepticism, a vein of cool, ironical
fantasy, and an irreverent critical spirit, which
has often been attacked as merely reductive and
irresponsible.[6] (Especially useful to More and
Rabelais was Lucian's way of describing the manners of fabulous peoples, so as to produce an
unsettling sense of relativity.) The Lucianic
mode might be epitomized as a serio-comic style,
in which the extent to which the writer is in
jest or earnest is often left deliberately unclear.
   There is one direct connection between this
serio-comic tradition and the *Dunciad*. During the
Renaissance a classical *genre* was revived which
was not especially Lucianic, although Lucian did
contribute to it. This *genre* has been given the
name *adoxography*: the rhetorical praise or defence
of things of doubtful value. The writing of such
perverse or paradoxical *encomia* had been a recog-

nized rhetorical exercise in antiquity, and was
enthusiastically taken up again in the Renaissance.
A bulky collection of such writings, in Latin,
appeared in Hanover in 1619, and was followed by
other editions; it was edited by Caspar Dornavius
and called *Amphitheatrum Sapientiae Socraticae Joco-
Seriae*.[7] It includes elaborate rhetorical praises
of such things as hair (and baldness), gout,
deafness, poverty, fleas, lice, and so on; Erasmus's *Praise of Folly* is included, since that work
belongs to this *genre*; so is Lucian's *Encomium of
the Fly*.[8] There are, interestingly, several poems
in praise of Nothing--interesting because they
form precursors of Rochester's famous poem *Upon
Nothing*, which is itself probably an important
formative influence on the *Dunciad*.[9] (Pope's imitation of it, *Upon Silence*, comes into the same
genre; and, as is well known, Pope helped to improve Wycherley's 'adoxographical' poem *A Panegyric
of Dulness*.) Also included in this collection are
several works of a rather different nature, which
treat indecent or 'scatological' subjects.[10]
Considerable verbal ingenuity is lavished on these
scurrilous *nugae*, and one is strongly reminded of
some of the effects of mock-heroic: the treatment
is ludicrously verbalistic, the tone earnest, the
style solemnly elevated and necessarily much
given to circumlocution. What further anticipates
Swift and Pope--and among Pope's poems the *Dunciad*
in particular--is the combination of scholastic
method with gross and indecent subjects. The result is a manner or tone which might be called a
learned puerility.

I remarked that the *Dunciad* can be seen as
Pope's Praise of Dulness, a work which, at however great a remove, owes something to *The Praise
of Folly*. Mr. Erskine-Hill has convincingly described Pope's ambiguity of response towards the
'world' of Dulness created in the *Dunciad*, and has
related Pope's Goddess Dulness to Erasmus's Folly.
Structurally, too, *The Praise of Folly* may have
helped Pope to organize his poem. Erasmus's
Folly is presented as a kind of universal principle: every one is in some sense a fool, and Eras-

mus's ironical understanding of the multiple applications of *folly* as he uses it allows him to
embark on a survey of mankind from which no walk
of life is exempt. Between Erasmus and Pope came
Rochester, whose poem *Upon Nothing*, for all its
brevity, is similarly all-inclusive or potentially so, since every one and everything contains the principle of 'nothingness'. Like Erasmus's Folly and Rochester's Nothing, Pope's Dulness is a fundamental principle of being, and the
phrase 'great Negative' which Rochester applied to
Nothing could equally be applied to Dulness. The
concept of Dulness becomes for Pope a structural
device which makes possible a certain kind of
poem: its inclusiveness allows him to treat a
wide variety of subjects so that in the *Dunciad*.
he managed to write a poem which impinges on much
more than its subject would seem to promise. F.
R. Leavis's phrase, 'a packed heterogeneity',
which occurs in his essay on the *Dunciad*, very
aptly characterizes it.[11] In one of Pope's prefatory pieces to the *Dunciad* he says: 'And the
third book, if well consider'd, seemeth to embrace the whole world.' *The Praise of Folly* also
embraces the whole world, and like the *Dunciad* it
could be indefinitely extended: the structure
is a capacious hold-all. The author does put an
end to it, but it is possible to imagine it
given repeated additional material, as Pope found
with his poem. In this respect--its tendency to
accumulate additional material--the *Dunciad* foreshadows two other works which share a relation
to the Lucianic Rabelaisian tradition: Sterne's
Tristram Shandy and Byron's *Don Juan*. Neither is
finished, and in theory both could be (and in a
sense were) extended for as long as the author
lived. In the case of *A Tale of a Tub* and the *Dunciad*, part of their power seems to derive from
the appeal, inherent in the subject-matter, of
formlessness: both authors are overtly hostile
to the chaotic threat embodied in their subject,
but both betray a strong interest, indeed fascination, in it. In this they are interestingly different from Sterne and Byron, who are frankly

delighted by the rule of accident, the unpredict-
able flow of things, which is perceived as the
principle of Nature, the inexhaustible source of
organic form. The attitudes of Swift and Pope
are more divided: hostile on the face of it, but
in their over-all treatment of the subject more
equivocal.

The point I want to stress is this. The
traditions and *genres* of writing which I have just
been referring to were of a kind to exert a two-
sided influence. They could be liberating, but
they could also be unstabilizing; they could help
a writer to realize his creative impulse, but
they might do so at the expense of his rational
equilibrium. His powers of judgement might be
compromised by a spirit of reckless, possibly
generous, irresponsibility.

III

A comparable influence, liberating but in
some ways unsettling, might be ascribed to the
mock-heroic kind itself, to which of course the
Dunciad belongs--if it belongs to anything.

It is in the first place remarkable that some
of the best imaginative writing from the Restoration to about 1730 is mock-heroic or burlesque
or in some way parodic in form. The mock-heroic
has been very fully discussed in terms of its
literary conventions, its comic use of epical
situations, characters, diction, and so on, but
the secret of its fascination remains not wholly
accounted for. These mocking parodic forms had
been available to English writers since the sixteenth century, but they have usually taken a very
subsidiary place in the literary scene. But in
the later seventeenth and early eighteenth centuries they seem to move to the centre of things:
they attract writers of power. The result is
such works as *Mac Flecknoe, A Tale of a Tub, The Battle
of the Books, Gulliver's Travels,* and *The Beggar's Opera,*
as well as, on a lower level, Cotton's *Virgil Tra-
vestie* and his versifications of Lucian, and such
burlesque plays as Buckingham's *Rehearsal,* Gay's

What D'ye Call It, and some of Fielding's farces.
Certainly no other period in English history
shows such a predilection for these forms. Why
were so many of the best writers of the time
drawn to mock-heroic and burlesque? No doubt it
is useless to look for a single comprehensive
answer, but a partial explanation may be sought
by considering the time, the age, itself.

The period from the Restoration to Pope's
death was one whose prevailing ethos was avowedly
hostile to some of the traditional uses of the
poetic imagination. It disapproved of the romantic and fabulous, and saw little reason for the
existence of fiction. 'The rejection and contempt of fiction is rational and manly': the
author is Dr. Johnson, writing in 1780,[12] but the
attitude was common, even prevalent, during
Pope's lifetime. The literary world into which
the young Pope grew up was, it seems fair to say,
relatively poor in imaginative opportunities.
The poets writing immediately before Pope were
without fables and without myths, except those
taken in an etiolated form from classical antiquity; they seemed content with verses that made
little demand on the imaginative life of their
readers. It is suggestive that in his final collection of poems, *Fables Ancient and Modern* (1700),
Dryden drew away from contemporary manners and
affairs with versions of Ovid, Boccaccio, and
Chaucer: the fabulous and romantic are readmitted
through translation and imitation. Otherwise
the literary scene as Pope must have viewed it as
a young man was, at its best, lucidly and modestly sensible; but in feeling and imagination it
was undeniably somewhat impoverished. What
characterizes the literature of the Restoration
is a brightly lit, somewhat dry clarity, a dogmatic simplicity; it is above everything the expression of an aggressively alert rational consciousness.

Something of this imaginative depletion can be
observed in the structure of single poems. If
we leave Milton aside, the poetry of the Restoration with most life in it suffers from a certain

formal laxity: there is brilliance of detail but
often a shambling structure. Parts are added to
parts in a merely additive way, with often little
concern for the whole: poems go on and on and
then they stop. The poets often seem too close
to actual social life, as if the poetic imagination had surrendered so much of its autonomous
realm that they were reduced to a merely journalistic role; their longer poems seem to lack
'inside'. At one time Milton thought of Dryden
as 'a good rimist, but no poet'. And T. S.
Eliot's words still seem true of much of Dryden's
verse: 'Dryden's words ... are precise, they
state immensely, but their suggestiveness is
often nothing.'
    In such a period the mock-heroic and burlesque
forms seem to minister to a need for complexity.
The mock-heroic, for example, gave the poet the
possibility of making an 'extended metaphor', a
powerful instrument for poetic thought--as opposed to thought of more rationally discursive
kinds. It allowed him entry into an imaginative
space in which his mythopoeic faculties could be
freed to get to work. And yet, while offering
him a means of escape from a poetry of statement,
from a superficially truthful treatment of the
world around him, it at the same time seemed to
guarantee his status as a sensible adult person
--as a 'wit'--since what arouses laughter in the
mock-heroic is precisely a perception of the
ludicrous incongruities between the heroic fabulous world of epic and the unheroic, non-fabulous
world of contemporary society. Presumably few
people nowadays think that the essence of mock-
heroic is really mockery of the heroic, but
neither is simply the reverse true: mockery, by
means of the heroic, of the unheroic contemporary
world. It would be truer to say that the mock-
heroic poet--at his best, at any rate--discovers
a relationship of tension between the two realms,
certainly including mockery of the unheroic present, but not by any means confined to that. It
might be nearer the full truth to think of him
as setting out to exploit the relationship be-

tween the two realms, but ending up by calling a
new realm, a new world, into being.[13] And this
new realm does not correspond either to the coherent imagined world of classical epic or to the
actual world in which the poet and his readers
live and which it is ostensibly the poet's intention to satirize. It is to some extent self-
subsistent, intrinsically delightful, like the
worlds of pastoral and romance. In various ways
it gratifies an appetite, perhaps all the more
satisfyingly for doing so without the readers'
conscious awareness. And in any case, mock-
heroic, with its multiple layers of integument,
its inherent obliquity, was temperamentally
suited to a man like Pope, who 'hardly drank tea
without a stratagem'.

Before coming to the *Dunciad* I should like to
glance at Pope's first great success in mock-
heroic, *The Rape of the Lock*. It takes 'fine ladies'
as its main satirical subject, and the terms in
which the satire works are explained in Ariel's
long speech in the first canto. Since the sylphs
are the airy essences of 'fine ladies', Ariel's
object is to impress such young ladies as Belinda
with a sense of their own importance and to confirm them in their dishevelled scale of values:

> Some secret Truths from Learned Pride con-
>   ceal'd,
> To Maids alone and Children are reveal'd:
> What tho' no Credit doubting Wits may give?
> The Fair and Innocent shall still believe.

Pope characteristically blurs his moral terms,
so that his own position as a man of good sense
is represented by the ironical phrases 'Learned
Pride' and 'doubting Wits', whereas the empty-
headed young girls have access to 'secret Truths'
they are "Fair and Innocent', they shall have
faith. Such faith abhors any tincture of good
sense, for fine ladies are characterized by an
absence of good sense. They are preoccupied with
their own appearance, with the outward forms of
society, and--it is suggested--with *amours*. 'Melt-

ing Maids' are not held in check by anything corresponding to sound moral principles; they are
checked only by something as insubstantial, or
as unreal, as their 'Sylph'. Mere female caprice
or whim prevents a young girl from surrendering
her honour to the importunity of rakes. Pope is
working on a double standard: as readers of the
poem we enjoy the fiction of the sylphs, but the
satire can only work if we are also men and women
of good sense who do not confuse fiction with
fact--so that we do not 'believe in' the sylphs
any more than we 'believe in' fairies. Judged
from this sensible point of view, the sylphs are
nothing, thin air. So in answer to Ariel's question, 'What guards the purity of melting Maids?'
our sensible answer is 'Nothing': if a young
lady rejects a man's improper proposal it is
simply because--she doesn't want to accept it: she
is restrained by her 'Sylph'. For the principles
of female conduct are not rational: they are, as
Ariel says, 'mystic mazes', and sometimes mere
giddy inconstancy will happen to keep a young
lady chaste.

> When *Florio* speaks, what Virgin could with-
>   stand,
> If gentle *Damon* did not squeeze her Hand?
> With varying Vanities, from ev'ry Part,
> They shift the moving Toyshop of their
>   Heart ...

and so to the conclusive irony:

> This erring Mortals Levity may call,
> Oh blind to Truth! the *Sylphs* contrive it all.

What is the nature of Pope's poetic interest
in 'fine ladies' in *The Rape of the Lock*? From the
standpoint of men of good sense--the 'doubting
Wits' of Ariel's speech--such women are silly,
vain, and ignorant. They are of course badly
educated: they may be able to read and write a
little, but their letters, ludicrously phrased

and spelt, will only move a gentleman to condes-
cending amusement. (As Gulliver found with the
Lilliputians: 'Their manner of writing is very
peculiar, being neither from the left to the
right, like the Europeans; nor from the right to
the left, like the Arabians; nor from up to down,
like the Chinese; but aslant, from one corner of
the paper to the other, like ladies in England.')
This at least is how women, or many of them, often appeared in *The Tatler* and *The Spectator*--and how
they appeared to Pope to the extent that he was a
satirist. However, simply because women were
less rational than men, they were also, from
another point of view, more imaginative because
more fanciful than their male superiors. They
were more credulous, more superstitious, more
given to absurd notions. For if gentlemen, or
'wits', were creatures of modern enlightenment,
women could be regarded as belonging to the fabulous dark ages. Accordingly what woman, or women
of this kind, provided for a poet like Pope, a
poet working in a *milieu* of somewhat narrow and
dogmatic rationalism, was a means of entry to a
delightful world of folly and bad sense. For although Pope as a satirist pokes fun at them, he
is yet as a poet clearly fascinated by them. Women are closer than men to the fantastic and
fabulous world of older poetry, such as that of
A Midsummer Night's Dream, and it is precisely the
'fantastic' nature of women that allows Pope to
create his fantastic, fairy-like beings, the
sylphs. *The Rape of the Lock* is full of the small
objects and appurtenances of the feminine world
which arouse Pope's aesthetic interest: such
things as 'white curtains', combs, puffs, fans,
and so on. This world of the feminine sensibility
is one which offers a challenge to the larger
world of the masculine reason. The man of good
sense might laugh at it, but he could not destroy
it; and to some extent he had to recognize an
alternative system of values.
     The subject I have been keeping in mind is the
more general one of the imaginative appeal of
mock-heroic, and what I have just said about the

poetic attraction of the feminine world applies
also, with certain modifications, to the attraction of the *low*. The age in which Pope lived
seems to have been markedly aware of the high
and the low in life as in literature. The high
level of polite letters, indeed the contemporary
cult of politeness, and the genteel social tone
of the Augustan heroic couplet seem to have co-
existed with a strong awareness of what they
left out below. That is to say, in this period
of somewhat exaggerated politeness, correctness,
rationalism, there existed a correspondingly
strong interest in the low, the little, the trivial, the mean, the squalid, and the indecent--to
the extent of giving all these things expression
in imaginative writing. The structure of mock-
heroic and burlesque forms provided a means of
getting at this kind of material and thus gratifying a desire which might otherwise have been
hard to reconcile with the poet's and his readers' dignity as sensible and adult men and women.
For all Pope's and Swift's different intentions,
one can discern something distinctly similar in
Pope's sylph-attended young ladies and Swift's
Lilliputians: Pope's young ladies have something
of the aesthetic fascination of children's dolls,
while the Lilliputians--as when the army parades
on Gulliver's handkerchief--call to mind in a
rather similar way the nursery world of toy
soldiers; they are both enchantingly *below* our
level. *The Rape of the Lock* and Gulliver's Voyage
to Lilliput are undoubtedly remarkable creative
efforts: in Pope's case his poem for a good many
of his readers (and not necessarily the undiscerning many) has represented the climax of his
fictive powers: it has an achieved roundness, a
plenitude, and an affectionate warmth, for the
absence of which nothing in his later poems com-
pensates. And yet in both works--this is a matter I shall take up later--the creative impulse
seems close to something childish or childlike
in the minds of their authors.

IV

It is easy enough to see how Pope came to
value the *little* in the form it took in his earlier mock-heroic poem: the feminine and the absurd.
More problematical is the use he makes of the *low*,
especially in the form it takes in the *Dunciad*:
the gross and the obscene. I want to consider
mainly the first three books, which are mock-
heroic in a way in which the fourth is not. Each
of these books treats a different aspect of Dulness as Pope imagined it, and does so through an
appropriate action or setting. The result is to
create in each book one or two large composite
images which--such is the interest with which
Pope invests them--are exciting, or disturbing,
or even exhilarating, to contemplate. However,
as I suggested earlier, we can be said to contemplate these images only obliquely, since what
engages the foreground of our attention is the
luxuriantly profuse detail of the poem's verbal
activity. Our minds are stimulated and energized
by a ceaseless flow of wit, word-play, allusion,
and so on, which exercise a control over us almost hypnotic--and particularly important is the
arresting use of proper names. Obliquely, however, we are made aware of these larger images,
and it is these that I want very tentatively to
investigate.
    Book One presents the Grub-street poet in his
setting: Grub-street, a night town of poverty,
hunger, mercenary writers, and urban squalor.
As usual Pope is at his happiest as a poet when
dealing with a body of material which had been
frequently used before: he can then treat it
allusively, confident that his readers will be
familiar with the *kind* of material he is alluding
to. Pope came at the end of forty or fifty years
of an Augustan tradition which had taken the
topic of bad mercenary poets as itself a poetic
subject; the result was some poetry of a startling
intensity. Pope could of course take for granted
the most famous of Grub-street poems, Dryden's
Mac Flecknoe; he would certainly have known, even

if some of his readers might not, Oldham's *Satyr
Concerning Poetry* and Swift's *Progress of Poetry*; while
Juvenal's Third Satire, which Oldham had imitated,
and which Pope quoted in one of his notes to the
Dunciad, supplied the authoritative classical version of the 'Cave of Poverty and Poetry'. Oldham's imitation of part of the Juvenal includes
the following:

> The moveables of *P----ge* were a Bed [Pordage]
> For him and's Wife, a Piss-pot by its side,
> A looking-glass upon the Cupboards Head,
> A Comb-case, Candlestick and Pewter-spoon,
> For want of Plate, with Desk to write upon:
> A Box without a Lid serv'd to contain
> Few Authors, which made up his *Vatican*:
> And there his own immortal Works were laid,
> On which the barbarous Mice for hunger prey'd....

Some lines from Oldham's *Satyr upon a Printer* contain more Grub-street imagery, and end with a
horrifying simile:

> May'st thou ne'er rise to History, but what
> Poor Grubstreet Penny Chronicles relate,
> Memoirs of *Tyburn* and the mournful State
> Of Cut-purses in *Holborn*'s Cavalcade,
> Till thou thy self be the same Subject made.
> Compell'd by Want, may'st thou print Popery,
> For which, be the Carts Arse and Pillory,
> Turnips, and rotten Eggs thy Destiny.
> Maul'd worse than *Reading*, *Christian*, or *Cellier*,
> Till thou, daub'd o'er with loathsome filth,
>   appear
> Like Brat of some vile Drab in Privy found,
> Which there has lain three Months in Ordure
>   drown'd.

Images such as those of the hack writer's garret,
the bookseller's stall or post--

> The meanest Felons who thro' *Holborn* go,
> More eyes and looks than twenty Poets draw:
> If this be all, go have thy posted Name

> Fix'd up with Bills of Quack, and publick
>   Sham;
> To be the stop of gaping Prentices,
> And read by reeling Drunkards, when they
>   piss ...14

--the whole underworld of prostitute, thief, and
gamester merge in Pope's mind with such images
as the following (from an ironical dispraise of
learning):

> Let *Bodley* now in its own ruins lie,
> By th'common Hangman burnt for Heresie.
> Avoid the nasty *learned* dust, 'twill breed
> More Plagues than ever Jakes or Dunghill did.
> The want of Dulness will the World undo,
> This learning makes us mad and Rebels too.15

The *Dunciad*'s original connection with Theobald,
the restorer of Shakespeare, entailed admitting
into the poem the dulness of learning--the world
of silent libraries, unread tomes, the brains of
scholars laden with unusable *data*--and mixing it
with the socially different *milieu* of Grub-street.
Indeed in the person of Theobald, as far as
Pope was concerned, the two worlds were actually
united: he was a learned emendator, treading in
Bentley's footsteps, but he also wrote pantomime
libretti to keep himself alive.
    This is the world which Pope so allusively
and economically re-creates in the first Book of
the *Dunciad*. The question arises: why does this
Grub-street imagery arouse such an intense
response? The Grub-street mythology, which
fuses together the concerns of 'high', polite
literature with material poverty and every sort
of personal deprivation, produced--one may con-
jecture--a peculiar thrill in Pope and his contemporaries, one which may still be felt, to some
extent, by a reader of his poetry. (A single
line in the *Epistle to Arbuthnot*--'Lull'd by soft
Zephyrs thro' the broken Pane'--brilliantly e-
vokes the whole of this mythology.) No doubt

merely to glimpse such misery, degradation, and
squalor produced a fascinated shudder in some
readers. But in Pope's handling there is more
to it than that. The condition of Grub-street's
inhabitants was, above all, one of deprivation:
a state of physical need combined with a state
of mental vacuity. We may consider the two con-
stituents separately.

Pope exposed himself to a good deal of adverse
criticism, on moral and humanitarian grounds, for
taking poverty as a subject for satire. He defended himself in various ways: by citing the
authority of Juvenal, or, more often, by claiming
that what he was attacking was the *pride* of dull
writers who had only their own lack of self-
knowledge or their dishonesty to blame for land-
ing themselves in a condition which might otherwise be pitiable. But these high-minded profes-
sions of Pope do not wholly carry conviction:
one may at least feel that there must have been
more to it than that. The literary treatment of
poverty in Pope and his predecessors seems to
have something in common with the harsh comic
treatment of hunger or even starvation which is
a common feature of Spanish literature of the
sixteenth and seventeenth centuries--the constant
stress on pangs of hunger, bellies emptily rumbling, and so on, which we find in Spanish drama
and picaresque fiction. Oldham, Pope, and the
others find the subject funny, but also--it
seems--in some way interesting and stimulating.

One of the aspects of the Grub-street setting
which they give marked attention to is that of
ludicrous physical discomfort: the material conditions of life press with a harsh and unwelcome
force on the hack writer's consciousness; the
unlovely objects which furnish his garret loom
large in his vision of the world--and the fact
that they do so is given mirthful emphasis for
us because the Grub-street hack is, after all,
attempting to write *poetry* in this setting: he is
'Lull'd by soft Zephyrs thro' the broken Pane',
or as Oldham put it:

> And there his own immortal Works were laid,
> On which the barbarous Mice for hunger prey'd.

What the Grub-street setting does is to force into violent antithesis the notions of body and
mind by showing the etherially spirited poet of
tradition yoked to a clumsy machine of a body
which constantly craves to be fed, clothed,
warmed, and cleaned. Such a poet drags out a
doleful existence--which we are invited to find
funny--in a world of unsympathetic *objects*, an
environment totally hostile to and unsuggestive
of mental and literary activity. The traditional
garret setting seems to make the writing of po-
etry--any poetry--absurd; it derides it. And it
derides it, it calls in question the necessity
of its existence, by insisting on the primacy of
matter, mere things, mere bodies. The Grub-
street myth is primarily a Restoration creation:
it has some classical prototypes, but it makes
its full appearance in English poetry in the
satires of Marvell, Rochester, Oldham, and others,
and it may be that its strong appeal is to be
related to the rise of the new philosophy with
its strong bias against the poetic and the
imaginative. Such poets as Oldham may have seen
in the reduced condition of the Grub-street poet
as they imagined him, a grotesque reflection of
the impoverishment of themselves. And so the
peculiarly radical nature of the challenge put
to the poet by the Grub-street myth was one to
arouse powerful and mixed feelings: an intense
curiosity (possibly unconscious of its own motive)
intense mirth, and perhaps a vague feeling of
alarm. There seems at times something almost
hysterical in the violent response of such a poet as Oldham.

But there is another side to the subject.
Poverty reduced the hack poet to a man struggling
for survival amidst unfriendly objects; and one
way in which Pope and his predecessors exploit
the Grub-street theme is to insist on the gross
materiality of *poems*, to focus attention on the
poem not as a mental artefact but as so many

pages of solid paper, something that can be eaten
by mice, burnt for fuel, used for 'wrapping Drugs
and Wares' (Oldham), lining trunks (Pope), or, as
Oldham put it, addressing the hack poet:

> Then who'll not laugh to see th' immortal Name
> To vile *Mundungus* made a Martyr flame?
> And all thy deathless Monuments of Wit,
> Wipe Porters Tails, or mount in Paper-kite?[16]

Both Oldham and Rochester degrade poetry further
even than this by zestfully comparing it to ex-
crement--a peculiarly Restoration conceit. Of
course the satirical target in such passages is
ostensibly *bad* poetry, but the satirical strategy
is such as to involve good poetry--poetry of
whatever quality--along with it. In the *Dunciad*
Pope too uses this theme, but with less intensity
than the Restoration satirists. The action of
Book One takes place, we may say, in the archetypal Grub-street night, with Cibber writing in
his garret surrounded by the fragments of his
literary efforts:

> Round him much Embryo, much Abortion lay,
> Much future Ode, and abdicated Play;
> Nonsense precipitate, like running Lead,
> That slipp'd thro' Cracks and Zigzags of the
>   Head ...

and later, in despair, he addresses some of his
literary works (his 'better and more christian
progeny') before consigning them to the flames:

> Ye shall not beg, like gratis-given Bland,
> Sent with a Pass, and vagrant thro' the land;
> Not sail, with Ward, to Ape-and-monkey climes,
> Where vile Mundungus trucks for viler rhymes;
> Not sulphur-tipt, emblaze an Ale-house fire;
> Not wrap up Oranges, to pelt your Sire!

--the last line one of Pope's brilliant effects
of agile concentration. Poems ('papers of verses') had frequently been made to wrap foodstuffs

in satires before Pope, but to make them wrap
oranges for theatre audiences to use as missiles
is a new refinement. Pope uses the theme of the
materiality of literary works with much less emotional involvement than his Restoration forebears,
but the topic still has enough life in it to
arouse him to considerable artistic excitement.
His treatment of Cibber here is less ferocious
than Oldham would have made it, but more elaborate and ingenious. And Pope's verse is of course
rhetorically orchestrated, shaped, and climaxed
in a fashion beyond Oldham's reach.

This aspect of the Grub-street setting has to
do with the hack poet's physical need, his uncom-
fortable awareness of his physical environment.
The other aspect I mentioned concerned the poet's
own *mental* poverty. To some extent what I have
said of the materiality of poetry has already
touched on this. For the bad poet's mental
vacuity, his mental dulness, is imagined in terms
of solid inert matter, heaviness, retarding fric-
tion, torpor, and so on, in a manner learnt from
Dryden's example in *Mac Flecknoe*. The whole topic
has been admirably treated by D. W. Jefferson.[17]
Like Dryden, Pope is keenly stimulated by images
of solidity and inertness--he has a remarkably
sensitive insight into insensitivity.

I am suggesting that images such as these of
the sordid and the grossly material are as exciting to Pope as they are repulsive. The deprived
social underworld of Grub-street presented a
challenge and stimulus to a poet who was placed
in a position of social comfort and even superiority; as did the spectacle of insensitivity to
a mind acutely sensitive. In both, the poet of
consciousness and wit can be said to be contemplating a form of the mindless. A further related aspect of Pope's treatment of Dulness might
be called the challenge of the unconscious to a
mind keenly conscious, perhaps even over-confident-
ly so. This is an area of my subject about which
I want to remain tentative, and which I will approach somewhat obliquely.

There is in the further dim recesses of the
Dunciad a region of Dulness, created for us by
hints and allusions, which is an important element in the imaginative impact of the poem. It
is there in Cibber's address to his literary
offspring:

> O! pass more innocent, in infant state,
> To the mild limbo of our Father Tate:
> Or peaceably forgot, at once be blest,
> In Shadwell's bosom with eternal rest!

as well as in single lines like that describing
the poets of Grub-street:

> Sleepless themselves, to give their readers
>   sleep

or the dunce's 'Gothic Library', where

> high above, more solid learning shone,
> The Classics of an Age that heard of none.

This is an elusive region, but recognizable to
anyone familiar with the poem: a vast dim hinter-
land of book-writing, book-reading, and book-
learning, not so much a dream of learning as a
nightmare of dead knowledge. This striking fantasy seems essentially a late-Renaissance phenomenon, something peculiar to a period not too far
removed from the first age of print to have altogether lost its sense of the power and objectivity
of printed books, but so late in the era of
humanism that its sense of the closing of a cycle
was very strong.[18] Milton had said that 'books
are not absolutely dead things', and that a good
book was 'the precious life blood of a master
spirit, embalmed and treasured up on purpose to a
life beyond life'. Pope, in effect, shows that
bad books too do not die, but if they do not
achieve the empyrean of fame they are at least
consigned to an eternity in limbo, a place of
soft, gently decaying verbal matter--'the mild
limbo of our Father Tate'. Pope is sounding the

great Augustan theme--it is of course a lasting
pre-occupation of humanism--of the use of knowledge: how to make knowledge live by making it
useful to the real business of living. Cibber,
about to burn his own literary productions, says
they are

> Soon to that mass of Nonsense to return,
> Where things destroy'd are swept to things
>   unborn

--and an obscure region is evoked where things
not dead, but dormant or only potentially alive,
maintain their phantom-like existence. They lurk
in a kind of lumber-room of the mind, useless and
irrelevant, in a manner comparable to the physical
fate of the dead in Rochester's powerful line:
'Dead, we become the Lumber of the World'.[19] (The
word _lumber_--'old furniture'---ike _frippery_--'old
clothes'--is a favourite with Augustan writers,
and is often given imaginative definition by the
opposite concept of _use_. Pope finds a place for
both words in the _Dunciad_.[20])
There is, I think, a strange intensity in
these glimpses into a limbo of the mind, not altogether explained by the Augustan commonplace
concerning useless knowledge. Pope seems to be
communicating here, however obscurely and momentarily, a sense of non-conscious life--a form of
vitality which is alien to the conscious mind and
felt to be a threat to it. It is of interest
that the word _unconscious_ first makes it appearance in English a few years before the _Dunciad_;[21]
and indeed Pope's own image in Book Two of an
'unconscious' pool is a suggestive one:

> No noise, no stir, no motion canst thou make,
> Th' unconscious stream sleeps o'er thee like
>   a lake.

In this connection--Pope's poetic interest in
mindlessness, which is one form of Dulness--
Lancelot Law Whyte's book _The Unconscious before
Freud_ (1962) is illuminating: its theme is 'the

development of European man from over-emphasis of
self-consciousness to recognition of the unconscious'.[22] Especially valuable in Whyte's book
is his anthology of sayings from writers of the
two and a half centuries before Freud. Pascal is
quoted: '... never does reason override the
imagination, whereas the imagination often un-
seats reason', and the remark has its value in
this context. Another, which would certainly
have been known to Pope, is from Dryden: '...
long before it was a play; when it was only a
confused mass of thoughts, tumbling over one
another in the dark; when the fancy was yet in
its first work, moving the sleeping images of
things towards the light....'[23] The *Dunciad* seems
to have a peculiarly rich commerce with this
twilight zone where intuitions have not yet been
polished and clarified into an acceptable good
sense. For what Pope as a deliberate satirist
rejects as dully lifeless his imagination communicates as obscurely energetic--states of being
densely, but often unconsciously, animated. Pope
himself was undoubtedly committed to defending
conscious mental alertness, vigilance, keen
critical activity. Yet the poem as a whole makes
us aware of the possibility of another tenable
attitude, the value of what the Cambridge Platonist Ralph Cudworth called, in speaking of the
mind's powers, 'a drowsy unawakened cogitation'.[24]
In *The Castle of Indolence* (to take a slighter poem
than the *Dunciad* and a far simpler case, but one
not far removed in time) Thomson eventually
works round to a useful moral recommending 'Industry', but what is agreed to be the best part
of the poem celebrates the allure of 'Indolence'.
Nearly a hundred years after the first *Dunciad*
Keats was to take the theme much further so as to
make plain the association of Indolence, or Dulness in one of its senses, with artistic creativity.

V

I take my last ambiguous image of Dulness from
a part of the poem which has hardly been the most

popular or appreciated: the second Book. This
Book, which describes the heroic games of the
dunces, is the most notorious part of the poem,
perhaps the most notorious part of all Pope's
works. Here the satire against the booksellers,
critics, patrons, and Grub-street writers takes
the form of making them go through ludicrous actions of a humiliating and even disgustingly
sordid nature. At least, this is one way of
looking at it--although a way which takes a rather external view of the actual working of the
poetry. For this is not, I think, what it feels
like to read. What the Book communicates is a
curious warmth, a gusto, even a geniality--which,
notably, G. Wilson Knight has testified to and
described.25 Certainly Pope lavished a good deal
of work on this Book, and most of it is admirably
written. He might have been expected to have
shied away from it himself when he revised the
Dunciad. But far from that, he carefully improved
it, and added to it, making it the second longest
of the four Books.

First of all, what is the dominant effect of
Book Two--apart from its indecency? Some of the
power of its imaginative conception comes from
the fact that the action now moves out of the
Grub-street garret into the more publicly exposed
setting of the City of London, but a city fan-
tastically simplified, seen as in dream. This is
London seen as Lud's-town--or Dul-town, as Pope
brings out in a couplet in the 1728 version (its
leaden thud was sacrificed in the recasting):

> Slow moves the Goddess from the sable flood,
> (Her Priest preceding) thro' the gates of Lud.

'Dul-town' is inhabited not by starving poets
but by vividly felt, if faceless, presences who
are sometimes infantile and sometimes maniac.
(The notion of an *infant* can be related to the
Dunciad's verbal and literary concerns through its
literal meaning: 'a person unable to speak or
use words'.)

Wilson Knight has remarked on the absence of
cruelty in this narrative of the games. On the
contrary, every one is having a wonderful time,
for within the imaginative world of the poem no
one is conscious of humiliation. These dunces
are, in fact, like unabashed small children--but
children viewed with the distance and distaste
of the Augustan adult. The world they inhabit is,
like that of early infancy, wholly given to feeling and sensation, and so all the activities are
of a simple physical nature: they run races, have
urinating, tickling, shouting, and diving compe-
titions, and finally vie with each other in keeping awake until 'the soft gifts of Sleep conclude
the day'. The poetic atmosphere is soft and
delicate, the feelings expressed by the dunces
playful, occasionally petulant, but essentially
affectionate. As a satirist Pope is of course
degrading his enemies: all the characters are
given the names of actual persons. Yet, as usual,
the poetry is doing something more interesting
than a narrowly satirical account would suggest.
What it is doing, in part, is creating a world
free of adult and social restraints. 'Here strip,
my children!' cries their mother Dulness at one
point, and they strut about naked, play games,
quarrel, and shout, as free of inhibition and
shame as any small infant. Pope evokes the unrestrained glee of childhood, its unthinking sensuality (as in the tickling match) and the deafening noise made by children at play:

> Now thousand tongues are heard in one loud
>   din;
> The monkey-mimics rush discordant in;
> 'Twas chatt'ring, grinning, mouthing, jabb'ring
>   all,
> And Noise and Norton, Brangling and Breval ...

The world of Book Two seems in many way a version of pre-literate infancy, and to enter it is
to experience a primitive sense of liberation.
Not only is it innocent; it is completely without self-consciousness: again Pope's poetic con-

cern is with a form of unconscious vitality. The
comparison of the dunces with small children,
however, is only implicit; it does not exhaust
the whole of the poetic image. The dunces are,
after all, not in fact children, and in so far
as they are adult they call to mind the inhabitants of Bedlam, madmen resembling small children
in being without restraint and without manners.
Bedlam is one of the places which Pope is careful to include on his simplified map of London:
in the first Book it is said to be close to the
'Cave of Poverty and Poetry' which is Cibber's
Grub-street residence. In this second Book the
implicit Bedlamite metaphor becomes more insistent. (One of the prints in the early editions of
A *Tale of a Tub* gives an intensely dismal picture
of Bedlam hospital: naked madmen lie chained on
filthy mattresses in a large cell, while being
peered at through grills by members of the public.)
     Let me give an example of a dunce who combines
qualities of infantility with the manic energy
of a madman. This is Blackmore in the shouting
competition:

     But far o'er all, sonorous Blackmore's strain;
     Walls, steeples, skies, bray back to him again.
     In Tot'nham fields, the brethren, with amaze,
     Prick all their ears up, and forget to graze;
     Long Chanc'ry-lane retentive rolls the sound,
     And courts to courts return it round and round;
     Thames wafts it thence to Rufus' roaring hall,
     And Hungerford re-echoes bawl for bawl.

It is as if this dunce has grown to a figure of
Brobdingnagian size, or as if the City has
shrunk to the dimensions of a toy-town with a
child standing astride over it. Aubrey Williams's
account of this passage is a good example of his
method. He shows that the place-names mentioned
here are chosen to mark Westminster's boundaries,
so that the voice of Blackmore the 'City Bard'
resounding all over Westminster represents the
invasion of the West End by dulness.[26] His com-

mentary is helpful and entirely convincing, but
such an account may have the effect of shielding
us from the full impact of the image as Pope has
conceived it. For the image of deafening, gigant-
esque noise--as of a giant *shouting* over London--
is, though comic, a disturbingly powerful one;
and although it has an allegorical meaning which
we should know, the image itself in all its rude
force ought, it seems to me, to come first. This
after all is what one remembers after reading the
Book: the games themselves, not what they 'stand
for'; the poetic fiction is primary.
   No doubt most readers of Pope will never do
other than shrink from this second Book. But if
one is willing to explore it, one beneficial result might be a clearer perception of Pope's
extraordinarily rich, but undoubtedly very
strange, sensibility. It seems possible that the
impression of an unusual degree of creative re-
lease given by such parts of the *Dunciad* as these
is due to Pope's being able to indulge intense
feelings of an infantile nature by taking advantage of the permissive decorum of mock-heroic.
There is a quality of complicity in the writing
--'Heav'n rings with laughter' (ii. 121), and
the mirth seems to include both poet and reader--
that makes it hard to bear in mind that, from
the 'satirical' point of view, such writing is
supposed to show Pope making a fierce retaliatory
attack on his enemies. But so often this other
point of view, which occasionally finds expression in Pope's own notes, seems to belong to a
quite different mood and spirit. One of Pope's
notes to the second Book opens in a tone of high
moral indignation: 'In this game is expos'd in
the most contemptuous manner, the profligate
licentiousness of those shameless scriblers....'
But the corresponding part of the poem reads:

   See in the circle next, Eliza plac'd,
   Two babes of love close clinging to her
      waist ...

The poetry, as Wilson Knight says, has a 'nature
tone', and it seems not altogether absurd to find

here a certain real tenderness--of course set
against the incongruously risible circumstances,
but none the less a modifying element in the full
poetic effect. In a similar way the account of
the mud-diving and the encounter with the mud-
nymphs is, as several critics have remarked,
strangely attractive, and has the effect of rob-
bing the huge open sewer of Fleet-ditch, the actual scene of the action, of its horrible offensive-
ness. The effect is quite un-Swiftian, not
nasty in the reading. In a related way such a
passage as the following achieves an inimitably
Popian beauty:

> Thro' Lud's fam'd gates, along the well-known
>   Fleet
> Rolls the black troop, and overshades the
>   street,
> 'Till show'rs of Sermons, Characters, Essays,
> In circling fleeces whiten all the ways:
> So clouds replenish'd from some bog below,
> Mount in dark volumes, and descend in snow.

This draws its vitality from its absorption of
'base' matter into forms pleasurable to contemplate and from an attitude to experience which
refuses to find anything repulsive or offensive:
the 'disagreeables' are evaporated.
   But the element of the obtrusively childish
and dirty in this part of the *Dunciad* remains an
issue to be faced. Pope often seems to have been
attracted to indecent or equivocal subjects, as
if he derived a stimulus from affronting conventional good taste: indeed, of all the considerable
English poets he remains perhaps the one with
the greatest power to shock--no doubt partly because the social restraints which make the sense
of shock possible are themselves powerfully represented in his verse. However we may respond
to this side of Pope, it does not seem helpful
to call it 'immature', since it may well have
been an indispensable part of his creative temperament. Indeed Pope might have been a less comprehensive poet, even a less balanced one, with-

out it. It has been suggested that during this
period 'various forms of play and irresponsibility
may have been a chief outlet for the poetic impulse';[27] and certainly without their disconcertingly childish side not only Pope but also his
fellow Scriblerians Swift and Gay would be considerably less forceful and original writers. Ambrose Philips's undistinguished, if innocuous,
little poems addressed to children (such as those
written for the Pulteney girls: one is dated
1724, another 1727, the years immediately preceding the first *Dunciad*) were mercilessly attacked
and parodied (e.g. by Henry Carey as well as by
Pope[28]), presumably because they contravened the
current assumption that childish feelings might
be indulged obliquely in comic and parodic forms
but not expressed directly in all their unwitty
vulnerability. For the Augustans, Pope included,
mock-heroic provided the perfect protective form
for the expression of childish feelings, since
(as I suggested earlier) its built-in critical
apparatus served to absolve the poet from a possible charge of too outrageous an irresponsibility.
Similarly such versicles as Henry Carey's and
Pope's Lilliputian Odes (written, for the most
part, in lines of two and three syllables respectively) take advantage of the Lilliputian fiction for writing of an undiluted frivolity.

VI

In what I have been saying I have been deliberately stressing one side of Pope's genius: the
peculiar *energy* of his poetry and its power to excite. I want finally to add a few remarks on
this subject from a rather different point of
view.
The *Dunciad* is so often discussed simply in
terms of its topics, its ideas, attitudes, literary conventions, etc., or its individual effects
of wit--its grotesque metaphors, its low puns,
its studiedly indecorous diction--that it might
seem that the poem as a whole was fully accounted
for. Yet something more fundamental seems to

escape such discussions: everything that can be
included under the idea of *form*--the over-all
shape of the poetic experience, the contributions
made by Pope's use of the couplet, the paragraph,
the episode and each Book of the poem. When Pope
is writing well, the verse moves with a strong
purposefully directed energy, the couplets are
pointed, the paragraphs draw to a climax, and the
individual Books each have a true conclusion--
they do not merely stop. The couplets, for example, are never allowed to succeed each other in a
merely additive way; instead they are held firmly
in place in the verse paragraph, and the paragraph itself often follows a large rhythmic curve
which makes possible a dynamic verse movement.
When read with a sympathetic mimetic co-operation,
such verse has an exceptional capacity to arouse
nervous excitement. However, this energy sometimes has an ambiguous effect, which may be such
that an account of the poem which stays too close
to its satirical paraphrasable meaning may distort the real effect of the poetry.

In his liking for exuberant or agitated movement, for vehement emphasis, and for intense
surface vivacity, Pope reveals himself as baroque
in sensibility; as he does in his nervous sense
of tempo, especially at those moments when he
gathers speed for an overwhelming climax.[29] Among
English poets in this one respect his true predecessor is Crashaw, whom Pope had read carefully
and used, although it is not necessary to suppose that he needed Crashaw to discover these
qualities in himself: there were numerous other
influences. But nowhere in seventeenth-century
English poetry except in the *Hymn to Saint Teresa*
and the magnificent, and in some ways curiously
Popian,[30] *Music's Duel*, can one find a comparable
verve and ardour, such an acute response to sen-
sory experience, or such a flamboyantly dynamic
sense of movement.

These qualities are to be found in all Pope's
greater poems, not least in the work he was engaged on immediately before the first *Dunciad*:
the translation of Homer. This, in its energy,

its sustained 'elasticity' (Pope's term[31]), and
in the way in which its personages are so often
posed in brilliant theatrically lit *tableaux*, can
certainly be seen as an outstanding example of the
late baroque sensibility in poetry. In a comparable way the fantastic action of the *Dunciad* also
allowed Pope to devise forms amenable to baroque
taste. Some baroque art seems designed to express movement or animation almost for its own
sake; and Dulness, as imagined by Pope--anarchic,
'busy, bold, and blind'--encouraged the invention
of such effects as those in the passage I have
already quoted:

> 'Till show'rs of Sermons, Characters, Essays,
> In circling fleeces whiten all the ways:
> So clouds replenish'd from some bog below,
> Mount in dark volumes, and descend in snow

--with its repeated swirling movement, an effect
which receives a number of variations:

> Not with more glee, by hands Pontific crown'd,
> With scarlet hats wide-waving circled round ...

and

> As man's Maeanders to the vital spring
> Roll all their tides, then back their circles
>   bring ...

The sensibility which took pleasure in these and
similar effects informs the entire poem, and,
despite all the personal and topical allusions
and all the brilliant local explosions of wit,
sets going (in the first three Books at least) a
powerful current of feeling; at times the larger
movements take on a demonic momentum. This may
be felt particularly in the concluding phases of
the Books, which are given an emphasis as if each
Book were a self-contained poem.[32] Throughout
his career the endings of Pope's poems are conspicuously strong and deeply felt: indeed some
of his poems sound at their conclusions an almost

apocalyptic note--a desire to relate the poetic
subject to ultimate ends. In the *Elegy to the
Memory of an Unfortunate Lady* the poet finally anticipates his own death, the end of time for himself, while in *Eloisa to Abelard* the heroine looks
forward to as far in the future as her story
will be read--which may again be interpreted as
the end of time. And *The Rape of the Lock* has an
ending whose startling power has to do with its
looking forward to the death of Belinda, and
again to an eternity made possible by poetry. In
the *Dunciad* the first and third Books both end on
sustained climactic movements; both record, in a
high incantatory strain, a visionary moment when
the order of things as they are, appears to be
dissolving to give place to a totally different
order. In the first version Book Three (originally, of course, the final Book) ends with the
uplifted strains of Settle's prophecy--in the
last line of which Pope's own name is introduced
--before entering upon the great Conclusion to
the whole poem. And this Conclusion is an ending
in the grandest possible sense: the end of Nature
itself.

The Conclusion to the *Dunciad* is uninterruptedly
solemn and sublime: indeed its sublimity may be
felt to be somewhat disconcertingly absolute.
It seems entirely in keeping with the mode of
the poem that we do not, perhaps, quite know how
to take it; and indeed in the first version a
note by Pope introduces a sense of wavering or
qualification into the reader's mind.[33] In the
same version the poem ends with a couplet which
'contains' the vision of 'Universal Darkness' and
consigns it to the realm of false dreams:

'Enough! enough!' the raptur'd Monarch cries;
And thro' the Ivory Gate the Vision flies.

But in the final version of 1743 the Conclusion
is no longer framed by this couplet, but ends
uncompromisingly with

> Thy hand, great Anarch! lets the curtain fall;
> And Universal Darkness buries All.

And there is no note here to suggest that the
poet is not fully committed to what his poem is
saying. The Conclusion has become a final,
grandiose, annihilating gesture, sublime but also
grotesque--for it is surely hugely disproportionate, not really prepared for in terms of the
poem's own fiction. Moreover it has the effect,
not uncommon in baroque paintings, of overflowing
the bounds of the frame so as to engulf the
spectator. Pope is of course cornering the
reader, forcing upon him an acknowledgement of
his responsibility, pulling him into the world
of the poem--by making the poem reach out to him.
But even here, it seems to me, where Pope is at
his greatest as a poet of prophecy and lament,
our feelings are not simple, nor simply tragic,
and in one part of our minds we move through the
Conclusion with a powerful sense of pleasure:
the emotional drive of the poem, its baroque af-
flatus, seem to require a consummation as absolute as this. Pope's imaginative desire for
completeness, for making an end, is here fused
with his poetic delight in images of cataclysmic
destruction. It is an important part of his
greatness as a poet that he could not only recognize, judge, and repudiate the anarchic but feel
within himself its vitality and excitement, and
communicate what he felt. So it is here in the
Conclusion. The poet at once succumbs to and
defies the power of Dulness; and what destroys
the world completes the poem.

APPENDIX

THE CONCLUSION TO THE *DUNCIAD*

It has apparently not been noticed that as a
poetic unit the Conclusion to the *Dunciad* was probably, though in a very general way, modelled on
Ovid's account of the coming of the Iron Age
(*Metamorphoses*, i. 125-50).

In Book One Pope had written of Dulness:

Here pleas'd behold her mighty wings outspread
To hatch a new Saturnian age of Lead. (27-8)

To which he appended a note: 'The ancient Golden
Age is by Poets stiled *Saturnian*: but in the
Chymical language *Saturn* is Lead. She is said
here only to be spreading her wings to hatch this
age; which is not produced completely till the
fourth book.' Pope here probably has in mind
Ovid's account of the four ages (Gold, Silver,
Brass, Iron), so that the Golden Age of Dulness
--Pope's 'new Saturnian age of Lead'--corresponds
to Ovid's last, and worst, Iron Age.
   The best-known version of the *Metamorphoses* in
English was that in heroic couplets (1626) by
George Sandys, whom Dryden had called 'the best
versifier of the former age' (*Preface to the Fables*).
Pope had read Sandys's translation as a child
and had 'liked [it] extremely' ('Spences's *Anec-
dotes*', ed. James Osborn, 1966, vol. i, 14).
Sandys translates the coming of the Iron Age as
follows (it is not, as it happens, a particularly
good speciment of his style):

   Next unto this succeeds the *Brazen Age*;
   Worse natur'd, prompt to horrid warre, and
        rage:
   But yet not wicked. Stubborn *Yr'n* the last.
   Then, blushlesse crimes, which all degrees
        surpast,
   The World surround. Shame, Truth, and Faith
        depart:
   Fraud enters, ignorant in no bad Art;
   Force, Treason, and the wicked love of gain.
   Their sails, those winds, which yet they knew
        not, strain:
   And ships, which long on loftie Mountains
        stood,
   Then plow'd th'unpractis'd bosome of the
        Flood.
   The Ground, as common earst as Light, or Aire,
   By limit-giving Geometry they share.

Nor with rich Earth's just nourishments con-
      tent,
For treasure they her secret entrailes rent,
The powerful Evill, which all power invades,
By her well hid, and wrapt in Stygian shades.
Curst Steele, more cursed Gold she now forth
      brought:
And bloody-handed Warre, who with both fought:
All live by spoyle. The Host his Guest be-
      trayes;
Sons, Fathers-in-law: 'twixt Brethren love
      decayes.
Wives husbands, Husbands wives attempt to kill.
And cruell Step-mothers pale poysons fill.
The Sonne his Fathers hastie death desires:
Foild Pietie, trod underfoot, expires.
Astraea, last of all the heavenly birth,
Affrighted, leaves the blood-defiled Earth.

(I have quoted from the edition of 1640, page 2.)
There is no doubt that Pope used Book One of the
Metamorphoses elsewhere in the Conclusion, since
his note to lines 637-8--

As Argus' eyes by Hermes' wand opprest,
Clos'd one by one to everlasting rest;

--refers to the source in *Metam*. i. 686-7, 713-
14.
   Ovid's description and Pope's Conclusion share
a concern with a rapid decline or degeneration
in human life. In structure too they have a good
deal in common: like so many of the great set-
pieces in the *Metamorphoses*, this one proceeds by
enumerating circumstances line by line, working
by accumulation to a climax--a procedure adapted
here by Pope. But only the first twenty-six
lines of Pope's Conclusion (627-52) are modelled
on Ovid: his final four lines, in which Dulness
is apostrophized, are his own invention:

Lo! thy dread Empire, CHAOS! is restor'd;
Light dies before thy uncreating word:
Thy hand, great Anarch! lets the curtain fall;
And Universal Darkness buries All.

The fact that Sandys's verse paragraph also fills
twenty-six lines suggests that Pope used Sandys,
rather than the original Latin, as a structural
model. Moreover Pope's lines 649-52 are close in
substance and tone to the last four of Sandys,
and in the case of one line (650)--which was, in
fact, added only in the final version--has one
identical word, also in the final position:

> *Religion* blushing veils her sacred fires,
> And unawares *Morality* expires.
> Nor *public* Flame, nor *private*, dares to shine;
> Nor *human* Spark is left, nor Glimpse *divine*!

Of course the effects made by Ovid's description and Pope's Conclusion are very different.
Pope transforms Ovid's description by substituting his own more abstractly metaphysical circumstances and building up to a far grander climax.
But quite as important is the placing of each
passage within the poem as a whole. In Pope's
hands the Ovidian set-piece is removed from its
place within the seemingly endless sequence of
the *Metamorphoses* to a position right at the end
of a long poem, unsoftened (in the final version)
by any narrative framework, and left to make its
full impact in all its massive abruptness.
  Pope's Conclusion (unlike Johnsons's in *Rasselas*
is a conclusion in which *everything* is concluded.
And just as the whole poem works up to the great
Conclusion, so the Conclusion itself works up to
the immensely resonant last line:

> And Universal Darkness buries All.

The line had an earlier form, in which Pope
tried out 'Dulness' and 'cover' in place of 'Dark-
nexx' and 'buries'. Sutherland also notes three
lines in Pope's *Iliad* which anticipate it (iv.
199, vi. 73--he wrongly cites 199--and xii. 80);
and Constance Smith in a note, 'An Echo of Dryden in Pope' (*Notes and Queries*, N.S. xii, 1965,
451), suggests as a closer parallel, line 117
in Dryden's 'Last Parting of Hector and Andro-
mache' from *Iliad*, vi:

    And Universal Ruine cover all

--only this parallel having the words *Universal*
and *cover* (which Pope had used in the 1728 *Dunciad*). Two other parallels that I would add are
from Crashaw's *Music's Duel*, 156:

    A full-mouth *Diapason* swallowes all

and from Creech's translation of Manilius's
Astronomicon (1697, p. 52):

    Earth would not keep its place, the *Skies* would
        fall,
    And universal Stiffness deaden All.

There are no doubt other examples of this form
of verse-sentence, with a similarly placed verb
and a final *All*. These lines are all concerned
with striving to accomplish something absolute
and final--to swallow, cover, deaden, bury, *all*;
their quasi-erotic energy is very characteristic
of baroque sensibility. Among the poets who
use this form of line, however, Pope achieves unquestionably the greatest effect. In his final
version of the *Dunciad*, by virtue of its perfect
phrasing and by being placed last in a long poem,
the line reaches what seems an ultimate degree of
intensity.

POPE'S ILLUSIVE TEMPLE OF INFAMY

Michael Rosenblum

One of the peculiarities of the modern sensibility is its admiration for works which are about themselves: poems about the writing of poetry, or even more familiar, novels about the writing (and the reading) of novels. We have known for a long time that *Tristram Shandy* is not an oddity, but only recently have we begun to think of it as in some ways the typical novel. A writer is self-conscious when he sees the activity in which he is engaged as problematic, and for us to be self-conscious seems to be more natural than to be un-self-conscious. If this is true, then I think satire can legitimately lay claim to being a genre suited to the modern taste because it was self-conscious a long time before modern exercises in literary introversion became fashionable.[1] From its beginnings, satire has been considered problematic as moral activity and as art.

The lyric poet need not justify his impulse to song, but the satirist does because he seems to choose to sing of the deformed, the vicious, and the absurd. The traditional charge against the

This essay first appeared in *The Satirist's Art*, ed. H. James Jensen and Malvin R. Zirker, Jr. (Bloomington: Indiana University Press, 1972), pp. 28-54.

satirist is that he expresses his own pathology
rather than the sickness that he claims to observe in the society around him. The satirist
is a man with a bias, in some striking cases literally thrown off balance by curvature of the
spine, a clubfoot, or affliction of the middle
ear. A more psychologically acute version of this
charge is that what the satirist pretends to discover in his target may well be a projection of
the same vice within himself. Kenneth Burke observes that "the satirist attacks in others the
weaknesses and temptations that are really within himself." Satire is then "an approach from
without to something within."[2]
     The satirist has ready answers for his cri-
tics, has in fact been elaborating and passing
down a defense of his art to succeeding generations of satirists. According to his own self-
portrait, he is the most moral of men, the sworn
enemy of vice and folly, the doctor who purges
and heals a sick society, the defender of civilization against its enemies. Moreover, he does
not choose to write satire: faced with the
spectacle of Augustan Rome or Augustan England
or twentieth-century Los Angeles, and the energy
and persistence of the knaves and fools who inhabit them, it is difficult not to write satire.
As Pope says, "Fools rush into my head, and so
I write."[3] The satirist finds it easy to don the
robes of virtue--what in Pope's case Maynard Mack
describes as the "now almost seamless garment
formed of ancient Rome and Twickenham and seventeenth-century retirement precedents, which signalized the posture of the honest satirist protesting a corrupt society."[4]
     Even if the satirist convinces us that his
work is morally justified, there is still the
question of whether it can be much good as art.
According to a long tradition satire is the bastard genre, a farrago, a mixed dish, a hastily
set down affair without the style and unity of
the more elevated genres. Horace asks is it
Lucillus' own fault or "his rugged themes that
denied him smoothness?" (Satires, I, X, 56-9),

and Pope makes that question the epigraph for his
"versification" of Donne's satires. The answer
often given is that the genre itself makes attention to formal values difficult. One doesn't re-
fine and polish when the times demand a bold,
truthful voice. Moreover, the nature of the subject matter imposes limitations: the poet may
know how to treat Aeneas, but what if his subject
is Curll or Colley Cibber? Speaking of the epic
games in Book II of *The Dunciad*, Pope points out
that "if we consider that the Exercises of his
Authors could with justice be no higher than *Tickling, Chatt'ring, Braying,* or *Diving*, it was no easy
matter to invent such Games as were proportion'd
to the meaner degree of *Booksellers* . . . with whom
it had been great impropriety to have joined any
but vile ideas . . ."[5] Satire's decorum demands
"vile ideas." The poet can only hope that what
Addison says of Virgil in *The Georgics* would be
true of him: he "tosses about his Dung with an
air of Majesty." Finally, how can a poem be expected to survive if it depends on the reader's
knowledge of particulars which are anything but
timeless? No matter, satire can be an inferior
genre artistically since morality is its primary
concern. It is permissible for Lucillus' stream
to be muddy. The satirist often even appears
willing to offer up his rough, fragmentary poem
as evidence of his moral seriousness. As Pope
says, "Truth guards the Poet, sanctifies the
line, / And makes Immortal, Verse as mean as
mine" (*Epilogue to the Satires: Dialogue II*).
    What satirists have said about themselves--
that they are moralists first and only incidentally artists--is reflected in scholarly criticism
of satire. According to this view, the satirist
is really a kind of rhetorician. No matter how
distorted the satirist's fictions, no matter how
obliquely he equates his fictional world with the
outside world, ultimately he is writing about
something which exists outside the frame of his
own work, something that "refers beyond the page"
to a situation that has a historical basis and
which he wants us to condemn: Thus according to

Sheldon Sacks "a satire is a work organized so
that it ridicules objects external to the fictional world created in it." Ronald Paulson argues that "however much mimesis or representation
is involved, the generic end is rhetorical."[6]
     If satire's reflexiveness, its concern with
its own form, makes it seem like a genre congenial to modern taste, the rhetorical view of satire makes it seem old-fashioned in that it runs
counter to a view of the relation of poetry to
the real world that has become orthodox in many
influential poetics. I'll use Northrop Frye's
distinction between "ornamental speech" and "persuasive speech," but I think a similar distinction
could be found in many other places. According
to Professor Frye "ornamental speech" and "persuasive speech" are "psychologically opposed to
each other, as the desire to ornament is essentially disinterested, and the desire to persuade
is essentially the reverse. In fact ornamental
rhetoric is inseparable from literature itself,
or what we have called the hypothetical verbal
structure which exists for its own sake. Persuasive rhetoric is applied literature, or the use
of literary art to reinforce the power of argument. Ornamental rhetoric acts on its hearers
statically, leading them to admire its own
beauty or wit; persuasive rhetoric tries to lead
them kinetically toward a course of action."[7]
It seems clear to me that in the view of the
critics I have been citing as well as some of
the satirists themselves, satire is persuasive
speech rather than ornamental speech. The satirist is interested in his work primarily for
its power to move his audience; no matter how
inventive the *personae* or ingenious the metaphors,
these literary devices exist only to persuade the
audience. This also means that the reader's
response to satire is correspondingly changed.
Instead of the disinterested contemplation of the
work in all its internal relations, the appropriate response is to translate the fictions back
into the world which they in some way comment
upon (Grand Academy of Lagado=the Royal Society),

and then if we are persuaded, we evaluate the
outside object in a new light (empirical experi-
ments=extracting sunbeams from cucumbers). We
are denied the centripetal movement of a purer
poetry, and are forced to shuttle back and forth
between two realms.

It might be possible to say that Dickens'
London is not, nor does it purport to be, the
"real" London as it existed outside the novel,
but rather a "vision" of London, incorporating
some of the historically recognizable features
of London, but existing in its own right.
(Though to the extent that we might consider
the Dickens of *Bleak House* a satirist, one might
argue that we are meant to see that Chancery=
the real Chancery). But we never could say the
same of Pope's or Swift's London--its existence
is not so self-contained; it takes it Cibbers
and Theobalds from history, what Mack calls "the
chronicle of the existing city." The dunces are
not hypothetical constructs to be observed dis-
interestedly. It may be true that other poets
never affirm anything and therefore never lie,
but the satirist is affirming something, albeit
negatively. The satirist's efforts are tied to
history, "the existing city," in a way that
other poets' efforts are not. Sidney's poet
makes a second nature, ranges freely within the
zodiac of his own wit, substituting for our brazen nature the golden world of his own invention;
but the satirist must stick with the brazen one
and try to make us feel its weight.

If he succeeds in making us feel its weight,
then we might try to do something about it; the
work will be "kinetic" and produce consequences
in the real world. Another poet has said that
poetry doesn't make anything happen in the world.
But satire does--as in the case of *The Drapier's
Letters,* which actually brought about the cancel-
lation of Wood's patent. Satire tries to make
us move back to the world; it may try to make
us forget there are two realms. Paulson has
argued that "as satire increases in rhetorical
effectiveness it draws less and less attention

to itself as satire; ultimately the most effective satire (given its generic aims) would be the
one that passed as something else. (The reader's
knowledge that he is reading satire makes him
more aware of formal matters and less concerned
about combatting evil.)"[8] He cites Swift's "Dying Statement" of Ebenezor Elliston, a counterfeit confession of a condemned criminal which
threatened to expose those colleagues who did
not reform. According to Walter Scott the crime
rate of Dublin actually went down. The natural
direction of satire then, "given its generic
aims," is toward illusionism, the foisting of
the art work into the real world. The satirist
disappears as he tries to smuggle his creations
into the real world. Swift disappears (taking
Partridge along with him) and leaves Bickerstaff
behind. The satirist has become what Hugh Kenner calls a counterfeiter, someone whose "real
purpose is to efface himself, like the Flauber-
tian artist, so that we will draw the conclusion
he wants us to about how his artifact came into
existence."[9]

An even more radical and challenging account
of the satirist's (or satire's) self-annihilating
tendencies is provided by Edward Said's argument
that for Swift the fact that a work survived as
a literary text was a sign of its failure. Swift
was interested in writing only as it is "stimulated by a specific occasion and planned in some
way to change it...Correct writing for him did
not merely conform to reality. It was reality;
or better still, it was an event necessitated by
other events, and leading to still other events."[10] Success as an event "would have meant
it extinction and dispersion in time past." If
we can extend what Said says of Swift to all
satire, then satire has only the most qualified
reason for its existence: it is, on the one hand,
a middle term suspended precariously between the
causes outside itself, the occasions which have
provoked it into existence, and on the other
hand, the consequences or events which it is
meant to provoke in the outside world. If the
satirist feels that he can no longer change

reality, make his art truly "kinetic," then he
might as well stop writing. In the footnote
attached to the end of the *Epilogue to the Satires:
Dialogue II*, Pope claims that he resolves to publish no more poems of the same kind. "Could he
have hoped to have amended any, he had continued
these attacks...." This little epilogue to the
Epilogue might be considered the satirist's farewell to his art.

   This seems to me as far as you can take the
view that the satirist is primarily a moralist,
a rhetorician concerned with the effects of his
art on history. Before satire as a genre disappears entirely, I would like to reverse the
direction in which we have been moving and pursue some of the implications of the opposing
view: that satire is ornamental rhetoric rather
than persuasive rhetoric, that it flaunts its
own artifice rather than conceals it, and that
it is concerned with the powers of the satirist
and the act of satire rather than with any situation which exists outside the satire. In this
view the satirist may pose as outraged moralist,
but that is only one of the conventional fictions
of satire. No matter what he may claim, the satirist is moved to write satire for the same reason the lyric poet is moved to song; he is not
trying to explore the substantive issues of
Ancients versus Moderns or the *Querelles des Femmes*,
or the doctrines of Leibniz. These serve only
as the occasions for the poem, and as an artist
he is grateful to them. The Tory wits keep attacking all the machinery of scholastic philosophy and logic not because they see these ways
of thinking as threats to society, but because
they realize that these vanishing enemies provide them with a perfect opportunity for the
display of their own kind of virtuosity. The
satirist doesn't really hate lawyers, quack doc-
tors, pedant philosophers, braggart soldiers,
antiquarians, opera singers, or even bad poets--
he just sees their artistic possibilities and is
drawn to them as the landscape painter is to
picturesque waterfalls. If this goes too far

and replaces the moralist's toga with the formal-
ist's velvet jacket, one might say that the satirist is "interested" in these phenomena in the
sense proposed by Austin Warren: "As its signal
advantage, burlesque, (with its allied forms,
satire and irony) allows a self-conscious writer
to attend to objects, causes, and persons in
which he is deeply interested, yet of which, in
part or with some part of him, he disapproves.
'Interest' is a category which subsumes love and
hate, approval and disapproval; often it is an
unequal, an unsteady mixture."[11]

Where this is not the case, where the writer
doesn't have the necessary detachment for the
contemplation of his subject, where the man with
a cause takes precedence over the artist, then
the result is a work like *The History of John Bull*.
The actual issues of the War of the Spanish
Succession, the peace negotiations leading to
the Treaty of Utrecht, the Union with Scotland
are important to Arbuthnot, and so the fictions
are threadbare and lifeless. Whatever the importance of the work for historians, for literature the work is dead, in much the same way
that Smollett's *Adventures of an Atom* is dead. The
rhetorician who wants to move his audience kinetically to action in the real world may use
irony or metaphor, but only within limits: brilliant as they are, the polemics of Junius are too
closely tied to history to be works of satire.
When Swift really wanted to make something happen
in the world, he was wise enough to play it fairly straight, leave out the fireworks of wit, and
distort the issues only minimally. Hence *The
Drapier's Letters*, which some critics would not consider satire.

If on the other hand we examine the great works
of satire we will see how unrhetorical they really are. Good rhetoric is never unclear or ambiguous, but good saitre can be--as the controversy
(surely not all of it fabricated, not all the result of historical misunderstanding) over the
"meaning" of Swift's masterpieces indicates. The
rhetorician's "meaning" is thinner and more easily

formulated, whereas the satirist's "meaning" in literature is dense.

Paulson in arguing for what I have called the rhetorical view of satire has claimed that "Satire's purpose ordinarily is not to create something new but to expose the real evil in the existing."[12] To that one might oppose what T.S. Eliot says of Ben Jonson: "But satire like Jonson's is great in the end not by hitting off its object, but by creating it; the satire is merely the means which leads to the aesthetic result, the impulse which projects a new world into a new orbit."[13] "A new world into a new orbit," not the old world distorted for rhetorical purposes. The satirist doesn't transform our brazen world upward into a golden world like other poets, but downward into an equally autonomous, equally aesthetic world of lead.

If the first view of satire led ultimately to the disappearance of the satirist and his art, the second ushers both back again in full glory. I think the possibility of reversing direction has been implicit in the notion of counterfeiting and illusionism. The point about counterfeiting, if I understnad Kenner's argument, is that for the wise reader it implies a counterfeiter. We look for traces of the controlling person, the real person, the real author, who is not counterfeit-- Swift, not Bickerstaffe. A real author is a presence, a live voice, and thus for Pope and Swift, different from the dead voices which surround them. I think the same is true of illusionism in art: it is easy to see that *trompe l'oeil* painting always calls attention to itself as artifice, as a triumph of the painter's art. It's only crows who try to peck at grapes. And it is only the gulls that get taken in by Swift's labyrinth peopled with mock Patridges. For the ones who share the irony, the men of wit and taste to whom Swift appeals in the Preface to *A Tale of a Tub*, the interest is in the maker of the maze. The real object is not to discredit Partridge so much as to show what the ingenious satirist can accomplish. For all their evasiveness, their impostures, the fictions of *Gulliver's Travels*, *A Tale of a Tub*, and *The Dunciad* return us to the figure of the satirist at work on the poem.

All this by way of introduction to *The Dunciad*, a work which culminates Pope's career, and which also brings to fulfillment the Scriblerean program of compiling the complete works of the unlearned. That project was first adumbrated in *A Tale of a Tub*, a panegyric upon modernism by an "author" whose other productions also anticipate *The Dunciad*: *A Character of the Present Wits in this Island*, *A Dissertation upon the Principal Productions of Grub Street*, and *A Description of the Kingdom of Absurdities*. In *The Art of Sinking in Poetry* Pope acknowledged "the extent, Fertility, and Populousness of our Lowlands of Parnassus" by codifying that realm's poetics, but it wasn't until *The Dunciad in Four Books* of 1743 that the comprehensive and definitive account of all the works of dullness was achieved. It may be also argued that *The Dunciad* is a culminating work of the satirist's art, a virtuoso demonstration of how the apparent limitations of the genre can be converted to artistic gain. *The Dunciad* is a work about dunces, but it is also a work about *The Dunciad*. It reveals satire's peculiar combination of private motivation and disinterestedness, moral rhetoric and autonomous poetry. It shows how the satirist may efface himself or assert his presence, how he can make his poem and the world interact, and how he can make a beautiful and enduring poem out of the ugly and transient materials with which he is forced to deal.

If, as Dr. Johnson informs us, Pope could make the taking of tea an occasion for stratagem, we shall not be surprised if the making of *The Dunciad* calls forth all the poet's "indirect and unsuspected methods." *The Dunciad* is an illusive poem in every way, a mocking, jeering, apparition intended to deceive the mental eye by its false prospects. Pope disorients the reader by misleading him about the work's mode of existence. A poem may be described with reference to four

coordinates: the work itself, its author, the
audience, and what M.H. Abrams, whose scheme I
am borrowing, calls "the universe." The work
has "a subject which directly or deviously is derived from existing things."[14] Pope constantly
shifts and plays upon each of these coordinates
and their possible relationships, so that the
limits of each term become something of a puzzle.
This is the kind of serious game exploring the
boundaries between art and reality that writers
of our own time have liked to play, but as Kenner shows in *The Counterfeiters*, it is a game which
Pope and Swift had perfected in the first half
of the eighteenth century.

It is not so easy to decide what the term
"the work itself" refers to when we speak of *The
Dunciad*. Certainly Pope's contemporary reader was
bound to be puzzled by the status of a poem ushered or smuggled into the world in such a way as
to produce anger or amusement depending on the
nature of the reader. The physical text itself--
what should be the most substantial aspect of the
work--proves to be a phantom. The title page of
the first edition claims that it is a London reprint of a prior Dublin edition, but that edition
never existed. It bears the name of a publisher
who did exist, but who probably had nothing to do
with the publication of the poem. The publisher's preface "prefixed to the first five imperfect editions of the *Dunciad in Three Books*," the
first item in the appendix to *The Dunciad Variorum*,
admits that the publication is unauthorized:
"How I came possest of it, [the manuscript] is
no concern of the Reader...If it provoke the
Author to give us a more perfect edition, I have
my end" (pp. 203-204). The advertisement to the
first separate edition of the *Fourth Book of the
Dunciad* is even less reassuring about the text:
"It was found merely by accident, in taking a
survey of the *Library* of a late eminent nobleman;
but in so blotted a condition, and in so many
detatch'd pieces, as plainly shewed it to be not
only *incorrect*, but *unfinish'd*" (pp. 410-411). That
is, the contemporary reader, having access only

to corrupt or possibly pirated editions of an
unfinished poem, would have to regard what he
was reading as only the roughest approximation
of the poet's intention. The repeated notices
that there is more to come force him to anticipate a newer, more up-to-date *Dunciad*. As early
in the poem as the preface of Martin Scriblerus
we are warned that the crowd scene in the second book indicates "the design to be more extensive than to bad poets only, and that we may
expect other Episodes...as occasion shall bring
them forth" (p. 51). The poem is a potential
poem, a work in progress as the original title
The Progress of Dulness suggests, a design in the
head of its creator; that design extends to
parts of the poem yet to be written which will
incorporate events in the outside world which
have not yet taken place.

The modern reader can of course assume that
there is no forthcoming completer *Dunciad*, but
he is forced to cope with all the versions of
the poem--*The Dunciad* of 1728, *The Dunciad Variorum*
of 1729, the *New Dunciad* of 1742, and *The Dunciad
in Four Books* of 1743 as well as all the many
revisions, insertions, and deletions that took
place in intervening editions. He also has the
additional burden, as Pope knew he would, of
trying to separate the mock-critical apparatus
from the genuine critical apparatus of his
scholarly editors. (In a letter he refers to
"my *Chef d'ouevre*, the Poem of Dulness, which
after I am dead and gone, will be printed with
a large Commentary, and lettered on the back,
Pope's Dulness.")[15] All of this makes *The Dunciad*
a remarkably difficult poem to possess. I don't
think that one can argue that since *The Dunciad* of
1743 represents Pope's final intentions, it sup-
plants the earlier versions. Pope wants the
reader to remember that there were earlier versions as he reads the last one, since the notes
often refer to changes which have been made.
Cibber's throne has only recently been vacated
by Theobald, whom "we have ordered...utterly to
vanish, and evaporate out of this work" (p. 252).

(But this "Notice" is posted conspicuously at
the very beginning of the poem lest the reader
forget Theobald.) Although that progress is now
complete, the poem is still a progress of Dullness, and the multiple versions of the poem (*Dunciad* A to *Dunciad* B in the Twickenham edition) are
meant to record and enact that process, just as
it is enacted in any one version of the poem.
     Authorship is something of a mystery--not the
minor mystery of who actually wrote the poem
(that was solved almost immediately despite Pope's
half-hearted but necessary attempts to conceal
his authorship), but rather how our notion of
authorship must be enlarged to account for a work
which seems to accumulate by means of a continuing collaboration between the poet, his friends,
his enemies, and anyone else who reads the poem
and wishes to join in. William Cleland's letter
to the publisher, which first appeared in the
quarto of 1729 and remained a part of the work
thereafter, invites the publisher to keep adding
to the text: "Such Notes as have occurr'd to me
I herewith send you; you will oblige me by inserting them amongst those which are, or will be,
transmitted to you by others: since not only the
Author's friends, but even strangers, appear in-
gag'd by humanity, to some care of an orphan of
so much genius and spirit, which its parent seems
to have abandoned from the very beginning, and
suffered to step into the world naked, unguarded,
and unattended" (p. 11). The invitation is extended to any reader in the advertisement to *New
Dunciad* of 1742:

     If any person be possessed of a more perfect
copy of this work, or any other fragments of
it, and will communicate them to the publisher,
we shall make the next edition more complete:
In which, we also promise to insert any *Criticisms* that shall be published (if at all to the
purpose) with the *Names* of the *Authors*; or any
Letters sent us (tho' not to the purpose)
shall yet be printed under the title of *Epistolæ
Obscurorum Virorum*; which, together with some

others of the same kind formerly laid by for
that end, may make no unpleasant addition to the
future impressions of this poem.[16]

As Sutherland points out this last invitation
satirizes Curll's methods of publication. But
the invitation also indicates Pope's method of
building up the poem by "over-dubbing" a babble
of real and mock voices: Martinus Scriblerus,
Bentley of the facetious notes, those puppets
through which the "two or three of my friends"[17]
who Pope claims wrote the notes speak (but who
are probably in turn puppets through which Pope
speaks), the puppet voice of William Cleland,[18]
through which Pope delivered an impassioned justification of himself, the semi-puppet "Warburton"
used for more solemn effects, and most of all the
voices of dunces as they respond to Pope's invitation or as gleaned from their own writings.
     Pope wants to distance himself from the poem
in order that the true "voice" of *The Dunciad*
will not be the angry, maligned poet, but a more
impersonal one, resonant and authoritative above
the din of dissonant mock-voices that sound in
the poem and the notes. This does not disguise
the fact that *The Dunciad* is among other things a
monumental paying off of scores, as Pope admits
when he writes to Swift that "this poem will rid
me of these insects" (2, 481, March 23, 1728).
At the same time, Pope's efforts at removing his
presence from the poem are balanced by his wish
to assert his presence. The passage I just quoted in which "Cleland" describes the poem as an
orphan "which its parent seems to have abandoned
from the very beginning and suffered to step into
the world naked, unguarded, and unattended" illustrates Pope's ambiguous relation to the poem:
instead of being an orphan, the poem is more like
the beloved child whom the parent only pretends
to relinquish, the better to supply his offspring
with stepparents, sponsors, and guardians to see
it safely into the world and protect it when the
parent is no longer on the scene. Hence Pope
repeatedly makes Swift another father of the poem:

"Do you care I shou'd say anything farther how
much the poem is yours?"[19] He makes use of the
indispensable noble lords to take the responsibility for the patent, and after the immediate
danger is over replaces them with the printer
Lawton Gilliver. Later on, William Warburton is
solicited to become editor, contributor to, and
protector of the poem: "I have a particular reason to make you Interest yourself in Me and My
Writings. It will cause both them and me to
make the better figure to Posterity" (4, 428,
November 27, 1742). Far from being an abandoned
orphan, the satire is a continuing presence in
the poet's life, and eventually becomes his claim
upon posterity.

The poet seems to withdraw from the work, but
as in the case of Cleland's letter (it is Pope
who writes it), he is most there when he seems
to have disappeared. This seems to me a characteristic stance of the satirist, who often de-
precates his own importance by asserting that
writing a satire is only making a response to an
occasion. Thus Pope claims that the "late Flood
of Slander" which resulted from the publication
of *The Peri-Bathos* "gave birth to *The Dunciad*." The
enthronement of Cibber in the 1743 version would
in the same way appear to be a response to Cibber's publication in 1742 of *A Letter from Mr. Cibber to Mr. Pope*. But both events, the actions of
the dunces and Cibber, may very well have been
engineered by Pope himself, who not only anticipated their response, but may have actually provoked it to justify the poem.[20] If one of the
occasions of *The Dunciad* is the "uncontrolled License of the Press" and the "Late Flood of Slander," then it is a flood which, at least in part,
the poet has instigated. Granted that Cibber and
the dunces exist out there in the universe, the
poet can nevertheless manipulate events to serve
an artistic purpose. The satirist pretends to be
taking candid snapshots from life, but practices
instead a very highly contrived portraiture: he
tricks his subjects into striking the poses in
which they are captured within the poem.

Pope is, at his most oblique and ingenious,
a practitioner of "indirect and unsuspected methods" in his deliberate complication of the relation between his poem and the universe, the
characters and events of history to which the
poem refers. Is it "document," the record of the
artist's confrontation of his historical situation
in order to shape the reader's response to that
situation, or is it "monument," "a richly solip-
sistic or playful edifice?"[21] The aspect of the
poem that concerns me now is the surprising way
in which it can serve as an illustration of both
extreme views of satire. Pope makes the question
of satire's capacity to mirror history or to mirror itself one of the important issues of the poem.
    The Dunciad would seem to be the perfect exam-
ple of how far a satirist can go in aligning his
poem with history. If ever a poem could be said
to be "the chronicle of the existing city," the
record of the literary and political world of
London in the first half of the eighteenth cen-
turn, it is *The Dunciad*-- or so the satirist would
have us believe. The poet may falsify information or he may reveal his biases in politics,
but the fact that he offers a *version* of history
doesn't alter our sense that his conception of
the poem is historical. In fact the poet is so
concerned that his work and outside events be
aligned that he is willing to keep changing his
poem so that it will keep up with history. If
someone dies, or makes his peace with Pope or
quarrels with him, or if Sir Thomas Hamner has
a new edition of Shakespeare ready for the
presses, these new developments must somehow be
registered by the poem, by an insertion, by a
new footnote, or an addition to an existing
footnote, or by a new version of the poem. Lines
115-118 in Book IV appear with the following
note: "These four lines were printed in a separate leaf by Mr. Pope in the last edition, which
he himself gave, of the Dunciad, with directions
to the printer, to put this leaf into its place
as soon as Sir T.H.'s Shakespear should be
published" (p. 352-3). Lines 247-250 in A, Book

I read: "Know, Settle, cloy'd with custard and
with praise,/Is gather'd to the Dull of antient
days,/Safe, where no criticks damn, no duns molest,/Where Gildon, Banks, and high-born Howard
rest" (p. 92). In editions of A from 1735c-1742
there is an additional couplet: "And high-born
Howard, more majestic sire/Impatient waits, till**
grace the quire" (p. 92). The ranks of the dull
of ancient days received some distinguished additions in the years that intervened between *Dunciad*
A and *Dunciad B*: Eusden died in 1730, Ned Ward in
1731, and best and most recent of all, Lord Hervey in 1743, just in time for a last minute
change in the text. Thus the corresponding lines
in *Dunciad B*, Book I, lines 293-298, read:

> Know, Eusden thirsts no more for sack or
>   praise;
> He sleep among the dull of ancient days;
> Safe, where no critics damn, no duns molest,
> Where wretched Withers, Ward, and Gildon rest,
> And high-born Howard, more majestic sire,
> With Fool of Quality compleats the quire.
>   (p. 291)

If somebody makes a suitable act of submission to
Pope he can be taken out of the poem, as in the
case of the poet originally referred to in *Dunciad*
A, III, line 146. The footnote to that line informs us how one can disappear from *The Dunciad*:
"But the person who suppos'd himself meant applying to our author in a modest manner, and with
declarations of his innocence, he removed the
occasion of his uneasiness. At the same time
'promising to do the like to any other who could
give him the same assurance, of having never writ
scurrilously against him'" (pp. 162-163). If you
can get out of the poem, you can also be dragged
into it, as in the case of Arnall, who was originally to have a place in the poem but who managed to talk Pope into omitting his name. He
appears in a later version because "since, by
the most unexampled insolence, and personal abuse
of several great men, the Poet's particular

friends, he most amply deserved a niche in the
Temple of Infamy..." (p. 312). The contents of
the poem, what is to be included or omitted, is
dictated not by inner logic and the organic form
of the whole, but simply by the course of events
in the world, in this case a minor literary figure's present state of grace with the poet. *The
Dunciad* is not a necessary whole whose integrity
is inviolable; on the contrary it is the only
masterpiece of literature whose contents are
negotiable.

If the poem is to be tied to external events
in this way, then it must necessarily be incomplete. Pope can no more finish his poem than
Tristram Shandy can complete the account of his
life. Just as the novelist discovers more circumstances that demand treatment, so the satirist
is besieged by new speciments of dullness. The
fiction of succession within the poem allows new
versions to be written: Dunce the second reigns
like Dunce the first; the line stretches backward
into the past, and also into the future. There
will always be new claimants for the throne.
There are new recognition scenes to be enacted
as Dullness acknowledges her own, and in turn,
her own loyal sons acknowledge her. More activities, especially those in the world of politics,[22] are revealed to be inspired by Dullness,
just as her sway extends over more and more of
London, England, and Europe, until finally she
does as prophesied embrace the whole world. The
Cibber enthronement does not really seem a new
direction in the poem, but rather a natural evolution of the fiction of succession, which allows
for multiple Dunciads. We know that poets often
revise poems making them better or worse, or that
poets can write sequels to their own poems, but
it is difficult to think of a continuing poem
like *The Dunciad* which has to be revised, expanded,
and updated to take into account the rush of
events in the outside world.

But the claim to historical authenticity is
an illusion. No matter how much the poem and
footnotes seem to refer to history, to reflect a

subject which "is derived from existing things,"
that is only one of the fictions of the poem. On
this point I can only repeat Aubrey Williams' argument that in the notes Pope systematically dis-
places history. The dunces are placed in "a curiously ambiguous realm of half-truth in which the
reader wanders, never quite sure as to the validity of what he reads, never certain what is
fact, what is make-believe."[23] The poem "simultaneously affirms and denies its historical connections at every moment..." (p. 76). "The Tibbald of *The Dunciad* is not quite the Theobald of
history" (p. 68). Of course the dunces don't
know that, and so they send in indignant correc-
tions which are incorporated into the next edition of the poem. Curll protests that he stood
in the pillory not in March but February, and
was moreover tossed in a rug, not a blanket. Ned
Ward claims that it is not true that he keeps a
public house in the City--rather he sells Port in
Moor-Fields. The dull are troubled that Cibber's
brazen, brainless brothers are made out of wood
and therefore should be called "blocks"; they
worry whether Theobald really was supperless,
or whether the statement that Curll's "rapid
waters in their passage burn" did actually "convey an idea of what was said to be Mr. Curll's
condition at that time."

What the wise reader sees (and like other
Scriblerean works, *A Tale of a Tub* and *The Bickerstaffe Papers*, the work has multiple aspects according to the nature of its audience)[24] is that
the dunces are only raw material for a poem.
They don't occasion the poem so much as become
occasions for the exercise of the satirist's art.
Pope everywhere asserts the priority of the poem
over history:

> For whoever will consider the Unity of the
> whole design, will be sensible, that the *Poem
> was not made for these Authors, but these Authors for
> the Poem:* And I should judge they were clap-
> p'd in as they rose, fresh and fresh, and
> chang'd from day to day, in like manner as

when the old boughs wither, we thrust new
ones into a chimney. (Appendix I pp. 205-
206)

For all their noise and activity, the dunces are
mute and passive, completely subject to the "design" of the poet, who is free to paste them in,
tear them out, or shuffle them about in the niches or slots that the poem contains. He manipu-
lates them in accord with the internal logic of
the poem, and is perfectly free to ignore their
"historical" identity. Thus line 118 in Book II
of *Dunciad* A is "Breval, Besaleel, Bond, the Varlets caught" (p. III), and in the corresponding
line in *Dunciad* B it is "Breval, Bond, Besaleel,
the varlets caught" (p. 301). Prosody is all.
A line in which asterisks are used to indicate
the name of a dunce, and the name is "Concanen."
The note attached to that line explains that
"this name was since inserted merely to fill up
the verse, and give ease to the ear of the reader."[25]
     Lines prepared for any dunce can be applied to
any other dunce. If Bentley can be moved into a
slot originally intended for Welsted ("Welsted
his mouth with classic flatt'ry opes" A II. 1.
197 [p. 124] becomes "Bentley his mouth with
classic flatt'ry opes" B II, 205 [p. 305]), then
Welsted in turn can get the line previously occupied by Oldmixon, with only a slight adjustment
needed for the extra syllable in Oldmixon's name:
"But Oldmixon the Poet's healing balm" (p. 125)
becomes "But Welsted most the Poet's healing
balm" (p. 306). This aspect of the poem disturbed Dr. Johnson, who thought it didn't make sense
to pretend that you can say the same thing of
different men.[26] This is of course the point:
the switch from Cibber to Theobald can be accomplished with a minimum of fuss, because like all
the other dunces, they are really all the same.
Going from Theobald to Cibber is only the distance
from "Now flames old Memnon, now Rodrigo burns"
(A I, 208, p. 87) to "Now flames the Cid, and now
Perolla burns" (B I, 250, p. 288). One need not
respect their individuality because they have

none: they are "phantoms," "Things," fictions:
"Reader! These also are not real persons...Thou
mays't depend on it no such authors ever lived:
all phantoms" (p. III). There were complaints
about the chronology of the poem because the
Gazetteers who are depicted had not "lived within
the time of the poem." Scriblerus replies that
"we may with equal assurance assert, these Gazetteers not to have lived since, and challenge all
the learned world to produce one such paper at
this day. Surely therefore, where the point is
so obscure, our author ought not to be censured
too rashly" (p. 311). In the same way Bickerstaffe had dismissed the question of the existence of Partridge as a "point merely speculative" in a scholarly argument.

By responding to the "random" initials in *The
Art of Sinking* they have confessed their own fic-
tionality, and thus the poet "had acquired such
a peculiar right over their Names as was necessary to his design" (p. 202). According to Ricardus Aristarchus, Cibber has made the same
mistake in acknowledging that he was in *The Dunciad*: "For no sooner had the fourth book laid open
the high and swelling scene, but he recognized
his own heroic Acts" (p. 261). Cibber has claimed that he would always be a buffoon and so "he
is become *dead in law*, (I mean the *law Epopaeian*)
and descendeth to the Poet as his property: who
may take him, and deal with him, as if he had
been dead as long as an old Egyptian hero; that
is to say, *embowel* and *embalm him for posterity*" (p.
265). All the other dunces are dead in the same
way and therefore fit subjects for the satirist
to make of them what he will.

There is no point in trying to reconstruct the
poem as history since the events and figures with
which it deals are so ephemeral, and therefore in
a way unreal. "Reality" may be better recorded
and interpreted by reading the poem, which is a
full and sufficient account of history. Not only
is the poem aligned with history; in some instances it anticipates history. Thus line 146 of A
III reads: "Lo Horneck's fierce, and Roome's

funereal face" (p. 162). According to the note
that accompanies the line, "These two are worth-
ily coupled, being both virulent Party-writers;
and one wou'd think prophetically, since immediately after the publishing of this Piece the former dying, the latter succeeded him in *Honour* and
Employment" (p. 163). Another instance of prophecy
is that couplet in A III associating two poets:
"Beneath his reign, shall Eusden wear the Bays,/
Cibber preside Lord Chancellor of Plays" (pp.186-
187). The note comments: "I have before observ'd
something like Prophecy in our Author. Eusden,
whom he couples with Cibber, no sooner died but
his place of Laureate was supply'd by Cibber, in
the year 1730..." (p. 187). Prophecy is not difficult since history is so predictable, a repetition of the same kinds of events; one knows
that Philips or Cibber will be promoted for wit.
Thus the poem can exhaust history. If the reader
takes the trouble to keep up with the dunces, he
will still not be enlightened, "since when he
shall have found them out, he will probably know
no more of the Persons than before" (p. 206).
The conjunction of Horneck and Roome, of Eusden
and Cibber conveys all the essential information
about each, and history can only confirm the
poet's intuition. The Lord Hervey of history is
unimportant; it is only when he completes the
quire, enters the pages of Pope's book, that he
has any significance. Pope and the reader are
not interested in who the dunce is, but only in
what can be made of him. This seems to me the
general issue in *The Dunciad*: how may the deeds of
dullness be converted into an act of wit?

Doctor Johnson was not impressed by Pope's
grotto; he thought it vain of the poet to pretend to have "extracted an ornament from an inconvenience." But perhaps the knack of extract-
ing an ornament from an inconvenience is one of
the qualifications of the satirist. Pope writes
to Swift that he hopes Ambrose Philips will be
promoted: "If they do not promote him, they'l
spoil a very good conclusion to one of my Satyrs,
where having endeavoured to correct the taste of

the town in wit, and criticisme, I end thus: But
what avails to lay down rules for Sense?/In ___'s
reign these fruitless lines were writ,/When A̅m̅-
brose Philips was preferr'd for wit!" (2, 332,
October 15, 1725). Swift replied with the same
resigned irony: "I would have the Preferment
Just enough to save your lines; let it be ever
so low, for your sake we will allow it to be
Preferment" (2, 343, November 26, 1725). If you
live in George's reign, and know that the lines
must therefore be fruitless, the best you can do
is to incorporate that couplet into a vast and
intricate structure.

Relatively early in Pope's career he wrote a
poem called *The Temple of Fame*, like *The Dunciad* a
poem in which the poet is granted a vision. In
the early poem, however, the poet celebrates
those names which "From Time's first Birth, with
Time it self shall last;/These ever new, nor
subject to Decays,/Spread, and grow brighter
with the Length of Days" (*Temple of Fame*, ll. 49-52).
In a footnote to lines 178 through 243 Pope says
that these great names were "describ'd in such
Attitudes as express their different Characters.
The Columns on which they are rais'd are adorn'd
with Sculptures, taken from the most striking
Subjects of their Works; which Sculpture bears a
Resemblance in its Manner and Character, to the
Manner and Character of their Writings" (p. 179).
When some ten years later Pope decided that the
times demanded a *Temple of Infamy*, he was able to
use the same method to celebrate those whose
names were already forgotten. The satirist is
one who knows the ornamental value of grotesque
sculpture when heroic sculpture is no longer
possible.

The epigraph which Pope attaches to the title
page of *Dunciad B* is from *The Metamorphoses* (XI, 58-
60). After Orpheus has been slain by the wild
women, the musician's head drifts out to the op-
en sea still singing. A monster gets ready to
pierce its lips and eyes but "Phoebus was quick-
er, for as the snake's tongue flickered/He glazed
the creature into polished stone,/And there it

stayed, smiling wide-open-jawed."[27]   If I'm not
being too heavy-handed about this, Orpheus is
the maligned Pope, the monster the potentially
dangerous Grubs, or Dullness herself at her moment of triumph.   Phoebus is the power of poet,
in this case "the power of satire," or more
specifically the Pope who writes *The Dunciad*. The
monster is transformed by the poem into an artifact, a piece of living staturary; though the
original menace presented by the gaping jaws
still shows clearly, the monster is now harmless.
By the writing of *The Dunciad* the dull and their
works are absorbed into a witty structure, a
frame is put around chaos, and the apparent disorder of the dunces is revealed in the end to
be a part of the poet's overarching design.
     The poem itself celebrates the triumph of
Dullness, but the making of the poem, the outside frame which is contributed by the notes
and the fictional situation which they imply,
suggests the forces of wit which are to contain
Dullness.   The poet has complete control over
the dunces; like Prospero[28] he can decide who
is going to be made to dance through the horse-
ponds, or who, like Aaron Hill, will be allowed
to jump out of the poem.   The notes and appendices are joyfully accumulated by the poet and
the partly imaginary circle of wits who are
allied with him.   The satirist is able to respond to any external circumstance: the correc-
tions and protests of the dull, the false readings supplied by Curll and Concanen, a pirated
edition--all these are incorporated into the
next edition of the poem.   The dunces are helpless and their works are fast disappearing: "As
for their writings, I have sought them (on this
one occasion) in vain, in the closets and libraries of all my acquaintance" ("A Letter to the
Publisher," p. 14).   The excerpts from the dunce's works which are made a part of the poem are
all "that could be saved from the general destruction of such works." "Of the *Persons* it was
judg'd proper to give some account; for since it
is only in this monument that they must expect
to survive, (and here survive they will, as long

as the English tongue shall remain such as it
was in the reigns of Queen ANNE and King GEORGE)
it seem'd but humanity to bestow a word or two
upon each, just to tell what he was, what he writ,
when he liv'd, or when he dy'd"("Advertisement,"
p. 8). The poem expresses the wish that the vanishing dunces and their equally ephemeral works
be significant only in that they are a part of a
poem which is not disappearing, but which is in
fact multiplying and permanent. The works of
the dunces are lost, but new versions of *The Dunciad* are found. The historical situation with
which the poem deals is blotted out by *The Dunciad*,
which transforms the threatening situation, the
monster, the inconvenience of the historical
pressure of the dunces into a work of art.

At the end of the *Temple of Fame* the "youthful
bard" acknowledges that he too is "a candidate
for praise." But he insists that he only seeks
"an honest fame," the kind of fame which would
seem to be difficult for a satirist to attain:

>   Or if no Basis bear my rising Name,
>   But the fall'n Ruins of Another's fame:
>   Then teach me, heav'n! to scorn the guilty
>   Bays;
>   Drive from my Breast that wretched lust of
>   Praise;
>   Unblemish'd let me live, or die unknown,
>   Oh grant an honest Fame, or grant me none!
>   (p. 188)

The poet of *The Dunciad* has found a way to deal
with the scruples of the youthful bard. The
older (and cleverer) poet has discovered that
the "fall'n ruins of another's fame" can make a
very fine foundation for his own constructions.
If not entirely "unblemished" the artful poet can
at least avoid "the guilty bays." He can combine
the negative and positive enterprise, make one
edifice serve as Temple of Infamy for his enemies
and a temple of fame for himself.

One last qualification: I have argued that
Pope tries to substitute the poem for history,
to transcend the occasions which have provoked

the poem by means of making the poem. In this
respect *The Dunciad* is a document, a record of
Pope's sense of his situation in history. But
if the poem expresses the wish that Dullness can
be controlled, it also expresses the anxiety that
Dullness cannot be contained by the poem. Even
when the poet sounds most secure he reveals his
doubt: *The Dunciad* is to be a monument which will
survive "as long as the English tongue shall remain such as it was in the reigns of Queen ANNE
and King GEORGE," but as Sutherland points out,
Pope had strong doubts about the permanence of
the English language. Is the vision recorded in
Book III a chimera of the dreamer's brain, a
vision passing through the Ivory gate, and thus
"wild, ungrounded, and fictitious?" Or is the
prophecy already coming true "in the writings of
some even of our most adored authors, in Divinity,
Philosophy, Physics, Metaphysics, etc...."? (p.
192). Pope had ended poems with visions of the
fall of a city before but in the Horatian poems
the poet has, to quote Professor Mack, "a place
to stand, an angle of vision," the secure ter-
rain provided by the garden and the grotto. But
in *The Dunciad* the poet is less insulated; he may
not be protected from the powers that he is ironically celebrating: "Ye Pow'rs! whose Mysteries
restor'd I sing,/To whom Time bears me on his
rapid wing,/Suspend a while your Force inertly
strong,/Then take at once the Poet and the Song"
(pp. 339-340). Is the vision of Dullness contained within the head of the poet, or is the
poet contained within Dullness--is it Alice's
dream or the Red King's?[29] The satirist may explore the abyss to show us what may happen if
we stray too far, but once having taken us there,
he may find it difficult to lead us out of it: it
may be difficult to show that compared to the
universal madness that is the human condition in
"The Digression on Madness," or the universal
dullness that is celebrated in *The Dunciad*, the
life of common forms, of wit, order, and civilization are still possible, and thus exempt from
the satirist's negative vision.[30]

ORDERING CHAOS: *THE DUNCIAD*

B. L. Reid

Even reluctant readers of Pope confess the
greatness of the end of *The Dunciad*. Most students of poetry would call those fifty lines,
in which the enormous yawn of the Goddess
Dulness speaks her final uncreating word and
completes the incursion of universal darkness,
the grandest thing in Pope and one of the triumphs of English genius. "Crowded thoughts and
stately numbers"[1] Samuel Johnson found there,
and the lines surely express power, intelligence, taste, grandeur of conception, mastery
of medium, ease and energy of movement:

> More had she spoke, but yawn'd--All Nature
>   nods:
> What Mortal can resist the Yawn of Gods?
> Churches and Chapels instantly it reach'd:
> (St. James's first, for leaden Gilbert
>   preach'd)
> Then catch'd the Schools; the Hall scarce
>   kept awake;
> The Convocation gap'd, but could not speak:
> Lost was the Nation's Sense, nor could be
>   found,

This essay first appeared in *Quick Springs of Sense*, ed. Larry S. Champion (Athens:
University of Georgia Press, 1974), pp. 75-96. Copyright 1974 by University
of Georgia Press.

678

While the long solemn Unison went round:
Wide, and more wide, it spread o'er all the
    realm;
Ev'n Palinurus nodded at the Helm:
The Vapour mild o'er each Committee crept;
Unfinish'd Treaties in each Office slept;
And Chiefless Armies doz'd out the Campaign;
And Navies yawn'd for Orders on the Main.
O Muse! relate (for you can tell alone,
Wits have short Memories, and Dunces none),
Relate, who first, who last resign'd to rest;
Whose Heads she partly, whose completely
    blest;
What Charms could Faction, what Ambition
    lull,
The Venal quiet, and entrance the Dull;
"Till drown'd was Sense, and Shame, and
    Right, and Wrong--
O sing, and hush the Nations with thy Song!
In vain, in vain--the all-composing Hour
Resistless falls: The Muse obeys the Pow'r.
She comes! she comes! the sable Throne
    behold
Of *Night* Primaeval, and of *Chaos* old!
Before her, *Fancy's* gilded clouds decay,
And all its varying Rain-bows die away.
Wit shoots in vain its momentary fires,
The meteor drops, and in a flash expires.
As one by one, at dread Medea's strain,
The sick'ning stars fade off th' ethereal
    plain;
As Argus' eyes by Hermes' wand opprest,
Clos'd one by one to everlasting rest;
Thus at her felt approach, and secret might,
Art after *Art* goes out, and all is Night.
See skulking *Truth* to her old Cavern fled,
Mountains of Casuistry heap'd o'er her head!
Philosophy, that lean'd on Heav'n before,
Shrinks to her second cause, and is no more.
Physic of Metaphysic begs defence,
And Metaphysic calls for aid on *Sense*!
See *Mystery* to *Mathematics* fly!

> In vain! they gaze, turn giddy, rave, and
>   die.
> *Religion* blushing veils her sacred fires,
> And unawares *Morality* expires.
> Nor *public* Flame, nor *private* dares to shine;
> Nor *human* Spark is left, nor Glimpse *divine!*
> Lo! thy dread Empire, CHAOS! is restor'd;
> Light dies before thy uncreating word:
> Thy hand, great Anarch! lets the curtain
>   fall;
> And Universal Darkness buries All.[2]

The effect is massive and horrific, literally stunning, as it is meant to be. The lines
make most of their point even in isolation,
freestanding. But that solitary impressiveness
is itself obscurely disturbing. Has Pope done
more than make a "moment" of Longinian sublimity? Do the ending and the main body of the
poem deserve each other? Is the conclusion a
true one, an honest rounding of a unified design? For the questions of the unity of this
big poem of four books and 1,754 lines, of the
part structure plays in its achievement, of the
size of the achievement itself are still vexed
and complicated.
     The dubieties as to structure are obvious
and significant: Pope's dithering with the
names of the individual dunces; the spurious
anonymity of the first versions; alterations in
the text and additions to the apparatus culminating in the "Variorum" three-book *Dunciad* of
1729; the addition to the "completed" poem,
thirteen years later, of a fourth book nearly
twice as long as any of the others; the mechanical dethronement there of Lewis Theobald in
favor of Colley Cibber as Prince of Dulness;
the continued absence of any true hero as a
figure of focus controlling the action within
the mock-epic form. None of this suggests any
great clarity in the original conception or any
firm purpose in the long piecemeal history of
the execution of the "design." Is the poem a
shape or an agglomeration, a more or less ef-

ficient set of accidents? And if the structure
is casual and fortuitous, are Pope's command
of satirical penetration, of scenic and dramatic movement, and of figurative precision
and logic powerful enough to order that loose-
ness into fluency and coherence? Nobody who
has compared the original and the revised versions of *The Rape of the Lock* will ever again
doubt Pope's artistic nerve or the altering and
synthesizing powers of his imagination, the
lordly command of purpose and medium that can
rebuild a "finished" work and raise it to a
higher order of excellence. And whereas *The
Dunciad* never achieves the seamless fabric of *The
Rape of the Lock* it does grow to a massive comeli-
ness of form thoroughly suited to its very different nature.

From Johnson on down, Pope's critics have
naturally compared his two mock-epics. It is
enchanting to watch the lobster-claw delicacy
with which Johnson handles the jewelwork of *The
Rape*: "the most airy, the most ingenious, and the
most delightful of all his compositions," he
called it; "the most exquisite example of ludicrous poetry."[3] Johnson treats *The Dunciad*, in
the main, respectfully but coolly: it is "one
of his greatest and most elaborate performan-
ces"; it "affords perhaps the best specimen
that has yet appeared of personal satire ludicrously pompous."[4] Among recent critics Geoffrey Tillotson's formulation I take to be decisive: "*The Dunciad*, like *MacFlecknoe*, is the ludicrous, grotesque, lifesize shadow cast by a
piece of an epic poem, *The Rape of the Lock*, an
exquisitely diminished shadow cast by an entire
epic, by the august epic form itself."[5] That
carries one a long way: *The Rape* (794 lines) is
a brilliant miniature of a complete grand original; *The Dunciad* mocks a fragment of the grand
original in terms of equivalent size. The
distinction means a fundamental difference in
scale, in the general manner of attack. The
satirical arithmetic of the two epical mock-
eries is very different, and so is the angle of
observation.

In *The Rape of the Lock* the subject is the absurdity of human vanity and pettiness, and Pope
observes his creatures and his scene from a position a bit raised and oblique. His figures
are slightly distanced by this slight removal,
but they are not really shrunk in size as in
Swift's kind of geometry--though there occurs an
insistent trivializing of the figures due to the
not-quite-present omnipresence of the tiny
sylphs, just barely not caught every so often
in a flicker at the corner of one eye. But the
real reduction of the persons and the action is
less a matter of size than of limitation, less
vertical than horizontal: an abstracting that
is achieved by narrowing the thing seen, by
applying a kind of fanatical tunnel vision. An
unspoken metaphor of concentration controls the
whole poem. We see only the world of the poem's
society because that *is* the world as limited and
redefined by the madly inflated social issue,
taking over life: a hermetic world, tiny passions making a great noise under a bell jar.
Pope's persons have no thought, no action, no
character that is not related to the ridiculous
affair of the rape of the lock. That is the
point. We see nothing but this world because it
is what is left, the trivial absolute created by
absolute vanity.
In *The Dunciad* we are in the same city but a
different world. Rather than control by a metaphor of concentration and exclusion, we are in
the hands of grandiosity, a burly, slovenly inclusiveness. The vision is extensive rather
than intensive. Instead of the fanatically
intensified, fastidiously neat mannikin world of
The Rape, a world folded inward, we see London
folded outward to become a race, a time, a landscape of the national mind, a culture preempted.
The master metaphor is that of seizure, of occupation, of dispossession and repossession:
a whole society hollowed out and replaced by its
antiself. As Tillotson says, it is all both
grotesque and lifesized. We move on the London
bricks and mud here, and we meet the swarming

citizens of Dulness's kingdom eye to eye. Except for the great Queen herself, that "ample
presence," they are not really larger than ourselves though they are, thank God, grosser, for
the moment. The mirror of vision in *The Dunciad*
is convex rather than concave. What we see is
ourselves unhealthily plumped out, a bit swol-
len and softened, with a certain pompous duct-
ility of outline and an air of inconsequential
busyness.

The basic difference in the shape and feeling
of the two poems rests then less upon the scale
of the persons observed than upon the arena of
their movement and the manner of their moving.
The theater of *The Rape of the Lock* is an elegant
drawing room approached by a narrow corridor
of river and city. There the lovely sillies
dance out a clear narrative-dramatic line,
sharply defined and brightly lit. They do it
beautifully, for they have nothing else to do.
Every movement is stylized and stylish, graceful, to the point of action, with no waste at
all. The theater of *The Dunciad* is the sprawl of
the city, folding out to seize, to "involve"
the whole Augustan world. The scene is crowded,
filthy, flaring, frenetic: a favorite word of
the text is "swarm." Here the dance is a disorderly cockney Kermess, observed by Hogarth or
Gilray. Movements are violent and awkward because they share no coherent impulse: the only
conscious purpose here is the gross chthonic
malevolence of Dulness herself, the force "inertly strong" of her implacable "deep Intent."
The Dunciad does not move in linear and progressive ways, along a line of "plot" as in *The
Rape of the Lock*. Movement is lateral, side-to-
side, echoic, repetitive, an agitation in place
at once clumsy and efficient; it winnows and
harrows the complex city scene as it moves to
accomplish not so much a plot as an action.

Shapeliness is a word one does not easily
associate with *The Dunciad*. Its knobby symmetry
is a very queer aesthetic phenomenon, and it
takes one a long time to find it and give it a

name. Certainly the sense of a developing
shape fulfilling a commanding purpose does not
dominate one's first readings of the poem.
What one feels first is a general hectic busyness of no clear point or tendency; numerous
single foci of satirical brilliance, varied and
scattered tableaux and processions; semidram-
atic burlesque episodes. Fairly soon we begin
to see that something big is going on but we
cannot quite say what it is: we still feel a
discrepancy between part and whole.

The peppering of the page with the initials
or names or pseudonyms of the individual dunces
is a famous difficulty, a litter of persons we
no longer know and can hardly be brought to
care about. This particularity of the names is
the first formidable barrier to a perception
of the big design of the action. With re-
readings the names come clearer and clearer and
mean less and less. Ultimately they lose identity and become so many counted neutral syllables. One sees the point then of Austin
Warren's assurance that the names of the dunces
are "annually replaceable"[6]: what matters is
not who a dunce was but what he stood for, his
intellectual character in Pope's view. When
the dunces have become types or symbols, an
effect will have been achieved that Pope did not
quite intend, I suspect, and he will have built
even better than he knew. *The Dunciad* is first
of all a profoundly occasional poem, and we
should be wrong to forget the fact. Pope was
attacking real persons for real or supposed injuries or errors, out of an animosity that was
private before it was public or general, particular before it was typological. Though it was
easier to say then than now, Johnson's description continues accurate: "personal satire ludicrously pompous."

But the poem is more than that, and the more
that it is is timeless. I think Pope knew that
too, for he made it so at great cost of labor
and genius. It is the structure, the design,
the ordering of the action, not the dunces nor

yet their annual replaceability, that turns the
poem toward the universal, and we need to try to
understand the means, chiefly those of the grand
figures, that accomplish this aggrandizement.
    If we turn back to the closing lines of *The
Dunciad* with which we began, we find in those
crowded thoughts and stately numbers the great
creeping, sweeping, annihilating gesture that
perfects the action of the poem. The action of
The Dunciad is just what Pope said it was in his
note of "Martinus Scriblerus of the Poem" attached to the *Variorum* of 1729: "the restoration
of the reign of Chaos and Night, by the ministry of Dulness their daughter." Chaos and
Night is to say shapeless and dark, the void,
the abyss. Pope's superb invention casts the
final movement of the poem in the trope of a
"Yawn *of extraordinary virtue*" (Argument to Book IV)
which spreads to paralyze and engulf the instru-
ments and institutions of church, state, and
art, the whole visible civility of the world.
    It is noteworthy that the yawn of Dulness
hushes even her own speech. In the grand last
scena that culminates her "progress" Dulness is
distributing prizes and making a state address
to her collected children, presenting her program to "MAKE ONE MIGHTY DUNCIAD OF THE LAND":

> Then blessing all, "Go Children of my care!
> To Practice now from Theory repair.
> All my commands are easy, short, and full:
> My Sons! be proud, be selfish, and be dull."
>   (IV, 579-582)

But her oration is interrupted by her own yawn:
"More she had spoke, but yawn'd ..." What she
speaks, then, is the yawn, the last "word," the
"uncreating word" before which "light dies": the
yawn is the word, or the word is the yawn-in
any case, the death of the mind. The iconography of the scene seems medieval, a kind of
abstract graphic absolute: the maw of Dulness
into which the yawn opens becomes among other
things a Hell Mouth. That gaping awfulness

emits a narcotic vapor and between them they
work the annihilation, the paralysis, and en-
gulfment. The line of movement is epidemic and
inclusive: "Wide, and more wide, it spread o'er
all the realm" (IV, 613); it misses nothing
living and significant. Churchmen, statesmen,
military men, artists, and learned men succumb
in turn. The Muse is called to read the catalog
of victims, to "sing, and hush the Nations with
thy Song" (IV, 626). But she too "obeys the
Pow'r" and lies mute. The triumph of Dulness
is proclaimed: "She comes! she comes! the sable
Throne behold / Of *Night* primaeval, and of *Chaos*
old!" (IV, 629-630). Her "Hour" is come and it
is "all-composing": an order and a paralysis,
at once a new construct and a negative absolute,
a life that is a death. Her composition is lit-
tered with the stunned forms of her victims:
"In vain! they gaze, turn giddy, rave, and die"
(IV, 648). The way is cleared for the terrible
last couplets.
     All of this is obvious enough, perhaps, and
all the more imposing for its union of clarity
and massiveness. What is less obvious, and
what I hope to document, is the fact that the
main lines of movement at the end of the poem
are true ends of ligaments of action and thought
that have girded and shaped the poem from the
outset. The stunning power of the Goddess, her
ability to drop curtains between sense and effective energy, and the "sick'ning" capitulation
of her subjects, are cases copiously proven by
the end of the awful comedy: the great yawn
both includes and concludes.
     First and last, *The Dunciad* is a poem of the
mind in trouble, intelligence and good will be-
set by implacable mindlessness. The mock-epic
form, by mocking, becomes itself the most inclusive metaphor of the work, and we must take
that as given. In his first lines, by brisk
and brilliant mockery of the myths of Eden and
the Golden Age, Pope establishes a context of
size and significance that is never lost. The
uncreating word speaks at the beginning as well

as at the end. Milton's Holy Spirit "dove-like satst brooding on the vast Abyss / And madst it pregnant"[7]: the divine will to life. Pope presents a gross malign fowl: "Here pleas'd behold her mighty wings out-spread / To hatch a new Saturnian age of Lead" (I, 27-28). In the anticreation of his epic proposition, the Goddess has "pour'd her Spirit o'er the land and deep" (I, 8) and "bade Britannia sleep" (I, 7). The miasma of her stupefying spirit, in vapors, veils, mists, fogs, excrements, pervades the poem, saturating the air we breathe.

Dulness is "Daughter of Chaos and eternal Night" (I, 12) and from them naturally takes her genetic equipment: she is "gross as her sire, and as her mother grave" (I, 14). Before the awakening of intelligence, "in eldest time, e'er mortals writ or read" (I, 9), Dulness had ruled over all, in "native Anarchy" (I, 16). Now, her sway having been interrupted by the march of mind, she moves to reinstate her power: "Still her old Empire to restore she tries" (I, 17). There is the subject of our epic action. Its ways of moving derive from the qualities of the Goddess's personal presence: "Laborious, heavy, busy, bold, and blind" (I, 15).

As the mock-epic form makes a comprehensive metaphor, so does the city. The city is London, and London is Britannia, and Britannia is the civilized world. The city is the theater of the arts of life: statecraft, religion, art, learning. It is the head and heart of the race, and it shows itself sick and vulnerable. The work of Dulness is to make a conquering "progress" through these kingdoms and establish her dominion, to "occupy" the city. She discovers or creates vacuums and fills them with her own vague and awful plenitude. Her ramshackle, rabble-engulfing progress is the axial movement of the poem, varied by pauses for complex posturings, disorderly agitations *in situ*, grotesque and vulgar *scenae*, audiences of the Goddess instated amid her thralls or holding levee over their drowsing forms in anticipation of

the great sleep that closes all. The general
rhythm and the pictorial logic, again, feel
vaguely and massively medieval: crude processions lapsing into crude tableaux, a big,
ugly, profane Book of Hours.

In fact most of Book I is composed of tableaux of one kind or another, clusters of persons, gestures, themes that establish an arena
and a climate for the action to come. The secret throne room of Dulness, where she "shines"
in "clouded Majesty" (I, 45), is appropriately
situated near the gates of the madhouse, Bedlam
Hospital. It is a cavernous, hollow place, full
of the howling winds that are "emblem of Music
caus'd by Emptiness" (I, 36), the retreat of
the nameless bards of Grub-street, wont to "escape in Monsters, and amaze the town" (I, 38),
taking protean shapes to startle and confound
the city audience. What the "cloud-compelling
Queen" (I, 79) contemplates "with self-applause"
(I, 82) is the "wild creation" (I, 82), the
chaos of unreason that her influence induces in
the world of art:

How hints, like spawn, scarce quick in
     embryo lie,
How new-born nonsense first is taught to cry,
Maggots half-form'd in rhyme exactly meet,
And learn to crawl upon poetic feet.
Here one poor word an hundred clenches makes,
And ductile dulness new meanders takes;
There motley Images her fancy strike,
Figures ill-pair'd, and Similies unlike.
She sees a Mob of Metaphors advance,
Pleas'd with the madness of the mazy dance:
How Tragedy and Comedy embrace;
How Farce and Epic get a jumbled race;
How Time himself stands still at her command;
Realms shift their place, and Ocean turns to
     land.
Here gay Description AEgypt glads with
     show'rs
Or gives to Zembla fruits, to Barca flow'rs;
Glitt'ring with ice here hoary hills are
     seen,

There painted vallies of eternal green,
In cold December fragrant chaplets blow,
And heavy harvests nod beneath the snow.
    (I, 59-78)

Ironically, what holds it all together is formlessness, the nonsense that vainglorious stupidity makes of form, discipline, tradition,
logic. The passage is a storehouse of images--
of incongruous conjunctions, swarming embryos,
busy indeterminate shapes, crowds of creatures
in frantic and indecisive movement--that go on
to control the poem. Fundamental is the idea
of endless ugly generation, the remorseless
will of mindlessness to spawn and survive.
    It is this line of her generation that the
Goddess inspects with peculiar satisfaction:
"She saw, with joy, the line immortal run, /
Each sire imprest and glaring in his son"
(I, 99-100). Her gaze sweeps to the worthy new
Prince, Cibber, as he sits "swearing and supperless" in an ectasy of frustration:

Then gnaw'd his pen, then dashed it on the
    ground,
Sinking from thought to thought, a vast
    profound!
Plung'd for his sense, but found no bottom
    there,
Yet wrote and flounder'd on, in mere despair.
Round him much Embryo, much Abortion lay,
Much future Ode, and abdicated Play;
Nonsense precipitate, like running Lead,
That slip'd thro' Cracks and Zig-zags of the
    Head;
All that on Folly Frenzy could beget,
Fruits of dull Heat, and Sooterkins of Wit.
    (I, 117-126)

He is moved finally to build a votive pyre of
his own writings and those he had plundered, and
to address a prayer to Dulness, whom he salutes
as "Great Tamer of all human art" (I, 163), and
begs to keep him "obliquely wadling to the mark

in view" (I, 172), to "spread a healing mist
before the mind" (I, 174), to hang on the
weights to keep his clockwork moving. He ig-
nites the heap and "the rowling smokes involve
the sacrifice" (I, 248). It is the first use
of this inconspicuous but important verb which
in its literal sense conveys the manner of Dulness's movement through the city and through
the mind. Dulness "whelms" the fire--another
of the verbs specified to her nature--then manifests herself to her chosen Prince. It is our
first full, if not clear, view of the Goddess
and it establishes once and for all her basic
nature and her way of working: her dreadful
ductile amplitude, her overbearing sufficiency,
her power to occupy a space and to substitute
her gross vague self for any former content or
emptiness:

> Her ample presence fills up all the place;
> A veil of fogs dilates her awful face:
> Great in her charms! as when on Shrieves and
>   May'rs
> She looks, and breathes herself into their
>   airs. (I, 261-264)

The grateful Prince is led to her throne
room and shown her state treasure of heaped
nonsense:

> Prose swell'd to verse, verse loit'ring
>   into prose:
> How random thoughts now meaning chance to
>   find,
> Now leave all memory of sense behind:
> How Prologues into Prefaces decay,
> And these to Notes are fritter'd quite away:
> How Index-learning turns no student pale,
> Yet holds the eel of science by the tail:
> How, with less reading than makes felons
>   scape,
> Less human genius than God gives an ape,
> Small thanks to France, and none to Rome or
>   Greece,

A vast, vamp'd, future, old, reviv'd, new
   piece,
"Twixt Plautus, Fletcher, Shakespear, and
   Corneille,
Can make a Cibber, Tibbald, or Ozell.
   (I, 274-286)

The book closes parodically as it began, with
the anointment and proclamation of the Beloved
Son, the burlesque Messiah: Cibber to be Poet
Laureate. The Queen then summons the first of
the poem's mad processions, the Holiday of
Misrule of the Mind:

Lift up your gates, ye Princes, see him come!
Sound, sound, ye Viols, be the Cat-call dumb!
Bring, bring the madding Bay, the drunken
   Vine;
The creeping, dirty, courtly Ivy join.
And thou! his Aid de camp, lead on my sons,
Light-arm'd with Points, Antitheses, and
   Puns.
Let Bawdry, Billingsgate, my daughters dear,
Support his front, and Oaths bring up the
   rear. (I, 301-308)

She looks ahead in rapture to the final perfection of her power when "all be sleep" (I, 318),
and the shouts of the acquiescent mob, "God
save king Cibber!" ricochet from point to point
and enroll the city in the cause of Dulness:
from the Chapel Royal, to White's gaming house,
to Drury Lane, to Mother Needham's brothel, to
the Devil Tavern in Fleet Street, to the bear-
gardens in Hockley Hole.
   The mock-epic simile that closes Book I,

So when Jove's block descended from on high
(As sings thy great forefather Ogilby)
Loud thunder to its bottom shook the bog,
And the hoarse nation croak'd, "God save King
   Log!" (I, 327-330)

692   REID

rounds the opening movement by presenting the
national voice choked and vulgarized by the
thick wash of stupidity. At the same time it
names the master element of Book II and a controlling figure of the entire poem, filth, assorted forms and densities of the miasma of the
mind that emanates from Dulness and is a sign
of her "ductile," "ample" presence: fogs, veils,
mists, clouds, opium, mud, drains, exrement,
polluted lakes and streams. Certainly these
essences imbue the "high heroic Games" (II, 18)
that comprise the action, again mainly a move-
ment-in-place, of the second book.
   The book opens on Cibber enthroned (again
flanking both Milton's and Pope's deities) and
we see that he has learned overnight how royalty behaves in the Kingdom of the Dull: "The
proud Parnassian sneer, / The conscious simper,
and the jealous leer, / Mix on his look"
(II, 5-7). He has swiftly acquired, too, some
of the Gorgon powers of the Queen: "All eyes
direct their rays / On him, and crowds turn
Coxcombs as they gaze" (II, 7-8). But the full
deadliness of this Incarnation and its malign
outreach into morality is better suggested by
Pope's comparison of Cibber to the burlesque
Roman Laureate Camillo Querno, "the Antichrist
of wit" (II, 16). The heralds' summons to the
games in Drury Lane draws forth the jumbled
swarm of Dulness's citizenry:

                        An endless band
   Pours forth, and leaves unpeopled half the
      land.
   A motley mixture! in long wigs, in bags,
   In silks, in crapes, in Garters, and in rags,
   From drawing rooms, from colleges, from
      garrets,
   On horse, on foot, in hacks, and gilded
      chariots. (II, 19-24)

The various contests, for their various tawdry
prizes, need not be recalled in detail, but
they do need to be recognized as common in kind,

and as archetypes of behavior in a mental kingdom so enthralled, so dispossessed and repos-
sessed as this. Booksellers, hacks, and critics expose their greed, their vanity and their
awkwardness without shame, indeed with besotted
eagerness, in movements appropriately laborious,
heavy, busy, bold, and blind. Filth is everywhere and in it the contestants joyfully slide,
sink, plunge, grope. Curll's headlong surge,
for example, "swift as a bard the bailiff
leaves behind" (II, 61), comes a cropper in the
lake his Corinna "chanc'd that morn to make"
(II, 70). As he "lies bewray'd" he directs his
prayer to Jove whose throne is a kind of celestial close-stool where "amus'd he reads, and
then returns the bills / Sign'd with that Ichor
which from Gods distils" (II, 91-92). His
petition preferred, Curll rallies and sweeps
on through his native element:

> Renew'd by ordure's sympathetic force,
> As oil'd with magic juices for the course,
> Vig'rous he rises; from th' effluvia strong
> Imbibes new life, and scours and stinks
>   along. (II, 103-106)

But of course the absolute of filth is the
diving contest held at the sewer mouth.

The plan of this book devoted to the serial
games is frankly and naturally episodic. Yet
the book possesses a curious and instructive
coherence. It is held together by the concord
of its discords: the dirt, the noise, the
ugliness, the blatancy and ineptitude that are
everywhere. The brilliant mockery of the epic
similes, here generally heavy or grotesque, is
a major factor in this unity. Here is Lintot's
gross gallop:

> As when a dab-chick waddles thro' the copse
> On feet and wings, and flies, and wades,
>   and hops;
> So lab'ring on, with shoulders, hands, and
>   head,

Wide as a wind-mill all his figures spread,
With arms expanded Bernard rows his state.
    (II, 63-67)

Here is Pope's analog of the din raised by the
"Monkey-mimics" as they try the "wound'rous
pow'r of Noise" (II, 222):

As when the long-ear'd milky mothers wait
At some sick miser's triple-bolted gate,
For their defrauded, absent foals they make
A moan so loud, that all the guild awake;
Sore sighs Sir Gilbert, starting at the bray,
From dreams of millions, and three groats to
    pay.
So swells each wind-pipe; Ass intones to Ass,
Harmonic twang! of leather, horn, and brass.
    (II, 247-254)

But it is in the episodic movement of Book
II that the "involvement" of the city is particularly dramatized, and that action works
strongly for unity. The topography of Pope's
similes of the braying asses and the defecating
Dutchman suggests the strategy of his design
here:

Walls, steeples, skies, bray back to him
    again.
In Tot'nam fields, the brethren, with amaze,
Prick all their ears up, and forget to graze;
Long Chanc'ry-lane retentive rolls the
    sound,
And courts to courts return it round and
    round;
Thames wafts it thence to Rufus' roaring
    hall,
And Hungerford re-echoes bawl for bawl.
    (II, 260-266)
....
As what a Dutchman plumps into the lakes,
One circle first, and then a second makes;
What Dulness dropt among her sons imprest
Like motion from one circle to the rest;

> So from the mid-most the nutation spreads
> Round and more round, o'er all the sea of
>   heads. (ii, 405-410)

What occurs in each case is a powerful "communication" from a center of malign energy, radiating
outward to occupy the city spaces and to take
physical and spiritual possession of the popu-
lace. The din raised by "sonorous Blackmore's
strain"(above) is stupefying, stunning the whole
city's sense. The epidemic movement of Dulness
takes several shapes and rhythms; the raucous
bouncing echo; the spreading circles of the
Dutchman's deposit; the wavelike progression of
sympathetic influence, as in the simile of the
nodding pines:

> Then mount the Clerks, and in one lazy tone
> Thro' the long, heavy, painful page drawl
>   on;
> Soft creeping, words on words, the sense
>   compose,
> At ev'ry line they stretch, they yawn, they
>   doze.
> As to soft gales top-heavy pines bow low
> Their heads bend with them as they cease to
>   blow;
> Thus oft they rear, and oft the head decline,
> As breathe, or pause, by fits, the airs di-
>   vine.
> And now to this side, now to that they nod
> As verse, or prose, infuse the drowzy God
>   (II, 387-396)

the cynosure effect of the enchanted crowds;
"turning coxcombs as they gaze" at Dulness's
shows; and a rolling, tumbling linear movement
that seems to lick up the city's streets and
the river's banks. Cibber's ecstatic vision
prefigures a condition perfected:

> "And oh! (he cry'd) what street, what lane
>   but knows,
> Our purgings, pumpings, blankettings, and
>   blows?

In ev'ry loom our labours shall be seen,
And the fresh vomit run for ever green!"

The "involving" force of this movement can be
shown by the single couplet that brings the
crowd back into the old City at the end of its
eastward return: "Thro' Lud's famed gates, a-
long the well-known Fleet, / Rolls the black
troop, and overshades the street' (II, 359-360).
   The movement of the fable itself, admittedly
hazy and desultory in the first two books, is
of course that of a mock Lord Mayor's Procession, east to west and back again, along Fleet
Street, the Strand, the Thames, from the City
to Westminster and return, bringing "the Smithfield Muses to the ear of Kings" (1, 2), bringing vulgarity to polite and learned life. The
progress of Dulness throws a long slovenly
noose about the heart of London, a garrotte
about the city's throat.[8] At the end of Book II
even the dunces are choked into silence; the
reading clerks subside into mutters; Centlivre
"felt her voice to fail" (II, 411). No head
can resist the opiate of Dulness, and prefigur-
ing, now gently, the end of the poem, "the soft
gifts of Sleep conclude the day" (II, 419). Dulness has begun her work of "hushing the Nations."
   Partly because it is the most static, the
action of Book III is the most orderly and homo-
geneous of the four books. Though the mental
eye moves with great range and agility here,
the angle of the artist's observation is single
and fixed, and the fictive theater is entirely
intracranial. But of course Cibber's is presented as a fairly hectic cranium. The action
is that of a vision, busy and complicated, of
the past and present history of Dulness and "a
glimpse, or Pisgah-sight of the future Fulness
of her Glory" (Argument to Book III). Cibber
is discovered in a posture that continues the
last movement of the preceding book, asleep like
a huge baby in the lap of Dulness in the sanctum
of her temple: a posture "of marvellous virtue,"
the Argument assures profane Madonna and Child,

forms a womb at the center of the concentric
circles of her kingdom, at the radial point of
her labyrinths. Attitude and atmosphere both
shield and inspire the snoring Prince:

> Him close she curtains round with Vapours
>   blue,
> And soft besprinkles with Cimmerian dew.
> Then raptures high the seat of Sense o'er-
>   flow,
> Which only heads refin'd from Reason know.
>   (III, 3-6)

Being refined from reason, Cibber's head is free
to wander "on Fancy's easy wing" to the Dunci-
adic underworld, where "a slip-shod Sibyl led
his steps along, / In lofty madness meditating
song" (III, 15-16).

     There is neither space nor need to canvass
these visions in detail. I am more concerned
with showing how the main fibers of the action
as a whole also shape the principal images of
the dreams, for in content they too are effectual actions. What dominates Cibber's first
view of the soporific realm of Bavius, for example, is another of Pope's swarming undiffer-
entiated multitudes:

> Millions and millions on these banks he
>   views,
> Thick as the stars of night, or morning dews,
> As thick as bees o'er vernal blossoms fly,
> As thick as eggs at Ward in Pillory.
>   (III, 31-34)

So Cibber's own history is treated as a type of
the endless genetic chain of the lineage of
stupidity: "Who knows how long thy transmigra-
ting soul / Might from Boeotian to Boeoötian
roll?" (III, 49-50). So too the rhythmical
outreach and ingestion of Dulness's malign plenitude is caught in a single swift and homely
simile:

> Or whirligigs, twirl'd round by skilful
>   swain,
> Suck the thread in, then yield it out again:
> All nonsense thus, of old or modern date,
> Shall in thee centre, and from thee circu-
>   late.   (III, 57-60)

So Cibber is invited to view the range of Dulness's power to encompass and smother: Earth's
wide extremes "her sable flag display'd, / And
all the nations cover'd in her shade!" (III,
71-72). All of this within the first seventy-
two lines of the book.
   It is this sense of inexorable progression
that unifies the series of visions unveiled by
Settle for the enraptured Prince. The march of
Dulness through space and time calls forth some
of Pope's grandest synoptic couplets:

> How little, mark, that portion of the ball,
> Where, faint at best, the beams of Science
>   fall:
> Soon as they dawn, from Hyperborean skies
> Embody'd dark, what clouds of Vandals rise!
> Lo! where Maeotis sleeps, and hardly flows
> The freezing Tanais thro' a waste of snows,
> The North by myriads pours her mighty sons,
> Great nurse of Goths, of Alans, and of Huns!
> See Alaric's stern port! the martial frame
> Of Genseric! and Attila's dread name!
> See the bold Ostrogoths on Latium fall;
> See the fierce Visigoths on Spain and Gaul!
> See, where the morning gilds the palmy shore
> (The soil that infant arts and letters bore)
> His conqu'ring tribes th' Arabian prophet
>   draws,
> And saving Ignorance enthrones by Laws.
> See Christians, Jews, one heavy sabbath keep,
> And all the western world believe and sleep.
>   (III, 83-100)

The phantasmagorias of present and future foretell the restoration of England to Dulness's
possession: "This fav'rite Isle, long sever'd

from her reign, / Dove-like, she gathers to her
wings again" (III, 125-126). The huge vision
now concentrates and grows more particular as
the scene returns to the occupation of the city
as the type of her triumph:

> Not with less glory mighty Dulness crown'd,
> Shall take thro Grub-street her triumphant
>   round;
> And her Parnassus glancing o'er at once,
> Behold an hundred sons, and each a Dunce.
>   (III, 135-138)

Settle's vision of the city arts, based on the
wild popular stage fare of the day, shows the
products of perfected unreason:

> Thence a new world, to Nature's laws unknown,
> Breaks out refulgent, with a heav'n its own:
> Another Cynthia her journey runs,
> And other planets circle other suns.
> The forests dance, the rivers upward rise,
> Whales sport in woods, and dolphins in the
>   skies;
> And last, to give the whole creation grace,
> Lo! one vast egg produces human race.
>   (III, 241-248)

Cibber's predicted conquest will "involve" the
city:

> Happier thy fortunes! Like a rolling stone,
> Thy giddy dulness still shall lumber on,
> Safe in its heaviness, shall never stray
> But lick up ev'ry blockhead in the way.
> Thee shall the Patriot, thee the Courtier
>   taste,
> And ev'ry year be duller than the last.
> 'Till rais'd from booths, to Theatre, to
>   Court,
> Her seat imperial Dulness shall transport.
>   (III, 293-300)

And finally Cibber is accorded the ensign of the
poppy, a new proclamation and acclamation, and
the book closes with enthusiastic prophecies of
general disaster to ensue.

It is impossible to say whether Pope realized
that the revised and expanded *Dunciad* would be
his last published work. But the great fourth
book, added after an interval of thirteen years
and including relics of other proposed but un-
attempted works, takes on special elevation and
poignancy in the context of the close of "this
long disease, my Life." One seems to hear swan
song airs particularly at the beginning and end
of the book. The second sentence, for example,
conveys both a continuing anathema and a weary
resignation:

> Ye Pow'rs! whose Mysteries restor'd I sing,
> To whom Time bears me on his rapid wing,
> Suspend a while your Force inertly strong,
> Then take at once the Poet and the Song.
>   (IV, 5-8)

The "sickness" of the sun seems to express not
only the Dog Star's "unpropitious Ray" (IV, 9)
but the poet's own mind and heart as once more
he sees the stubborn daughter of Chaos and old
Night ever ready "to blot out Order, and extinguish Light" (IV, 14). The voice of the heart-
broken priest, always audible within the ventri-
loquism of the Tory satirists, sounds with special resonance here. It is a bitter joke, the
new invocation in Miltonic parody that opens
Book IV, begging only a little light, "one dim
Ray" (IV, I), just enough "as half to shew,
half veil the deep Intent" (IV, 4). The full
view is too awful to bear. And in this book
treating the "consummation of all" (Argument to
Book IV) even the prayer of the poet is addressed to Chaos and Night as powers confirmed in
state.

The fourth book is altogether a court scene,
and as such relatively static, mostly lateral
in movement. The panoramas and processions move

toward a central point, "by sure Attraction led,/
And strong impulsive gravity of Head" (IV, 74-
75), to the throne where Dulness sits with her
head in a cloud and her "Laureat son" still lol-
ling in her lap, and there they caper and freeze
into tableaux, convenient to the yawn that will
engulf them and their betters at the end. The
throne of Dulness is evidently now the throne of
the kingdom, and the jumbled *scena* of the opening
view shows her situated at the peak of a heaped
pyramid of vanquished and spurned disciplines of
the mind: "Beneath her foot-stool, *Science* groans
in Chains, / And *Wit* dreams Exile, Penalties, and
Pains. / There foam'd rebellious *Logic*, gagg'd
and bound" (IV, 21-23). The catalog fills
twenty-three lines.

With the Goddess fixed on her throne, her
swarming disciples cluster busily "conglob'd"
about their "Centre." The "rolling," "involving" movement of the mobs through the city is
more intense than ever in Book IV, though its
effect is more centripetal than processional
now, converging on the Queen, moving toward the
eye rather than past it. Here is the general
picture:

> The gath'ring number, as it moves along,
> Involves a vast involuntary throng,
> Who gently drawn, and struggling less and
>   less,
> Roll in her Vortex, and her pow'r confess.
>   (IV, 81-84)

And even when the rowdy scene is more or less
fixed, the disorderly local movement of "crowds
on crowds" as one or another party presses for
attention continues the rhythm of dispossession
and possession. Here is the mass of black-gown-
ed academics, for example: "Prompt at the call,
around the Goddess roll / Broad hats, and hoods,
and caps, a sable shoal: / Thick and more thick
the black blockade extends" (IV, 189-191). And
the rout of travelled fops who displace them:
"In flow'd at once a gay embroider'd race, /
And titt'ring pushed the Pedants off the place
(IV, 274-275).

With the mincing "Harlot form" of Opera, the
first of the serial petitioners of Book IV,
Pope plays an interesting variant on his theme
of unbalanced and inefficient movement: not
merely awkward this time, but an incoherent and
meretricious prettiness with no musculature and
no tensile strength, no body and no brain. "*O
Cara! Cara!*" she trills, glancing scornfully at
the prostrate Muses;"silence all that train: /
Joy to great Chaos! let Division reign..." (IV,
53-54). The successive petitioners are archetypes of vanity and anti-intellectualism, per-
verters of faith and reason, purveyors of egotism, triviality, and false doctrine. They
achieve a hectic unity by their common tendency
to special pleading, partial views, short and
straitened programs to which they adhere with
obsessed enthusiasm. Opera's punning imperative, "Let Division reign," could stand as a
rubric for the whole book.

These spokesmen perform at greater length
and in stricter oratorical modes than those of
earlier books, with heavier gravity and more
extended resonance, and the effect is that of a
ponderous and ominous thickening of spiritual
and intellectual crisis. The schoolmasters
boast of their "narrowing" potency, their enmity to dubiety and speculation, their command
of rote learning and formulaic language by
which they "hang one jingling padlock on the
mind":

Plac'd at the door of Learning, youth to
    guide,
We never suffer it to stand too wide.
To ask, to guess, to know, as they commence,
As Fancy opens the quick springs of Sense,
We ply the Memory, we load the brain,
Bind rebel Wit, and double chain on chain,
Confine the thought to exercise the breath;
And keep them in the pale of Words till
death.   (IV, 153-160)

The university men, led by "that awful Arist-
arch" Bentley, handle language and learning in
more sophisticated forms of the same false values.   "The critic Eye, that microscope of Wit, /
Sees hairs and pores, examines bit by bit" (IV,
233-234):   woods are lost in trees, wholes are
drowned under a shoal of parts. As sworn servants of Dulness, they use the instrument of
language in her obfuscatory and stultifying
spirit:

> ...For thee explain a thing till all men
>   doubt it,
> And write about it, Goddess, and about it:
> So spins the silkworm small its slender
>   store,
> And labours till it clouds itself all o'er.
>   (IV, 251-254)

The pedants are "pushed off the place" by the
"gay embroider'd race" of continental travelers,
led by "Whore, Pupil, and lac'd Governor from
France" (IV, 272), a "finished" youth with his
harlot and his bear-leader, who assures the
Queen that "Europe he saw, and Europe saw him
too"[9] (IV, 294). If the young man showed any
prospect of English yeomanly sturdiness, it has
been sloughed in a tide of continental perfumes.
As he "saunter'd Europe round, / And gather'd
ev'ry Vice on Christian ground" (IV, 311-312),
he has

> ...Dropt the dull lumber of the Latin store,
> Spoil'd his own language, and acquir'd no
>   more,
> All Classic learning lost on Classic ground;
> And last turn'd *Air*, the Echo of a Sound!
>   (IV, 319-322)

It is in this sense that the young man is Dulness's "accomplish'd Son" (IV, 282). The Governor presents the youth and his consort to the
Queen with the prophecy that they will fit smoothly
into the endless genetic chain of Dulness:

"So may the sons of sons of sons of whores..."
(IV, 332). The Queen receives them gladly,wraps
them in her veil, and "frees from sense of Shame"
(IV, 336). The extravagances of the Virtuosi--
of coins, flowers, insects--who follow move the
Goddess to an ecstatic apocalyptic vision:

> O! would the Sons of Men think their Eyes
> And reason giv'n them but to study *Flies!*
> See Nature in some partial narrow shape,
> And let the Author of the Whole escape:
> Learn but to trifle; or, who most observe,
> To wonder at their Maker, not to serve.
>   (IV, 453-458)

"Be that my task," promptly offers a "gloomy
Clerk, / Sworn foe to Myst'ry, yet divinely
dark" (IV, 459-460), speaking for free thinkers
and mechanic philosophers who have perverted
reason to be an enemy of both revelation and
experience:

> Let others creep by timid steps, and slow,
> On Plain Experience lay foundations low,
> By common sense to common knowledge bred,
> And last, to Nature's Cause thro' Nature
>   led.
> All-seeing in thy mists, we want no guide,
> Mother of Arrogance, and Source of Pride!
> We nobly take the high Priori Road,
> And reason downward, till we doubt of God.
>   (IV, 465-472)

So the demonstrations of Book IV, and hence
of the poem, come to a point in absolute Ego,
the ultimate vulgarity. Enthralled and fixed
in Self, the dunces are ready to be swept up
in the harvesting yawn of Dulness. In a book
that treats largely of the misuse of reason
and of language its vehicle, the yawn that
speaks the uncreating word, the antilogos, the
anticreation, is the powerful and suitable conclusion. And the yawn rightly concludes the
poem as a whole.

It is no use to argue for a neat or obvious
unity in *The Dunciad*. It is not a well-made work.
It is a big harsh poem with a lot of violent
work to do, which it does with some waste and
awkwardness that are incidents of its energy,
defects of its virtues. Its unity is not that
of straightforward narrative march toward a
dramatic end always in view, as in *The Rape of the
Lock*. One can force out of the scenario of the
four books a specious linear sequence of a more
traditional sort: perhaps Coronation, Celebration, Consecration, Consummation, if we wish
to be fancy about it. But the alignment of the
four books is less linear and progressive than
parallel and iterative: they are laid not end
to end but side by side. But I insist that the
poem does march forward, a unity, and the yawn of
Dulness does reach upward and outward to enclose
the ends of all four books. The unifying movement is that of common cause, of energy, of
passion, of intellectual outrage that emerges in
visions that have the insistent recurrence of
nightmare and merge finally into a single vision,
sufficiently apocalyptic.

Size is of the essence in *The Dunciad*: the size
of the issue, of the scene, of the fictive
events. I have tried to suggest the unity that
comes from the proper iteration of images specified to function, especially images of movement
appropriate to the nature of Dulness, and more especially her movement through the city of the
mind. After the great yawn and the awful No-
thing-filled silence that follows, perhaps the
strongest lingering effect is that of sheer
size, size as significance: of a giant ethical
and aesthetic displacement, of the robustness
of Pope's vision and the prodigality of his gesture in writing this poem. The effect may lead
one to think back over his work as a whole--past
our bemusement with his frail childlike figure,
his addiction to the tiniest of stanza forms,
and the filigree delicacy of his most famous
poem--to recognize that his satirical grasp, his
way of seizing and moving a subject, had always

been direct and stout. Even in *The Rape of the
Lock*, is not the sensibility, the manner and spirit of attack, fundamentally robust and large-
minded? Looking at Pope from our own day one
thinks how nice it would be to have him back:
our times could use him.

THE *DUNCIAD* AS MOCK-BOOK

William Kinsley

   Pope's *Dunciad* has long been recognized as a
many-splendored monster that feeds on the meat
it mocks. Pope follows knowingly, wittily, and
rationally the techniques that the Dunces follow
unknowingly, solemnly, and irrationally. In Dulness' new world, "Farce and Epic get a jumbled
race"--but Pope's own poem is an offspring of the
same mésalliance. The Dunces produce bathos by
accident, Pope by design. They produce poetic
chaos, he reproduces their chaos in a way that
transforms it into an unusually rich and complex
poetic order. Like Nabokov's Sebastian Knight,
he is "an angel mimicking a tumbler pigeon."
Whetted on each other in Pope's poetic workshop
and unerringly reaimed, the Dunces' dull spears
transfix their owners.[1] This method complements
the more straightforward one of condemning the
Dunces by juxtaposing them with the epic and religious masterpieces of the Western tradition,
that is, by showing at the same time what the
Dunces *don't* do.
   If we consider the poem as a mock-book, both
methods will come into play. On one hand, the

This essay first appeared in *Huntington Library Quarterly* 35 (1971), 29-47.

epic values and Pope's cultural values in general
are embodied in books; on the other, bookmaking
is a characteristic activity of Dunces. These
facts enable Pope not only to satirize all aspects of contemporary book production and consump-
tion but also to exploit Duncical bookmaking procedures for his own satiric purposes. Thus, just
as the poem is a mock-epic with some of the grandeur of a true epic, so it is at once a book and
a mock-book, or parody of a book.[2] There is nothing accidental about this; not only does Pope
mock prefaces, footnotes, and other bookish im-
pedimenta, but as my friend Joseph Keogh once
pointed out, he carries this mockery to the point
of having a mock proof-sheet leaked to Cibber
before the 1743 version was printed.[3]

In the history of Western civilization the
book has served as a focal point for many com-
plexes of ideas and attitudes. Three of these
are especially important for the *Dunciad*. Most
generally, the book was an incarnation of wisdom
and a metonym for learning and culture. Second,
since literature was a counterpart of reality in
aesthetic theories based on mimesis ("Nature and
Homer were, he found, the same")[4] and since literature existed almost exclusively in books, the
book itself was thought of as a mirror of nature.
(In the Middle Ages the terms of this comparison
had been reversed: the created universe was
thought of as a kind of book in which God, its
author, revealed himself to man just as he did in
the Book of Scripture.) Third, since in Pope's
time virtually all books were printed, the book
can be a symbol as well as a carrier of the mental habits fostered by the domination of printing
as a means of learning and communication. It is
probably impossible to determine the precise
importance of each of these traditions of the
book in the consciousness (or subconsciousness)
of Pope and his readers, or to determine the
exact degree of literal force remaining for them
in the many metaphors involved, but I hope to
show that such ideas were prominent enough to
form a significant part of the amazingly rich

and diverse materials out of which Pope fashioned
his *Dunciad*.

From its invention until the nineteenth century the book, first in manuscript and later
printed, was highly and almost universally respected, if not venerated, as the single most
important means of preserving and transmitting
knowledge.[5] The books in the *Dunciad*, from this
point of view, are obviously everything that
books should not be: they are repositories of
dullness and nonsense, not of wisdom. We can in-
fuse poetic life into this truism by recalling a
well-known passage in Milton's *Areopagitica*:

For books are not absolutely dead things, but do
contain a potency of life in them to be as active
as that soul was whose progeny they are; nay,
they do preserve as in a vial the purest eff cacy
and extraction of that living intellect that bred
them....a good book is the precious lifeblood of
a master spirit, embalmed and treasured up on
purpose to a life beyond life.[6]

A similar idea appears in Davenant's *Gondibert*.
The hero and his companion visit Astragon's
library,

> Where, when they thought they saw in well
>   sought Books,
>   Th'assembled souls of all that Men held wise,
> It bred such awful rev'rence in their looks,
>   As if they saw the buryd writers rise.[7]

In Pope's time we find this idea in Swift's *Battle of the Books*; and in the *Memoirs of Martinus Scriblerus*, Martin, "casting his eyes around on the
Books that adorned his room, broke forth in this
pathetic Apostrophe. O ye Spirits of Antiquity,
who yet live in those sacred leaves!"[8]
This image of course appears by negation in
the immovable folios that clutter the scene of
the *Dunciad*, in the asbestine "sheet of Thulè"
that extinguishes Cibber's sacrificial fire,[9] in

the book-induced sleep that concludes the mock-
epic games. In the world of the *Dunciad* the letter kills, and there is no spirit to give life.
Just as Dulness is both Gravity and Pertness,
however, so Milton's idea is present by exaggeration and perversion as well as by negation.
Books and their parts take on a magical, bestial,
or demonic life of their own. "A winged volume"
flies swiftly to the hand of a sorcerer (III.234;
p. 331). A pun can endow a sorry specimen of a
printed page with the life and movement of an
equally sorry human one: Dulness "saw slow
Philips creep like Tate's poor page" (I.105; p.
277), and gives another Page her word (IV.30; p.
343). Another poem seethes with life--the larval
life that flourishes in dead flesh:

> Maggots half-form'd in rhyme exactly meet,
> And learn to crawl upon poetic feet.
> (I.61-62; p. 274)

"Maggots" are whims or crotchets as well as the
larvae of flies, and the term "feet" operates
like "page" in the preceding quotation, mingling
art and life to the confusion and corruption of
both. Finally, in a parody of classical ideas
of reincarnation that also echoes the images of
Milton and Davenant, souls of dead poets

> Demand new bodies, and in Calf's array,
> Rush to the world, impatient for the day.
> (III.29-30; p. 321)

Brown and Mears, the booksellers who unbar the
gates for them, hardly fulfill Milton's qualifications: "he who is made judge to sit upon the
birth or death of books, whether they may be
wafted into this world or not, had need to be a
man above the common measure" (*Areopagitica*, p.
734). In the world of the *Dunciad* we find neither real books nor humankind, but a sort of monstrous *tertium quid*, part book (bound in calfskin),
part author (since "calf" is a slang term for
fool), and informed by a dead soul. These dead

souls are incarnated in the *Dunciad* in another way
also, since it is they who, according to the fiction of the poem, have produced the pedantic prefaces and notes that encumber the text.

For the *Dunciad*, the most important aspect of
the tradition is probably the image of the created world as the Book of Nature which, like the
Book of Scripture, reveals God to man if it is
properly read. A medieval commonplace, this
image appears frequently in such Renaissance
writers as Donne, Bacon, and Milton, and survives
vigorously into the eighteenth century. In *Paradise Lost* Raphael tells Adam,

> To ask or search I blame thee not, for
>   Heav'n
> Is as the Book of God before thee set,
> Wherein to read his wond'rous Works.
> (VIII.66-68)

With an ethical rather than epistemological emphasis, James Thomson wishes to

>   meditate the book
> Of Nature, ever open, aiming thence
> Warm from the heart to learn the moral song.[10]

Joseph Trapp proclaims,

> With holy Fear I read Thy sacred Word;
> And where I could not understand, ador'd ...
> Thy Book of Nature too both Day and Night
> I read, and study'd with sincere Delight.[11]

These examples may seem conventional and un-
inspired compared to similar images from the
Renaissance, and it is true that they do not seem
to be informed by the almost mystical sense of
analogy that we find in the earlier age. But the
image was given a new impetus in the eighteenth
century by the physico-theologians, who began to
use the new discoveries of science systematically
in an attempt to proclaim the existence and glory

of God. John Ray's popular treatise has a characteristic title: *The Wisdom of God Manifested in the
Works of the Creation* (1st ed., 1691, 6th ed., 1714).
For Ray and his fellows, science was an exegetical tool with which to improve one's reading of
the Book of Nature. William Derham quotes with
approval St. Bernard's aphorism that "mundus
codex est Dei, in quo jugiter legere debemus."[12]
Elaborating the metaphor, a popularizer tells his
readers that they should not confine their studies
to "the capitals in nature's mighty volume"
(bears, elephants, etc.) but should also be "master of the little letters likewise."[13] Another
religious motive for reading the Book of Nature
was the obscurity of Scripture and the acrimonious disputes which had sprung up among its readers. John Locke was not alone in feeling that
the "legible characters of [God's] works and
providence" in the world might provide a surer
way than Scripture to the knowledge of God;[14]
even Donne gave qualified approval to a similar
idea of Raymond de Sebonde.[15]

    The secular side of this tradition, however,
was probably more important for Pope himself.
The discovery he attributes to Virgil, that Nature and Homer are the same, was his own discovery
also. We need to remember that for Pope and his
readers Homer, like other classics, existed primarily in books that included not only the text
but also a copious commentary. (The idea that
"Homer" was a strolling bard or group of bards
whose works were stitched together by others had
made its appearance in Pope's time,[16] but it had
not yet affected significantly the way Homer was
read or understood. The early disintegrators,
knowing nothing of the real conditions of oral
epic composition that have been revealed to us by
Milman Parry and Albert B. Lord[17] and judging
from criteria derived unconsciously from print
culture, concluded that if Homer were not a literate individual he couldn't have produced a book
and therefore wasn't much of a poet. Homer's
defenders replied that he must have been a literate individual, since the *Iliad* and the *Odyssey*

were obviously unified books.) The metaphorical
identity of Nature and Homer, and by extension of
Nature and all good writing, pervades the *Essay
on Criticism* and implies, of course, that human
poetry is also in some sense a Book of Nature.[18]
A similar conception may have encouraged the
early Greek allegorical interpreters of Homer.
Since Homer had long been the literary equivalent
of their whole world, critics felt compelled to
find in him everything that a nascent science was
beginning to discover or speculate about in the
cosmos.[19]

For the Augustans there was no real opposition
between the sacred and secular branches of this
tradition. On the contrary, the Augustans tended
to fuse them. As Earl Wasserman has often pointed out, the Renaissance habit of Christianizing
pagan authors by means of moral and allegorical
interpretations lasted well into the eighteenth
century, and this syncretic tendency is also apparent in the characteristic metaphors of the
period. Cowley in "The Resurrection" speaks of
"*Virgils* sacred *work*," which, like "all th'*harmonious Worlds* on high," will perish only on the Last
Day. Homer was a favorite target for Christianizing interpretations of all kinds in the later
seventeenth century, and some critics went to
the extent of virtually identifying him with
Moses.[20] In the manuscript of the *Essay on Criticism*, Pope associates Homer very closely with the
Bible:

Nor is it *Homer nods* , but *We* that *dream*,
In *Sacred Writ* where Difficulties rise,
'Tis safer far to *fear* than *criticize*.[21]

In the final version, of course, Nature, "still
divinely bright," is itself almost deified, and
Homer's status rises accordingly.[22]

In a climate of thought like this, the critic,
the scientist, and the scriptural exegete become
collaborators, and their jobs all become different varieties of reading. The resulting analogies
kaleidoscope into many configurations. If a pro-

per reading of Homer can lead one to an understanding of Nature herself, the critic's dignity, as
well as the poet's, is enormously enhanced; but
the critic's responsibilities are correspondingly
grave, since bad reading may not merely misinterpret a work of art but also guide both the critic
and his readers *away* from Nature. Similarly, bad
poetry may lead an undiscerning critic into a "*glaring Chaos* and *wild Heap* of *Wit*," equally far from
the order of Nature.[23] Conversely, Nature illuminates Homer; as has been said of a modern heir
of much of Pope's outlook, "*Ulysses* is a book of
life, a microcosm which is a small-scale replica
of the universe, and the methods which lead to an
understanding of the latter will provide a solution of the obscurities in *Ulysses*."[24] If the
critic brings to his reading a mechanistic or
otherwise impoverished conception of Nature, his
interpretation of his text will suffer accordingly. Likewise with his attitude toward language:
the main fault of Bentley's emendations, always
based prosaically on "clear syntax, strict logic,
and normal usage,"[25] is that there is more in
Horace, let alone Homer and Milton, than is dreamt
of in Bentley's philology. The scriptural exegete must also be able to read the Book of Nature.
Misinterpretations of Genesis, says William Whiston, are "the effects of ignorance of the frame
of the World, and of the stile of Scripture; of an
unacquaintedness with the *Works*, and thence an inability of judging concerning the *Word of God* relating to them."[26] On the other hand, the Book
of Nature may have to be "digested" into a human
written book before the intellect can fully assimilate it.[27] The implication that poetry, by reflecting Nature, can lead its readers to God is
made explicit by Sir William Davenant:

Poesy, which like contracted *Essences* seems the
utmost strength & activity of Nature, is as all
good Arts subservient to Religion ... And as
Poesy is the best Expositor of Nature, Nature being misterious to such as use not to consider,
so Nature is the best Interpreter of God, and
more cannot be said of Religion.[28]

This particular network of analogical correspondences is one example of the kind of thought
patterns that Earl Wasserman has called "cosmic
syntaxes." (Others include the Great Chain of
Being, man as microcosm of the universe, and the
body politic.) Wasserman goes on to point out
that the eighteenth-century poet "could afford to
think of his art as imitative of 'nature,' since
these patterns were what he meant by 'nature.'"[29]
Similarly it is not surprising that Robert Boyle
chose the clock in Strasbourg Cathedral as the
model for the cosmos in his argument from design,
since, as Derek J. Price has shown, such clocks
were originally only minor appendages of far
more complicated clockwork mechanisms designed
explicitly as man-made models of the cosmos and
having no utilitarian purpose at all.[30] Some of
the astronomical imagery in the *Essay on Man* may
have been inspired by Pope's familiarity with
Whiston's *Copernicus,* a fairly elaborate astronomical model designed primarily to demonstrate
eclipses.[31] In relation to our present concerns,
it was quite natural for Pope's predecessors and
contemporaries to think of Nature as a book, since
they examined it with minds and sensibilities
formed to a great degree by books. Without sub-
scribing, like Mallarmé, to the view that each
individual's language *is* his reality, we can see
how this particular kind of book-language helped
to form the Augustan world picture.

The importance of all this for the *Dunciad* is
that the poem is permeated by these analogies, but
they are inverted or perverted in the way that
the epic tradition and the rest of human culture
are perverted at the hands of the Dunces. If
Nature and Homer are the same, if Scripture and
Nature are the twin books of God's revelation,
then the *Dunciad* is in one sense the same as the
irrational "new world" it describes; among other
things, it is a poem upon Nothing, an attempt to
give an earthly habitation and a name to nonbeing,
the Revelation of Dulness and Satan. One of
Pope's earliest poetic exercises, it will be recalled, was "On Silence," imitated from Rochester's

"Upon Nothing" (TE, VI, 17-19). The *Dunciad* is an imitation of the *Iliad* and the *Aeneid*, poems about the whole cosmos and cornerstones of Western civilization; but it is also an imitation of the *Margites*, a poem long since "uncreated," if indeed it ever existed.[32] Everything and nothing are both always present in the poem, but their relationship changes through time; as the poem proceeds, Dulness captures more and more, until at the end, when she controls everything, she reduces it immediately to nothing.[33] If, for Davenant, good poetry can lead the reader through Nature to God, the poetry of the Dunces can lead him to the devil. If the encyclopedic knowledge of epics and the Bible "is regarded sacramentally, as a human analogy of divine knowledge,"[34] the *Dunciad* tries to emulate Satanic ignorance and error. Where medieval encyclopedias were usually organized as commentaries on the six days of Creation, the *Dunciad* runs in the opposite order, toward uncreation. If the Bible is a visible representation of the invisible Book of Life or Register of the Elect, the *Dunciad* is, as Anthony Raspa says of Donne's *Ignatius His Conclave*, "the Register of the damned or the evil."[35] Pope complicates and enriches his book metaphor by using another art, the theater, as the metaphorical basis of the "new world" of Dulness, so that a sensational and commercialized stage becomes all the world; the *codex mundi* includes a *theatrum mundi*, and in Pope's mind the implications of the latter metaphor had long been cosmic, not just earthly.[36]

Thus the *Dunciad* is the mock-book of a whole cosmos gone wrong, and may be contrasted to other mock-books such as *A Tale of a Tub* or *Pale Fire*, which concentrate on portraying the way the addled individual minds of their putative authors or editors (the "Hack" and Charles Kinbote) project their own disordered images onto the world. From this point of view these books are expressive, whereas the *Dunciad* is mimetic; and this is another way of saying that the *Dunciad*, text and notes taken together, has many "authors." But Pope, like Swift and Nabokov, of course knows that he is also writing a real book, and the norms of the book condemn the mock-book just as the Holy Spirit condemns Dulness. Here we see another contrast with *A Tale of a Tub*: Swift's work, partly because it is always focused on the process of authorship, is a much more detailed and thoroughgoing parody of the form of the book than is the *Dunciad*, but it does not bring into play so many of the positive metaphorical associations of the tradition of the book.

As with the poem, so with the notes and prefaces, though their relation to the book tradition is somewhat more complex and involved. First of all, the *Dunciad* is not the only one of his poems for which Pope provided notes, and John Butt has shown that Pope's reason for this self-annotation was his conviction that he was already a modern classic.[37] This procedure in turn rests on a belief that a classic is a classic not only by virtue of its intrinsic worth but also by virtue of the recognition of that worth by generations of readers and critics. Notes and commentaries are a visible index of that recognition. In translating the *Iliad*, therefore, Pope "regards it as his duty to embody in his work the tradition of epic scholarship as well as epic poetry."[38] In other words, notes become almost as much a generic requirement of the successful classic as invocations to the muse are of the epic, and the form of the book asserts itself in yet another way. From this point of view, the *Dunciad* as book has useful real notes, and as mock-book it has ludicrously inept and overgrown mock-notes.[39]

This is straightforward enough, but Pope's campaign against pedantry introduces complications. For one thing, the presence of copious notes is by no means a guarantee that the book so annotated is a classic; one of Pope's major objects of attack is the scholar who wastes his time and energy providing vast commentaries for negligible authors. Such real notes on virtual nonbooks show pseudo-criticism at its worst. But if such critics turn their attention to Homer or Horace, they succeed no better, since their com-

mentary steadfastly ignores the qualities that
make these writers important. This amounts to
writing mock-notes about real books. Both of
these operations occur in the mock-notes to the
Dunciad: as a poem about Nothing, it attracts the
kind of commentators who "poach in Suidas for
unlicens'd Greek";[40] as a poem about Nature, it
attracts the kind of mind that cannot distinguish between Nature and Nothing. Both operations are of course present at once in any given
mock-note, an indication that for Pope they are
essentially the same operation.

Printing concerns us here because, first of
all, by Pope's time virtually all books were
printed and the Book of Nature was thought of as
a printed book, and second, because the process
and some of the consequences of printing are an
important theme of the *Dunciad*. Our investigation
here must rely to some degree on conjecture and
intuition, since, as such modern students of
communications as Marshall McLuhan and Walter J.
Ong have shown, the users of a given medium of
communication are often unaware of the thought-
patterns fostered, or even imposed, by the medium. A few texts do exist, however, which make
explicit something of what Pope's contemporaries
felt about printing. One N. Billingsley wrote
of Gutenberg somewhat as Pope later wrote of
Newton, praising the year

> Wherein God pleased to unbosom Night,
> The Art of Printing being brought to Light.[41]

In a similar vein, someone in France call printing "cette seconde délivrance de l'homme." In
Spectator 166, Addison explicitly makes printing
analogous to the Creation:

Aristotle tells us, that the World is a Copy or
Transcript of those Ideas which are in the Mind
of the first Being; and that those Ideas which
are in the Mind of Man, are a Transcript of the
World: To this we may add, that Words are the

Transcript of those Ideas which are in the Mind
of Man, and that Writing or Printing are the
Transcript of Words.
 As the supreme Being has expressed, and as it
were printed his Ideas in the Creation, Men express their Ideas in Books, which by this great
Invention of these latter Ages may last as long
as the Sun and Moon.[42]

Writing from Williamsburg, Virginia, in 1730, J.
Markland celebrates the typesetter's work in
terms that echo Ovid's creation story in the *Metamorphoses*, Dryden's in *A Song for St. Cecilia's Day*,
and the myth of Amphion, as a new world of print
springs into being:

> For this the careful *Artist* wakes,
> And o'er his countless Brood he stands,
>   His numerous Hoards,
>   Of *speechless* Letters, *unform'd* Words,
> *Unjointed* Questions, and *unmeaning* Breaks,
> Which into Order rise, and Form, at his
>   Commands.
>   . . . .
> With less Expence of Care and Thought
>   Did th'antient *Sage* surmise
> The *Frame*, (thus Epicurus taught)
> And *Order* of the Earth to rise.[43]

In these passages printing is clearly associated
with order, light, knowledge, and divinity. The
idea of types as embodiments of energy and power
appears also, particularly in Markland, but is
more striking when the types are compared to
soldiers:

> First, carv'd on blocks, his ruder handmaids
>   stood,
> But soon for metal chang'd th'ignoble wood;
> Till, free to break the rank, or form the line,
> For various use they variously combine.[44]

Sterling also prophesies, in terms that perhaps
unconsciously echo the *Dunciad*, that printing will
"sway the whole creation in thy right" (p. 150).

The educational reforms of Peter Ramus and his
followers in the sixteenth century had given
printing another, more subliminal, role in the
human consciousness. "On the one hand everything,
even physics, is conceived of as some kind of
operation on a [printed] text. But on the other
hand, the operation does not seem to respect sufficiently the mysterious nature of verbal expression.... Literary expression is allowed to masquerade as physical reality."[45] The mind thus
came to be thought of as a sort of printer's font,
from which one selected "elements" of discourse
the way a typesetter selects types, and "the
printed page [corresponds] to methodized discourse."[46]

Ramism had of course ceased to be a coherent
program long before the eighteenth century, and
it is hard to say precisely what degree of unconscious influence its assumptions still had. Pope
himself was probably not directly affected by it,
thanks to his irregular education, but certain
aspects of the *Dunciad* suggest that he was aware
of it. On the other hand, his voracious and solitary reading in childhood must have made him
aware of another power of printed books, the power
to enthrall and hypnotize. He could hardly have
escaped the temptation, to which Don Quixote suc-
cumbed, of taking for reality the printed world
of his own library.[47]

Another curious attempt to reduce Nature to
print, perhaps the most radically Ramist of all,
is relevant to the *Dunciad*: John Wilkins' *Essay
towards a Real Character, and a Philosophical Language*
(London, 1668). Wilkins' "real character" was a
system of writing designed to express directly
the nature of the thing or concept it represented. Each kind of substance, accident, relation,
etc., had its own graphic sign; and preliminary
to this the whole world of both thought and reality had been elaborately analyzed, classified, and
diagramed.[48] Wilkins transcribed the Lord's
Prayer and the Creed into his character and interpreted each word exhaustively.

Wilkins' goal was a printed version of the kind of natural language that is the subject of Plato's *Cratylus* and that Adam was thought to have spoken before the Fall, a language in which the *sound* of each word reveals the full nature of its referent--in other words, a language in which there is a natural and inevitable connection between word and thing.[49] Wilkins also devised a spoken language, but it was secondary to the printed character, which chould be learned without any reference to it at all (p. 385). The interesting thing from our point of view is that the components of Wilkins' character, in their mobility, repeatability, and combinability, are so clearly based on printer's types. There are hundreds and thousands of words and things, but only a few types. What Wilkins did, unconsciously no doubt, was to analyze reality and break it up the way a printer distributes type from a forme, and then to reconstitute it again on a printed page. As McLuhan has said of a different enterprise, Baconian technology, Wilkins was trying to put out the Book of Nature in a revised edition.[50] The old letters, based on the words that Locke and others so distrusted and dating back to prehistory, were good only for stories; to reflect reality, the resources of the printing press were needed.

The static, improverished conception of reality that such a method produces (or vice versa) is obvious. Wilkins' method leads him to conclude, for example, that there are many fewer species than are commonly thought to exist, "not a hundred sorts of Beasts, nor two hundred of Birds" (p. 162).[51] Following the thought patterns we have noticed before, he then turns his attention to the Book of Scripture, using this radical new conclusion to support the historicity of Noah's ark. Another indication of Wilkins' static, print-influenced way of looking at things appears in his assignment of nouns only, not verbs, to the class of "integrals" or principal words, a verb being "really no other than an *Adjective*, and the *Copula sum* affixed to it or conteined in it."[52]

The extent to which Wilkins and his *Essay* remained a live issue in the early eighteenth century
is hard to determine. It is worth noting that
his supporters were often opponents of Pope or
Swift. Wotton gives the *Essay* high praise, and
Bentley mentions it favorably in passing.[53] As
an object of satire, Wilkins appears in both *The
Battle of the Books*, as a modern engineer (p. 237),
and in the *Dunciad* (IV.452). An anonymous key-
writer also finds him in Gulliver's third voyage:

(the Customs and Manners of the *Laputians* very
much resemble the *Lunarians* of Bishop *Wilkins*, alluding also to another Book wrote by that Prelate
in Folio, intitled, *The Real Character*) ... And the
Scheme proposed for entirely abolishing all *Words*,
and talking by *Things*, may be farther Illustrated
by consulting Bishop WILKINS's *Real Character* ... *ut
supra.*[54]

The printed Laputan words look suspiciously like
Wilkins' characters, and the operation of the
frame like the recombining of movable types.
Thus Swift seems to be satirizing both Wilkins
and printing, or more precisely, their interaction: the assumption that a mechanical operation
plus a real character can lead to universal
knowledge. These various references are enough,
I think, to justify our including Wilkins in the
general satiric ambience of the *Dunciad*. Our main
interest in the *Essay*, however, lies in the clarity with which it illustrates the way the printing
press could penetrate the consciousness of a
scientist so deeply that he interpreted reality
according to its norms.[55]
    In his preface to the *Dunciad*, Martinus Scrib-
lerus tells us that "our Poet ... lived in those
days, when (after providence had permitted the
Invention of Printing as a scourge for the Sins
of the learned) Paper also became so cheap, and
printers so numerous, that a deluge of authors
cover'd the land" (TE, V, 49). This sort of complaint had of course been repeated by every hack
who ever set pen to paper, and the metaphor of

the Deluge is hardly original; but this is another Duncical cliché that Pope is going to enliven
for his own ends, and the association of printing
with destruction announces an important theme of
the poem. Here the kind of energy that we have
seen associated with print produces cancerous
overgrowths: the notes crowd the poem off the
page, prefaces and appendices reproduce their
kind to the seventh generation, and the presses,
like the mechanical word-frame in Lagado, clatter
on long after any rational mind has ceased to
direct them. The only god in this machine is the
"Divinity without a *Nous*," "Wrapt up in Self, a
God without a Thought," in whose image the Dunces
are made (IV.244, 485). Markland's Amphion-like
typesetter has turned sorcerer's apprentice. The
social outlook and universal scope of the *Dunciad*
are emphasized again by comparison with the individual focus of *A Tale of a Tub*, at the end of
which a single pen, the Hack's, is moving on, impelled by the "Ghost of Wit," writing about Nothing long after his real subject is exhausted.
    One feature of the "new world" of the *Dunciad*
is a new letter, Bentley's digamma:

    Roman and Greek Grammarians! know your Better:
    Author of something yet more great than Letter;
    While tow'ring o'er your Alphabet, like Saul,
    Stands our Digamma, and o'er-tops them all.
                        (IV.215-218; pp. 363-364)

Again, we may note the overgrowth--a double let-
ter--and the way the metaphor compares the letter
to a human being. Pope's note gives the whole
enterprise the air of an acrobatic performance
when he describes the Digamma as "one Gamma set
upon the shoulders of another." This kind of invention and the physical conquest it implies form
the appropriate final achievement of someone who
begins by proclaiming "words we teach alone."
The importance assigned to the individual letter
is also characteristic of printing, where each
letter is physically separated from its fellows
until it is locked up in the forme. It is worth

noting also that Saul, besides being of towering
stature, was an enemy of David--poet, prophet,
musician, and later king himself--and that Saul's
wrath was most strongly roused precisely by
David's attempt to soothe his "evil spirit" by
singing to a harp (1 Samuel xviii-xix). Saul
persecuted David, George II promoted Cibber.

Since typography provided a physical means far
more effective than any earlier one of "extending
the dimensions of the private author in space and
time,"[56] it is not surprising that Dulness and
her votaries, vain egomaniacs all, latched onto
it eagerly. The overgrowth of the *Dunciad* is also
an image of this aspect of print. There was
plenty of Dulness in the Middle Ages, as Pope
would be the first to affirm, but the self-effacing
manuscript authors of those days had remained a-
nonymous to an astonishing degree, and in any
case a single individual's influence was greatly
limited by the conditions of manuscript reproduction. Typography fostered individualism and
authorial self-consciousness, and gave the author
greatly increased power, once he had access to a
press, to blanket the country with his thought
and art, for good or ill. The possibility of
such power, along with the opportunity for financial gain, tempted many to become authors who
would otherwise have followed some other trade.
The almost hypnotic power of print to attract
readers brought up under its influence increased
the chances of success for the hacks.[57]

Language in general is a means of exteriorizing
one's "innerness," of communicating it to others
--"speake, that I may see thee," writes Ben Jonson, for language "springs out of the most retired and inmost parts of us, and is the Image
of the Parent of it, the mind."[58] Writing and
print of course make Jonson's visual metaphor
literal, and probably influenced his choice of it.
In *A Tale of a Tub*, this conception is degraded to
a mechanical transfer of contents from one receptacle to another: "what tho' his *Head* be empty,
provided his *Common-place-Book* be full" (p. 148).
The empty brain may be easily reconstituted, how-

ever, by three daily drops of an elixir made of boiled books. This "*will dilate it self about the Brain (where there is any) in fourteen Minutes, and you immediately perceive in your Head an infinite Number of* Abstracts, Summaries, Compendiums, Extracts, Collections, Medulla's, Excerpta quaedam's, Florilegia's *and the like, all disposed into great Order, and reducible upon Paper*" (pp. 126-127). No brain was ever more conditioned by print than the Hack's: his view of reality, his mind, his writing, and his reading are perfect mirrors of each other as he prints out his Book of Chaos.

In the *Dunciad*, Jonson's idea enriches the theological aspect of the satire. According to St. Augustine and other patristic writers, every man bears (or should bear) an image of the Trinity in his own mind: "the very act of conceiving truth is but an image within us of the Word's conception by the Father in the bosom of the Trinity."[59] Milton called a good book "reason itself,... the image of God" (*Areopagitica*, p. 720). The Dunces' minds are of course images not of God's mind but of Dulness's, and thus ultimately of Satan's:

> In each she marks her Image full exprest,
> But chief in BAYS's monster-breeding breast.
>   (I.107-108; p. 277)

Thus, by writing and printing, what they are really doing is scattering Satan's image through the land, incarnating him in paper and ink and turning the printshop into an idol factory. The new world of the *Dunciad* is created by a similar process; instead of the transcriptions of the Divine Ideas that Addison saw in the Creation, this new world is a printout of Cibber's vagaries, as Settle shows him:

> "Son; what thou seek'st is in thee! Look, and find
> Each Monster meets his likeness in thy mind."
>   (III.251-252; p. 332)

The audience comes under attack here also.
"Since readers are as vain as authors, they crave
to view their own conglomerate visage and, therefore, demand the dullest wits to exert themselves
in ever greater degree as the collective audience
increases."[60] This mirroring process is not
static; it produces a continual metamorphosis, as
readers are remade in less and less divine images:

> All eyes direct their rays
> On him, and crowds turn Coxcombs as they gaze.
> His Peers shine round him with reflected grace,
> New edge their dulness, and new bronze their
>   face.
>   (II.7-10; p. 296)

Here the active agent is Cibber and his writings,
and the audience remains passive and malleable;
Cibber is a kind of Medusa, turning his peers into new brothers like the statues that grace Bedlam gates (I.32).   What Pope is revealing here is
the dark obverse of the process by which the
Spectator, to cite the most successful example, was
able to enlist the mass audience in support of
its attacks on folly and bad manners.   Any reader
of the *Spectator* who was guilty of the fault described in the issue of the paper he was reading
felt the paper's whole readership watching him
with disapproval;[61] the readers of the Dunces'
productions view their own dullness with complacency.
     For all its attacks on printing as an agent
of Dulness, however, the *Dunciad* is itself very
much a product of print culture and print technology, which, like other aspects of his milieu,
Pope knew how to use for his own ends.   One of
the most important benefits of printing for him
was its rigid spatial separation of text and
commentary.   It enabled him to provide, in Hugh
Kenner's words, "an Attic column of verse standing on a thick pedestal of miscellaneous learning,"[62] whereas marginal glosses, the manuscript
equivalent of footnotes, always had a fateful
tendency to creep into the text and lodge there.

Once the spatial separation is firmly established,
Pope is free to set up many kinds of ironical
relationships between text and commentary; he can
allow the Dunces to be half-wrong, entirely wrong,
or even right on occasion, and sometimes obtuse
but illuminating in spite of themselves. For an
example of the latter, see "Theobald's" and Scriblerus' attempt to emend *ears* to *years* in "By his
broad shoulders known, and length of ears" (1729
version, III.28; p. 153). As William Empson
points out, though without giving Pope credit for
being aware of what he was doing, this note in
fact emphasizes Settle's long-eared stupidity.[63]
In a similar way, "Bentley" tries to emend *Solo*
to *Opera* in "With nothing but a Solo in his head"
(IV.324; p. 375) on the grounds that "nothing but
a Solo" is tautological, thereby making sure that
no reader will miss the super-vacuity of the grand
tourist.

This spatial fixity of printing, which makes
Wilkins' view of reality so schematized and lifeless, is useful to Pope in other ways too. Along
with his metamorphoses of proper names into
grotesque things ("Something betwixt a Heideggre
and owl"), it helps him dehumanize his Dunces and
reduce them from living persons to comic devices.
They are "types" in two senses, removable and replaceable at the will of the poet-compositor.
Once fixed in their places on the page, they seem
to be products of the press rather than sons of
human parents. Like Swift's Hack, they are what
they have written. Thus the medium reinforces
Pope's principle that the *"Poem was not made for
these Authors, but these Authors for the Poem"* (p. 205).

Even within the notes there are certain clash-
es between form and content that are similar to
the mock-heroic disparities. As a form, the
footnote suggests scholarship, mature consideration, and a certain relative permanence. But the
matter of many of the notes is drawn from gazettes,
newspapers, and fly-by-night libels. Thus the
whole wrangling world of Georgian journalism is
subsumed into the poem, the relatively decorous
quarrels of scholars are mocked by the billingsgate of journalists, and all varieties of Dunces

--critics, journalists, poets--are endowed with
an ironic artistic immortality. The notes also
benefit from the almost inevitable propensity of
an attack to produce a reply; much of their
material comes from attacks on earlier versions
of the poem or on *Peri Bathous*, which seems to have
begun the process. Thus Pope implies that the
Dunciad, like a sacred book, can assimilate all
future commentary into itself.

    We end where we began, with the awareness that
Pope is using for his own ends, and with full
understanding, techniques and media that have
betrayed or numbed his contemporaries. Pope may
have shared one of Blake's visions--"I was in a
Printing house in Hell, & saw the method in which
knowledge is transmitted from generation to
generation"[64]--but the source of his glory is
that he was able to build a poetic heaven in hell's
despite, to reclaim Pandemonium from Dulness and
make it sing the glory of the Word.

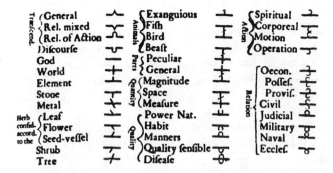

The Differences are to be affixed unto that end which is on the left
fide of the Character, according to this order;

The Species fhould be affixed at the other end of the Character according to the like order.

And whereas feveral of the Species of Vegetables and Animals, do
according to this prefent conftitution, amount to more than Nine, in
fuch cafes the number of them is to be diftributed into two or three
Nines, which may be diftinguifhed from one another by doubling
the ftroke in fome one or more parts of the Character; as fuppofe after
this manner, ⌐ ⌐.   If the firft and moft fimple Character
be made ufe of, the Species that are affixed to it, will belong to the firft
combination of *Nine*; if the other, they will belong according to the
order of them, unto the fecond Combination.

Thofe Radicals which are paired to others uppon account of *Oppo-*
fition, may be exprefled by a Loop, or (o) at the left end of the Character, after this manner, o⌐

Thofe that are paired upon the account of *Affinity*, are to be exprefled by the like Mark at the other end of the Character, thus, ⌐o

| 1 | 2 | 3 | 4 5 | 6 | 7 | 8 | 9 | 10 | 11 |

Our Parent who art in Heaven, Thy Name be Hallowed, Thy

| 12 | 13 | 14 | 15 | 16 | 17 | 18 | 19 | 20 | 21 | 22 | 23 | 24 | 25 | 26 |

Kingdome come, Thy Will be done, so in Earth as in Heaven, Give

| 27 | 28 | 29 | 30 | 31 | 32 | 33 | 34 | 35 | 36 | 37 | 38 | 39 | 40 | 41 | 42 | 43 |

to us on this day our bread expedient and forgive us our trespasses as

| 44 | 45 | 46 | 47 | 48 | 49 | 50 | 51 | 52 | 53 | 54 | 55 | 56 | 57 | 58 |

we forgive them who trespass against us, and lead us not into

| 59 | 60 | 61 | 62 | 63 | 64 | 65 | 66 | 67 | 68 | 69 | 70 |

temptation, but deliver us from evil, for the Kingdome and the

| 71 | 72 | 73 | 74 | 75 | 76 | 77 | 78 | 79 | 80. |

Power and the Glory is thine, for ever and ever, Amen. So be it.
                              Eee2   1. (⌣|)

___

Parent   2. (↲) This next Character being of a bigger proportion, must therefore represent some *Integral* Notion. The Genus of it, *viz.* (↲) is appointed to signifie *Oeconomical Relation*. And whereas the Transverse Line at the end towards the left hand, hath an affix, making an acute Angle, with the upper side of the Line, therefore doth it refer to the first Difference of that Genus, which according to the Tables, is relation of Consanguinity : And there being an Affix making a right Angle at the other end of the same Line, therefore doth it signifie the second Species under this Difference, *viz. Direct ascending*, by which the Notion of *Parent* is defined. And this being originally a Noun of Person, doth not the need therefore Transc. Note of Person to be affixed to it. If it were to be rendred Father in the strictest sense, it would be necessary that the Transcendental Note of *Male* should be joyned to it, being a little hook on the top, over the middle of the Character, after this manner (↲.) The word Father in the most Philosophical and proper sense of it, denoting a *Male Parent*. And because the word Parent is not here used according to the strictest sense, but Metaphorically; therefore might the Transcendental Note of *Metaphor*, be put over the head of it, after this manner, (↲.) But this being such a Metaphor as is generally received in other Languages, therefore there will be no necessity of using this mark.

"WAFTING VAPOURS FROM THE LAND OF DREAMS":
VIRGIL'S FOURTH AND SIXTH ECLOGUES AND
THE *DUNCIAD*

Traugott Lawler

That Pope was fond of Virgil's *Eclogues*, especially in his youth, is clear. One thinks not
only of the *Pastorals* with their prefixed "Discourse," but also of *Messiah* ("A Sacred Eclogue,
in Imitation of Virgil's Pollio"), parts of *Windsor Forest*, including its epigraph, and incidental
allusions in other works such as the *Essay on
Criticism* or *To Mr. Addison*. He had, indeed, like
Spenser and Milton, some sense of the classic
progress of the poet's career, moving from the
Pastorals through the "georgic" *Windsor Forest* to
the translation of Homer--or, perhaps, to the *Dunciad*. The genres are of course not mutually exclusive; in the classic career each form may re-
capitulate an earlier form, pastoral for example
making its appearance in the Pallantean scenes in
the *Aeneid*, in Book 6 and elsewhere of the *Faerie
Queene*, and everywhere in Milton's Paradise. One
does not, however, ordinarily imagine Pope's fondness for pastoral as spilling over into the *Dunciad*. The fresh world of the *Eclogues*, only occasionally touched by Rome, seems alien to its sor-

This essay first appeared in *SEL* 14 (1974), 373-86.

731

did urban scene. Nor do the *Eclogues* seem to provide a satiric norm; the Virgilian standard from
which the actions in the *Dunciad* veer is the *Aeneid*.
     Yet the truth is that Pope's notes to the *Dun-
ciad* identify no fewer than seventeen allusions
to the *Eclogues*. Some of these involve mere local
strategies, a momentary contrast between Virgil's
dignified beauty and some low dunceish action or
stance; but the fact that nine of those seventeen
allusions, plus several more not annotated, belong to Eclogues 4 and 6 suggests that at least
those two may have some strong bearing, some profound and central influence. In fact, several
possible inferences spring to mind: that Eclogue
4 is related to Eclogue 6; further, that these
two poems helped shape the *Dunciad*, and should be
recognized as "sources" for it; or, best, that
studying these two poems may help us interpret,
not only the individual passages where the allusions appear, but the whole *Dunciad*. This essay
is an attempt to support those inferences. It
proceeds by describing Eclogue 4 and relating it
to the *Dunciad*, then by describing Eclogue 6 and
discussing its complex relationship both to
Eclogue 4 and to the *Dunciad*; then by assessing in
somewhat larger terms what these relationships
mean.
     The fourth, the famous "Messianic" eclogue, is
so familiar that it hardly needs summarizing:
briefly, it speaks prophetically of the imminent
return, symbolized in the birth of an unnamed
child, of the golden age of Saturn: "redeunt
Saturnia regna" (6). The main body of the poem
is a prophetic account of the several stages of
this gradual return, coinciding with the child's
gradual growth to maturity. It ends with a series
of exhortations addressed to the child, urging
him to come and inaugurate the happy time.
     The relationship of this poem to the *Dunciad* is
fundamental: the plot of the *Dunciad*, as announced
at the start, is a parodic version of the "plot"
of Eclogue 4. Dulness spreads her wings to
"hatch a new Saturnian age of Lead" (I,28), to
bring about a return to the pristine state of

"native Anarchy" (I,16).[1] Pope's poem is about
this return. Virgil's poem, of course, is a
lyric prophecy, Pope's a narrative: in Book IV
of the *Dunciad*, the return is actually achieved,
the Saturnian age ushered in, as "Universal
Darkness buries All." But though Pope thus goes
eventually beyond Eclogue 4, and though the exi-
gencies of narrative demand that he seek models
elsewhere for particular episodes, Virgil's poem
remains the source of its basic idea.

What I am saying seems to contradict Aubrey
Williams' demonstration that the "action" of the
Dunciad is a "progress," the transferral of the
seat of Dulness from the City to Westminster, in
imitation of the transferral of Troy to Latium in
the *Aeneid*.[2] Williams is surely right, but his
argument seems to me to be incomplete, and to
fail to make an important distinction between spatial and temporal progress. The largest action
in the *Dunciad* is the establishment *in time* of the
age of Saturn; the geographical progress of the
seat of Dulness is a smaller action inside this
or a metaphor for it. Williams (p. 17) rightly
quotes Pope's warning "From the Publisher to the
Reader," prefixed to the 1728 version, about "the
frequency of his allusions to *Virgil*, and a *labor'd*
(not to say *affected*) *shortness* in imitation of him,"
but errs, I think, by applying this warning exclusively to the *Aeneid*: the warning may suggest,
he says, "that the *Dunciad* is a labored and affected, though highly condensed, imitation of the
Aeneid," as if "Virgil" and *Aeneid* were interchangeable. The *Aeneid* is primarily a spatial poem in its central action; Eclogue 4 is exclusively temporal. Part of the difficulty one has in
assigning an "action" to the *Dunciad* comes from
the fact that it, too, is primarily temporal
rather than spatial. Though it gives, in Books I
and II, an account of the progress of Dulness
from the City to Westminster, the bringing of
"the Smithfield Muses to the Ear of Kings," and,
in Book III, of the *translatio studii* westward to
England, and though in Book IV Dulness' levee
seems to take place at the Court of St. James's,

the more important progress is the establishment
in time of Dulness' reign, the Saturnian age. The
apocalyptic closing passage describing the onset
of Universal Darkness has no local reference: its
events are purely temporal. The Saturnian age is
prophesied in Book 6 of the *Aeneid*, but the "action" of that poem remains the spatial transfer
of Trojan civilization; the most fundamental
Virgilian model for the action of the *Dunciad* is
Eclogue 4. The *Aeneid* provides the model for the
narrative working-out of the prophecy, but Eclogue
4 provides the widest framework of the prophecy
itself. I do not want to question the overwhelming, detailed presence of the *Aeneid*, but only to
insist that Eclogue 4 is present, too, much more
briefly and even peripherally--but "peripherally"
must be understood to mean "at the outer edges,"
at beginning and end, "providing the circumference." It "encompasses" the poem, the *Aeneid*
fills it.[3]

Yet, though Eclogue 4 does not fill the poem,
neither is its relevance confined to the large
frame. Particular reminiscences of it are fairly
frequent. Let me first mention briefly a few
minor ones, then discuss several that are more
central. At III, 141 the line addressed to Cibber's son, "With all thy Father's virtues blest,
be born!" echoes not only the general injunction
to the child at the end of Eclogue 4 but the
particular phrase "patriis virtutibus" in l. 17.
At IV, 61 the line "Another Phoebus, thy own
Phoebus, reigns" translates directly Virgil's
"tuus iam regnat Apollo" (10). Again in Book III,
lines 241ff., beginning "Thence a new world to
Nature's laws unknown, / Breaks out refulgent,"
though they refer only to bizarre stage effects
in contemporary plays, have the visionary pastoral air, and match the vision of a natural world
freed from "Nature's laws" in Eclogue 4, 28-30:

> Molli paulatim flavescet campus arista,
> Incultisque rubens pendebit sentibus uva,
> Et durae quercus sudabunt roscida mella.

(Then a slow flush of tender gold shall mantle
    the great plains,
Then shall grapes hang wild and reddening on
    thorn-trees,
And honey sweat like dew from the hard bark of
    oaks.)[4]

Indeed, it is in Book III, where Settle is
prophesying the return of Dulness' reign, that
one is most directly aware of Eclogue 4. Anchises'
prophecy in *Aeneid* VI and Michael's in *Paradise Lost*
XI-XII are the narrative bases of this episode,
and yet Eclogue 4 is also in the background, particularly since it is a reversion, not a progress,
that is being foretold. In Settle's final burst,
for example, "Proceed, great days! 'till Learning
fly the shore" (333), not only does the first
phrase come from Eclogue 4, as a note tells us,
but the new primitiveness that the flight of
learning will bring about recalls and debases the
gathering simplicity Virgil prophesies.
    Lines 319-320 are particularly interesting, for
they provide a hint of a deeper relationship to
Eclogue 4, a rationale for all the verbal echoes.
"This, this is he, foretold by ancient rhymes: /
Th'Augustus born to bring Saturnian times." I
am interested in the word "born" in particular.
The source Pope gives for the lines is *Aeneid* VI,
791-794:

Hic vir, hic est, tibi quem promitti saepius
    audis,
Augustus Caesar, divi genus, aurea condet
Saecula qui rursus Latio regnata per arva
Saturno quondam.

(And here, here is the man, the promised one
    you know of--
Caesar Augustus, son of a god, destined to rule
Where Saturn ruled of old in Latium, and there
Bring back the age of gold.)

"Bring Saturnian times," however, is much closer
to the specific thought of Eclogue 4 than to this

passage, where the times are called "golden," not
"Saturnian," and merely localized in the region
where Saturn once reigned. And since Saturn only came to Italy after he was dethroned by Jupiter, there is not even a veiled reference to the
ancient *Saturnia regna*. "Foretold by ancient
rhymes" echoes Dryden's translation of Eclogue 4
(1. 5): "foretold by sacred rhymes." More importantly, the word "born" has no counterpart in the
Aeneid passage: we are not invited there to dwell
on Augustus' birth, only his maturity. The ambience of "born" is Eclogue 4, its suggestion
that Cibber is to be associated with the miraculous child. It is in Eclogue 4 that Saturnian
times are specifically associated with a birth:

> redeunt Saturnia regna,
> iam nova progenies caelo demittitur alto.
> Tu modo nascenti puero, quo ferrea primum
> desinet ac toto surget gens aurea mundo,
> casta fave Lucina. (6-10)

> (The Golden Age
> Returns, and its first-born comes down from
>   heaven above.
> Look kindly, chaste Lucina, upon this infant's
>   birth,
> For with him shall hearts of iron cease, and
>   hearts of gold
> Inherit the whole earth.)

Birth is the controlling image of Eclogue 4, mother and child its central figures. Lucina,
goddess of childbirth, is its presiding genius.
The birth of the child heralds the birth of the
golden age: "magnus ab integro saeclorum *nascitur*
ordo" (5). Its first effect is to spark a series
of births in the natural world: the earth, another mother figure, *fundet*, will bring forth a-
bundantly gifts of flowers for the child, spreading its fertility to the very cradle that holds
him: "ipsa tibi blandos fundent cunabula flores"
(23). Animals, too, succumb to the maternal
urge: the breasts of goats fill with milk, oxen
find lions more childlike:

Ipsae lacte domum referent distenta capellae
ubera, nec magnos metuent armenta leones.
                              (21-22)

(Goats shall walk home, their udders taut
    with milk, and nobody
Herding them: the ox will have no fear of the
    lion.)

As Virgil goes on to speak of the adolescence
and maturity of the child, the fertile earth
takes over the central role of bearer: "omnis
feret omnia tellus" (39). At the end, the simple
relationship of mother and child returns:

Incipe, parve puer, risu cognoscere matrem--
matri longa decem tulerunt fastidia menses.
                              (60-61)

(Begin, dear babe, and smile at your mother to
    show you know her--
This is the tenth month now, and she is sick
    of waiting.)

Reuben Brower[5] has shown how Pope makes use of
Virgil's promising boy in his portrait in Book
IV of the "dauntless infant" just back from the
grand tour, finding particularly in the line
"Europe he saw, and Europe saw him too" an ironic
allusion to Virgil's "divisque videbit / permix-
tos heroas, et ipse videbitur illis" (15-16). It
seems to me that Eclogue 4 is also behind another
dauntless infant, behind, indeed, the whole
mother-son relationship of Dulness and Cibber.
Grotesque images of birth swarm around Dulness,
as here in the description of her cave:

Here she beholds the Chaos dark and deep,
Where nameless Somethings in their causes
    sleep,
'Till genial Jacob, or a warm Third day,
Call forth each mass, a Poem, or a Play:

How hints, like spawn, scarce quick in embryo
    lie,
How new-born nonsense first is taught to cry,
Maggots half-form'd in rhyme exactly meet,
And learn to crawl upon poetic feet. (I, 55-62)

Dulness "marks her Image full exprest" in Cibber,
eyes him "with transport" as she remembers her
own youth (I, 107, 111). He too is surrounded
with hideous births: "Round him much Embryo,
much Abortion lay / ... Fruits of dull Heat, and
Sooterkins of Wit" (I, 121-126). Cibber himself
is the great Sooterkin. Dulness celebrates their
intimate relationship at the end of Book I:

The Goddess then, o'er his anointed head,
With mystic words, the sacred Opium shed.
And lo! her bird, (a monster of a fowl,
Something betwixt a Heideggre and owl,)
Perch'd on his crown. "All hail! and hail
    again,
My son! the promis'd land expects thy reign.
Know, Eusden thirsts no more for sack or
    praise;
He sleeps among the dull of ancient days;
Safe, where no Critics damn, no duns molest,
Where wretched Withers, Ward, and Gildon rest,
And high-born Howard, more majestic sire
With Fool of Quality compleats the quire.
Thou Cibber! thou, his Laurel shalt support,
Folly, my son, has still a Friend at Court.
Lift up your gates, ye Princes, see him come!
Sound, sound ye Viols, be the Cat-Call dumb!
Bring, bring the madding Bay, the drunken Vine;
The creeping, dirty, courtly Ivy join.
And thou! his Aid de camp, lead on my sons,
Light-arm'd with Points, Antitheses, and Puns.
Let Bawdry, Bilingsgate, my daughters dear,
Support his front, and Oaths bring up the rear:
And under his, and under Archer's wing,
Gaming and Grub-street skulk behind the King.
    "O! when shall rise a Monarch all our own,
And I, a Nursing-mother, rock the throne,
'Twixt Prince and people close the Curtain
    draw,

Shade him from Light, and cover him from Law;
Fatten the Courtier, starve the learned band,
And suckle Armies, and dry-nurse the land:
'Till Senates nod to Lullabies divine,
And all be sleep, as at an Ode of thine."

Dulness exploits an intricate combination of
noble precedents here. The owl, for instance, is
descended from both Venus' doves and the Holy
Spirit; "the promis'd land expects thy reign"
calls up both Christ and Aeneas, and especially
since Eclogue 4 has always been associated with
Christ, also its "Tuus iam regnat Apollo." It
is her closing lines, however, as they envision a
an eternal childhood for Cibber, an eternal young-
motherhood for herself, that recall Eclogue 4
most fully. We do not know of Aeneas' childhood,
and the infancy of Christ is eclipsed by his
maturity; only in Eclogue 4 is the reigning savior
destined to remain eternally a child, for though
his growth is envisioned, that is the only clear
image we have of him.[6] Dulness, a "Nursing-
mother," will "rock" Cibber's throne as a mother
rocks her infant's cradle; he is "Prince," not
king, whom she will shade from light and "cover"
--he will be always kicking the covers off. She
will "suckle" and "dry-nurse" to the sound of
"Lullabies" till "all be sleep." Cibber, in
short, is a child who will bring about a millenial
reign. And the general infancy, to which armies,
senates, "the land" are all reduced, is a parodic
counterpart of Virgil's rejuvenated land, a different sort of return to a primordial condition.
Pope, having followed Eclogue 4 for the large
movement of his "plot," draws also on its imagery
of infancy and motherhood for the details of its
working-out. And as Cibber disappears from the
poem after Book III, the "glorious youth" fresh
from Europe in Book IV takes over his role: no
part of the poem is without its *parvus puer*.
    I am not arguing that Eclogue 4 plays any ex-
clusive role in the formation of the image of
Dulness and Cibber, or that recognizing its role
will produce some revolutionary reassessment of

its meaning. The most important thing to grasp
is that Dulness and Cibber pervert the ordinary
sweet relationship of mother and son that we know
primarily from life as well as from such famous
pairs as Thetis and Achilles, Venus and Aeneas,
Mary and Jesus, or even Pope and his own mother
in the closing lines of *Arbuthnot*, but that also
receives one of its great celebrations in
Eclogue 4; they take their place with such other
malevolent boys and their mamas as Grendel and
his dam, Milton's Sin and Death, or Uriah Heep
and his 'umble parent. What I am arguing is
that the various clear individual echoes of
Eclogue 4 throughout the poem are complemented
and given fuller meaning by an integration of
its imagery into one of the basic images of the
Dunciad. Cibber is both more ridiculous and more
threatening as a modern incarnation of Virgil's
miraculous infant.

*   *   *

   Eclogue 6 presents a more elusive and complex
problem, both in itself and in its relation to
Pope's poem. Its matter is as follows. Two boys
fetter Silenus in his sleep in order to force him
to sing to them. He complies, rather generously
and humorously, and sings a brief history of the
world, starting with its creation. In his song
the world deteriorates quickly from the golden
age ("Saturnia regna," 41) into a series of scenes
of grotesquerie and pain: Prometheus tortured,
Hylas abandoned by the Argonauts, Pasiphae besti-
ally impassioned, Scylla become a monster, Tereus
and Philomela. In the midst of these Silenus
sets the benign story of how Gallus the poet was
honored by Apollo and the Muses. Silenus ends
his song as evening comes, and the boys depart.
   Scholars have ordinarily taken Eclogue 6 as
complementary to 4, providing a record of history
as degeneration in contrast to the regeneration
that 4 celebrates. Brooks Otis presents this
view in cogent detail; the poem, he says, shows
through a series of brief "neoteric" allusions
to mystic material, how *amor indignus* (the phrase

is from Eclogue 10.10), "demented love," beginning
with Pasiphae, has consistently brought about a
degeneration from the golden age. He acknowledges that Virgil is being very complimentary to
Gallus, but argues that "he is none the less indicating in a poetical way two alternative conceptions of human destiny as well as of literary
purpose. The neoteric and elegiac poetry of
Cinna, Parthenius, and Gallus was not adapted to
an age in which violent and criminal disorder
called for moral restoration. Virgil himself had
been neoteric or Alexandrine in his poetical past:
he, like his dear friend Gallus, had written and
was writing of *amor indignus*; but a new situation
was now demanding a broader, bigger, more serious
kind of poetry,"[7] which Virgil provided in
Eclogue 4.

I do not think that Otis, when he implies that
Virgil rejects the "conception of human destiny"
of 6 for that of 4, has found the best way of
defining the relationship that clearly exists between the two poems. He rightly recognizes that
the lines about Gallus are a stumbling block to
his argument, but then he seems to stumble on it
anyhow. There are other obstacles, too, to reading the poem as the report of an inadequate view
of history in comparison to that of 4. But before discussing Eclogue 6 more fully, it will be
useful to see how often and in what ways it is
employed in the *Dunciad*.

Eclogue 6 has no such obvious fundamental role
in the *Dunciad* as Eclogue 4. On the other hand,
lines from it are explicitly parodied more frequently and at greater length. In IV, 493ff.,
Thomas Gordon, Commissioner of Wine Licenses,
appears as Silenus, rising from "bowzy" sleep to
speak, shaking from his pipe "the seeds of fire"
("semina ... ignis," 6, 32-33). The line about
Pasiphae, "Et fortunatam, si numquam armenta
fuissent" (45), is parodied at III, 117-118:
"That once was Britain--Happy! had she seen / No
fiercer sons, had Easter never been." These are
incidental allusions. In Book II occur the central usages: Silenus' vignette of Hylas left be-

hind by his fellows appears three times, and the
whole story of Gallus and the Muses is the basis
for Smedley's reappearance from the river bed.
These need close study.
   Here is Virgil's Hylas:

> His adiungit, Hylan nautae quo fonte relictum
> Clamassent, ut litus "Hyla, Hyla" omne sonaret.
> (43-44)

> (And Hylas--how the Argonauts left him beside
>   a spring,
> Then shouted for him till the whole shore was
>   echoing "Hylas! Hylas!")

And here are Pope's imitations in Book II. As
Lintot overcomes Curll in the footrace: "Here
fortun'd Curl to slide; loud shout the band / And
Bernard! Bernard! rings thro' all the Strand" (73-
74). (Did Pope marvel at the coincidence that
enabled him to pun on "Strand," or was it that
street-name that led him to the allusion? In any
case the allusion has the effect of reawakening
one to the literal meaning of the street-name,
and so illustrating how multiple are the ways in
which in the world the Dunces inhabit the beautiful has been reduced to the crass.) When Smedley
dives into Thames and fails to reemerge:

> Next Smedley div'd; slow circles dimpled o'er
> The quaking mud, that clos'd, and op'd no more.
> All look, all sigh, and call on Smedley lost;
> Smedley in vain resounds thro' all the coast.
> (291-294)

And when Smedley finally returns, he relates how
"the Mud-nymphs suck'd him in" and "Vy'd for his
love in jetty bow'rs below, / As Hylas fair was
ravish'd long ago" (335-336). At this point,
through the agency of Smedley, the story of Hylas
blends into the story of Gallus:

> Thence to the banks where rev'rend Bards repose,
> They led him soft; each rev'rend Bard arose;

```
    And Milbourn chief, deputed by the rest,
    Gave him the cassock, surcingle, and vest.
    "Receive, (he said) these robes which once
        were mind,
    Dulness is sacred in a sound divine." (347-352)
```

This is Virgil's account:

```
    Tum canit errantem Permessi ad flumina Gallum
    Aonas in montis ut duxerit una sororum,
    Utque viro Phoebi chorus adsurrexerit omnis;
    Ut Linus haec illi divino carmine pastor
    floribus atque apio crinis ornatus amaro
    dixerit: "Hos tibi dant calamos, en accipe,
        Musae,
    Ascraeo quos ante seni, quibus ille solebat
    Cantando rigidas deducere montibus ornos.
    His tibi Grynei nemoris dicatur origo,
    Ne quis sit lucus quo se plus iactet Apollo."
                                            (64-73)
```

```
    (And then he sang how Gallus, at large by the
        streams of Permessus,
    Met one of the Muses, who led him to the
        Aonian hills
    Where the whole choir of Apollo stood up to
        honour him,
    A mortal; and that divine poet of pastoral,
        Linus,
    Wearing his wreath of flowers and bitter par-
        sley leaves,
    Said to Gallus, "the Muses give you this pipe
        --accept it--
    Which long ago they gave to Hesiod; and he
        played it
    So well, his music drew downhill the obstinate
        ash-trees.
    Sing, to this pipe, the story of the Grynean
        wood,
    And not one grove on earth will Apollo be so
        proud of.")
```

What happens in Pope's poem is the same thing
that happens in Virgil's. Smedley disappears as

Hylas and reemerges as Gallus (with an intermediate stage in which his relation to Hylas is rendered less firm, begun, so to speak, to be severed,
by being treated in a simile rather than in a
direct allusion). Similarly in Eclogue 6 Gallus
is, as it were, the continuation or reincarnation
of Hylas: Hylas disappears from his companions
and from the poem by a spring (we know, though
Virgil does not say, that a nymph ravished him);
Gallus enters the poem wandering by the river
Permessus and encountering a Muse. This connection is important, for the lines on Gallus are at
once central to the meaning of the poem and yet
apparently foreign to its subject. Without the
couplet on Hylas they would enter the poem with
too rude an abruptness; when Hylas disappears he
leaves an empty shore, a void in the poem which
Gallus fills. The transmutation or metamorphosis
of Hylas into Gallus is also a transmutation of
feeling, from desolation into rich joy, from the
painful cry "Hyla! Hyla!" of his baffled companions into the magical singing of Hesiod and Gallus. This transmutation qualifies the "degenera-
tive" movement of the poem; it is because of
Gallus that one cannot read the poem as presenting history as degeneration.

What Otis and others perhaps fail to take into
account is the importance of form in the poem.
It is certainly true that its content is a series
of incidents of corrupt love that mark stages of
disintegration from the golden age; yet it is
more proper to say that its subject-matter is *how
Silenus sang* that series. The ultimate subject-
matter is poetry, not degenerate love: that
is why Virgil keeps renewing the indirect discourse with phrases like "his adiungit," "tum
canit," "refert." Silenus sings so well, in
fact, that one is much more aware of Pasiphae as
a lyric symbol than as a demented lover.8 This
is how the suddenly benign episode of Gallus fits
in: the air of divinity with which that episode
surrounds poetry and the poet reminds us that
what the Orphic Silenus (cf. 1. 30) is doing is
creating something beautiful out of those tales

of madness and pain. When Gallus inherits the pipe from Linus he makes a new beginning, starts a new reign: the lines stress the ability of art to create, and so oppose the "degenerating" movement of the poem with an image of regeneration. The poem contains three major and two minor images of the poet: Virgil himself, Silenus, and Gallus, and also Linus and Hesiod: each of the main three is "touched" in some way by Apollo. These creators stand out against destroyers like Tereus or Scylla; if the instrument of regeneration in 4 is politics as wielded by the divine child, the instrument of regeneration in 6 is poetry. The regeneration envisioned, or rather, put forth in the texture of the verse itself, is less grand than that in 4 but more palpable.[9]

Hylas and Gallus combined, then, are emblematic of the magical, transcendent quality of poetry: Gallus undergoes an experience that translates Hylas' muteness and the Argonauts' ineffective shouts into the wonder-working music of Hesiod. It is easy enough to see how all this applies to Smedley. In the *Dunciad* poetry not only fails to overcome degeneration but is seen as itself the most potent of corrupters. The parade of singers, Virgil, Silenus, Gallus, Hesiod, Linus, Orpheus, Apollo himself, is replaced by a parade of dunces. Eclogue 4 presents a "good" image of regeneration, a return to a Golden Age, which Pope takes as a model for the evil image of regeneration in the *Dunciad*, a return to a leaden age; similarly, Eclogue 6 presents an image of degeneration overcome by poetry, which Pope takes as a model for the account in the *Dunciad* of poetry leading to and abetting degeneration. Eclogue 6 is about poetry creating, the *Dunciad* about poetry destroying. Unlike Gallus, Smedley learns nothing from his underworld journey.

The Smedley passage, even though it is part of a series of mock-epic games, may thus with more accuracy be called "mock-pastoral" than mock-epic. Just as the failure being satirized in mock-epic finds its meaning in comparison to epic success,

Smedley's failure to profit from his journey
works because of the pastoral success of Gallus.
And in the light of the fundamental relevance to
it of Eclogue 4, the mock-pastoral aspect of the
Dunciad takes on far wider significance. In
general it seems to me to be important that the
genre of the poem be recognized as quite as much
mock-pastoral as mock-epic. Of course the abstract distinction we are accustomed to make between pastoral and epic is not so total in reality, as the "epic strain" of Eclogue 4 may show.
Yet there are many particular differences, and
the special relevance to the *Dunciad* that pastoral
has over epic is that poetry itself so often forms
the subject of pastoral poetry. All the characters of the *Eclogues* are poets; what earns disapproval in the pastoral world is not cowardice or
evil-doing but poor singing. Similarly the Dunces
are evil not because they fail to be heroic but because they fail to be creatively poetic. This
suggests how central the Smedley episode is: it
is less brilliantly funny than some of the other
events in Book II, the race between Curll and
Lintot for instance, but it is more important than
they are because more directly about poetic failure. Though the grander underworld visit of
Cibber in Book III is based on the *Aeneid*, this
lesser pastoral visit prepares for that and allies it to the specific question of poetic regeneration: Cibber follows Smedley's example and
fails to be revitalized. One may recollect also
that Settle's final words in Book III are a return
to the pastoral idiom of Eclogue 4. Thus the
mock-epic of Book III works within a pastoral
framework that keeps the specific issue of poetic
ability to the fore.
   Another effect of pastoral on the poem is more
complicated. Though Pope parodies Virgil, he
manages at the same time to transfer into his poem a good deal of the beauty of Virgil's descriptions. Virgil's image of Hylas is full of lyric
beauty: the shore is at once desolate and alive,
bereft of Hylas but filled with his name, repeated, a futile utterance, a thin vestige of his

living presence. Those effects are still present
in these lines: "All look, all sigh, and call
on Smedley lost; / Smedley in vain resounds thro'
all the coast." When Smedley relates

> How young Lutetia, softer than the down,
> Nigrina black, and Merdamante brown,
> Vy'd for his love in jetty bow'rs below,
> As Hylas fair was ravish'd long ago, (333-336)

though we do not ignore what "Merdamante" means,
it does not seem to me that much of the Virgilian
beauty fades. It changes: for desolation we
have warm life, we see Hylas from a new perspective; but there is beauty nonetheless. The vile-
ness of *lutum* and *merde* is absorbed in the lovely-
sounding names; "black" and "jetty" do not fill
the mind with images of murk and filth but of the
luminously reflective surface of ebony or black
marble. The figure of "Hylas fair" gives the
depth of contrast to these darkly brilliant colors. Furthermore, the source of all this lyric-
ism is apparently Smedley himself--like Silenus
"he relates" this (331),

> Then sung, how shown him by the Nut-brown
>   maids
> A branch of Styx here rises from the Shades,
> That tinctur'd as it runs with Lethe's streams,
> And wafting Vapours from the Land of dreams,
> (As under seas Alphaeus' secret sluice
> Bears Pisa's off'rings to his Arethuse)
> Pours into Thames. (337-343)

For an extended moment, and despite the continuation of double-entendres relating to sewerage,
mock-pastoral shades into genuine pastoral. The
Virgilian allusions lend a lyric tone to both
Pope's voice and Smedley's.
   What is the effect of this? Is Pope acknowledging a certain bizarre attractiveness in the
poetry of the dunces, suggesting, as H. H. Erskine-
Hill has urged, something "surrealistically awe-
inspiring or beautiful as well as ridiculous and

offensive"[10] in their world? One hesitates to
assert that. Better to say that the pastoral
style enables Pope to ridicule the dunces further
by proving that he can write beautifully as well
as satirically. This beauty calls attention to
Pope's brilliance at the expense of the dunces.
He shows what a true poet, like a ringmaster with
a herd of elephants, can do with gauche materials.
Smedley himself could never have done what Pope
and Virgil together do for him.

   Thus from the most expansive to the most local
level, from conception to diction, Virgil's twin
pastoral poems bring us nearer to the genesis
and meaning of the *Dunciad*. Eclogue 4 provides a
mother and son who will bring about a regenerative return to the age of Saturn. Eclogue 6 complements Eclogue 4 by presenting various particular images of the regenerative power of poetry.
Since the *Dunciad* is about how bad poetry causes
degeneration, or how the poetry of the dunces
will bring on the Saturnian age of lead, Pope
was able to add an inversion of 6 to his inversion of 4, to employ the pair of poems as a complex unit, as Virgil employs them. Smedley's
underworld journey in the sewer is, in this
light, a central incident in the poem. In it
Pope employs the Hylas-Gallus image ironically to
indicate how the dunces fail in their poetry to
overcome or transcend degeneration; and as he
does so he mocks them further by charging his
lines with some of the delicately beautiful diction of pastoral poetry.

THE *DUNCIAD* ILLUSTRATIONS

Elias F. Mengel

No one, to my knowledge, has made a study of
the seven plates I bring together here from editions of the *Dunciad* up through the final version
of 1743. Of the possible reasons for this neglect I would advance two. First, these engravings present a number of puzzling details which
make for difficulties in interpretation. Second,
for the most part they seem more tangential or
extraneous to the poem than illustrative of it.
No doubt many readers have been inclined to dismiss them as enigmatic trifles in which Pope himself had no hand.
We know that three of the plates were engraved
by Peter Fourdrinier after the designs of Pope's
friend William Kent, but the remaining four are
unsigned. It is possible that Pope himself drew
the designs for some of these.[1] Although we will
probably never know whether any of the unsigned
engravings come from Pope's own hand, in the
light of what we do know about his care in the
printing of his work, and in the production of
the critical apparatus, the notes of "various
commentators," for this particular work, I think

This essay first appeared in *Eighteenth-Century Studies* 7 (1973-4), 161-178.

Figure 1

Figure 2

we must assume that he is responsible for all the
Dunciad prints. Even if he himself did not design
any, he must have directed the artists or, at the
very least, approved the designs submitted to him.
A study of the prints will show that they are as
much a part of the poem as its apparatus. Just
as the apparatus criticus serves in part to parody the learned tomes of Dulness, so one function
of the illustrations is to mock her ornamental
volumes in which "by sculpture made for ever
known, / The page admires new beauties, not its
own" (1728 I, 119-20). The main purpose of the
illustrations, however, is to confirm visually
the satiric mode of the poem and to picture certain scenes in it. The Kent/Fourdrinier headpieces to Books II and III, for example, illustrate particular passages in these books in such
a way that "images reflect from art to art" (*Epistle to Jervas*, 20), but, more generally, all the
prints reflect the mock-heroic style of the poem
by pictorial confrontation of the high with the
low. The visual equivalents or approximations of
the poem's epic background are the mock heraldic,
the decorated initial letter, the ornate picture
frame, and, in one instance, the framelike use of
a line of Latin. The low subjects of the illustrations are those of the poem itself: the owl
and the ass, the dunces and their works, the
poem's second hero Colley Cibber.[2]
     Figure 1 is the owl frontispiece to the 1728
Dunciad (Griffith 198). In the poem a kind of owl
is the bird of the goddess Dulness: "And lo! her
Bird (a monster of a fowl! / Something betwixt a
H[eidegger] and Owl) / Perch'd on his crown"
(1728 I, 233-35).[3] In Figure 1 this owl, perched
on select dunce publications, is ironically magnified into a heraldic animal with a motto scroll
in its beak. The motto/title *Dunciad* is now the
war cry of Dulness in her "immortal war with Wit."
The six dunce authors appearing here as books
are all represented in the poem itself: reading
from bottom to top of the pile, Colley Cibber's
plays (with a pun on "plays"), the Duchess of
Newcastle, the works of John Dennis (with a pun

on "works"), Ogilby "the *great*" (1728 I, 111), the
"Shakespeare Restored" of the poem's first hero
Theobald, and two of Sir Richard Blackmore's
epics, *Prince Arthur* and *King Arthur*. It may well be
that Blackmore's epics top the pile in reference
to his victory in Book II: "All hail him victor
in both gifts of Song, / Who sings so *loudly*, and
who sings so *long*" (1728 II, 245-46). But what
really seems to determine the position of each
dunce on the pile is merely the size and shape
of his book used as building block--"Volumes,
whose size the space exactly fill'd" (1728 I,
107). And just as Pope speaks in Appendix I of
the *Dunciad Variorum* of "the inevitable removal of
some Authors, and the insertion of others in their
Niches," so in the owl frontispiece of Griffith
219 "Gildon and Woolston ag[st]x[t] [against Christi-
anity]" takes the place of "P. & K. Arthur" and
"Blackmore" of "Newcastle." Likewise, in the
owl frontispiece of Griffith 405 "Dennis's Works"
is replaced by "Oldmix[on's] Hist[ory] of Stuart
F[amily]," and in the ass engraving (Figure 2) of
Griffith 373 the newspaper "Baker's Journal" in
the lower right corner is replaced by "The Free
Briton." The dunces and their productions are
interchangeable parts.
    In the poem Theobald demonstrates this reduc-
tion of dunce books to blocks "fit to erect altars to Dulness" (I, 135*n*.). Like the Baron in
The Rape of the Lock, he constructs his altar by
treating books "in the most literal sense," as
Swift's Bookseller advises in *The Battle of the Books*.
They are "only certain Sheets of Paper, bound up
in Leather":

    Of these twelve volumes, twelve of amplest
        size,
    Redeem'd from tapers and defrauded pyes,
    Inspir'd he seizes: These an altar raise:
    An hecatomb of pure, unsully'd lays
    That altar crowns; a folio Common-place
    Founds the whole pyle, of all his works the
        base:

Quarto's, octavo's shape the lessening pyre,
And last, a *little* Ajax tips the spire.
(1728 I, 125-32)

Like Theobald's, the pile of books in Figure 1 is
an altar to Dulness. The traditional Greco-Roman
form and the monstrous owl parody an altar to
Athene and her owl. Dulness, pretending to be
Wit, is worshipped in her place.[4]

Moreoever, we see in the owl and altar taken
together an emblem of the stupidity and incoherence of Dulness. It is typical of the goddess to
commit an egregious breach of decorum by planting
an owl from the medieval art of heraldry on a
classical altar built of modern blockheads. Such
a mixture exemplifies those mindless and chaotic
productions of Dulness in which she takes so much
satisfaction: "There motley *Images* her fancy
strike, / *Figures* ill-pair'd, and *Similes* unlike"
(1728 I, 53-54).

The Ogilby volume, like a Newcastle folio, is
"stamp'd with arms" (1728 I, 112), a chevron between three martlets. This emblazonment functions
as visual equivalent of the mock-heroic, desig-
nating the dunce pretentiousness of Ogilby.[5] The
ornate pattern enclosing the seal no doubt mocks
those sumptuous volumes for which Ogilby was
famous and which "on Out-side merit but presume"
(I, 135). In a note on 1729 I, 121 ("Ogilby
the *great*") Pope quotes from Winstanly, *Lives of the
Poets*: "His translations of *Homer* and *Virgil*, done
to the life, and with such excellent Sculptures! and
(what added great grace to his works) he printed
them all on *special good Paper*, and in a *very good
Letter*."

At the bottom of the frontispiece the imprint
reads: "Dublin; Printed; London; Reprinted for
A. Dodd." This is double subterfuge. First, it
implies that the poem is from the hand of an
Irish dunce, one more Mac Flecknoe, "from Ireland
let him reign." Bolingbroke alludes to the stock
identification of Ireland as the modern Boeotia
when in a letter to Swift (February 1727/8) he
reports on the state of the *Dunciad* in manuscript:

"In the mean time his [Pope's] *Dulness* [*The Progress of Dulness* was the original title of the poem] grows and flourishes as if he was there [in Dublin] already."[6] Second, "Reprinted for A. Dodd" refers to Mrs. Anne Dodd, who, since she published trivial poems, tales, and miscellaneous pieces, might well be expected to reprint an Irish poem. But, as Sutherland states, just as there was no Dublin edition of the poem prior to the London one of 18 May 1728, so Mrs. Dodd "was never in any sense the publisher of the poem."[7] "A. Dodd" (or "A. Dod" in the imprint of Figure 2) must therefore be a red herring. But it is also possibly a play on "adod" (a favorite interjection of Old Bellair in Etherege's *Man of Mode*, equivalent to "egad") and on "a doddard" (dotard, dunce).[8] This production of an Irish dunce is published by an English one, as is only fit.

Figure 2 is the title page of the 1729 Variorum edition (Griffith 211). The ass is referred to in Appendix VI ("Of the Poet Laureate") in the 1743 *Dunciad* as "that noble one ... whose portraiture makes so great an ornament of the *Dunciad*." Characteristically the ass "carries Loads, and feeds on Thistles," as Swift describes its proper "Trade" in *The Beasts Confession* (1732). That the ass chews thistles ts proverbial, but the association of the thistle with satire, on which the point of the emblem partly depends, is not so well known. Swift connects the thistle with dunce satire in the following passage from the Preface to *A Tale of a Tub*:

> Besides, most of our late Satyrists seem to lye under a sort of Mistake, that because Nettles have the Prerogative to Sting, therefore all *other Weeds* must do so too. I make not this Comparison out of the least Design to detract from these worthy Writers: For it is well known among *Mythologists*, that *Weeds* have the Pre-eminence over all other Vegetables; and therefore the first *Monarch* of this Island [James I], whose Taste and Judgment were so acute and refined, did very wisely root out the *Roses* from the Collar of the *Order*, and plant the *Thistles*

in their stead as the nobler Flower of the two.
For which Reason it is conjectured by profounder Antiquaries, that the Satyrical Itch, so prevalent in this part of our Island, was first
brought among us from beyond the *Tweed*. Here may
it long flourish and abound; May it survive and
neglect the Scorn of the World, with as much
Ease and Contempt as the World is insensible to
the Lashes of it. May their own Dulness, or
that of their Party, be no Discouragement for
the Authors to proceed; but let them remember,
it is with *Wits* as with *Razors*, which are never
so apt to *cut* those they are employed on, as
when they have *lost their Edge*.

Later we shall see that Swift had other grounds,
apart from the Scotch thistle, on which to make
his connection between the Scots and dunce satire.
Here his point that the dunce satirist only hurts
himself can be applied to the ass chewing the
thistle: if he tries to bite he is bit. Congreve
makes the same point in the prologue to *Love for
Love*:

> We've something too, to gratify ill nature
> (If there by any here) and that is Satire--
> Though Satire scarce dares grin, 'tis grown so
>   mild,
> Or only shows its teeth, as if it smiled.
> As asses thistles, poets mumble wit,
> And dare not bite for fear of being bit.
>   (31-36)

The implication in the emblem would seem to be
that the dunces who have assaulted Pope on the
score of *Peri Bathous* and the 1728 *Dunciad*, for all
their rage, are ineffectual. Dryden in *Mac Flecknoe* had described this kind of mumbling, bumbling
satire in lines that demonstrate by contrast his
own "keen Iambics":

> With whate'er gall thou sett'st thyself to
>   write,
> Thy inoffensive satires never bite.

In thy felonious heart though venom lies,
It does but touch thy Irish pen, and dies.
                              (199-202)

And in *The Medal* he has a passage that provides a
gloss on the scene before us:

    The man who laugh'd but once, to see an ass
    Mumbling to make the crossgrain'd thistles
        pass,
    Might laugh again, to see a jury chaw
    The prickles of unpalatable law.   (146-49)

Even the humorless would burst out laughing at
the sight of these asses stubbornly persisting in
their attempts at satire. For them, in contrast
to the wits, *difficile est saturam scribere.*
Whereas the books in the owl frontispiece are
arranged according to their size and shape, here
they are treated as a load for a beast of burden,
and ironically distributed according to their
pretentiousness. Thus, reading from the top, we
see three "highbrow" works comparable to those
making up the altar in Figure 1: Welsted's poetry, Ward's works, and the works of Dennis (this
last carried over from the owl frontispiece).
These, as serious stuff, are separated from the
rest by an open space. The puns on "works" and
"plays," found also in the altar of Figure 1, confirm this separation of superior from inferior
dulness. Theobald's plays (rather than his
"Shakespeare Restored") head the lower productions, followed by Oldmixon and by Eliza Haywood's novels, with her *Secret History of ... the
Court of Caramania* (1727) singled out for infamy.
Last of all come the literally ephemeral newspapers, *Mist's Journal, British Journal, Pasquin, London
Journal, Daily Journal, Baker's Journal, Flying Post*, etc.
As in the owl frontispiece all the dunce authors
figure in the poem itself, and the newspapers,
except for *Pasquin,* the *London Journal*, and *Baker's
Journal*, are included in Appendix II: "A list of
Books, Papers, and Verses, in which our Author
was abused, printed before the Publication of the

Dunciad: With the true Names of the Authors."
These newspapers are weighted down by the more
solid dulness of the bound volumes, but some have
flown out of the ass's pannier, as the *Flying Post*
illustrates.

Here the owl of Dulness, although not the
heraldic bird of Figure 1, is still "high on a
throne of its own labors reared." That it is
carried over from the 1728 frontispiece but much
reduced by comparison with the ass may indicate
that the original *Dunciad*, for which it seems to
stand, is now all but obliterated by the critical
apparatus of the Variorum. The heavy load on the
plodding ass makes an especially apt emblem for
the learned lumber with which Scriblerus, Bentley,
and their kind have weighed down the poem.

The picture is "framed" by a motto from Horace,
Epistles II, i, 269: *Deferor* (for *deferar*) *in vicum /
vendentem thus et odores*. The ironic incongruity of
the beast of burden with the Latin quotation resembles the coupling of learned allusion, with
the Latin in footnotes, and rural realism in
Gay's *Shepherd's Week*. In the passage from which
the line is taken Horace speaks with witty exaggeration, under the figure of his funeral, of
the danger in allowing himself to be flattered by
a bad poet:

> Not for me attentions that are burdensome, and
> I want neither to be displayed anywhere in
> wax, with my features misshaped, nor to be
> praised in verses ill-wrought, lest I have to
> blush at the stupid gift, and then, along with
> my poet, outstretched in a closed chest, be
> carried into the street where they sell frank-
> incense and perfumes and pepper and everything
> else that is wrapped in sheets of useless pa-
> per.[9]

The passage reveals Pope's attitude towards the
dunces: he can dismiss their blame as innocuous
but he dreads their praise. As he was to put it
in *Arbuthnot*:

>   One Flatt'rer's worse than all;
> Of all mad Creatures, if the Learn'd are right,
> It is the Slaver kills, and not the Bite.
> A Fool quite angry is quite innocent;
> Alas! 'tis ten times worse when they *repent*.
>   (104-8)

He deals with the dunces in this poem, not because their attacks have hurt him, but because
he can keep them at a distance, and thus avoid
the degradation Horace fears, only by putting
them in their place.[10]
     More particularly, the motto points to the
great distance separating Pope the satirist from
these venal lampooners and puffers: "I am
brought down into the street where they sell perfume and stench." In writing to Warburton about
a new attack on him by Cibber, Pope speaks of
"Flatteries" as "Perfumes" and of "Railing" as
"Stink" (*Correspondence*, IV, 492). Pope is forced
to stoop from Parnassus to Grubstreet in order
to silence those scribblers who sell their flattery and slander.
     I take the building in the background to repre-
sent a baker's shop; the objects on the top level
seem to be pies, those on the lower one loaves of
bread. They are there to illustrate the satiric
commonplace that worthless writing ends up mere
paper: "Martyrs of pies, and relics of the bum."
Left with the works of Swift on his hands, Lintot
"sent them with a Load of Books, / Last *Monday* to
the Pastry-cooks" (*Verses on the Death of Dr. Swift*,
259-60). Pope, in his version of the passage
from which the motto is taken, specifies other
ignominious uses:

> And when I flatter, let my dirty leaves
> (Like Journals, Odes, and such forgotten things
> As Eusden, Philips, Settle, writ of Kings)
> Cloath spice, line trunks, or flutt'ring in a
>   row,
> Befringe the rails of Bedlam and Sohoe.
>   (*Imitations of Horace*, Ep.II,i,415-19)

THE
DUNCIAD.

BOOK the First.

OOKS and the MAN I sing,
the first who brings
The Smithfield Muses to the
Ear of Kings.
Say great Patricians! since your
selves inspire

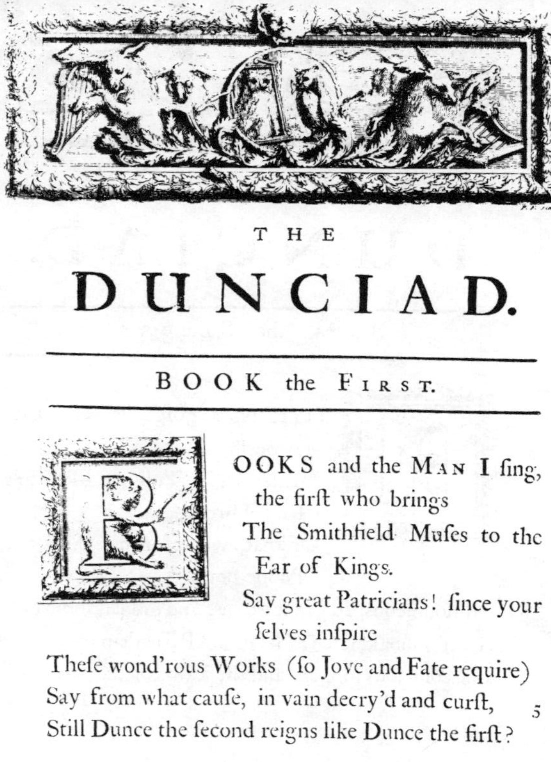

These wond'rous Works (so Jove and Fate require)
Say from what cause, in vain decry'd and curst,
Still Dunce the second reigns like Dunce the first? 5

Figure 4

THE
DUNCIAD.

BOOK the FIRST.

NEMO ME IMPVNE LACESSIT

Figure 3

THE

DUNCIAD.

BOOK the SECOND.

IGH on a gorgeous feat, that far outfhone
Henley's gilt Tub, or Fleckno's Irifh Throne,
Or that, where on her Curls the Public pours
All-bounteous, fragrant grains, and golden fhow'rs:
Great Tibbald fate: The proud Parnaffian fneer,
The confcious fimper, and the jealous leer.

Figure 5

THE

DUNCIAD.

BOOK the THIRD.

UT in her Temple's laft recefs
inclos'd,
On Dulnefs' lap th'Anointed head repos'd.
Him clofe fhe curtain'd round with vapors blue,
And foft befprinkled with Cimmerian dew.
Then raptures high the feat of fenfe o'erflow,
Which only heads refin'd from reafon know.

Figure 6

And Theobald intends to save his works from such
a fate by burning them:

"Adieu my children! better thus expire
Un-stall'd, unsold; thus glorious mount in
  fire
Fair without spot; than greas'd by grocer's
  hands,
Or shipp'd with Ward to ape and monkey lands,
Or wafting ginger, round the streets to go,
And visit alehouse where ye first did grow."
                           (I, 197-202)

Such is the Progress of Dulness: the dull work,
returning as waste paper to the very alehouse
which gave it birth, comes full circle.
     Figure 3 is the mock heraldic headpiece to
Book I of the Variorum (Griffith 211).[11] The
motto, *Nemo me impune lacessit*, is not only that of
Scotland but also that of the Order of the
Thistle, the distinctively Scottish order of
knighthood. The motto refers specifically to the
thistle, which no one picks with impunity. Together with the thistle and asses, carried over
from Figure 2, it announces the theme of dunce
satire. As in Figure 2, both the owl and the
ass appear, but here the owl is featured. His
scowl, repeated in the flanking asses, confirms
the threatening motto: no one attacks *him* with
impunity. Yet the fool's cap and bells turns
the threat to ridicule. The dunce who blusters
is twice a dunce. The motto itself is turned to
irony since Pope has attacked, and is now attacking, the dunces with perfect impunity. The
scowling owl may point specifically to "furious"
Dennis ("And all the Mighty Mad in Dennis rage"
[I, 104]). In the *Essay on Criticism* Dennis *"stares,
Tremendous!* with a *threat'ning Eye"* (586). Taken
together the angry beasts represent the impotent
rage of the whole dunce tribe upon the publication of the *Peri Bathous* and the 1728 *Dunciad*. As
in Figure 2, the ass ears are pricked up to show
their "length of ears" (III, 28); to display
their badge of asininity they "prick all their
ears up" (II, 250).

We have already noted Swift's connection between the Scots and impotent satire. The owl of
Figure 3 calls up two satiric *topoi* applicable to
the Scots which contribute to this association.
In Section VIII of the *Tale* Swift makes use of the
first of these in referring to Scotland as " Σκοτία,
or the *Land of Darkness*." Like Ireland, it belongs
to Dulness. In this connection we recall that
Scotland produced Duns Scotus, the eponym for the
race of dunces. The second commonplace about the
Scots, to which Swift alludes in making the
satirical itch endemic in Scotland, is that they
are *genus irritabile*. That it was good sport to put
the gullible and irascible Scot in a rage is revealed by a slang sense of "Scot" noted by the
OED in a single example dated 1812: "J.H. Vaux
Flash Dict., *Scot*, a person of an irritable temper,
who is easily put in a passion, which is often
done by the company he is with, to create fun,
such a one is declared to be a fine *Scot*."

Figures 4, 5 and 6 are the headpieces, respectively, to Books I, II, and III of Griffith
372, an edition of the *Dunciad* which formed part
of the collected works of Pope published in 1735.
These elaborate engravings are by Peter Fourdrinier
after William Kent. Kent, a friend of Pope, is
probably best known as an architect and landscape gardener, but he was also an artist who had
illustrated editions of Pope, Gay, and Thomson.[12]
W. K. Wimsatt identifies Fourdrinier as a pupil
of Picart at Amsterdam who came to England in
1720, and was known especially for architectural
engraving. He did the plates for the volume of
Palladio brought out by Kent's patron and Pope's
friend the Earl of Burlington.[13] In all three of
these *Dunciad* plates the ironic contrast of the
ornate frames with the low scenes they contain
effects a visual equivalent of the mock-heroic
style of the poem. These headpieces appear to be
diminished history paintings (Kent was a history
painter), and their base subjects magnified to
biblical/classical status.

Figure 4, unlike the two other headpieces, is
more in the nature of a frontispiece to the poem

than an illustration of particular passages in it.
Accordingly, it picks up the owl and the ass of
the preceding illustrations. In the centered
medallion a foppish owl with a bow around its
neck is regarding itself in a mirror. This is a
visual translation of "owl-glass" (from Till
Eulenspiegel), or buffoon, depicting the ridiculous vanity of the dunces. Here ugliness is aim-
ing at the applause of beauty, as Fielding puts
it. To the left of the medallion are two asses,
the bridled one playing a harp and softly braying (or snoring, having sung himself to sleep).
There is an animal head, possibly a boar, as
ornament on the harp. To the right of this ass
is another with large thick spectacles, writing
in a book. These are the tame and decorous asses
of solid dulness. To the right of the medallion
are the wild, unbridled ones of pert, impudent
dulness. One ass is playing a harp topped appropriately with a ram's head. Behind it is another
with lifted head aggressively and loudly braying.
And behind it the hindquarters of yet a third,
kicking and farting under its lifted tail: "Its
proper Pow'r to hurt, each Creature feels, /
Bulls aim their horns, and Asses lift their heels"
(*Imitations of Horace*, Sat. II, i, 85-86). Clearly
these are manifestations of dunce satire.

The thistles emblematic of dunce satire appear
here both in the picture and in its frame. Directly above the medallion, on the frame, is
the upturned haughty face of a satyr, disdainful
of the scene below. The decorated initial letter
of the poem's first line exhibits a bespectacled
animal holding a book. This I take to be a mole
blindly trying to read, witty emblem of dunce
persistence. In his section on Kent, Wimsatt
notes a drawing of a *"Dunciad*-like" subject: an
owl holding in its bill a kind of hornbook. This
is either the work of Kent or of his pupil Lady
Burlington (pp. 122-23).

Figure 5 is the only one of these three headpieces lacking the "W.K. inv:," having only "P.
F. sculp:" on the right. Like Figure 4 it shows
a centered medallion (or, more precisely, a

medal, as we shall see). An old man in clerical
gown is pilloried, and an eight-pointed star is
placed above his head. On the border of the
medal at the top appears the motto *Ad Summa*, and
at the bottom *Inveniam Viam Aut Faciam*. This is
John "Orator" Henley whose history is given in a
long note to III, 195, the end of which reads:

> After having stood some Prosecutions, he
> turned his Rhetorick to Buffoonry upon all
> publick and private occurrences. All this
> passed in the same room; where sometimes he
> broke Jests, and sometimes that Bread which he
> call'd the *Primitive Eucharist*. This wonderful
> person struck Medals, which he dispersed as
> Tickets to his subscribers: The device, a
> Star rising to the Meridian, with this Motto,
> AD SUMMA; and below, INVENIAM VIAM AUT FACIAM.

In Book II Henley is mentioned only twice: "Henley's gilt Tub" (2) and "My Henley's periods"
(338). However, the pillory of the medal and the
cudgels and knotted cords on either side of it
illustrate the following passage in Book II and
establish in the headpiece the theme of dunce
punishment:

> Earless on high, stood un-abash'd Defoe,
> And Tutchin flagrant from the scourge, below:
> There Ridpath, Roper, cudgell'd might ye view;
> The very worsted still look'd back and blue.
> (139-42)

Kent must have chosen Henley to pillory because
with his insignia of medals and mottos, star and
clerical gown he could be easily depicted and
identified. There is possibly yet another sign
in the headpiece pointing to the punishment of
the dunces. The cudgels and chamberpots on the
right might be lying on a blanket. If so, there
is an allusion to the two couplets following the
two just quoted:

Himself [Curll] among the storied Chiefs he
    spies,
As from the blanket high in air he flies,
"And oh! (he cry'd) what street, what lane,
    but knows
Our purgings, pumpings, blanketings and blows?"
                    (143-46)

On the left we see the evidence of the crimes
for which the dunces are punished: a sheet with
Journal printed on it and "reams abundant" (86)
of dunce wastepaper.
    The other objects establish the corollary but
ironic theme of dunce rewards, that is, the
prizes Dulness gives her sons in the games of
Book II. Three of these are specified in the
following lines of the goddess:

"Who flings most filth, and wide pollutes
    around
The stream, be his the Weekly Journals, bound.
A pig of lead to him who dives the best.
A peck of coats a-piece shall glad the rest."
                    (267-70)

On the right of the medal we see three volumes
on the open one of which is printed *Weekly Journals*.
On the left what looks at first like a volume
must be the pig of lead, and near it, presumably,
the peck of coals (although this might be a bas-
ket of fruit or ancient eggs for those in the
pillory). Again on the right are two other
prizes: a large drum ("And his this Drum, whose
hoarse heroic base / Drowns the loud clarion of
the braying Ass" [225-26]), and two chamberpots
commemorating the pissing contest ("This China-
Jordan, let the chief o'ercome / Replenish, not
ingloriously, at home" [157-58]).
    The decoration of the initial letter H is mock
heraldic. On the caduceus of Mercury, standing
for Wit, is stuck a fool's cap and bells wreathed
with bays, the perfect emblem for Duncery, or Wit
Mocked. In the middle of each side of the frame
is a surly male face with a suggestion of the
satyr's horns.

Figure 6, the headpiece to Book III, illustrates
the passages attacking farces and pantomimes in
that book. We can well understand Kent's choice
of subject: these passages of grotesque description call out for illustration. At the center
is a dragon with what could be the wings of an
owl and the ears of an ass. Much like a medieval
depiction of Satan eating sinners, it is devour-
ing, head first, in its fiery furnace of a maw a
harlequin figure who is also a sorcerer, to judge
from his wand and book of magic symbols on the
ground: "He look'd, and saw a sable Sorc'rer
rise, / Swift to whose hand a winged volume flies"
(229-30). To the left of the monstrous dragon-
owl-ass we see what appears to be another winged
dragon excreting or giving birth to a harlequin
head first. The tail of this dragon is so wound
about his torso and head that the harlequin appears to form part of its tail:

   "Yet lo! in me [Settle] what authors have to
      brag on!
   Reduc'd at last to hiss in my own dragon.
   Avert it, heav'n! that thou [Theobald] or
      Cibber e'er
   Should wag two serpent tails in Smithfield
      fair."   (287-90)

On the right is another harlequin birth from a
huge egg: "And last, to give the whole creation
grace, / Lo! one vast Egg produces human race"
(243-44). A note on this last verse explains
that "in another of these Farces Harlequin is
hatch'd upon the Stage, out of a large Egg." The
center and left are so shaded as to indicate
flames whereas the right side is filled with the
rays of the sun. The juxtaposed flames and rays
illustrate the crazy chronology of dunce productions which can represent at one and the same
time the destruction and the creation of the
world:

   Till one wide Conflagration swallows all.
      Thence a new world, to Nature's laws unknown,
   Breaks out refulgent, with a heav'n its own.
                        (236-38)

The frame seems to confirm the impression that
the central monster is a hybrid dragon, owl, and
ass, since on it we see a dragon with open maw
and bulging eyes, two ass heads, and the head of
an angry owl. The thistles reappear on the right
and left of the scroll-work frame. Thus this
illustration for the last book of the Variorum
recapitulates all three of the recurrent images
in the illustrations.

Griffith 372 also has two tailpieces by Fourdrinier after Kent. One showing a boar at a
watering trough appears twice (at the end of
Book III, p. 54, and after the last note to Book
I, p. 115). The other, an eagle flying off with
what seems to be a goose in its beak, appears at
the end of "A Declaration," p. 56. I have not
reproduced these two engravings since it seems to
me likely that they were not made expressly for
the *Dunciad*: these particular animals do not figure in the poem itself and I cannot connect the
two pictures with any of its passages or themes.
It may be that these tailpieces were included as
generally illustrative of the animal imagery of
the *Dunciad*.[14]

Figure 7, with the royal arms of Great Britain,
first appeared in the revised *Dunciad* of 1743
(Griffith 578). Since the coat of arms is royal,
it may be seen as representing the climactic expression of the mock heraldic treatment in the
illustrations. The new hero Cibber required a
new emblem, and nothing less than the royal arms
would do justice to his imperious impudence and
his claim to be King of Dunces. Until one begins
to examine it closely, this royal coat of arms
appears to be a standard official block. Although
he does regard it with some doubt, Sutherland is
inclined, on the whole, to accept the coat as
authentic:

> Apart from the absence of GR on the royal
> arms, and a suspiciously human expression on
> the lion's face, there seems to be little in
> the coat of arms to suggest that it was not
> being used "by authority."[15]

By A U T H O R I T Y.

𝕭Y virtue of the Authority in Us vested by the Act for subjecting Poets to the power of a Licenser, we have revised this Piece, where finding the stile and appellation of King to have been given to a certain Pretender, Pseudo-Poet, or Phantom, of the name of TIBBALD; and apprehending the same may be deemed in some sort a Reflection on Majesty, or at least an insult on that Legal Authority which has bestowed on another person the Crown of Poesy: We have ordered the said Pretender, Pseudo-Poet, or Phantom, utterly to vanish and evaporate out of this work: And do declare the said Throne of Poesy from henceforth to be abdicated and vacant, unless duly and lawfully supplied by the LAUREATE himself. And it is hereby enacted, that no other person do presume to fill the same.

Figure 7

Anno Regni

G E O R G I I II.

I E G I S

Magnæ Britanniæ, Franciæ, & Hiberniæ,

D E C I M O Q U A R T O.

At the Parliament begun and holden at *Westminster*, the Fourteenth Day of *January*, *Anno Dom.* 1734, in the Eighth Year of the Reign of our Sovereign Lord *G E O R G E* the Second, by the Grace of God, of *Great Britain*, *France*, and *Ireland*, King, Defender of the Faith, *&c.*

And from thence continued by several Prorogations to the Eighteenth Day of *November*, 1740, being the Seventh Session of this present Parliament.

L O N D O N,
Printed by *John Baskett*, Printer to the King's most Excellent Majesty. 1741.

Figure 8

Following tradition, the lion face of the authentic royal arms suggests a human face (see Figure
8), but that of Figure 7 is human to such a degree
that it seems to invite identification yet at the
same time to defy it. There is an innuendo in
Warburton's mock critique entitled *Ricardus Aristarchus of the Hero of the Poem* (in Griffith 578) that
the face belongs to Cibber:

> *Bravery*, the second attribute of the true
> Hero, is Courage manifesting itself in every
> limb; while, in its correspondent virtue in
> the mock Hero [Impudence], that Courage is all
> collected into the *Face*. ... his *Face* 'more
> known (as he justly boasteth) than most in the
> kingdom.'

Further on in the piece he refers to the "*erect
face*" of Cibber. This italicized insistence on
Cibber's face (with a play on "face" as impudence) looks like a clue to the lion's face. But
since the crowned lion represents both the King
and the king of poets, its face must hint at
George and Colley both. As sometimes in the poem
itself, to use Maynard Mack's expression, "the
image of Cibber blurs into the image of George
II."16

There is a noticeable difference in the treatment of the Garter buckle (below the *Honi* of the
motto) in the authentic and in the counterfeit
arms. Here the buckle clearly forms the monogram GƆ, a G for George and a reversed C for
Colley. This coupling of these two kings of Brentford would appear to be Pope's substitution for
the missing GR on the proclamation, noted by
Sutherland. If this is indeed a cipher of George
and Colley, it reflects Pope's fusion of the two
in I, 6: "Still Dunce the second reigns like
Dunce the first." George II has succeeded George
I (1727), Cibber has succeeded Eusden as the
Laureate (1730), and now George and Colley dispute the title of First Dunce of the Land. The
two are identified, not only in the figure of the
royal lion and in the poem ("'God save king
Cibber!' mounts in ev'ry note" [I, 320]), but

also, repeatedly, in the text of the proclamation
by such phrases as "the style and appellation of
KING" (with its implication that both the King
and the Laureate are counterfeit), "a Reflection
on *Majesty*," "the *Crown of Poesy*," and "the said
Throne of Poesy." Moreover, a close look at the
arms will reveal that the monogrammatic linking
of the C and G is also slyly suggested in both
the lion's crown and the large central one.

The sham document is signed "ƆC. Ch." Sutherland notes that Pope's editors have ignored "this
cryptic signature."[17] I read it as two C's, the
first reversed, thus forming a monogram of Colley
Cibber which can also be read as X: The illiterate Cibber has set his mark to his proclamation.[18]
The "Ch." would then stand for Chancellor as in
III, 324: "Our Midas [Cibber] sits Lord Chancellor of Plays" ("Cibber preside Lord-Chancellor
of Plays" [A III, 320]). Sutherland, however,
presents another candidate:

> The "Ch." presumably stands for "Chamber-
> lain," since it was the Lord Chamberlain who
> had the power loosely referred to in Pope's
> mock-proclamation--if he is thinking of the
> Licensing Act of 1737, which, however, con-
> cerned *dramatic* poets. The Lord Chamberlain
> in 1743 was Charles, second Duke of Grafton,
> whose father was a natural sone of Charles II.
> Charles II had a monogram made of two capital
> C's interlocked, the first C being reversed;
> and as his grandson was also a Charles the
> signature may be intended to recall the royal
> monogram.[19]

Sutherland's reading is surely right, but right
only in part since Pope covers no less than
three dunces with this one cipher. As it was
this Grafton who made Cibber laureate to George
II, the official, the poet, and the king are all
three lumped together and branded illiterate.[20]
This threefold illiteracy seems confirmed in the
arms by the X (the saltire, or cross of St.
Andrew, patron of Scotland) on all three crowns.
And on the unicorn's crown the ƆC motif can be
seen in the treatment of the fleur-de-lys: Ɔ/C.

The wording of the proclamation identifies
Cibber and the King, but the fact that this royal
document is counterfeit and that Cibber has given
himself "the style and appellation of KING" indicates that, like the usurping Georges, Cibber has
usurped the throne of duncedom as well as that of
poetry, and he will bear no brother near either
one. Moreover, the wording also confuses Grafton
and Cibber in such a way as to reveal that Cibber
has stolen his "authority" from Grafton. The
first phrase, "By virtue of the Authority in Us
vested by the *Act for subjecting Poets to the power of
a Licenser*," unequivocally refers to one of Grafton's
functions as Chamberlain, but the following
clause, although still descriptive of Grafton's
power, also alludes to Cibber's practice of fitting up old plays, to use his own language (I,
132*n.*), like those of Shakespeare (I, 134*n.*).
Such is his mad presumption that it will stop at
nothing: revising Shakespeare, revising the *Dunciad* to make himself Pope's chief dunce, even
forging a royal proclamation to establish forever
the fact that he, and only he, is King of Dunces.
The absolutely authoritarian tone of the piece
certifies Cibber as sole author, and, just as he
commands Theobald to *"vanish* and *evaporate"* out of
the poem, so he pushes the King and his minister
into the background of the proclamation. Aristarchus describes Cibber's jealousy of the poem's
rival hero Theobald:

> The good Scriblerus indeed, nay the World it-
> self might be imposed on in the late spurious
> editions, by I can't tell what *Sham-hero,* or
> *Phantom*: But it was not so easy to impose on
> HIM whom this egregious error most of all con-
> cerned. For no sooner had the fourth book laid
> open the high and swelling scene, but he re-
> cognized his own heroic Acts: and when he came
> to the words,
>   *Soft on her lap her Laureat son reclines,*
> (though *Laureat* imply no more than *one crowned with
> laurel,* as befitteth any Associate or Consort
> in Empire) he ROAR'D (like a Lion) and VINDICA-
> TED HIS RIGHT OF FAME.

So in the lion rampant of the arms Cibber emerges
first and foremost. And in his royal proclamation Grafton and George himself appear only as
"phantoms," like Theobald in the poem, all three
revised out of their roles by the overwhelming
vanity of Cibber.

If the lion's face is "suspiciously human," so
are his genitals, and those of the unicorn as well.
Moreover, both phalluses are erect and pointing
ironically to the motto of the Garter, *Honi soit
qui mal y pense*. The satiric point here is the sexual notoriety shared by George and Colley. George
II kept several mistresses, but in this vice too
he is eclipsed by Colley, who shamelessly reveals
his promiscuity in the autobiography ("And has
not *Colly* still his Lord, and Whore?" [*Arbuthnot*,
97]). The Garter motto, then, when it is read as
Cibber's own, turns sharply satiric. In the
Advertisement to the Reader (initialed by Warburton
but probably by Pope) which immediately precedes
the proclamation, the last sentence reads in part:
"This person was one, who from every Folly (not
to say Vice) of which another would be ashamed,
has constantly derived a *Vanity*." For Aristarchus,
however, since Love becomes Debauchery in the
mock Hero, the lust of the old Cibber is a "standing ornament" to the *Dunciad*: "The man is sure
enough a Hero, who has his Lady at fourscore."

As for the other, royal motto, *Dieu et mon droit*,
from the mouth of Cibber it comes out blasphemy
as well as *lèse majesté*: "We generally find," says
Aristarchus, "this kind of courage in so high and
heroic a degree, that it insults not only Men,
but Gods."

In one way of looking at them the *Dunciad* illustrations satirize the visual aids of Dulness
in such works as

> on Out-side merit but presume,
> Or serve (like other Fools) to fill a room;
> Such with their shelves as due proportion hold,
> Or their fond Parents drest in red and gold;
> Or where the pictures for the page attone,
> And Quarles is sav'd by Beauties not his own.
>   (I, 135-40)

As we have seen, however, a closer look reveals
that these mock emblems also reflect the wit of
the poem in such a way as to make the pictures at
one with the page.

NOTES

BUTT,   Pope: The Man and The Poet
 1. *Correspondence*, ed. Sherburn, IV, 381.
 2. Ibid., IV, 490.
 3. Ibid., II, 110.
 4. *Epilogue to the Satires*, II, 74-93.
 5. *Remarks on the Life and Writings of Dr Jonathan Swift*, fifth
edition, 1752, p. 158.
 6. *Correspondence*, III, 166.
 7. Ibid., III, 168.
 8. Ibid., I, 185-6.
 9. Ibid., I, 269.
 10. *Epistle to Miss Blount, With the Works of Voiture*, ll. 57-80.
 11. *The Yale Review*, XLI (1951), 80-92.

GOLDBERG,   Integrity and Life in Pope's Poetry
 1. *Literary Criticism of Alexander Pope*, ed. Bertrand A. Goldgar, Lincoln, Neb., 1965, p. 161.
 2. Ibid., p. 108.
 3. *The Poems of Alexander Pope*, ed. John Butt, London, 1963,
p. 433. Henceforth cited as *Poems*.
 4. See 'Soliloquy, or Advice to an Authour', in *Characteristics*, ed. J. M. Robertson, 2 vols., 1900; repr. Gloucester,
Mass., 1963, I, 101-234, esp. p. 211. Also p. 136: 'The
moral artist who can thus imitate the Creator, and is thus
knowing in the inward form and structure of his fellow-crea-
ture, will hardly, I presume, be found unknowing in himself...'.   Cf. Walter Jackson Bate, 'The Sympathetic Imagination in Eighteenth-Century English Criticism', *ELH*, XII (1945),
144-64.
 5. 'Personae', in *Restoration and Eighteenth-Century Literature*,
ed. Carroll Camden, Chicago, 1963, p. 33.
 6. *Lives of the English Poets*, ed. G. B. Hill, 3 vols., Oxford, 1905, III, 217.
 7. 'The Muse of Satire', *Yale Review*, n.s. XLI (1951-2),
88. Cf. Donald Greene, "'Dramatic Texture' in Pope", in *From Sensibility to Romanticism*, ed. Frederick W. Hilles and Harold Bloom,
New York, 1965, pp. 31-53.
 8. My argument in this paper develops some points made
in an earlier article, 'Alexander Pope', *Melbourne Criticial
Review*, No. 7 (1964), 49-65.
 9. *Literary Criticism* (ed. Goldgar), p. 123.
 10. *The Dunciad* I, 186 (p. 729).
 11. 'The "Fall" of China and *The Rape of the Lock*', *Philological
Quarterly*, XLI (1962), 424. (The article is reprinted in
Essential Articles for the Study of Alexander Pope, ed. Maynard Mack,
rev. and enl. edn, Hamden, Conn., 1968).
 12. *Poems*, p. xxvi.
 13. Cf. Patricia Meyer Spacks, *An Argument of Images: The
Poetry of Alexander Pope*, Cambridge, Mass., 1971, Chap. 3.
 14. *The Poems of Alexander Pope*, Vol. III, i: *An Essay on Man*, ed.
Maynard Mack, London, 1950, p. lxx.
 15. cf. the discussion of Pope's 'oscillations' in Peter
Dixon, *The World of Pope's Satires*, London, 1968, Chaps. 8 and 9.

16. *Alexander Pope: The Poetry of Allusion*, Oxford, 1959, pp. 206ff., 241.
17. *Biographia Literaria*, ed. J. Shawcross, 2 vols., Oxford, 1907, II, 20.
18. Ibid., II, 12.
19. Ibid.
20. 'The Second Satire of the Second Book of Horace, Paraphrased', line 180 (*Poems*, p. 624).
21. Pope's tone earlier, in his correspondence, is significantly different from that of the Imitation of Horace, Bk I, Ep. i; see, e.g., *Correspondence of Alexander Pope*, ed. George Sherburn, 5 vols., Oxford, 1956, I, 185-6, 201-3 (on inconsistency and activity); II, 141 (on retirement); II, 315 (on folly).
22. *The Garden and the City*, Toronto, 1969.
23. Ibid., p. 234, n. 4.
24. 'The First Satire of the Second Book of Horace, Imitated', lines 51-2, 14 (*Poems*, pp. 615, 614).
25. For a different view of the *Epilogue to the Satires*, see Thomas R. Edwards, *Imagination and Power*, London, 1971, pp. 106ff.
26. 'Epistle II: To a Lady', line 2 (*Poems*, p. 560). Cf. the prose argument to the poem: 'the Characters of *Women* . . . are yet more inconsistent and incomprehensible than those of Men' (p. 559).
27. This last point is discussed quite suggestively by Patricia Spacks in *An Argument of Images*, Chaps. 2 and 4.
28. *Lives* (ed. Hill), III, 174-5.
29. Cf. Shaftesbury, 'Soliloquy', in *Characteristics* (ed. Robertson), I, 197-212, and Montaigne, 'Of the Inconstancy of our Actions', in *Essays*, II, i.
30. *Essay on Man*, II, 133-4 (*Poems*, p. 520).
31. On the background meanings of 'ruling passion', see Mack's Introduction to the *Essay on Man*, pp. xxxviff.; Bertrand A. Goldgar, 'Pope's Theory of the Passions: the Background of Epistle II of the *Essay on Man*', *Philological Quarterly*, XLI (1962), 742-3; and Benjamin Boyce, *The Character-Sketches in Pope's Poems*, Durham, N.C., 1962, Chap. 6. The similarity of Pope's sense of 'character' and Shakespeare's is briefly mentioned by Reuben Brower, *The Poetry of Allusion*, pp. 298 and 301; cf. p. 305 on the 'sensitive point' in Pope himself, where 'taste' and moral judgment meet.
32. Benjamin Boyce (*Character-Sketches*, p. 82) briefly notes some of the qualities that distinguish Pope's portraits: his remarkable 'inward' sense of character; his continuous interest in human 'inconsistency'--i.e. in the nature of the individual's unique identity (pp. 96, 114, 125); and the 'intensely emotional perception' that unifies the details in his finest 'Characters' so that 'the imagination can accept [the result] as a dynamic organism' (p. 128).

33. It is worth noticing that the central metaphor of
'veterans' was absent from the first version of these lines,
which began, 'Not as the World its pretty Slaves rewards':
see *The Poems of Alexander Pope*, Vol. III, ii; *Epistles to Several
Persons (Moral Essays)*, ed. F. W. Bateson, London, 1951, p. 67,
note to lines 243-8.
34. Reuben Brower has noted the structural likeness to
The Temple of Fame (see *The Poetry of Allusion*, p. 354); but the
central insight echoes the early lines on Dulness for
Wycherley's *Panegyrick on Dulness* (*Poems*, pp. 272-3), and the
ending that of the early *Messiah*.
35. Several illuminating discussions of *The Dunciad* have
appeared in the last decade or so: Murray Krieger, 'The
"Frail China Jar" and the Rude Hand of Chaos', *Centennial
Review*, V (1961), 176-94; H. H. Erskine-Hill, 'The "New
World" of Pope's *Dunciad*', *Renaissance and Modern Studies*, VI (1962),
49-67; Tony Tanner, 'Reason and the Grotesque: Pope's
Dunciad', *Critical Quarterly*, VII (1965), 145-60; Emrys Jones,
'Pope and Dulness', *Proceedings of the British Academy*, LIV (1968),
231-63. (The first three are reprinted in *Essential Articles*,
ed. Maynard Mack, 1968).
36. 'The "Romanticism" of Pope's Horace', *Essays in Criticism*,
X (1960), 390-404.
37. *The Structure of Complex Words*, London, 1952, p. 96.
38. *The Central Self*, London, 1968.
39. *English Literature in Our Time and the University*, London,
1969, p. 106. The view of Pope implicit in this passage
seems cruder than that in Leavis's earlier (and classic)
essays on Pope in *Revaluation* and *The Common Pursuit*.
40. London, 1972.
41. *In Search of Cultural History*, Oxford, 1969, esp. pp. 42ff.

PAULSON, Satire, and Poetry, and Pope
1. "Satire, moralizing and allegory," as a recent critic
of pastoral poetry has written, "are merely the inborn tendencies of pastoral rendered overt and explicit" (Peter V.
Marinelli, *Pastoral* [London, Metheun, 1971], p. 12).
2. I am indebted in my description of Pope's pastorals
to Martin C. Battestin, "The Transforming Power: Nature and
Art in Pope's Pastorals," *Eighteenth-Century Studies*, II (1969),
183-204.
3. Wycherley's satire is "dramatic," but there is, of
course, a sense in which protagonists like Manly may have
influenced Pope's less dramatic mode; and the same may be
true of Swift's poetic apologias.
4. For a somewhat different view of metamorphosis in
Pope, see Ralph Cohen, "Transformation in *The Rape of the
Lock*," *Eighteenth-Century Studies*, II (1969), 205-24.
5. Pope also drawns upon Polyphemus' lament in Theocritus'
eleventh idyll, upon which he also drew for the "Summer"
pastoral (both of which were also dedicated to physicians).

6. See E.R. Wasserman, "The Limits of Allusion in *The Rape of the Lock*," *Journal of English and Germanic Philology*, LXV (1966), 425-44.

7. See William Frost, "*The Rape of the Lock* and Pope's Homer," *Modern Language Quarterly*, VIII (1947), 342-54.

8. The Baron's speech about his conquering steel is a less direct version of Clarissa's passage about time: it is after all Time that will "strike to Dust th' Imperial Tow'rs of Troy," and his term "steel" covers a scythe as well as a scissors or sword. He and Clarissa together represent the real world, which, however, only has the effect of stimulating further rage in Belinda.

9. *The Temple of Fame* suggests why, in his few statements on satire, Pope spent so much time arguing for particular against general satire. Only in the first are real, living people involved--those who appear in the Temple--as opposed to generalized vices and follies, by stigmatizing which the satirist merely allows the record to remain perverted and untrue concerning the people who commit these vices.

10. Rather like Galatea, who in Ovid was also the speaker, Eloisa is a person with two demands upon her love; and these tend to be related to the two demands of Acis and Polyphemus. Pope shows how it feels to be the person--here victim--caught between love for one man and the jealous demands of another. The Ovidian episode included both the narrative of Galatea and the love-lament and roaring rage of Polyphemus, and the power (and ambiguity) of *Eloisa to Abelard* derives partly at least from the embodiment of both of these agonies in one speaker.

11. Murray Krieger, "Eloisa to Abelard: The Escape from Body or the Embrace of Body," *Eighteenth-Century Studies*, III (1969-70), 30.

12. In passing, we should mention Pope's translation of Chaucer's "Prologue of the Wife of Bath" (1713), which is also concerned with a sensuous woman's attempt to reconcile her real urge toward the love of men with the Church's teachings and the laws about marriage; she enacts the Popean drama in her own figure, a comic Eloisa who has had her lovers and now only needs to justify her conduct.

13. "Cleopatra" is probably by Pope, but it should be noted that it was not acknowledged by him during his lifetime.

14. See E.R. Wasserman, "Pope's Ode for Musick," *English Literary History*, XXVIII (1961), 163-86.

KENNER, Pope's Reasonable Rhymes
1. Quintilian, *Inst. Orat.* IX.iiii.73ff. "A poor trick" is the Loeb translator's rendition.

2. For his strictures on the "troublesom and modern bondage of Rimeing" see his headnote, "The Verse," first prefixed to the 1668 edition of *Paradise Lost*.

3. See the note signed "P." prefixed to *Spring* in the
1736 edition of Pope's *Works*.
4. See Hugh Kenner, *The Pound Era* (Berkeley & Los Angeles,
1971), pp. 109-10. The ascription of primitive speech to
thunder dates from Herder's *Ursprung der Sprache* (1772).
5. William Carlos Williams, *Collected Earlier Poems* (Norwich, Conn., 1951), pp. 241-42. The poem dates from 1922.
6. See Hugh Kenner, *The Counterfeiters* (New York, 1973),
pp. 80-84.
7. See W.K. Wimsatt Jr., "One Relation of Rhyme to Reason," in *The Verbal Icon* (Lexington, Ky., 1954), pp. 153-66.
Wimsatt's pioneer treatment underlies the present essay. Cf.
his mention (p. 157) of the stress-shifts which over a 300-
year period deprived the language of many rhymes accessible
to Chaucer.
8. Wimsatt, pp. 158-65, lists Pope's devices for making
rhymes seem less obvious.
9. John Wilkins, *An Essay Towards a Real Character and a
Philosophical Language* (London, 1668).
10. Swift, *Gulliver's Travels*, Bk. III, ch. 5.
11. Preface to the *Dictionary*.
12. Barbara Shapiro, *John Wilkins, 1614-1672* (Berkeley & Los
Angeles, 1969), p. 221. Her outline (pp. 207-23) of Wilkins'
and other schemes for a Philosophical Language is a convenient historical summary.
13. Wilkins, *Real Character*, citations from the unpaginated
"Contents" (s.v. Part I, ch. v) and "Epistle to the Reader."
14. Wilkins, p. 414.
15. Examples from Wilkins, p. 415. For the antitheses
which underlie so much Augustan poetry, Wilkins employed a
code of prefixed vowels. "Thus if (Da) be put to signifie
God, then (ida) must signifie that which is opposed, namely
Idol. If (Dab) be *Spirit*, (odab) will be *Body*. If (Dad) be
Heaven, (odad) will signifie Hell" (Wilkins, p. 416). Thus
Milton's subject is the war between Dad and odad. The Persons of the Trinity, by the way, are the First, Second and
Third Differences of the Genus D*a*, *God*, namely D*a*b, d*a*d and
D*a*g. When we address God the Father, however, His Godhead
gives way to His status as Second Species (parent) of first
difference (consanguinity) of the Genus *Co* (Oeconomical Relations), hence *coba*, which a sibilant affix will turn into its
opposite *cobas*, Son (Wilkins, pp. 428-29).

BATTESTIN, The Transforming Power: Nature and Art in Pope's
Pastorals
1. *The Dunciad*, IV, l. 16. Quotations from Pope are from
the Twickenham Edition, general ed. John Butt (London and
New Haven). Specific volumes used are the following: *Pastoral
Poetry and An Essay on Criticism*, eds. E. Audra and Aubrey Williams
(1961); *The Dunciad*, ed. James Sutherland (1943); *An Essay on
Man*, ed. Maynard Mack (1950); *The Rape of the Lock and Other
Poems*, ed. Geoffrey Tillotson (1940); *Minor Poems*, eds. Norman
Ault and John Butt (1954).

2. In *The True Intellectual System of the Universe* (1678), for example, Ralph Cudworth echoes Plotinus in comparing the world to "a dramatick poem" and God to the "skilful drama- tist" who connects our actions and His designs "into good coherent sense, and will at last make it appear, that a thread of exact justice did run through all, and that rewards and punishments are measured out in geometrical proportion" (2nd ed. [1743], II, 879-880). On the relation between Nat- ure, the perfect artifact, and Art, the imperfect imitation of Nature, see *ibid.*, I, 155-158.

3. Cf. Sir Thomas Browne's observation that in Eden Nature was not at variance with Art, nor Art with Nature, "they being both servants of [God's] Providence" (*Religio Medici*, Pt. I, sec. 16; *Works*, ed. Geoffrey Keynes [London, 1928], I, 22).

4. See Kermode's introductions to *English Pastoral Poetry from the Beginnings to Marvell* (London, 1952) and to the Arden Edition of *The Tempest*, 5th ed. (London, 1954); and Tayler's *Nature and Art in Renaissance Literature* (New York, 1964).

5. Northrop Frye offers a succinct account of the Christ- ian humanist tradition defining the relationship of art to the "two levels of nature": "The traditional view of the relation of art to nature, as enunciated by Aristotle, broadened by the late Classical rhetoricians, and developed by Christianity, preserves a distinction that is much less clear in Pope. In this view there are two levels of nature. The lower one is the ordinary physical world, which is the- ologically 'fallen'; the upper is a divinely sanctioned order, existing in Eden before the Fall, and mirrored in the Classical and Boethian myth of the Golden Age.... The upper world is the world of 'art' ... and poetry, for all its Renaissance defenders, is one of the most important of the educational and regenerative agents that lead us up to the world of art" ("Nature and Homer," *Texas Quarterly*, I [1958], 192-204). Though, as Frye believes, the distinction between the two levels of Nature may be blurred in Pope, it is none the less real and functional.

6. See, in particular, J.E. Congleton, *Theories of Pastoral Poetry in England, 1684-1798* (Gainesville, Fla., 1952).

7. From "Milton," *Lives of the English Poets*, ed. George Birkbeck Hill (Oxford, 1905), I, 163.

8. *An Epistle to Dr. Arbuthnot* (1734), l. 340.

9. The metaphorical dimensions of Spenser's calendar structure have been explicated by S.K. Heninger, Jr., "The Implications of Form for *The Shepeardes Calender*," *Studies in the Renaissance*, IX (1962), 309-321. Heninger shows that in the Renaissance the calendar was an emblematic device implying the "Pythagorean tetrad," a theory of universal Order which saw the world as a synthesis of the four elements with cor- respondences in all spheres of life: the four humours, the four ages of man, the four seasons, etc. That Pope was wide- ly read in Pythagorean theory at this stage of his career is

doubtless questionable; certainly, however, he had sensed
the significance of Spenser's form in relating "the great
and little worlds."

10. The standard account of this concept from Heraclitus
through the Church fathers is Leo Spitzer, "Classical and
Christian Ideas of World Harmony," *Traditio*, II (1944), 409-
464, and III (1945), 307-364. For its relevance to Pope
(and to Denham), see Earl R. Wasserman, *The Subtler Language*
(Baltimore, 1959), chs. III-IV, and Maynard Mack, Introduction to the Twickenham Edition of the *Essay on Man*, pp. xxxiv-
xxxv.

11. See *Paradise Lost* (1674), IV, ll. 264-268, and *Paradise
Regained* (1671), II, ll. 25-26.

12. *Essay on the Writings and Genius of Pope* (1756), p. 10.

13. "Pope," *op. cit.*, III, 225.

14. "Pope's *Ode for Musick*," *ELH*, XXVIII (1961), 163-186.

15. In this respect, Pope's view of the redemptive, idealizing function of poetry--or at least of pastoral and
georgic--seems closer than we have supposed to that of the
Renaissance. One recalls Sidney, for example, who in a
famous passage in his *Apologie* (1595) had asserted: "Onely
the Poet, disdayning to be tied to any such subiection [to
Nature], lifted up with the vigor of his owne invention,
dooth growe in effect into another nature, in making things
either better than Nature bringeth forth, or, quite anewe,
formes such as never were in Nature...." "Nature," he continued, "never set forth the earth in so rich tapistry, as
divers Poets have done, neither with so pleasant rivers,
fruitful trees, sweet smelling flowers, nor whatsoever els
may make the too much loved earth more lovely. Her world is
brasen, the Poets only deliver a golden." (Ed. Evelyn S.
Shuckburgh [Cambridge, 1891], p. 8.)

16. See Theocritus, *Idyll I*; Virgil, *Eclogue III*; and Spenser's "August."

17. In his note to line 39, Pope observed that Colin Clout
was "the name taken by *Spenser* in his Eclogues, where his
mistress is celebrated under that of *Rosalinda*."

18. "Pope," *op. cit.*, III, 224.

19. See, for instance, Reuben Arthur Brower, *Alexander
Pope: The Poetry of Allusion* (Oxford, 1959), ch. I, and Giorgio
Melchiori, "Pope in Arcady: The Theme of *Et in Arcadia Ego* in
his Pastorals," *English Miscellany: A Symposium of History, Literature and the Arts*, XIV (1963), 83-93.

20. Tayler, pp. 8, 176.

21. Quoted by F.R. Leavis in "Pope," *Revaluation: Tradition
and Development in English Poetry* (New York, 1947), p. 84.

SPACKS, Imagery and Method in *An Essay on Criticism*

1. Letter to Murray, March 1821; quoted in G. Wilson
Knight, *Laureate of Peace: On the Genius of Alexander Pope* (New
York: Oxford Univ. Press, 1955), p. 140.

2. *Speculations: Essays on Humanism and the Philosophy of Art*, ed.
Herbert Read (New York: Harcourt, Brace, N.D.), p. 134 [first
publ. 1924].

3. Discussed by Aubrey Williams in his introduction to *An Essay on Criticism*, Alexander Pope, *Pastoral Poetry and An Essay on Criticism*, ed. E. Aubra and Aubrey Williams, The Twickenham Ed. of the Poems of Alexander Pope, I (New Haven, Conn.: Yale Univ. Press, 1961), 212-218.

4. Its various meanings have been discussed by Williams (cited above) and by William Empson, "Wit in the Essay on Criticism," *The Structure of Complex Words* (Norfolk, Conn.: New Directions, 1951), pp. 84-100, and E.N. Hooker, "Pope on Wit: The *Essay on Criticism*," *The Seventeenth Century ... By Richard Foster Jones and Others Writing in His Honor* (Stanford, Calif.: Stanford Univ. Press, 1951), pp. 225-246.

5. Alexander Pope, *The Iliad of Homer*, ed. Maynard Mack, The Twickenham Ed. of the Poems of Alexander Pope, VII, VIII (New Haven: Yale Univ. Press, 1967), note to *Iliad* III, 7; VII, 188.

6. Maynard Mack, in his introduction to Pope's Homer, points out the identification (Twickenham Ed., VII, xlvi-xlvii), as does Williams in his introduction to the *Essay on Criticism* (Twickenham Ed., I, 214).

7. Pope's Preface to the *Iliad*, Twickenham Ed., VII, 9.

8. Jacob H. Adler, "Balance in Pope's *Essays*," *ES*, XLIII (1962), 438-439.

9. Twickenham Ed., I, 224.

10. Donald Greene, "'Logical Structure' in Eighteenth-Century Poetry," *PQ*, XXXI (1952), 330.

11. *The Augustans*, ed. Maynard Mack (Englewood Cliffs, N.J.: Prentice-Hall, 1961), pp. 22-23.

12. Discussed by Maynard Mack in *The Augustans* and by William Bysshe Stein, "Pope's 'An Essay on Criticism': The Play of Sophia," *BR*, XIII (1965), 73-86.

13. "'First Follow Nature': Strategy and Stratification in *An Essay on Criticism*," *JEGP*, LV (1956), 604-617.

14. *The Mirror and the Lamp: Romantic Theory and the Critical Tradition* (New York: Norton, 1958).

15. Richard Harter Fogle supports this point in connection with some of Pope's Coleridgean metaphors. See his "Metaphors of Organic Unity in Pope's *Essay on Criticism*," *TSE*, XIII (1963), 51-58.

16. Note to *Iliad* XIV, 457; Twickenham Ed., VIII, 186.

17. In *Spectator* 253, 20 Dec. 1711.

18. *The Works of John Sheffield ... Duke of Buckingham*, 2nd ed., 2 vols. (London, 1729), I, 128-129.

19. Rosemond Tuve, *Elizabethan and Metaphysical Imagery* (Chicago: Univ. of Chicago Press, 1947), p. 183.

20. *The Dunciad*, ed. James Sutherland, The Twickenham Ed. of the Poems of Alexander Pope, V (New Haven: Yale Univ. Press, 1963), 205-206.

21. Caroline F.E. Spurgeon, *Shakespear's Imagery and What It Tells Us* (New York: Macmillan, 1936), p. 9.

22. Thomas R. Edwards, Jr., *This Dark Estate: A Reading of Pope* (Berkeley: Univ. of California Press, 1963), p. 18.

23. Williams identifies a source of this idea in Quintilian. Twickenham Ed., I, 231.
24. Note to *Iliad* V, 1054; Twickenham Ed., VII, 317.
25. *Structure of Complex Words*, p. 84.
26. Letter to Wycherley, 10 April 1706; *The Correspondence of Alexander Pope*, ed. George Sherburn, 5 vols. (Oxford: Clarendon Press, 1956), I, 16.
27. Letter to Cromwell, 17 Dec. 1710; *Correspondence*, I, 109-110.
28. Letter to Wycherley, 20 Nov. 1707;*Correspondence*, I, 34.
29. *Elizabethan and Metaphysical Imagery*, p. 61.

MORRIS, Virgilian Attitudes in Pope's *Windsor-Forest*
1. *Guardian* No. 40 (1713), in *The Prose Works of Alexander Pope*, ed. Norman Ault (Oxford, 1936), p. 98. All quotations from Pope's poetry refer to the eleven-volume Twickenham Edition of *The Poems of Alexander Pope* (New Haven, 1939-69), under the general editorship of John Butt. *Windsor-Forest* (1713) appears in the volume *Pastoral Poetry and An Essay on Criticism*, ed. E. Audra and Aubrey Williams (1961).
2. From an early version of Pope's "Epistle to Mr. Jervas," quoted by Norman Ault, *New Light on Pope* (1949; rpt. Hamden, Conn., 1967), p. 73.
3. *Lives of the English Poets*, ed. George Birkbeck Hill (Oxford, 1905), III, 224.
4. Audra and Williams, eds., *Pastoral Poetry*, p. 132.
5. *Alexander Pope: The Poetry of Allusion* (Oxford, 1959), pp. 61-62. The best account to date is in John Chalker's *The English Georgic: A study in the development of a form* (Baltimore, 1969). Chalker's scope is too broad, however, to permit him to develop a detailed reading of *Windsor-Forest*.
6. In Joseph Spence, *Observations, Anecdotes, and Characters of Books and Men*, ed. James M. Osborn (Oxford, 1966), I, 21.
7. *An Essay on Translated Verse* (1684), in *Critical Essays of the Seventeenth Century*, ed. J.E. Spingarn (1908-09; rpt. Bloomington, Ind., 1957), II, 300. Longinus' recommendation, in Chapter 11 of Boileau's translation, is quoted by Dryden in his Preface to *Troilus and Cressida* (1679)(*Essays of John Dryden*, ed. W.P. Ker [1900; rpt. New York, 1961], I, 206).
8. Lines 402-405. All translations are from Dryden's *The Works of Virgil* (London, 1697).
9. In Spence, *Anecdotes*, I, 24.
10. *The Insistence of Horror: Aspects of the Supernatural in Eighteenth-Century Poetry* (Cambridge, Mass., 1962), p. 142.
11. See, for example, Thomas Otway's "Windsor Castle," in *Minor English Poets 1660-1780*, comp. David P. French (New York, 1967), I, 520.
12. The figure is based upon Edwin Abbott's *A Concordance to Pope* (1875; rpt. New York, 1965), which excludes Pope's translations. Book Five of Pope's version of the *Iliad*, a book almost wholly devoted to violent and frenzied warfare, uses the word "fury" at least twelve times and the adjective

"furious" at least ten, while the following description and
explication of a standard pictorial emblem of Fury emphasizes
the menacing irrationality latent in the idea of *furor*: "A
Man shewing Madness in his Looks, his Eyes tied with a Fillet, in a Posture as if he had a Mind to throw a Bundle of
Arms bound up, in a short Habit. The Fillet denotes the
Understanding *lost*, when Madness has Domination, for Madness
is the *Blindness* of the Mind. The Arms signifie that Fury
is ever *arm'd* for Revenge. The short Garment shews that he
respects neither *Decency* nor *good Manners*" (*Iconologia: or,
Moral Emblems, by Caesar Ripa* [London, 1709], p. 30--an adaptation of Ripa's original text published in 1595).

13.   Robert M. Schmitz, *Pope's Windsor Forest 1712: A Study of
the Washington University Holograph*, Washington Univ. Studies,
No. 21 (St. Louis, 1952), p. 32.

14.   Ibid., p. 40.

15.   Preface to *The Iliad* (1715), in *Prose Works*, ed. Ault,
p. 231. Pope may have recalled Dryden's discussion of Virgilian subjectivity in the preface to *Annus Mirabilis* (1667)
(*Essays of John Dryden*, ed. Ker, I, 15-16).

16.   *Virgil: A Study in Civilized Poetry* (1963; corr. edn. Oxford, 1966), pp. 49-50.

17.   *The Subtler Language: Critical Readings of Neoclassic and
Romantic Poems* (Baltimore, 1959), p. 131.

18.   *The Poetic Workmanship of Alexander Pope* (1955; rpt. New
York, 1966), p. 173.

19.   From a poem by Fr. Knapp prefixed to the 1717 edition
of Pope's *Works*. The Longinian version of *enargeia* appears
in chapter 13 of Boileau's translation. Boileau subtitled
the chapter "*Des Images*."

20.   Thomas R. Edwards, Jr., "The Colors of Fancy: An
Image Cluster in Pope," *MLN*, 73 (1958), 485-489.

21.   Audra and Williams, eds., *Pastoral Poetry*, p. 161, n.
115. The commentators are William Warburton and Joseph
Wharton.

22.   Quoted by Audra and Williams, eds., *Pastoral Poetry*,
p. 186, n. 366.

23.   *The Poetry of the "Aeneid": Four Studies in Imaginative Unity
and Design* (Cambridge, Mass., 1965), p. 192.

24.   In Spence, *Anecdotes*, I, 196. Osborn notes the
parallel in Chetwood.

25.   John H. Miller, "Pope and the Principle of Reconciliation," *TSLL*, 9 (1967), 185-192.

26.   *The Subtler Language*, p. 164.

27.   Ed., *An Essay on Man* (New Haven, 1950), p. lxiii.

28.   *Guardian* No. 61 (1713), in *Prose Works*, ed. Ault, p.
109. Pope quotes approvingly Plutarch's view that man's
humanity should be extended "thro' the whole Order of Creatures, even to the meanest: Such Actions of Charity are the
Over-flowings of a mild Good nature on all below us." The
essay proves that in 1713 Pope had already articulated the
position regarding charity and hunting which appears in *An
Essay on Man*.

29. *The Poetry of Alexander Pope: Laureate of Peace* (1955; rpt. London, 1965), p. 22.

30. Schmitz, *Windsor Forest 1712*, p. 47. Schmitz cites the phrase from verses included in Pope's letter to John Caryll on November 29, 1712.

ROGERS, 'The Enamelled Ground': the Language of Heraldry and Natural Description in *Windsor-Forest*

1. The most important discussion of the poem is that of Earl R. Wasserman, *The Subtler Language* (Baltimore, 1964), pp. 101-168; see also pp. 45-47. Briefer but useful accounts may be found in Maynard Mack, 'On Reading Pope', *College English*, VII (1946), 263-73; John Robert Moore, '*Windsor-Forest* and William III', *MLN*, LXVI (1951), 451-54; Reuben A. Brower, *Alexander Pope: The Poetry of Allusion* (Oxford, 1959), pp. 49-62; Thomas R. Edwards, Jr., *This Dark Estate* (Berkeley, 1963), pp. 5-12. I have also consulted the Twickenham Edition of *Pastoral Poetry and the Essay on Criticism*, ed. E. Audra and A. Williams, (London, 1961), abbreviated here as 'TE'; and R. M. Schmitz, *Pope's Windsor Forest 1712* (St. Louis, 1952).

2. Norman Ault, 'Mr. Alexander Pope: Painter', *New Light on Pope* (London, 1949), pp. 68-100.

3. Text and line numbering follow TE, pp. 148-94.

4. TE, pp. 151-52.

5. Cf. Wasserman, pp. 143-51.

6. TE, p. 136.

7. Information on heraldry and its terminology is drawn from a variety of standard sources, notably William Dugdale, *The Antient Usage of Arms*, ed. T.C. Banks (London, 1811); and Joseph Edmondson, *A Complete Body of Heraldry* (London, 1780). Definitions are taken chiefly from Edmondson, but precise references are not supplied as there is no pagination.

8. It is true that such terms are not uncommon elsewhere: e.g. Thomas Parnell's 'A Night-Piece on Death' has *sable* and *azure, gold* and *silver*, within a few lines. But Parnell also uses '*Scutcheons*', a specifically heraldic word, which indicates that his own poem was strongly influenced by the armorial lexicon.

9. On this section see Wasserman, p. 146ff.

10. *Springing* is the term used in heraldry of beasts such as a stag, equivalent to *rampant* as applied to beasts of prey. *Preying*, incidentally, is itself a heraldic posture, used of eagles and like birds. See Randle Home, *The Academy of Armory, or the Storehouse of Armory and Blazon* (Chester, 1688), II, 143.

11. See *The Rape of the Lock*, III, 25-100.

12. Brower, pp. 53-54, cites Elwin's observation that *painted* does not properly apply to the pheasant's wings. He adds that 'Pope was looking ... at a picture in language consecrated to such descriptive uses through literary tradition, since "painted" goes back via Milton and via Dryden's translation to the *pictae volucres* of the *Georgics*'. Yes: but not only literary tradition is involved in the 'consecrating' process.

13. 'Laid down on his Belly, and the foremost feet
stretched out': Home, *op. cit.* That is exactly a game-dog's
posture at the juncture Pope describes.
14. TE, p. 164, notes that *rowze* (line 150) is a technical
hunting term. It is also an expression used in heraldry
with a slightly different connotation (Home, II, 228-29).
15. TE, p. 178.
16. 'A Grove is a green pleasant place set with trees'--
Home, II, 46.
17. Cited in TE, p. 186.
18. TE, p. 387.
19. Another example is *bend* (379, 384), which happens to
be one of the basic terms in heraldry.
20. *The Correspondence of Alexander Pope*, ed. G. Sherburn (Oxford, 1956), I, 172.
21. See Home, II, 225-32, on eagles, the most commonly
represented bird in armorial designs.
22. Wasserman, p. 139.
23. G.M. Trevelyan, *The Peace and the Protestant Succession*
(London, 1965), p. 198. Jersey was named as an envoy for
the Utrecht negotiations, but died of an apoplexy before
they could start.
24. See Elizabeth Handasyde, *Granville the Polite* (London,
1933), pp. 113-118. That Granville was notorious for seeking out honours 'the Herald finds out for him' is clear from
a pamphlet called *The Lives of Roger Mortimer ... and of Robert,
Earl of Oxford* (London, 1711), p. 7.
25. TE, p. 175.
26. Pope actually uses 'Clarion' in *The Temple of Fame*,
line 402. Both this poem and the almost contemporaneous
Messiah contain a good deal of armorial language.
27. It might be added that Matthew Prior wrote the preamble to at least two patents for newly created peers; and
that Swift is thought to have translated the preamble to the
patent granted to Harley in 1711. Another of the twelve
peers created along with Landsowne was Lord Bathurst, later
a close friend of Pope. The supporters to his arms were
stags, often styled in heraldry harts (see line 84).
28. The phrase cited is that of Moore, loc. cit. He uses
it of a passage suppressed by Pope, but I believe it is
accurate in respect of the poem as printed.
29. *Correspondence*, I, 168.
30. Home, II, 255.
31. To take a single instance: TE, p. 163, remarks of
the word 'Tyrants' applied to pikes (146) that 'the epithet
was common'. More to the purpose, it was a recognised emblematic usage--see Home, II, 369.
32. I borrow this phrase from G. Wilson Knight, *The Poetry
of Alexander Pope: Laureate of Peace* (London, 1955), pp. 79-110.
33. It is worth recalling that one of Pope's main sources
was Camden, himself Clarencieux King of Arms. As for contemporary interest in heraldry, Dugdale's biography appeared
in 1713; whilst there was enough demand for a new version of

Ashmole's work on *The Order of the Garter* in 1715. That Pope knew the earlier editions is possible but not certain. Samuel Kent's *Grammar of Heraldry* dates from 1716.

LANDA, Pope's Belinda, The General Emporie of the World, and the Wondrous Worm

1. *The Critical Works of John Dennis*, ed. E. N. Hooker (Baltimore, 1943), II, 513-14.

2. *Ibid.*, II, 334, 335.

3. See Hugo M. Reichard, "The Love Affair in Pope's *Rape of the Lock*," PMLA, 69 (1954), 887-902; Aubrey Williams, "The 'Fall' of China and The Rape of the Lock," PQ, 41 (1962), 412-25; Cleanth Brooks, "The Case of Miss Arabella Fermor: A Re-Examination," *Sewanee Review*, 51 (1943), 505-24 (also in his *The Well Wrought Urn*, 1947); Rebecca P. Parkin, "Mythopoeic Activity in the *Rape of the Lock*," ELH, 21 (1954), 30-38. The essays by Williams and Brooks are reprinted in *Essential Articles for the Study of Alexander Pope*, ed. Maynard Mack (1964).

4. All quotations from *The Rape of the Lock* are from *The Rape of the Lock and Other Poems*, ed. Geoffrey Tillotson, Twickenham Edition (London, 1940), Vol. II.

5. *A Panegyric to My Lord Protector, of the Present Greatness, and Joint Interest, of his Highness, and the Nation* (London, 1655), Stanzas 14 and 15.

6. Donald F. Bond, *The Spectator: Edited with an Introduction and Notes* (Oxford, 1965), No. 69, I, 294-96. In 1674 John Evelyn, in *Navigation and Commerce: Their Original and Progress*, anticipated Addison's passage: "Thus Asia refreshes us with spices, recreates us with perfumes, cures us with drugs, and adorns us with jewels; Africa sends us ivory and gold; America, silver, sugar, and cotton; France, Spain, and Italy, give us wine, oyl, and silk; Russia warms us in furs; Sweden supplies us with copper; Denmark and the Northern tracts, with masts and material for shipping." *The Miscellaneous Writings of John Evelyn, Esq., F.R.S.*, ed. William Upcott (London, 1825), p. 362.

7. *The Poetical Works of Edward Young* (Boston, 1894), II, 204.

8. *The Causes of our Present Calamities in reference to the Trade of the Nation fully Discovered* (London, 1695-96), p. 2.

9. For the lines as Pope quoted them in his letter to Caryll, see *The Correspondence of Alexander Pope*, ed. George Sherburn (Oxford, 1956), I, 157. Thomas Tickell, *A Poem on the Prospect of Peace* (London, 1713), p. 9.

10. "Whig Panegyric Verse: A Phase of Sentimentalism," in *Backgrounds of English Literature, 1700-1760* (Minneapolis, 1953), pp. 104-44.

11. John Edwards, "That Decay of Trade and Commerce, and Consequently of Wealth, is the Natural Product and Just Penalty of Vice in a Nation," in *Sermons on Special Occasions and Subjects* (London, 1698), p. 156.

12. Pp. 5-7. Catcott and the other clergymen who drew the parallel between Tyre and London pointed out, of course,

that Tyre was an object lesson for Londoners, that despite
its wealth and magnificence Tyre fell as a result of pride
and sin.
    13. [James Ralph], *Clarinda, Or the Fair Libertine: A Poem in
Four Cantos* (London, 1729), pp. 37-38.
    14. Sir Richard Blackmore, "The Nature of Man" (1711), in
A Collection of Poems (London, 1718), p. 224.
    15. The quality of the verse is apparent in these charac-
teristic lines:

> Ev'n Boots and Spurs have grac'd Heroick Verse;
> *Butler* his Knight's whole Suit did well rehearse,
> King *Harry's* Codpiece stands upon record,
> And every Age will Precedents afford.
>
> Then on my Muse, and sing in Epick Strain,
> The Petticoat--thou shalt not sing in vain;
> The Petticoat will sure reward thy Pain.
> Will all this Skill its secret Virtues tell;
> A Petticoat shou'd still be handl'd well.

    16. See C. Willett, and Phillis Cunnington, *Handbook of Eng-
lish Costume in the Eighteenth Century* (London, 1957), p. 106 and
passim.
    17. *The Spinster: in Defence of the Woollen Manufactures, No. 1*
(1719), in *Tracts and Pamphlets by Richard Steele*, ed. Rae Blan-
chard (Baltimore, 1944), p. 552.
    18. *The Weavers' Complaint Against the Callico Madams* (1719),
quoted in *A Calendar of British Taste from 1600 to 1800*, ed. E. F.
Carritt (London, 1948), p. 183.
    19. *England's Interest and Improvement, Consisting in the Increase
of the Store and Trade of this Kingdom* (1673), in *Early English
Tracts on Commerce*, ed. J. R. McCulloch (Cambridge, Eng., 1952),
p. 232.
    20. Ibid., p. 233. In *Tatler*, No. 149 (1 Sept. 1713),
ascribed to John Gay, we find him telling us that "as Horace
advises that all new-minted words should have a Greek derivation to give them an indisputable authority, so I would
counsel all our improvers of fashion always to take the hint
from France, which may as properly be called the fountain of
dress, as Greece was of literature."
    21. Fortrey, p. 231.
    22. See, for example, *The General Remarks on Trade*, Nos. 222
and 223 (25-28, 28-30 July 1707), a London newspaper written
by Charles Povey, who repeats Fortrey's figures on the annual
loss to England from such importations as fans, girdles,
masks, looking glasses, feathers, pins, needles, tortoise-
shell combs, and other mercery ware.
    23. *Britannia Languens, or A Discourse of Trade: Shewing the Grounds
and Reasons of the Increase and Decay of Land-Rents, National Wealth,
and Strength* (1680) in Mc Culloch, *Early English Tracts*, p. 421.
    24. Henry Barham, *An Essay Upon the Silk-Worm* (London, 1719),
p. 151.

25. Ibid.
26. Nicholas Geffe, *The Perfect Use of Silk-Wormes, and their Benefit. With the Exact Planting and Artificiall Handling of Mulberrie Trees whereby to Nourish Them, and How to Feed the Wormes and to Winde off the Silke* ... *Done out of the French Original of D'Olivier de Serres* ... *into English* (London, 1607), A^2 recto. Geffe adds to the tract by Serres "A Discourse of His Owne, of the Meanes and Sufficiencies of England, for to have Abundance of Fine Silk, by Seeding of Silkwormes within the Same." He pleads that the English should not avoid "such a golden fleece" (p. 10). Two years after the appearance of Geffe's work James I authorized the planting of mulberry trees in what later became known as Mulberry Garden. The king had hopes of stimulating the manufacture of silk in England, but Mulberry Garden soon became a place of public entertainment, much mentioned in Restoration drama and frequented by Pepys and Evely, who refer to it in their diaries.
27. Geffe, A^4 recto.
28. Ibid.
29. *Antidote Against Atheism*, 2d ed. (London, 1755), Ch. viii, "The Usefulness of Animals an Argument of Divine Providence," p. 116.
30. *Virgo Triumphans* (London, 1650), p. 38.
31. Hill's "Essay on the Silkworm" appeared in *Essays for the Month of January, 1717* .... *By a Society of Gentlemen. For the Universal Benefit of the People of England* (London, 1717), Essay v, p. 7 and passim.
32. *The Art of Dress* (London, 1717), p. 17.
33. *The Art of Dancing, Written in the Year 1728* (London, 1729), p. 8.
34. *Clarinda*, p. 37.
35. *Nature Display'd* (London, 1727), p. 73.
36. *Prose works of Jonathan Swift*, ed. Herbert Davis (Oxford, 1941), xi, 164-65.
37. *Philosophical Account* (London, 1721), pp. 139-40. Bradley devotes Chs. xii and xiii to "the Papilionaceous or Butterfly Kind."
38. *Review*, Vol. I [IX], No. 43 (8 Jan. 1713).
39. [? Jocelyn], *An Essay on Money & Bullion* (London, 1718), p. 17. See also *Some Considerations on the Nature and Importance of the East India Trade* (1728): "Providence in its infinite goodness designed to make life as easy and as pleasurable as possible, and gave us reason to find out arts, and to make them subservient to our delight and happiness" (p. 71). In another study I have treated the lady of fashion (and Belinda, briefly) in a different economic context. This study, titled "Of Silkworms and Farthingales and the Will of God," will appear in *Studies in the Eighteenth Century: Papers Presented at the Second David Nichol Smith Seminar, Canberra, 1970,* ed. R. F. Brissenden (1971). It may be considered complementary to this present study.

WIMSATT, Belinda Ludens: Strife and Play in *The Rape of the Lock*
1. *Homo Ludens* (Boston, 1955), pp. 5, 18.
2. "*Homo Ludens* Revisited," *Yale French Studies*, Issue 41, p. 56.
3. *Journals* (Boston , 1909-14), VI, 18.
4. *Philosophical Investigations*, tr. G. E. M. Anscombe (New York, 1970), p. 32e, 67.
5. *Critique of Judgment*, tr. J. C. Meredith (Oxford, 1911), 45.
5. *Ibid.*, 45, 46.
7. Expanded into a book, *Les Jeux et les hommes* (1958, 1967) [*Man, Play, and Games*, tr. Meyer Barash (New York, 1961)].
8. *On the Aesthetic Education of Man*, Letter 27.
9. Caillois' alignment of *agōn*, *alea*, *mimicry*, and yet another thing, *ilinx* (the vertigo of the roller coaster or ferris wheel), as four ways of escape from reality, and hence as four species of play, is a tidy unification which stands a little to one side of my own purpose.
10. In another essay in *Yale French Studies*, 1968, a member of the French Department at the University of Chicago, Bruce Morrissette, examines games as the centers of structures in the game-like fictions of Robbe-Grillet.
11. George Steiner, *Extraterritorial: Papers on Literature and the Language Revolution* (New York, 1971), produces some ringing evocations from Nabokov, Zweig, and other chess sources (pp. 47-57).
12. *Le Royal Jeu de l'Hombre et du Piquet* (Paris, 1685). The English version includes a substantial quotation from Pope.
13. See especially F. W. Bateson, 1 March 1941, p. 108.
14. On the supposition that the Baron had the Queen of spades, two or three diamonds, and one or two low hearts or two low clubs (but *not* both hearts and clubs), and that his diamonds would take one or two tricks and then lead into the third player's hand, so that the Baron would throw his low heart or hearts or low club or clubs on a last trick or tricks won by the third player with a diamond or diamonds-- on this supposition, the score would be 4-3-2₇ again a win for Belinda--different only in a nonessential way from her 5-4 win if she led her King of hearts (or King of clubs) on the fifth trick.
15. "Epic Mockery," *Touchstone*, 2 (1965), 23-28.
16. George Lord, in a letter.

WASSERMAN, The Limits of Allusion in *The Rape of the Lock*

1. Virgil's words are recorded as an apothegm by Macrobius (*Saturnalia*, V, 16) and Erasmus (*Adagia*, III, 5, 81).
2. Ovid, *Metamorphoses*, II, 146: "consiliis, non curribus, utere nostris." See also Addison's comments on this in the notes to his translation.
3. *Aeneid*, II, 237, 488; V, 140; XI, 832.
4. Cf. *Essay on Criticism*, ll. 181-82.

5. *Aeneid*, V, 663, VII, 431, VIII, 93; Ovid, *Met.*, III, 639, VI, 511; Lucan, III, 511; etc.

6. *Aeneid*, II, 653; Livy, V, 22, 8; 36, 6; XXII, 43, 9; Ovid, *Heroides*, III, 43; Valerius Flaccus, IV, 252.

7. E.g., Ovid, *Met.*, VIII, 144; Livy, XXXVII, 31, 6. Incidentally, it is likely that "And beauty draws us with a single Hair" (II, 28) derives from the Vulgate version of Canticles 4:9 ("vulnerasti cor meum in uno oculorum tuorum et in uno crine colli tui") rather than from any of the sources cited in the Twickenham edition.

8. *Odyssey*, XIII, 519-20. In his note to these lines Pope again discussed Homer's designation of time "from the dining of the labourer" (referring to *Iliad*, XI, 119) and "from the rising of the judges."

9. Euripides, *Hippolytus*, ll. 1424-25; Herodotus, IV, 34; Callimachus, *Hymn. in Delum*, ll. 295 seq.; Valerius Flaccus, VIII, 1 seq.; Pausanias, I, 43, 4, II, 32, 1; Lucian, *De dea Syria*, l. 60.

10. *Thebaid*, II, 253 seq.

11. Another major source was Julius Pollux' *Onomasticon*, III, 3. For a characteristically learned note on the subject, see that by Ezechiel Spanheim in *In Callimachi Hymnos Observationes*, ed. T. J. Graevius (1697), II, 507.

12. Dennis, *Critical Works*, ed. E. N. Hooker II, (Baltimore, 1943), 350.

13. And by the age generally: see, e.g., Gay, "On a Lap-Dog."

14. Dennis, II, 338. In preparing his defenses against the men Ariel properly recognizes that the order of importance is the lock, Shock, and Belinda's petticoat, to which he assigns fifty sylphs (II, 115-23). The Baron's rape of the social sign of maidenhood involves an assault on neither the toy husband nor Belinda's virginity.

15. See, e.g., the annotations on Matt. 11:25 by Nicolas de Lyre, Benedictus Aretius, Gulielmus Estius, Johannes Piscator, David Pareus, and Daniel Whitby.

16. *Moralia*, 472 C.

17. Juvenal, II, 10. Hence Sterne's character La Fosseuse in the court of the Queen of Navarre.

18. For this sense of *res*, see Martial, XI, 44. In his "Sober Advice from Horace" Pope translated Horace's "magno prognatum deposco consule CUNNUM" as "A Thing descended from the Conqueror" (l. 90), and in a mock-note on Horace's line 36 he explained that Horace's "cunnus albus" does not mean "a *white* or *grey Thing*, but a Thing under a *white* or *grey Garment*, which thing may be either black, brown, red, or particoloured." See also Alexander Burnet, *Achilles Dissected* (London, 1733), pp. 13-14. One will also recall Sterne's distinction between the *Argumentum Tripodium*, "which is never used but by the woman against the man," and the *Argumentum ad Rem*, which "is made use of by the man only against the woman" (*Tristram Shandy*, I, xxi).

19. See, e.g., Apuleius, *Metamorphoses*, XI, 20, 24.
20. *Ibid.*, XI, 9.
21. *Ad Lucilium epistolae moralis*, XCV, 48.
22. *Civitas dei*, VI, 10.
23. Laurens Beyerlinck, *Magnum theatrum* (1687). See also Joannes David, *Duodecim specula deum* (1610), emblem 5.
24. Hofmann, *Lexicon universale*, s.v. *speculum*.
25. See, e.g., Augustine and Bellarmine.
26. Cf. "Watch all their ways, and all their actions guide" (II, 88).
27. Richard Seymour, *The Court Gamester* (London, 1719), p. I.
28. *Aeneid*, XI, 504: "solaque Tyrrhenos equites ire obvia contra."
29. *Aeneid*, XI, 792-95, 583. In addition, Pope's note on V, 64, draws attention to "the Opera of Camilla" as the source of Sir Fopling's dying words. Since Sir Fopling's speech means that his murderess, a nymph attending Belinda, is to be identified with Tulla, handmaid to Camilla, Belinda is again implicitly equated with Camilla.
30. In his copy of Dennis' *Remarks on Mr. Pope's Rape of the Lock* (1728), at the point where Dennis questions the purpose of Umbriel's descent, Pope entered a marginal note that mentions Alecto and Amata; and when Dennis complained that Belinda was at the height of the spleen even before the descent of Umbriel, Pope, referring to *Aeneid*, VII, 345, wrote, "So was Ama[ta] before Foemi[neae] ardentem cu[raeque] coque[bant]." See the annotation as recorded in the Twickenham edition, II, 374. Boileau, incidentally, had also adapted the Alecto episode to generate the wars in *Le Lutrin*.
31. *Spectator*, No. 515.
32. Tristram Shandy was not, of course, the first to write a chapter on noses of this sort, and he admitted his debt to the "Prologue Facecieux sur le Nez" in *Les Fantaisies de Bruscambille* (1618). Swift was merely adapting a popular maxim when he wrote, "...if there be a Protuberancy of Parts in the *Superior* Region of the Body, as in the *Ears* and *Nose*, there must be a *Parity* also in the *Inferior*" (*Tale of a Tub*, sect. XI; see also his "Answer to D--n J--n"). See also Middleton, *Chaste Maid in Cheapside*, I.ii.67: "she's a tumbler, 'a faith, the nose and belly meet."

John Dennis again proves a close but naive reader. When the Baron, overcome by the sneeze, warns Belinda, "Boast not my Fall.... / Thou by some other shalt be laid as low," Dennis recognizes the "bawdy Quibble" but complains: "we heard nothing before of the Baron's lying low. All that we heard is that by a dextrous Toss of this *modest Virgin*, his Nostrils were fill'd with Snuff. So that he seems here to say the same thing to her that *Nykin* says to *Cocky* in the *Old Batchelor*: 'I have it in my Head, but you will have it in another Place'" (*op. cit.*, II, 348).
33. Despite his obtuseness, Dennis had no difficulty in reading accurately this adaptation of the ancient hero's

ideal death on the battlefield: "That is to say, 'He wish'd
for nothing more than to fight with her, because he desired
nothing more than to lie with her'" (*op. cit.,* II, 347).
34.   "Omne animal post coitum tristis."   But the Baron,
after all, is a hero, a demigod.
35.   Ovid, *Ars amatoria,* II, 725-26.
36.   *Ibid.,* III, 449-50:   "'Restore my robe!' the robbed
girls often cry.   'Restore my robe!' their voices echo over
the entire forum."
37.   Statius, *Sylvae,* I, 2, 113; II, 1, 26; V, 5, 29; Silius
Italicus, IV, 755; Pliny, *Panegyric,* IV, 7; etc.
38.   "At regina gravi iamdudum saucia cura / vulnus alit
venis, et caeco carpitur igni."
39.   "Sane bene *regina,* quia contra dignitatem amor suscep-
tus gravior esse solet."
40.   Quintilian glossed Dido's words as follows: "Quam-
quam enim de matrimonio queritur Dido, tamen huc erumpit
eius affectus, ut sine thalamis vitam non hominum putet, sed
ferarum" (*Inst. Orator.,* IV, 2).   On "more ferae" Ascensius
commented: "ad morem beluarum ferarum, quae propter feritatem
conjugium vitant.   Homo autem, est animal sociale: et ita
quadrat ei conjugium: sed infeliciter amans, praefert vitam
ferarum vitae suae."   Ruaeus, more succinctly: "Id est
solitariam vitam degere, et minime sociabilem, et quasi
feram."
41.   "To Mr. Pope."   No doubt Parnell took his clue from
the illustration in the 1714 edition of *The Rape of the Lock*
which shows cupids attending Belinda at her toilet and
satyrs at the edge of the group.
42.   Pope also drew on Catullus' poem for III, 171-78.
43.   In a footnote Pope called attention to the parallel
between Umbriel watching the final contest (V, 53-54) and
Minerva watching "during the Battle of Ulysses with the
Suitors"; and the irony in Pope's introducing the agent of
Spleen in this manner is made evident by Pope's note on the
Homeric passage which allegorizes Minerva as "the courage
and wisdom which was exerted by Ulysses in the destruction
of the Suitors" (*Odyssey,* trans. Pope, XXII, 246 n.).   Belinda
is also fighting off suitors; but, in view of her identification with Dido and Berenice, who wish for the return of lover
and husband, we might note the additional ironic fact that
Ulysses, unlike Belinda, drives off the suitors so that he
might regain his wife.
44.   Nolueram, Polytime, tuos violare capillos:
              Sed juvat hoc precibus me tribuisse tuis,
              Talis eras modo tonse Pelops, positisque nitebas
              Crinibus, ut totum sponsa videret ebur.
                                          (Martial, XII, 86)
45.   "Polytimus tonsus factus est cum cogitaret de ducenda
uxore."   Calderinus' interpretation is based in part on
Martial, XII, 76:   "Festinat Polytimus ad puellas."

KALMEY, Pope's *Eloisa to Abelard* and "Those Celebrated Letters"

    1. *Lives of the English Poets*, ed. George Birkbeck Hill (Oxford: Clarendon Press, 1905), III, 235-36. For a brief history of the lives of Heloise and Abelard, see the Twickenham Edition of *The Rape of the Lock and Other Poems*, ed. Geoffrey Tillotson, 3rd ed. (London, 1962), pp. 411-13. All quotations from *Eloisa to Abelard* are taken from this edition, hereafter cited as *Twick. Ed.*
    2. See Henry Pettit, "Pope's *Eloisa to Abelard*: An Interpretation," in University of Colorado Studies: Series in Language and Literature, No. 4 (July 1953), pp. 67-74, especially pp. 73-74; and Thomas R. Edwards, Jr., *This Dark Estate: A Reading of Pope* (University of California Press, 1963), p. 23. See also Reuben Arthur Brower, *Alexander Pope: The Poetry of Allusion* (Oxford: Clarendon Press, 1959), pp. 74-84. For a different and more suggestive view, see Brendan P. O Hehir, "Virtue and Passion: The Dialectic of *Eloisa to Abelard*," Texas Studies in Literature and Language, II (1960), 219-32. After my essay had been written, James E. Wellington, ed., *Alexander Pope: Eloisa to Abelard* (Miami, Fla., 1965), hereafter cited as Wellington ed., published his view that Eloisa "is one of the poet's *personae*, an identity created for the purpose of dramatizing truth, rather than a fully individualized creation" (p. 60). If Professor Wellington is correct, then Pope's Eloisa, and necessarily the whole poem, lacks the integrity of "a fully individualized creation." My essay implicitly seeks to refute Professor Wellington's judgment of Pope's creation.
    3. Brower, p. 83.
    4. For the popularity of Drayton's *Englands Heroicall Epistles*, see *Twick. Ed.*, p. 294.
    5. Etienne Gilson, *Heloise and Abelard*, trans. L. K. Shook (University of Michigan Press, 1960), pp. ix-x.
    6. *Twick. Ed.*, p. 318.
    7. Hughes' translation was an immediate success in Pope's time. Four editions had appeared by 1722, and seven by 1743. I quote from the 4th ed., 1722. I retain Hughes' Anglicized spelling "Heloise" to distinguish the person in the medieval letters and their later translations from Pope's Eloisa of his poem. Cf. *Twick Ed.*, "Note on the Text," p. 315. Part of Hughes' 1713 translation of the *Letters* has been reprinted in the Wellington ed., pp. 63 ff. Regrettably, Professor Wellington has chosen to omit all Abelard's letters from his reprinting of Hughes' translation. This omission (cf. Wellington ed., textual note, p. 63) severely limits the utility of his edition and reprinting, for as it will be noted, Pope makes extensive and crucial use of Abelard's letters in his poem. All six letters, as translated by Hughes, are readily available in The Temple Classics edition, *The Love Letters of Abelard and Heloise* (London, 1901).
    8. See *Twick. Ed.*, pp. 295-98; Emile Audra, *L'Influence française dans l'oeuvre de Pope* (Paris, 1931), pp. 399-426;

Robert K. Root, *The Poetical Career of Alexander Pope* (Princeton, 1938), pp. 94-96; John Joseph Deeney, "A Critical Study of Alexander Pope's *Eloisa to Abelard*," unpubl. diss. (Fordham, 1961), pp. 1-25; Lawrence S. Wright, "A History of the Letters of Abelard and Heloise in French and English," unpubl. diss. (Harvard, 1930); Wellington ed., pp. 20-24.

9.   See, for example, *Twick. Ed.*, p. 297, and Wellington ed., pp. 20-24.

10.   Hughes, "Preface," sig. A3v; quoted in *Twick. Ed.*, p. 298.

11.   *Petri Abelardi ... et Heloisae conjugis ejus ... Opera*, 2 vols. (Paris, 1616).   Richard Rawlinson's edition of the Latin letters, *P. Abaelardi ... et Heloissae ... epistolae* (London, 1718), was published after *Eloisa to Abelard*; there is no evidence that Pope saw Rawlinson's edition before publication.   Cf. *Twick. Ed.*, p. 298.

12.   Gilson, *Heloise and Abelard*, p. 96.

13.   Cf. Abelard in his *Historia calamitatum* (Letter I); "Wherefore also is it said to Him rightly in all circumstances; 'Thy will be done." (trans. C. K. Scott Moncrieff [New York, 1926], p. 49).   And Heloise (Letter IV):   "In whatever little corner of heaven God puts me, that will satisfy me" (trans. H. O. Taylor, *The Mediaeval Mind*, 4th ed. [Cambridge, Mass., 1951], II, 46).

14.   Roger de Rabutin, Comte de Bussy, *Les Lettres de Messire Roger de Rabutin, Comte de Bussy* (Paris, 1697).

15.   *Twick. Ed.*, p. 297.

16.   *Twick. Ed.*, p. 295.   See Edmund Gosse, "A Nun's Love Letters," *Fortnightly Review*, new ser., XLIII (1888), 506-17.

17.   Audra, *L'Influence francaise*, pp. 412-22.

18.   See articles, "Abelard," "Heloise," "Foulques," and "Paraclete."

19.   N. F. Du Bois, *Histoire des amours et infortunes d'Abelard et d'Eloise, avec la traduction des lettres*, 5th ed. (The Hague, 1711).   Cf. Audra, *L'Influence francaise*, p. 417.

20.   In Hughes' translation, Heloise and Abelard show their awareness of their sin by invoking an analogy of themselves with Adam and Eve.   Heloise writes: "'Twas Woman which threw down the first Man from that Glorious Condition in which Heaven had placed him.   She who was created in order to partake of his Happiness, was the sole Cause of his Ruin" (pp. 180-1).   Abelard replies: "Such is the Lot of the Posterity of Adam, that they should always have something to suffer, because they have forfeited their Primitive Happiness" (p. 218).

21.   My italics.

22.   *Twick. Ed.*, p. 308, n. 1; Audra, *L'Influence francaise*, pp. 438-9.

23.   Cf. Abelard's conviction that he and Heloise "retired from the World to sanctify our selves ..." (p. 201).

24.   Cf. St. Thomas Aquinas, *Summa theologica*, literally translated by Fathers of the English Dominican Province (New York, 1947), IIa-IIae, Q. 83, A. 15.

25. St. Thomas Aquinas, *Summa theologica*, IIa-IIae, Q. 20, AA. 1-3.
26. In Hughes' translation, this sentence concludes with a question mark that distorts its manifest syntax and sense.

JACK, The Elegy as Exorcism: Pope's 'Verses to the Memory of an Unfortunate Lady'
1. *The Correspondence of Alexander Pope*, ed. George Sherburn, 5 vols (1956) (hereafter cited as *Correspondence*), I, 416. 'Butt now I have named such a person', Caryll continues, 'Mrs. Cope occurrs to my mind.'
2. *Ibid.*, I, 419.
3. *Ibid.*, II, 528.
4. *Memoirs of the Life and Writings of Alexander Pope, Esq.* (1745), I, 75.
5. *Ibid.*, 75, 76.
6. *The Works of Alexander Pope Esq.* (1751), I, 265n.
7. *Correspondence*, II, 367-8.
8. Pp. 249, 253. The passages quoted from the 2nd edn (in which the title becomes *An Essay on the Genius and Writings of Pope*) are from p. 247 and pp. 333-4. The italics are mine.
9. *The Life of Alexander Pope, Esq.*, 135-133.
10. *Lives of the English Poets by Samuel Johnson*, ed. George Birkbeck Hill (1905), III, 100, 226, 101. The definition of suicide is from the *Dictionary*.
11. *The Gentleman's Magazine*, LIV (November 1784), 807. Walpole's comment occurs in a letter first published by Cunningham and not yet included in the Yale edition. It is given in vol. XIII (1905) of Mrs Paget Toynbee's edition, pp. 230-2. The passage from Hawkins is to be found in his edition of *The Works of Samuel Johnson*, IV (1787), 113n.
12. Photograph and transcription most kindly provided by Mr W. S. Lewis. Warton's note is in Vol. I (1797) of *The Works of Alexander Pope, Esq., with notes and Illustrations by Joseph Warton and others*, 336n.
13. I am very much indebted to Miss Meryl Jancey, the Deputy County Archivist, for searching the Hereford records for me, and to my friend Dr Nicholas Cox for his investigations at the Public Record Office.
14. *The Works of Alexander Pope*, ed. William Lisle Bowles, I (1806), xxxi-ii, xxxiv.
15. 'The Life of Alexander Pope', second part, *The Athenaeum*, 15 July 1854 (no. 1394), 876c: reprinted in *The Papers of a Critic, selected from the writings of the late Charles Wentworth Dilke* (1875), I, 128.
16. *The Works of Alexander Pope*, with introductions and notes by the Rev. Whitwell Elwin, II (1871), 203-4.
17. Pp. 133-4.
18. *An Essay*, 253.
19. *The Early Career of Alexander Pope* (1934), 202-3.
20. *Correspondence*, II, 367n.
21. The Twickenham Edition, II (1940), 331-4.

22. 'Who she was outside the poem (if she existed) will
perhaps never be known', he remarks in *Alexander Pope: the
poetry of allusion* (1959), p. 64, while on p. 66 he writes:
'Pope's difficulties ... may have come from trying to write
a heroic epistle about a private affair, or perhaps about no
affair whatever.'

23. Brower, *op. cit.*, 64.

24. The Twickenham Edition, vol. I (1961), ed. E. Audra
and Aubrey Williams, 47.

25. *Joseph Spence, Observations, Anecdotes, and Characters of Books
and Men,* ed. James M. Osborn (1966), I, 226. The word 'elegy'
is often ambiguous, as most writers on the subject point
out, notably Joseph Trapp (see n.30, below). None of the
elegies of Tibullus deals primarily with death, and only one
or two of Ovid's do.

26. *Ibid.*, 234.

27. *Poetices Libri Septem* (1561), Book III, cxxii-iii, as
translated in *Milton's 'Lycidas',* ed. Scott Elledge (1966),
109-10.

28. *Observations on the Faerie Queene* (1754), 166n., cited by
Tillotson. Cf. lines 19-22 of Jonson's poem:
       Shee was the Lady *Jane,* and *Marchionisse*
     Of *Winchester*; the Heralds can tell this:
     Earle *Rivers* Grand-Child - serve not formes, good
                                              Fame,
        Sound thou her Vertues, give her soule a Name
  with lines 69-72 of Pope's 'Elegy':
     So peaceful rests, without a stone, a name,
     What once had beauty, titles, wealth, and fame.
     How lov'd, how honour'd once, avails thee not,
     To whom related, or by whom begot.

29. 'I desire ... that you will cause the space for the
initial letter to the Dedication to the Rape of the Lock to
be made of the size of those in Trapp's Praelectiones':
Correspondence, I, 394. The letter seems to have been written
early in 1717.

30. *Lectures on Poetry ... Translated from the Latin* (1742), 165.
Trapp's lectures were first published in Latin, in three
volumes, in 1711, 1715 and 1719. The lecture 'De Elegia'
occurs in the second volume (pp. 66-75), and first appeared,
therefore, a year or two before Pope seems to have written
this poem.

31. My quotations are from the Oxford Standard Authors
edition, edited by Herbert Davis (1966). When I quote line
39 I correct the obvious misprint 'These' to 'There'.

32. *Correspondence,* I, 107. As Sherburn points out (*ibid.*,
22 n.3), a letter which Pope printed as addressed to Walsh,
in 1735, seems to have been 'fabricated' from the Cromwell
letter which is genuine. The letter addressed to Walsh
slightly elaborates certain points.

33. *An Essay,* 250.

34. *Correspondence,* I, 24. The same is true of the other
monosyllabic line, 33: Cold is that breast which warm'd
the world before.

35. *Lectures*, 169.
36.   It has usually been taken for granted that 'foreign'
has its most common modern meaning, as it sometimes has in
Pope (e.g. *Epilogue to the Satires*, I, 155, 'foreign Gold').
Elsewhere, however, he uses the word to mean 'belonging to
or coming from another district, county, society, etc." (*Oxford English Dictionary*, 6.b), as in the second Moral Essay, *To A
Lady*, ll. 223-4:
        For foreign glory, foreign joy, they roam;
        No thought of peace or happiness at home.
The proximity of the words 'friends', 'domestic' and 'strangers' could support the older meaning of the word.   The
Oxford English Dictionary notes that the word is often 'opposed
to *domestic*'.
37.   *Correspondence*, I, 107.
38.   *Eighteenth Century Verse & Prose*, ed. Louis I. Bredvold,
Alan D. McKillop and Lois Whitney, 3rd edn prepared by John
M. Bullitt (New York, 1973), 542.   My objection to the view
that there are two speakers in Pope's poem is not that it is
inherently improbable but that it is not true.   Minturno
distinguishes between three types of elegy on the basis of
the speaker of the poem: 'sive se ipsum poeta, sive alterum
fingit, qui queratur, et quod triste, luctuosumve est, ex-
primat ... Mixtum autem hoc dicendi genus cum sit, poeta nunc
suam tenet, nunc alienam summit personam ... Quod vero
plerumque fit, est ubi nemo alius, quam poeta ipse loquatur':
De Poeta (Venice, 1559), 407-.   The speaker of the last eight
lines of 'Lycidas' is different from the speaker of the rest,
so that it is to be considered as belonging to the mixed
kind.   In the elegies of the Italian Latinist Ioannes Iovianus
Pontanus, *De Tumulis*, which Pope is certain to have known
(three of his poems are included in the second volume of
Selecta Poemata Italorum, which he edited in 1740, although none
of them happens to be an elegy in our sense of the word),
there are sometimes several speakers within a single poem.
I.v, for example, is divided between Viator, Genius   and
Sacerdos.
39.   Colin Macleod, *Times Literary Supplement*, 7 November 1975,
1326.   Scaliger observes that 'A discourse of consolation
... can proceed only from a friend.   For this reason the
rule of the ancient writers was that the comforter also must
show grief and must magnify the atrocity of the event'
(Elledge, *op. cit.*, 110).   Critics who believe that Pope's
Elegy is 'about' Mrs Weston, Mrs Cope or Lady Mary have made
him 'magnify' matters to an unusual degree, as none of these
ladies was dead.

I should like to thank Dr Howard Erskine-Hill for his kindness in reading and commenting on this essay.

ERSKINE-HILL, The Medal Against Time: A Study of Pope's
epistle *To Mr Addison**
     *   I wish to make acknowledgement here to my colleague
Dr. Sydney Anglo, with whom I have often discussed the background to this poem of Pope, and who has read and criticized
this article in draft.
     1.   The Elizabethan satirist Joseph Hall wrote admiringly
of the age of Augustus in Latin Literature: 'Who had but
liued in *Augustus* daies / T'had beene some honour to be
crown'd with Bayes' (*Virgidemiarum*, VI, i, 11.205-6; *Collected
Poems*, ed. Arnold Davenport, 1949, p. 93) but clearly regarded
his own age as in no way Augustan. Jonson, however, in his
comedy *The Poetaster* (1601), cast himself in the role of
Horace and presented the literary quarrels of his own London
in terms of Augustan Rome; Cleveland addressed Jonson as the
'English *Horace*' (Jonson, *Works*, ed. C. H. Herford and Percy
Simpson, 1925-52, xi, p. 338) and Crites, in Dryden's *An
Essay on Dramatic Poesy*, recognized him as 'a professed imitator
of Horace' (*Essays of John Dryden*, ed. W. P. Ker, 1900, i, p. 43).
Sir Thomas Higgons, in his 'Ode on the Death of Mr. *Abraham
Cowley*' (1667), reflected that: 'If he had flourish'd when
Augustus sway'd, / Whose peacefull Scepter the whole World
obey'd, / Account of him *Mecoenas* would have made' and Sir
John Denham went further: '*Horace* his wit and *Virgil's* state,
/ He did not steal, but emulate' (*The Works of Mr. Abraham
Cowley*, Ninth Edition, 1700, n.p.). Oldham, on his death,
was hailed by Thomas Andrews as: '*Virgil* in Judgement, *Ovid*
in Delight, / An easy Thought with a *Meonian* Flight; / Horace
in Sweetness, Juvenal in Rage' (*The Remains of Mr. Oldham in Verse
and Prose*, 1684, n.p.), while the death of Waller, in 1687,
was received with even more fulsome praise, involving even
grander comparisons with Augustan Rome and Ancient Greece.
Sir Thomas Higgons is once more lavish of comparison: '*Athens*
and *Rome*, when Learning flourish'd most, / Could never such
a Finish'd Poet boast: / Whose matchless softness in the
English Tongue / Out-does what *Horace*, or *Anacreon* Sung', but
he is supported by no less a person than the neoclassical
critic Thomas Rymer, who affirmed that Waller 'This Northern
Speech refin'd to that degree, / Soft *France* we scorn, nor
envy *Italy*: / But for a fit Comparison must seek / In *Virgil's*
Latin, or in *Homer's* Greek' (*Poems to the Memory of ... Edmund
Waller ... By Several Hands*, 1688, 11. 5-8, p. 1; 11. 62-65, p. 7).
     2.   In the first instance, see Nicholas Rowe's dedication
of his *Ulysses* to Lord Godolphin (1704); in the second,
Francis Atterbury's *Preface to the Second Part of Mr. Waller's Poems*,
1690 (*Poems*, ed. G. Thorn Drury, 1893, i, p. xix) and Joseph
Warton's *Essay on the Genius and Writings of Pope*, 1756-82, i, pp.
160-61, 189-91.
     3.   Pope never explicitly speaks of himself as such, but
comes close to it in the Advertisement to his *Epistle to Augustus* (1737): '*The Reflections of Horace, and the Judgements past in
his Epistle to Augustus, seem'd so seasonable to the present Times,*

that I could not help applying them to the use of my own Country' (The
Poems of Alexander Pope, general editor John Butt, 1939-61; iv,
ed. John Butt, 1939, p. 191. All subsequent references to
Pope's poetry are to this edition). In addition to this,
Pope's literary ideals are Augustan (cf. *An Essay on Criticism*,
1711, ll. 181-200, 643-86; *Poems*, i, pp. 261-63, 311-17) and
he strove to follow Walsh's advice to be the first great 'correct' English poet (Joseph Spence, *Anecdotes, Observations, and
Characters, of Books and Men*, 1820, p. 52), that is, to obey the
precepts and emulate the practice of the Ancients in general
and the Roman Augustans in particular. In different ways
Pope did indeed emulate both Virgil and Horace. His *Pastorals*
and *Messiah* are in the mode of Virgil's *Eclogues*; his *Windsor
Forest* of the *Georgics*; his *Homer* of the *Aeneid*; Virgilian
epic is also powerfully recalled in *The Rape of the Lock*. An
Essay on Criticism is in a mode deriving ultimately from
Horace's *De Arte Poetica*, though Vida and Boileau do of course
intervene. Pope plays an Augustan role, perhaps most clearly, in his *Imitations of Horace*, where, as in the writing, so
in the very printing, the reader is invited to witness the
proud parallel-and-contrast that the poet sets up between
himself and his own age, and Horace and Augustan Rome.

4. The whole of Settle's prophecy in *The Dunciad*, Bk. iii,
is relevant to Pope's conception of barbarism and of the
Dark Ages; especially important passages are *Dunciad* (1729):
iii, ll. 65-130, 315-56 (*Poems*, v, pp. 156-61, 186-93). It
is l. 117 which alludes to the Renaissance in Britain, while
ll. 315-18, 329, 335 in particular, with their deeply ironical echoes of Virgil's Fourth Eclogue and of Pope's own
Messiah, confirm the poet's conceit of the inverted Renaissance.

5. ll. 681-704; *Poems*, i, pp. 316-20. Pope then proceeds
to describe how the Renaissance, driven from Rome, moved
north over the Alps to France, and gained just a foothold
('among the *sounder Few*'--l. 719) in Britain.

6. For details of the composition and publication of the
epistle see *Poems*, vi, pp. 205-6. All but ll. 5-10, 63-72
were probably written in 1713, and the poem was certainly intended to be prefixed, as was eventually the case, to Addison's *Dialogues Upon the Usefulness of Ancient Medals*. It had this
place of honour in the great 1721 edition of Addison's *Works*
(i, pp. 431-33) and was printed with other important epistles
in vol. ii of the 1735 edition of Pope's *Works*, and of subsequent editions until his death. In Warburton's definitive
edition of Pope's *Works* (1751) it appeared as a fifth *Moral
Essay*. Clearly it had been hard to fit the poem into the new
arrangement of Pope's epistles in that edition, and its extremely tenuous connection with the *Moral Essays* proper was
exploited as a last resort (*Works*, ed. William Warburton,
1751, iii, pp. 294-99). In the Twickenham Edition the
epistle is banished to the volume of minor poems. While the
position Warburton gave the poem was unsatisfactory, it is
notable that he resisted the convenient idea of relegating

it to his *Miscellaneous Pieces in Verse* in vol. vi. He seems
to have felt--rightly in my view--that the epistle deserved
a more significant status. It is good to see that this has
been accorded it in the recent single-volume Twickenham
Edition of Pope's *Poems* (ed. John Butt, 1963, pp. 215-16).
    7. Much the longest of the three dialogues (Addison,
Miscellaneous Works, ed. A. C. Guthkelch, 1914, ii, pp. 299-
376--all subsequent references are to this edition) is devoted to this last subject; it was to be taken up in greater
detail, and in a more ambitious series of dialogues, by
Joseph Spence in his *Polymetis* (1747). There is a short account of this work in Austin Wright, *Joseph Spence: A Critical
Biography*, 1950, ch. v.
    8. ll. 1-5; *Poems*, vi, p. 202.
    9. Cf. Du Bellay, *Antiquitez de Rome*, 1559, Sonnet iii, and
Spenser's version (*The Ruines of Rome: by Bellay*, 1591, iii);
also *Antiquitez*, vii, viii, xxvii; Spenser, *Faerie Queene*, VII,
vii, 47; Shakespeare, Sonnets xii (l. 10), xv (l. 11), xix,
lxiv and lxv.
    10. ll. 1-9. Du Bellay, *Poésies Françaises et Latines*, ed.
E. Courbet, 1918, ii, p. 267. Spenser, in his *Ruines of Rome*,
rendered the figure: '*Rome* now of *Rome* is th'onely funerall'.
It is a striking and memorable conceit. That it too may
have become a commonplace is suggested by the fact that James
Howell uses it in a letter from Rome, in his *Epistolae Ho-
Elianae* (1645). His source was certainly either Du Bellay or
Spenser, since the whole argument of Sonnet xviii of the
Antiquitex appears, unacknowledged, in another part of the
same letter. (James Howell, *Epistolae Ho-Elianae: The Familiar
Letters*, Bk. i, Sect. i, Letter xxxviii: *To Sir* William St.
John, *Knight, from* Rome. Ed. Joseph Jacobs, 1890, pp. 85-86.)
    11. *De Remediis utriusque Fortunae*, I, xcvi (*Opera*, Basle, 1554,
p. 99).
    12. Migne, *PL*, xxv, p. 75. The other place where Jerome
speaks of Rome as the sepulchre of its own people was first
noticed in this connection by Joseph Warton (*The Works of Alexander Pope, Esq.*, 1797, iii, p. 303; *Poems*, vi, p. 206); it is
from Epistola cxxx: *Ad Demetriadem*, 5: 'Nescis misera, nescis
cui virginitatem tuam debeas. Dudum inter barbaras tremuisti
manus, aviae matrisque sinu, et palliis tegebaris. Vidisti
te captivam, et pudicitiam tuam, non tuae potestatis. Hor-
ruisti truces hostium vultus: raptas virgines Dei gemitu
tacito conspexisti. Urbs tua, quondam orbis caput, Romani
populi sepulcrum est; et tu in Libyco littore, exulem virum,
exul ipsa accipies." (Migne, *PL*, xxii, 1109.)
    13. ll. 5-10 were added to the poem in 1726 (*Poems*, vi,
p. 205); they subtilize Pope's attitude to Rome, as already
expressed, into one more balanced and human. Pope was always
on his guard against magnificence raised at the expense of
the less fortunate (see George Sherburn, ed., *The Correspondence of Alexander Pope*, 1956, II, p. 239; also *To Bathurst*, ll.
219-33; *Poems*, III, ii, p. 108).

14. ll. 9-10; *Poems*, vi, p. 203. Warburton's note is apposite, though it perhaps exaggerates the effect of Pope's
lines: 'By these Gods he means the Tyrants of Rome, to whom
the Empire raised Temples. The epithet, *admiring*, conveys a
strong ridicule; that passion, in the opinion of Philosophy,
always conveying the ideas of ignorance and misery, which can
never approach the Deity.
          Nil admirari prope res est una, Numici,
          Solaque quae possit facere et servare beatum.
Admiration implying our ignorance of other things; *pride*, our
ignorance of ourselves.' (*Works*, ed. Warburton, 1751; quoting
here from the revised edition of 1766, iii, p. 357).
15. It is useful to remember here the original title of
Pope's imitation of Virgil's Fourth Eclogue: 'Messiah.   A
Sacred Eclogue, *compos'd of several Passages of Isaiah the Prophet.*
Written in Imitation of Virgil's Pollio.' (*Poems*, i, p. 103.)
Pope is not an Augustan at the expense of being a Christian.
16. Sherburn, *op. cit.*, i, pp. 118-19; also *An Essay on Criticism*, ll. 687-96; *Poems*, i, pp. 204-5.
17. ll. 11-14; *Poems*, i, p. 203. Pope is expressing traditional Renaissance sentiments; cf. Vasari, *Lives*, Introduction;
translated by Mrs. Jonathan Foster, 1850-55, i, pp. 20-23.
18. ll. 15-18; *Poems*, i, pp. 203, 206. T.O. Mabbot has
pointed out that Vespasian and Titus shared the same official
names on inscriptions.
19. *Iconologia*, Padua, 1611, pp. 234-35. See Rudolf Wittkower, 'Chance, Time and Virtue', this *Journal*, I, p. 318,
for the significance of the rectangular form. See also *Iconologia: Or, Moral Emblems, by Caesar Ripa* ..., London, 1709, pp.
38-39, where this form is missing, and where the book is replaced by a shield.
20. ll. 690, 695; *Poems*, i, pp. 317, 319.
21. *Of The Advancement of Learning*, i; *Works*, ed. Spedding, El-
lis and Heath, 1870, iii, p. 318.
22. For full discussion of the distinction between History
and Antiquities see Arnoldo Momigliano, 'Ancient History and
the Antiquarian', this *Journal*, XIII, pp. 285-315. For Pope's
own personal interest in Roman antiquities, see Joseph
Spence, *op. cit.*, pp. 204-5. It is interesting to note that
Pope's aunt and godmother, Christiana Cooper, bequeathed to
him her books, pictures *and medals* [my italics]. (Joseph
Hunter, *Pope: His Descent and Family Connections*, 1867, p. 41.)
23. *Of The Advancement of Learning*, ii; *ed. cit.*, iii, p. 334.
Here, as in *An Essay on Criticism* (see n. 21 above), the image
of the 'deluge' seems to suggest an almost universally ob-
literating power but one which, nevertheless, expresses the
will of God. The implication may be that everything necessary for humanity survived the Dark Ages, just as Noah and
his ark survived the Flood.
24. *Antiquitez de Rome*, Sonnet xxx, l. 14; *ed. cit.*, ii, p.
280.
25. Hubert Goltz (1526-83), the antiquarian, spent several
years surveying the medals in the cabinets of the European

collectors, before commencing his series of major works on
the antiquities and history of the ancient world.   A passage
in which he refers to his *Historia Siciliae et Magnae Graeciae*
(1576) conveys the importance of medals to his task, and also his sense of excitement and discovery in the work.   'SING-
VLAREM laboris mei & diligentiae, Marce Fuggere, fructum
capio, quòd hoc tempore, veluti post longam saeculorum seriem,
ab obliuione atque silentio Siciliae & Magnae Graeciae memo-
riam, res gestas, situm, descriptionémque ex antiquitatis
arcanis, & numismatum epigrammatúmque monumentis restituerim;
& antiqua, quibus illae floruerunt, ornamenta renouarim.'
(*Thesaurus Rei Antiquariae,* 1579, Epistola Dedicatoria, n.p.).
Cf. Addison, *Dialogue,* i; *ed. cit.,* ii, p. 291: 'You here see
the copies of such Ports and triumphal Arches as there are
not the least traces of in the places where they once stood.
You have here the models of several ancient Temples, though
the Temples themselves, and the Gods that were worshipped in
them, are perished many hundred years ago. Or if there are
still any foundations or ruines of former edifices, you may
learn from Coins what was their Architecture when they stood
whole and entire.   These are buildings which the *Goths* and
Vandals could not demolish, that are infinitely more durable
than stone or marble, and will perhaps last as long as the
earth it self.   They are in short so many real monuments of
Brass.'
    26. See Momigliano, 'Ancient History and the Antiquarian',
this *Journal,* XIII, pp. 295-307. John Evelyn put the case
succinctly when he wrote of '... these small pieces of
Metal, which seem to have broken and worn out the very
Teeth of Time, that devours and tears in pieces all things
else.' (*Numismata. A Discourse of Medals, Antient and Modern,* 1697,
p. 2.)
    27. The full title of the work, on first publication,
was: *Introduction à l'histoire par la connoisance des médailles*. It
was reprinted in 1667, translated into Latin in 1683, and
reprinted in 1695 (from which edition I quote) under the
title of *Histoire des Médailles*. The eighteenth-century numis-
matist De la Bastie described this treatise as 'propre à en
donner les notions générales, & a faciliter l'étude de cette
Science [Numismatics] ... Ces Traductions & ces Editions
différentes, prouvent asséz combien un Livre de cette ex-
péce, étoit regardé comme nécessaire. Cependant on trouva
l'Ouvrage de Patin un peu trop abregé ...' (Louis Jobert, *La
Science des Médailles ... avec des Remarques Historiques & Critiques*
[by J. Bimard de la Bastie], 1739, i, xvi-xvii). Addison,
in his *Dialogues*, alludes to Patin on medals, but it is not
clear to which work he refers (*Miscellaneous Works*, ii, p. 285).
    28. *Histoire des Médailles*, 1695, pp. 11-12. See also Louis
Jobert, *La Science des Médailles*, 1692; reference is to the
English translation, as *The Knowledge of Medals*, 1697, p. 66.
Subsequent references are to this edition.

29. *Histoire des Médailles*, pp. 1-3; Addison, *Dialogues*, i; *Miscellaneous Works*, ii, p. 291.

30. ll. 19-30; *Poems*, vi, p. 203.

31. See L. D. Ettlinger, 'The Pictorial Source of Ripa's "Historia"', this *Journal*, XIII, pp. 322-33.

32. It is in fact the second of the two medals engraved by Addison (*Miscellaneous Works*, ii, pp. 370-72; Series iii, Nos. 13 and 14) to which Pope may be alluding in his reference to 'sad Judaea' in l. 26 (*Poems*, vi, p. 203).

33. *Antiquitez de Rome*, Sonnet vii, ll. 9-11; *ed. cit.*, ii, p. 269.

34. Both senses of the word are given as current in the earlier eighteenth century by *OED*.

35. *Works*, ed. Warburton, 1751; revised edition of 1766, iii, p. 358. I would differ from Warburton, however, when he states that the phrase is 'a ridicule' on the title of Orbis Romanus; the whole poetic context, with its emphasis on pity at fallen grandeur, would seem to preclude ridicule at this point. See also Obadiah Walker, *The Greek and Roman History Illustrated by Coins and Medals*, 1692, pp. 139-40.

36. Epistola lx: *Ad Heliodorum*, 16; *Commentariorum in Ezechielem Prophetam*: Liber Primus. Migne, *PL*, xxii, 600; xxv, 16.

37. *Dialogues*, ii; *Miscellaneous Works*, ii, pp. 311-19.

38. *Ibid.*, ii, pp. 318-19. See also Obadiah Walker, *op. cit.*, p. 80.

39. See fig. 154 of *Iconologia: or, Moral Emblems*, by Caesar Ripa ... London, 1709 (an English emblem book based on but not identical with Ripa's *Iconologia*), for an emblem of 'Rome Eternal': 'A Figure standing with a Helmet; in her left Hand a Spear, with a triangular Head; in her right a Globe, upon which stands a Bird with a long Beak; a little Shield at her Feet; and a Serpent in a Circle, denotes *Eternity*. The Bird is the *Phoenix*, out of whose Ashes springs another' (pp. 39-40).

40. Cf. Du Bellay, *Antiquitez de Rome*, Sonnet xxvii: 'Ces vieux fragmens encor servent d'examples. / Regarde apres, comme de jour en jour / Rome fouillant son antique sejour, / se rebastist de tant d'oeuvres divines:' (ll. 8-11; *ed. cit.*, ii, p. 279), and Charles Patin, *Histoire des Médailles*: 'La magnificence de leurs Temples, la beauté de leurs Arcs triomphaux ... passent aujourd'hui pour des chef-d'oeuvres inimitables. Cependant le Temps jaloux de leu gloire a derobé ce qu'ils avoyent de plus precieux, & il acheve tous les jours de ruiner ce que le fer & le feu nous en ont laissé de reste. Peu de Statues ont evités ces mesmes disgraces, les Medailles seules ont esté sauvées de ce débris, & leur nombre les a conservées jusques à nous' (pp. 2-3).

41. *The Rape of the Lock*, Canto i, ll. 121-48; *Poems*, ii, pp. 155-58.

42. ll. 29-30; *Poems*, vi, p. 203.

43. See n. 21 above.

44. *Antiquitez de Rome*, Sonnet xxx, ll. 12-14; Sonnet xxvii (lines quoted in n. 40 above); *ed. cit.*, ii, pp. 280, 279.

For evidence of Pope's own fascination with antiquarian
studies, see the reference in n. 22 above.
  45. *Epistolae de Rebus Familiaribus et Variae*, ed. Fracassetti,
Florence, 1859-63; ii, p. 520.
  46. *La Science des Médailles: Nouvelle ed.*, Paris, 1739, pp. iii-
iv. This treatise was first published in 1692, reprinted in
1693, published in Latin in 1695 and in English in 1697 as
The Knowledge of Medals. A second English edition appeared in
1715. Addison is almost certain to have known this work,
since his *Guardian* paper No. 96 (*The Error in Distributing
Modern Medals*) was appended to this second English edition
(pp. 152-6). Pope probably knew it for the same reason (in
ll. 53-62 of *To Mr Addison* he seems to allude to *Guardian*, No.
96) though possibly not before the poem was first drafted.
De la Bastie described the treatise in his Preface to the
1739 edition, as 'le meilleur qu'on ait fait jusqu'à présent,
pour rendre l'étude de ces Monumens Antiques plus facile,
plus utile, & plus agréable' (p. xviii). It is noteworthy
that De la Bastie, in an anecdote in his Preface, seems to
recall the imagined power of medals to inspire to greatness:
'Alphonse Roi d'Arragon & de Naples, Prince plus célébre encore par son amour pour les Lettres que par ses Victoires,
fit chercher avec soin des Médailles dans toute l'Italie, &
il plaça la suite qu'il en avoit formée, & qui étoit asséx
considérable pour ce tems-là, dans une cassette d'yvoire
qu'il faisoit porter par-tout avec lui' (I, iv). The English
translator was probably Obadiah Walker, whose own treatise
The Greek and Roman History Illustrated by Coins and Medals was published in 1692.
  47. E.g. pp. 14-15: 'On y reconnoit la Couronne civique,
la triomphale, la murale, la navale ... dont ils recompen-
soyent en differentes occasions le merite de leurs Heros.
Rien n'y manque de ce qui peut augmenter l'amour qu'on doit
avoir pour les grandes actions, & pour s'exciter d'autant
plus à la vertu'; p. 269 (*Epistre Au Roy*): 'Le plus beau sujet
de la Peinture est l'Histoire qu'elle embellit, & qu'elle
rend presente à nos yeux; elle fait revivre la continence de
Scipion, & la generosité de Camille, & nous exprimant ces
beaux passages de l'histoire avec tout les ornemens qui leurs
sont deus, Elle nous donne autant d'amour pour ceux dont les
grandes actions en ont donné la matiere, que d'horeur pour
ceux qui ce sont rendus illustres par leur crimes ... l'Histoire dans les Livres divertit d'une autre maniere, & fournit
des exemples plus circonstanciez & plus suivis. Enfin les
Medailles achevent cet assortiment, & nous donnent en abregé
ce que les Tableaux & l'Histoire ne nous exposent qu'en une
plus grande estenduë'; pp. 6-7: '... cependant il se trouve,
faisant reflexion sur ces deux differentes inclinations, de
Medailles & de Tableaux, qu'ayant en commun le dessein & la
representation des plus grandes d'entres les actions humaines,
tandis que ceux-ci ne servent que pour le plaisir, & sont
souvent l'effet de la seule imagination du Peintre: Les

autres fournissent encore une utilité considerables dans la
societé des hommes, puis qu'elles prouvent ce qu'elles repre-
sentent, & que sans elles, la Peinture n'a pas d'authorité.'
    48. *The Knowledge of Medals*, p. 30: 'Nothing shews the deso-
lation of the Empire more than the Universal loss of all
good Arts, which appears in this of Engraving, which is no
more than a miserable scratching of the Metal'; p. 31: 'The
small care of the Emperors took of their Medals after the
three first Centuries, may be very well admired. For after
that time, we find not one footstep of the *Roman* Majesty;
there being none but little Medals without Relief, or
Thickness, till *Theodosius's* time; and after the Division of
the Empire when he died, nothing but Misery and Poverty.
No more curious Heads or Reverses, the Characters, Language,
Figures, and Legend all barbarous; so that no body troubled
themselves to collect them, and they are thereby become almost as scarce, as they are deformed.' Cf. Addison, *Dialogues*, iii; *Miscellaneous Works*, ii, p. 392.
    49. *The Knowledge of Medals*, p. 78. The passage continues:
'As for instance, we see on a Medal of *Augustus* two Hands
joyned, clasping a *Caduceus* betwixt two *Cornucopia's*; this is
the Body: the word *Pax* there engraven, is to denote the
Peace which that Prince had given to the State, by reconciling it to *M. Antony*, which had restored Felicity and
Plenty to it. Whereas those very two Hands on the Medals
of *Balbinus* and *Pupienus* have this Legend, *Amor mutuus Augustorum*,
expressing thereby the good Understanding between the two
Colleagues in governing the Empire' (p. 79). The metaphor
of the soul and body for the Legend and Figure is common in
the literature of devices; see, e.g., Thomas Blount, The
Art *Of making* Devises, ... *First Written in French by Henry
Estienne* ..., 1646, pp. 11, 13 and 18; Camden's *Remaines of a
Greater Worke, Concerning Britaine* ..., 1605, p. 158; Samuel
Daniel, *The Worthy tract of Paulus Iouius*, 1585₇ n.p.
    50. For a full exposition and historical account of this
doctrine, see E. H. Gombrich, '*Icones Sybolicae*: The Visual
Image in Neo-Platonic Thought', this *Journal*, XI, pp. 163-188,
especially p. 174.
    51. *Iconologia: Or, Moral Emblems*, 1709, Preface, n.p. Cf.
Evelyn, *Numismata*, p. 66. The writer of this preface also may
have remembered the more eloquent statement of the power of
the visual image in Thomas Blount's The Art *Of making* Devises
(see n. 49 above), pp. 13-14: '*Bargagli* saith with good reason, That a *Devise* is nothing else, but a rare and particular way of expressing ones self; the most compendious, most
noble, most pleasing, and most efficacious of all other that
humane wit can invent. It is indeed most compendious, since
by two or three words it surpasseth that which is contained
in the greatest Volumes. And as a small beame of the Sun is
able to illuminate and replenish a Cavern (be it never so
vast) with the rayes of its splendor: so a *Devise* enlightens
our whole understanding, & by dispelling the darknesse of

Errour, fills it with a true Piety, and solid Vertue. It is
in these Devises as in a Mirrour, where without large Tomes
of Philosophy and History, we may in a short tract of time,
and with much ease, plainly behold and imprint in our minds,
all the rules both of Morall and Civill life; tending also
much to the benefit of History, by reviving the memory of
such men, who have rendred themselves illustrious in all
sorts of conditions, and in the practice of all kinds of
Vertue.' In his Epistle Dedicatory, Blount claimed to be the
first writer on this subject in English, except for a 'small
parcell of it in *Camdens* Remaines', but he had forgotten, or
did not know, Samuel Daniel's translation of the dialogue of
Paulus Jovius (see no. 49 above).

  52. 11. 31-34; *Poems*, vi, p. 203. Cf. Addison, *Dialogues*,
i; *Miscellaneous Works*, ii, p. 284.
  53. See no. 21 above.
  54. 11. 35-44; *Poems*, vi, pp. 203-4. It was this passage
that Warburton used to justify the inclusion of *To Mr. Addison* in the *Moral Essays* group (see n. 6 above).
  55. Addison, *Dialogues*, i; *Miscellaneous Works*, ii, p. 291;
Jobert, *The Knowledge of Medals*, pp. 129-30: 'The value of the
Medal is yet augmented by another Beauty, that Nature has
only given, and Art hitherto cannot counterfeit: 'Tis a Varnish that a certain Earth gives the Metal, and covers some
with an Azure almost as fine as that of the *Turkish* Stone;
others with a true Vermilion, and others with a certain
bright and polisht Brown, excelling that of our Copper-Fig-
ures beyond comparison, and never deceiving the Eye even of
those that do but moderately understand it, extremely sur-
passing all that Sal-Armoniack mixt with Vinegar is able to
give. The common Varnish is a curious Green, that fixes it
self upon the delicatest Strokes without defacing them, and
more exactly than the finest Enamel upon the Metals to which
we apply it. The Copper only is susceptible of it: For the
green Rust upon Silver Medals only spoils it, and must be
taken off with Vinegar, or Juice of Lemons, if you have the
Medal valuable.' Pope mocks a similar, though more eccentric
attitude, in the slapstick comedy of the *Memoirs of ... Martinus
Scriblerus*, I, iii, ed. Kirby-Miller, 1950, pp. 102-3. Cf.
also *The Dunciad*, iv, 347-96; Poems, v (Revised Ed.), pp. 377-
81.
  56. *Poems*, vi, p. 207; 11. 39, 40 and 44[n]. Medals of Pescennius are mentioned by Patin as particularly rare: 'Je
donnerai icy l'example de la plus rare Medaille de bronze
qui soit au monde. Elle represente *Pescennius Niger*, dont le
regne fut si court, & la demeure si eloignée de l'Italie,
qu'il ne faut pas s'estonner si les Medailles en sont si
rares en tous metaux' (p. 180), and Jobert notes that '...
the Latin *Otho* of the large size in Copper is inestimable...'
(p. 15).
  57. *Epistolae De Rebus Familiaribus et Variae*, ed. cit., ii, 60-62;
see in this Canzone stanzas 1-3 and 7-8 especially.

810 NOTES TO PAGES 302-306

58. See n. 40 above.
59. ll. 699-700; *Poems*, i, p. 319.
60. ll. 45-52; *Poems*, vi, p. 204.
61. Addison, *Dialogues*, i; *Miscellaneous Works*, ii, pp. 291-92.
62. Louis Jobert, *The Knowledge of Medals*, p. 130; see n. 55 above.
63. Addison, *Dialogues*, i; *Miscellaneous Works*, ii, pp. 293-99; and the whole of *Dialogue ii*. Cf. also *Dialogue i*; *Miscellaneous Works*, ii, p. 285 and n. 47 above for further discussion of medals and painting.
64. ll. 20, 24, 32; *Poems*, vi, pp. 156-57.
65. Addison, *Works*, 1721, iv, pp. 135-37. The same argument occurs in *Dialogues iii* (*Miscellaneous Works*, ii, pp. 380-81) and Patin had drawn attention to the same point (*L'Histoire des Médailles*, pp. 45-46). Pope's allusion here would seem to be primarily to the *Guardian* paper, since only this contains a definite proposal that Britain should adopt the Roman practice. Addison does, however, perhaps allude to his own *Guardian* paper when, in *Dialogue iii*, Eugenius is made to say: 'I have often wondered that no nation among the moderns has imitated the ancient *Romans* in this particular ... But where Statesmen are ruled by a spirit of faction and interest, they can have no passion for the glory of their country, nor any concern for the figure it will make among posterity ...' and Cynthio replies: 'We shall think ... you have a mind to fall out with the Government, because it does not encourage Medals.' (*Miscellaneous Works*, ii, p. 380).
66. Addison, *Works*, iv, p. 136. Cf. Louis Jobert, *The Knowledge of Medals*, p. 110.
67. Addison, *Works*, iv, p. 137.
68. See no. 65 above.
69. Addison alludes to the French *Académie* in *Dialogue iii* (*Miscellaneous Works*, ii, p. 390): 'One might expect, methinks, to see the Medals of that nation [France] in the highest perfection, when there is a society pensioned and set apart on purpose for the designing of them.' See L.-F. Alfred Maury, *L'Ancienne Académie des Inscriptions et Belles-Lettres*, Paris, 1864, pp. 28-29, 428, 449, and Frances Yates, *The French Academies of the Sixteenth Century*, 1947, pp. 301-3. The academy was officially constituted in 1701 under the title of 'L'Académie Royale des inscriptions et médailles.' It was laid down that '... L'Académie s'appliquera à faire des médailles sur les principaux événements de l'histoire de France; elle travaillera à l'explication de toutes les médailles, médaillons, pierres et autres raretés antiques et modernes, du cabinet de Sa Majesté, comme aussi à la description de toutes les antiquités et monuments de la France.' (Maury, p. 28.)
70. Cf. Patin, *L'Histoire des Médailles*, pp. 111-113, especially the following: 'Ces barbares se contenterent de faire courir pour Monoye, des pieces malfaites, dont on ne peut expliquer les caracteres & les types. Ils se servoient mesme d'or tres-bas, & il n'y avoit pas quelquefois le quart de

fin. C'est sans doute grand dommage que leur nonchalance
nous ait fait ignorer leur histoire, par le peu de monumens
que nous en avons, & qui ne suffisent pas pour nous en infor-
mer. La ruine de l'Empire Romain a fait l'establissement
des Monarchies d'aujourd'huy, & nous sçaurions toutes les
particularitez de leurs origines, si on avoit continué de
faire des Monoyes & des Medailles, comme dans les six Siecles
precedens' (p. 113).
    71. *Miscellaneous Works*, ii, p. 389.
    72. *Ibid.*, ii, p. 379; *The Dunciad*, 1729, iii, pp. 71-74 and
note; *Poems*, v, p. 156.
    73. ll. 53-62; *Poems*, vi, p. 204.
    74. Pope imagines a series of medals devoted to great
philosophers, just as different series were devoted to consuls, cities, kings, emperors, deities and so forth. The
jump from Plato to Bacon derives some of its boldness from
its confident departure from the conventional categories of
'Ancient' and 'Modern' in contemporary numismatics--this,
says Jobert, 'is the first Notion of the Art, on which depends their [i.e. the medals'] esteem and value. The Ancients are all those that were coined within the Third and
Ninth Age of *Jesus Christ*; the Modern which have been made
within these last Three hundred Years: For, as for those we
have after *Charlemagne* till that time, the Curious will not
vouchsafe to collect them ...' (*The Knowledge of Medals*, p. 3).
    75. At the head of the 'Preface *de l'Edition de* 1715'; p.
xxxv. It may perhaps be thought surprising that Pope's
tremendously exalted compliment to Addison should have been
retained after the estrangement between the two men in 1715.
The answer is probably that the *idea* of a modern counterpart
to an Augustan original is of more importance to the poem
than the name itself. *To Mr Addison* is a poem of ideas not
personalities; it would not, by its nature, have demanded
revision in the light of personal developments. The compliment, nevertheless, seems exaggerated and implausible to
modern ears. It would not have done so to a contemporary.
Addison's reputation, not only as a writer of prose but also
as a poet in Latin and English, could not well have stood
higher at this time. In addition to this, Addison had recently held the Secretaryship of State for the Southern Department, one of the highest political offices in the land.
He thus exemplified in his own person that close alliance of
political power and literary excellence (Augustus's patronage of Virgil and Horace) which has always been an important
part of the conception of an Augustan Age. Both these points
are well demonstrated by contemporary reactions to Addison's
promotion to high office, in 1717: 'who would have expected
to have seen the Head of the Poets a Secretary of State?
However, he has the character of an incorrupt man, which is
no little matter now a days.' The French Ambassador commented: 'Mr. Addisson un homme d'esprît es tres poli mais
imaginés vous ce qu'on auroit dit in France si l'on eut fait

Mr. Racine Secretaire d'Etat.' (Peter Smithers, *The Life of Addison*, 1954, p. 367.)

   76. *Poems*, vi, p. 205.

   77. ll. 63-72; *Poems*, vi, p. 204.

   78. It may be that at some stage Pope and Addison looked to Craggs to implement the proposal on medals in *Guardian*, No. 96, and that they envisaged the offices of the monarch's Secretaries of State being recorded on coins, just as those of the Roman consuls had been. See, however, E. H. Gombrich, 'Renaissance and Golden Age', this *Journal*, XXIV, pp. 306-9, for traditional use of the concept of the Golden Age in Renaissance dedication and panegyric. Pope had of course published his own version of Virgil's Fourth Eclogue in 1712 (see n. 15 above). James Craggs is, indeed, here paid a compliment almost as exalted as that to Addison. There are several reasons why Pope may have thought this appropriate. First, Craggs had succeeded Addison as Secretary of State; the last lines of the epistle were almost certainly composed when he was in office. Secondly, Addison's collected *Works*, in which the *Dialogues* together with Pope's poem were to make their first official appearance, was to be dedicated to Craggs. (Though both Addison and Craggs died before publication, the dedication was retained.) Thirdly, Craggs appears to have had not only an extremely frank and pleasing personality, which won him good opinions from all sides, but also a genuine desire to help men of letters and to promote the arts. He had to this end offered Pope a pension of £300 a year, which the poet refused (Spence, *op. cit.*, p. 307). Addison's own tribute, from the letter which was to become the dedication of his *Works*, is perhaps the most telling: 'I have no time to lay out in forming such Compliments as would but ill suit that Familiarity between us, which was once my greatest pleasure and will be my greatest Honour hereafter. Instead of them, accept of my hearty Wishes, that the great Reputation you have acquired so early may increase more and more; and that you may long serve your Country with those excellent Talents, and unblemished Integrity, which have so powerfully recommended you to the most gracious and amiable Monarch that ever filled a Throne. May the Franknesse and Generosity of your Spirit continue to soften and subdue your Enemies, and gain you many Friends, if possible, as Sincere as your self.' (*The Letters of Joseph Addison*, ed. Walter Graham, 1941, pp. 406-7.) Pope expressed a high opinion of Craggs in his letters; and his friend Robert Digby, in a letter probably written on 30 July 1720, playfully suggested that Pope's intimacy with Craggs heralded a return of 'the figurative moral golden-age' and a 'revival of the polite arts' (Pope, *Correspondence*, ii, pp. 73 and 51).

   79. Cf. Dryden, *Astrea Redux*, ll. 292-322, and *Absalom and Achitophel*, ll. 1026-31; *Poems*, ed. James Kinsley, 1958, i, pp. 23-24, 243.

80. *Miscellaneous Works*, ii, pp. 316-17.
81. 'Therefore we shall call only those words the Legend which go round the Medal, and which serve to explain the Figures that are upon the Field.' Jobert, *The Knowledge of Medals*, p. 71.
82. *The Fourth Pastoral. Or, Pollio*, ll. 5-8; *Poems of John Dryden*, ed. Kinsley, ii, p. 887.
83. Spence, *op. cit.*, p. 204.
84. l. 30; *Poems*, vi, p. 203.
85. *An Essay on Criticism*, l. 318; *Poems*, i, p. 274.
86. l. 62; *Poems*, vi, p. 204.
87. ll. 23-30; *Poems*, vi, p. 203.
88. ll. 197-204; *Poems*, III, ii, p. 151.

MAHAFFEY, Timon's Villa: Walpole's Houghton
1. *A Master Key to Popery, or A True and Perfect Key to Pope's Epistle to the Earl of Burlington*, printed in the "Twickenham" edition of *The Poems of Alexander Pope*, III-ii, *Epistles to Several Persons*, ed. F.W. Bateson, 2d ed. (London and New Haven, 1961), Appendix C, p. 183. This is the edition of the *Poems* cited throughout.
In the preparation of this essay I have incurred many obligations: to Professor Ernest C. Mossner of The University of Texas, whose encouragement and criticism have been my mainstay from the inception to the completion of the work, and who headed the doctoral committee before whom I presented the argument in November 1962; to Professor Maynard Mack of Yale, who not only read the manuscript in semifinal draft and made valuable suggestions for its emendation but graciously lent his support to forward its publication. I am indebted also to the staffs of The University of Texas Library, especially to Miss Kathleen Blow, Chief Reference Librarian; the Henry E. Huntington Library; the Cambridge University Library; and the Fitzwilliam Museum. Other obligations are acknowledged at the appropriate places in the notes.
2. *The Correspondence of Alexander Pope*, ed. George Sherburn (Oxford, 1956), III, 259, 262-263.
3. *Ibid.*, 254-257.
4. "Timon's Villa and Cannons," *Huntington Library Bulletin*, No. 8 (October 1935), 131-152.
5. Vol. II, *Early Georgian, 1715-1760* (London, 1955), 16.
6. Sherburn takes no definite stand on this question, only remarking that the *Epistle to Burlington* should "in general" be read "not for its personalities but for the sound esthetic principles that it enumerates." For the opinion that Timon satirizes a type rather than an individual person, see Bateson, *Poems* III-ii, xxvi-xxxii, 146-154nn., and Appendix C; also Benjamin Boyce, *The Character-Sketches in Pope's Poems* (Durham, N.C., 1962), p. 14.
7. 26 July 1734, *Correspondence*, III, 419.
8. *Early Georgian*, pp. 72-86.
9. In many cases these are the same. The *Dunciad Variorum*, with notes identifying the dunces, had been published in April 1729.

10. J. H. Plumb, *Sir Robert Walpole*, Vol. II, *The King's Minister* (London, 1960), p. 331.

11. "On Seeing a Portrait of Sir Robert Walpole," *Letters and Works of Lady Mary Wortley Montagu*, 3d ed. (London, 1861), II, 483-484.

12. John Lord Hervey, *Memoirs of the Reign of George the Second* (London, 1848), I, 30-46; Plumb, *The King's Minister*, pp. 162-169.

13. The play is described on the title page as "Reviv'd from Mountfort, with Alterations."

14. *Political Ballads Illustrating the Administration of Sir Robert Walpole*, ed. Milton Percival (Oxford, 1916), pp. 14-16, 56-58.

15. Plumb, *The King's Minister*, pp. 90, 113.

16. *Ibid.*, pp. 85-87; *Aedes Walpolianae: or, a Description of the Collection of Pictures at Houghton-Hall in Norfolk*, 2d ed. (London, 1752).

17. Plumb, *The King's Minister*, p. 90.

18. 21 July 1731, in *Lord Hervey and His Friends*, ed. Earl of Ilchester (London, 1950), pp. 73-74.

19. *Aedes Walpolianae*, p. 73. Penshurst and the tradition it represented are discussed in G. R. Hibbard's "The Country House Poem of the Seventeenth Century," *Essential Articles for the Study of Alexander Pope*, ed. Maynard Mack (Hamden, Conn., 1964), pp. 401-437.

Edward Harley, second Earl of Oxford, was also critical of Houghton and its lantern. The lantern, he said, was "very ugly," and "not really big enough for the room it hangs in." Hist. MSS. Comm., *Portland*, VI, 161. In 1750 Lord Chesterfield bought "the famous lanthorn, that produced so much Patriot wit; and very likely some of his Lordship's." Horace Walpole to Horace Mann, 25 July 1750, *Correspondence*, ed. W. S. Lewis (New Haven, 1937--), XX, 163.

20. *Lord Hervey and His Friends*, pp. 70-72. Correction "yᵉ chaise-party" for "of chaise-party" from manuscript copy in the Bristol Papers, West Suffolk County Record Office.

21. From a clipping pasted onto p. 10 of the Cambridge University copy of Isaac Ware's *Plans, Elevations, and Sections; Chimney-Pieces, and Cielings of Houghton in Norfolk*, (London, 1760), presented to the University 1 November 1810 by the Rev. Baily Wallis.

The Duke's visit to Houghton began on 2 November, according to the *Monthly Intelligencer*. See also *Daily Journal*, 15 November 1731; *Lord Hervey and His Friends*, pp. 102-107, 121; Sir Thomas Robinson to Lord Carlisle, 9 December 1731, Hist. MSS. Comm., *Fifteenth Report*, Appendix, Part VI, *The Manuscripts of the Earl of Carlisle, preserved at Castle Howard*, p. 85.

22. See also *Craftsman*, 19 July 1729; *The Norfolk Congress; or A full and true Account of the Hunting, Feasting, and Merrymaking of Robin and his Companions*, reprinted in *Craftsman*, 1731, III, Appendix, 317-322; *The Norfolk Congress Versified* (1728); "A New Norfolk Ballad by Sir Francis Walsingham's Ghost," *Daily Journal*, 17 November 1730, reprinted in Percival, *Political Ballads*, pp. 38-39.

23. *Aedes Walpolianae*, p. 37; Plumb,*The King's Minister*, pp. 81-85.
24. To Lord Carlisle, 9 December 1731, Hist. MSS. Comm., *Carlisle*, p. 85.
25. Plumb, *The King's Minister*, p. 83 n.
26. *Early Georgian*, p. 72.
The domes, according to Hervey, "were obstinately raised by the master, and covered with stones in defiance of all the virtuosi who ever gave their opinions about it." *Lord Hervey and His Friends*, p. 71. Horace Walpole adds that his father "used to say that he had taken the idea of the towers from Osterly-park, near Brentford." *Aedes Walpolianae*, p. 37.
Campbell had no part in these alterations and, perhaps significantly, did not oversee construction. Horace Walpole speaks slightingly of him in *Anecdotes of Painting* --a further hint that there was trouble between Sir Robert and his architect. Campbell died in 1729. *Craftsman*, 20 September 1729.
27. *Poems*, IV, 11. 185-186.
28. *Anecdotes of Painting*, in *The Works of Horatio Walpole, Earl of Orford*, (London, 1798), III, 484-485.
29. *On Modern Gardening*, in *Works*, II, 535.
30. *Plans, Elevations, and Sections*.
31. Hist. MSS. Comm., *Carlisle*, p. 85. Both Hervey and Horace Walpole give the garden area as twenty-three acres.
32. *Vitruvius Britannicus: or, The British Architect*, III (London, 1725), Pl. 27-28.
33. The same phrase, interestingly enough, is used by Horace Walpole in recounting an exchange of witticisms between Thomas Wyndham and another critic of Sir Robert: "Going to see Longleat, built by Sir John Thynne, steward to the Protector Somerset, and the man who showed the house (which by the way is a town in comparison) saying, 'It is a large house, but we don't pretend that it rivals Houghton,' Windham replied, 'No--yet I believe Mr Jenkins' (my father's steward) 'has not built such an one.'" This bit of repartee, according to Horace, occurred at "the height of the clamour" against Sir Robert, presumably before 1736, when Jenkins died. *Correspondence*, XXVIII, 302-303 and nn.
34. Hist. MSS. Comm., *Carlisle*, p. 85. Hervey also comments on the disadvantageous situation of Houghton: "The soil is not fruitful, there is little wood, and no water: absolutely none for ornament, and all that is necessary for use forced up by art." *Lord Hervey and His Friends*, pp. 70-71.
35. *Aedes Walpolianae*, p. 44; Hussey, *Early Georgian*, p. 78.
36. Hussey, *Early Georgian*, p. 83.
37. Pope's note to 1. 95, 1735 octavo and later editions.
38. Ware, *Plans, Elevations, and Sections*, p. 7; Hussey, *Early Georgian*, p. 76.
39. J. H. Plumb, *Sir Robert Walpole*, Vol. I, *The Making of a Statesman* (London, 1956), p. 82; "The Walpoles: Father and Son," *Studies in Social History: A Tribute to G. M. Trevelyan* (London, 1955), p. 197.
40. *Poems*, III-ii, Appendix A, "Who Was Atossa?"

41. Sir Thomas Robinson writes of the north wing, the last to be built, as containing "a very magnificent hall for a chapel," as though it were not finished. Hist. MSS. Comm., *Carlisle*, p. 85.

42. This is not a part of the Timon character, but of a generalized portrait of the prodigal. Even in the delineation of the type, however, there are strokes recognizable as personal satire.

43. To Lady Mar, 31 October 1723, *Letters and Works*, I, 473.

44. Plumb, *The King's Minister*, pp. 94-98.

45. P. 152 n.

46. *Poems*, IV, 303 n.

47. *Aedes Walpolianae*, p. 39 n.; Plumb, *The Making of a Statesman*, pp. 88, 205; *The King's Minister*, p. 81 n.

48. 7 July 1742, *Correspondence*, XVII, 487.

49. Ware, *Plans, Elevations, and Sections*; Hussey, *Early Georgian*, p. 84. Sir Thomas Robinson luckily never wearied of detail. On 9 December 1731 he told Lord Carlisle, "There is only one dining room to be finished which is to be lined with marble." Hist. MSS. Comm., *Carlisle*, p. 85.

50. Pope last mentions dining at Sir Robert's in a letter to William Fortescue, dated 7 June 1730. *Correspondence*, III, 112.

51. Gay had been a commissioner of the State Lottery until sometime in 1731. His place may have been the one given to Leonard Welsted on 18 May 1731. Memoir by John Nichols in *The Works in Verse and Prose, of Leonard Welsted, Esq.* (London, 1787), pp. xi-xii.

52. Butt published the *Master Key* in *Pope and His Contemporaries: Essays Presented to George Sherburn*, ed. James L. Clifford and Louis A. Landa (Oxford, 1949).

53. *Poems*, III-ii, xxx, 175.

54. *Correspondence*, III, 255-256.

55. *Poems*, III-ii, 177-179.

56. *Memoirs*, I, 47.

57. It is surprising that "Orator" (John) Henley escaped mention here, for he, like some of the others, qualified as both Walpole's hireling and Pope's dunce, and he was the first to print the calumny concerning Pope's ingratitude to Chandos. It appeared in his *Hyp-Doctor*, a paper frequently at the service of the government, on 21 December 1731, the day before Pope's defense in the *Post-Boy*. Sherburn, *HLB* (October 1935), 133 n.

58. This is the familiar boast that Pope's pen is neither bought nor bribed. Pope parodied this "Rule of Macchiavel" in a letter to Fortescue, 23 September 1735: "If I have any other very extraordinary thing to tell you, it is this, that I have never since returned Sir R.W.'s visit. The truth is, I have nothing to ask of him; and I believe he knows that nobody follows him *for nothing*." *Correspondence*, II, 323.

59. *Poems*, III-ii, 183-188.

60. Pope gives a turn to Dodington's characterization of himself (in *An Epistle to The Right Honourable Sir Robert Walpole*,

1726), "In Power, a Servant; out of Power, a Friend," implying that this deserter is typical of Sir Robert's sycophant-
ic guests.
   61. *Poems*, III-ii, xxxii.
   62. *Ibid.*, 144 n.
   63. Sir James Prior, *Life of Edmond Malone, Editor of Shakespeare, with Selections from His Manuscript Anecdotes* (London, 1860),
p. 368.
   64. *Poems*, III-ii, lvii-lviii and frontispiece. Professor
Maynard Mack has called my attention to a recent work which
questions the attribution to Hogarth, but the evidence, I
think, is not conclusive. See *Hogarth's Graphic Works*, Ronald
Paulson, comp. (New Haven, 1965), I, 299-300.
   65. *HLB* (October 1935), 151.
   66. Most of Pope's friends were either Tories or Whigs
out of place, and Burlington also joined this latter group
in 1733, when he went into opposition to the Walpole administration.
   67. The *Daily Courant* for 8 July 1731 carries the full text
of the presentment.
   68. *Lord Hervey and His Friends*, pp. 124-125. The copy is
misdated 21 December 1732 instead of 1731.
   69. *Ibid.*, p. 66 and n.
   70. The two letters to Lady Kaye are among the Dartmouth
MSS. in the William Salt Library, Stafford. For his kind
permission to use the papers and to quote from them, I am
indebted to the Earl of Dartmouth, and for assistance in using the papers, to Mr. F. B. Stitt, Librarian.
   Excerpts from the Letters are printed in Hist. MSS. Comm.,
Eleventh Report, Appendix, Part V, *Manuscripts of the Earl of Dartmouth*, p. 328.
   71. The first had appeared on 3 January 1731/2, and the
second 10 February 1731/2. *Poems*, III-ii, 176 n.
   72. *Ibid.*, 186.
   73. Sherburn, *HLB* (October 1935), 140-141.
   74. Welsted, *Works*, p. 197.
   75. I am indebted to Professor Maynard Mack for the phrase
and for sharpening my thinking on this point.
   76. Under the heading "Mr. Pope's Epistle on Taste censur'd
and defended" (II, 555) appear two letters, side by side,
the first an abbreviated version of Pope's letter in the *Post-
Boy*, and the second, addressed "To A--P-pe, *Esq.*" Pope's
critic ostensibly attacks the satire of Timon as personal,
calling attention to the ambiguity of Pope's remarks concerning the personal element; what he actually does is to point
up the satire: "By the Word *just* you must mean *like* ; and by
unjust injurious: For the more *just* (like) a *personal* Reflection is, so much the more *unjust* (injurious) it must be. So
that these *inconsidering* Men seem to reason very right." This
is the same device that Pope employs in the *Master Key*.

GIBSON, Three Principles of Renaissance Architectural Theory
in Pope's *Epistle to Burlington*
   This work was supported, in part, by the Ohio State University Development Fund through its Faculty Summer Fellow-
ship program, and by a grant from the Penrose Fund of the
American Philosophical Society. I should like to express my
gratitude for both of these grants.
   1. A. Lynn Altenbernd, "On Pope's 'Horticultural Romanticism'," *Journal of English and Germanic Philology*, LIV (1955),
477.
   2. Among the most helpful recent discussions of the *Epistle* illustrating these various approaches are: G. R. Hibbard, "The Country House Poem of the Seventeenth Century,"
Journal of the Warburg and Courtauld Institutes, XIX (1956), 159-
174; Kathleen Mahaffey, "Timon's Villa: Walpole's Houghton,"
Texas Studies in Literature and Language, IX (1967), 193-222; Edward Malins, *English Landscaping and Literature, 1660-1840* (London,
1966), pp. 37-41 Earl Wasserman, *Pope's "Epistle to Bathurst":
A Critical Reading* (Baltimore, 1960), pp. 37-39.
   3. All references to the *Epistle to Burlington* in the text
of this paper are from F. W. Bateson's edition of the *Epistles
to Several Persons* in the *Twickenham Edition of the Poems of Alexander
Pope*, Vol. III. ii, 2nd ed. (London, 1961).
   4. Wasserman, p. 37.
   5. Robert G. Shafer, "Cannons No Canon: Pope's *Epistle
to Burlington*," *Papers of the Michigan Academy of Science, Arts and
Letters*, XLV (1960), 409.
   6. The epithet is F.W. Bateson's, p. xxvi.
   7. Hibbard, p. 173.
   8. The passage is quoted in *An Essay on Harmony as it relates
chiefly to Situation and Building*, 2nd ed. (London, 1739), p. iii.
For the attribution of the work to Gwynn see H. M. Colvin,
A Biographical Dictionary of English Architects (London, 1954), p.
254. The publication date of the first edition of the *Essay*
is unknown.
   9. "Alciphron, or The Minute Philosopher," Dialogue III.
9, in *Works of George Berkeley*, ed. Alexander Campbell Fraser
(Oxford, 1871), II, 120.
   10. Anthony Ashley Cooper, Third Earl of Shaftesbury,
"Miscellaneous Reflections," Miscellany III, Ch. ii, in
Characteristics, ed. John M. Robertson, 1900 (Gloucester, Mass.,
1963), II, 267.
   11. Shaftesbury, II, 267n-268n; Vitruvius, *De Architectura*,
IV.ii. 5-6.
   12. Philander's commentary on Vitruvius, well known in
eighteenth-century England, is included in the then widely-
used edition of Vitruvius by J. De Laet (Amsterdam, 1649).
For another typical use of the same sources for the same purpose see John Dalton, "Some Thoughts on Building and Planting," in *A Descriptive Poem* (London, 1755), ll. 40-55, and his
note, p. 34.

13. Robert Morris, *An Essay in Defence of Ancient Architecture* (London, 1728), pp. 34-35; cf. Morris, *Lectures on Architecture* (London, 1734, 1736), pp. 55-57.

14. John Gilbert Cooper, "Letters Concerning Taste," 3rd ed., 1757, in *Essays on Taste*, The Augustan Reprint Society, Publ. No. 30 (Los Angeles, Calif., 1951), p. 51.

15. *De Architectura*, I. ii. 5, ed. and trans. by Frank Granger (London and Cambridge, Mass., 1931), I, 27, 29.

16. Granger, I, 26n.

17. Vitruvius, I. ii. 5-7; Granger, I, 29, 31.

18. Sebastiano Serlio, *Tutte L'Opere D'Architettura et Prospettiva*, Bk. IV, "L'Avttore ai Lettori," and chs. vi, vii, viii, facsim., Venice, 1619 (Ridgewood, N.J., 1964), fols. 126r, 139r, 158v, 169r.

19. Daniele Barbaro, *I Dieci Libri Dell'Architettura Di M. Vitruvio* (Venice, 1629), p. 35.

20. Pietro Cataneo, *I Quattro Primi Libri De Architettura*, IV. i, facsim., Venice, 1554 (Ridgewood, N.J., 1964), fol. 47r.

21. Henry Wotton, *Reliquiae Wottonianae* (London, 1651), pp. 304-305; cf. Andrea Palladio, *Four Books of Architecture*, II.i, trans. Isaac Ware, facsim., London, 1738 (New York, 1965), p. 37; John Evelyn, "An Account of Architects and Architecture," in his translation of *A Parallel of the Antient Architecture with the Modern*, by Roland Fréart de Chambray (London, 1664), p. 101.

22. Evelyn, "Dedication to Sr John Denham," *Parallel*, n.p.

23. Morris, *Lectures*, p. 81.

24. See for example Palladio's discussions of his designs for villas, II. xiii-xv.

25. Morris, *Lectures*, Part the Second, pp. v-vi; cf. pp. 136-37.

26. Vitruvius, I. ii. 8, iv. 1-12, vi.

27. Leon Battista Alberti, *Ten Books on Architecture*, I. iii-vi, IV. ii, V. xiv-xvii, trans. James Leoni, 1726, ed. Joseph Rykwert (London, 1955).

28. Andrew Boorde, *A Dyetary of Helth*, ed. F. J. Furnivall, E.E.T.S. (1870), pp. 223-35.

29. Palladio, II. xii.

30. *The Diary of John Evelyn*, ed. F. S. deBeer, 6 vols. (Oxford, 1955), III, 112.

31. *The Correspondence of Alexander Pope*, ed. George Sherburn, 5 vols. (Oxford, 1956), II, 109-110.

32. Walter G. Hiscock, *John Evelyn and His Family Circle* (London, 1955), p. 50.

33. See Pope's note on l. 96, Bateson, p. 146n.

34. "A Master Key to Popery," Bateson, Appendix C, p. 177.

35. For a good summary of the ideal life of virtue, study, contemplation, and hospitality that a decorous villa is to promote, see Palladio, II. xii.

36. Cf. ll. 75-76.

37. From Pope's note to l. 155, Bateson, p. 152n.

38. From Pope's letter to William Fortescue, 21 September 1736, *Correspondence*, IV, 34.
39. *The Spectator*, ed. Gregory Smith, 4 vols. (Everyman Library, 1945), III, 288; Fréart, *Parallel*, trans. Evelyn, pp. 10-11.
40. *Spectator*, III, 289-290. Contrast with "greater air" Pope's ironically ambiguous epithet "stupendous air" (1. 101).
41. Morris, *Defence*, pp. 1-4.
42. Morris *Lectures*, pp. 101-102.
43. Alberti, I. ix, V. xiv, and Rykwert, p. 242; Palladio, II. xii; Rudolft Wittkower, *Architectural Principles in the Age of Humanism*, 3rd ed. (London, 1962), pp. 74-75.
44. Albert, V. xiv. 100.
45. Morris, *Defence*, p. 13.
46. Alberti, V. xvii. 109; Palladio, II. xii-xv.
47. See Pope's note to 11. 195-204, Bateson, p. 155n.
48. Morris, *Defence*, pp. 4-6.
49. Morris, *Lectures*, pp. 101-102.

REVERAND, *Ut pictura poesis*, and Pope's "Satire II, i"

1. In addition to Hagstrum's book, see the following for discussions of pictorial and painterly elements in Pope: Norman Ault, "Mr. Alexander Pope: Painter," in *New Light on Pope* (London, 1949), pp. 68-100; Robert J. Allen, "Pope and the Sister Arts," in *Pope and His Contemporaries*, ed. James L. Clifford and Louis A. Landa (Oxford, 1949), pp. 78-89; D. S. Bland, "Pope's Colour-Sense: A Comment," *DUJ*, 47 (1955), 104-9; Chester F. Chapin, *Personification in Eighteenth-Century English Poetry* (New York, 1955), pp. 116-30; Benjamin Boyce, *The Character-Sketches in Pope's Poems* (Durham, N.C., 1962); James Sambrook, "Pope and the Visual Arts," in *Alexander Pope*, ed. Peter Dixon (Athens, Ohio, 1972), pp. 143-71; Hagstrum, "Verbal and Visual Caricature in the Age of Dryden, Swift, and Pope," in *England in the Restoration and Early Eighteenth Century*, ed. H. T. Swedenberg, Jr. (Berkeley, 1972), pp. 173-95.
2. The text for all references to Pope's poems is that of *The Poems of Alexander Pope*, gen. ed. John Butt, Twickenham ed., 6 vols. (London, 1939-62).
3. *The Garden and the City* (Toronto, 1969), p. 66.
4. Edwards, *This Dark Estate: A Reading of Pope* (Berkeley, 1963), pp. 80-95; Weinbrot, *The Formal Strain: Studies in Augustan Imitation and Satire* (Chicago, 1969), pp. 154-57; Weinbrot, "On the Discrimination of Augustan Satires," from *Proceedings of the Modern Language Association Neoclassicism Conferences, 1967-68*, ed. Paul J. Korshin (New York, 1970), pp. 5-12. The quotations cited in this paragraph are from *This Dark Estate*, p. 93, and *The Formal Strain*, p. 157. For other readings of the poem that view Pope as the victor in the argument, see: John M. Aden, *Something Like Horace: Studies in the Art and Allusion of Pope's Horatian Satires* (Nashville, Tenn., 1962), pp. 7-13; Mack, *The Gar-*

den and the City, pp. 66-69, 177-87; Thomas E. Maresca, *Pope's Horatian Poems* (Columbus, Ohio, 1966), pp. 37-72.

5. "Satire, Poetry, and Pope," from *English Satire: Papers Read at a Clark Library Seminar, January 15, 1972* (Los Angeles, 1972), pp. 55-106; see especially p. 81. Reuben A. Brower, in *Alexander Pope: The Poetry of Allusion* (Oxford, 1959), mentions the "splendidly pictorial metaphors" that characterize this Pope passage, but Brower does not pursue the point (pp. 287-88).

6. Kames, *Elements of Criticism*, 2nd ed. (Edinburgh, 1762), III, 65.

7. For a thorough discussion of the Renaissance uses of this motif and theme, see Erwin Panofsky, *Hercules am Scheidewege und andere antike Bildstoffe in der neueren Kunst* (Leipzig-Berlin, 1930); E. Tietze-Conrat, "Notes on Hercules at the Crossroads," *JWCI*, 14 (1951), 305-9; Theodor E. Mommsen, "Petrarch and the Story of the Choice of Hercules," *JWCI*, 16 (1953), 178-92. For a discussion of the relevance of this motif to Dryden, see Hagstrum, *The Sister Arts*, pp. 190-97.

8. Hagstrum, *The Sister Arts*, p. 149.

9. See Hagstrum, *The Sister Arts*, plates VII-B, VII-A, and VI for reproductions of these depictions.

10. Chapin, *Personification*, p. 62.

11. First published in Antwerp, 1607; the text used for all references is that of the 3rd edition, published in Brussels, 1683. For evidence of this book's popularity, see Mario Praz, *Studies in Seventeenth-Century Imagery*, 2nd ed. (Rome, 1964), pp. 523-24.

12. *Joseph Spence: Observations, Anecdotes, and Characters of Books and Men*, ed. James M. Osborn, 2 vols. (Oxford, 1966), I, 228 (No. 541). This anecdote is dated 1739, but of course Pope could have read this book at any point before he made this comment to Spence. Had there been an edition of van Veen's book in the late 1730s, the anecdote might suggest that Pope was commenting on a book just published, but there is no 1730s edition of the work (except for a Spanish edition of 1733).

13. This book contains two virtually identical figures which closely resemble van Veen's Virtue; in one case, the figure is Virtue (emblem 44); in the other case, as the text makes clear, the figure represents Minerva (emblem 24). For other depictions of Virtue that display some of the features van Veen uses--helmet, spear, *parazonium*, etc.--and that thus demonstrate that van Veen's Virtue is traditional rather than exceptional, see the following: the Rubens and Carracci paintings already mentioned (Hagstrum, *The Sister Arts*, plates VII-B, VII-A); Joannes Sambucus, *Emblemata, et Aliquot Nummi Antiqui Operas* (Antwerp, 1566), pp. 120, 193; Geoffrey Whitney, *A Choice of Emblemes and Other Devises* (Leyden, 1586), pp. 44, 222 (copies of de Jonge, emblem 44, and Sambucus, p. 120, respectively); see also Panofsky, *Hercules am Scheidewege*, illustrations 56 (Ph. Trière), 60 (Anonymous, after Jan Saenredam), 62 (Th. van Thulden), 77 (S. Gribelin), 82 (Pompeo

Battoni), 83 (Anton Tischler), 89 (Giuseppe Diamantini),
and 93 (G. Vallet).
    14. *Cicero: Tusculan Disputations*, ed. and trans. J. E. King,
rev. ed., Loeb Classical Library, Vol. 18 (1945; rpt. Cambridge, Mass., 1971), pp. 194-96 (*Disputations* II, xviii, 43).
    15. George Howe and G. A. Harrer, A *Handbook of Classical
Mythology* (New York, 1947), p. 294; M. A. Dwight, in *Grecian
and Roman Mythology*, 2nd ed. (New York, 1849), calls Virtue the
"personification of manly valor" (p. 290).
    16. A common proverb that dates from roughly the same
period as the van Veen book embodies the same idea: "He
that sows Virtue reaps fame." See Morris Palmer Tilley, A
*Dictionary of the Proverbs in England in the Sixteenth and Seventeenth
Centuries* (Ann Arbor, Mich., 1950), p. 699.
    17. Cited by Mommsen, "Petrarch and the Choice of Hercu-
les," p. 190. Petrarch, *Apologia contra cuiusdam Galli Calumnias*,
in *Atti della R. Accademia di Archeologia, Lettere e Belle Arti*, ed.
E. Cocchia, NS 7 (Naples, 1920), 148.
    18. Rollenhagen, *Nucleus Emblematum selectissimorum* (Arnheim,
1611), No. 6.
    19. The same motif of Virtue elevated is repeated in the
background of the emblem, where Virtue, again carrying a man
heavenward, appears in a cloud floating above three mortals
on the ground. See also Guillaume de La Perrière, *La Morosophie
de Guillaume de la Perrière* (Lyons, 1553), No. 17. This emblem,
depicting Virtue unrecognized by her blind admirers, shows
Virtue atop a rock, surrounded by six men, all blindfolded,
at ground level. Although the purpose of this emblem is
different from that of van Veen's, the same suggestion of
Virtue's elevated status and inherent superiority emerges.
One might add that in the Hercules representations, the way
of Virtue is toward her temple high atop a hill, distinctly
elevated above and superior to the worldly concerns for
which Voluptas pleads; see, for example, Panofsky, *Hercules am
Scheidewege*, illustrations 82 (Pompeo Battoni), 84 (C. Faucci).
    20. See especially Maresca, *Pope's Horatian Poems*, pp. 37-72;
Brower, *The Poetry of Allusion*, pp. 282-318.
    21. Sambucus, *Emblemata*, p. 148. Van Veen also plays with
the motif, using a triumphal chariot in two emblems (pp. 3,
41), one of which is entitled "Le Glorieux Triomphe de la
Vertu" (p. 3). Virtue herself does not actually appear in
this engraving, but the text makes it clear that this is "le
char de la Vertu."
    22. Hogarth too, as Paulson has pointed out, displayed a
fascination for the Virtue-Vice motif and painted numerous
versions, or inversions, of the Choice of Hercules. See
Paulson, *Hogarth: His Life, Art, and Times*, 2 vols. (New Haven,
1971), I, 271-76, 417-20; II, 45, 201-2, 393-95.

ATKINS, Pope and Deism: A New Analysis
    1. *Heav'n's First Law: Rhetoric and Order in Pope's* Essay on
Man (DeKalb, 1967). Kallich says, e.g., that Pope's principal articles of confession in the *Essay* are "in their orientation deistic" (p. 5) and that certain images demonstrate
his "distaste for zeal in religion and preference for the
moderation of natural religion and ethical deism" (p. 117).
    2. *The Rise of Modern Paganism*, Vol. I (New York, 1966) of
The Enlightenment: An Interpretation; see p. 382: "[In France]
Pope's most deist poems were also his most widely read and
most frequently imitated." Scholars specializing in Pope's
work--especially in the United States--tend to be apologet-
ic and try to water down the charge of deism; see Maynard
Mack in his introduction to Vol. III-i of the Twickenham
ed. of the *Poems* (New Haven, 1950). But books on general
topics, when confronted with this question, follow Leslie
Stephen's lead in finding--or assuming--Pope to be a deist.
See Stephen, *History of English Thought in the Eighteenth Century*
(1876; repr. New York, 1962); D. G. James, *The Life of Reason*
(London, 1949); Norman Sykes, *From Sheldon to Secker: Aspects of
English Church History, 1660-1768* (Cambridge, Eng., 1959); Frank-
lin L. Baumer, *Religion and the Rise of Scepticism* (New York,
1960); Gerald R. Cragg, *Reason and Authority in the Eighteenth
Century* (Cambridge, Eng., 1964).
    In any case, testifying to the interest in questions re-
garding Pope's religion is the fact that articles on Pope's
religious views appear in nonprofessional as well as scholarly journals. See, e.g., Patrick Cruttwell, "Pope and His
Church," *Hudson Review*, XIII (1960-61), 392-405; Nancy K.
Lawlor, "Pope's *Essay on Man*: Oblique Light for a False Mirror," *Modern Language Quarterly*, XXVIII (1967), 305-315. For
discussion of the latter, see below, n. 43. A recent book
by Douglas H. White is not concerned with such labels as
"deist" but with comparison of Pope's statements in the *Essay
on Man* and views of other writers on the same or similar
points: *Pope and the Context of Controversy: The Manipulation of
Ideas in* An Essay on Man (Chicago, 1970).
    3. See, e.g., White, p. 16, and E. C. Mossner, *Bishop
Butler and the Age of Reason* (New York, 1936). One may note
that Archbishop Tillotson was called by many a deist.
    4. Quoted in Mossner, p. 73, from the *Memoirs of Joseph
Priestley* (1806).
    5. *Modern Philology*, XXIX (1932), 281-299. See Roland N.
Stromberg, "Lovejoy's 'Parallel' Reconsidered," *Eighteenth-
Century Studies*, I (1967), 381-395.
    6. Arthur Friedman, "Pope and Deism (*The Dunciad*, IV, 459-
92)" in *Pope and His Contemporaries: Essays Presented to George
Sherburn*, ed. James L. Clifford and Louis A. Landa (1949;
repr. New York, 1968), p. 89.
    7. From the introduction to the *Essay on Man* in *The Poems
of Alexander Pope*, III-i; hereafter cited as Mack. My debt to
Professor Mack throughout this essay is obvious and considerable.

8. See Mack, esp. pp. xv-xxii.

9. There was some questioning of relatively minor points in the poem. See Mack, xvi-xvii, and Robert W. Rogers, *The Major Satires of Alexander Pope*, Ill. Studies in Lang. and Lit., 40 (Urbana, 1955), p. 95; see also Robert Donald Spector, "Pope's Reputation as a Deist," *Notes and Queries*, CXCVII (1952), 318.

10. Cited in Mack, p. xviin.

11. E. Audra, *L'Influence francaise dans l'oeuvre de Pope* (Paris, 1931), p. 92, and Robert W. Rogers, "Critiques of the *Essay on Man* in France and Germany, 1736-1755," *Journal of English Literary History*, XV (1948), 176-193. Incidentally, after Crousaz's essay in 1737, the Jesuit publication retracted its opnion and condemned the poem's theology.

12. Mack, p. xxiii. And see Spence's note, alluded to there.

13. Crousaz tried to associate the doctrines of Pope's poem with Leibnitzian philosophy and Spinozism. See Mack, pp. xx, xxvii. See also C. A. Moore, "Did Leibniz Influence Pope's *Essay*?," *Journal of English and Germanic Philology*, XVI (1917), 84-102. It should be noted that Pope explicitly rejected the doctrines of Spinoza and Leibnitz; see the Pope-Louis Racine letters.

14. Mark Pattison, "Pope and His Editors," in *Essays* (Oxford, 1889), II, 350-395.

15. For a lively but unscholarly and often inaccurate defense of Pope, see Francis Beauchesne Thornton, *Alexander Pope: Catholic Poet* (New York, 1952).

16. George Sherburn, *The Early Career of Alexander Pope* (Oxford, 1934), Ch. i.

17. Spence says that Pope "mentioned then, and at several other times, how much (or rather how wholly) he himself was obliged to [Bolingbroke] for the thoughts and reasonings in his moral work, and once in particular said that beside their frequent talking over the subject together, he had received (I think) seven or eight sheets from Lord Bolingbroke in relation to it, as I apprehended by way of letters, both to direct the plan in general, and to supply the matter for the particular epistles"; in *Observations, Anecdotes, and Characters of Books and Men*, ed. James M. Osborn (Oxford, 1966), I, 138; hereafter cited as Spence. See also Osborn's appendix, "Bolingbroke and the *Essay on Man*," II, 632-633.

18. Mack, pp. xxivff and Appendix A, p. 169.

19. Lord Bathurst told Hugh Blair that the *Essay* "was originally composed by Lord Bolingbroke in prose, and that Mr. Pope did no more than put it into verse: that he had read Lord Bolingbroke's manuscript in his own hand-writing; and remembered well, that he was at a loss whether most to admire the elegance of Lord Bolingbroke's prose, or the beauty of Mr. Pope's verse" (quoted in Osborn's appendix in Spence, II, 632). Lord Bathurst repeated the story. Joseph Warton in 1780 writes: "Lord Bathurst repeatedly assured me, that

he had read the whole scheme of the Essay on Man, in the
handwriting of Bolingbroke, and drawn up in a series of propositions, which POPE was to versify and illustrate" (An Essay on the Genius and Writings of Pope, 4th ed. [London, 1782],
II, 62).
   20. Works, ed. W. Elwin and W. J. Courthope (London, 1871-
89), VII, 245; hereafter cited as Elwin-Courthope.
   21. Works (London, 1809), V, 73.
   22. Works (London, 1811), XII, 335. See Mack, pp. xiv-xvn,
and John Laird, Philosophical Excursions into English Literature
(Cambridge, Eng., 1946), p. 37, for the opinion that Bolingbroke's statement is not malicious but rather indicative of
the difference in convictions and interests of the two men.
   23. See Mack, pp. xxix-xxxi; Laird, pp. 40-42, 50-51.
   24. Elwin-Courthope, II, 276.
   25. Philip Dormer Stanhope, 4th earl of Chesterfield, Letters and Other Pieces, ed. Richmond P. Bond (New York, 1935),
p. 317.
   26. Joseph Warton, Pope's Works (London, 1797), III, 10.
See also Elwin-Courthope, II, 276.
   27. Richardsoniana (London, 1776), p. 265; quoted in Mack,
p. xxv. Note Mack's interpretation of Richardson's comment.
Warburton had, after all, given an impossibly pietistic reading to the Essay on Man.
   28. The "irreconcilability" of these passages to orthodox
theology is pointed to by Patrick Cruttwell in the essay
mentioned in n. 2.
   29. The text of the Essay on Man used throughout is the
Twickenham edition as cited in n. 2.
   30. The opening 4 lines are used as illustration of Pope's
deism by Baumer (see n. 2), pp. 56-57. For an answer to
such charges see Thornton, esp. p. 274.
   31. White, passim, finds a number of significant similarities between Pope and the Cambridge Platonists.
   32. See Mossner, esp. pp. 146-155. Note too the optimism
in Henry More's Psychathanasia (esp. Bk. III, canto iv, sts.
16-22). See also White, pp. 185-187.
   33. See Michael Macklem, The Anatomy of the World (Minneapolis, 1958), esp. pp. 58-80, for the reaction against Hobbes,
particularly in Archbishop King.
   34. See, e.g., Sermons, I, No. 6. See also White, pp.
128-132, 189.
   35. A letter to Servatius Rogenus (1534), quoted in Ernst
Cassirer, The Platonic Renaissance in England, trans. James P.
Pettegrove (Austin, 1953), p. 20, from Works of Erasmus, ed.
P. S. Allen (Oxford, 1906), I, 567ff. See also a letter to
Colet (1499) in Allen, I, 246ff.
   36. Life and Recently Discovered Writings, ed. William Lee
(London, 1869), II, 128-130. Of course, The Spectator eschewed theology for morality.
   37. From Moral and Religious Aphorisms, quoted in Cassirer,
p. 32.

38. From *A Sermon before the House of Commons, March 31, 1647,* quoted in Cassirer, pp. 33-34.

39. See, esp., Cassirer, pp. 8-24.

40. Ibid., p. 35. See also Louis Capéran, *Le problème du salut des infidèles: essai historique* (1912; repr. Toulouse, 1934). That at least some Catholics believed heathens could be saved is apparent in Dominique Bouhours's *Life of St. Francis Xavier,* as translated by Dryden: *The Works of John Dryden,* ed. Sir Walter Scott, rev. George Saintsbury (Edinburgh, 1882-93), XVI, 339-340.

41. Friedman, p. 92.

42. See Cassirer, esp. pp. 24, 41.

43. Nancy K. Lawlor, in the essay cited above (n. 2), maintains that deism does in fact appear in the *Essay on Man.* She finds deism "throughout the four epistles"; as evidence she cites such facts as that "there is no direct claim for the need of supernatural revelation," that "there is no mention of Christ," and that "there is no expressed concern for the fate of the soul after death" (pp. 308-309). It is precisely this failure to discriminate carefully among positions, to note exactly what deists said and what Pope said, that has so long clouded the issues regarding Pope's religious position. Lawlor goes on to argue for a tension between deism and Christianity in the *Essay* and to conclude, in finding the poem in agreement with Thomist doctrine, that Pope tries to reveal a course that both deism and revealed religion share. The *Essay on Man* defends, she says, revealed religion. I trust my effort here generally will serve as a reply to her arguments. For further rebuttal of her last two pieces of "evidence" for deism in the *Essay,* see White, esp. p. 125.

44. "Anglican Apologetics and the Idea of Progress, 1699-1745," *Modern Philology,* XXXI (1934), 282.

45. *Deism and Natural Religion: A Source Book* (New York, 1967), p. x.

46. White, p. 11, n. 4.

47. In Charles Blount, Charles Gildon, and others, *The Oracles of Reason* (London, 1693), p. 210. Some recent studies of Dryden provide valuable insight into the muddied waters of late 17th- and early 18th-century religious thought. See Phillip Harth, *Contexts of Dryden's Thought* (Chicago, 1968); Sanford Budick, *Dryden and the Abyss of Light: A Study of Religio Laici and The Hind and the Panther* (New Haven, 1970).

48. *Christianity as Old as Creation: or, The Gospel, A Republication of the Religion of Nature* (London, 1730), p. 332.

49. As "A. W." says in "Of Natural Religion, as opposed to Divine Revelation," "Natural Religion is the Belief we have of an eternal intellectual Being, and of the Duty which we owe him, *manifested to us by our Reason,* without Revelation or positive Law" (in *Oracles of Reason,* p. 197; italics mine.)

50. Tindal, p. 157.

51. *The Two First Books of Philostratus, concerning the Life of Apollonius Tyaneus* (London, 1680), Bk. I, Ch. v, ill. 6, p. 20.

52. "A Summary Account of the Deists Religion" in *The Oracles of Reason*, pp. 92-93.

53. Tindal, p. 20.

54. Ibid., p. 164.

55. It is important to distinguish the deistic position on reason from that of the Cambridge Platonists, who seem on a cursory reading at least to view reason in much the same light. But actually the differences are great. The basic Cambridge Platonist position on reason in religious matters is apparent in Benjamin Whichcote's statement that "there can be no faith without reason, nor yet any higher reason without faith" (quoted in John Tulloch, *Rational Theology and Christian Philosophy in England in the Seventeenth Century* [London, 1872], II, 116). The Platonists maintain that religion fosters rather than extinguishes reason. They are hardly willing to go so far as the deists. In *An Elegant and Learned Discourse of the Light of Nature* Nathaniel Culverwel says that his purpose is "to give unto *Reason* the things that are *Reasons*, and unto *Faith* the things that are *Faiths*" ([London, 1652], p. 175). And on the point which the deists spent so much effort trying to refute, Culverwel maintains that there are indeed matters of faith which are above reason, but not contrary to it. It should also be noted that Robert Boyle, who was not a Cambridge Platonist, wrote *A Discourse of Things above Reason.* Further, John Locke, often called a deist, is to be clearly distinguished from Toland and others who went so far in arguing reason's capabilities. See *The Reasonableness of Christianity*, ed. I. T. Ramsey (Stanford, 1958). Ramsey's introduction is particularly valuable on this point.

56. Tindal, e.g., pp. 164, 183, 198-199, 332. Tindal implies that the notion of things being "above reason" is owing to priestcraft (pp. 198-199).

57. *An Essay concerning the Use of Reason in Propositions, the Evidence Whereof Depends upon Human Testimony* (London, 1707), pp. 24-25.

58. Ibid., p. 29.

59. Ibid., p. 34.

60. *English Deism: Its Roots and Its Fruits* (Grand Rapids, 1934), p. 15.

61. Mossner, p. 39.

62. Mack, p. xxvi. See also Phillip Harth's discussion in *Contexts of Dryden's Thought* of the similar division in various Christian treatises of the 17th century.

63. Quoted in Mossner, p. 27.

64. Thornton, p. 196.

65. *The Religion of Nature Delineated* (London, 1750), p. 95.

66. John Toland, *Christianity Not Mysterious: or A Treatise Shewing, that There Is Nothing in the Gospel Contrary to Reason, nor above It: and that No Christian Doctrine Can Be Properly Call'd a Mystery* (London, 1696), p. 57.

67. Rogers, *The Major Satires of Alexander Pope*, p. 55.

68. *Deism: An Anthology*, ed. Peter Gay (Princeton, 1968), p. 13.
69. See the present writer's "Dryden and the Clergy," Diss. Virginia 1969.
70. Lawlor interprets these extremes, without justification, it seems to me, as Christianity and deism. She finds Pope to be interested in "a Christian unity that few people dreamed of before the present day" (p. 308).
71. *The Correspondence of Alexander Pope*, ed. George Sherburn (Oxford, 1956), I, 454; hereafter cited as *Correspondence*.
72. Ibid., II, 171-172.
73. See, for instance, the letters of Aug. 20, Oct. [date approximate], Nov. 10, 1716, to Lady Mary Wortley Montagu and the letter of Aug. 27, 1714, to Edward Blount.
74. Pope was no stern-faced Christian, of course. He could ridicule priests. His "Roman Catholick Version of the First Psalm" offended many because of its liberties with Scripture. But that Pope poked fun at aspects of Christianity does not necessarily mean that he was anti-Christian. Many apparently sincere Christians have taken such liberties; an obvious example is Swift. Further, as the Twickenham editors suggest, Pope's "First Psalm" is probably a parody, not of the Bible, but of Sternhold's popular versifications.
75. *Correspondence*, I, 118.
76. Ibid., I, 454.
77. Spence, I, 82.
78. *Correspondence*, I, 453-454.
79. Thornton, p. 8.
80. Sherburn, *The Early Career of Alexander Pope*, Ch. ii.
81. Mossner, p. 27.
82. Ibid., p. 19.
83. On the question of Pope's not leaving the Catholic Church, one must admit that to have done so would have been to invite trouble and many accusations.
84. See Vol. I of the Twickenham ed. of the *Poems* (Pastoral Poetry *and* An Essay on Criticism), ed. E. Audra and Aubrey Williams (New Haven, 1961), 304*n*.

FABIAN, On The Literary Background of the *Essay on Man*: A Note on Pope and Lucretius
1. Cf. *Correspondence of Alexander Pope*, ed. George Sherburn (Oxford: 1956), III, 37 and 81.
2. *Alexander Pope: The Poetry of Allusion* (Oxford: 1959), pp. 206-39.
3. *Correspondence*, III, 312.
4. *Ibid.*, III, 433.
5. *Works*, ed. David Mallet (1754; repr. Hildesheim: 1968), III, 317.
6. Brower, *Alexander Pope,* p. 207, rejects this possibility.
7. *Observations, Anecdotes, and Characters of Books and Men*, ed. James M. Osborn (Oxford: 1966), I, 135 (no. 305).

8. *An Essay on the Genius and Writings of Pope* (ed. 1806), II, 120.

9. *Div. Inst.*, III, 13-16.

10. Cf. the foreword to his 1563 edition of Lucretius.

11. On "overcoming" Lucretius, cf. for example, Dennis, *Critical Works*, ed. Edward Niles Hooker (Baltimore: 1943), II, 120; on Coleridge, cf. his letter of May 30, 1815, *Collected Letters*, ed. Earl Leslie Griggs (Oxford: 1959), IV, 574.

12. I, 1-2. Quotations from the printed text are from the Twickenham edition, III, i.

13. The manuscripts are quoted according to photocopies of the originals; they are reproduced in *An Essay on Man: Reproduction of the Manuscript in the Pierpont Morgan Library and the Houghton Library, with the Printed Text of the Original Edition*: Introduction by Maynard Mack (Oxford: Printed for Presentation to the Members of the Roxburghe Club, 1962).

14. Cf. Manfred Erren, "Untersuchunger zum antiken Lehrgedicht" (Diss. Freiburg im Breisgau: 1956).

15. Griffith, no. 294 and 307.

16. On Pope's criticism of the *Georgics*, III, 10 ff. cf. Spence, *Anecdotes*, I, 229 (no. 543). Cf. also Lucretius IV, 1 ff. and the parallel in I, 927.

17. Cf. the beginning of Blackmore's *Creation*.

18. *Correspondence*, III, 249.

19. *Serm.* II, 1, 71-4.

20. Cf. Baxter Hathaway, "The Lucretian 'Return upon Ourselves' in Eighteenth-Century Theories of Tragedy," *PMLA*, 62 (1947), 672-89.

21. Cf. Aubrey L. Williams, *Pope's* Dunciad: A *Study of Its Meaning* (London: 1955), p. 19, note 1.

22. *Poems*, ed. James Kinsley (Oxford: 1958), II, 669.

23. *Ibid.*, I, 395.

24. *Ibid.*, I, 403. The original in the text edited by Cyril Bailey (Oxford: ed. 1957) reads:

> Suave, mari magno turbantibus aequora ventis,
> e terra magnum alterius spectare laborem;
> non quia vexari quemquamst iucunda voluptas,
> sed quibus ipse malis careas quia cernere suave est.
> suave etiam belli certamina magna tueri
> per campos instructa tua sine parte pericli.
> sed nil dulcius est, bene quam munita tenere
> edita doctrina sapientum templa serena,
> despicare unde queas alios passimque videre
> errare atque viam palantis quaerere vitae,
> certare ingenio, contendere nobilitate,
> noctes atque dies niti praestante labore
> ad summas emergere opes rerumque potiri.
> o miseras hominum mentis, o pectora caeca!
> qualibus in tenebris vitae quantisque periclis
> degitur hoc aevi quodcumquest!

25. *Anthropologie in pragmatischer Hinsicht*, § 58.

26. The satirical element in Lucretius is often overlooked. Cf. for example Clyde Murley, "Lucretius and the History of Satire," *Transactions and Proceedings of the American Philological Association*, 70 (1939), 380-95, and B. Lavagnini, "Motivi diatribici in Lucrezio e in Giovenale," *Athenaeum*, 25 (1947), 83-88.

27. Fragment 35 (translation by Capelle); Jean Bollack, "Lucretius and Empedocles," *Neue Rundschau*, 70 (1959), 656-86.

28. In the Pierpont Morgan manuscript Pope associated each of the opening verses with projected epistles. Cf. George Sherburn, "Pope at Work," *Essays on the Eighteenth Century Presented to David Nichol Smith* (1945; repr. New York, 1963).

29. *Collected Writings*, ed. David Masson (London: 1897), XI, 92 f.

30. Mary Clair Randolf, "'Candour' in XVIIIth-Century Satire," *Review of English Studies*, 20 (1944), 45-62.

31. Pope to Spence (1730): "These two lines ['Laugh where we must...'] contain the main design that runs through the whole." *Anecdotes*, I, 131 (no. 299).

HOTCH, The Dilemma of an Obedient Son: Pope's *Epistle to Dr. Arbuthnot*

1. All quotations from *An Epistle to Dr. Arbuthnot* are from the text in *The Twickenham Edition of the Poems of Alexander Pope*, IV, ed. John Butt, 2nd ed. (London: Methuen, 1961).

2. For the beginning of the attack on Pope, in connection with his poem "To the Ingenious Mr. Moore, Author of the Celebrated Worm Powder," see George Sherburn, *The Early Career of Alexander Pope* (Oxford: Clarendon Press, 1934), pp. 175-77.

3. *The Character of the Poet: Wordsworth in "The Prelude"* (Princeton: Princeton Univ. Press, 1971), p. 6.

4. "A True Character of Mr. Pope" (1716), in *The Critical Works of John Dennis*, ed. Edward Niles Hooker (Baltimore: Johns Hopkins Press, 1943), II, 105.

5. "Rhetoric and the Appreciation of Pope," *Modern Philology*, 37 (1939-40), 25.

6. A summary of these and other charges may be found in J. V. Guerinot, *Pamphlet Attacks on Alexander Pope, 1711-1744: A Descriptive Bibliography* (New York: New York Univ. Press, 1969), pp. xxix-xxxvi.

7. The parallels to baptism and the blind man in the Gospel of John are discussed by Thomas E. Maresca, *Pope's Horatian Poems* (Columbus: Ohio State Univ. Press, 1966), pp. 95-99. The blind man and Achilles parallels are noted by Elias F. Mengel, "Patterns of Imagery in Pope's *Arbuthnot*," in *Essential Articles for the Study of Alexander Pope*, ed. Maynard Mack (Hamden, Conn.: Archon Books, 1968), p. 571. Neither of these critics, however, suggests that there is anything in the lines that modifies the obvious import of these parallels.

8. *The Garden and the City: Retirement and Politics in the Later Poetry of Pope, 1731-1743* (Toronto: Univ. of Toronto Press, 1969), p. 26.

9. Ibid., p. 25.
10. Cf. *The Correspondence of Alexander Pope*, ed. George Sherburn (Oxford: Clarendon Press, 1956), III, 424 n. 1.
11. *An Essay on the Genius and Writings of Pope* (1756), 5th ed. (London, 1806), II, 262-63.

HUNTER, Satiric Apology as Satiric Instance: Pope's *Arbuthnot*

1. *Verses Address'd to the Imitator of the First Satire of the Second Book of Horace. By a Lady* (London, 1733). Another edition, entitled *To the Imitator* and virtually identical except for the omission of one couplet, was also published in 1733. *Epistle* was published the same year.
2. Lines 151-214 and 289-304 had earlier been published, in a slightly different form, and a version of ll. 406-19 existed as early as 1731; see John Butt's introduction to Twick. Ed., IV, esp. pp. xxiii-xxiv. For a convincing argument that the Huntington and Morgan manuscripts of *Arbuthnot* are pre-1733, see Professor Butt's "Pope's Poetical Manuscripts," *Proceedings of the British Academy*, XL (1954), 23-39 and plates.
3. The best critical reading of *Arbuthnot* is by Thomas Maresca (*Pope's Horatian Poems* [Columbus, 1966], pp. 73-116), who shows Pope's alliance with a Christianized classical tradition of moral satire. Though our emphases differ, I am encouraged by our general agreement about the intention of the poem and about some of its rhetorical procedures. For other examinations of the poem, see especially Elias F. Mengel, Jr., "Patterns of Imagery in Pope's *Arbuthnot*," *PMLA*, LXIX (1954), 189-97; Elder Olson, "Rhetoric and the Appreciation of Pope," *MP* XXXVII (1939-40), 13-35; Reuben Brower, *Alexander Pope: The Poetry of Allusion* (Oxford, 1959), pp. 293-302, and Thomas R. Edwards, *This Dark Estate*, Perspectives in Criticism, No. II (Berkeley and Los Angeles, 1963), pp. 102-10.

4. Pope's relation to Juvenal has often been underrated; for a perceptive account of Pope's tonal and procedural alliances with Juvenal, see Edwards, cited in the preceding note.
5. See Robert C. Elliott, *The Power of Satire: Magic, Ritual, Art* (Princeton, 1960).
6. *Popp* has often been ascribed to Lady Mary, and Pope apparently thought she wrote it. The "attack" was evidently fictively conceived as a kind of sick joke deriding Pope's physical defects.
7. See *Verses on the Death of Dr. Swift*, ll. 455-74.
8. In his *First Satire of the Second Book of Horace Imitated* (February 1733) Pope had self-effacingly imagined this criticism of his own poetry:

> The Lines are weak, another's pleas'd to say,
> Lord *Fanny* spins a thousand such a Day. (ll. 5-6)

Hervey took Fanny to be himself, even though Pope used the
name elsewhere to stand for other poets or types; and it is
apparently these lines which generated Hervey's hatred of
Pope. Interestingly enough, the manuscript of this poem
(in the Berg Collection of the New York Public Library) shows
that Pope wrote the line originally to describe someone else.
    9. The last line thrusts at Pope's father (see Pope's
note to l. 381 of *Arbuthnot*), who was often described in London lampoons as a hatter or some sort of tradesman. The
father's inability to create alludes again to Pope's physical deformity.
    10. For accounts of the London lampoon wars of the 30's,
see W. L. MacDonald, *Pope and His Critics* (London, 1951), pp.
153 ff., and especially Robert W. Rogers, *The Major Satires of
Alexander Pope*, Illinois Studies in Language and Literature,
Vol. XL (Urbana, 1955), Appendices D and E.
    11. Butt, "Pope's Poetical Manuscripts," n. 2. I am
grateful to the Henry E. Huntington Library and the Pierpont
Morgan Library for permission to examine the early manuscripts of *Arbuthnot*, and to the Emory University Research
Council for travel funds.
    12. Philip Pinkus, "Satire and St. George," *Queen's Quar-
terly*, LX (1963), 30-40.
    13.. See Geoffrey Tillotson, *Augustan Studies* (London, 1961),
esp. pp. 42-45.
    14. Pope may have taken his suggestion here from the sup-
pressed (and perhaps unconscious) sexual imagery in the
second couplet of *Verses*:
              Where ribaldry to satire makes pretence
              And modern scandal rolls with ancient sense.
                                            (ll. 3-4)
    15. W. K. Wimsatt, "One Relation to Rhyme to Reason:
Alexander Pope," *MLQ*, v (1944), 323-38; his argument here
implies that Pope's usually careful relation of rhyme to reason dramatizes the departures and casts blame for them upon
the subjects under discussion; the Pope-elope example is his,
though I have slightly altered his interpretation.
    16. Pope's footnote to this passage should, I believe, be
construed as part of the poem's text. Here Pope attempts
one of his most elaborate and difficult-to-read devices--a
pun where the reader must supply missing parts of the equation. "The Story," says Pope, "is told by some, of his
Barber, but by Chaucer of his Queen." Ironic irrelevance
underscores contemporary relevance; here is scholarly detail
to connect Minister and Barber (whose trade symbol was a *pole*
on the street *wall*). The safe pretense of antiquarian
interest guards the guide to meaning. Such use of footnotes
as integral parts of the text has received too little critical attention.
    17. Richard Savage, *The Modern Reasoners* (London, 1734), pp.
4-5. For a similar passage describing the aural oppression
of Augustan England, see James Bramston, *The Man of Taste*
(London, 1733), p. 13.

18. Pope's development of the ear metaphor may owe some
of its power to Swift (*A Tale of a Tub*) and may glance at the
corruption of oral tradition, both poetical and theological.
The relevant classical context seems to be Persius, Satire
I, where the ear imagery also carries suggestions of perversion.

19. See note to ll. 289-304 of Twick. Ed., IV. His couplet about misreaders who confuse terms--

> Who reads but with a Lust to mis-apply,
> Make Satire a Lampoon, and Fiction, Lye
> (ll. 301-322)

--has no counterpart in the 1732 squib.

20. The tension between triviality and significance is
like (in reverse) that exploited in *The Rape of the Lock*, where
the central events of the poem betray the triviality of
modern life at the same time as they remind of potential
significances. See Aubrey L. Williams, "The 'Fall' of China
and *The Rape of the Lock*," PQ, XLI (1962), 412-25.

21. For a typical use of the image, see Fieldings' *Modern
Husband*, I.viii. Pope may be thinking of the monarch butterfly, which is supposed to live only one day, but I have been
unable to discover whether this term and legend were current
in 1735.

22. Pope also puns on these words elsewhere; see, for
example, his extensive play in *Sober Advice from Horace* (1734).

23. For an interesting account of contemporary beliefs
about bedbugs, see Robert Southall, *A Treatise on Buggs* (2nd
ed., London, 1730). The scientific and pseudoscientific
facts offered by Southall suggest that Pope characteristically had chosen his image with great care and a full awareness of its ramifications for his contemporaries.

24. The force of Pope's images here derives in part from
inverting traditional ideas of poetic "inspiration." These
scribblers, says Pope, are vehicles spoken through by powers
of evil, not by a divine muse.

25. As an amphibian, the toad is a dramatically successful symbol, not only in received moral terms, but as a perverted philosophic animal extension of the characteristic
vacillation of Sporus. Pope's satire is sharp and precise;
the term amphibian had long been standard to describe man's
proper place in creation, but Sporus, like the other dunces
in *Arbuthnot*, misunderstands the implications of the term,
trying to be amphibious between sexes, not between orders.
The device here, and the implications of it, are like Pope's
strategy in showing what classical imitation amounts to for
the dunces.

26. Pope's increasing glances at Juvenal in his Horatian
imitations make the same point. In *Arbuthnot*, Pope appears
to echo Juvenal in several places; see especially Juvenal's
Third Satire.

27. Pope's naming of Addison may glance at the political
circumstances preceding Addison's death--when Addison's

political advice in the *Old Whig* infuriated many of his acquaintances, including Steele. Tacitus' view of Vestinus
Atticus combines the same praise and blame as Pope's portrait. Vestinus had been considered untrustworthy by his
peers and was not let into the conspiracy against Nero, but
he nevertheless died stoically when Nero, falsely informed,
sent to have him punished.

28. I take it that Pope here implies, on one level, that
duncical pens portray toads as beautiful creatures, but only
succeed in emphasizing their misplaced pride.

29. The analogue to Nero's misjudging of Atticus and to
the choice of Cibber as laureate is perhaps implicit. It
may be worth remarking that Pope omitted from his Atticus
portrait two earlier lines about Addison which would have
thoroughly involved Addison in the complicity of evil:

> Who when two Wits on rival themes contest,
> Approve them both, but likes the worst the best.

The lines refer to Addison's preference of Tickell's *Iliad*
over Pope's. I should guess that Pope's desire to be just
to Addison here overwhelmed even his artisitc commitment.

30. William Pulteney, Earl of Bath (under pseudonym of
Caleb D'Anvers), *A Proper Reply to a Late Scurrilous Libel* (London,
1731), p. 6. Pulteney treats Hervey as an hermaphrodite,
and in one rather amusing passage describes him as a Petrar-
chan lady (p. 10).

31. See the bust pictured in Hervey, *Memoirs of the Reign of
George the Second* (London, 1844).

32. See Pope's prefatory statement that his satires produce no injury *"since a Nameless Character can never be found out,
but by its Truth and Likeness."* Here Pope facetiously exaggerates
his fairness, but nevertheless points up a fundamental difference between his method and that of the London lampooners.

33.   My humble verse demands a softer theme,
             A painted meadow, or a purling stream.
                                   (*A Letter from Italy*, ll. 165-66)

Pope's alteration of one word shifts the evocative range to
fit his own context, but the line retains a tonal quality
that gently teases Addison, possibly Hervey, and certainly
Pope's own early work.

34. *Verses* describes Pope in this way:

> Who but must laugh, this bully when he sees,
> A puny insect shiv'ring at a breeze?   (ll. 79-80)

then elaborates the insect imagery, though not very imaginatively. Like Pope in the Addison line quoted above, Hervey
tries to carry the line by changing one significant word
("Master" to "bully"), but close comparison of each change
suggests the difference in the way the poets understand allusive technique. Pope's modification of Addison ("Meadow"
to "mistress") surprises the original context, but is thoroughly absorbed into Pope's context. Hervey's modification
is simple name-calling; as in his allusion to the Fall, Hervey has gone to a relevant fountain (for Hervey regarded the

Timon portrait as an attack on the Duke of Chandos), but
making the "Master" a "bully" is not irony in its subtlest
form.
  35. For documentation of this search, see the Earl of
Ilchester, *Lord Hervey and His Friends, 1726-38* ([London, 1950],
p. 241), though Lord Ilchester proposes a different explanation. Dion Cassius had been translated into English thirty
years earlier, but I have found no evidence that this translation was widely known. If Pope's joke did indeed annoy
Hervey, the irony is thus a double one.
  Pope added the name "Sporus" in the April 1735 edition;
the first edition of *Arbuthnot* used "Paris."
  36. For a statement of this view see G. Wilson Knight, *The
Burning Oracle* ([London, 1959], p. 188), though I should note
Professor Knight's generally corrective effect on criticism
which then viewed Pope as almost exclusively particular and
splenetic in his satiric portraits. For a sound brief statement of the relation between historical particular and
general application see Maynard Mack, "The Muse of Satire"
(*Yale Review*, XLI [1951], 80-92); and for an excellent detailed
discussion of how Pope shifts the emphasis beyond particulars
see Earl R. Wasserman, *Pope's Epistle to Bathurst* ([Baltimore,
1960], pp. 56-57).

SITTER, The Argument of Pope's *Epistle to Cobham**

  * I wish to thank the trustees and staff of the William
Andrews Clark Library for generous financial and intellectual
support during the preliminary research for this and other
studies. I am particularly grateful to Professor Aubrey L.
Williams of the University of Florida for patient tutelage.
  1. *The Epistle to Cobham* follows immediately after the *Essay
on Man* in the 1735 *Works*. Pope tends to be even more careful
than usual in arranging his epistolary poetry of the 1730's,
most likely because his projected "magnum opus," of which
the *Essay* and "Ethic Epistles" were to be parts, made him
especially attentive to the cumulative effect of poem
upon poem. The remark to Swift (discussed more fully later
in this essay) dates from January 31, 1733 (*Correspondence*,
ed. George Sherburn [Oxford, 1956], III, 348).
  2. Bowles's opinion is most easily consulted in the Elwin-Courthope edition of *The Works of Pope* (London, 1871-1889),
III, 49-51; see also F. W. Bateson's Introduction to his edition of the *Epistles to Several Persons* (Vol. III-ii of the
Twickenham edition, London and New Haven, 2nd ed., 1961),
p. xxi.
  3. Pope discussed his "new hypothesis, that a prevailing
passion in the mind is brought with it into the world, and
continues till death" with Spence in May, 1730 (*Observations,
Anecdotes and Characters*, ed. James Osborne [Oxford, 1966], I,
130). Its exposition in the *Essay on Man* is not of direct
concern to the present essay, but important background stud-

ies include Maynard Mack's Introduction to Vol. III-i of the
Twickenham edition (especially pp. xxvi-xl), Bertrand Goldgar,
"Pope's Theory of the Passions," *PQ*, 41 (1962), 730-743, and
Douglas H. White, *Pope and the Context of Controversy* (Chicago,
1970), pp. 144-172. Though made nearly a century ago, Leslie Stephen's pronouncement on the use of the ruling passion
in the *Ep. to Cob.* has been echoed frequently in modern criticism: "This theory ... is sufficiently striking for his
purpose; but it rather turns up at intervals than really
binds the epistle into a whole. But the arrangement of his
portrait gallery is really unsystematic; the affectation of
system is rather in the way" (*Alexander Pope* [New York, 1880],
pp. 183-184). For similar views see Reuben Brower, *The Poetry
of Allusion* (Oxford, 1959), pp. 260-265, Thomas R. Edwards,
This Dark Estate (Berkeley and Los Angeles, 1963), pp. 46-55.
Also of interest are Thomas A. Stumpf, "Pope's *To Cobham, To a
Lady,* and the Traditions of Inconstancy," *SP*, 67 (1970), 339-
358, and especially Benjamin Boyce, *The Character-Sketches in
Pope's Poems* (Durham, N.C., 1962), pp. 105-130.

    4. Warburton's transpositions in the editions of 1744
and 1751 are discussed by Bateson, pp. 6-12. These changes
were considered authoritative until the Twickenham edition.
For readers wishing to compare the two versions in more detail the Warburton text is still readily available in W. K.
Wimsatt's paperback anthology of the *Selected Poetry and Prose,*
2nd ed. (New York, 1972).

    5. "Here I am, like Socrates, distributing my morality
among my friends, just as I am dying. (On sending about him
some of his Ethic Epistles as presents, about three weeks before we lost him)" (Spence, I, 261-262). William B. Piper's
essay on "The Conversational Poetry of Pope" (*SEL*, 10 [1970],
505-524) and Frederick M. Keener's chapter on the Moral Essays in *An Essay on Pope* (New York and London, 1974) seem to me
the only commentaries which sufficiently emphasize the stress
and disagreement in Pope's major epistles. Piper does not
discuss the *Ep. to Cob.,* but his general view of the epistles
published between 1733 and 1738 is pertinent: "The greatest
of these poems are those in which the conversational advance
toward common sense is submitted to the most dynamic stress,
that is, those in which the divisive force of the topics and
the varieties of social opinion are most vividly realized"
(515). Keener describes Pope as "defending himself against
the peer's impetuous disdain for the bookish man" (76) and as
the "poet who patiently develops and holds to his own moral
vision even when, as in the epistles to Cobham and Bathurst
especially, it differs from that of his friends" (82).

    6. Having read more than four hundred of Rochefoucauld's
epigrams, the English reader of Pope's day would encounter
the following maxim against all others: "Maxims are to the
Minds, just what a staff is to the Body, when a man cannot
support himself by his own Strength. Men of sound Sense that
see things in their full and just Proportions, have no need

of General Observations to help them out" (*Moral Maxims and Reflections* [London, 1694], Part IV, xi, 171-172).

7. *The Garden and the City* (Toronto, 1969), pp. 204-205.

8. *Letters of John Keats*, ed. Hyder Edward Rollins (Cambridge, Mass., 1958), I, 193-194.

9. Pope's indebtedness to the introspective psychologizing of Montaigne and Charron has often been noted: first (and wryly) by Pope himself at l. 146, second (and ponderously) by Warburton in his note to this line, more recently (and dubiously) by Bateson, p. 27n. See Anthony Levi, *French Moralists: The Theory of the Passions, 1585 to 1649* (Oxford, 1964), for a useful commentary on the introspective tradition which culminates in Pascal and Malebranche; Chapters 3 and 8 are especially helpful. The most memorable expression of man's paradoxical nature is of course Pope's own introduction to the second epistle of the *Essay on Man*.

10. Warburton placed the couplet beginning, "On human actions ..." *before* the lines on the rapidity of "Life's stream" (ll. 31ff.) and, more importantly, before the passage casting doubt on the "optics seeing." The effect is to lessen Pope's assault on the observer's "reason."

11. June 7, 1733, *Corr.*, III, 374.

12. The connection between the inconsistency of man as subject and as object is stated forcefully by Charron: "So little is any of us the same; and so much harder is it to sound and know Man perfectly than any other Creature whatsoever: For he is full of doubles and trickings; the closest, cunningest, and most counterfeit part of the Creation. He hath a tousand little Closets and false Doors, where he hides, and comes out again; sometimes a Man, sometimes a monster..." (*Of Wisdom*, tr. Stanhope, 2nd ed. [London, 1707], I, 330). The inconsistency of the observer himself is the most difficult to see clearly: "Like the eyes of men in *Jaundice*, or the *Prisms*, that refract and vary the Rays, that fall upon the Organs of our outward Sense, so does the Soul alter its Objects too; and the present Constitution of it is the *Medium*, thro' which they must pass to us.... Thus our Thoughts are like our Clothes, that keep us warm, with a Heat which is none of their own, but such as we first gave them, and they keep it" (I, 172). Pope and Charron seem to share the conviction that introspection is not the road to but the escape from solipsism.

13. *The Search after Truth*, tr. T. Taylor (London, 1700), p. 44. For Pope's approving reference to Malebranche see his letter to Swift of Sept. 15, 1734, *Corr.* III, 433.

14. If one accepts Ernst Cassirer's account of dominant psychologies in the late 17th and early 18th centuries, Pope's emphasis on the mind as activity would align him with Leibniz (and Wolff and Condillac) rather than Locke. (See *The Philosophy of the Enlightenment* [Princeton, 1951], pp. 12-25, 93-133.) But without constructing systematic philosophies, many moralists well before the German Enlightenment had in-

sisted upon defining the soul in terms of action, however
negatively. Charron, e.g., states flatly that "The Soul indeed *cannot live* idle, for to be doing something is its very
Essence; and hence it is, that for fear of lying quite unac-
tive, it ... will study to cheat and deceive itself ... rather than be out of business" (I, 133-134). Jacques Esprit
uses the Heraclitian river to argue by analogy that man "is
never in the same situation" from one moment to the next,
and this condition of flux is attributed to "internal" as
well as "foreign" causes (*Discourse on the Deceitfulness of Humane
Virtues*, tr. William Beauvoir [London, 1706], pp. 4-5). Esprit's imagery, as well as his argument, may have influenced
Pope's passage on "Life's stream" (ll. 29-40).
   15. Pierre Nicole, *Moral Essays* (London, 1677-1682), III,
4, 49-50; cf. Isaac Watts, *Doctrine of the Passions Explain'd and
Improv'd* (1732), pp. 112-113, 118, 121, and William Law, *A
Serious Call to a Devout and Holy Life* (1729), pp. 101, 167, 169-
170. (Boyce [chap. 4] has discussed Law's more technical
influences on Pope's character-sketches.)
   16. Feb. 16, 1733, *Corr.* III, 347. The composition dates
of the *Ep. to Cob.* have never been precisely determined. All
that is certain is that Pope sent Cobham a near-final draft
in Nov., 1733, two months before publications and that Cobham had seen a "brouillion" of it sometimes earlier (*Corr.*,
III, 391). But a letter of April of the same year may provide a more precise date: "I have but last week finished
another of my Epistles, in the order of the system" (*Corr.*,
III, 366). While the epistle referred to cannot be identified certainly as the poem to Cobham, the identification is
plausible. At this time Pope had not yet acknowledged the
Essay on Man to Swift and he had already reported the completion of the *Ep. to a Lady* two months earlier.
   17. This allusion to Bacon occurs in "The Design" to the
Essay on Man, first published with the poem in April, 1734.
   18. Pope refers to the eventual *Essay on Man*, and perhaps
some or all of the *Epistles to Several Persons*, in these terms
in a letter to Swift of Nov. 28, 1729, *Corr.*, III, 81.
   19. Milton's inhibiting effect on 18th-century poetry has
been discussed by Walter Jackson Bate, *The Burden of the Past
and the English Poet* (Cambridge, Mass., 1970), and Harold Bloom,
The Anxiety of Influence (New York, 1973).
   20. It might also be argued that this premise is relevant
to the external perspective of much traditional satire; see
Martin Price, *To the Palace of Wisdom* (Carbondale, Ill., 1964),
pp. 16-17.
   21. For Pope's adoption of Montaigne's essay, "*De l'incon-
stance de nos actions*," see Spence, I, 142, and Bateson, p. 16n.
As is often the case, Charron echoes Montaigne closely in
arguing that one "can have no true Judgment made of him, but
from what he does in private and alone .... We must know his
Temper and usual department, for all the rest is Fiction and
Constraint" (I, 478); Charron's conclusion is categorical:

"For the Motive and Cause is the Life and Soul of all, and
gives both Being and Denomination to the whole Action. This
is the only mark we have to judge by" (II, 50; cf. I, 12,
164, 328-329; II, 2-3, 48-49). Rochefoucauld's distinction
between deeds and intentions--"Though an Action be never so
Glorious in it self, it ought not to pass for Great, if it
be not the Effect of Wisdom and good Design" (p. 42, max.
clxi)--suggests both the suspicion of heroic narratives and
the tendency toward intentional psychology in more religious writers. Nicole speaks of the "infinite number of hidden notions and considerations" which may lie behind actions
(I, 311-312; cf. III, 123-124); Esprit criticizes the "Lev-
ity of judging" displayed by most observers (and particularly the recorders of "heroic" actions) who do not "dive into
the hidden cause of humane Actions" (Preface to *Discourses*,
sig. A4); and Law's character-sketches are offered as case
studies in the "*chief* and *ruling* tempers" dominating the inner life of his exempla (pp. 13-14, and especially Chapters
III, VII-IX, XIII).
    22. *Ep. to Bath.*, 116. The subject of greed is revivified
in other ways as well, particularly through a "subtler language" which combines Horatian observation and Christian
homily. See Earl R. Wasserman, *Pope's "Epistle to Bathurst": A
Critical Reading with an Edition of the Manuscripts* (Baltimore,
1960), pp. 11-55.
    23. Spence, I, 130.
    24. Bloom's "Manifesto to Antithetical Criticism" consti-
tutes a brief "interchapter" in *The Anxiety of Influence*.
    25. Spence, I, 131-132.

EHRENPREIS, The Cistern and the Fountain: Art and Reality
in Pope and Gray
    1. Preface to *Love of Fame, The Universal Passion* (London,
1728), sig. A2.
    2. In both the life of Pope and the review of Soame
Jenyns.
    3. Particularly in the Preface to the edition of Shake-
speare.
    4. Empson in *Seven Types of Ambiguity*, Leavis in *Revaluation*,
Strachey in *Pope*.
    5. "Rhetoric and the Appreciation of Pope," MP, XXXVII
(1939), 13-35.
    6. For these identifications see F. W. Bateson's edition
of Pope's *Epistles to Several Persons* (III, pt. ii, Twickenham
ed.).
    7. Letter of January 18, 1733/4, in Historical Manuscript
Commission, *XV Report*, Appendix, pt. vi, p. 97.
    8. Young, *Universal Passion*, satire VI, p. 155.
    9. For my discussion of the metaphors drawn from paint-
ing I am indebted to Jean H. Hagstrum's *The Sister Arts: The
Tradition of Literary Pictorialism and English Poetry from Dryden to
Gray* (Chicago, 1958), pp. 236-40, and to Robert J. Allen's

"Pope and the Sister Arts" in *Pope and His Contemporaries: Essays Presented to George Sherburn*, ed. James A. Clifford and Louis A. Landa (Oxford, 1949), pp. 78-88.

10. See H. M. Margoliouth's discussion in his edition of Marvell's *Poems and Letters* (Oxford, 1927), I, 268-70, 289.

11. Young, *Universal Passion*, satire VI, p. 141.

12. Hagstrum, *Sister Arts*, pp. 236-40.

13. *Ibid.*

14. On Pope's interest in painting and his connection with Jervas, see George Sherburn, *The Early Career of Alexander Pope* (Oxford, 1934). For the correspondence between Jervas and Pope, see the first volune of Sherburn's edition of Pope's *Correspondence* (Oxford, 1956). I refer particularly to *The Early Career*, pp. 69 and 102-3; the *Correspondence*, I, 189, 239, 315, 332. See also Morris R. Brownell, *Alexander Pope and the Arts of Augustan England* (Oxford, 1978), pp. 1-67, especially pp. 61-64.

15. See Mr. Bateson's note to I, 107; Pope's *Correspondence*, I, 189, and II, 21-22; and Pope's *Minor Poems*, Twickenham ed., VI, ed. John Butt, 211-12.

16. Bateson, ed., *Epistles to Several Persons*, pp. ix-xvi, 40-44.

17. Charlotte E. Crawford, "What Was Pope's Debt to Edward Young?" *ELH*, XIII (September 1946), 161.

18. Young, *Universal Passion*, satire V, p. 113; satire VI, pp. 155-56. Cf. Crawford, "Pope's Debt," p. 167. The ridicule of the stereotype-maker is also found in the *Epistle to Cobham*, II, 87-92. The end of *To Augustus* is, I suppose, the last refinement of the theme.

19. The reference in l. 198 to "honest Mah'met," a servant to George II, seems intended to strengthen the innuendoes.

20. Cf. Mr. Bateson's comment, p. xlviii, on the accuracy of the poem. Pope's allluions to Martha Blount in his letters, and the contrast he draws between her and Lady Suffolk, are remarkably close to his language in the poem; see his *Correspondence*, III, 349, 434-34, 450, and IV, 187.

21. Young, *Universal Passion*, satire IV, p. 71.

22. *Ibid.*, satire III, p. 49.

23. *Ibid.*, satire III, pp. 54-55.

24. *Ibid.*, satire IV, p. 63.

25. *Ibid.*, satire III, pp. 56-60.

26. Though Gray's influence on Wordsworth hardly wants demonstration--particularly in connection with his taste for mountains--I should like to call attention to the note, in the Selincourt-Darbishire ed. of *The Prelude* (Oxford, 1959), on Book V, ll. 581-601, of the 1805 text.

27. In the life of Gray.

28. Letter of July 2, 1770--the day Gray signed his will.

29. See the sixth paragraph of the 1800 preface and Coleridge's headnote to the poem.

ADEN, That Impudent Satire: Pope's *Sober Advice*

1. **The** poem has been woefully neglected and misjudged.
Omitted from the editions by Warburton (1751) and **E**lwin-
Courthope (1871-89), as well as from Mark Pattison's edition
of the *Satires and Epistles* (1872), it has only recently been
restored to the editorial canon by the Twickenham edition
(1939). To the extent that it has been noticed at all, it
has been regarded variously as an unserious "exercise in
playful ribaldry" (R. K. Root, *The Poetical Career of Alexander
Pope*, Princeton, 1938, p. 240n.), as a "somewhat libidinous"
stratagem to enhance the receptivity of the *Arbuthnot* (R. W.
Rogers, *The Major Satires of Alexander Pope*, Illinois, 1955, p.
71), as "gloriously comic" in its description of bashful
Jenny, but embarrassingly equivocal in its authorial duplicity (G. Tillotson, *Pope and Human Nature*, Oxford, 1958, pp. 117,
222-23), as a "fairly nasty imitation" of Horace's original,
"insinuating and, in the notes if not in the text, pornographic" (Reuben Brower, *Alexander Pope, The Poetry of Allusion*,
Oxford, 1959, p. 293), as "racy," exploring "the perversity
of cultivated lust," but not to "be taken very solemnly"
(Thomas R. Edwards, Jr., *This Dark Estate: A Reading of Pope*,
Berkeley & Los Angeles, 1963, p. 84; see also pp. 100-101),
and, most recently, as "a quickly written *jeu d'esprit*, in
which he [Pope] could blissfully forget about his painfully
created public persona in order to amuse himself, his close
friends, and his readers" (Leonard Moskovit, "Pope's Purposes in *Sober Advice*," *PQ*, XLIV [1965], p. 199). There is no
notice of the poem in W. L. Macdonald'd *Pope and His Critics*
(London, 1951), or, curiously enough, in J. W. Tupper's "A
Study of Pope's Imitations of Horace," *PMLA*, XV (1900), 181-
215.

2. See R. H. Griffith, *Alexander Pope, A Bibliography* (London, 1922, 1962), I, 253 (headnote) and entry No. 347, pp.
262-63. The publication date was 28 December, the publisher
was T. Boreman, and the poem was offered as "Imitated in the
Manner of Mr. Pope." In 1738 T. Cooper reissued it under
the title "A Sermon against Adultery: Being Sober Advice
From Horace ..." (Griffith, No. 507).

3. See George Sherburn, *The Correspondence of Alexander Pope*
(Clarendon Press, 1956), III, 413 n. Italics mine. Other
changes include the omission of the phrases "Sober Advice"
and "Sermon against Adultery," as well as the Bentleyan
footnotes, their place being taken by the removal of the
Latin text from facing pages to the foot of the page. See
Griffith, No. 507.

4. Warburton and Elwin-Courthope. See above, n. 2, and
cf. the "Note on the Text" in the Twickenham edition of the
Imitations of Horace, ed. John Butt (London, 1939), IV, 72.

5. Mid 1734 is Sherburn's dating, from Bolingbroke's
letter to Swift 27 June of that year See *Corr.* III, 413 and
n. 2. It is tempting, however, to associate the composition

with an earlier date, 20 March 1732/3, when Pope wrote to
Caryll, "I've done another of Horace's Satires since I wrote
to you last, and much in the same space of time as I did the
former [*i.e.*, *Sat.* II. i] ...." Sherburn (*Corr.* III, 358, n. 5)
regards this new satire as Horace II. ii ("What, and how
great, the Virtue and the Art"), though Butt (Twickenham ed.,
IV, xxiv), who also takes mid-1734 as the composition date
of S. A., says, "It would be difficult to say which *Imitation*
Pope was referring to; not to [*Sat.* II. ii], one must suppose,
for to this he refers unmistakably as a poem just completed
in a letter to Swift dated April 2, 1733, 'this week, *exer-
citandi gratia*, I have translated, or rather parodied, another
of Horace's, in which I introduce you advising me about my
expenses, housekeeping, &c.'" This letter, which Sherburn
dates 20 April (*Corr.* III, 365), he supposes simply mistakes
the matter, and he maintains that Pope is referring to the
poem announced in the letter to Caryll, *i.e.*, *Sat.* II. ii
(*Corr.* III, 336, n. 6). But there is clearly room for doubt,
and nothing in the evidence precludes the possibility that,
in the letter to Caryll, Pope was referring to *Sober Advice*.
That he would not divulge to Caryll what he later disclaimed
to him is true, but then he did not divulge which of the
satires he had imitated, only that he had imitated another.
That he would be unlikely to let an interval of nearly two
years lapse between composition and publication is no argument either, for he let an interval slightly longer lapse
between the composition and publication of *To a Lady*. The
earlier dating of *Sober Advice* would not only put it closer to
the composition of *To a Lady*, to which it bears interesting
resemblances, but also to Bentley's *Paradise Lost* (1732), his
announced intention of doing an edition of Homer, and his
second trial at Ely House, which was over by April, 1734
(See R. C. Jebb, *Bentley*, Harper, 1902, pp. 115, 145).
   6. Sherburn, *Corr.*, III, 413-14.
   7. *Ibid.*, p. 424 n.
   8. For the quotations from the letters, see *ibid.*, pp.
446, 447, 450, 451. It is instructive to notice, by the
way, the terms Pope applies to the composition as over
against his equivocations about it. He calls it a *satire* (not,
as Mr. Moskovit has terms it, a "libel"), a piece of *poetry*,
a *sermon* (perhaps punningly), and *Ludicrous* (it is "obscene"
only "if you please").
   9. Sherburn, *Corr.* III, 446 n.
  10. Rogers, *Major Satires*, p. 71.
  11. Not only *Satires* II. i and II. ii, but the *Ethic Epistles* as well, are richly laced with lampoon.
  12. *Epistle to Arbuthnot*, vv. 281-82.
  13. For an impressive recent demonstration of this fact,
see Alvin Kernan, *The Cankered Muse* (Yale, 1959).
  14. "Imitation also permitted him to say more daring
things about personalities and institutions than he might
otherwise have ventured to assert in times when authority

was not inclined to tolerate severe criticism: it offered a
convenient evasion in the event of trouble." Rogers, p. 78.

15. *Epilogue to the Satires*, Dialogue ii, vv. 181-84.

16. Judged by the standards of satire, including that of
the eighteenth century, and by comparison with Horace himself, Bolingbroke was more nearly right about Pope's "decency" than the complainants on that score. Beside *est qui /
Inguen ad obscaenum subductis usque facetus* (vv. 25-26) bashful
Jenny with her "Fore-Buttocks," which have scandalized many,
though they pleased Tillotson, seems decent enough after
all. Pope will retain, as his age was wont, Horace's *permin-
xerunt* (Horace, 44; Pope, 56), but he tones down *Accidit, ut
cuidam* TESTIS, CAUDAMQUE SALACEM ..." (45) to "One bleeds
in Person" (58). He has Horatian authority (*mutonis*) for
"that honest Part that rules us all" (87), and he renders
cunnum by the popular and yet decently ambiguous term "Thing."
His "rise" (88), latent in the idea of *muto*, gains additional
support from Horace's *mea cum conferbuit ira* (also rendered,
later, by "Or when my pulse beat highest," v. 91). The embellishment of Horace's *Quid responderet? Magno patre nata puella
est* (72)--put in terms of venereal embarrassment--is characteristically witty, not smutty: "What would you answer?
Could you have the Face, / When the poor Suff'rer humbly
mourn'd his Case, / To cry 'You weep the Favours of her
GRACE?" (93-95). In the passage which follows (96-105) he
elaborates Horace's "moral" and ventures another metaphor
for *muto* --"God's good Thing." Horace's *dum futuo* (127) is
given the perfectly decent expression "in the Fact." We
shall have further ocaasion, in the text, to see how Pope
translates Horace's blunt Latin into witty periphrasis. As
for the Bentleyan footnotes, Professor Moskovit has admirably met the objection that these are pornographic. By the
token of the *persona* there represented, these notes, as he
shows (pp. 198-99), belong not to Pope, but to the pedant,
to whom they are altogether appropriate.

17. *An Essay on Man* (Twickenham edition, ed. Maynard Mack),
pp. 7-8.

18. Rogers, p. 52. Brower (p. 207 ff) differs with Rogers' view of the *Essay on Man* as Lucretian, insisting rather
upon its affinity with the "Horatian diatribe-epistle."

19. Cf. Rogers, p. 58, and F. W. Bateson, ed., *Epistles to
Several Person* (Twickenham), p. xxi.

20. See Rogers, pp. 38-39.

21. See n. 5, above.

22. If we count the adaptation of Donne's Fourth Satire
("The Impertinent"), along with *Qui fit, Maecenas* and *Unde et
quo Catius*, which Pope told Spence (*Anecdotes*, ed. S. W.
Singer, 1820, pp. 297-98) he had imitated or translated before *Sat.* II. i, but which have not survived, Pope imitated
only seven of Horace's eighteen satires: I.i (lost), ii
(*Sober Advice*), ix ("The Impertinent") and II.i (*Sunt quibus in
satura*), ii (*Quae Virtus et quanta*), iv (lost), and vi (*Hoc erat*

in votis: in part only, and in the manner of Swift).

23. *Cobham* is perhaps too close to *An Essay on Man*, from
which it takes its more nearly abstract stance and manner.
See Bateson's remarks, Twickenham ed., p. xxxiv. It is this
difference, and the greater likeness to the *Epistle to a Lady*,
which incline me, along with other reasons, to favor an
earlier date for the composition of *Sober Advice*.

24. All quotations from the poem are taken from the Twickenham text, ed. John Butt. This line, incidentally, and its
idea are very nearly repeated in *To a Lady*, v. 113: "Woman
and Fool are two hard things to hit." The basic formula recurs in Cobham (v. 183): "Women and Fools must like him or
he dies." Here is another argument for the kinship of these
poems.

25. It should be remarked, however, that in respect of
status some of Pope's women in *Sober Advice* may hark from a
different inspiration than *To a Lady*. One suspects that Moll
(and Jack), Peg and Jenny derive from the lower world of
Swift's burlesque and lampoon. Cf. "They keep at Stains the
old blue Boar, / Are Cat and Dog, and Rogue and Whore."
("The Progress of Love," vv. 99-100, in *The Poems of Jonathan
Swift*, ed. Harold Williams, 2nd edition, 1958, I, 225).

26. He addressed *Sober Advice* "To the Young Gentlemen about
Town."

27. I am aware that in the last analysis substance and
form are inseparable, but I distinguish them for convenience
of discussion.

28. Moskovit (*op. cit.*, p. 197) criticizes the adaptation
for neglecting "unity of theme and logical continuity," ob-
jecting that the opening section (vv. 1-26), "with its prevailing topic of avarice combined with female sexual promiscuity, has little to do with the remainder of the poem, which
deals with foolish or harmful extremes in satisfying male
sexual passion." Pope, he thinks, starts off with "an obviously creative technique of imitation," from which he declines
into "a nearly translational one." It is already apparent
that I disagree with such a view. The femininizing of Horace's opening is not only consistent in the ways I have remarked above, but also (and partly for those reasons) with
the poem itself, as a whole. Here is a foretaste of the
"big game" (*matronam*) which Horace and Pope rebuke us for so
foolishly and rashly aspiring to when we would be safer and
therefore saner to content ourselves with "Frigates of the
second Rate." Women--high or low--are, after all, what it
is all about. And avarice, as much as lust, is a part of
their culpability in the crime. Pope displays, in reality,
a high level of sophistication and sense of design in his
adaptation; and, as I hope to show, a great deal of wit in
rendering his poem something more than a mere translation.

29. Moskovit has remarked a number of Pope's adaptations:
op. cit., pp. 195-96, 198. To his citations of Pope's partic-
ularizations of Horace may be added these: *hoc genus omne*--"all

the Court ... and half the Town" (3); *hic, ille, hunc* (41-44)
--"Monsieur" and "good Sir *George*" (53, 55); *quid vis tibi,*
etc. (69)--"Sir *Robert!* or Sir *Paul!*" (88); *Altera* --Mother
Needham's (133); *Cantat*--"as *Sucklyn* sings" (139). Substitu-
tions are many, as already noted, including, in addition,
Bathurst (158) for *Philodemus* and Liddel, Jefferys, and
Onslow (178) for *Fabio*.

30. Does Pope, in addition, play upon the first word of
Horace's *cur atque parentis* for Con's opening exclamation, "A
sneaking Dog I hate?"

31. V. 129. Cf. the annotation recorded in the Twickenham ed., p. 85: "a famous Stay-maker of this name [Cozens]
... stiffens the *double entendre* here meant...." It ought not
to go unremarked, either than in this line Pope gives us an
Alexandrine to go with the "obstacles by dozens" of the preceding line.

32. Vv. 39-44. Cf. Swift's "An Excellent New Ballad" on
the same subject (*Poems*, ed. Harold Williams, II, 516 ff.).

33. *Monsieur* is, of course, the 18th century Rémond, and
Sir George, presumably, Sir G. Oxenden. See Twickenham ed.,
pp. 79-80, notes.

34. V. 62. Italics mine. Maritime imagery for the sex
and for sexual activity is common in Restoration comedy. Cf.
Ariana and Gatty, of Courtall and Freeman, in Etherege's
She wou'd if she cou'd, II, i, 73 ff. Also the sailing metaphor
in Vanbrugh's *Relapse*, III, ii. And Mirabell's classic des-
cription of the entry of Millamant, *The Way of the World*, II, v.
For the word *frigate* as applied to a woman, see, *s.v.*, Eric
Partridge, *Dictionary of Slang and Unconventional English*, 1961.

35. For Charles' habit of judging with his own eyes, see,
e.g., the *Mémoires de la Vie du Comte de Gramont*. For further instances of the Restoration accent in *Sober Advice*, see n. 16,
above.

36. See *scut* in Eric Partridge, *Shakespeare's Bawdy* (Dutton
Paperback, 1960).

37. Twickenham ed., p. 86 n.

38. Vv. 151-52. Horace's own *tentigine* (118) seems susceptible of double meaning.

39. Other, less witty and in some cases less certain,
doubles entendres occur in vv. 9 ("pay'd it down"), 74 ("draw
him in"), 81 ("push'd ... on"), 86 ("shut out ... let in"),
147-48 (*re* the "flowing Bowl?"), 150 ("Bedford-head" = bed's
head?), 175 ("deep Tranquility"), and 177 ("the Dev'll in
Hell").

SCHONHORN, Pope's *Epistle to Augustus*: Notes toward a Mythology

1. Aubrey L. Williams, *Pope's "Dunciad"* (London, 1955), p.
142.

2. The *locus classicus* of this approach to Pope is Professor
Earl Wasserman's review of the first volume of the Twickenham Pope, *PQ*, XLI (1962), 616-622. See also his "The Limits

of Allusion in *The Rape of the Lock*," *JEGP*, LXV (1966), 425–
444; David R. Hauser, "Pope's Lodona and the Uses of Mythology," *SEL*, VI (1966), 465–482; Jay Arnold Levine, "Pope's
Epistle to Augustus, Lines 1–30," *SEL*, VII (1967), 427–451.
Professor Levine also remarks about the degree of Pope's
subtlety: "Pope had to observe consummate delicacy in order
to protect himself..." (p. 428).

  3. The unusual number of notes in *To Augustus* should have
invited critical suspicion earlier; there are twenty-one in
all, a surprising increase over the one and three which
Pope's readers found in his Horatian imitations published
before and after *To Augustus* in May, 1737. *The Second Epistle
of the Second Book*, published in April, has only two, though
Pope added another to the 1738 reprint; *The Sixth Epistle of the
First Book*, published Jan. 1738, has one. Even the carefully
shaped *Epistle to Arbuthnot*, with its fourteen glosses--I am
counting those in the first edition of 1734--falls much below the number in *To Augustus*, and the former's are more in
the nature of proofs of the scurrilous falsehood of Pope's
libelling enemies, whereas the latter's, as I will try to
show, are of a different order.

  4. Citations are from *Imitations of Horace*, The Twickenham
Edition, ed. John Butt, 2nd ed. (London, 1953).

  5. E. K. Broadus, *The Laureateship* (Oxford, 1921), Ch. I.

  6. See Dryden's comments in *Essays*, ed. W. P. Ker (New
York, 1961), II, 260. Pope's own parody of the celebration
and his ridicule of the titleholder in 1729 rise above the
comic precisely because he is aware of the ritualistic importance of the institution; see his "Of the Poet Laureate," in
The Dunciad, The Twickenham Edition, ed. James Sutherland, V,
412–417.

  7. For the political content of the poem, see Levine,
and Manuel Schonhorn, "The Audacious Contemporaneity of Pope's
Epistle to Augustus," *SEL*, VIII (1968), 431–443.

  8. *The Dunciad*, ed. Sutherland, V, 294n. There is also an
epigram on laureates attributed to Pope, printed in the
octavo edition of the *Dunciad* of 1743, which strengthens this
contemporary response to the Devil Tavern: "When Laureates
make Odes, do you ask of what sort? / Do you ask if they're
good, or are evil? / You may judge--From the Devil they come
to the Court, / And go from the Court to the Devil." See
Minor Poems, The Twickenham Edition, ed. Norman Ault and John
Butt, VI, 402.

  9. Broadus, *The Laureateship*, p. 43n. It might be noted
that Davenant occupies a significant place in Pope's sketch
for the history of English poetry; see *The Works of Thomas Gray*,
ed. T. J. Matthias (London, 1814), II, vii.

  10. For Eusden and Settle, see the Biographical Appendix
of *Imitations of Horace*, IV, 359, 385; for Philips, see my note
in *N&Q*, n.s. XIV (1967), 406–407.

  11. *Fog's Journal*, Dec. 6, 1735, reprinted in the *London Magazine*, IV (1735), 663.

12. *Works of Alexander Pope*, ed. Joseph Warton (London, 1797),
IV, 148n.
13. I am not unaware of the ambiguities in the contemporary use of Augustus or Augustan; see Levine, pp. 428-434;
and J. W. Johnson, "The Meaning of 'Augustan,'" *JHI*, XIX
(1959), 507-522.
14. *The World of Pope's Satires* (London, 1968), pp. 2-3.
15. For Swift's delighted comment on the gift of these
lines, see *Correspondence of Alexander Pope*, ed. George Sherburn
(Oxford, 1956), IV, 56.
16. Justice and Mercy as attributes of monarchy are other
commonplaces of the age. See, for example, James I, *The Trew
Law of Free Monarchies*, in *Workes* (London, 1616), p. 194; Ben
Jonson, *Discoveries*, in *Works*, ed. C. H. Herford and P. & E.
Simpson (Oxford, 1947), VIII, 600. Also Edward O. Smith, Jr.,
"The Elizabethan Doctrine of the Prince as Reflected in the
Sermons of the Episcopacy, 1559-1603," *HLQ*, XXVIII (1964),
1-17. Especially important for my developing argument would
be the goddess Astraea seen as a combination of Justice and
Mercy; see Sir John Davies, *Hymnes to Astraea*, in *Complete Poems*,
ed. A. B. Grosart (London, 1876), I, 151. In Pope's "Plan
of a Epic Poem," the Supreme God with whom the second book
begins is also a composite of Justice and Mercy; see *Works of
Alexander Pope*, ed. Warton, IV, 362. It must also be noted
that the projection of Swift as the embodiment of proper
monarchy is supported and enhanced by his possession of the
mystic light of kingship and his obvious similarity to the
Christ-like Man of Ross; see *Epistles to Several Persons*, The
Twickenham Edition, ed. F. W. Bateson, III, ii, 113-116.
17. Donald Torchiana, "Brutus: Pope's Last Hero," *JEGP*,
LXI (1962), 853-867.
18. A. E. Parsons, "The Trojan Legend in England," *MLN*,
XXIV (1929), 256.
19. Aaron Thompson, *The British History, Translated into English
from the Latin of Jeffrey of Monmouth* (London, 1718), p. 24.
While this was the first complete English translation of
Geoffrey's *Historia Regum Britanniae*, there had been a transla-
tion of the prophecies of Merlin from the *Historia* seventy
years earlier; see Charles Bowie Millican, "The First English
Translation of the *Prophecies of Merlin*," *SP*, XXVIII (1931), 720-
729
20. For the backgrounds to the Merlin legend see William
E. Mead's introduction to Henry B. Wheatley, *Merlin, or the
Early History of King Arthur: A Prose Romance* (London, 1899; Early
English Text Society), Vol. I. Friedrich Brie, "Pope's
Brutus," *Anglia*, LXIII (1939), 152, mentions the figure of
Merlin in connection with the Brutus legend. Curiously
there is no mention of the Merlin heritage nor of its func-
tion in the Brutus myth in Professor Torchiana's article
cited above.
21. Ernest Jones, *Geoffrey of Monmouth: 1640-1800*, Univ. of
Cal. Pub. in English, V (1944), 359. The most detailed treat-

ment of Merlin's genesis and prophecies in the *Historia* is
to be found in J. S. P. Tatlock, *The Legendary History of Britain*
(Berkeley and Los Angeles, 1950), Chs. V, XVII. See also
Lucy Alan Paton, "Notes on Merlin in the *Historia Regum Britan-
niae* of Geoffrey of Monmouth," MP, XLI (1943), 88-95, which
details the distinctive British quality of Geoffrey's seer.
"The credit of really introducing the political prophecy into
England belongs to Geoffrey" (Rupert Taylor, *The Political
Prophecy in England* [New York, 1911], p. 8).
    22. Cola di Rienzo, *Epistolario*, ed. A. Gabrielli (Rome,
1890), pp. 120, 126, 131, 210, cited in Frances Yates, "Queen
Elizabeth as Astraea," *Journal of the Warburg and Courtauld Institutes*,
X (1947), 36.
    23. For Merlin in the *Faerie Queene*, see Book III, Canto
iii; Book I, Canto x. Also Edwin Greenlaw, *Studies in Spenser's
Historical Allegory* (Baltimore, 1932); and Roberta Brinkley,
Arthurian Legend in the Seventeenth Century (Baltimore, 1932), Ch.
I.
    24. *Arthurian Legend*, p. 6. Miss Brinkley cites a number of
contemporary texts on pp. 7 and 9 which assert James as the
actual fulfillment and consummation of the prophecies of
Merlin.
    25. Jones, *Geoffrey of Monmouth*, pp. 376, 377, 359; Brinkley,
Arthurian Legend, pp. 55, 74.
    26. James Westfall Thompson, *A History of Historical Writing*
(New York, 1942), I, 626-627. See also Philip Styles,
"Politics and Historical Research in the Early Seventeenth
Century," in *English Historical Scholarship in the Sixteenth and
Seventeenth Centuries*, ed. Levi Fox (London, 1956), pp. 55-56.
    27. Brinkley, *Arthurian Legend*, pp. 79, 80.
    28. See Dryden's Dedication to Halifax in *Works*, ed. Scott-
Saintsbury (London, 1884), VIII, 129-130. Note Scott's
surmise, VIII, 127: "We may therefore conclude that the
piece, as originally written, had a strong political tendency, and probably abounded with these ingenious parallels by
which Dryden, with dexterity far exceeding that of every
other writer, could draw, from remote or distant events, a
moral directly applicable to those of his own time."
    29. Dryden, "A Discourse Concerning the Original and Pro-
gress of Satire," in *Essays*, ed. Ker, II, 38.
    30. *Works*, ed. Scott-Saintsbury, VIII, 193. For echoes of
the lines of Philidel, the "Airy Spirit" in *King Arthur*, in
Pope, see *The Rape of the Lock*, The Twickenham Edition, ed.
Geoffrey Tillotson, II, 78. I owe this note to Reuben A.
Brower, "Dryden and the 'Invention' of Pope," in *Restoration
and Eighteenth-Century Literature. Essays in Honor of Alan Dugald
McKillop*, ed. Carroll Camden (Rice University, 1963), p. 219.
    31. See, for example, Richard Blackmore, *Prince Arthur*
(London, 1695), pp. 150-153. Blackmore's Christianizing of
the Virgilian epic form and the Geoffrey materials precludes
any use of Merlin and necromancy. Not ghosts or pagan magi-
cians but the angels Raphael and Gabriel speak to Arthur, to

support him in his Aeneas-like, Brutus-like wanderings, and
to prophesy his return to Albion-England and the throne;
see pp. 16, 115. Prior, in a New Year's Ode to William,
propels the Star of Nassau to a classical pantheon of illustrious forebears which includes Aeneas, "Sire of the LATIAN,
and the BRITISH Throne..." (*The Literary Works of Matthew Prior*,
ed. H. Bunker Wright and Monroe K. Spears [Oxford, 1959], I,
181).

32. See, for example, Prior, "An Ode, Humbly Inscrib'd
to the Queen. On the Glorious Success of Her Majesty's Arms,
1706" in *Works*, Wright-Spears ed., I, 231, 239-240.

33. "A Famous Prediction of Merlin, the British Wizard,"
in *Prose Writings*, ed. Herbert Davis (Oxford, 1957), II, 165-
170. There is no indication that Johnson was aware that it
was a hoax. See *Letters of Samuel Johnson*, ed. R. W. Chapman
(Oxford, 1952), II, 384; *Lives of the Poets*, ed. G. B. Hill
(Oxford, 1905), III, 14. See also the editor's note to
"Merlin" in *Poems of Jonathan Swift*, ed. Harold Williams, 2nd
ed. (Oxford, 1958), I, 102.

34. For example: "477, the *British Merline* now wrote," one
of the important dates since the creation of the world,
cited in *Perkins: A New Almanack For the Year of Our Lord God, 1734*.
It might also be noted that Jeremy Collier's "corrected and
enlarged" edition of Moreri's *Great Historical, Geographical,
Geneological and Poetical Dictionary* (London, 1701; 2nd ed. rev.)
includes a citation to Merlin, which disputes the credulous
and skeptical approach and points the reader to Geoffrey's
Elizabethan supporters. Moreri's monumental *Dictionary* was
cited by Prior in 1721 as a kind of general handbook of
knowledge which a common reader could easily consult (*Works*,
Wright-Spears ed., I, 589; II, 1008). To turn to the end of
the century, the lengthy chronology of significant dates at
the end of the 1773 3dition of the famous Robert Ainsworth
English-Latin Dictionary also notes: "477 *Merlinus* Britannicus."

35. *The London Stage: 1660-1800, Part 3: 1729-1747*, ed. Arthur H.
Scouten (Carbondale, 1961), I, 440. I have not seen a copy
of Theobald's pantomine but there is a notice of publication
in the Monthly Catalogue for December of the *London Magazine*,
III (1734), 671.

36. (London, 1735).

37. "In 1733, Queen Caroline set up a grotto in the Royal
Hermitage as a sort of scientific hall of fame, in which the
busts of Newton, Locke, Boyle, Wollaston, and Samuel Clark
were placed to remind visitors of the achievements of science
and physico-theology," William Powell Jones, *The Rhetoric of
Science* (Berkeley, 1966), pp. 99-100.

38. *Gentleman's Magazine*, V (1735), 331.

39. For these debates between the *Craftsman* and the government dailies, see the *Gentleman's Magazine*, V (1735), 498, 532-
535, 660, 671, 715-716. For accounts of Merlin in the *Faerie
Queene* see the *Gentleman's Magazine*, V (1735), 660; and the

London Magazine, IV (1735), 608. In addition, the *Gentleman's Magazine*, V (1735), 671, gave the account of Merlin from Harrington's *Orlando Furioso*, noting that fables of his life and death were difficult to believe, "But concerning his Life, that there was such a Man, a great Counsellor of K. *Arthur*, I hold it certain...." For the view that the glory of George's reign eclipsed that of the Augustan Age, see the pro-Government *Daily Gazetteer* article reprinted in the *Gentleman's Magazine*, VI (1736), 81.

40. See Jane Brereton, *Merlin: A Poem* (London, 1735); and John Nixon, *Merlin: A Poem* (London, 1736). I am indebted to Prof. David Foxon of Oxford University for aid in locating these poems. "Merlin's Prophecy" from Brereton's poem was reprinted in the March 1736 issue of the *Gentleman's Magazine*, VI, 160. Nixon's poem was given a bathetic restatement in prose in the *Grub Street Journal* for March 11, 1736. I should also point out that the prophecies of Merlin were given immediate and wide circulation by Curll with the publication of *The Rarities of Richmond*, which also contained Thomas Heywood's *Life of Merlin*, published in 1641. Curll's volume was advertised as published in Nov. 1735; see the *Gentleman's Magazine*, V (1735), 684.

41. *The London Stage*, I, lxxxiii-lxxxiv; cxxi-cxxii. Thomas Gray, detailing the London theatrical season to Horace Walpole, spends the greater part of his letter on *King Arthur*; see *The Correspondence of Gray, Walpole, West, and Ashton*, ed. Paget Toynbee (Oxford, 1915), I, 57-59.

42. The additional speeches are explained as "ALTERATIONS upon the Revival of this OPERA" (*Merlin: or, The British Inchanter* [London, 1736], p. 34).

43. *Ibid.*

44. *Ibid.*

45. Sig. A3v.

46. "Secretum Iter," in *Aspects of the Eighteenth Century*, ed. Earl Wasserman (Baltimore, 1965), p. 209.

47. See, for example, Blackmore, *Prince Arthur*, p. xii: "And tho' the above-cited Geofrey of Monmouth is indeed a Fabulous Author, yet his Authority, especially considering that there was such a War like Prince as Arthur is a sufficient Foundation for an Epick Poem." Cf. Prior: "*That this* BRUTE, *Fourth or Fifth from* AENEAS, *settled in* ENGLAND, *and built* LONDON, *which he call'd* Troja Nova, *or* Troynovante, *is a Story which* (I think) *owes it's Original if not to* GEOFFRY *of* Monmouth, *at least to the* Monkish *Writers; yet is not rejected by Our great* CAMDEN, *and is told by* MILTON, *as if* (at least) *He was pleas'd with it; though possibly He does not believe it: However it carries a Poetical Authority, which is sufficient for our Purpose. It is as certain that* BRUTE *came into* ENGLAND, *as that* AENEAS *went into* ITALY; *and upon the Supposition of these Facts,* VIRGIL *wrote the best Poem that the World ever read, and* SPENSER *paid Queen* ELIZABETH *the greatest Compliment*" (Works, Wright-Spears ed., I, 231). See also Jacob, *Brutus the Trojan*, sig. A5r.

48. *Correspondence*, I, 425. Pope's fragment can be read in *Minor Poems*, VI, 404.

49. John Nichols, *Literary Anecdotes of the Eighteenth Century* (London, 1812), VI, 13. Gay was instrumental in this action of Oct. 1728; see *Anecdotes*, VI, 84n, 106.

50. Schonhorn, "Audacious Contemporaneity." Significantly, two serious defenses of Geoffrey were published immediately before Pope's imitation: Francis Hutchinson, *A Defense of the Antient Historians, with a Particular Application of it to the History of Ireland and Great Britain* (Dublin, 1734); and Francis Drake, *Eboracum: or, The History and Antiquities ... of York* (London, 1736). Hutchinson catalogues a good deal of support, mostly ecclesiastical, for the reality of Brutus and the reliability of Geoffrey; see pp. 38-39, 91-95. Copious extracts from his preface were read by Londoners in *The Present State of the Republick of Letters* for Dec. 1734. Giffard's *Merlin*, I should note here, was chosen to begin the 1736 theatrical season at Lincoln's Inn Fields and was staged four more times before the end of the year (*London Stage*, II, 602-604; 625-626).

51. *The Breaking of the Circle* (New York, 1962), p. 92.

52. Frances Yates, "Queen Elizabeth As Astraea," p. 32. A summary of the legend of Astraea and the myth of the Golden Age can be found in Arthur O. Lovejoy and George Boas, *A Documentary History of Primitivism and Related Ideas* (Baltimore, 1935), I, Ch. ii.

53. Tatlock, *Legendary History*, pp. 403-418. See also Edmond Faral, *La Legende Arthurienne* (Paris, 1929), II, 49-67.

54. Brinkley, *Arthurian Legend*, p. 12. Of extreme significance is the merging of Astraea and British prophecy in a pageant play produced by the students of Gray's Inn in 1588; see *The Misfortunes of Arthur*, Tudor Facsimile Texts (London, 1911). I owe this citation to Miss Yates's article. British prophecy, Merlin, and "The golden veine of SATVRNES age" come together also in Jonson's *Speeches at Prince Henry's Barriers*, in *Works*, ed. Herford-Simpson, VII, 323-336.

55. Sees H. T. Swedenberg, Jr., "England's Joy: *Astraea Redux* in its Setting," *SP*, L (1953), 30-44.

56. *Works*, Scott-Saintsbury ed., VII, 239. It is worth noting that in this retrospective review of a golden age restored to England, the verse on the title page and inscribed on the stage frontispiece over the figure of the King is from *Aeneid*, VI, 620, a central passage in the section describing Aeneas' descent into Hades where he hears Anchises' prophecy of the coming reign of Augustus and an age of gold.

57. *Ibid.*, VII, 256.

58. *Ibid.*, VII, 281.

59. See, for example, Prior, "A Pindarique on His Majesties Birth-Day" (*Works*, Wright-Spears ed., I, 96-98). Prior's *Carmen Seculare, For the Year 1700. To the King*, which was sung before William on New Year's Day, 1700, not only re-

peats the legend on Astraea's return in William's reign but
is introduced with an epigraph from Virgil's Eclogue IV, of
the revival of Saturnian times and a coming age of gold
(*Works*, I, 161, 170). Three years later, with the accession
of Anne, the same Eclogue was translated to exult in the
death of Whiggish influence in the Church and the return of
a High Church progeny ushering in a different age of gold;
see *The Golden Age from the Fourth Eclogue of Virgil* (London, 1703).
There is a note on this poem by A. J. Sambrook, "William
Walsh and *The Golden Age from the Fourth Eclogue of Virgil* (1703),"
MP, LXIV (1967), 324-325. Nearly all of the seventeenth-
century translations of the Eclogue talk about the "blest
Maid" but Astraea is specifically named by Joseph Warton in
his translation; see Christopher Pitt, *Virgil's Works Translated*
(London, 1753), I, 89. For the ease with which the connection could be made in George I's reign see the *Weekly Journal:*
or, British Gazetteer, Sept. 21, 1723 (p. 2662).
    60. *A Translation of the Second Book of HORACE's Epistles* ... (Dub-
lin, 1731), sigs. A2v-Blr.
    61. Brereton, *Merlin*, p. 10. The reader should not over-
look the persistent reinforcement of the whole Astraea-Gold-
en Age idea not only via the translations and close imitations of the Virgil poems but in the incidental productions
of obscure writers of the day; for example, the Poetical
Essays column of the *London Magazine* for June 1735 has a poem
by J. W. on "The Golden Age," asking for a return to happier
times and a reforming spirit for the ills of the present day.
    62. It should be unnecessary to recall here the signifi-
cant use to which Pope put the myth of Astraea nd the coming
of a Golden Age in his *Messiah. A Sacred Eclogue, in Imitation of
Virgil's Pollio*. And one should not overlook the Messianic
culmination of *Windsor Forest*, with its ecstatic vision of the
return of Justice and Peace in Anne's time. See Hauser,
"Pope's Lodona and the Uses of Mythology." Perhaps our growing awareness of Pope's classical and Renaissance orientation
and the mythopoeic nature of his poetry will enable us to see
that his mythic patterns in their infinity variety are the
soul and form of his work. Pope, it would seem, has been
loosely lumped with his Augustan mimics in recent mythic examinations of the age's literature. See, for example,
Douglas Bush, *Science and English Poetry* (New York, 1950), p.
80; and Albert J. Kuhn's unpublished dissertation, "Conceptions of Mythology and their Relations to English Literature,
1700-1830" (Johns Hopkins Univ., 1954), pp. 2-3, 11, which
dismisses the Augustan sensibility when confronted with mythic referents.

GABRINER, Pope's "Virtue" and the Events of 1738
    1. Joseph Warton, in the 1797 ed. of Pope's *Works*, thought
this passage "perhaps the noblest ... in all his works, without any exception whatever" (IV, 317). W. L. Bowles, Pope's
next editor, was of the opinion that "more dignified and im-

pressive numbers, more lofty indignation, more animated appeals, and more rich personifications never adorned the page of the Satiric Muse" (*Works* [London, 1806], IV, 334). W. J. Courthope considered that "the splendid picture of the Triumph of Vice (reaches) ... the highest pitch of indignation" (*Works* [London, 1881], III, 453), and John Butt, Pope's most recent editor, terms the passage "one of the grandest ... of his later poetry" (*Twickenham Ed.* [London, 1939], IV, xxxix).

2. Details of the poem's first appearance are cited in R. H. Griffith, *Alexander Pope, a Bibliography* (Austin, Texas, 1927), no. 484--hereafter listed in the text as *Griffith.*

3. The leading figures of the day amused themselves filling in the blanks and margins with the correct names in their copies of Pope, some of which survive. Elwin transcribed the following memorandum taken from Lord Orrery's copy of Pope: "Whatever names appear here in manuscript were never communicated by the author, but are merely the guess work of idle hours, and may be deemed the echoes and recoils of busy town whispers" (*The Works of Alexander Pope*, ed. William John Courthope and Whitwell Elwin [London, 1881], III, 18). Of "Dialogue I" Courthope wrote in 1881 that "this satire requires to be read very carefully, as almost every phrase has a double allusion, and the marvellous skill of the workmanship is only appreciated when the irony is thoroughly understood." Butt, above (IV, xxxix), reminds us of Pope's conviction that general satire is useless, and that living examples must be made if reform is to be effected.

4. Pope himself added the title "Epilogue to the Satires" to both "Dialogues" in 1740. See Butt, IV, 94, above.

5. George Sherburn, ed., *The Correspondence of Alexander Pope* (Oxford, 1956), IV, 178, May 17-19, 1739--hereafter cited as *Corr.* After 1738, Pope's writing was confined to some minor pieces, an unpublished fragment entitled "One Thousand Seven Hundred and Forty," and the revisions and additions used in the final *Dunciad* of 1743.

6. James M. Osborn, "Pope, The Byzantine Empress, and Walpole's Whore," *Review of English Studies*, VI (1955), 372-82. Osborn's statement that "in a memorandum of a conversation with Pope in 1756, Spence recorded that Phryne ... was a jibe at 'Miss Skerrett'" (p. 375), is probably inaccurately punctuated. The memorandum may have been jotted down by Spence in 1756, but Pope had died twelve years earlier.

7. Osborn suggests the allusion was probably "passed by unrecognized by the general public but caviare to the 'cognoscenti'," p. 379.

8. In a note to the "Epistle to Dr. Arbuthnot" in the *Twickenham Ed.* Butt agrees with Courthope that Warburton on very doubtful authority titled "Arbuthnot" the "Prologue to the Satires;" the natural candidate both in chronology and content for this distinction is the "First Satire of the Second Book."

9. See Pope's letter to John Caryll, Sept. 27, 1732, where he writes that his studies are directed toward a good end, "the advancement of moral and religious vertue, and the discouragement of vicious and corrupt hearts" (*Corr.* III, 316). The *Essay on Man* deals with vice and virtue only in terms of ethical philosophy.

10. Henry St. John, Viscount Bolingbroke, is the "Statesman out of Place" of l. 126 and the "*St. John*" of l. 127. A chief minister under Queen Anne, he allied himself with the Pretender at her death, and with the advent of the Hanoverians was banished by an Act of Attainder that was partially repealed in 1723, when he was allowed to return to his estates from France, though barred from Parliament. His influence on Pope was very great, particularly during the 1730's, when the *Essay on Man* and the Horatian poems were written. The "Chief out of War" (l. 126) is Charles Mordaunt, 3rd Earl of Peterborough, Pope's fellow gardening-enthusiast who, although not active politically, was responsible for military successes in Spain that glorified Bolingbroke's ministry under Anne. Pope's "Grotto," an underground chamber beneath the Twickenham road that divided his property, was the object of much aesthetic attention; Pope stocked it with rare minerals from all over the British isles. In the early 1730's the Grotto became an Opposition meeting place, which function Pope memorialized in verses sent to Bolingbroke in Sept., 1740. For the significance of the Grotto to Pope as a poet, see further Chapter 2, "The Shadowy Cave," of Maynard Mack's *The Garden and the City: Retirement and Politics in the Later Poetry of Pope*, 1731-1743 (Univ. of Toronto Press, 1969).

11. Pope wrote to Swift on Feb. 16, 1733 that the motive of the poem was "about a score of lines towards the latter end, which you will find out" (*Corr.* III, 348). Although he does not specify the lines, the passage quoted above is almost certainly among those intended.

12. Addison Ward, "The Tory View of Roman History," *Studies in English Literature* IV (1964), 413.

13. *The Discourses of Niccolo Machiavelli*, trans. and introd. Leslie J. Walker (London, 1950), I, 101.

14. See J. R. Sutherland, "The Circulation of Newspapers and Literary Periodicals, 1700-30," *The Library*, 4th ser., XV, no. 1. Usage in the 1730's divides "Virtue" into three categories. "Moral virtue" broadly refers to ethics and ethical character. "Publick virtue" usually means spirited political idealism in Opposition (often Parliamentary opposition) to Walpole, while "private virtue" refers to the character and honesty imputed to the personal lives of those so opposed.

15. No. 320, Aug. 19, 1732.

16. *Ibid.* and No. 436, Nov. 9, 1734.

17. No. 413, June 1, 1734. Implicit here is the common view of Walpole, who was reputed to hold as a "general rule, that there is really no such thing as virtue, and that every

man will do every thing, if you will but pay him his price"
(Alexander, Earl of Marchmont to the Earl of Stair, Dec. 10,
1736 in George Henry Rose, ed., *Marchmont Papers* [London, 1831],
II, 76).

18. No. 413, June 1, 1734.

19. *The Discourses of Niccolo Machiavelli*, op. cit., chap. XVII,
p. 257.

20. Henry St. John, Viscount Bolingbroke, *The Idea of a
Patriot King* (1749; rpt. Sydney Jackman, ed., U.S.A., 1965),
p. 39.

21. *Ibid.*

22. *Ibid.*, p. 86.

23. Quoted in Rose Mary Davis, *The Good Lord Lyttleton: A
Study in 18th Century Politics and Culture* (Bethlehem, Pa., 1939),
p. 108--taken from Hagley MSS., I, 208-9.

24. *Corr.*, IV, 424. The letter is addressed to Orrery's
wife.

25. *Ibid.*, 260, Sept. 3, 1740. For a similar example see
Pope to Marchmont, p. 271, Oct., 1740.

26. Horace Walpole, *Letters*, ed. Mrs. Paget Toynbee (Oxford, 1903-5), II, 63.

27. June 30, 1735 and May 17, 1738. Pope's enemy, Lord
Hervey, the Walpole-supporter and court favourite whose *Memoirs* are a chief source for the social and political history
of the period, gives us a very interesting example of the
ministerial view of the then current distinction between
"Virtue" and "Vice." Writing to Henry Fox from St. James'
on Dec. 2, 1735, he reports "My Lord Ch(esterfield) ... says
that his kinsman (Lord Stanhope) is too fond of Greek and
Roman virtue to join the degenerate vices of the majority of
a modern English Senate." He then adds, "There is really
nothing I am so sick of hearing repeated from the lips of
our modern Patriots, as the encomiums upon the wisdom of our
ancestors and the virtue of the Romans. I would be glad to
know for which age of our ancestors they would like to change
the circumstances of the present? Or if they would choose
to have England resemble Rome in the time of what they must
call that of it's great virtue.--that is, when it was miser-
ably poor, without any trade, involved in perpetual wars
abroad, and torn by conflicting factions of the nobility and
commonalty at home. For my own part I like extremely to
read of those times, but to live in these: and think of such
virtue as I do of his Lordship's understanding, that it makes
an excellent figure in words, though it is of small use in
practice" (*Lord Hervey and his Friends*, 1726-38, ed. Earl of Ilchester [London, 1950], p. 242)--yet another example of the
continuing war between the "Moderns" and "Ancients"! An
example of Walpole's vain attempts to wrest the term from the
Opposition is a pamphlet written by one of his hirelings
entitled *The ministerial Virtue; or, Long-Suffering extoll'd in a great
Man*, advertised in the *Gentleman's Magazine* of September, 1738
(Vol. VIII, p. 496)--the date is worth note.

28. Joseph Spence, *Observations, Anecdotes, and Characters of Books and Men: Collected from Conversation*, ed. James M. Osborn (Oxford: Clarendon Press, 1966), I, 143, no. 321a.

29. Pope's "case" had to do with the clamour raised by the portrait of Timon in the "Epistle to Burlington," published in Dec. 1731. Pope was afraid of a similar reaction to the more outspoken "Epistle to Bathurst," which he had suppressed and then published in Jan., 1733, using, as Butt suggests (*Twickenham Ed.*, IV, xiv), the "First Satire of the Second Book" as a "rear-guard" justification of the two.

30. W. T. Laprade, *Public Opinion and Politics in Eighteenth-Century England* (New York, 1936), p. 341. Stair lost his post as a result of this attempt.

31. *Corr.*, III, 372, May 28, 1733.

32. *London Evening Post*, Oct. 4-7, 1735.

33. *Corr.*, IV, 5, March 25, 1736.

34. Pope's March publication was the minor "First Ode of the Fourth Book of Horace, to Venus" (*Griffith* no. 443). Another cause for excitement was the publication in April of Richard Glover's anti-government epic, "Leonidas," which enjoyed an immediate and unparalleled popularity for a poem of its length. Lyttleton, who reviewed it in the April 9, 1737 issue of *Common Sense*, wrote that the "whole Plan and Purpose" of the poem is "to shew the Superiority of Freedom over Slavery; and how much Virtue, Publick Spirit, and the Love of Liberty are preferable both in their Nature and Effects, to Riches, Luxury, and the Insolence of Power." Even Swift, who habitually complained of hearing no "news" from London, wrote Pope to find out something about the "Mr. Glover, who writ the Epic Poem called Leonidas, which is reprinting here, and hath great vogue" (*Corr.*, IV, 72, May 31, 1737). After the Opposition collapse a year later, Glover (1712-85) quickly passed into relative obscurity.

35. Beginning in March the ministry had introduced in the Lords a bill of penalties against the city of Edinburgh for its alleged role in the murder of Capt. Porteus; it was finally sent to the Commons on May 16th, where it was opposed so strenuously that the majority in favour was only six; on June 13th it became law, but only upon the attachment of debilitating amendments (*Cobbett's Parliamentary History* [London, 1811], X, 317, 319--hereafter cited as *Parl. Hist.*); however, the intended irony of the "Epistle to Augustus" seems not to have been noticed.

36. Philip Dormer Stanhope, 4th Earl of Chesterfield, *Letters*, ed. Bonamy Dobree (London, 1932), II, no. 608, Nov. 12, 1737.

37. Laprade, *Public Opinion and Politics*, p. 391.

38. *Marchmont Papers*, pp. 91, 93.

39. Alexander Ewald, *Sir Robert Walpole: A Political Biography, 1676-1745* (London, 1878), p. 323.

40. Harold Williams, ed., *The Correspondence of Jonathan Swift* (Oxford, 1963-5), V, 78, Dec. 6, 1737.

41. Osborn in "Pope, the Byzantine Empress, and Walpole's Whore," cited above, writes that "evidence in the Stuart Papers suggests that about this time Pope was also intriguing with friends of the Pretender" p. 375, n. Further evidence for this contention may be seen in G. H. Jones, "The Jacobites, Charles Molloy, and *Commonsense*," *Review of English Studies*, n.s. IV (1953), 144-7.

42. *Parl. Hist.*, X, 467.

43. *Marchmont Papers*, p. 96.

44. *Ibid.*, p. 98.

45. *Ibid.*

46. *Parl. Hist.*, X, 635.

47. Lyttleton, the "Boy Patriot" leader, had been for months the subject of a heated newspaper "war" in which his "Virtue," figure and debating abilities were the chief points of contention. Pope's phrase, "active in debate," is a partisan blow in this controversy, as is the line "Still true to Virtue, and as warm as true."

48. The court, no less than the ministry which represents it, is suspect: "Adieu to Virtue if you're once a Slave: / Send her to Court, you send her to her Grave" (ll. 118-9).

49. Rev. Henry Paton, ed., *Report on the Manuscripts of the Right Honourable Lord Polwarth*, Vol. V, 1725-1780 (*Historical Manuscripts Commission*   London, 1961), no. 67, document no. 215, March 28, 1738, p. 148.

50. *Parl. Hist.*, X, 727.

51. *Corres.*, IV, 93.

52. *A Collection of the Parliamentary Debates in England* (London, 1741), XVI, 1738-39, pp. 456-7.

53. *Ibid.*, p. 438.

54. *Ibid.*, p. 471.

55. *The Siege of Damascus* , a tragedy.

56. *Marchmond Papers*, II, p. 101.

57. *Parl. Hist.*, X, 867.

58. The poem was "more popular than the bookseller had anticipated and went through three issues, totalling perhaps 4,000 copies, a large initial sale for such a publication" (Griffiths, *Alexander Pope, a Bibliography*, II, ii, 383). Walpole's *Gazetteer*, with a good sense of the poem's timing, political disposition and popularity, devoted the entire front page of its May 26 issue to a long, highly critical review. On May 30th the paper again attacked Pope in a poem which praises Horace at the expense of Pope's imitations. After "Dialogue II" was published, the paper offered to the public a little dialogue of its own in the issue for August 24th: Speaking of Pope, "B." observes: "I thought so virtuous a Person would be of no side, but the Side of Virtue." "A." replies: "He is of the Side of the Patriots:--And is not that the same thing?" As late as May, 1739, Pope could still complain to Swift: "The Ministerial Writers rail at me" (*Corr.*, IV, 178, May 17-19, 1739).

59. *Corr.*, III, 348, Feb. 10, 1733.

60. *Corr.*, IV, 109, July 6, 1738.
61. *Ibid.*, 126, Sept. 8, 1738.
62. *Ibid.*, 142, c. Nov. 1, 1738.
63. *Ibid.*, 165, Feb. 6, 1738/9.
64. *Ibid.*, 169, March 27, 1739.
65. *Ibid.*, 178, May 17-19, 1739.
66. *Ibid.*, 208, Dec. 12, 1739 and 220, Jan. 19, 1739/40.
67. *Ibid.*, 227, Feb. 29, 1739/40. Polwarth is now 3rd Earl of Marchmont, but here Pope still addresses him by his courtesy title.
68. *Ibid.*, 249, June 22, 1740. The dead Tory leader is Sir William Wyndham.
69. *Ibid.*, 257, Aug. 14, 1740. On Sept. 3, however, Pope sent Bolingbroke the commemmorative "Verses on a Grotto" (*Corr.*, IV, 262); still, the poem's glance is retrospective, and holds no brief for the future.
70. *Ibid.*, 289, Oct. 27, 1740.
71. *Gentleman's Magazine*, XI, 546, Oct., 1741.
72. *Corr.*, IV, 351, July 18, 1741.
73. *Ibid.*, 364, Oct. 10, 1741.
74. *Ibid.*, 368, Nov. 3, 1741.
75. *Ibid.*, 369, Nov. 7, 1741.
76. *Ibid.*, 387, Feb. 8, 1741/2.
77. *Ibid.*, 404, July 18, 1742, to Warburton. See also Pope's remark to Bethel: "The Turn of affairs here has by no means made me think better of the situation of it, than before..." 396, May 21-23, 1742.
78. *Ibid.*, 406, July 23, 1742.
79. *Ibid.*, 429, Dec. 1, 1742 (the date is Sherburn's guesswork).
80. *Ibid.*, 431, Dec. 8, 1742.
81. *Ibid.*, 437, Jan. 13, 1742/3.
82. *Ibid.*, 398, May 27, 1742.

JONES, Pope and Dulness
1. *Augustan Satire* (1952), 134.
2. 'The "New World" of Pope's *Dunciad*', *Renaissance and Modern Studies*, vi (1962); reprinted in *Essential Articles for the Study of Alexander Pope*, ed. Maynard Mack (1964).
3. See Theodor E. Mommsen, 'Petrarch's Conception of the Dark Ages', *Speculum*, xvii (1942), 226-42; quoted by Erwin Panofsky, *Renaissance and Renascences in Western Art* (Stockholm, 1960), 10.
4. For example, the third of Oldham's *Satires upon the Jesuits* was modelled on George Buchanan's Latin satire against the Franciscans, *Franciscanus*. See *Poems on Affairs of State*, ii, 1678-81, 44, ed. Elias F. Mengel, Jr. (Yale, 1965).
5. See Aubrey Williams and H. H. Erskine-Hill, op. cit.
6. The use made of Lucian by Erasmus and More is fully discussed in H. A. Mason's *Humanism and Poetry in the Early Tudor Period* (1959).

7. See A. S. Pease, 'Things without Honor', *Classical Philology*, xxi (1926), 27-42; quoted by Charles Osborne McDonald, *The Rhetoric of Tragedy* (Massachusetts, 1966), pp. 89 ff.

8. Pope's insect-winged Sylphs perhaps owe something to Lucian's Fly. Lucian's *Podagra* (Gout) formed the basis of a poem, *The Triumphs of the Gout*, by Pope's contemporary Gilbert West.

9. V. de Sola Pinto suggested a connection between the two poems in 'John Wilmot, Earl of Rochester and the Right Veine of Satire', *Essays and Studies*, 1953. Dornavius's collection includes Passerat's *Nihil*, which was quoted in full (apparently from memory) by Johnson in his *Life of Rochester*.

10. Such things as *Podicis encomium, Latrinae querela*, and *Stercoris encomium*, and several pages each under the titles *Problemata de Crepitu Ventris* and *De Peditu Eiusque Speciebus*.

11. 'The *Dunciad*', in *The Common Pursuit* (1952), p. 95.

12. *The Life of Addison*.

13. This is the argument of H. H. Erskine-Hill.

14. From Oldham's *Satyr Concerning Poetry*. Quotations from Oldham are from the 1710 edition.

15. From an elegy on Oldham by T. Wood, dated 1684, in *Remains of Oldham*, 1710. Pope uses the phrase 'learned dust' in *Dunciad*, iii. 186, a parallel not noted by Sutherland.

16. There was a strong element of realism in this topic. Cf. an observation by T.J.B. Spencer: 'The demand for waste paper, for a variety of domestic and other uses, has, until comparatively recent times, been heavy and continuous and urgent and far in excess of the supply. The consequences for English literature have been serious.' ('Shakespeare v. The Rest: The Old Controversy', *Shakespeare Survey*, xiv (1961), 81.)

17. 'Aspects of Dryden's Imagery', *Essays in Criticism*, iv (1954), 20-41.

18. Marshall McLuhan ends *The Gutenberg Galaxy* (1962) with a discussion of the *Dunciad*. He declares that 'the first age of print introduced the first age of the unconscious', p. 245.

19. From *The latter End of the Chorus of the second act of Seneca's Troas, translated* (*Poems*, ed. Pinto, 49). The couplet quoted above is, as Sutherland points out, adapted by Pope from the same poem:

> And to that Mass of Matter shall be swept,
> Where things destroy'd, with things unborn are kept...

20. For a late example (1791) of *lumber* in a context concerning the use of learning, cf. Boswell's summing up of Johnson's character at the end of his *Life*: 'But his superiority over other learned men consisted chiefly in what may be called the art of thinking, the art of using his mind; a certain continual power of seizing the useful substance of all that he knew, and exhibiting it in a clear and forcible manner; so that knowledge, which we often see to be no bet-

ter than lumber in men of dull understanding, was, in him,
true, evident, and actual wisdom.'
    21. According to the *O.E.D. unconscious* is first recorded in
1712: Sir Richard Blackmore uses it several times in his
poem *The Creation*, of which the seventh Book is concerned with
the operations of the human mind.
    22. Whyte's book is quoted by McLuhan, op. cit., p. 245.
    23. From an epistle To Roger, Earl of Orrery, prefixed to
The Rival Ladies (1664) (*Of Dramatic Poesy and Other Critical Essays*,
ed. George Watson, 1962, vol. 1, 2).
    24. Quoted by Whyte, op. cit., p. 96.
    25. Wilson Knight notes that 'there is a strange and hap-
py absence of the sadistic. The comedy is not precisely
cruel: the duncas are all happy, are not shown as realizing
their absurdity, and are allowed to maintain a certain physic-
cal, though ludicrous, dignity'. He further comments on
Pope's 'delicate emotional and sensuous touch, felt in the
softness, the nature-tone, of the whole atmosphere'. See
Laureate of Peace (1954), pp. 61, 62. In his essay on the *Dunciad*, in a discussion of a passage in Book Four, F. R. Leavis
remarks on 'the predominant feeling, which, in fact, might
fairly be called genial'.
    26. Op. cit., pp. 36-8.
    27. William K. Wimsatt, Jr. and Cleanth Brooks, *Literary
Criticism: A Short History* (New York, 1957), p. 217, n. 2.
    28. Pope refers to Philips's 'Infantine stile' in his
note to 1728 *Dunciad*, iii. 322. Chapter xi of *The Art of Sinking in Poetry* (1727) had dealt with 'The Infantine', 'where a
Poet grows so very simple, as to think and talk like a child'.
Cf. also Pope's reference to Philips in a letter to Swift,
14 December 1725 (*Correspondence*, ii. 350, ed. George Sherburn).
    29. One of the most impressive of such climactic move-
ments, the conclusion to the *Epilogue to the Satires*, *Dialogue I*
--the 'triumph of Vice'--was compared by Joseph Warton to a
painting by Rubens.
    30. The account of the tickling contest in Book Two of the
Dunciad possibly owes something to *Music's Duel*. Pope perhaps
remembered Crashaw's reference to tickling: 'that tickled
with rare art / The tatling strings' (47-8). Pope's line
212, 'And quick sensations skip from vein to vein' may recall
Crashaw's 'then quicke returning skipps / And snatches this
againe' (32-3), while his phrase 'the pleasing pain' (211)
is reminiscent of some of Crashaw's peculiar interests.
    31. Cf. *Dunciad*, i. 186.
    32. Book Two is an exception: it cannot end with a power-
ful climax, since it shows the dunces falling asleep--al-
though the falling asleep is in itself an elaborate set-
piece.
    33. 1728 *Dunciad*, iii. 337.

ROSENBLUM, Pope's Illusive Temple of Infamy
  1. W. B. Carnochan's *Lemuel Gulliver's Mirror for Man* (Berkeley, 1968) has presented Swift as the self-conscious satirist. According to Carnochan *Gulliver's Travels* is "of all
satires, the most self-aware. It illustrates a paradox that
has for better or worse established itself in the modern
mind: that great art is typically, perhaps even necessarily,
its own subject, is about itself" (p. 13). The necessary
self-consciousness of the satirist is one of the implications of Robert C. Elliott's *The Power of Satire: Magic, Ritual,
Art* (Princeton, 1960).
  2. Kenneth Burke, *Attitudes Twoards History* (Boston, 1961),
pp. 49-50.
  3. "The First Satire of the Second Book of Horace Imitated," *The Poems of Alexander Pope*, ed. John Butt (New Haven,
1966), p. 614, l. 14. I have used this edition, a one-
volume edition of the Twickenham text, for all Pope's poetry
other than *The Dunciad.*
  4. Maynard Mack, *The Garden and the City* (Toronto, 1969),
p. 193.
  5. *The Dunciad,* ed. James Sutherland (New Haven, 1953), p.
107. I have used this edition (the Twickenham) for all references to *The Dunciad.* "A" or "B" indicates references to
the A (1729) or B (1743) texts in this edition.
  6. Sheldon Sacks, *Fiction and the Shape of Belief* (Berkeley,
1967), p. 26, and Ronald Paulson, *The Fictions of Satire* (Baltimore, 1967), p. 3. Edward Rosenheim in *Swift and the Satirist's Art* (Chicago, 1958) argues that "satire cannot be fully
effective if we fail to understand what the satirist genuinely believes and wishes us to believe about the issues reflected in his work. When we identify his victim, we establish the 'true' direction of his assault, locating his final
target in the realm of actuality. Fiction serves a satiric
purpose only when we are aware of the manner and extent of
its departure from authentic fact and belief" (pp. 179-80).
Although Sacks, Paulson, and Rosenheim do not have the same
view of satire, I do not think I misrepresent their positions
in saying that they share a broadly rhetorical view of
satire. An exception to the prevailing rhetorical view is
John Clark's *Form and Frenzy in Swift's "Tale of a Tub"* (Ithaca,
1970), a work which I saw only after writing this paper.
  7. Northrop Frye, *The Anatomy of Criticism* (Princeton,
1957), p. 245.
  8. Paulson, p. 152.
  9. Hugh Kenner, *The Counterfeiters* (Bloomington, Ind., 1968),
p. 30.
  10. Edward Said, "Swift's Tory Anarchy," *Eighteenth Century
Studies*, 3 (Fall 1969), pp. 51, 54.
  11. Austin Warren, "Pope," *Essential Articles for the Study of
Alexander Pope*, ed. Maynard Mack (Hamden, 1968), p. 87.
  12. Paulson, p. 5.

13. T. S. Eliot, *Essays on Elizabethan Drama* (New York, 1956), p. 80.

14. M. H. Abrams, *The Mirror and the Lamp* (New York, 1958), p. 6.

15. *The Correspondence of Alexander Pope,* ed. George Sherburn (Oxford, 1956), 2:468.

16. Sutherland, p. 411.

17. Pope writes to Caryll on April 8, 1729 about *The Dunciad*: "The other book is written (all but the poem) by two or three of my friends, and a droll book it is" (3:31). On May 30, 1729 he says: "My friends who took so much pains to comment upon it, must come off with the public as they can" (3:36). And again, more emphatically: "As to the Notes, I am weary of telling a great Truth, which is, that I am not Author of 'em" (3:165). Despite Pope's insistence on this "great truth" his modern editor remains unconvinced: "There seems to be no escaping the conclusion, therefore, that when Pope decided to published the *Dunciad* with Notes Variorum it was he himself (with Savage acting, perhaps, as a sort of secretary) who worked through his four volumes of *Libels,* Jacob's *Poetical Register,* Winstanley's *Lives of the Poets,* and other works of reference or abuse" (Sutherland, xxvii).

18. "Beyond lending his name to it, Cleland had probably not much more to do with writing the Letter than Mrs. Anne Dodd had with publishing it" (Sutherland, xxv).

19. "Do you care I shou'd say any thing farther how much that poem is yours? Since certainly without you it had never been. Would to God we were together for the rest of our lives! The whole weight of Scriblers would just serve to find us amusement, and not more" (Pope to Swift, 2:522). Sherburn is skeptical: "Pope is somewhat too eager to involve Swift with himself as an ally against the Dunces."

20. I am relying on two of Sutherland's conjectures here. The first, that Pope intended the publication of *Peri Bathous* as "a sort of ground bait for the subsequent sport of the *Dunciad*" (xvi), seems to have won fairly wide acceptance. The second is more speculative but still plausible: that Pope "arranged that a spurious proof sheet of the revised *Dunciad* should be 'stolen' from the printer's and sent to [Cibber]," to provoke Cibber into writing something like *A Letter from Mr. Cibber to Mr. Pope* (Sutherland, xxxiv).

21. The terms are Geoffrey Hartman's in "Toward Literary History," *Daedalus* (Spring 1970), 356.

22. Mack has demonstrated the increasingly political nature of the references in Pope's revisions: "Small changes in successive texts of the three book *Dunciad* had already for some years been deepening its political complexion" (p. 150). "In general, then, both by added notes and added or revised lines, Pope made the political intent of the *New Dunciad* of 1742 yet more explicit in Book IV of 1743 which it became. At the same time, to the Variorum *Dunciad* of 1729,

which provided Books I-III, he added a vein of political innuendo that was not originally present" (p. 155).
23. Aubrey Williams, *Pope's Dunciad* (Baton Rouge, 1955), p.
62. A good deal of what I have to say in this essay is a
restatement in different terms of the argument of William's
third chapter, "The Variorum Dunciad."
24. "In the meantime his *Dulness* grows and flourishes as
if he was there already. It will indeed be a noble work:
the many will stare at it, the few will smile, and all his
Patrons from Bickerstaffe to Gulliver will rejoice, to see
themselves adorn'd in that immortal piece" (Bolingbrooke and
Pope to Swift, February 1727/8, 2:472).
25. The line is "True to the bottom, see Concanen creep"
(A II, p. 137, l. 287). Pope is probably responding to Concanen's assertion that another line in which Pope had used
asterisks referred to the King and Queen. The line is A II,
287: "Thy dragons Magistrats and Peers shall taste."
Pope's note to the line reads: "It stood in the first edition with blanks, *Thy dragons* *** and ***. *Concanen* was sure,
'they must needs mean no-body but the *King* and *Queen*, and said
he would insist it was so, till the Poet clear'd himself by
filling up the blanks otherwise agreeably to the context,
and consistent with his *allegiance*'" (p. 184).
26. "By transferring the same ridicule from one to another, he destroyed its efficacy; for, by shewing that what he
had said of one he was ready to say of another, he reduced
himself to the insignificance of his own magpye, who from
his cage calls cuckold at a venture" (*Lives of the Poets* [Lon-
don, 1959], 2:288).
27. Horace Gregory, trans., *The Metamorphoses* (New York,
1960), pp. 300-301.
28. Mack in his concluding sentence makes the figure of
Prospero the final emblem for Pope's relation to his subjects: "Under his magisterial wand, like the wrecked voyag-
ers in *The Tempest*, lords and rich men, ministers and society-
wenches, kings, courtiers, Quakers, clowns, and good Ralph
Allens move through the paces of an intricate satirical bal-
let, which combines the features of reality and dream" (p.
236).
29. The poem has been read by critics as expressing either the wish (to control dullness) or the fear (that it can't
be contained). Thus, Alvin Kernan in *The Plot of Satire* (New
Haven, 1965) has argued that Pope "has so arranged his poem
that this ultimate expansion is at once a contraction. At
the very moment that dullness becomes everything, everything
becomes nothing, for dullness is finally nothingness, vacuity, matter without form or idea" (p. 115). On the other
hand Thomas Edwards, Jr. glosses these lines (B IV 5-8) in
this way: "The critical intelligence that made the poem
possible must bow before the irresistible onslaught of *nature*
--a nature no longer seen as a synonym for light and order
but as a label for a ceaseless mutability destroying all that

makes life dignified or even possible" ("Light and Nature:
A Reading of the Dunciad" in Mack, *Essential Articles*, p. 785).
    30.   Elliott has suggested the negative tendencies of
"major satire": "Let the conscious intent of the artist be
what it will, the local attack cannot be contained: the
ironic language eats its way in implication through the most
powerful-seeming structures" (*Power of Satire*, p. 274). "The
pressure of his [Swift's] art works directly against the ostensibly conservative function which it appears to serve.
Instead of shoring up foundations, it tears them down. It
is revolutionary" (pp. 274-5).

REID,   Ordering Chaos *The Dunciad*
    1.   "Life of Pope," *Rasselas, Poems, and Selected Prose*, ed.
Bertrand H. Bronson (New York, 1958), p. 400.
    2.   *The Dunciad*, ed. James Sutherland (London, 1943), pp.
605-607.   All future references will be to this edition and
will be given in parentheses in the text.
    3.   "Life of Pope," pp. 317-318, 319.
    4.   "Life of Pope," pp. 340, 399.
    5.   *On the Poetry of Pope*, 2nd ed. (Oxford, 1950), p. 55.
    6.   "Alexander Pope," *Rage for Order: Essays in Criticism*
(Ann Arbor, 1959), p. 50.
    7.   *Paradise Lost*, I, 21-22.
    8.   The map on pp. 34-35 of *Pope's "Dunciad": A Study of Its
Meaning*, by Aubrey L. Williams (Baton Rouge, 1955), is a great
help in visualizing these matters.
    9.   One may recall the American recruiting poster: "Join
the Marines and Let the World See You!"

KINSLEY,   The *Dunciad* as Mock-Book
    1.   Hugh Kenner discusses the *Dunciad* from this angle in
"The Man of Sense as Buster Keaton," *Virginia Quarterly Review*,
XLI (1965), 82-86; revised in *The Counterfeiters* (Bloomington,
Ind., 1968).   See also Aubrey L. Williams, *Pope's "Dunciad": A
Study of Its Meaning* (London, 1955), p. 55.   My whole essay
owes a great deal to this excellent study.
    2.   For an interesting discussion of Swift's *Tale of a Tub*
as a parody of the book, see Kenner, *Flaubert, Joyce, and Beckett:
The Stoic Comedians* (Boston, 1962), pp. 37-44.
    3.   James Sutherland, Introduction, *The Dunciad*, Twicken-
ham Edition of the *Poems*, ed. John Butt (London and New Haven,
1939-67), V, xxxiv.   All quotations of Pope's poems are from
this edition, hereafter referred to as TE.   On the false
proof-sheet, see also Joseph Spence, *Observations, Anecdotes,
and Characters of Books and Men*, ed. James M. Osborn (Oxford,
1966), Nos. 253, 331, 332.
    4.   *Essay on Criticism*, 1. 135; TE, I, 255.
    5.   See the chapter on "The Book as Symbol" in Ernst
Robert Curtius, *European Literature and the Latin Middle Ages* (New
York and Evanston, 1963).   An opposing tradition, represented
by Ecclesiastes with "Of making many books there is no end,
and much study is a weariness of the flesh" and Callimachus

with "A big book is a great evil," also flourished but was less significant.

6. Milton, *Complete Poems and Major Prose*, ed. Merritt Y. Hughes (New York, 1957), p. 720.

7. William Davenant, *Gondibert* (London, 1651), II.v.37. Pope seems to have known the poem well. See Spence, *Anecdotes*, No. 440.

8. *A Tale of a Tub, The Battle of the Books*, etc., ed. A. C. Guthkelch and D. Nichol Smith (Oxford, 1958), p. 222; *Memoirs*, ed. Charles Kerby-Miller (New Haven, 1950), p. 147.

9. 1743 version, I.257-260; TE, V, 289. Unless otherwise indicated, I quote from this ("B") version.

10. *Autumn*, ll. 670-672. The image appears also in *Summer*, ll. 192-196.

11. *Thoughts upon the Four Last Things ... Part II. Judgement* (London, 1734), ll. 380-388.

12. Introduction, *Physico-Theology*, 10th ed. (London, 1742), p. 2.

13. Henry Baker, *The Microscope Made Easy* (London, 1743); quoted in William Powell Jones, *The Rhetoric of Science* (London, 1966), p. 16. Jones cites many other uses of "the Book of Nature" in the 18th century, as does C. A. Patrides for earlier periods in *Milton and the Christian Tradition* (Oxford, 1966), pp. 68-70.

14. *Essay concerning Human Understanding* III.ix.23.

15. *Essays in Divinity*, ed. Evelyn M. Simpson (Oxford, 1952), pp. 7-8. Basil Willey points out that Bishop Butler finally tried to rebut deistic attacks on the obscurity of the Bible by emphasizing the obscurity and illegibility of the Book of Nature (*The Eighteenth Century Background* [London, 1949], pp. 77-82).

16. I owe this information to Martin C. Battestin; see his notes to *Joseph Andrews*, Riverside ed. or Wesleyan ed., II, i. For a full discussion, see Donald M. Foerster, *Homer in English Criticism: The Historical Approach in the Eighteenth Century* (New Haven, 1947), Chs. 1-3. My parenthetical account here is somewhat oversimplified.

17. Albert B. Lord, *The Singer of Tales* (Cambridge, Mass., 1960).

18. These attitudes may perhaps be seen more clearly if contrasted to the viewpoint of Mallarmé, which derives in part from the same sources but is more individualistic and absolute. Mallarmé seems at times to want to write, all by himself, a book that would replace the universe by rendering it obsolete: "le monde existe pour aboutir à un livre." See Jacques Scherer, *Le "Livre" de Mallarmé* (Paris, 1957), especially pp. 22 ff., 46-52, 138-143.

19. Robert Scholes and Robert Kellogg, *The Nature of Narrative* (New York, 1968), p. 118.

20. Noémi Hepp, "Les Interprétations Religieuses d' Homère au XVIIe Siècle," *Revue des Sciences Religieuses*, XXXI (1957), 36, 41.

21. *Pope's Essay on Criticism 1709*, ed. Robert M. Schmitz (St. Louis, 1962), p. 42, ll. 202-204 of MS. Emile Audra and Aubrey Williams may be making Pope's innuendo too explicit when they say that he "calls" Homer sacred writ (TE, I, 205n).

22. Line 70; TE, I, 246. John M. Aden draws out the implications of this passage in "'*First* Follow Nature': Strategy and Stratification in *An Essay on Criticism*," *JEGP*, LV (1956), 604-617.

23. *Essay on Criticism*, l. 292; TE, I, 272.

24. Stuart Gilbert, *James Joyce's Ulysses* (New York, 1955), p. 42.

25. Jebb's expression, quoted by Harold Richard Joliffe, *The Critical Methods and Influence of Bentley's* Horace (Chicago, 1939), p. 5.

26. "A Discourse ... of the Mosaick History of the Creation," p. 40; bound with *A New Theory of the Earth*, 3rd ed. (London, 1722).

27. Donne, *Essays in Divinity*, p. 7.

28. "Preface to *Gondibert*," *Critical Essays of the Seventeenth Century*, ed. J. E. Spingarn (Oxford, 1908-09), II, 48. Osborn suggests that Pope may have had this passage in mind while working on the *Essay on Criticism* (Spence, *Anecdotes*, No. 350n).

29. *The Subtler Language* (Baltimore, 1959), p. 11.

30. Boyle, *Works* (London, 1772), II, 39; Price, *Science since Babylon* (New Haven and London, 1961), p. 29. Boyle's unawareness of the clock's origin of course makes his choice all the more significant.

31. Marjorie Nicolson and G. S. Rousseau, *"This Long Disease, My Life": Alexander Pope and the Sciences* (Princeton, 1968), pp. 158-160, 225.

32. TE, V, 48-49.

33. Alvin B. Kernan, *The Plot of Satire* (New Haven and London, 1965), pp. 119-120.

34. Northrop Frye, *Anatomy of Criticism* (Princeton, 1957), p. 57.

35. "Theology and Poetry in Donne's *Conclave*," *ELH*, XXXII (1965), 481. Pope may not have been aware of this particular refinement of Biblical allegorizing; but it remains available for our appreciation of his poem, since he was working in the same general tradition.

36. See George Sherburn, "Pope and 'The Great Shew of Nature,'" in R. F. Jones et al., *The Seventeenth Century: Studies in the History of English Thought and Literature from Bacon to Pope* (Stanford, 1965), pp. 306-315; Nicolson and Rousseau, *Pope and the Sciences*, pp. 193-195.

37. "Pope's Poetical Manuscripts," in *Essential Articles for the Study of Alexander Pope*, ed. Maynard Mack (Hamden, Conn., 1964), pp. 507-508.

38. TE, VII, xci. Is there a pun in the first "epic"?

39. Recent critics who quite rightly emphasize the fictional role of the notes sometimes tend to ignore their

quite straightforward complementary role of elucidating a
poem that was obscure even to Swift.
40. *Dunciad* IV.228; TE, V, 365.
41. Quoted by F. Burges in *Some Observations on the Use and
Original of the Noble Art and Mystery of Printing* (Norwich, Eng.,
1701); *Harleian Miscellany* (1745), III, 149.
42. Ed. Donald F. Bond (Oxford, 1965), II, 153-154. Addison goes on to quote Cowley's verses about Virgil's sacred
work cited above.
43. *Typographia: An Ode on Printing*, pp. 10-11, 13. This poem
also praises the governor of Virginia for fostering printing, and its final line deserves preservation: "Where *GOOCH*
administers, *AUGUSTUS* reigns."
44. *A Poem on the Invention of Letters, and the Art of Printing*, reprinted in Henry Lemoine, *History, Origin, and Progress, of the
Art of Printing* (London, 1797), p. 153. The poem is attributed
to one James Sterling (*Literary History of the United States*, ed.
Robert E. Spiller et al. [New York, 1949], I, 52-53). It is
worth noting that both Markland and Sterling wrote their poems in the colonies, where printing presses were much rarer
than in the mother country. Lemoine reprints an intriguing
passage from Sterling's preface of 1758: "His [the author's]
intimacy with Mr. Pope obliged him to tell that great poet,
above twenty years before, that it was peculiarly ungrateful
in him, not to celebrate such a subject as the *Invention of
Letters*, or to suffer it to be disgraced by a meaner hand"
(p. 149).
45. Walter J. Ong, S.J., "Ramist Classroom Procedure and
the Nature of Reality," *SEL*, I (1961), 40.
46. Walter J. Ong, S.J., *Ramus, Method, and the Decay of Dialogue* (Cambridge, Mass., 1958), p. 310.
47. See Ian Watt, *The Rise of the Novel* (Harmondsworth, 1968),
pp. 203-208; and Maynard Mack's discussion of the "rapture"
with which the young Pope read Ogilvy's Homer (TE, VII, ccxxi-
ccxxii).
48. There is a good discussion of the *Essay*, with several
facsimile pages, in Paul Cornelius, *Languages in 17th- and Early
18th-Century Imaginary Voyages* (Geneva, 1965), pp. 89-97. The
Scolar Press has announced a facsimile of the whole *Essay*.
See Plates for Wilkins' forty principal characters and his
discussion of the sign for "Father."
49. He takes care to point out, however, that he does not
aspire to a knowledge of the "immediate form" or essence of
each being (p. 289).
50. *The Gutenberg Galaxy: The Making of Typographic Man* (Toronto,
1962), p. 185.
51. John Ray, the best scientist among the physico-theologians, collaborated with Wilkins but criticized his system
for falsifying reality in this way. Wilkins wanted to keep
his character simple enough so that it could at least be
transcribed phonetically within the limitations of the Roman
alphabet, whereas Ray wanted to elaborate the character with-

out regard for the language in an attempt to make it reflect
the complexity of reality as closely as possible. Any such
attempt, of course, must remain an uneasy compromise between
simplification of reality and unmanageable complexity of
symbolism. See Benjamin DeMott, "Science vs. Mnemonics:
Notes on John Ray and John Wilkins," *Isis*, XLVIII (1957), 3-12.

52. *Essay*, pp. 298-299, 303; Otto Funke, "On the Sources
of John Wilkins' Philosophical Language," *English Studies*, XL
(1959), 212-213.

53. Wotton, *Reflections upon Ancient and Modern Learning*; Spingarn, III, 226; Bentley, Preface to *A Dissertation upon the
Epistles of Phalaris* (London, 1699), p. xciii. Other admirers
included Sprat, Leibnitz, Bolingbroke, and the *Athenian Oracle*;
see Clark Emery, "John Wilkins' Universal Language," *Isis*,
XXXVIII (1948), 182-183.

54. *The Flying Island, &c. Being a Key to Gulliver's Voyage to
Laputa....In a Third Letter to Dean Swift* (London, 1726), pp. 11,
22. This key and the others, one for each voyage, purport
to be the work of "Corolini Di Marco." Joseph Keogh called
this key to my attention, and the University of Toronto
Library provided a microfilm.

55. A word about Leibnitz, the best-known seeker after a
"caractéristique universelle," may be in order here. At one
time or another Leibnitz considered many different schemes,
but in spite of his admiration for Wilkins he never followed
him very closely. Most of his proposals were either a kind
of symbolic logic, concentrating on the reasoning process
rather than on the world of reality, or were modified versions of the pictograph or ideogram. His "caractéristique"
was conceived of as developing alongside his Book of Nature,
the "Encyclopédie"; each would help improve the other, and
together they would finally produce universal knowledge.
See Louis Couturat, *La logique de Leibniz d'après des documents in-
édits* (Paris, 1901), Chs. 3 and 4, especially pp. 108-118.

56. McLuhan, *Gutenberg Galaxy*, p. 131.

57. Someone, quite likely Pope himself, wrote a letter to
the *Spectator* marvelling at the appetite of readers for any
kind of printed news, whatever the matter--strayed horses,
advertisements, foreign battles, anything (No. 452; ed. Bond,
IV, 92). For the question of authorship, see also p. 114.

58. *Timber, or Discoveries*; Spingarn, I, 41.

59. Etienne Gilson, *The Christian Philosophy of St. Augustine*
(London, 1961), p. 222.

60. McLuhan, *Gutenberg Galaxy*, p. 259.

61. See Philip Stevick, "Familiarity in the Addisonian
Familiar Essay," *College Composition and Communication*, XVI (1965),
169-173, and my "Meaning and Format: Mr. Spectator and His
Folio Half-Sheets," *ELH*, XXXIV (1967), 492-493.

62. *Flaubert, Joyce, and Beckett*, p. 40.

63. *Seven Types of Ambiguity*, 3rd ed. (New York, 1955), p. 100.

64. *The Marriage of Heaven and Hell*, Pls. 15-17; *Complete Writings*, ed. Geoffrey Keynes (London, 1957), p. 154.

LAWLER, "Wafting Vapours from the Land of Dreams": Virgil's
Fourth and Sixth Eclogues and the *Dunciad*
    1. All Quotations from the *Dunciad* are from the 1742 ver-
sion, in four books, ed. James Sutherland, the *Twickenham Edition of the Poems of Alexander Pope*, Volume V, 2nd. ed. (London
and New Haven, 1953). Let me record here my debt to A. Bart-
lett Giamatti, Michael Holahan, and Michael O'Loughlin, from
whose criticism of drafts of this essay I have profited
greatly. It was written in memory of Francis A. Drumm.
    2. Cf. Aubrey Williams, *Pope's* Dunciad, *A Study of its Mean-
ing* (London, 1955), Chapter One, passim.
    3. Of course, the return to the age of Saturn is a com-
monplace, and has a long history outside of Eclogue 4. It
also merges importantly at the end of the *Dunciad* with the
Christian notion of apocalypse. Yet it still seems right
to refer the idea as it is expressed in the *Dunciad* explicitly
to Eclogue 4, primarily because of the several direct allusions to it that I am about to examine, but also because of
its historical preeminence in Golden-Age literature, and
further because of Pope's special fondness for it as expressed in *Messiah* and in his prophecy of "Albion's Golden
Days" at the end of *Windsor Forest*, a passage that may well
be included in the parody here.
    4. Both text and translation of Virgil's *Eclogues* are
quoted from *The Eclogues and Georgics of Virgil*, translated by C.
Day Lewis (Garden City, N.Y., 1964). The *Aeneid* is quoted
from *P. Vergili Maronis Opera*, ed. F. A. Hirtzel (Oxford, 1900);
its translation from *The Aeneid of Virgil*, translated by C. Day
Lewis (Garden City, N.Y., 1953).
    5. *Alexander Pope: The Poetry of Allusion* (Oxford, 1959), pp.
30-32.
    6. Pope's *Messiah*, of course, makes use of Eclogue 4 to
create an image of Christ as child-Savior. Most allusions
to Eclogue 4 in the *Dunciad* thus allude as it were automatic-
ally also to *Messiah*. This fact, like the notion of the
Apocalypse, and the traditional Christian interpretation of
Eclogue 4, helps absorb Pope's use of it into a Christian
framework.
    7. Brooks Otis, *Virgil: A Study in Civilized Poetry* (Oxford,
1963), p. 140.
    8. Virgil is here relying on the positive side of Silenus:
the inspired truth of his music, the ironic wisdom that enabled Socrates to be compared to him. He was also regarded
as a good father to the satyrs; this aspect too is recognized
in his easy patronization of the boys Chromis and Mnasyllus
who fetter him to make him sing; cf. *The Oxford Classical Dictionary* (Oxford, 1949), p. 797. His other aspect, the old
drunkard, is present at first but slips away as his song
asserts its magic. The Dunces are Sileni without kindness,
wisdom, or melodic power; or rather Sileni whose wisdom has
been converted into black art. When Thomas Gordon appears
as Silenus in Book IV, it is to introduce to Dulness first

the "Youth," with their "trifling head and contracted heart,"
then her "Magus," a "Wizard old," who extends his cup to
Dulness. Here again, duncery not only effaces the positive
magical power of the poet; it perverts it into malign art.
The Silenus of *Dunciad* IV is the destructive opposite of Virgil's creative singer.
    9. Otis, pp. 136-137, argues that the "broader scope"
promised in the opening lines of Eclogue 4 is to be referred
explicitly to the modest adoption of a "slender reed" at the
opening of 6. He is right, but I do not think that the contrast works only in favor of 4. The reader of 4 may feel
the grander strain in relation to 6; but the reader of 6 may
feel that the more modest regeneration it envisions is a corrective to what is pretentious, too vatic, in 4. If in 4
Virgil is moving beyond the simplicities of 6, in 6 he is
equally well moving back into history from the unreality of
4. The poems qualify each other; they exist in equilibrium.
Another aspect of 6 which Otis overlooks as he contrasts
its history of "degeneration" to the "regenerative" impulse
of 4 is Silenus' benevolence and easy good humor, qualities
which soften not only the harsh trick of the boys in fetter-
ing him but also the decadence of much of his subject-matter.
Of course I cannot prove that Pope read Eclogue 6 as an
assertion of the redemptive power of poetry; yet his allusions to it are so sensitively poetic that he clearly felt
that power, and responded to it as a poem and not as an outline of history. And the genial tone is obvious.
    10. "The 'New World' of Pope's *Dunciad*," *Renaissance and Modern*
Studies, 6 (1962), 47-67; reprinted in Maynard Mack, ed.,
Essential Articles for the Study of Alexander Pope (Hamden, Connecticut, 1964), pp. 739-760; the passage quoted is on p. 748.

MENGEL, The *Dunciad* Illustrations
    1. Sherburn notes that in the inventory of Pope's goods
taken at his death there is an item of seventeen drawings by
him found in the garret (*The Correspondence of Alexander Pope*, ed.
George Sherburn, 5 vols. [Oxford, 1956], I, 187, n.2).
Spence records that "Mr. Pope learned to draw of Jervas for
a year and a half." Actually he took lessons from about
March 1713 to February 1714 (*Joseph Spence: Observations, Anecdotes,*
and Characters of Books and Men, ed. James M. Osborn, 2 vols.
[Oxford, 1966], I, 46).
    2. All quotations of Pope's poetry are from the Twicken-
ham Edition, but for the 1728 version of the *Dunciad*, Elwin-
Courthope (IV, 263-97) is used. All *Dunciad* quotations
not marked 1728 are from Volume V of the *Twickenham Edition of*
the Poems of Alexander Pope, ed. James Sutherland, 3rd ed. rev.
(New Haven and London, 1963). Figure 8 is from the Library
of Congress copy (HJ 7761/.A5/1740). The other plates are
reproduced by permission of the Beinecke Rare Book Library,
Yale University. For each of these I give the Griffith number of the edition from which it is taken (R. H. Griffith,

Alexander Pope: a Bibliography, 2 vols. [Austin, Texas, 1922-1927]).

3. Pope's note to the line in the Variorum (I, 244) reads: "A H-r.] A Strange Bird from Switzerland." John James Heidegger was a Swiss who from 1728 to 1734 collaborated with Handel to produce operas in London. In the 1734 revision of Fielding's *The Author's Farce* Heidegger appears as "Count Ugly from the Opera House in the Haymarket." Sutherland (p. 444) affirms that his notorious ugliness is the "main reason" for Heidegger's mention in the *Dunciad*. But for Pope, as for Fielding, Heidegger's ugliness would be at least as much moral as physical. Pope would no doubt see him primarily as pimp for that "harlot form" (IV, 45) the Italian opera. Fielding, who dedicated *The Masquerade* to "C---t H--D----R" in 1728, in 1734 has him boast of his masquerades to the Goddess of Nonsense and claim the title of "Surintendant des plaisirs d'Angleterre" (*The Author's Farce*, ed. Charles B. Woods [Lincoln, Nebraska, 1966], pp. 99, 103-4).

4. A correspondent in *N&Q*, 2nd ser. 2 (1856), 182 writes that he "found the following epigram on a fly-leaf in the *Dunciad*, 8vo. edition, 1729. The copyist states that it appeared in *The Daily Gazetteer*, about 18 Dec. 1738:
'Pallas for Wisdom priz'd her favorite Owl,
Pope for its Dulness chose the self-same Fowl:
Which shall we choose, or which shall we despise,
If Pope is witty, Pallas is not wise.'"

5. Papworth has three columns of families with the chevron between three martlets, but Ogilby is not one of them (John W. Papworth, *An Alphabetical Dictionary of Coats of Arms ... Ordinary of British Armorials* [London, 1874], I, 399-400).

6. *Correspondence*, II, 472. In a letter to Swift (?January 1727/8) Pope makes the joke at his own expense: "And it grieves me to the soul that I cannot send you my chef d'oeuvre, the Poem of Dulness, which after I am dead and gone, will be printed with a large Commentary, and letterd on the back, *Pope's Dulness*" (*Correspondence*, II, 468).

7. Sutherland, p. xix.

8. In Griffith 216 and 217 the imprint of the 1729 Variorum reads "A. Dob." instead of "A. Dod." Like Mrs. Dodd, Mrs. Dob was a London publisher of the time (Griffith I, 170). Just as "dod" is short for "doddard," so "dob" is probably from "dobby," dotard.

9. *Horace: Satires, Epistles and Ars Poetica*, trans. H. R. Fairclough, Loeb Classical Library (Cambridge, Mass., 1961).

10. Cf. Pope to Swift, 23 March 1727/8: "As the obtaining the love of valuable men is the happiest end I know of this life, so the next felicity is to get rid of fools and scoundrels; which I can't but own to you was one part of my design in falling upon these Authors, whose incapacity is not greater than their insincerity, and of whom I have always found (if I may quote myself)

That each bad Author is as bad a Friend.
This poem will rid me of those insects" (*Correspondence*, II,
481).
    11. This headpiece may have been designed by Kent. Pope
writing to Burlington on 23 December 1728 remarks in connection with a book which was probably the Variorum *Dunciad*:
"These are what Mr. Kent sent me some days since." As Sherburn notes, "The first page of the volume has a head-piece
that looks much like Kent's work, and he may have submitted
other designs to Pope" (*Correspondence*, II, 533n).
    12. For an account of Kent see W. K. Wimsatt, *The Portraits
of Alexander Pope* (New Haven, 1965), 107-36. Kent did illustrations and ornaments for Gay's *Poems* (1720), for his *Fables*
(1727), and for Thomson's *Seasons* (1730). For a study of the
Kent illustrations for the *Seasons* see Ralph Cohen, *The Art of
Discrimination: Thomson's "The Seasons" and the Language of Criticism*
(Berkeley, 1964), 259-65. In 1725 he contributed fifty designs for Pope's *Odyssey*, and in 1734 six head and tail pieces
for Gilliver's edition of *An Essay on Man* (Wimsatt, *Portraits of
Pope*, 111).
    13. Wimsatt, *Portraits of Pope*, 126.
    14. For the same reason--that they were not made express-
ly to illustrate the *Dunciad*--I have excluded printer's ornaments from my study. Some of these seem chosen for ironic
effect. In Griffith 206 a cupid shooting an arrow and a
vase of flowers both occur several times, certainly highly
inappropriate ornaments for a satire. I have, however, seen
two others which relate specifically to the *Dunciad*: in Griffith 204 a female figure of Justice, blindfolded and with
sword and balance (see A I, 50-52) and in Griffith 225 a lion crowned and with a human face (see Figure 7).
    15. Sutherland, 252.
    16. Maynard Mack, *The Garden and the City: Retirement and Politics
in the Later Poetry of Pope, 1731-1743* (Toronto, 1969), 161.
    17. Sutherland, 252.
    18. Cf. Dryden's preface to *All for Love*: "For my part, I
would wish no other revenge, either for myself or the rest
of the poets, from this rhyming judge of the twelve-penny
gallery, this legitimate son of Sternhold, than that he would
subscribe his name to his censure, or (not to tax him beyond
his learning) set his mark."
    19. Sutherland, 252.
    20. Cf. Swift to Pope, 20 April 1731: "You know favor is
got by two very contrary qualitys, one is by fear, the other
by ill taste; as to Cibber if I had any inclination to excuse the Court I would alledge that the Laureats place is
entirely in the Lord Chamberlain's gift; but who makes Lord
Chamberlains is another question. I believe if the Court
had interceded with D. of Grafton for a fitter man, it might
have prevailed" (*Correspondence*, III, 192).